9-2B FIFO inventory profit, $285
9-3B Gross margin: Average, $54,520; FIFO, $55,170; LIFO, $53,870
9-4B No check figure
9-5B Gross margin, $154,000
9-6B Net income: 19X4, $31 mil.; 19X5, $34 mil.; 19X6, $39 mil.
9-7B Estimated cost of ending inventory, $367,400
9-8B Ending inventory, at cost, $37,281
9-9B FIFO ending inventory, $890
DP Net income without purchase: FIFO, $25,200; LIFO, $22,200. Net income with purchase: FIFO, $25,200; LIFO, $15,000
FSP Net purchases, $1,800.5 mil.

10-1A Depr.: Land improve., $2,805; Home office bldg., $22,459; Garage, $1,519; Furniture, $25,144
10-2A Depr. for 19X6: SL, $7,000; UOP, $7,560; DDB, $321; SYD, $2,000
10-3A Depreciation expense, balance Dec. 31, 19X5, before closing, $7,688
10-4A No check figure
10-5A Cost of new truck, $18,578
10-6A No check figure
10-1B Depr.: Land improve., $2,277; Office bldg., $16,936; Storage bldg., $1,065; Furniture, $14,625
10-2B Depr. for 19X5: SL, $15,750; UOP, $11,250; DDB, $414; SYD, $5,250
10-3B Depreciation expense, Dec. 31, 19X3, balance before closing, $2,683
10-4B No check figure
10-5B Cost of new truck, $16,807
10-6B No check figure
DP Net income, Frycer Company $38,000 more than Bergdahl Company
FSP No check figure

11-1A No check figure
11-2A No check figure
11-3A Total liabilities, $283,926
11-4A Salary Expense, $10,170
11-5A Total annual cost for employee, $58,682
11-6A 3. Cash payment, $12,889; 4. Cash payment, $11,788
11-7A Net pay, $1,740
11-1B No check figure
11-2B No check figure
11-3B Total liabilities, $317,035
11-4B Wage Expense, $15,639
11-5B Total annual cost for employee, $68,274
11-6B 3. Cash payment, $55,545; 4. Cash payment, $40,264
11-7B Net pay, $1,480

DP No check figure
FSP No check figure

12-1A No check figure
12-2A No check figure
12-3A No check figure
12-4A Gross profit, installment method, $18,000
12-5A Net income, year 3, $60,200
12-6A Income, 19X8, percentage-of-completion method, $854,000
12-7A Correct net income, 19X5, $42,100
12-1B No check figure
12-2B No check figure
12-3B No check figure
12-4B Gross profit, installment method, $204,900
12-5B Net income, year 3, $
12-6B Income, 19X6, percentage-of-completion method, $942
12-7B Correct net income,
DP Net income, $
FSP No check figure

13-1A
13-2A 1.d. Leitmer, $27,000; Mu
13-3A 4. Lake capital at ⅛ interest, $30,000; 5. Lake capital at 15% interest, $34,500
13-4A 5. Debit Golden, Capital, $29,000
13-5A 1.d. Disbursement of cash to partners: Yagoda, $3,100; Kelly, $2,400; Dobbs, $0
13-6A Disbursements to: Morales, $6,000; Goldberg, $8,000
13-1B 2. Total assets, $111,600
13-2B 1.d. Hogan, $42,500; Stanford, $37,500; Reichlin, $52,000
13-3B 3. Newton's capital at ⅛ interest, $60,000; 5. Newton's capital at 10% interest, $34,000
13-4B 5. Debit Herron, Capital, $60,600
13-5B 1.d. Disbursement of cash to partners: Monet, $0; Dixon, $14,625; Palma, $5,375
13-6B Disbursements: Bell, $2,625; Pastena, $1,375
DP No check figure

14-1A Total stockholders' equity, $91,000
14-2A Total stockholders' equity: Lopez, $155,000; Monroe, $585,000
14-3A Total stockholders' equity, $221,570
14-4A Total yearly pref. dividends to pay

to avoid paying dividends in arrears, $22,500,000
14-5A 2. 19X3 dividends: Preferred, $2,000; Common, $32,000
14-6A Book value per share: Preferred, $28.20; Common, $7.16
14-7A Total assets, $683,000
14-1B Total stockholders' equity, $177,500
14-2B Total stockholders' equity: Baker, $94,000; Wang, $397,000
14-3B Total stockholders' equity, $324,320
14-4B Total yearly pref. dividends to pay to avoid paying dividends in arrears, $212,080
14-5B 2. 19X3 dividends: Preferred, $42,500; Common, $222,500
14-6B Book value per share: Preferred, $56.45; Common, $4.80
14-7B Total assets, $378,000
DP Total stockholders' equity: Plan 1, $405,200; Plan 2, $380,200
FSP No check figure

15-1A No check figure
15-2A Total stockholders' equity, Dec. 31, 19X2, $808,700
15-3A Total stockholders' equity, Dec. 31, 19X6, $321,500; Total stockholders' equity, Dec. 31, 19X7, $339,600
15-4A Earnings per share, $3.25; Total stockholders' equity, Sept. 30, 19X6, $618,000
15-5A Retained Earnings balance, Dec. 31, 19X3, $114,000; Earnings per share, $.30
15-6A 2. Debit to Retained Earnings, $28.3 mil.; 4. Treasury Stock, ending balance, $222.2 mil.; 7. Earnings per share, $1.95
15-7A Earnings per share for net income, $.97
15-1B No check figure
15-2B Total stockholders' equity, Dec. 31, 19X4, $561,400
15-3B Total stockholders' equity, Dec. 31, 19X8, $443,000; Total stockholders' equity, Dec. 31, 19X9, $513,000
15-4B Total stockholders' equity, June 30, 19X5, $509,000
15-5B Retained Earnings balance, June 30, 19X4, $94,000; Earnings per share, $2.85
15-6B 2. Debit to Retained Earnings, $1.3 mil.; 4. Treasury Stock, ending balance, $213.5 mil.; 7. Earnings per share, $4.46
15-7B Earnings per share for net income, $2.89
DP No check figure
FSP No check figure

ROUTE TO: (I*STAR 7)

ROUTE TO: (I*STAR 7)

06 - IS VISTA CAPSIL SUPPORT AREA
MICHELLE D THOMSON

ACCOUNTING
LOMA Edition

This book is a special edition of Horngren and Harrison's **Accounting** that has been prepared for use in LOMA's FLMI Insurance Education Program. As such, this edition contains only chapters 1–15 and Appendices A, B, and C of the regular 28-chapter edition of that text. FLMI students should disregard any references in this special edition to material covered in chapters 16 through 28 or Appendices D and E in the regular edition. Students should consult the current FLMI Program Booklet to determine the correct FLMI reading/study assignment for this course.

PRENTICE HALL SERIES IN ACCOUNTING
Charles T. Horngren, Consulting Editor

AUDITING: AN INTEGRATED APPROACH, 4/E
Arens/Loebbecke

KOHLER'S DICTIONARY FOR ACCOUNTANTS, 6/E
Cooper/Ijiri

INTERMEDIATE ACCOUNTING, 2/E
Danos/Imhoff

FINANCIAL STATEMENT ANALYSIS, 2/E
Foster

FINANCIAL ACCOUNTING: PRINCIPLES AND ISSUES, 3/E
Granof

COST ACCOUNTING: A MANAGERIAL EMPHASIS, 6/E
Horngren/Foster

ACCOUNTING
Horngren/Harrison

INTRODUCTION TO FINANCIAL ACCOUNTING, Third Revised Edition
Horngren/Sundem

INTRODUCTION TO MANAGEMENT ACCOUNTING, 7/E
Horngren/Sundem

ADVANCED MANAGEMENT ACCOUNTING, 2/E
Kaplan/Atkinson

GOVERNMENT AND NONPROFIT ACCOUNTING THEORY & PRACTICE, 3/E
Freeman/Shoulders/Lynn

A NEW INTRODUCTION TO FINANCIAL ACCOUNTING, 2/E
May/Mueller/Williams

AUDITING PRINCIPLES, 5/E
Stettler

BUDGETING, 5/E
Welsch

ACCOUNTING
LOMA Edition

Charles T. Horngren
Stanford University

Walter T. Harrison, Jr.
Baylor University

Published for the FLMI Insurance Education Program
Life Management Institute – LOMA

Prentice Hall
A Division of Simon & Schuster
Englewood Cliffs, New Jersey 07632

Accounting: LOMA Edition is a special edition of **Accounting,** by Charles T. Horngren and Walter T. Harrison, Jr. (copyright Prentice Hall, 1989) comprised of the first 15 chapters of Horngren/Harrison, **Accounting.**

Production editor: Esther S. Koehn
Development editor: Stephen Deitmer
Acquisitions editor: Joseph Heider
Interior design: Linda Conway
Cover design: LOMA's Graphics Dept.
Manufacturing buyer: Ed O'Dougherty

For our wives, Joan and Nancy

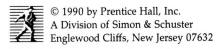

© 1990 by Prentice Hall, Inc.
A Division of Simon & Schuster
Englewood Cliffs, New Jersey 07632

Printed in the United States of America
10 9 8 7 6 5 4 3 2 1

ISBN 0-13-005273-6

Prentice Hall International (UK) Limited, *London*
Prentice Hall of Australia Pty. Limited, *Sydney*
Prentice Hall Canada Inc., *Toronto*
Prentice Hall Hispanoamericana, S.A., *Mexico*
Prentice Hall of India Private Limited, *New Delhi*
Prentice Hall of Japan, Inc., *Tokyo*
Simon & Schuster Asia Pte. Ltd., *Singapore*
Editora Prentice Hall do Brasil, Ltda., *Rio de Janeiro*

Brief Contents

Contents

Part Three
Accounting for Noncash Assets and Liabilities 309

Part Four
Generally Accepted Accounting Principles 461

Part Five
Accounting for Partnerships and Corporations 495

Appendices

Glossary *G-1*

Index *I-1*

Foreword

LOMA is proud to present this special edition of Horngren and Harrison's **Accounting** for use in the FLMI Insurance Education Program. This edition of the text is part of the assigned reading for FLMI Course 7 — Accounting in Life and Health Insurance Companies — and includes only the first 15 chapters of the regular edition of the Horngren and Harrison text. The LOMA edition of **Accounting** is designed to provide FLMI students with a background in basic financial accounting practices in order to prepare them for the material in the insurance accounting segment of FLMI Course 7.

Accounting has more exercises and problems than any other leading textbook in the field. Developed over a five-year period, **Accounting** was carefully class-tested at 65 colleges and universities before being offered in the FLMI Program. The book contains many fine learning aids. For example, each chapter includes:

- learning objectives, which appear both at the beginning of every chapter and in the margin beside relevant chapter material
- detailed chapter summaries
- self-study questions with answers and page number references to the text that supports each answer
- lists of key terms, each referenced by the page number on which the term is discussed

Most chapters also include summary problems with detailed solutions. These problems generally appear in the middle and at the end of each chapter and provide students with immediate feedback on what they have learned. A complete glossary appears at the end of the book. And, as an extra feature, the four-color format makes this book easier and more interesting to read than most accounting texts.

A number of individuals in LOMA's Life Management Institute deserve special thanks for their efforts toward helping us secure this customized edition. Robert J. Bowsher, FLMI, ALHC, reviewed over 25 texts in helping us select Horngren and Harrison's **Accounting.** Ernest L. Martin, Ph.D., FLMI, Director, Examinations Department, also reviewed several texts included in our list of final candidates. Robert D. Land, FLMI, helped coordinate with Prentice Hall production on the special LOMA edition. William H. Rabel, Ph.D., FLMI, CLU, Senior Vice President, provided much support and leadership.

LOMA would also like to thank Maura M. Vill, Corporate Sales Account Executive; Terri Peterson, Accounting Editor; and Esther S. Koehn, Production Editor at Prentice Hall, for their assistance and cooperation on behalf of this special edition.

Dennis W. Goodwin, FLMI
Manager, Curriculum Department
Life Management Institute — LOMA

The Class-Test Edition

To ensure that we have delivered to you a completely error-free text, we extended the development process of **Accounting** and established the *Prentice Hall Class-Testing Program.* Over sixty community colleges and universities—listed below—participated. Instructors at these educational institutions taught their students from our limited first printing of **Accounting.** *Each chapter* of Accounting has been thoroughly checked by your colleagues and their students. Any errors found by instructors or students and sent to Prentice Hall have been corrected in this second printing—the *Class-Test Edition.* Copies of the first printing have been destroyed.

The authors and the publisher wish to thank the following people—your colleagues and their students—for participating in the *Prentice Hall Class-Testing Program.*

Fred Baird and his students
Austin Community College

Gordon Bell and his students
Florida Atlantic University

Walter Berry and his students
Old Dominion University

Allen B. Bess and his students
University of Evansville

Earl Biggett and his students
Edison Community College

David Blummer and his students
West Virginia Northern Community College

Arthur Braza and his students
Dean Junior College

Philip Brown and his students
Harding University

Charles Buckley and his students
University of Scranton

Sarah Brown and her students
University of North Alabama, University Station

Eric Carlsen and his students
Kean College

Ray Carreon and his students
Fullerton College

Barbara Carter and her students
Pensacola Junior College

Matthew Coyne and his students
Dominican College

Billie Cunningham and her students
Collin County Community College

Deborah Davis and her students
Hampton University

Larry C. Davis and his students
Southwest Virginia Community College

Fred Dial and his students
Stephen F. Austin University

David Doran and his students
West Virginia University

Steve Driver and his students
Horry-Georgetown Technical College

William Eberle and his students
Community College of Philadelphia

Anthony Falgioni and his students
State University of New York, Fredonia

Russell Ferrara and his students
Bryant College

Patrick J. Flynn and his students
Baldwin Wallace College

Marilyn Fuller and her students
Paris Junior College

Mohammed Gaber and his students
State University of New York, Plattsburgh

Lucille Genduso and her students
Nova University

James Genseal and his students
Joliet Junior College

Joyce Griffin and her students
Kansas City Community College

Tom Harrison and his students
Baylor University

Ruby Hayes and her students
Virginia State University

Delmer Hylton and his students
Wake Forest University

George Johnson and his students
Norfolk State University

Becky Jones and her students
Baylor University

Mike Kalphat and his students
Barry University

James Krause and his students
University of Tampa

Ken Larson and his students
Adelphi University

Joan Lawrence and her students
Fairmont State College

Carl Leggett and his students
Valdosta State College

Larry Lipner and his students
Barry University

Ken Mark and his students
Kansas City Community College

Frances McNair and her students
Mississippi State University

Tony Merlonghi and his students
Napa Valley College

Patty Mills and her students
Indiana State University

Bill Nalepka and his students
University of Arkansas

Lee Nicholas and his students
University of Northern Iowa

William Olson and his students
Wagner College

Ed Pauley and his students
West Virginia State College

Grace Peng and her students
Muskingum Area Technical College

Ida Pound and her students
College of Alemeda

Fabiola Rubio and his students
El Paso Community College

Dan Rutz and his students
West Virginia Institute of Technology

Wallace Satchell and his students
St. Phillips College

Walter Schimpf and his students
Dowling College

David Schmedel and his students
Amarillo College

William Shaver and his students
J. Sargeant Reynolds Community
College

Lee E. Stokes and his students
Wake Forest University

Norman Sunderman and his students
Angelo State University

Robin Turner and her students
University of North Carolina,
Greensboro

James Walden and his students
Sinclair Community College

Bea Wallace and her students
University of Texas

Connie Wedemeyer and her students
McClennan Community College

David Weiner and his students
University of San Francisco

Betsy Willis and her students
Baylor University

The Business Context of
ACCOUNTING

To enhance our presentation of accounting, we set out to create a business context for the student. As accounting educators, we know that students benefit from perceiving accounting as more than mere numbers set apart from the rest of their lives and education. We have constructed this business context in two ways.

(1) As often as possible, we have integrated real-world companies and their data into our text and assignment material. Students reading about companies familiar to them find the material more interesting and also develop a deeper appreciation for accounting's importance in today's business world. We have not used boxes to set aside this real-world material. Our references to the world of business are woven into our text narrative.

(2) When information drawn from real companies would be too advanced for introductory students, we have illustrated the accounting point at hand by using realistic examples, building a framework of relevance that makes learning the topic more inviting for the student.

The following list presents only a sampling of how our narrative creates a business context in Chapter 1, *Accounting and Its Environment*. We invite readers to examine this chapter and other chapters to see how we incorporate the world of business throughout the entire book.

Chapter 1

p. 1. A student's decision about which college to attend depends in part on accounting information, including the costs and benefits of various education choices.

p. 2. Investors and creditors use accounting information reported in *The Wall Street Journal, Business Week, Forbes,* and *Fortune.*

p. 4. Private accountants may work for a local department store, the McDonald's restaurant chain, or the Eastman Kodak Company.

p. 5. Price Waterhouse estimated that it took 630,720 hours—72 years of nonstop work—to complete one audit.

p. 7. Procter & Gamble and General Electric are leaders in budgeting. Motorola, Bank of America, and 3M Company have internal auditors.

p. 9. To illustrate the entity concept, the income from Mazzio's personal business dealings is distinguished from his pizzeria's operations.

p. 12. Gary Lyon, CPA, is introduced. His accounting practice is used to illustrate proprietorships throughout Chapters 1 through 4.

p. 20. Campus Apartment Locators, owned by Jill Smith, is the subject of a *Summary Problem for Your Review,* which asks students to record transactions and prepare financial statements.

p. 25. In Exercise 1-2, students use the accounting equation to analyze the first month's events for the medical practice of Gloria Hill, M.D.

p. 26. Exercise 1-5 uses the business of Fadal Travel Agency to focus on income statement preparation.

p. 27. Stevens Interiors in Problem 1-1A provides the data with which students analyze transactions and prepare financial statements.

p. 28. In Problem 1-2A, Zane Jones, attorney, opens up his own law office. Students are tested on the entity concept, transaction analysis, and the accounting equation using his business.

p. 36. The *Decision Problem* centers on whether to loan money to Butler Department Store or to Nielsen Home Decorators.

p. 37. The *Financial Statement Problem* requires students to turn to the actual balance sheet of Gulf+Western Inc., which appears in Appendix C, and asks them to write the accounting equation at October 31, 1987. Many chapters feature a *Financial Statement Problem,* which ties the chapter's topic directly to Gulf+Western's actual financial statements.

Preface

Accounting: LOMA Edition provides full introductory coverage of financial accounting. In content and emphasis, instructors will find that **Accounting** is in the mainstream for courses in introductory accounting. This book focuses on the most widely used accounting theory and practice. This text and its supplements supply the most effective tools available for learning fundamental accounting concepts and procedures.

Clarity and Accuracy

Two themes have directed our writing of this text—*clarity* and *accuracy*. We believe that we have produced the clearest prose, learning objectives, exhibits, definitions, and assignment material for courses in principles of accounting. Students will find this book easy to study. We have assumed that students have no previous education in accounting or business.

The contributions of technical reviewers, general reviewers, and class testers and their students have guided us in writing an accurate text. We and the publishers have sought input on our work from an unprecedented number of accounting educators and students in order to publish a book that meets your strict demands for accuracy.

Distinctive Features

Accounting offers many features that make this text special and superior.

1. **Accounting** has more—and better—exercises and problems than the leading competitors. Exercises and problems tie directly with the text in terminology, setup, and difficulty level. They progress from simple to complex, from short to long.
2. The emphasis on real-world examples promotes student interest.
3. The four-color design enlivens and eases learning. A strong program of visual features—exhibits and tables—helps reinforce the text. Note that the two-tone beige color in exhibits denotes financial statements. The green color in exhibits is used with ledgers, journals, work sheets, and the like. The learning objectives appear with a purple tint at the chapter's opening and in the text. Key headings appear in blue.
4. Appendix A: Mathematical Presentations, presents the mathematical operations essential to accounting. Students may refer to this appendix to refresh their knowledge of necessary math skills.

5. Appendix B: Reversing Entries, offers instructors the opportunity to teach reversing entries. This appendix is presented in a standard text chapter format, complete with learning objectives and assignment material.

Chapter Organization

1. Each chapter begins with *Learning Objectives,* which also appear in the margin, keyed to the relevant chapter material.

2. Most chapters offer two *Summary Problems for Your Review.* Each *Summary Problem* includes its fully worked-out solution. These features, which generally appear at the halfway point and at the end of each chapter, provide students with immediate feedback and serve as key review aids.

3. Each chapter presents three important tools for student review. A text *Summary* recaps the chapter discussion. *Self-Study Questions* allow students to test their understanding of the chapter. The text that supports the answer is referenced by page number, and the answers appear on the last page of the chapter. *Accounting Vocabulary* presents the key terms introduced in the chapter, referenced by page number. A complete Glossary, also with terms keyed by page number, appears at the end of the book.

4. *Assignment Material* is more varied and plentiful than in competing texts. *Questions* (covering the major definitions, concepts, and procedures) may be assigned as homework or used to promote in-class discussion. **Accounting** has more exercises and more problems than the competitors. *Exercises,* identified by topic area, cover the full spectrum of the chapter text. These "short problems" allow instructors to cover a wide range of topics in a limited time. *Problems,* also identified by topic area, come in A and B sets. The two sets allow instructors to vary assignments from term to term and to solve the A or B problem in class and assign the related problem for homework. Those exercises and problems that can be solved using the Lotus® 1-2-3 or Microsoft Excel templates are designated by a computer disk.

5. Each chapter presents a *Decision Problem,* which helps students to develop critical thinking skills. Analysis, interpretation, and determining a course of action are ordinarily required.

6. Most chapters feature a *Financial Statement Problem.* In these problems, the chapter's subject matter is directly linked to the actual financial statements of Gulf+Western Inc., which appears in Appendix C. As students progress through the course, they will grow increasingly comfortable with the real-world financial report of a large company.

The Supplements Package

We have a far-reaching, highly developed package of teaching and learning tools to supplement the text. A team of twenty-seven contributors, five editors, five coordinators, and dozens of reviewers devoted hundreds of hours to perfecting the supplements. The coordinators are professional accounting teachers who worked with the contributors and editors to ensure maximum instructional value, accuracy, and consistency with the text and within the supplements package. All of the supplements are uniquely useful, and fuller descriptions of them are available in the *Annotated Instructor's Edition* and from the publisher's representatives.

Resources for the Instructor

Annotated Instructor's Edition
Solutions Manuals
Test Bank and Achievement Tests
Prentice Hall Test Generator Version 3.0
Telephone Test-Preparation Service
Solutions & Teaching Transparencies
Electronic Transparencies
Instructor's Resource Package

Resources for the Student

Study Guide
Videos
Manual and Computerized Practice Sets
Software Packages

Acknowledgments

The authors and publisher wish to thank our many reviewers, whose contributions have meant so much to this project:

Neal Adkins
Marshall University

Harold Averkamp
University of Wisconsin, Whitewater

James Barnhart
Ball State University

Martin Batross
Franklin University

Deborah Boswell
University of North Carolina, Greensboro

David Bourque
Middlesex College

Nancy Boyd
Middle Tennessee State University

Lloyd Buckwell, Jr.
Indiana University, Northwest

Eric Carlson
Kean College

Janet Cassagio
Nassau Community College

Judith Cassidy
Louisiana State University

Leo Chiantelli
Shasta College

Judith Considine
Rutgers University, New Brunswick

James F. Cook
University of Texas at Arlington

Judith Cook
Grossmont Community College

Pauline Corn
Virginia Polytechnic Institute

Art Croisette
Saddleback College

Joyce Dean
Baylor University

Walter Doehring
Genesee Community College

Kathy Dow
Boston University

Richard Fern
Eastern Kentucky University

Joseph Ford
Mesa Community College

Louis H. Gilles
USC—Coastal Carolina College
(Retired)

Max Godwin
Southwest Texas State University

Edward Gordon
Triton College

Diane Green
Sam Houston State University

Don Green
State University of New York,
Farmingdale

Raymond Green
Texas Tech University

B. B. Griffith
Odessa College

Nancy Grzesik
Chesapeake Business Institute

Larry Hagler
Mississippi State University

Gloria Halpern
Montgomery College, Rockville

Gaylon Halverson
University of Northern Iowa

Joseph Hampton
American University

Dorothy Dean Harris
J. Sargeant Reynolds Community College,
Parham

Linda Herrington
Community College of Allegheny County

Carl High
New York City Technical College

George Holdren
University of Nebraska, Lincoln

Cynthia Holloway
Tarrant County Junior College

W. Clyde Hopkins
Memphis State University

Fred A. Jacobs
Georgia State University

Letha Jeanpierre
DeAnza College

Becky Jones
Baylor University

Edward Kelly
Delaware Technical and Community
College

Sandra Knecht
Florida Community College

Anthony Krzystofik
University of Massachusetts, Amherst

Kris Lawyer
North Carolina State University

Albert Lew
Wright State University

Dale Martin
Wake Forest University

Dianna Matthew
Ball State University

Emily Miklis
Cuyahoga Community College

Helen Miller
Baylor University

Michael Milliren
Milwaukee Area Technical College

John Minch
Cabrillo College

Jane Murden
University of North Carolina, Greensboro

Ravi C. Narayan
Northern Virginia Community College

Lois Anne New
Sam Houston State University

Mary Ann Prater
Clemson University

Agnes Price
University of North Carolina, Greensboro

Patrick Reihing
Nassau Community College

Arthur T. Roberts
University of Baltimore

Scott Sandstrom
College of the Holy Cross

Nathan Schmukler
C. W. Post

Janice Shields
University of Maine, Orono

Paul J. Shinal
Cayuga Community College

Ben Shlaes
Des Moines Area Community College

Robert Spear
University of North Carolina, Charlotte

Beverly Terry
Central Piedmont Community College

Phyllis Webster
University of North Carolina, Greensboro

Robert Wennagel
College of the Mainland

Betsy Willis
Baylor University

Deanne Winiarski
Western Carolina University

Ray Winn
El Paso Community College

Among the many people at Prentice Hall who helped to publish this book are Linda Albelli, Sara Colacurto, Linda Conway, Stephen Deitmer, Lisa Garboski, Deborah Garvin, Jackie Hartwick, Joseph Heider, Irene Hess, Jeanne Hoeting, Dennis Hogan, Joanne Jimenez, Gary June, Esther Koehn, Susanna Lesan, Raymond Mullaney, Asha Rohra, Susan Seuling, Beth Stoll, Jacqueline Vernaglia, and Julie Warner. Elsie Young likewise deserves our thanks.

Charles T. Horngren
Stanford, California

Walter T. Harrison, Jr.
Waco, Texas

Accounting and Its Environment

Accounting has been called "the language of business." Perhaps a better term is "the language of financial decisions." The better you understand the language, the better you can manage the financial aspects of living. Personal financial planning, investments, loans, car payments, income taxes, and many other aspects of daily life are based on accounting. A recent survey indicates that business managers believe it is more important for college students to learn accounting than any other subject. Other surveys show that persons trained in accounting and finance make it to the top of their organizations in greater numbers than persons trained in any other field. Indeed, accounting is an important subject.

Decisions and Accounting

Do you make decisions that have a financial impact? Your answer is undoubtedly yes. Regardless of your roles in life — student, head of household, investor, manager, politician — you will find a knowledge of accounting helpful. The major purpose of this book is to help you learn to use accounting information to make informed decisions. Individuals who can do so have a great advantage over those who cannot.

As a student you must decide whether to attend a community college, a four-year college, or a university. And how are you going to finance your education? To make these decisions you weigh the costs and benefits of the various educational choices. These decisions are largely accounting matters. Accounting is also used to form a financial picture of businesses that range from a corner pharmacy to giant companies such as IBM and General Motors. Being able to understand their financial statements will help you make wise investment decisions.

OBJECTIVE 1
Define Accounting

What Is Accounting?

Accounting is the system that measures business activities, processes that information into reports, and communicates these findings to decision makers. **Financial statements** are the documents that report on an individual's or an organization's business in monetary amounts.

Is our business making a profit? Should we start up a new line of women's clothing? Are sales strong enough to warrant opening a new branch outlet? The most intelligent answers to business questions like these use accounting information. Decision makers use the information to develop sound business plans. As new programs affect the business's activities, accounting takes the company's financial pulse beat. The cycle continues as the accounting system measures the results of activities and reports the results to decision makers.

Bookkeeping is a procedural element of accounting as arithmetic is a procedural element of mathematics. Increasingly, people are using computers to do much of the detailed bookkeeping work at all levels—in households, business, and organizations of all types. Exhibit 1-1 illustrates the role of accounting in business.

OBJECTIVE 2
Identify users of
accounting information

Users of Accounting Information

Most of the material in this book describes business situations, but the principles of accounting apply to the financial considerations of individuals as well. The following sections discuss the range of people and groups who use accounting information.

Individuals.　People use accounting information in day-to-day affairs to manage their bank accounts, to evaluate job prospects, to make investments, and to decide whether to rent or to buy a house.

Businesses.　Managers of businesses use accounting information to set goals for their organizations, to evaluate their progress toward those goals, and to take corrective action if necessary. Decisions based on accounting information may include which building and equipment to purchase, how much merchandise inventory to keep on hand, and how much cash to borrow.

Investors and Creditors.　Investors provide the money that businesses need to begin operations. To decide whether to help start a new venture, potential investors evaluate what income they can reasonably expect on their investment. This means analyzing the financial statements of the new business. Those people who do invest monitor the progress of the business by analyzing the company's financial statements and by keeping up with its developments in the business press—for example, *The Wall Street Journal, Business Week, Forbes,* and *Fortune.* Accounting reports are a major source of information for the business press.

EXHIBIT 1-1 *The Accounting System: The Flow of Information*

Before making a loan, potential lenders determine the borrower's ability to meet scheduled payments. This evaluation includes a projection of future operations, which is based on accounting information.

Government Regulatory Agencies. Most organizations face government regulation. For example, the Securities and Exchange Commission (SEC), a federal agency, requires businesses to disclose certain financial information to the investing public. The SEC, like many government agencies, bases its regulatory activity in part on the accounting information it receives from firms.

Taxing Authorities. Local, state, and federal governments levy taxes on individuals and businesses. The amount of the tax is figured using accounting information. Businesses determine their sales tax based on their accounting records that show how much they have sold. Individuals and businesses compute their income tax based on how much money their records show they have earned.

Nonprofit Organizations. Nonprofit organizations—such as churches, most hospitals, government agencies, and colleges, which operate for purposes other than to earn a profit—use accounting information in much the same way that profit-oriented businesses do. Both profit organizations and nonprofit organizations deal with budgets, payrolls, rent payments, and the like—all from the accounting system.

Other users. Employees and labor unions may make wage demands based on the accounting information that shows their employer's reported income. Consumer groups and the general public are also interested in the amount of income that businesses earn. For example, during times of fuel shortages consumer groups have charged that oil companies have earned "obscene profits." On a more positive note, newspapers report "improved profit pictures" of companies as the nation emerges from an economic recession. Such news, based on accounting information, is related to our standard of living.

The Development of Accounting Thought _____

Accounting has a long history. Some scholars claim that writing arose in order to record accounting information. Account records date back to the ancient civilizations of China, Babylonia, Greece, and Egypt. The rulers of these civilizations used accounting to keep track of the cost of labor and materials used in building structures like the great pyramids.

Accounting developed further as a result of the information needs of merchants in the city-states of Italy during the 1400s. In that commercial climate the monk Luca Pacioli, a mathematician and friend of Leonardo da Vinci, published the first known description of double-entry bookkeeping in 1494.

The pace of accounting development increased during the Industrial Revolution as the economies of developed countries began to mass-produce goods. Until that time, merchandise had been priced based on managers' hunches about cost, but increased competition required merchants to adopt more sophisticated accounting systems.

In the nineteenth century, the growth of corporations, especially those in the railroad and steel industries, spurred the development of accounting. Corporation owners—the stockholders—were no longer necessarily the managers of their business. Managers had to create accounting systems to report to the owners how well their businesses were doing.

The role of government has led to still more accounting developments. When the federal government started the income tax, accounting supplied the concept of "income." Also, government at all levels has assumed expanded roles in health, education, labor, and economic planning. To ensure that the information that it uses to make decisions is reliable, the government has required strict accountability in the business community.

OBJECTIVE 3

Identify different aspects of the accounting profession

The Accounting Profession _____

Positions in the field of accounting may be divided into several areas. Two general classifications are *public accounting* and *private accounting*. **Public accountants** are those who serve the general public and collect professional fees for their work, much as doctors and lawyers do. Their work includes auditing, income tax planning and preparation, and management consulting. These specialized accounting services are discussed in the next section. Public accountants are a small fraction (about 10 percent) of all accountants. Those public accountants who have met certain professional requirements are designated as **Certified Public Accountants (CPAs).**

Private accountants work for a single business, such as a local department store, the McDonald's restaurant chain, or the Eastman Kodak Company. Charitable organizations, educational institutions, and government agencies also employ private accountants. The chief accounting officer usually has the title of controller, treasurer, or chief financial officer. Whatever the title, this person usually carries the status of vice-president.

Some public accountants pool their talents and work together within a single firm. Most public accounting firms are also called *CPA firms* because most of their professional employees are CPAs. CPA firms vary greatly in size. Some are small businesses, and others are medium-sized partnerships. The largest CPA firms are worldwide partnerships with over 2,000 partners. Such huge firms are necessary because some of their clients are so large and their operations are so complex. For instance, Price Waterhouse, one of the eight largest American CPA firms, has reported that its annual audit of one particular client would take one accountant 630,720 hours of effort—that equals 72 years of nonstop work! Another Price Waterhouse client owns 300 separate corporate entities. All their records are combined into a single set of financial statements. Such time-consuming tasks make a large staff of accountants a necessity.

The eight largest American accounting firms, often called the Big Eight, are, in alphabetical order,

Arthur Andersen & Co.   Ernst & Whinney

Arthur Young & Co.   Peat Marwick Main & Co.

Coopers & Lybrand   Price Waterhouse & Co.

Deloitte Haskins & Sells   Touche Ross & Co.

Although these firms employ only about 12 percent of the 200,000 CPAs in the United States, they audit the financial statements of approximately 85 percent of the 2,600 largest corporations. The top partners in large accounting firms earn about the same amount as the top managers of other large businesses.

Exhibit 1-2 shows the accounting positions within public accounting firms and other organizations. Of special interest in the exhibit is the upward movement of accounting personnel, as the arrows show. In particular, note how accountants may move from positions in public accounting firms to similar or higher positions in industry and government. This is a frequently traveled career path. Because accounting deals with all facets of an organization—such as purchasing, manufacturing, marketing, and distribution—it provides an excellent basis for gaining broad business experience.

Accounting Organizations and Designations _____

The position of accounting in today's business world has created the need for control over the professional, educational, and ethical standards for accountants.

The *American Institute of Certified Public Accountants (AICPA)* is the national

EXHIBIT 1-2 *Accounting Positions within Organizations*

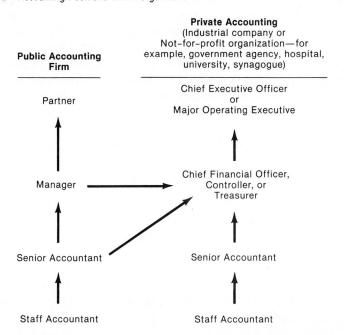

professional organization of CPAs. A CPA is a professional accountant who earns this title through a combination of education, qualifying experience, and an acceptable score on a written national examination that takes approximately three days. The AICPA prepares and grades the examination and gives the results to the individual states, which then issue licenses that enable qualifying people to practice accounting as CPAs. CPAs must also be of high moral character and must conduct their professional practices according to a code of professional conduct. Other nations have similar arrangements, but some use the designation *Chartered Accountant* in place of *Certified Public Accountant.*

The AICPA also develops accounting and auditing principles. The Auditing Standards Board of the AICPA formulates generally accepted auditing standards, which govern the way CPAs perform audits. The AICPA publishes a monthly professional journal, the *Journal of Accountancy.*

State societies of CPAs are professional organizations, much like the AICPA, whose jurisdictions are limited to their respective states. Each state has a state board of accountancy, which administers the state laws that regulate the practice of accounting within its borders. State boards of accountancy, not the AICPA, issue CPA certificates to qualifying individuals.

The *Financial Accounting Standards Board (FASB)* is the body that formulates **generally accepted accounting principles (GAAP).** These principles, which we discuss later in this chapter, are the most important accounting guidelines. The FASB also issues documents called *financial accounting standards*, which are to financial accounting what government laws are to our general conduct. The FASB, composed of seven members, is governed by the Financial Accounting Foundation and is not a part of the AICPA or any other organization.

The *National Association of Accountants (NAA)* focuses on the practice of management accounting, the branch of accounting that is designed to help manage a business. A *CMA*—Certified Management Accountant—earns this designation much as a CPA does but under the direction of the NAA. The NAA publishes the journal *Management Accounting.*

Like the NAA, the *Financial Executives Institute (FEI)* is active in management accounting. The FEI's journal is the *Financial Executive.*

The *CIA*—Certified Internal Auditor—receives this designation from the *Institute of Internal Auditors (IIA).* This organization publishes the journal *The Internal Auditor.*

The *American Accounting Association (AAA)* focuses on the academic and research aspects of accounting. A high percentage of its members are professors. The AAA publishes a quarterly journal, *The Accounting Review.*

The *Securities and Exchange Commission (SEC)* is an agency of the United States government with the legal power to set and enforce accounting and auditing standards. The SEC has delegated much of this authority to the private sector (through the FASB and the AICPA).

The *Internal Revenue Service (IRS)*, another federal agency, has the responsibility of enforcing the tax laws and of collecting the revenue needed to finance the operations of the government. Since it focuses primarily on taxes, the IRS's main impact is on taxation.

Specialized Accounting Services

Because accounting affects people in many different fields, public accounting and private accounting include specialized services.

Public Accounting

Auditing is the accounting profession's most significant service to the public. An audit is the independent examination that assures the reliability of the accounting reports that management prepares and submits to investors, creditors, and others outside the business. In carrying out an audit, CPAs from outside a business examine the business's financial statements. If the CPAs believe that these documents are a fair presentation of the business's operations, the CPAs give a professional opinion stating that the firm's financial statements are in accordance with generally accepted accounting principles, which is the standard. Why is the audit so important? Creditors considering loans want assurance that the facts and figures the business submits are reliable. Stockholders, who have invested in the business, need to know that the financial picture management shows them is complete. Government agencies need accurate information from businesses.

Tax accounting has two aims: complying with the tax laws and minimizing taxes to be paid. Because income tax rates range as high as 28 percent for individuals and 34 percent for corporations, reducing income tax is an important management consideration. Tax work by accountants consists of preparing tax returns and planning business transactions in order to minimize taxes. CPAs advise individuals on what types of investments to make and on how to structure their transactions.

Management consulting is the catchall term that describes the wide scope of advice CPAs provide to help managers run a business. As CPAs conduct audits, they look deep into a business's operations. With the insight they gain, they often make suggestions for improvements in the business's management structure and accounting systems. (We discuss these areas of accounting in the next section.) Management consulting is the fastest-growing service provided by accountants.

Private Accounting

Cost accounting analyzes a business's costs to help managers control expenses. Traditionally, cost accounting has emphasized manufacturing costs, but it is increasingly concerned with the cost of selling the goods. Good cost accounting records guide managers in pricing their products to achieve greater profits. Also, cost accounting information shows management when a product is not profitable and should be dropped.

Budgeting sets sales and profit goals and develops detailed plans—called budgets—for achieving those goals. Many companies regard their budgeting activities as one of the most important aspects of their accounting systems. Some of the most successful companies in the United States have been pioneers in the field of budgeting—Procter & Gamble and General Electric, for example.

Information systems design identifies the organization's information needs, both internal and external. It then develops and implements the system to meet those needs. Accounting information systems help control the organization's operations. Flow charts and manuals that describe the various functions of the business and the placement of responsibility with specific employees are parts of system design.

Internal auditing is performed by a business's own accountants. Many large organizations—Motorola, Bank of America, and 3M among them—maintain a staff of internal auditors. These accountants evaluate the firm's own accounting and management systems. Their aim is to improve operating efficiency and to ensure that employees and departments follow management's procedures and plans.

EXHIBIT 1-3 *Accounting*

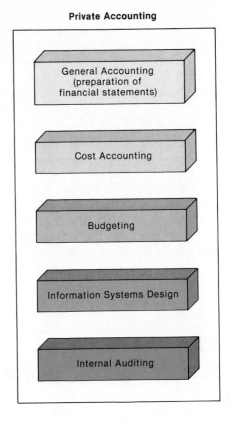

Exhibit 1-3 summarizes these accounting specializations. They may also be grouped under the headings financial accounting and management accounting.

Financial accounting provides information to people outside the firm. Creditors and stockholders, for example, are not part of the day-to-day management of the company. Likewise, government agencies, such as the SEC, and the general public are external users of a firm's accounting information. Chapters 2 through 15 of this book deal primarily with financial accounting.

Management accounting generates confidential information for internal decision makers, such as top executives, department heads, college deans, and hospital administrators.

Types of Business Organizations

OBJECTIVE 4

Identify the three different types of business organizations

Businesses take one of three forms of organization, and in some cases the accounting procedures depend on the organization form. Therefore, you should understand differences between a proprietorship, a partnership, and a corporation.

A **proprietorship** has a single owner, called the proprietor, who is usually also the manager. Proprietorships tend to be small retail establishments and individual professional businesses, such as those of physicians, attorneys, and accountants. From the accounting viewpoint each proprietorship is distinct from its proprietor. Thus the accounting records of the proprietorship do *not* include records of the proprietor's personal affairs.

A **partnership** joins two or more individuals together as co-owners. Each owner is a partner. Many retail establishments, as well as some professional organizations of physicians, attorneys, and accountants, are partnerships. Most partnerships are small and medium-sized, but some are gigantic, running to 2,000 partners. Accountants treat the partnership as a separate organization, distinct from the personal affairs of each partner.

A **corporation** is a business owned by **stockholders.** The business becomes a corporation when the state approves its articles of incorporation. A corporation is a legal entity, an "artificial person" that conducts its business in its own name. Like the proprietorship and the partnership, the corporation is also an organization with existence separate from its owners.

Accounting Concepts and Principles _____

Accounting practices rest on certain guidelines. The rules that govern how accountants measure, process, and communicate financial information fall under the heading GAAP, which stands for generally accepted accounting principles. Among these rules are the *entity concept,* the *reliability principle,* and the *cost principle.*

The Entity Concept

The most basic concept in accounting is that of the **entity.** An accounting entity is an organization or a section of an organization that stands apart from other organizations and individuals as a separate economic unit. From an accounting perspective, sharp boundaries are drawn around each entity so as not to confuse its affairs with those of other entities.

Consider Mazzio, a pizzeria owner whose bank account shows a $20,000 balance at the end of the year. Only half of that amount — $10,000 — grew from the business's operations. The other $10,000 arose from the sale of the family motorboat. If Mazzio follows the entity concept, he will account for the money generated by the business — one economic unit — separately from the money generated by the sale of an item belonging not to the business but to himself — a second economic unit. This separation makes it possible to view the business's operating result clearly. The owner knows that the pizzeria did not bring in much money. To make the pizzeria more profitable, Mazzio probably must make some operating changes.

Suppose he disregards the entity concept and treats the full $20,000 amount as income from the pizzeria's operations. He will be misled into believing that the business has performed twice as well as it has. The steps needed to improve the business will likely not be taken.

Consider GM, a huge organization made up of its Chevrolet, Buick, Oldsmobile, Cadillac, and Pontiac divisions. GM management considers each division as a separate accounting entity, and the following example shows why. Suppose sales in the Buick division are dropping drastically. GM would do well to come up with an immediate solution to the problem. But if sales figures from all five divisions are treated as a single lump-sum amount, then management will not even know the company is not selling enough Buicks.

Other accounting entities include professional organizations such as a law firm, a doctor's practice, a hospital, a church or synagogue, a college or university, and a family household. Each entity may have a number of subentities. For example, universities have various colleges like law and business as subentities. Each subentity should be accounted for separately.

OBJECTIVE 5
Apply accounting concepts and principles to business situations

In summary, business transactions should not be confused with personal transactions. Similarly, the transactions of different entities should not be accounted for together. Each entity should be evaluated separately.

The Reliability (or Objectivity) Principle

Accounting records and statements are based on the most reliable data available so that they will be as accurate and as useful as possible. This is the *reliability principle*. Reliable data are verifiable. They may be confirmed by any independent observer. Ideally, then, accounting records are based on information that flows from activities that are documented by objective evidence. Without the reliability principle, also called the objectivity principle, accounting records would be based on whims and opinions and would be subject to dispute.

Suppose that you start a stereo shop, and in order to have a place for operations, you transfer a small building to the business. You believe the building is worth $55,000. To confirm its value, you hire two real estate professionals, who appraise the building at $47,000. Is $55,000 or $47,000 the more reliable estimate of the building's value? The real estate appraisal of $47,000 is, because it is supported by independent, objective observation.

The Cost Principle

The *cost principle* states that assets and services that are acquired should be recorded at their actual cost (also called historical cost). Even though the purchaser may believe the price paid is a bargain, the item is recorded at the price paid in the transaction.

Suppose your stereo shop purchases some stereo equipment from a supplier who is going out of business. Assume you get a good deal on this purchase and pay only $2,000 for merchandise that would have cost you $3,000 elsewhere. The cost principle requires you to record this merchandise at its actual cost of $2,000, not the $3,000 that you believe the equipment to be worth.

The cost principle also holds that the accounting records should maintain the historical cost of an asset for as long as the business holds the asset. Why? Because cost is a reliable measure. Suppose your store holds the stereo equipment for six months. During that time, stereo prices increase, and the equipment can be sold for $3,500. Should its accounting value—the figure "on the books"—be the actual cost of $2,000 or the current market value of $3,500? According to the cost principle, the accounting value of the equipment remains at actual cost, $2,000.

As we continue to explore accounting, we will discuss other principles that guide accountants.

OBJECTIVE 6	**The Accounting Equation**

OBJECTIVE 6
Use the accounting equation to describe an organization

Accountants measure business activities and process those data to turn out financial statements. Their basic tool is the accounting equation. The accounting equation shows the equality of assets and claims to assets, called equities:

$$\text{ASSETS} = \text{EQUITIES}$$

Assets are the economic resources a business owns that are expected to be of benefit in the future. Cash, office supplies, merchandise, furniture, land, and building are examples.

Equities are the legal and economic claims to the assets. For example, a creditor who has loaned money to a business has a claim—a legal right, in fact—to a part of the assets until the business pays the debt. Also, the owner of the business has a claim to those assets that he or she has invested in the business. Equities logically divide into two categories: claims owing to people outside the business (the creditors), and claims held by people inside the business (those who own it).

"Outsider" claims. These are economic obligations—debts—payable to outsiders, and they are called **liabilities.** Debts owed to banks and lenders, for example, are liabilities. These outside parties are called *creditors.*

"Insider" claims. These claims belong to the owner of the business, and they are called **owner's equity,** or **capital.**

Adding these two categories—liabilities and owner's equity—to the accounting equation gives us:

Liabilities plus owner's equity equals total equities, so we can express the accounting equation in its most common form and the one that we will use throughout the book:

ASSETS = LIABILITIES + OWNER'S EQUITY

Let's take a closer look at the elements that make up the accounting equation. Suppose you run a business that supplies meat to fast-food restaurants. Some customers may pay you in cash when you deliver the meat. Cash is an asset. Other customers may buy on credit and promise to pay you within a certain time after delivery. This promise is also an asset because it is an economic resource that will benefit you in the future when you receive cash from the customer. This promise is called an **account receivable.** If the promise that entitles you to receive cash in the future is written out, it is called a **note receivable.** All receivables are assets.

The fast-food restaurant's promise to pay you for the meat it purchases on credit creates a debt for the restaurant. This liability is an **account payable,** which means that the debt is not written out. Instead it is backed up by the reputation and the credit standing of the restaurant and its owner. A written promise of future payment is called a **note payable.** All payables are liabilities.

Owner's equity is the amount of the assets that remains after subtracting liabilities. A rearrangement of the accounting equation shows this relationship:

ASSETS − LIABILITIES = OWNER'S EQUITY

Accounting for Business Transactions

In accounting terms, a **transaction** is any event that *both* affects the financial position of the business entity *and* may be reliably recorded. Many events may affect a company, including (1) elections, (2) economic booms and recessions, (3) purchases and sales of merchandise inventory, (4) payment of rent, (5) collection of cash from customers, and so on. However, the accountant records only events with effects that can be measured reliably as transactions.

Which of the above five events would the accountant record? The answer is events (3), (4), and (5) because their dollar amounts can be measured reliably. Dollar effects of elections and economic trends cannot be measured reliably, so they would not be recorded even though they may affect the business more than events (3), (4), and (5).

To illustrate accounting for business transactions, let's assume that Gary Lyon has recently become a CPA and opens his own accounting practice. Because the business has a single owner, it is called a proprietorship.

We now consider eleven events and analyze each in terms of its effect on the accounting equation of Gary Lyon's accounting practice. Transaction analysis is the essence of accounting.

Transaction 1.   Gary Lyon invests $50,000 of his money to begin the business. Specifically, he deposits $50,000 in a bank account entitled Gary Lyon, CPA. The effect of this transaction on the accounting equation of the business entity is

Assets	=	Liabilities +	Owner's Equity	Type of Owner's Equity Transaction
Cash			Gary Lyon, Capital	
(1) +50,000			+50,000	Owner investment

OBJECTIVE 7

Use the accounting equation to analyze business transactions

The first transaction increases both the assets, in this case Cash, and the owner's equity of the business, Gary Lyon, Capital. The transaction involves no liabilities of the business because it creates no obligation for Lyon to pay an outside party. To the right of the transaction we write "Owner investment" to keep track of the reason for the effect on owner's equity.

Note that the amount on the left side of the equation equals the amount on the right side. This equality must hold for every transaction.

Transaction 2.   Lyon purchases land for a future office location, paying cash of $20,000. The effect of this transaction on the accounting equation is

	Assets		=	Liabilities + Owner's Equity	Type of Owner's Equity Transaction
	Cash	+ Land		Gary Lyon, Capital	
(1)	50,000			50,000	Owner investment
(2)	−20,000	+ 20,000			
Bal.	30,000	20,000		50,000	
	50,000			50,000	

The cash purchase of land increases one asset, Land, and decreases another asset, Cash, by the same amount. After the transaction is completed, Lyon's business has cash of $30,000, land of $20,000, no liabilities, and owner's equity of $50,000. Note that the sums of the balances (which we abbreviate Bal.) on each side of the equation are equal. This equality must always exist.

Transaction 3.   Lyon buys stationery and other office supplies, agreeing to pay $500 within thirty days. This transaction increases the assets and the liabilities of the business. Its effect on the accounting equation is

	Assets				Liabilities +	Owner's Equity	
	Cash	+ Office Supplies +	Land		Accounts Payable +	Gary Lyon, Capital	
Bal.	30,000		20,000	=		50,000	
(3)		+500			+500		
Bal.	30,000	500	20,000		500	50,000	
		50,500				50,500	

The asset affected is office supplies, and the liability is called an account payable. The term *payable* signifies a liability. Since Lyon is obligated to pay $500 in the future, but signs no formal promissory note, we record the liability as an Account Payable, not as a Note Payable. We say that purchases supported by the general credit standing of the buyer are made on *open account*.

Transaction 4. The purpose of business is to increase assets and owner's equity through **revenues,** which are amounts earned by delivering goods or services to customers. Revenues increase owner's equity because they increase the business's assets but not its liabilities. As a result, the owner's interest in the assets of the business increases.

Exhibit 1-4 shows that owner investments and revenues increase the owner's equity of the business.

The exhibit also indicates the types of transactions that decrease owner's equity. Owner withdrawals are those amounts removed from the business by the owner. Withdrawals are the opposite of owner investments. Expenses are the cost of doing business and are the opposite of revenues. Our illustration will also show how to account for expenses and withdrawals. Gary Lyon earns service revenue by providing professional accounting services for his clients. Assume he earns $5,500 and collects this amount in cash. The effect on the accounting equation is an increase in the asset Cash and an increase in Gary Lyon, Capital, as follows:

	Assets				Liabilities +	Owner's Equity	Type of Owner's Equity Transaction
	Cash	+ Office Supplies +	Land		Accounts Payable +	Gary Lyon, Capital	
Bal.	30,000	500	20,000	=	500	50,000	
(4)	+ 5,500					+ 5,500	Service revenue
Bal.	35,500	500	20,000		500	55,500	
		56,000				56,000	

This revenue transaction caused the business to grow, as shown by the increase in total assets and total equities.

Transaction 5. Lyon performs services for a client who does not pay immediately. In return for his accounting services, Lyon receives the client's promise to pay the $3,000 amount within one month. This promise is an asset to Lyon, an account receivable because he expects to collect the cash in the future. In accounting, we say that Lyon performed this service *on account*. When the business performs service for a client or a customer, the business earns revenue regardless of whether it receives cash immediately or expects to collect cash later. This

EXHIBIT 1-4   *Transactions That Increase and Decrease Owner's Equity*

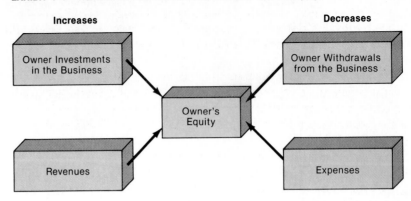

$3,000 of service revenue is as real to Lyon's business as the $5,500 of revenue that he collected immediately in the preceding transaction. Lyon records an increase in the asset accounts receivable and an increase in owner's equity as follows:

		Assets				Liabilities +	Owner's Equity	Type of Owner's Equity Transaction
	Cash	+ Accounts Receivable	+ Office Supplies	+ Land		Accounts Payable +	Gary Lyon, Capital	
Bal.	35,500	0	500	20,000	=	500	55,500	
(5)		+3,000					+ 3,000	Service revenue
Bal.	35,500	3,000	500	20,000		500	58,500	
		59,000					59,000	

Again, this revenue transaction caused the business to grow.

Transaction 6.   In earning revenue a business incurs expenses. **Expenses** are decreases in owner's equity that occur in the course of delivering goods or services to clients. Expenses decrease owner's equity because they use up the business's assets. Expenses include office rent, salaries paid to employees, newspaper advertisements, and utility payments for light, electricity, gas, and so forth. During the month, Lyon pays $2,700 in cash expenses: office rent, $1,100; employee salary, $1,200 (for a part-time assistant); and total utilities, $400. The effect on the accounting equation is

		Assets				Liabilities +	Owner's Equity	Type of Owner's Equity Transaction
	Cash	+ Accounts Receivable	+ Office Supplies	+ Land		Accounts Payable +	Gary Lyon, Capital	
Bal.	35,500	3,000	500	20,000	=	500	58,500	
(6)	− 2,700						− 1,100	Rent expense
							− 1,200	Salary expense
							− 400	Utilities expense
Bal.	32,800	3,000	500	20,000		500	55,800	
		56,300					56,300	

Because expenses have the opposite effect of revenues, they cause the business to shrink, as shown by the smaller amounts of total assets and total equities.

Each expense should be recorded in a separate transaction. Here, for simplicity, they are recorded together. Note that even though the figure $2,700 does not appear on the right-hand side of the equation, the three individual expenses add up to a $2,700 total. As a result, the "balance" of the equation holds, as we know it must.

Businesspeople, Gary Lyon included, run their businesses with the objective of taking in more revenues than they pay out in expenses. An excess of total revenues over total expenses is called **net income, net earnings,** or **net profit.** If total expenses are greater than total revenues, the result is called a **net loss.**

Transaction 7. Lyon pays $400 to the store from which he purchased $500 worth of office supplies in Transaction 3. In accounting, we say that he pays $400 *on account.* The effect on the accounting equation is a decrease in the asset Cash and a decrease in the liability Accounts Payable as follows:

	Cash	+	Accounts Receivable	+	Office Supplies	+	Land	=	Accounts Payable	+	Gary Lyon, Capital
				Assets					Liabilities +		Owner's Equity
Bal.	32,800		3,000		500		20,000		500		55,800
(7)	− 400								−400		
Bal.	32,400		3,000		500		20,000		100		55,800
			55,900							55,900	

The payment of cash on account has no effect on the asset Office Supplies because the payment does not increase or decrease the supplies available to the business.

Transaction 8. Lyon remodels his home at a cost of $30,000, paying cash from his personal funds. This event is a *nonbusiness* transaction. It has no effect on Lyon's accounting practice and therefore is not recorded by the business. It is a transaction of the Gary Lyon *personal* entity, not the Gary Lyon, CPA, *business* entity. We are focusing now solely on the business entity, and this event does not affect it. This transaction illustrates an application of the *entity concept.*

Transaction 9. In Transaction 5, Gary Lyon performed service for a client on account. Lyon now collects $1,000 from the client. We say that Lyon collects the cash *on account.* Lyon will record an increase in the asset Cash. Should he also record an increase in service revenue? No, because Lyon already recorded the revenue when he earned it in Transaction 5. The phrase "collect cash on account" means to record an increase in Cash and a decrease in the asset Accounts Receivable. The effect on the accounting equation is

	Cash	+	Accounts Receivable	+	Office Supplies	+	Land	=	Accounts Payable	+	Gary Lyon, Capital
				Assets					Liabilities +		Owner's Equity
Bal.	32,400		3,000		500		20,000		100		55,800
(9)	+ 1,000		−1,000								
Bal.	33,400		2,000		500		20,000		100		55,800
			55,900							55,900	

Total assets are unchanged from the preceding transaction's total. Why? Because Lyon merely exchanged one asset for another. Also, total equities are unchanged.

Transaction 10.   An individual approaches Lyon about selling a parcel of the land owned by the Gary Lyon, CPA, entity. Lyon and the other person agree to a sale price of $6,000, which is equal to Lyon's cost of the land. Lyon's business sells the land and receives $6,000 cash, and the effect on the accounting equation is

							Liabilities +	Owner's Equity
			Assets			=		
	Cash	+ Accounts Receivable	+ Office Supplies +	Land			Accounts Payable +	Gary Lyon, Capital
Bal.	33,400	2,000	500	20,000			100	55,800
(10)	+ 6,000			− 6,000				
Bal.	39,400	2,000	500	14,000			100	55,800
			55,900					55,900

Transaction 11.   Lyon withdraws $2,100 cash from the business for personal use. The effect on the accounting equation is

							Liabilities +	Owner's Equity	Type of Owner's Equity Transaction
			Assets			=			
	Cash	+ Accounts Receivable	+ Office Supplies +	Land			Accounts Payable +	Gary Lyon, Capital	
Bal.	39,400	2,000	500	14,000			100	55,800	
(11)	− 2,100							− 2,100	Owner withdrawals
Bal.	37,300	2,000	500	14,000			100	53,700	
			53,800					53,800	

Lyon's withdrawal of $2,100 in cash decreases the asset Cash and also the owner's equity of the business.

Does this withdrawal decrease the business entity's holdings? The answer is yes because the cash withdrawn is no longer available for business use after Lyon spends it on food, clothing, home mortgage payments, and so on. The withdrawal does *not* represent a business expense, however, because the cash is used for personal affairs unrelated to the business. We record this decrease in owner's equity as Withdrawals. Another acceptable title is Drawing.

Evaluating Business Transactions _____

Exhibit 1-5 summarizes the 11 preceding transactions. Panel A of the exhibit lists the details of the transactions, and Panel B presents the analysis. As you study the exhibit, note that every transaction maintains the equality:

ASSETS = LIABILITIES + OWNER'S EQUITY

EXHIBIT 1-5 *Analysis of Transactions of Gary Lyon, CPA*

Panel A—Details of transactions

1. Lyon invested $50,000 cash in the business.
2. Paid $20,000 cash for land.
3. Purchased $500 of office supplies on account payable.
4. Received $5,500 cash from clients for accounting service revenue earned.
5. Performed accounting service for a client on account, $3,000.
6. Paid cash expenses: rent, $1,100; employee salary, $1,200; utilities, $400.
7. Paid $400 on the account payable created in Transaction 3.
8. Remodeled his personal residence. This is not a business transaction.
9. Received $1,000 on the account receivable created in Transaction 5.
10. Sold land for cash equal to its cost of $6,000.
11. Withdrew $2,100 cash for personal living expenses.

Panel B—Analysis of transactions

	Cash	Accounts + Receivable +	Office Supplies +	Land		Accounts Payable +	Gary Lyon, Capital	Type of Owner's Equity Transaction
			Assets			**Liabilities**	**Owner's Equity**	
(1)	+50,000						+50,000	Owner investment
Bal.	50,000						50,000	
(2)	−20,000			+20,000				
Bal.	30,000			20,000			50,000	
(3)			+500			+500		
Bal.	30,000		500	20,000		500	50,000	
(4)	+ 5,500						+ 5,500	Service revenue
Bal.	35,500		500	20,000		500	55,500	
(5)		+3,000					+ 3,000	Service revenue
Bal.	35,500	3,000	500	20,000		500	58,500	
(6)	− 2,700				=		− 1,100	Rent expense
							− 1,200	Salary expense
							− 400	Utilities expense
Bal.	32,800	3,000	500	20,000		500	55,800	
(7)	− 400					−400		
Bal.	32,400	3,000	500	20,000		100	55,800	
(8)	Not a business transaction							
(9)	+ 1,000	−1,000						
Bal.	33,400	2,000	500	20,000		100	55,800	
(10)	+ 6,000			− 6,000				
Bal.	39,400	2,000	500	14,000		100	55,800	
(11)	− 2,100						− 2,100	Owner withdrawal
Bal.	37,300	2,000	500	14,000		100	53,700	

53,800 = 53,800

Financial Statements

The analysis of the transactions complete, what is the next step in the accounting process? How does an accountant present the results of the analysis? We now look at the **financial statements.** These business documents report financial information about the entity to persons and organizations outside the business.

The primary financial statements are the (1) balance sheet, (2) income statement, (3) statement of owner's equity, and (4) statement of cash flow. In this chapter, we discuss and illustrate the first three statements.

The **balance sheet** lists all the *assets, liabilities,* and *owner's equity* of an entity as of a specific date, usually the end of a month or a year. The balance sheet is like a snapshot of the entity. For this reason, it is also called the **statement of financial position.**

The **income statement** presents a summary of the *revenues* and *expenses* of an entity for a specific period of time, such as a month or a year. The income statement, also called the **statement of operations,** is like a moving picture of the entity's operations during the period. The income statement holds perhaps the most important single piece of information about a business—its net income, which is revenues minus expenses. If expenses exceed revenues, the result is a net loss for the period.

The **statement of owner's equity** presents a summary of the changes that occurred in the owner's equity of the entity during a specific time period, such as a month or a year. Increases in owner's equity arise from investments by the owner and net income earned during the period. Decreases result from withdrawals by the owner and from a net loss for the period. Net income or net loss comes directly from the income statement. Investments and withdrawals by the owner are capital transactions between the business and its owner, so they do not affect the income statement.

Each financial statement has a heading, which gives the name of the business—in our discussion, Gary Lyon, CPA, the name of the particular statement, and the date or time period covered by the statement. A balance sheet taken at the end of year 19X4 would be dated December 31, 19X4. A balance sheet prepared at the end of March 19X7 is dated March 31, 19X7.

An income statement or a statement of owner's equity covering an annual period ending in December 19X5 is dated For the Year Ended December 31, 19X5. A monthly income statement or statement of owner's equity for September 19X9 has in its heading For the Month Ended September 30, 19X9, Month Ended September 30, 19X9, or For the Month of September 19X9.

Exhibit 1-6 illustrates all three statements. Their data come from the transaction analysis in Exhibit 1-5. We are assuming the transactions occurred during the month of April 19X1. Study the exhibit carefully, because it shows the relationships among the three financial statements.

Observe the following in Exhibit 1-6:

1. The *income statement* for the month ended April 30, 19X1
   a. Reports all *revenues* and all *expenses* during the period. Revenues and expenses are reported only on the income statement.
   b. Reports *net income* of the period if total revenues exceed total expenses, as in the case of Gary Lyon's accounting practice for April. If total expenses exceed total revenues, the result is a net loss.

2. The *statement of owner's equity* for the month ended April 30, 19X1
   a. Opens with the owner's capital balance at the beginning of the period.

EXHIBIT 1-6   *Financial Statements of Gary Lyon, CPA*

Gary Lyon, CPA
Income Statement
Month Ended April 30, 19X1

Revenues:		
Service revenue		$8,500
Expenses:		
Salary expense	$ 1,200	
Rent expense.........................	1,100	
Utilities expense	400	
Total expenses		2,700
Net income...........................		$5,800

①

Gary Lyon, CPA
Statement of Owner's Equity
Month Ended April 30, 19X1

Gary Lyon, capital, April 1, 19X1............	$ 0
Add: Investments by owner	50,000
Net income for the month	5,800
	55,800
Less: Withdrawals by owner................	2,100
Gary Lyon, capital, April 30, 19X1...........	$53,700

②

Gary Lyon, CPA
Balance Sheet
April 30, 19X1

Assets		Liabilities	
Cash	$37,300	Accounts payable......	$ 100
Accounts receivable	2,000	**Owner's Equity**	
Office supplies	500		
Land	14,000	Gary Lyon, capital	53,700
		Total liabilities and	
Total assets...........	$53,800	owner's equity	$53,800

b. Adds *investments by the owner* of the business and also adds *net income* (or subtracts *net loss,* as the case may be). Net income (or net loss) comes directly from the income statement, which includes the effect of all the revenues and all the expenses for the period (see the first arrow).

c. Subtracts *withdrawals by the owner.*

d. Ends with the owner's capital balance at the end of the period.

3. The *balance sheet* at April 30, 19X1, the end of the period
   a. Reports all *assets,* all *liabilities,* and *owner's equity* of the business at the end of the period. No other statement reports assets and liabilities.

   b. Balances. That is, total assets equal the sum of total liabilities plus total owner's equity. This balancing feature gives the balance sheet its name. It is based on the accounting equation.
   c. Reports the owner's ending capital balance, taken directly from the statement of owner's equity (see the second arrow).

Summary Problem for Your Review

Jill Smith opens an apartment-locator business near a college campus. She is the sole owner of the proprietorship, which she names Campus Apartment Locators. During the first month of operations, May 19X1, Smith engages in the following transactions:

a. Smith invests $20,000 of personal funds to start the business.
b. She purchases on account office supplies costing $350.
c. Smith pays cash of $8,000 to acquire a lot next to the campus. She intends to use the land as a future building site for her business office.
d. Smith locates apartments for clients and receives cash of $1,900.
e. She pays $100 on the account payable she created in transaction b.
f. She pays $2,000 of personal funds for a vacation for her family.
g. She pays cash expenses for office rent, $400, and utilities, $100.
h. The business sells office supplies to another business for its cost of $150.
i. Smith withdraws cash of $1,200 for personal use.

Required

1. Record the preceding transactions in terms of their effects on the accounting equation of Campus Apartment Locators. Use Exhibit 1-5 as a guide, but show balances only after the last transaction.
2. Prepare the income statement, statement of owner's equity, and balance sheet of the business after recording the transactions. Use Exhibit 1-6 as a guide.

SOLUTION TO REVIEW PROBLEM

Panel A.   Details of transactions

a. Smith invested $20,000 cash to start the business.
b. Purchased $350 of office supplies on account.
c. Paid $8,000 to acquire land as a future building site.
d. Earned service revenue and received cash of $1,900.
e. Paid $100 on account.
f. Paid for a personal vacation, which is not a business transaction.
g. Paid cash expenses for rent, $400, and utilities, $100.
h. Sold office supplies for cost of $150.
i. Withdrew $1,200 cash for personal use.

Panel B. Analysis of transactions

	Assets					Liabilities +	Owner's Equity	Type of Owner's Equity Transaction
	Cash	+	Office Supplies +	Land		Accounts Payable +	Jill Smith, Capital	
(a)	+20,000						+20,000	Owner investment
(b)			+350			+350		
(c)	− 8,000			+8,000				
(d)	+ 1,900				=		+ 1,900	Service revenue
(e)	− 100					−100		
(f)	Not a business transaction							
(g)	− 500						− 400	Rent expense
							− 100	Utilities expense
(h)	+ 150		−150					
(i)	− 1,200						− 1,200	Owner withdrawal
Bal.	12,250		200	8,000		250	20,200	
		20,450					20,450	

Financial Statements of Campus Apartment Locators

Campus Apartment Locators
Income Statement
Month Ended May 31, 19X1

Revenues:		
Service revenue		$1,900
Expenses:		
Rent expense	$400	
Utilities expense......................................	100	
Total expenses		500
Net income		$1,400

Campus Apartment Locators
Statement of Owner's Equity
Month Ended May 31, 19X1

Jill Smith, capital, May 1, 19X1	$ 0
Add: Investments by owner.....................................	20,000
Net income for the month..............................	1,400
	21,400
Less: Withdrawals by owner	1,200
Jill Smith, capital, May 31, 19X1	$20,200

Campus Apartment Locators
Balance Sheet
May 31, 19X1

Assets		Liabilities	
Cash.....................	$12,250	Accounts payable	$ 250
Office supplies..............	200	**Owner's Equity**	
Land.....................	8,000		
		Jill Smith, capital	20,200
		Total liabilities	
Total assets	$20,450	and owner's equity	$20,450

Summary

Accounting is a system for measuring, processing, and communicating financial information. As the "language of business," accounting helps a wide range of decision makers.

Accounting dates back to ancient civilizations, but its importance to society has been greatest since the Industrial Revolution. Today, accountants serve as CPAs, CMAs, or CIAs in all types of organizations. They offer many specialized services for industrial companies, including general accounting, cost accounting, budgeting, system design, and internal auditing. CPAs in public practice deal with auditing, tax planning and preparation, and management consulting.

The three basic forms of business organization are the proprietorship, the partnership, and the corporation. Whatever the form, accountants use the entity concept to keep the business's records separate from the personal records of the people who run it.

Generally accepted accounting principles—GAAP—guide accountants in their work. Among these guidelines are the entity concept, the reliability principle, and the cost principle.

In its most common form, the accounting equation is

$$\text{ASSETS} = \text{LIABILITIES} + \text{OWNER'S EQUITY}$$

Transactions affect a business's assets, liabilities, and owner's equity. Therefore, transactions are analyzed in terms of their effect on the accounting equation.

The *financial statements* communicate information for decision making by the entity's managers, owners, and creditors and by government agencies. The *income statement* presents a moving picture of the entity's operations in terms of revenues earned and expenses incurred during a specific period. Total revenues minus total expenses equal net income. Net income or net loss answers the question, How much income did the entity earn, or how much loss did it incur during the period? The *statement of owner's equity* reports the changes in owner's equity during the period. The *balance sheet* provides a photograph of the entity's financial standing in terms of its assets, liabilities, and owner's equity at a specific time. It answers the question, What is the entity's financial position?

Self-Study Questions

Test your understanding of the chapter by marking the best answer for each of the following questions:

1. To become a CPA, a person must *(p. 6)*
   a. Graduate from college with a master's degree
   b. Obtain four years of accounting experience
   c. Pass a national examination
   d. Pass an accounting examination that differs from state to state
2. The organization that formulates generally accepted accounting principles is *(p. 6)*
   a. American Institute of Certified Public Accountants (CPAs)
   b. Internal Revenue Service
   c. Financial Accounting Standards Board
   d. National Association of Accountants
3. Which of the following forms of business organization is an "artificial person" and must obtain legal approval from a state to conduct business? *(p. 9)*
   a. Law firm   c. Partnership
   b. Proprietorship   d. Corporation
4. The economic resources that a business owns and expects to be useful to the enterprise are called *(p. 10)*

    a. Assets   c. Owner's equity
    b. Liabilities   d. Receivables

5. A business has assets of $140,000 and liabilities of $60,000. How much is its owner's equity? *(p. 11)*
    a. $0   c. $140,000
    b. $80,000   d. $200,000

6. The purchase of office supplies (or any other asset) on account will *(p. 13)*
    a. Increase an asset and increase a liability
    b. Increase an asset and increase owner's equity
    c. Increase one asset and decrease another asset
    d. Increase an asset and decrease a liability

7. The performance of service for a customer or client and immediate receipt of cash will *(p. 13)*
    a. Increase one asset and decrease another asset
    b. Increase an asset and increase owner's equity
    c. Decrease an asset and decrease a liability
    d. Increase an asset and increase a liability

8. The payment of an account payable (or any other liability) will *(p. 15)*
    a. Increase one asset and decrease another asset
    b. Decrease an asset and decrease owner's equity
    c. Decrease an asset and decrease a liability
    d. Increase an asset and increase a liability

9. The business document that reports assets, liabilities, and owner's equity is called the *(p. 18)*
    a. Financial statement   c. Income statement
    b. Balance sheet   d. Statement of owner's equity

10. The financial statements that are dated for a time period (rather than a specific time) are the *(p. 18)*
    a. Balance sheet and income statement
    b. Balance sheet and statement of owner's equity
    c. Income statement and statement of owner's equity
    d. All financial statements are dated for a time period.

Answers to the Self-Study Questions are at the end of the chapter.

Accounting Vocabulary

Accounting, like many other subjects, has a special vocabulary. It is important that you understand the following terms. They are explained in the chapter and also in the glossary at the end of the book.

accounting *(p. 2)*, account payable *(p. 11)*, account receivable *(p. 11)*, asset *(p. 10)*, auditing *(p. 7)*, balance sheet *(p. 18)*, budgeting *(p. 7)*, capital *(p. 11)*, certified public accountant (CPA) *(p. 4)*, corporation *(p. 9)*, cost accounting *(p. 7)*, entity *(p. 9)*, equities *(p. 11)*, expense *(p. 14)*, financial accounting *(p. 8)*, financial statements *(p. 18)*, generally accepted accounting principles (GAAP) *(p. 6)*, income statement *(p. 18)*, information systems design *(p. 7)*, internal auditing *(p. 7)*, liability *(p. 11)*, management accounting *(p. 8)*, net earnings *(p. 15)*, net income *(p. 15)*, net loss *(p. 15)*, net profit *(p. 15)*, note payable *(p. 11)*, note receivable *(p. 11)*, owner's equity *(p. 11)*, partnership *(p. 8)*, private accountant *(p. 4)*, proprietorship *(p. 8)*, public accountant *(p. 4)*, revenue *(p. 13)*, statement of financial position *(p. 18)*, statement of operations *(p. 18)*, statement of owner's equity *(p. 18)*, stockholder *(p. 9)*, transaction *(p. 11)*.

ASSIGNMENT MATERIAL

Questions

1. Distinguish between accounting and bookkeeping.
2. Identify five users of accounting information and explain how they use it.
3. Where did accounting have its beginning? Who wrote the first known description of bookkeeping? In what year?
4. Name two important reasons for the development of accounting thought.
5. Name three professional titles of accountants. Also give their abbreviations.
6. What organization formulates generally accepted accounting principles? Is this organization a government agency?
7. Name the three principal types of services provided by public accounting firms.
8. How do financial accounting and management accounting differ?
9. Give the name(s) of the owner(s) of a proprietorship, a partnership, and a corporation.
10. Why is the entity concept so important to accounting?
11. Give four examples of accounting entities.
12. Briefly describe the reliability principle.
13. What role does the cost principle play in accounting?
14. If *assets* = *liabilities* + *owner's equity*, then how can *liabilities* be expressed?
15. Explain the difference between an account receivable and an account payable.
16. What role do transactions play in accounting?
17. What is a more descriptive title for the balance sheet?
18. What feature of the balance sheet gives this financial statement its name?
19. What is another title of the income statement?
20. Which financial statement is like a snapshot of the entity at a specific time? Which financial statement is like a moving picture of the entity's operations during a period of time?
21. What information does the statement of owner's equity report?
22. Give two synonyms for the owner's equity of a proprietorship.
23. What piece of information flows from the income statement to the statement of owner's equity? What information flows from the statement of owner's equity to the balance sheet?

Exercises

Exercise 1-1 *Transaction analysis*

Indicate the effects of the following business transactions on the accounting equation. Transaction *a* is answered as a guide.

a. Paid $90 cash to purchase office supplies.

   Answer: Increase asset (Office Supplies)
   Decrease asset (Cash)

b. Performed legal service for a client and received cash of $2,000.
c. Paid monthly office rent of $700.
d. Invested cash of $1,800 in the business.
e. Performed legal service for a client on account, $650.
f. Purchased on account office furniture at a cost of $500.

g. Received cash on account, $400.

h. Paid cash on account, $250.

i. Sold land for $12,000, which was our cost of the land.

Exercise 1-2   *Transaction analysis; accounting equation*

Gloria Hill opens a medical practice to specialize in child care. During her first month of operation, January, her practice, entitled Gloria Hill, M.D., experienced the following events:

Jan. 6   Hill invested $135,000 in the business by opening a bank account in the name of Gloria Hill, M.D.

9   Hill paid cash for land costing $90,000. She plans to build an office building on the land.

12   She purchased medical supplies for $2,000 on account.

15   On January 15, Hill officially opened for business.

15–31   During the rest of the month she treated patients and earned service revenue of $6,000, receiving cash.

15–31   She paid cash expenses: employee salaries, $1,400; office rent, $1,000; utilities, $300.

28   She sold supplies to another physician for cost of $500.

31   She paid $1,500 on account.

Required

Analyze the effects of these events on the accounting equation of the medical practice of Gloria Hill, M.D. Use a format similar to that of Exhibit 1-5 in the chapter, with headings for Cash; Supplies; Land; Accounts Payable; and Gloria Hill, Capital.

Exercise 1-3   *Accounting equation*

Compute the missing amount in the accounting equation of each of the following three entities:

	Assets	Liabilities	Owner's Equity
Entity A	$?	$41,800	$26,400
Entity B	85,900	?	34,000
Entity C	63,700	29,800	?

Exercise 1-4   *Business organization, balance sheet*

Presented below are the balances of the assets and liabilities of Stark Delivery Service as of September 30, 19X2. Also included are the revenue and expense figures of the business for September.

Delivery service revenue	$3,500	Delivery equipment	$9,500
Accounts receivable	900	Supplies	600
Accounts payable	750	Note payable	5,000
D. Stark, capital	?	Rent expense	500
Salary expense	1,000	Cash	650

Required

1. What type of business organization is Stark Delivery Service? How can you tell?

2. Prepare the balance sheet of Stark Delivery Service as of September 30, 19X2. Not all amounts are used. Recall that only assets, liabilities, and owner's equity appear on the balance sheet.

Exercise 1-5   *Income statement*

Presented below are the balances of the assets, liabilities, owner's equity, revenues, and expenses of Fadal Travel Agency at December 31, 19X3, the end of its first year of business. During the year W. Fadal, the owner, invested $20,000 in the business.

Note payable	$30,000	Office furniture	45,000
Utilities expense	5,800	Rent expense	21,000
Accounts payable	3,300	Cash	3,600
W. Fadal, capital	27,100	Office supplies	4,800
Service revenue	108,000	Salary expense	29,000
Accounts receivable	9,000	Salaries payable	2,000
Supplies expense	4,000	Property tax expense	1,200

Required

1. Prepare the income statement of Fadal Travel Agency for the year ended December 31, 19X3. Not all amounts are used. Recall that only revenues and expenses appear on the income statement.
2. What was the amount of the proprietor's withdrawals during the year?

Exercise 1-6   *Business transactions*

For each of the following items, give an example of a business transaction that has the described effect on the accounting equation:

a. Increase an asset and increase owner's equity.
b. Increase an asset and increase a liability.
c. Increase one asset and decrease another asset.
d. Decrease an asset and decrease owner's equity.
e. Decrease an asset and decrease a liability.

Exercise 1-7   *Business organization, transactions, and net income*

The analysis of the transactions that United Rentals engaged in during its first month of operations follows. The company buys equipment that it rents out to earn rent revenue. The owners of the business made only one investment to start the business and no withdrawals.

	Cash	+	Accounts Receivable	+	Rental Equipment	=	Accounts Payable	+	Partners' Capital
a.	+65,000								+65,000
b.					+100,000		+100,000		
c.	+ 1,600								+ 1,600
d.			+150						+ 150
e.	−10,000						− 10,000		
f.			+850						+ 850
g.	+ 150		−150						
h.	− 2,000								− 2,000

Required

1. What type of business organization is United Rentals? How can you tell?
2. Describe each transaction.
3. If these transactions fully describe the operations of United Rentals during the month, what was the amount of net income or net loss?

Exercise 1-8   *Accounting equation*

Milstead Supply balance sheet data, at May 31, 19X2, and June 30, 19X2, were as follows:

	May 31, 19X2	June 30, 19X2
Total assets	$150,000	$195,000
Total liabilities	109,000	131,000

Required

Below are three assumptions about investments and withdrawals by the owner of the business during June. For each assumption, compute the amount of net income or net loss of the business during June 19X2.

a.   The owner invested $25,000 in the business and made no withdrawals.
b.   The owner made no additional investments in the business but withdrew $12,000 for personal use.
c.   The owner invested $8,000 in the business and withdrew $12,000 for personal use.

Exercise 1-9   *Transaction analysis*

Bliss Stone Masonry, a proprietorship, recorded the following events. State whether each event (1) increased, (2) decreased, or (3) had no effect on the total assets of the business. Identify any specific asset affected.

a.   Paid cash on accounts payable.
b.   Purchased machinery and equipment for a manufacturing plant; signed a promissory note in payment.
c.   Performed service for a customer on account.
d.   Bliss, the owner, withdrew cash from the business for personal use.
e.   Received cash from a customer on account receivable.
f.   Bliss used personal funds to purchase a swimming pool for his home.
g.   Sold land for a price equal to the cost of the land; received cash.
h.   Borrowed money from the bank.
i.   Cash purchase of land for a future building site.
j.   Bliss increased his cash investment in the business.

Problems   *(Group A)*

Problem 1-1A   *Transaction analysis, accounting equation, financial statements*

Margaret Stevens owns and operates an interior design studio called Stevens Interiors. The following amounts summarize the financial position of her business on August 31, 19X2:

	Assets			=	Liabilities	+	Owner's Equity
	Cash	+	Accounts Receivable	+	Land	=	Accounts Payable	+	Margaret Stevens, Capital
Bal.	1,250		1,500		12,000		8,000		6,750

During September 19X2 the following events occurred:

a. Stevens inherited $15,000 and deposited the cash in the business bank account.
b. Performed services for a client and received cash of $700.
c. Paid off the beginning balance of accounts payable, $8,000.
d. Purchased supplies on account, $500.
e. Collected cash from a customer on account, $800.
f. Invested personal cash of $1,000 in the business.
g. Consulted on the interior design of a major office building and billed the client for services rendered, $2,000.
h. Recorded the following business expenses for the month:
   1. Paid office rent—$900.
   2. Paid advertising—$100.
i. Sold supplies to another business for $150, which was the cost of the supplies.
j. Withdrew cash of $1,800 for personal use.

Required

1. Record the effects of the above transactions on the accounting equation of Stevens Interiors. Adapt the format of Exhibit 1-5. You need to add a column for Supplies.
2. Prepare the income statement of Stevens Interiors for the month ended September 30, 19X2. List expenses in decreasing order by amount.
3. Prepare the statement of owner's equity of Stevens Interiors for the month ended September 30, 19X2.
4. Prepare the balance sheet of Stevens Interiors at September 30, 19X2.

Problem 1-2A *Entity concept, transaction analysis, accounting equation*

Zane Jones practiced law with a large firm, a partnership, for five years after graduating from law school. Recently he resigned his position to open his own law office, which he operates as a proprietorship. The name of the new entity is Zane Jones, Attorney.

Jones recorded the following events during the organizing phase of his new business and its first month of operations. Some of the events were personal and did not affect his law practice. Others were business transactions and should be accounted for by the business.

May 4   Jones received $50,000 cash from his former partners in the law firm from which he resigned.
May 5   Jones deposited $50,000 cash in a new business bank account, entitled Zane Jones, Attorney.
May 6   Jones paid $300 cash for letterhead stationery for his new law office.
May 7   Jones purchased office furniture for his law office. Jones agreed to pay the account payable, $5,000, within six months.
May 10   Jones sold 500 shares of IBM stock, which he and his wife had owned for several years, receiving $75,000 cash from his stockbroker.
May 11   Jones deposited the $75,000 cash from sale of the IBM stock in his personal bank account.
May 12   A representative of a large company telephoned Jones and told him of the company's intention to transfer its legal business to the new entity of Zane Jones, Attorney.
May 29   Jones finished court hearings on behalf of a client and submitted his bill for legal services, $4,000. Jones expected to collect from this client within two weeks.
May 30   Jones paid office rent expense, $1,000.
May 31   Jones withdrew $2,500 cash from the business for personal living expenses.

Required

1. Classify each of the preceding events as one of the following:
   a. Personal transaction *not* to be accounted for by the proprietorship of Zane Jones, Attorney.

   b. Business transaction to be accounted for by the proprietorship of Zane Jones, Attorney.

   c. Business-related event but *not* a transaction to be accounted for by the proprietorship of Zane Jones, Attorney.

2. Analyze the effects of the above events on the accounting equation of the proprietorship of Zane Jones, Attorney. Use a format similar to Exhibit 1-5.

Problem 1-3A   *Balance sheet*

The bookkeeper of Dorman Home Builders prepared the balance sheet of the company while the accountant was ill. The balance sheet contains numerous errors. In particular, the bookkeeper knew that the balance sheet should balance, so he plugged in the owner's equity amount needed to achieve this balance. However, the owner's equity amount is not correct. All other amounts are accurate.

Dorman Home Builders
Balance Sheet
Month Ended July 31, 19X3

Assets		Liabilities	
Cash	$ 2,000	Accounts receivable	$ 3,000
Office supplies	1,000	Service revenue	35,000
Land	22,000	Property tax expense	800
Advertising expense	500	Accounts payable	8,000
Office furniture	10,000	**Owner's Equity**	
Note payable	16,000		
Rent expense	4,000	Owner's equity	8,700
Total assets	$55,500	Total liabilities	$55,500

Required

1. Prepare the correct balance sheet as of July 31, 19X3. Compute total assets and total liabilities. Then take the difference to determine correct owner's equity.
2. Identify the accounts listed above which should *not* be presented on the balance sheet and state why you excluded them from the correct balance sheet you prepared for Requirement 1.

Problem 1-4A   *Business transactions and analysis*

Larkin Company was recently formed. The balance of each item in the company's accounting equation is shown below for May 10 and for each of nine following business days.

	Cash	Accounts Receivable	Supplies	Land	Accounts Payable	Owner's Equity
May 10	$ 6,000	$4,000	$1,000	$ 8,000	$4,000	$15,000
11	11,000	4,000	1,000	8,000	4,000	20,000
12	6,000	4,000	1,000	13,000	4,000	20,000
15	6,000	4,000	3,000	13,000	6,000	20,000
16	5,000	4,000	3,000	13,000	5,000	20,000
17	8,000	1,000	3,000	13,000	5,000	20,000
18	16,000	1,000	3,000	13,000	5,000	28,000
19	13,000	1,000	3,000	13,000	2,000	28,000
22	12,000	1,000	4,000	13,000	2,000	28,000
23	8,000	1,000	4,000	13,000	2,000	24,000

Required

Assuming a single transaction took place on each day, describe briefly the transaction that was most likely to have occurred, beginning with May 11. Indicate which accounts were affected and by what amount. No revenue or expense transactions occurred on these dates.

Problem 1-5A *Balance sheet, entity concept*

Jan Gibson is a realtor. She buys and sells properties on her own, and she also earns commission as a real estate agent for buyers and sellers. She organized her business as a proprietorship on November 24, 19X4. Consider the following facts as of November 30, 19X4:

a. Gibson owed $100,000 on a note payable for some undeveloped land that had been acquired by her business for a total price of $160,000.
b. Gibson's business had spent $15,000 for a Century 21 real estate franchise, which entitled her to represent herself as a Century 21 agent. Century 21 is a national affiliation of independent real estate agents. This franchise is a business asset.
c. Gibson owed $120,000 on a personal mortgage on her personal residence, which she acquired in 19X1 for a total price of $170,000.
d. Gibson had $10,000 in her personal bank account and $12,000 in her business bank account.
e. Gibson owed $1,800 on a personal charge account with Neiman-Marcus Specialty Department Store.
f. Gibson acquired business furniture for $17,000 on November 25. Of this amount, her business owed $6,000 on open account at November 30.
g. Office supplies on hand at the real estate office totaled $1,000.

Required

1. Prepare the balance sheet of the real estate business of Jan Gibson, Realtor, at November 30, 19X4.
2. Identify the personal items given in the preceding facts that would not be reported on the balance sheet of the business.

Problem 1-6A *Income statement, statement of owner's equity, balance sheet*

Presented below are the amounts of (a) the assets and liabilities of Johnson Service Company as of December 31 and (b) the revenues and expenses of the company for the year ended on that date. The items are listed in alphabetical order.

Accounts payable	$ 19,000	Note payable	85,000
Accounts receivable	12,000	Property tax expense	4,000
Advertising expense	11,000	Rent expense	23,000
Building	180,000	Salary expense	53,000
Cash	10,000	Salaries payable	1,000
Furniture	20,000	Service revenue	200,000
Interest expense	9,000	Supplies	3,000
Land	65,000		

The beginning amount of Ray Johnson, Capital, was $150,000, and during the year Johnson withdrew $65,000 for personal use.

Required

1. Prepare the income statement of Johnson Service Company for the year ended December 31 of the current year.

2. Prepare the statement of owner's equity of the company for the year ended December 31.

3. Prepare the balance sheet of the company at December 31.

Problem 1-7A   *Transaction analysis for an actual company*

A recent balance sheet of Levi Strauss & Company, the world's largest seller of jeans and casual pants, is summarized as follows, with amounts in thousands. For example, Cash of $263,389,000 is presented as $263,389.

Levi Strauss & Company
Balance Sheet
November 25, 19XX
(thousands)

Assets		Liabilities	
Cash.....................	$ 263,389	Notes payable	$ 83,361
Accounts receivable........	339,798	Accounts payable	229,453
Merchandise inventories....	387,660	Other liabilities	300,847
Property, plant, and equip...	330,455	Total liabilities	613,661
Other assets	99,800		
		Owner Equity............	807,441
		Total liabilities and owner	
Total assets..............	$1,421,102	equity	$1,421,102

During December, the company had the following transactions and events (amounts in thousands):

a. Received cash investments from owners, $18.

b. Received special equipment from an owner as an investment in the company. The value of the equipment was $40.

c. Borrowed cash, signing a note payable, $100.

d. Purchased equipment for cash, $125.

e. Purchased inventories on account, $90.

f. Paid cash on account (to reduce accounts payable), $54.

g. Sold equipment to another company on account, $14. The equipment had cost $14.

h. Discovered that the president of the United States was going to wear Levi blue jeans while giving his State of the Union address next January.

i. Collected cash on account from customers, $84.

Required:

1. Showing all amounts in thousands, analyze the December transactions of Levi Strauss. Use a format similar to Exhibit 1-5.

2. Prove that assets = liabilities + owner equity after analyzing the transactions.

(Group B)

Problem 1-1B   *Transaction analysis, accounting equation, financial statements*

Maury Cheng owns and operates an interior design studio called Cheng Designers. The following amounts summarize the financial position of his business on April 30, 19X5:

	Assets			=	Liabilities	+	Owner's Equity
	Cash +	Accounts Receivable +	Land	=	Accounts Payable +		Maury Cheng, Capital
Bal.	720	2,240	23,100		4,400		21,660

During May 19X5 the following events occurred:

a. Cheng received $12,000 as a gift and deposited the cash in the business bank account.
b. Paid off the beginning balance of accounts payable, $4,400.
c. Performed services for a client and received cash of $1,100.
d. Collected cash from a customer on account, $750.
e. Purchased supplies on account, $120.
f. Consulted on the interior design of a major office building and billed the client for services rendered, $5,500.
g. Invested personal cash of $1,700 in the business.
h. Recorded the following business expenses for the month:
   1. Paid office rent—$1,200.
   2. Paid advertising—$860.
i. Sold supplies to another interior designer for $80, which was the cost of the supplies.
j. Withdrew cash of $2,400 for personal use.

Required

1. Record the effects of the above transactions on the accounting equation of Cheng Designers. Adapt the format of Exhibit 1-5. You need to add a column for Supplies.
2. Prepare the income statement of Cheng Designers for the month ended May 31, 19X5. List expenses in decreasing order by amount.
3. Prepare the statement of owner's equity of Cheng Designers for the month ended May 31, 19X5.
4. Prepare the balance sheet of Cheng Designers at May 31.

Problem 1-2B   *Entity concept, transaction analysis, accounting equation*

Rhonda Sperry practiced law with a large firm, a partnership, for ten years after graduating from law school. Recently she resigned her position to open her own law office, which she operates as a proprietorship. The name of the new entity is Rhonda Sperry, Attorney and Counselor.

Sperry recorded the following events during the organizing phase of her new business and its first month of operations. Some of the events were personal and did not affect the law practice. Others were business transactions and should be accounted for by the business.

July 1   Rhonda sold 1,000 shares of Procter & Gamble stock, which she had owned for several years, receiving $88,000 cash from her stockbroker.
July 2   Rhonda deposited the $88,000 cash from sale of the Procter & Gamble stock in her personal bank account.
July 3   Rhonda received $135,000 cash from her former partners in the law firm from which she resigned.
July 5   Rhonda deposited $130,000 cash in a new business bank account entitled Rhonda Sperry, Attorney and Counselor.
July 6   A representative of a large company telephoned Rhonda and told her of the company's intention to transfer its legal business to the new entity of Rhonda Sperry, Attorney and Counselor.
July 7   Rhonda paid $550 cash for letterhead stationery for her new law office.

July 9 Rhonda purchased office furniture for the law office, agreeing to pay the account payable, $11,500, within three months.

July 23 Rhonda finished court hearings on behalf of a client and submitted her bill for legal services, $2,100. She expected to collect from this client within one month.

July 30 Rhonda paid office rent expense, $1,900.

July 31 Rhonda withdrew $3,000 cash from the business for personal living expenses.

Required

1. Classify each of the preceding events as one of the following:
   a. Personal transaction *not* to be accounted for by the proprietorship of Rhonda Sperry, Attorney and Counselor.
   b. Business transaction to be accounted for by the proprietorship of Rhonda Sperry, Attorney and Counselor.
   c. Business-related event but *not* a transaction to be accounted for by the proprietorship of Rhonda Sperry, Attorney and Counselor.
2. Analyze the effects of the above events on the accounting equation of the proprietorship of Rhonda Sperry, Attorney and Counselor. Use a format similar to Exhibit 1-5.

Problem 1-3B *Balance sheet*

The bookkeeper of Reynolds Construction Company prepared the balance sheet of the company while the accountant was ill. The balance sheet contains numerous errors. In particular, the bookkeeper knew that the balance sheet should balance, so he plugged in the owner's equity amount needed to achieve this balance. However, the owner's equity amount is not correct. All other amounts are accurate.

Reynolds Construction Company
Balance Sheet
Month Ended October 31, 19X7

Assets		Liabilities	
Cash	$ 1,400	Notes receivable	$11,000
Advertising expense	300	Interest expense	2,000
Land	31,600	Office supplies	800
Salary expense	2,200	Accounts receivable	1,600
Office furniture	4,700	Note payable	20,000
Accounts payable	3,000	**Owner's Equity**	
Utilities expense	1,100		
		Owner's equity	8,900
Total assets	$44,300	Total liabilities	$44,300

Required

1. Prepare the correct balance sheet as of October 31, 19X7. Compute total assets and total liabilities. Then take the difference to determine correct owner's equity.
2. Identify the accounts listed above that should *not* be presented on the balance sheet and state why you excluded them from the correct balance sheet you prepared for Requirement 1.

Problem 1-4B *Business transactions and analysis*

Kluzewski Company was recently formed. The balance of each item in the company's accounting equation is shown below for February 8 and for each of nine following business days.

	Cash	Accounts Receivable	Supplies	Land	Accounts Payable	Owner's Equity
Feb. 8	$3,000	$7,000	$ 800	$11,000	$3,800	$18,000
12	5,000	7,000	800	11,000	3,800	20,000
14	6,000	6,000	800	11,000	3,800	20,000
17	6,000	6,000	1,100	11,000	4,100	20,000
19	3,000	6,000	1,100	11,000	4,100	17,000
20	1,900	6,000	1,100	11,000	3,000	17,000
22	7,900	6,000	1,100	5,000	3,000	17,000
25	7,000	6,000	1,100	5,000	2,100	17,000
26	6,800	6,000	1,300	5,000	2,100	17,000
28	1,700	6,000	1,300	10,100	2,100	17,000

Required

Assuming a single transaction took place on each day, describe briefly the transaction that was most likely to have occurred, beginning with February 12. Indicate which accounts were affected and by what amount. No revenue or expense transactions occurred on these dates.

Problem 1-5B *Balance sheet, entity concept*

Drew Beaty is a realtor. He buys and sells properties on his own, and he also earns commission as a real estate agent for buyers and sellers. He organized his business as a proprietorship on March 10, 19X2. Consider the following facts as of March 31, 19X2:

a. Beaty had $5,000 in his personal bank account and $9,000 in his business bank account.
b. Office supplies on hand at the real estate office totaled $1,000.
c. Beaty's business had spent $15,000 for an Electronic Realty Associates (ERA) franchise, which entitled him to represent himself as an ERA agent. ERA is a national affiliation of independent real estate agents. This franchise is a business asset.
d. Beaty owed $38,000 on a note payable for some undeveloped land that had been acquired by his business for a total price of $70,000.
e. Beaty owed $65,000 on a personal mortgage on his personal residence, which he acquired in 19X1 for a total price of $90,000.
f. Beaty owed $950 on a personal charge account with Sears, Roebuck and Co.
g. He had acquired business furniture for $12,000 on March 26. Of this amount, Beaty's business owed $6,000 on open account at March 31.

Required

1. Prepare the balance sheet of the real estate business of Drew Beaty, Realtor, at March 31, 19X2.
2. Identify the personal items given in the preceding facts that would not be reported on the balance sheet of the business.

Problem 1-6B *Income statement, statement of owner's equity, balance sheet*

Presented below are the amounts of (a) the assets and liabilities of Bryant Repair Service as of December 31 and (b) the revenues and expenses of the company for the year ended on that date. The items are listed in alphabetical order.

Accounts payable	$ 14,000	Note payable	31,000
Accounts receivable	6,000	Property tax expense	2,000
Building	18,000	Rent expense	14,000
Cash	4,000	Salary expense	38,000
Equipment	26,000	Service revenue	110,000
Interest expense	4,000	Supplies	13,000
Interest payable	1,000	Utilities expense	3,000
Land	8,000		

The beginning amount of Mike Bryant, Capital, was $12,000, and during the year Bryant withdrew $32,000 for personal use.

Required

1. Prepare the income statement of Bryant Repair Service for the year ended December 31 of the current year.
2. Prepare the statement of owner's equity of the company for the year ended December 31.
3. Prepare the balance sheet of the company at December 31.

Problem 1-7B   *Transaction analysis for an actual company*

A recent balance sheet of Xerox Corporation, the manufacturer of copiers and other office equipment, is summarized as follows, with amounts in thousands. For example, Cash of $266,600,000 is presented as $266,600.

Xerox Corporation
Balance Sheet
December 31, 19XX
(thousands)

Assets		Liabilities	
Cash.	$ 266,600	Notes payable	$1,985,500
Accounts receivable.	1,466,900	Accounts payable	390,300
Merchandise inventories. . . .	1,469,800	Other liabilities	2,107,600
Land, buildings, and equip. .	2,659,700	Total liabilities	4,483,400
Other assets	3,953,700		
		Owner Equity.	5,333,300
		Total liabilities	
Total assets.	$9,816,700	and owner equity.	$9,816,700

During January, the company had the following transactions and events (amounts in thousands):

a. Received cash investment from owners, $37.
b. Purchased inventories on account, $400.
c. Paid cash on account (to reduce accounts payable), $136.
d. Sold inventory to another company on account, $670. The equipment had cost $670.
e. Learned that a national television news program would show members of Congress using Xerox copy machines as part of a senate investigation. The value of this advertisement to the company is estimated to be $1,000.

f. Borrowed cash, signing a note payable, $550.
g. Purchased equipment for cash, $380.
h. Collected cash on account from customers, $289.
i. Received special equipment from an owner as an investment in the company. The value of the equipment was $119.

Required

1. Showing all amounts in thousands, analyze the January transactions of Xerox. Use a format similar to Exhibit 1-5.
2. Prove that assets = liabilities + owner equity after analyzing the transactions.

Decision Problem

Using Financial Statements to Evaluate a Request for a Loan

The proprietors of two businesses, Butler Department Store and Susan Nielsen Home Decorators, have sought business loans from you. To decide whether to make the loans, you have requested their balance sheets.

Butler Department Store
Balance Sheet
August 31, 19X4

Assets		Liabilities	
Cash	$ 1,000	Accounts payable	$ 12,000
Accounts receivable	14,000	Note payable	18,000
Merchandise inventory	85,000	Total liabilities	30,000
Store supplies	500		
Furniture and fixtures	9,000	**Owner's Equity**	
Building	90,000		
Land	14,000	Roy Butler, capital	183,500
		Total liabilities and	
Total assets	$213,500	owner's equity	$213,500

Susan Nielsen Home Decorators
Balance Sheet
August 31, 19X4

Assets		Liabilities	
Cash	$11,000	Accounts payable	$ 3,000
Accounts receivable	4,000	Note payable	18,000
Office supplies	1,000	Total liabilities	21,000
Office furniture	6,000	**Owner's Equity**	
Land	19,000		
		Susan Nielsen, capital	20,000
		Total liabilities and	
Total assets	$41,000	owner's equity	$41,000

Required

1. Based solely on these balance sheets, which entity would you be more comfortable loaning money to? Explain fully, citing specific items and amounts from the balance sheets.
2. In addition to the balance sheet data, what other financial statement information would you require? Be specific.

Financial Statement Problem

Identifying Items from a Company's Financial Statements

This and similar problems in succeeding chapters focus on the financial statements of an actual company (Gulf+Western Inc.). As each problem is solved, readers gradually strengthen their understanding of actual financial statements in their entirety.

Refer to the Gulf+Western financial statements in Appendix C, and answer the following questions.

1. How much in cash (including cash equivalents) did Gulf+Western have on October 31, 1987?
2. What were total assets at October 31, 1987? At October 31, 1986?
3. Write the company's accounting equation at October 31, 1987, by filling in the dollar amounts:

ASSETS = LIABILITIES + OWNER EQUITY

4. Identify total revenues and net revenues for the year ended October 31, 1987. (Net revenues means total revenues after certain subtractions.)
5. How much net income (net earnings) did Gulf+Western experience for the year ended October 31, 1987?

Answers to Self-Study Questions

1. c	3. d	5. b	7. b	9. b
2. c	4. a	6. a	8. c	10. c

2

Recording Business Transactions

LEARNING OBJECTIVES

After studying this chapter, you should be able to

1 Define and use all new terms in the chapter

5 Prepare a trial balance

2 Apply the rules of debit and credit

6 Record revenues and expenses

3 Record transactions in the journal

7 Analyze transactions without a journal

4 Post from the journal to the ledger

Chapter 1 illustrates how to account for business transactions by analyzing their effects on the accounting equation. That approach emphasizes accounting concepts, but it becomes unwieldy in day-to-day business if many transactions occur. In large businesses—such as a chain of department stores—hundreds or even thousands of transactions occur hourly. In practice, then, accountants use a different approach to handle accounting information. This chapter focuses on processing accounting information as it is actually done in practice.

The Account

OBJECTIVE 1

Define and use all new terms in the chapter

The basic summary device of accounting is the **account.** This is the detailed record of the changes that have occurred in a particular asset, liability, or owner's equity during a period of time. Each account appears on its own page. For convenient access to the information in the accounts the pages are grouped together in a single book called the **ledger.** When you hear reference to "keeping the books" or "auditing the books," the word *books* refers to the ledger. The ledger may be a bound book, a loose-leaf set of pages, or a computer record.

In the ledger, the accounts are grouped in three broad categories, based on the accounting equation:

ASSETS = LIABILITIES + OWNER'S EQUITY

Assets

Those economic resources that will benefit the business in the future are *assets*. The following asset accounts are common to many firms.

Cash.   The Cash account shows the cash effects of a business's transactions. Cash means money and any medium of exchange that a bank accepts at face value. Cash includes currency, coins, money orders, certificates of deposit, and checks. The Cash account includes these items whether they are kept on hand, in a safe, in a cash register, or in a bank.

Notes Receivable.   A business may sell its goods or services in exchange for a promissory note, which is a written pledge that the customer will pay the business a fixed amount of money by a certain date. The Notes Receivable account is a record of the promissory notes that the business expects to collect in cash.

Accounts Receivable.   A business may sell its goods or services in exchange for an oral or implied promise for future cash receipt. Such sales are made on credit (on account). The Accounts Receivable account includes these amounts.

Prepaid Expenses.   A business often pays certain expenses in advance. Prepaid expenses are assets because they will be of future benefit to the business. The ledger holds a separate asset account for each prepaid item. Prepaid Rent and Prepaid Insurance are prepaid expenses that occur often in business. Office Supplies are also accounted for as prepaid expenses.

Land.   The Land account is a record of the land that a business owns.

Building.   A business's buildings — office, warehouse, garage, and the like — appear in the Building account.

Equipment, Furniture and Fixtures.   A business has a separate asset account for each type of equipment — Office Equipment and Store Equipment, for example. The Furniture and Fixtures account shows the cost of this asset. Other asset categories and accounts will be discussed as needed. For example, many businesses have an Investments account for their investments in other companies.

Liabilities

Recall that a *liability* is a debt. A business generally has fewer liability accounts than asset accounts because a business's liabilities can be summarized under relatively few categories.

Notes Payable.   This account is the opposite of the Notes Receivable account. Notes Payable records the amounts that the business must pay because it signed a promissory note to purchase goods or services.

Accounts Payable.   This account is the opposite of the Accounts Receivable account. The oral or implied promise to pay off debts arising from credit purchases of goods appears in the Accounts Payable account. Such a purchase is said to be made on account. Other liability categories and accounts are added as needed. Taxes Payable, Wages Payable, and Salary Payable are accounts that appear in many ledgers.

Owner's Equity

The claim that the owner has on the assets of the business is called *owner's equity.* In a proprietorship or a partnership, owner's equity is often split into separate accounts for the owner's capital balance and the owner's withdrawals.

Capital. This account shows the owner's claim to the assets of the business. After total liabilities are subtracted from total assets, the remainder is the owner's capital. The balance of the capital account equals the owner's investments in the business plus its net income and minus net losses and owner withdrawals. In addition to the capital account, the following accounts also appear in the owner's equity section of the ledger.

Withdrawals. When the owner withdraws cash or other assets from the business for personal use, its assets and its owner's equity both decrease. The amounts taken out of the business appear in a separate account entitled Withdrawals, or Drawing. If withdrawals were recorded directly in the capital account, the amount of owner withdrawals would be merged with owner investments. To separate these two amounts for decision making, businesses use a separate account for Withdrawals. This account shows a *decrease* in owner's equity.

Revenues. The increase in owner's equity from delivering goods or services to customers or clients is called *revenue.* The ledger contains as many revenue accounts as needed. Gary Lyon's accounting practice would have a Service Revenue account for amounts earned by providing accounting service for clients. If the business loans money to an outsider, it will also need an Interest Revenue account. If the business rents a building to a tenant, it will need a Rent Revenue account. Increases in revenue accounts are *increases* in owner's equity.

Expenses. The cost of operating a business is called *expense.* Expenses have the opposite effect of revenues, so they decrease owner's equity. A business needs a separate account for each category of its expenses, such as Salary Expense, Rent Expense, Advertising Expense, and Utilities Expense. Expense accounts are decreases in owner's equity.

Exhibit 2-1 shows how asset, liability, and owner's equity accounts can be grouped into the ledger. Typically, each account occupies a separate sheet.

Double-Entry Bookkeeping

Accounting is based on double-entry bookkeeping, which means that accountants record the *dual effects* of a business transaction. We know that each transaction affects two accounts. For example, Gary Lyon's $50,000 cash investment in his accounting practice increased both the Cash account and the Capital account of the business. It would be incomplete to record only the increase in the entity's cash without recording the increase in its owner's equity.

Consider a *cash purchase of supplies.* What are the dual effects of this transaction? The purchase (1) decreases cash and (2) increases supplies. A *purchase of supplies on credit* (1) increases supplies and (2) increases accounts payable. A *cash payment on account* (1) decreases cash and (2) decreases accounts payable. All transactions have at least two effects on the entity.

EXHIBIT 2-1   *The Ledger (Asset, Liability, and Owner's Equity Accounts)*

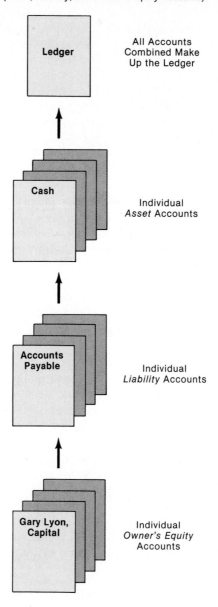

The T-Account

How do accountants record business transactions in the accounts? The account format used for most illustrations in this book is called the T-account. It takes the form of the capital letter "T." The vertical line in the letter divides the account into its left and right sides. The account title rests on the horizontal line. For example, the Cash account of a business appears in the following T-account format:

Cash	
Left side	**Right side**
Debit	*Credit*

The left side of the account is called the **debit** side, and the right side is called the **credit** side. Often beginners in the study of accounting are confused by the words *debit* and *credit*. To become comfortable using them, simply remember this:

$$\text{debit} = \text{left side}$$

$$\text{credit} = \text{right side}$$

Even though *left side* and *right side* are more descriptive, *debit* and *credit* are too deeply entrenched in accounting to avoid using.[1]

Increases and Decreases in the Accounts _____

The type of an account determines how increases and decreases in it are recorded. Increases in *assets* are recorded in the left (the debit) side of the account. Decreases in assets are recorded in the right (the credit) side of the account. Conversely, increases in *liabilities* and *owner's equity* are recorded by *credits*. Decreases are recorded by debits.

This pattern of recording debits and credits is based on the accounting equation:

$$\text{ASSETS} = \text{LIABILITIES} + \text{OWNER'S EQUITY}$$

Notice that assets are on the opposite side of the equation from liabilities and owner's equity. This explains why increases and decreases in assets are recorded in the opposite manner from liabilities and owner's equity. It also explains why liabilities and owner's equity follow the same pattern: they are on the same side of the equal sign. Exhibit 2-2 shows the relationship between the accounting equation and the rules of debit and credit.

To illustrate the ideas diagrammed in Exhibit 2-2, reconsider the first transaction from the preceding chapter. Gary Lyon invested $50,000 in cash to begin his accounting practice. Which accounts of the business are affected? By what amounts? On what side (debit or credit)? The answer is that Assets and Capital would increase by $50,000, as the following T-accounts show.

Assets	=	Liabilities	+	Owner's Equity
Cash				**Gary Lyon, Capital**
Debit for Increase, 50,000				Credit for Increase, 50,000

EXHIBIT 2-2 *Accounting Equation and the Rules of Debit and Credit*

Accounting Equation:	Assets		=	Liabilities		+	Owner's Equity	
Rules of Debit and Credit:	Debit for Increase	Credit for Decrease		Debit for Decrease	Credit for Increase		Debit for Decrease	Credit for Increase

---

[1] The words *debit* and *credit* have a Latin origin (*debitum* and *creditum*). Pacioli, the Italian monk who wrote about accounting in the fifteenth century, used these terms.

The amount remaining in an account is called its *balance.* This initial transaction gives Cash a $50,000 debit balance and Gary Lyon, Capital a $50,000 credit balance.

The second transaction is a $20,000 cash purchase of land. This transaction affects two assets: Cash and Land. It decreases Cash (a credit) and increases Land (a debit), as shown in the T-accounts:

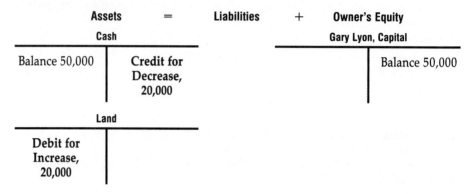

After this transaction, Cash has a $30,000 debit balance ($50,000 debit balance − $20,000 credit amount), Land's debit balance is $20,000, and the Capital account has a $50,000 credit balance.

Transaction 3 is a $500 purchase of office supplies on account. This transaction increases the asset Office Supplies and the liability Accounts Payable, as shown in the following accounts:

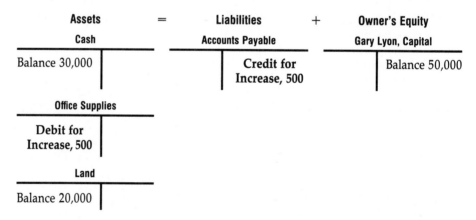

Accountants create accounts as needed. The process of writing a new T-account in preparation for recording a transaction is called *opening the account.* For Transaction 1, we opened the Cash account and the Gary Lyon, Capital account. For Transaction 2, we opened the Land account, and for Transaction 3, Office Supplies and Accounts Payable.

Accountants could record all transactions directly in the accounts as we have shown for the first three transactions. However, that way of accounting is not practical because it does not leave a clear record of each transaction. Suppose you need to know what account was debited and what account was credited in a particular transaction. Looking at each account in the ledger does not answer this question because double-entry accounting always affects at least two accounts. Therefore, you may have to search through all the accounts in the ledger to find both sides of a particular transaction. To avoid this waste of time, accountants keep a record of each transaction and then transfer this information into the accounts.

The Debit-Credit Language of Accounting _____

As we have seen, *debit* means "left side" and *credit* means "right side." We say "Debit Cash for $1,000," which means to place $1,000 on the left side of the cash account. We record "a $500 debit to Accounts Payable" by entering the $500 in the left side of this account, which signals a decrease in a liability. When we speak of "crediting a liability account for $750," we mean to increase the account's balance by recording $750 on the right side of the account.

In everyday conversation, we sometimes use the word *credit* in a sense that is different from its technical accounting meaning. For example, we may praise someone by saying, "She deserves credit for her good work." In your study of accounting forget this general use. Remember that *debit means left side* and *credit means right side.* Whether an account is increased or decreased by a debit or credit depends on the type of account (see Exhibit 2-2).

Recording Transactions in Journals _____

In actual practice, accountants record transactions first in a book called the **journal.** A journal is a chronological record of the entity's transactions. In this section, we describe the recording process and illustrate how to use the journal and the ledger.

The recording process follows these five steps:

1. Identify the transaction from source documents, such as bank deposit slips, sales receipts, and check stubs.
2. Specify each account affected by the transaction and classify it by type (asset, liability, or owner's equity).
3. Determine whether each account is increased or decreased by the transaction.
4. From the rules of debit and credit, determine whether to debit or credit the account.
5. Enter the transaction in the journal, including a brief explanation for the journal entry. It is customary to write the debit side of the entry first and the credit side next.

We have discussed steps 1, 2, 3, and 4. Step 5, "Enter the transaction in the journal," means to write the transaction in the journal. This step is also called "making the journal entry," "preparing the journal entry," or "journalizing the transaction." A major part of learning accounting is learning how to make journal entries.

Let's apply the five steps to journalize the first transaction of the accounting practice of Gary Lyon, CPA—the $50,000 cash investment in the business.

Step 1. The source documents are the bank deposit slip and Lyon's $50,000 check, which is drawn on his personal bank account.

Step 2. *Cash* and *Gary Lyon, Capital* are the accounts affected by the transaction. Cash is an asset account, and Gary Lyon, Capital is an owner's equity account.

Step 3. Both accounts increase by $50,000. Therefore, debit Cash: it is the asset account that is increased. Also, credit Gary Lyon, Capital: it is the owner's equity account that is increased.

Step 4. Debit Cash to record an increase in this asset account. Credit Gary Lyon, Capital to record an increase in this account.

OBJECTIVE 3
Record transactions in the journal

Step 5.   The journal entry is

Date	Accounts and Explanation	Debit	Credit
Apr. 2	Cash	50,000	
	Gary Lyon, Capital		50,000
	Initial investment by owner.		

Note that the journal entry includes (a) the date of the transaction, (b) the title of the account debited (placed flush left) and the title of the account credited (indented slightly), (c) the dollar amounts of the debit (left) and credit (right) — dollar signs are omitted in the money columns, and (d) a short explanation of the transaction.

A helpful hint: To get off to the right start when analyzing a transaction, you should first pinpoint its effects (if any) on cash. Did cash increase or decrease? Then find its effect on other accounts. Typically, it is much easier to identify the effect of a transaction on cash than to identify the effect on other accounts.

The journal offers information that the ledger's T-accounts do not provide. Each journal entry shows the complete effect of a business transaction. Let's examine Gary Lyon's initial investment. The Cash account shows a single figure, the $50,000 debit. We know that every transaction has a credit, so in what account will we find the corresponding $50,000 credit? In this simple illustration, we know that the Capital account holds this figure. But imagine the difficulties an accountant would face trying to link debits and credits for hundreds of daily transactions — without a separate record of each transaction. The journal answers this problem and presents the full story for each transaction.

The journal can be a loose-leaf notebook, a bound book, or a computer listing. Exhibit 2-3 shows how a journal page might look with the first transaction entered.

In these introductory discussions we temporarily ignore the date of each transaction in order to focus on other details.

Posting from the Journal to the Ledger

Posting means transferring the amounts from the journal to the appropriate accounts in the ledger. Debits in the journal are posted as debits in the ledger, and credits in the journal as credits in the ledger. The initial investment transaction of Gary Lyon is posted to the ledger as shown in Exhibit 2-4.

EXHIBIT 2-3   *The Journal*

	Journal		Page 6
Date	**Accounts and Explanation**	**Debit**	**Credit**
Apr. 2	Cash	50,000	
	Gary Lyon, Capital		50,000
	Initial investment by owner.		

EXHIBIT 2-4 *Journal Entry and Posting to the Ledger*

Panel A—Journal Entry:

	Accounts and Explanation	Debit	Credit
Debit:	Cash	50,000	
Credit:	Gary Lyon, Capital		50,000
	Initial investment by owner.		

Panel B—Posting to the Ledger:

Cash

→ 50,000 |

Gary Lyon, Capital

| 50,000 ←

> **OBJECTIVE 4**
> Post from the journal to the ledger

Flow of Accounting Data

Exhibit 2-5 summarizes the flow of accounting data from the business transaction to the ledger.

EXHIBIT 2-5 *Flow of Accounting Data*

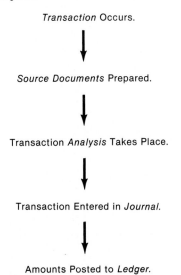

Transaction Occurs.

↓

Source Documents Prepared.

↓

Transaction *Analysis* Takes Place.

↓

Transaction Entered in *Journal.*

↓

Amounts Posted to *Ledger.*

Illustrative Problem _____

In this section, we illustrate transaction analysis, journalizing, and posting. We continue the example of Gary Lyon, CPA, and account for six of his early transactions.

Transaction Analysis, Journalizing, and Posting

1. *Transaction:* Lyon invested $50,000 to begin his accounting practice.

   Analysis: Lyon's investment in the business increased its asset cash; to record this increase, debit Cash.

   His investment also increased the owner's equity of the entity; to record this increase, credit Gary Lyon, Capital.

   Journal Entry:
   ```
   Cash ...................................  50,000
        Gary Lyon, Capital .................        50,000
   Initial investment by owner.
   ```

   Ledger Accounts:

Cash		Gary Lyon, Capital	
(1) 50,000			(1) 50,000

2. *Transaction:* He paid $20,000 cash for land as a future office location.

   Analysis: The purchase increased the entity's asset land; to record this increase, debit Land.

   The purchase decreased cash; therefore, credit Cash.

   Journal Entry:
   ```
   Land ...................................  20,000
        Cash .............................         20,000
   Paid cash for land
   ```

   Ledger Accounts:

Cash		Land	
(1) 50,000	(2) 20,000	(2) 20,000	

3. *Transaction:* He purchased $500 office supplies on account payable.

   Analysis: The credit purchase of office supplies increased this asset; to record this increase, debit Office Supplies.

   The purchase also increased the liability accounts payable; to record this increase, credit Accounts Payable.

   Journal Entry:
   ```
   Office Supplies .........................  500
        Accounts Payable...................        500
   Purchased office supplies on account.
   ```

   Ledger Accounts:

Office Supplies		Accounts Payable	
(3) 500			(3) 500

4. *Transaction:* He paid $400 on the account payable created in the preceding transaction.

Analysis: The payment decreased the asset cash; therefore, credit Cash. The payment also decreased the liability, accounts payable; to record this decrease, debit Accounts Payable.

Journal Accounts Payable. 400
Entry: Cash   400
    Paid cash on account.

Ledger
Accounts:

Cash				Accounts Payable		
(1)	50,000	(2)	20,000	(4) **400**	(3)	500
		(4)	**400**			

5. *Transaction:* He remodeled personal residence. This is not a business transaction of the accounting practice, so no journal entry is made.

6. *Transaction:* Lyon withdrew $2,100 cash for personal living expenses.

Analysis: The withdrawal decreased the entity's cash; therefore, credit Cash.

The transaction also decreased the owner's equity of the entity and must be recorded by a debit to an owner's equity account. Decreases in the owner's equity of a proprietorship that result from owner withdrawals are debited to a separate owner's equity account entitled Withdrawals. Therefore, debit Gary Lyon, Withdrawals.

Journal Gary Lyon, Withdrawals. 2,100
Entry: Cash   2,100
    Withdrawal of cash by owner.

Ledger
Accounts:

Cash				Gary Lyon, Withdrawals	
(1)	50,000	(2)	20,000	(6)	**2,100**
		(4)	400		
		(6)	**2,100**		

As each journal entry is posted to the ledger, it is keyed by date or by transaction number. In this way, a trail is provided through the accounting records so that any transaction can be traced from the journal to the ledger and, if need be, back to the journal. This linking allows the accountant to locate efficiently any information needed.

Ledger Accounts after Posting

We next illustrate how the accounts look when the amounts of the preceding transactions have been posted. The accounts are grouped under the accounting equation's headings.

Note that each account has a balance figure. This amount is the difference between the account's total debits and its total credits. For example, the balance in the Cash account is the difference between the debits, $50,000, and the credits, $22,500 ($20,000 + $400 + $2,100). Thus the balance figure is $27,500. The balance amounts are not journal entries posted to the accounts, so we set an account balance apart by horizontal lines.

If the sum of an account's debits is greater than the sum of its credits, that account has a debit balance, as the Cash account does here. If the sum of its credits is greater, that account has a credit balance, as Accounts Payable does.

Assets	=	Liabilities	+	Owner's Equity

Cash

(1) 50,000	(2) 20,000
	(4) 400
	(6) 2,100
Bal. 27,500	

Accounts Payable

(4) 400	(3) 500
	Bal. 100

Gary Lyon, Capital

	(1) 50,000
	Bal. 50,000

Office Supplies

(3) 500	
Bal. 500	

Gary Lyon, Withdrawals

(6) 2,100	
Bal. 2,100	

Land

(2) 20,000	
Bal. 20,000	

Trial Balance

A **trial balance** is a list of all accounts with their balances. It provides a check on accuracy by showing whether the total debits equal the total credits. A trial balance may be taken at any time the postings are up to date. Exhibit 2-6 is the trial balance of the general ledger of Gary Lyon's accounting practice after the first six transactions have been journalized and posted.

The word *trial* is well chosen. The list is prepared as a *test* of the accounts' balances. The trial balance shows the accountant whether the total debits and total credits are equal. In this way it may signal accounting errors. For example, if only the debit (or only the credit) side of a transaction is posted, the total debits will not equal the total credits. If a debit is posted as a credit or vice versa, debits and credits will be out of balance. For example, if the $500 debit in Office Supplies

OBJECTIVE 5

Prepare a trial balance

EXHIBIT 2-6 *Trial Balance*

Gary Lyon, CPA
Trial Balance
April 30, 19X1

Account Titles	Balance	
	Debit	Credit
Cash..............................	$27,500	
Office supplies.....................	500	
Land.............................	20,000	
Accounts payable		$ 100
Gary Lyon, capital.................		50,000
Gary Lyon, withdrawals.............	2,100	
Total.......................	$50,100	$50,100

is incorrectly posted as a credit, total debits will be $49,600 and total credits will be $50,600. The trial balance alerts the accountant to such errors in posting.

Some errors may not be revealed by the trial balance. For example, a $1,000 cash payment for supplies may be credited to Accounts Payable instead of to Cash. This error would cause both Cash and Accounts Payable to be overstated, each by $1,000. However, because an asset and a liability are overstated by the same amount, the trial balance would still show debits equal to credits. Also, if an accountant erroneously recorded a $5,000 transaction at only $500, the trial balance would show no error. However, total debits and total credits would both be understated by $4,500 (that is, $5,000 − $500).

Summary Problem for Your Review

On August 1, 19X5, Liz Shea, opens a business that she names Shea's Research Service. She will be the sole owner of the business, so it will be a proprietorship. During the entity's first ten days of operations, the following transactions take place:

a. To begin operations, Shea deposits $50,000 of personal funds in a bank account entitled Shea's Research Service.
b. Shea pays $40,000 cash for a small house to be used as an office. (Debit an asset account entitled Building.)
c. Shea purchases $250 in office supplies on credit (that is, on account).
d. Shea pays cash of $6,000 for office furniture. (Debit Office Furniture.)
e. Shea pays $150 on the account payable she created in transaction *c*.
f. Shea withdraws $1,000 cash for personal use.

Required

1. Prepare the journal entries to record these transactions. Key the journal entries by letter.
2. Post the entries to the ledger.
3. Prepare the trial balance of Shea's Research Service at August 10, 19X5.

SOLUTION TO REVIEW PROBLEM

Requirement 1

ACCOUNTS and EXPLANATION	Debit	Credit
a. Cash	50,000	
Liz Shea, Capital		50,000
Initial investment by owner.		
b. Building	40,000	
Cash		40,000
Purchased building for an office.		
c. Office Supplies	250	
Accounts Payable		250
Purchased office supplies on account.		

d. Office Furniture 6,000
      Cash 6,000
    Purchased office furniture.

e. Accounts Payable..................................... 150
      Cash 150
    Paid cash on account.

f. Liz Shea, Withdrawals................................. 1,000
      Cash 1,000
    Withdrew cash for personal use.

Requirement 2

Assets

Cash				Office Supplies		
(a)	50,000	(b)	40,000	(c)	250	
		(d)	6,000			
		(e)	150	Bal.	250	
		(f)	1,000			
Bal.	2,850					

Office Furniture		Building	
(d)	6,000	(b)	40,000
Bal.	6,000	Bal.	40,000

Liabilities

Accounts Payable			
(e)	150	(c)	250
		Bal.	100

Owner's Equity

Liz Shea, Capital		Liz Shea, Withdrawals		
	(a) 50,000	(f)	1,000	
	Bal. 50,000	Bal.	1,000	

Requirement 3

Shea's Research Service
Trial Balance
August 10, 19X5

	Balance	
Account Title	**Debit**	**Credit**
Cash.............................	$ 2,850	
Office supplies	250	
Office furniture	6,000	
Building	40,000	
Accounts payable..................		$ 100
Liz Shea, capital..................		50,000
Liz Shea, withdrawals..............	1,000	
Total	$50,100	$50,100

Details of Journals and Ledgers _____

In order to focus on the main points of journalizing and posting, we purposely omitted certain essential data. In actual practice, the journal and the ledger provide additional details that create a "trail" through the accounting records for future reference. For example, an accountant may need to verify the date of a transaction or to determine whether a journal entry has been posted to the ledger. Let's take a closer look at the journal and the ledger.

Journal.   Exhibit 2-7, Panel B, presents the journal format most often used by accountants. The top of the journal holds the journal title. Note also that the journal page number appears in the upper-right corner.

As the column headings indicate, the *journal* displays the following information:

1. The *date,* which is most important because it indicates when the transaction occurred. The year appears first. It is not necessary to repeat it for each journal entry. The year appears only when the journal is started or when the year has changed. Note that the year appears with an X in the third column. We present the year in this way because the dates we choose are for illustration only. Thus 19X1 is followed by 19X2, and so on. We will use this format throughout the book. Like the year, the month is entered only once. The second date column shows the day of the transaction. This column is filled in for every transaction.
2. The *account title* and explanation of the transaction. You are already familiar with this presentation from Exhibit 2-3.
3. The *posting reference,* abbreviated Post. Ref. How this column helps the accountant becomes clear when we discuss the details of posting.
4. The *debit* column, which shows the amount debited.
5. The *credit* column, which shows the amount credited.

Ledger.   Exhibit 2-7, Panel C, presents the *ledger* in T-account format. Each account has its own page in the ledger. Our example shows Gary Lyon's Cash account. This account maintains the basic format of the T-account but offers more information.

The account title appears at the top of the page. Note also the account number at the upper-right column. Each account has its own identification number. We will look later at how accountants assign account numbers.

The column headings identify the ledger account's features.

1. The date.
2. The item column. This space is used for any special notation.
3. The journal reference column, abbreviated Jrnl. Ref. The importance of this column becomes clear when we discuss the mechanics of posting.
4. The debit column, with the amount debited.
5. The credit column, with the amount credited.

Posting _____

We know that posting means moving information from the journal to the ledger accounts. But how do we handle the additional details that appear in the journal and the ledger formats that we have just seen? Exhibit 2-7 illustrates the steps in

EXHIBIT 2-7 *Details of Journalizing and Posting*

Panel A—Illustrative Transactions

Date	Transaction
April 2, 19X1	Gary Lyon invested $50,000 in his
	accounting practice.
3	Paid $500 cash for office supplies.

Panel B—Journal

Page 1

Date	Accounts and Explanation	Post Ref.	Debit	Credit
19X1				
Apr. 2	Cash	11	50,000	
	Gary Lyon, Capital	31		50,000
	Initial investment			
3	Office Supplies	13	500	
	Cash	11		500
	Purchased office supplies.			

① ② ③ ④

Panel C—Ledger

Cash   Account No. 11

Date	Item	Jrnl. Ref.	Debit	Date	Item	Jrnl. Ref.	Credit
19X1				19X1			
Apr. 2		J.1	50,000	Apr. 3		J.1	500

Office Supplies   Account No. 13

Date	Item	Jrnl. Ref.	Debit	Date	Item	Jrnl. Ref.	Credit
19X1							
Apr. 3		J.1	500				

Gary Lyon, Capital   Account No. 31

Date	Item	Jrnl. Ref.	Debit	Date	Item	Jrnl. Ref.	Credit
				19X1			
				Apr. 2		J.1	50,000

full detail. Panel A lists the first two transactions of Gary Lyon, CPA; Panel B presents the journal; and Panel C shows the ledger.

Since the flow of accounting data moves from the journal to the ledger, the accountant first records the journal entry, as shown in Panel B. The transaction data are given in Panel A, except for the Post. Ref. number. Let's trace the arrows to follow the details of posting.

Arrow 1 traces the date, Apr. 2, 19X1, from the journal to the ledger account Cash.

Arrow 2 begins at the journal's page number, Page 1, and ends in the journal reference column, Jrnl. Ref. of the ledger. The *J.1* entry in that column stands for "Journal (page) 1." Why bother with this detail? If an accountant is using the Cash account and needs to locate the original journal entry, the journal page number tells where to look.

Arrow 3 indicates that the accountant posts the debit figure—$50,000 in this journal entry—as a debit figure in the account.

Arrow 4 points to a posting detail. Once the accountant has posted a dollar figure to the appropriate account, that account's number is entered in the journal's Post. Ref. column. This step indicates that the information for that account has been posted from the journal to the ledger. A blank Post Ref. column for a journal entry means that the entry has not yet been posted to the ledger account.

Having performed these steps for the debit entry, the accountant then posts the credit entry to the ledger. After posting, the accountant draws up the trial balance, as we discussed earlier.

Four-Column Account Format

The ledger accounts illustrated in Exhibit 2-7 are in two-column T-account format, with the debit column placed left and the credit column placed right. The T-account clearly distinguishes debits from credits and is often used for illustrative purposes that do not require much detail.

Another standard format has four amount columns, as illustrated for the Cash account in Exhibit 2-8. The first pair of amount columns are for the debit and credit amounts, and the second pair of amount columns are for the account's balance. This four-column format keeps a running balance in the account and for this reason is used more often in actual practice.

In the exhibit, Cash has a debit balance of $50,000 after the first transaction is posted and a debit balance of $49,500 after the second transaction.

EXHIBIT 2-8 *Account in Four-Column Format*

					Balance	
Account Cash					**Account No.** 11	
Date	**Item**	**Jrnl. Ref.**	**Debit**	**Credit**	**Debit**	**Credit**
19X1						
Apr.2		J.1	50000		50000	
3		J.1		500	49500	

Chart of Accounts _____

As you know, the general ledger contains the business's accounts grouped under the headings Assets, Liabilities, Owner's Equity, Revenues, and Expenses. To keep track of their accounts, organizations have a **chart of accounts,** which lists all the accounts and their account numbers. These account numbers are used as posting references, as illustrated by arrow 4 in Exhibit 2-7. It is easier to write the account number, 11, in the posting reference column of the journal than to write the account title, Cash. Also, this numbering system makes it easy to locate individual accounts in the ledger.

Assets are usually numbered beginning with 1, liabilities with 2, owner's equity with 3, revenues with 4, and expenses with 5. The second digit in an account number indicates the position of the individual account within the category. For example, Cash may be account number 11, which is the first asset account. Accounts Receivable may be account number 12, the second asset account. Accounts Payable may be account number 21, the first liability account. All accounts are numbered using this system.

Many organizations have so many accounts that they use three- or four-digit account numbers. For example, account number 101 may be Cash on Hand, account number 102 may be Cash on Deposit in First National Bank, and account number 103 may be Cash on Deposit in Lakewood Bank.

The chart of accounts for Gary Lyon, CPA, appears in Exhibit 2-9. Notice that the account numbers jump from 13 to 17. Gary Lyon realizes that later he may need to add other supplies accounts—for example, Tax Forms Supplies. Any additional supplies account would logically appear after Office Supplies, and Tax Forms Supplies might be account number 14.

Normal Balances of Accounts _____

Accountants speak of an account's *normal balance,* which refers to the side of the account—debit or credit—where *increases* are recorded. This term also refers to the usual balance—debit or credit—in the account. For example, Cash and all

EXHIBIT 2-9   *Chart of Accounts—Accounting Practice of Gary Lyon, CPA*

Balance Sheet Accounts:

Assets	Liabilities	Owner's Equity
11 Cash	21 Accounts Payable	31 Gary Lyon, Capital
12 Accounts Receivable	22 Notes Payable	32 Gary Lyon, Withdrawals
13 Office Supplies		
17 Office Furniture		
19 Land		

Income Statement Accounts:

Revenues	Expenses
41 Service Revenue	51 Rent Expense
	52 Salary Expense
	53 Utilities Expense

EXHIBIT 2-10 *Normal Balances of Balance Sheet Accounts*

Assets	=	Liabilities	+	Owner's Equity
Normal Bal. Debit		Normal Bal. Credit		Normal Bal. Credit

other assets usually have a debit balance, so assets are *debit-balance* accounts. On the other hand, liabilities and owner's equity usually have a credit balance, so they are *credit-balance* accounts. Exhibit 2-10 illustrates the normal balances of assets, liabilities, and owner's equity.

An account that normally has a debit balance may occasionally have a credit balance. This indicates a negative amount of the item. For example, Cash will have a temporary credit balance if the entity overdraws its bank account. Similarly, the liability Accounts Payable—normally a credit balance account—will have a debit balance if the entity overpays its account. In other instances, the shift of a balance amount away from its normal column indicates an accounting error. For example, a credit balance in Office Supplies, Office Furniture, or Buildings indicates an error because negative amounts of these assets cannot exist.

As we have explained, owner's equity usually contains several accounts. In total, these accounts show a normal credit balance for the owner's equity of the business. Each individual owner's equity account has a normal credit balance if it represents an *increase* in owner's equity (for example, the Capital account). However, if the individual owner's equity account represents a *decrease* in owner's equity, the account will have a normal debit balance (for example, the Withdrawals account).

Additional Owner's Equity Accounts: Revenues and Expenses

The owner's equity category includes two additional types of accounts: revenues and expenses. As we have discussed, **revenues** are increases in owner's equity that result from delivering goods or services to customers. **Expenses** are decreases in owner's equity due to the cost of operating the business. Therefore, the accounting equation may be expanded as follows:

ASSETS = LIABILITIES + OWNER'S EQUITY

(CAPITAL − WITHDRAWALS) + (REVENUES − EXPENSES)

Revenues and expenses appear in parentheses because their impact on the accounting equation arises from their effect on owner's equity. If revenues exceed expenses, the net effect—revenues minus expenses—is net income, which increases owner's equity. If expenses are greater, the net effect is a net loss, which decreases owner's equity.

We can now express the *rules of debit and credit* in final form as shown in Exhibit 2-11, Panel A. Panel B shows the *normal balances* of the five types of accounts.

EXHIBIT 2-11 *Rules of Debit and Credit and Normal Balances of Accounts*

Panel A—Rules of Debit and Credit:

Assets		=	Liabilities		+	Capital	
Debit for Increase	Credit for Decrease		Debit for Decrease	Credit for Increase		Debit for Decrease	Credit for Increase

Withdrawals

Debit for Increase	Credit for Decrease

Revenues

Debit for Decrease	Credit for Increase

Expenses

Debit for Increase	Credit for Decrease

Panel B—Normal Balances:

Assets	Debit
Liabilities	Credit
Owner's equity-overall	Credit
Capital	Credit
Withdrawals	Debit
Revenue	Credit
Expenses	Debit

All of accounting is based on these five types of accounts. You should become very familiar with the related rules of debit and credit and the normal balances of accounts.

Typical Account Titles

Thus far we have dealt with a limited number of transactions and accounts to introduce key concepts. Actual businesses engage in more transactions, requiring more accounts. Additional transactions are recorded in the same manner, with accounts added to the analysis as needed. The following summary describes some of the more common accounts grouped by financial statement and account category. As you work exercises and problems in this and future chapters, you will find these descriptions useful.

Income Statement—Revenues and Expenses

Revenues

Service revenue: Revenue earned by performing a service (accounting service by a CPA firm, laundry service by a laundry, and so forth).

Sales revenue: Revenue earned by selling a product (sales of hardware by a hardware store, food by a grocery store, and so forth).

Expenses

Rent expense: Expense for office rent and the rental of office equipment or the rental of any other business asset.

Salary or wage expense: Expense of having employees work for the business.

Utilities expense: Expense of using electricity, water, gas, and other items provided by utility companies.

Supplies expense: Expense of using supplies such as stationery, stamps, paper clips, staples, and so forth.

Advertising expense: Expense of advertising the business.

Interest expense: Expense of using borrowed money.

Property tax expense: Expense for property tax on business land and buildings.

Balance Sheet—Assets, Liabilities, and Owner's Equity

Assets

Cash: Money on hand and in the bank

Accounts receivable: Claim on open account against the cash of a client or a customer. (Open account means that no promissary note exists to support the receivable.)

Note receivable: Claim against the cash of another party, supported by a promissory note signed by the other party. (*All receivables are assets, and any account with* receivable *in its title is an asset.*)

Merchandise inventory: Merchandise that an entity sells in its business (such as clothing by a department store, stereos by a stereo shop, and so forth).

Office supplies: Stationery, stamps, paper clips, staples, and so forth.

Office furniture: Desks, chairs, file cabinets, and so forth.

Office equipment: Typewriters, calculators, and other equipment used in a business office. A business may have other types of equipment, such as delivery equipment or store equipment.

Building: Building used in a business.

Land: Land on which a business building stands.

Liabilities

Account payable: Liability to pay cash to another party on open account.

Note payable: Liability to pay cash to another party, supported by a signed promissory note.

Salary or wage payable: Liability to pay an employee for work. (*Most liabilities have the word* payable *in the account title, and any account with* payable *in its title is a liability.*)

Owner's Equity

Gary Lyon, Capital: The interest of the owner of the business in its assets. (This account title bears the name of the owner.)

Gary Lyon, Withdrawals: The owner's withdrawals of assets from the business for personal use.

Illustrative Problem _____

Let's account for the revenues and expenses of the accounting practice of Sara Nichols, Attorney for the month of July 19X1. We follow the same steps illustrated earlier: analyze the transaction, journalize, post to the ledger, and prepare the trial balance. Revenue accounts and expense accounts work just like asset, liability, and owner's equity accounts. Each revenue and each expense account has its own page in the ledger and its own identifying account number.

OBJECTIVE 6

Record revenues and expenses

Transaction Analysis, Journalizing, and Posting

1. *Transaction:* Sara Nichols invested $10,000 cash in a business bank account to open her law practice.

   Analysis: The asset cash is increased; therefore debit Cash.
   The owner's equity of the business increased; therefore, credit Sara Nichols, Capital

   Journal Entry:
   Cash 10,000
       Sara Nichols, Capital 10,000
   Invested cash in the business.

   Ledger Accounts:

Cash		Sara Nichols, Capital	
(1) 10,000			(1) 10,000

2. *Transaction:* Nichols performed service for a client and collected $3,000 cash.

   Analysis: The asset cash is increased; therefore, debit Cash.
   The revenue service revenue is increased; credit Service Revenue.

   Journal Entry:
   Cash 3,000
       Service Revenue 3,000
   Performed service and received cash.

   Ledger Accounts:

Cash		Service Revenue	
(1) 10,000			(2) 3,000
(2) 3,000			

3. *Transaction:* Nichols performed service for a client and billed the client for $500 on account receivable. This means the client owes the business $500 even though the client signed no formal promissory note.

   Analysis: The asset accounts receivable is increased; therefore, debit Accounts Receivable.
   The revenue service revenue is increased; credit Service Revenue.

   Journal Entry:
   Accounts Receivable 500
       Service Revenue 500
   Performed service on account.

Ledger Accounts:

Accounts Receivable	Service Revenue
(3) 500	(2) 3,000
	(3) 500

4. *Transaction:* Nichols performed accounting service of $700 for a client, who paid $300 cash immediately. Nichols billed the remaining $400 to the client on account receivable.

   Analysis: The assets cash and accounts receivable are increased; therefore, debit both of these asset accounts.

   The revenue service revenue is increased; credit Service Revenue for the sum of the two debit amounts.

   Journal Entry:
   Cash 300
   Accounts Receivable 400
       Service Revenue......................... 700
   Performed service for cash and on account.

   Note: Because this transaction affects more than two accounts at the same time, the entry is called a *compound entry*. No matter how many accounts a compound entry affects—there may be any number—total debits must equal total credits.

   Ledger Accounts:

Cash	Accounts Receivable
(1) 10,000	(3) 500
(2) 3,000	(4) 400
(4) 300	

Service Revenue
(2)   3,000
(3)   500
(4)   700

5. *Transaction:* Nichols paid the following cash expenses: office rent, $900; employee salary, $1,500; and utilities, $500.

   Analysis: The following expenses are increased: Rent Expense, Salary Expense, and Utilities Expense. They should each be debited.

   The asset cash is decreased; therefore, credit Cash for the sum of the three expense amounts.

   Journal Entry:
   Rent Expense 900
   Salary Expense............................ 1,500
   Utilities Expense......................... 500
       Cash 2,900
   Paid cash expenses.

   Ledger Accounts:

Cash		Rent Expense
(1) 10,000	(5) 2,900	(5) 900
(2) 3,000		
(4) 300		

Salary Expense	Utilities Expense
(5) 1,500	(5) 500

6. *Transaction:*   Nichols received a telephone bill for $120 and will pay this expense next week.

   Analysis: Utilities expense is increased; therefore, debit this expense. The liability accounts payable is increased; credit this account.

   Journal Entry:
   Utilities Expense............................. 120
       Accounts Payable....................... 120
   Received utility bill.

   Ledger Accounts:

Accounts Payable			
	(6)	120	

Utilities Expense			
(5)	500		
(6)	120		

7. *Transaction:*   Nichols collected $200 cash from the client established in Transaction 3.

   Analysis: The asset cash is increased; therefore, debit Cash.
   The asset accounts receivable is decreased; therefore, credit Accounts Receivable.

   Journal Entry:
   Cash 200
       Accounts Receivable 200
   Received cash on account.

   Note: This transaction has no effect on revenue; the related revenue is accounted for in transaction 3.

   Ledger Accounts:

Cash			
(1)	10,000	(5)	2,900
(2)	3,000		
(4)	300		
(7)	200		

Accounts Receivable			
(3)	500	(7)	200
(4)	400		

8. *Transaction:*   Nichols paid the telephone bill that was received and recorded in transaction 6.

   Analysis: The liability accounts payable is decreased; therefore, debit Accounts Payable.

   The asset cash is decreased; credit Cash.

   Journal Entry:
   Accounts Payable............................ 120
       Cash 120
   Paid cash on account.

   Note: This transaction has no effect on expense because the related expense was recorded in transaction 6.

   Ledger Accounts:

Cash			
(1)	10,000	(5)	2,900
(2)	3,000	(8)	120
(4)	300		
(7)	200		

Accounts Payable			
(8)	120	(6)	120

9. *Transaction:*   Nichols withdrew $1,100 cash for personal use.

Analysis:	The withdrawal decreased owner's equity; therefore, debit Sara Nichols, Withdrawals.
	The asset cash decreased; credit Cash.
Journal Entry:	Sara Nichols, Withdrawals 1,100
	Cash 1,100
	Withdrew for personal use.

Ledger Accounts:

Cash				Sara Nichols, Withdrawals	
(1) 10,000	(5)	2,900		**(9) 1,100**	
(2) 3,000	(8)	120			
(4) 300	**(9)**	**1,100**			
(7) 200					

Ledger Accounts After Posting

Assets

Cash				Accounts Receivable			
(1) 10,000	(5)	2,900	(3)	500	(7)	200	
(2) 3,000	(8)	120	(4)	400			
(4) 300	(9)	1,100	Bal.	700			
(7) 200							
Bal. 9,380							

Liabilities

Accounts Payable			
(8) 120	(6)	120	
	Bal.	0	

Owner's Equity

Sara Nichols, Capital		Sara Nichols, Withdrawals	
	(1) 10,000	(9) 1,100	
	Bal. 10,000	Bal. 1,100	

Owner's Equity

Revenue

Service Revenue		
	(2)	3,000
	(3)	500
	(4)	700
	Bal.	4,200

Expenses

Rent Expense		Salary Expense		Utilities Expense	
(5) 900		(5) 1,500		(5) 500	
Bal. 900		Bal. 1,500		(6) 120	
				Bal. 620	

Trial Balance

Sara Nichols, Attorney
Trial Balance
July 31, 19X1

Account Title	Balance	
	Debit	Credit
Cash..................................	$ 9,380	
Accounts receivable	700	
Accounts payable		$ 0
Sara Nichols, capital....................		10,000
Sara Nichols, withdrawals	1,100	
Service revenue........................		4,200
Rent expense..........................	900	
Salary expense.........................	1,500	
Utilities expense	620	
Total.............................	$14,200	$14,200

Analytical Use of Accounting Information _____

OBJECTIVE 7

Analyze transactions
without a journal

What dominates the accountant's analysis of transactions: the accounting equation, the journal, or the ledger? The *accounting equation* is most fundamental. In turn, the ledger is more useful than the journal in providing an overall model of the organization. Accountants and other businesspersons must often make quick decisions without the benefit of a complete accounting system: journal, ledger, accounts, and trial balance. For example, the owner of a company may be negotiating the purchase price of another business. For a quick analysis of the effects of transactions, accountants often skip the journal and go directly to the ledger. They compress transaction analysis, journalizing, and posting into one step. This type of analysis saves time that may be the difference between a good business decision and a lost opportunity.

Let's take an example to see how it works. For instance, the first revenue transaction—Sara Nichols performed accounting service for a client and collected cash of $3,000—may be analyzed be debiting the Cash account and crediting the Service Revenue account directly in the ledger in the following manner:

Cash		Service Revenue	
3,000			3,000

With this short cut, the accountant can see immediately the effect of the transaction on both the entity's cash and its service revenue. Modern computer-assisted accounting systems often have this "journal-less" feature. These systems can also produce the essential data for individual transactions, such as the date, the transaction amount, and the accounts affected.

Summary Problem for Your Review

The trial balance of Tomassini Computer Service Center on March 1, 19X2, lists the entity's assets, liabilities, and owner's equity on that date.

	Balance	
Account Title	Debit	Credit
Cash.............................	$26,000	
Accounts receivable	4,500	
Accounts payable		$ 2,000
L. Tomassini, capital...................		28,500
Total...........................	$30,500	$30,500

During March the business engaged in the following transactions:

1. Tomassini borrowed $45,000 from the bank. He signed a note payable in the name of the business.
2. He paid cash of $40,000 to a real estate company to acquire land.
3. He performed service for a customer and received cash of $5,000.
4. He purchased supplies on credit, $300.
5. He performed customer service and earned revenue on account, $2,600.
6. He paid $1,200 on account.
7. He paid the following cash expenses: salaries, $3,000; rent, $1,500; and interest, $400.
8. He received $3,100 on account.
9. He received a $200 utility bill that will be paid next week.
10. Tomassini withdrew $1,800 for personal use.

Required

1. Open the following accounts, with the balances indicated, in the ledger of Tomassini Computer Service Center. Use the T-account format.

    Assets—Cash, $26,000; Accounts Receivable, $4,500; Supplies, no balance; Land, no balance

    Liabilities—Accounts Payable, $2,000; Note Payable, no balance

    Owner's Equity—Larry Tomassini, Capital, $28,500; Larry Tomassini, Withdrawals, no balance

    Revenues—Service Revenue, no balance

    Expenses—(none have balances) Salary Expense, Rent Expense, Utilities Expense, Interest Expense

2. Journalize the preceding transactions. Key journal entries by transaction number.
3. Post to the ledger.
4. Prepare the trial balance of Tomassini Computer Service Center at March 31, 19X2.
5. Compute the net income or net loss of the entity during the month of March. List expenses in order from the largest to the smallest.

SOLUTION TO REVIEW PROBLEM

Requirement 1

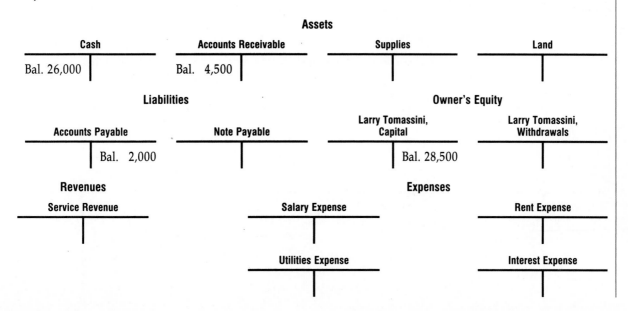

Requirement 2

Accounts and Explanation	Debit	Credit
1. Cash...	45,000	
Note Payable..................................		45,000
Borrowed cash on note payable.		
2. Land...	40,000	
Cash..		40,000
Purchased land for cash.		
3. Cash...	5,000	
Service Revenue		5,000
Performed service and received cash.		
4. Supplies...	300	
Accounts Payable		300
Purchased supplies on account.		
5. Accounts Receivable...............................	2,600	
Service Revenue		2,600
Performed service on account.		
6. Accounts Payable	1,200	
Cash..		1,200
Paid on account.		
7. Salary Expense	3,000	
Rent Expense.....................................	1,500	
Interest Expense	400	
Cash..		4,900
Paid cash expenses.		
8. Cash...	3,100	
Accounts Receivable...........................		3,100
Received on account.		
9. Utilities Expense	200	
Accounts Payable		200
Received utility bill.		
10. Larry Tomassini, Withdrawals......................	1,800	
Cash..		1,800
Withdrew for personal use.		

Requirement 3

Assets

Cash			
Bal. 26,000	(2)	40,000	
(1) 45,000	(6)	1,200	
(3) 5,000	(7)	4,900	
(8) 3,100	(10)	1,800	
Bal. 31,200			

Accounts Receivable		
Bal. 4,500	(8)	3,100
(5) 2,600		
Bal. 4,000		

Supplies	
(4) 300	
Bal. 300	

Land	
(2) 40,000	
Bal. 40,000	

Liabilities

Accounts Payable

(6)	1,200	Bal.	2,000
		(4)	300
		(9)	200
		Bal.	1,300

Note Payable

(1)	45,000
Bal.	45,000

Owner's Equity

Larry Tomassini, Capital

Bal.	28,500

Larry Tomassini, Withdrawals

(10)	1,800
Bal.	1,800

Revenues

Service Revenue

(3)	5,000
(5)	2,600
Bal.	7,600

Expenses

Salary Expense

(7)	3,000
Bal.	3,000

Rent Expense

(7)	1,500
Bal.	1,500

Utilities Expense

(9)	200
Bal.	200

Interest Expense

(7)	400
Bal.	400

Requirement 4

Tomassini Computer Service Center
Trial Balance
March 31, 19X2

Account Title	Balance Debit	Credit
Cash..................................	$31,200	
Accounts Receivable.....................	4,000	
Supplies..............................	300	
Land.................................	40,000	
Accounts Payable......................		$ 1,300
Note Payable..........................		45,000
Larry Tomassini, Capital.................		28,500
Larry Tomassini, Withdrawals.............	1,800	
Service Revenue.......................		7,600
Salary Expense........................	3,000	
Rent Expense.........................	1,500	
Utilities Expense......................	200	
Interest Expense......................	400	
Total.................................	$82,400	$82,400

Requirement 5 Net income for the month of March

Revenues:		
Service revenue		$7,600
Expenses:		
Salary expense	$3,000	
Rent expense	1,500	
Interest expense	400	
Utilities expense	200	
Total expenses		5,100
Net income		$2,500

Summary

The *account* can be viewed in the form of the letter "T." The left side of each account is its *debit* side. The right side is its *credit* side. The *ledger,* which contains a record for each account, groups and numbers accounts by category in the following order: assets, liabilities, owner's equity, revenues, and expenses.

Assets and *expenses* are increased by debits and decreased by credits. *Liabilities, owner's equity,* and *revenues* are increased by credits and decreased by debits. The side—debit or credit—of the account in which increases are recorded is that account's normal balance. Thus the normal balance of assets and expenses is a debit, and the normal balance of liabilities, owner's equity, and revenues is a credit. Withdrawals, which decreases owner's equity, normally has a debit balance. *Revenues,* which are increases in owner's equity, have a normal credit balance. *Expenses,* which are decreases in owner's equity, have a normal debit balance.

The accountant begins the recording process by entering the transaction's information in the *journal,* a chronological list of all the business's transactions. The information is then posted—transferred—to the *ledger* accounts. Posting references are used to trace amounts back and forth between the journal and the ledger. Businesses list their account titles and numbers in a chart of accounts.

The *trial balance* is a summary of all the account balances in the ledger. When *double-entry accounting* has been done correctly, the total debits and the total credits in the trial balance are equal.

We can now trace the flow of accounting information through these steps:

Business Transaction → **Source Documents** → **Journal Entry** →
Posting to Ledger → **Trial Balance**

Self-Study Questions

Test your understanding of the chapter by marking the best answer for each of the following questions.

1. An account has two sides called the *(p. 42)*
   a. Debit and credit   c. Revenue and expense
   b. Asset and liability   d. Journal and ledger
2. Increases in liabilities are recorded by *(p. 43)*
   a. Debits   b. Credits

3. Why do accountants record transactions in the journal? *(p. 45)*
    a. To ensure that all transactions are posted to the ledger
    b. To ensure that total debits equal total credits
    c. To have a chronological record of all transactions
    d. To help prepare the financial statements
4. Posting is the process of transferring information from the *(p. 46)*
    a. Journal to the trial balance c. Ledger to the financial statements
    b. Ledger to the trial balance d. Journal to the ledger
5. The purchase of land for cash is recorded by a *(p. 48)*
    a. Debit to Cash and a credit to Land
    b. Debit to Cash and a debit to Land
    c. Debit to Land and a credit to Cash
    d. Credit to Cash and a credit to Land
6. The purpose of the trial balance is to *(p. 50)*
    a. Indicate whether total debits equal total credits
    b. Ensure that all transactions have been recorded
    c. Speed the collection of cash receipts from customers
    d. Increase assets and owner's equity
7. What is the normal balance of the Accounts Receivable, Office Supplies, and Rent Expense accounts? *(p. 58)*
    a. Debit b. Credit
8. A business has Cash of $3,000, Notes Payable of $2,500, Accounts Payable of $4,300, Service Revenue of $7,000, and Rent Expense of $1,800. Based on these data, how much are its total liabilities? *(p. 59)*
    a. $5,500 c. $9,800
    b. $6,800 d. $13,800
9. The earning of revenue that is not received in cash is recorded by a *(pp. 60, 61)*
    a. Debit to Cash and a credit to Revenue
    b. Debit to Accounts Receivable and a credit to Revenue
    c. Debit to Accounts Payable and a credit to Revenue
    d. Debit to Revenue and a credit to Accounts Receivable
10. The account credited for a receipt of cash on account is *(p. 62)*
    a. Cash c. Service Revenue
    b. Accounts Payable d. Accounts Receivable

Answers to the Self-Study Questions are at the end of the chapter.

Accounting Vocabulary

account *(p. 39)*,   chart of accounts *(p. 56)*,   credit *(p. 43)*,   debit *(p. 42)*,   journal *(p. 45)*,
ledger *(p. 39)*,   posting *(p. 46)*,   trial balance *(p. 50)*.

ASSIGNMENT MATERIAL _____

Questions

1. Name the basic summary device of accounting. What letter of the alphabet does it resemble, and what are its two sides called?
2. Is the following statement true or false? Debit means decrease and credit means increase. Explain your answer.
3. Write two sentences that use the term *debit* in different ways.

4. What are the three *basic* types of accounts? Name two additional types of accounts. To which one of the three *basic* types are these two additional types of accounts most closely related?

5. Suppose you are the accountant for Smith Courier Service. Keeping in mind double-entry bookkeeping, identify the *dual effects* of Mary Smith's investment of $10,000 cash in her business.

6. Briefly describe the flow of accounting information. (Hint: See the diagram in the chapter summary.)

7. To what does the *normal balance* of an account refer?

8. Complete the table by indicating the normal balance of the five types of accounts.

Account Type	Normal Balance
Assets	_____
Liabilities	_____
Capital	_____
Revenues	_____
Expenses	_____

9. What does posting accomplish? Why is it important? Does it come before or after journalizing?

10. Label each of the following transactions as increasing owner's equity (+), decreasing owner's equity (−), or as having no effect on owner's equity (0). Write the appropriate symbol in the space provided.

    _____ a. Investment by owner   _____ e. Cash payment on account
    _____ b. Revenue transaction   _____ f. Withdrawal by owner
    _____ c. Purchase of supplies on   _____ g. Borrowing money on a note
              credit   payable
    _____ d. Expense transaction   _____ h. Sale of services on account

11. What four steps does posting include? Which step is the fundamental purpose of posting?

12. Rearrange the following accounts in their logical sequence in the ledger:

    Notes Payable   Cash
    Accounts Receivable   Jane East, Capital
    Sales Revenue   Salary Expense

13. What is the meaning of the statement, Accounts Payable has a credit balance of $1,700?

14. Jack Brown Campus Cleaners launders the shirts of customer Bobby Baylor, who has a charge account at the cleaners. When Bobby picks up his clothes and is short on cash, he charges it. Later, when he receives his monthly statement from the cleaners, Bobby writes a check on Dear Old Dad's bank account and mails the check to Jack Brown. Identify the two business transactions described here. Which transaction increases Jack Brown's owner's equity? Which transaction increases Jack Brown's cash?

15. Explain the difference between the ledger and the chart of accounts.

16. Why do accountants prepare a trial balance?

17. What is a compound journal entry?

18. The accountant for Bower Construction Company mistakenly recorded a $500 purchase of supplies on account as a $5,000 purchase. He debited Supplies and credited Accounts Payable for $5,000. Does this error cause the trial balance to be out of balance? Explain your answer.

19. What is the effect on total assets of collecting cash on account from customers?

20. What is the advantage of analyzing and recording transactions without the use of a journal? Describe how this "journal-less" analysis works.

Exercises

Exercise 2-1 *Analyzing transactions*

Analyze the following transactions in the manner shown for the October 1 transaction:

Oct. 1 Paid monthly rent expense of $700. (Analysis: The expense rent expense is increased; therefore, debit Rent Expense. The asset cash is decreased; therefore credit Cash.)

    4 Received $350 cash on account from a customer.

    8 Performed service on account for a customer, $1,100.

  12 Purchased office furniture on account, $620.

  19 Sold for $19,000 land that had cost this same amount.

  24 Purchased building for $48,000; signed a note payable.

  27 Paid the liability created on October 12.

Exercise 2-2 *Journalizing transactions*

Garner Service Company engaged in the following transactions during March 19X3, its first month of operations:

Mar. 1 Lynn Garner invested $40,000 of cash to start the business.

    2 She purchased supplies of $200 on account.

    4 She paid $15,000 cash for land to use as a future building site.

    6 She performed service for customers and received cash, $2,000.

    9 She paid $100 on accounts payable.

  17 She performed service for customers on account, $1,600.

  23 She received $1,200 cash from customer on account.

  31 She paid the following expenses: salary, $1,200; rent, $500.

Required

Record the preceding transactions in the journal of Garner Service Company. Key transactions by date and include an explanation for each entry, as illustrated in the chapter. Use the following accounts: Cash; Accounts Receivable; Office Supplies; Land; Accounts Payable; Lynn Garner, Capital; Service Revenue; Salary Expense; Rent Expense.

Exercise 2-3 *Posting to the ledger and preparing a trial balance*

1. After journalizing the transactions of Exercise 2-2, post the entries to the ledger, using T-account format. Key transactions by date as in the following example. Label the balance of each account *Bal.*

Lynn Garner, Capital	
	Mar. 1 40,000

2. Prepare the trial balance of Garner Service Company at March 31, 19X3.

Exercise 2-4 *Describing transactions and posting*

The journal of Scholes Company appears at the top of the next page.

Required

1. Describe each transaction. Example: Aug. 5—Cash sale.
2. Post the transactions to the ledger using the following account numbers: Cash, 11; Accounts Receivable, 12; Supplies, 13; Accounts Payable, 21; Sales Revenue, 41; Rent

Journal   **Page 5**

Date	Accounts and Explanation	Post Ref.	Debit	Credit
Aug. 5	Cash...................................		850	
	Sales Revenue			850
9	Supplies		270	
	Accounts Payable			270
11	Accounts Receivable		2,100	
	Sales Revenue			2,100
14	Rent Expense..........................		900	
	Cash.................................			900
22	Cash.................................		1,400	
	Accounts Receivable			1,400
25	Advertising Expense		350	
	Cash.................................			350
27	Accounts Payable		270	
	Cash.................................			270
31	Utilities Expense		220	
	Accounts Payable			220

Expense, 51; Advertising Expense, 52; Utilities Expense, 53. Use dates, journal references, and posting references as illustrated in Exhibit 2-7. You may write the account numbers as posting references directly in your book unless directed otherwise by your instructor.

3. Compute the balance in each account after posting. The first debit amount of $850 is posted to Cash as an example:

Cash
|||
Aug. 5 J.5   850 |

Exercise 2-5   *Preparing a trial balance*

The accounts of Norman Realty Company are listed below with their normal balances at September 30, 19X4. The accounts are listed in no particular order.

Account	Balance
Ken Norman, capital	$48,800
Advertising expense......................	650
Accounts payable.........................	1,300
Sales commission revenue.................	16,000
Land	23,000
Note payable	25,000
Cash	7,000
Salary expense	3,000
Building.................................	45,000
Rent expense.............................	2,000
Ken Norman, withdrawals	4,000
Utilities expense	400
Accounts receivable	5,500
Supplies expense	300
Supplies	250

Required

Prepare the company's trial balance at September 30, 19X4, listing accounts in proper sequence, as illustrated in the chapter. Supplies comes before Building and Land. List the expense with the largest balance first, the expense with the next largest balance second, and so on.

Exercise 2-6   *Journalizing transactions*

The first five transactions of Hoyt Repair Service have been posted to the company's accounts as follows:

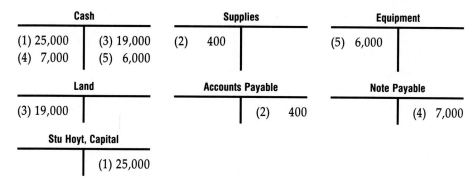

Cash		Supplies		Equipment	
(1) 25,000	(3) 19,000	(2) 400		(5) 6,000	
(4) 7,000	(5) 6,000				

Land		Accounts Payable		Note Payable	
(3) 19,000			(2) 400		(4) 7,000

Stu Hoyt, Capital	
	(1) 25,000

Required

Prepare the journal entries that served as the sources for the five transactions. Include an explanation for each entry as illustrated in the chapter.

Exercise 2-7   *Preparing a trial balance*

Prepare the trial balance of Hoyt Repair Service at September 30, 19X4, using the account data from the preceding exercise.

Exercise 2-8   *Correcting errors in a trial balance*

The trial balance of Walker Enterprises at November 30, 19X9, does not balance:

Cash	$ 6,000	
Accounts receivable	2,000	
Supplies	600	
Land	46,000	
Account payable		$ 3,000
Claudia Walker, capital		42,000
Service revenue		6,500
Salary expense	1,700	
Rent expense	800	
Utilities expense	300	
Total	$57,400	$51,500

Investigation of the accounting records reveals that the bookkeeper:

1. Recorded a cash revenue transaction by debiting Cash for the correct amount of $5,000 but failed to record the credit to Service Revenue.
2. Posted a $1,000 credit to Accounts Payable as $100.
3. Did not record utilities expense or the related account payable in the amount of $200.
4. Understated Cash and Claudia Walker, Capital, by $400 each.

Required

Prepare the correct trial balance at November 30, complete with a heading. Journal entries are not required.

Exercise 2-9 *Recording transactions without a journal*

Open the following T-accounts: Cash; Accounts Receivable; Office Supplies; Office Furniture; Accounts Payable; Lisa Lenski, Capital; Lisa Lenski, Withdrawals; Service Revenue; Salary Expense; Rent Expense.

Record the following transactions directly in the T-accounts without using a journal. Use the letters to identify the transactions.

a. Lisa Lenski opened an accounting firm by investing $10,000 cash and office furniture valued at $7,400.
b. Paid monthly rent of $1,500.
c. Purchased office supplies on account, $800.
d. Paid employee salary, $1,800.
e. Paid $400 of the account payable created in *c*.
f. Performed accounting service on account, $1,700.
g. Withdrew $2,000 for personal use.

Exercise 2-10 *Preparing a trial balance*

After recording the transactions in Exercise 2-9, prepare the trial balance of Lisa Lenski, CPA, at May 31, 19X7.

Problems   *(Group A)*

Problem 2-1A *Analyzing and journalizing transactions*

Paramount Theater Company owns movie theaters in the shopping centers of a major metropolitan area. Its owner, Robert Preston, engaged in the following business transactions:

Dec. 1   Preston invested $100,000 personal cash in the business by depositing this amount in a bank account entitled Paramount Theater Company.
      2   Paid $55,000 cash to purchase land for a theater site.
      5   Borrowed $300,000 from the bank to finance the construction of the new theater. Preston signed a note payable to the bank in the name of Paramount Theater Company.
      7   Received $20,000 cash from ticket sales and deposited this amount in the bank. (Label the revenue as Sales Revenue.)
     10   Purchased supplies for the older theaters on account, $1,700.
     15   Paid theater employee salaries, $2,800, and rent on a theater building, $1,800.
     15   Paid property tax expense on theater building, $1,200.
     16   Paid $800 on account.
     17   Withdrew $2,000 from the business to take his family to a nearby resort.

Paramount uses the following accounts: Cash; Supplies; Land; Accounts Payable; Notes Payable; Robert Preston, Capital; Robert Preston, Withdrawals; Sales Revenue; Salary Expense; Rent Expense; Property Tax Expense.

Required

1. Prepare an analysis of each business transaction of Paramount Theater Company, as shown for the December 1 transaction:

Dec. 1 The asset Cash is increased. Increases in assets are recorded by debits; therefore, debit Cash.

The owner's equity of the entity is increased. Increases in owner's equity are recorded by credits; therefore, credit Robert Preston, Capital.

2. Prepare the journal entry for each transaction. Explanations are not required.

Problem 2-2A *Journalizing transactions, posting to T-accounts and preparing a trial balance*

Gwen Kraft opened a law office on September 3 of the current year. During the first month of operations, the business completed the following transactions:

Sep. 3 Kraft transferred $25,000 cash from her personal bank account to a business account entitled Gwen Kraft, Attorney.

4 Purchased supplies, $200, and furniture, $1,800, on account.

6 Performed legal services for a client and received $1,000 cash.

7 Paid $15,000 cash to acquire land for a future office site.

10 Defended a client in court, billed the client, and received his promise to pay the $900 within one week.

14 Paid for the furniture purchased September 4 on account.

15 Paid the secretary's salary, $600.

16 Paid the telephone bill, $120.

17 Received partial payment from client on account, $700.

20 Prepared legal documents for a client on account, $800.

24 Paid the water and electricity bills, $110.

28 Received $1,500 cash for assisting a client sell real estate.

30 Paid secretary's salary, $600.

30 Paid rent expense, $500.

30 Withdrew $2,000 for personal use.

Required

Open the following T-accounts: Cash; Accounts Receivable; Supplies; Furniture; Land; Accounts Payable; Gwen Kraft, Capital; Gwen Kraft, Withdrawals; Service Revenue; Salary Expense; Rent Expense; Utilities Expense.

1. Record each transaction in the journal, using the account titles given. Key each transaction by date. Explanations are not required.
2. Post the transactions to the ledger, using transaction dates as posting references in the ledger. Label the balance of each account *Bal.*, as shown in the chapter.
3. Prepare the trial balance of Gwen Kraft, Attorney, at September 30 of the current year.

Problem 2-3A *Journalizing transactions, posting to accounts in four-column format, and preparing a trial balance*

The trial balance of the accounting practice of Rob Cheng, CPA, at February 14, 19X3, is shown at the top of the next page.

During the remainder of February, Cheng completed the following transactions:

Feb. 15 Cheng collected $2,000 cash from a client on account.

16 Performed tax services for a client on account, $700.

18 Paid utilities, $300.

20 Paid on account, $1,000.

21 Purchased supplies on account, $100.

21 Withdrew $1,200 for personal use.

21 Paid for a swimming pool for private residence, using personal funds, $13,000.

22   Received cash of $2,100 for audit work just completed.
28   Paid rent, $800.
28   Paid employees' salaries, $1,600.

Rob Cheng, CPA
Trial Balance
February 14, 19X3

Account Number	Account	Debit	Credit
11	Cash...	$ 4,000	
12	Accounts receivable	11,000	
13	Supplies......................................	800	
14	Land...	18,600	
21	Accounts payable		$ 3,000
31	Rob Cheng, capital		29,000
32	Rob Cheng, withdrawals	1,200	
41	Service revenue................................		6,200
51	Salary expense.................................	1,600	
52	Rent expense..................................	800	
53	Utilities expense	200	
	Total.......................................	$38,200	$38,200

Required

1.   Record the transactions that occurred during February 15 through 28 in *page 3* of the journal. Include an explanation for each entry.

2.   Open the ledger accounts listed in the trial balance, together with their balances at February 14. Use the four-column account format illustrated below. Enter *Bal.* (for previous balance) in the Item column, and place a check mark (✓) in the journal reference column for the February 14 balance, as illustrated for Cash:

Account   Cash   Account No. 11

| | | Jrnl. | | | Balance | |
Date	Item	Ref.	Debit	Credit	Debit	Credit
Feb. 14	Bal.	✓			4,000	

Post the transactions to the ledger, using dates, account numbers, journal references, and posting references.

3.   Prepare the trial balance of Rob Cheng, CPA, at February 28, 19X3.

Problem 2-4A   *Journalizing, posting to T-accounts, and preparing a trial balance*

Flaten Delivery Service completed the following transactions during its first month of operations:

a.   Dick Flaten, the proprietor of the business, began operations by investing $5,000 cash and a truck valued at $10,000 in the business.

b.   Paid $200 cash for supplies.

c.   Used a company credit card to purchase $50 fuel for the delivery truck. (Credit Accounts Payable).

d.   Performed delivery services for a customer and received $600 cash.

e. Completed a large delivery job, billed the customer $2,000, and received a promise to be paid the $2,000 within one week.

f. Paid employee salary, $800.

g. Received $900 cash for performing delivery services.

h. Purchased fuel for the truck on account, $40.

i. Received $2,000 cash from a customer on account.

j. Paid for advertising in the local newspaper, $170.

k. Paid utility bills, $100.

l. Purchased fuel for the truck, paying $30 with a company credit card.

m. Performed delivery services on account, $200.

n. Paid for repairs to the delivery truck, $110.

o. Paid employee salary, $800, and office rent, $200.

p. Paid $120 on account.

q. Withdrew $1,900 for personal use.

Required

1. Record each transaction in the journal, using the account titles given. Key each transaction by letter. Explanations are not required.

2. Open the following T-accounts: Cash; Accounts Receivable; Supplies; Delivery Truck; Accounts Payable; Dick Flaten, Capital; Dick Flaten, Withdrawals; Delivery Service Revenue; Salary Expense; Rent Expense; Advertising Expense; Fuel Expense; Repair Expense; Utilities Expense. Post the transactions to the ledger, keying transactions by letter. Label the balance of each account *Bal.*, as shown in the chapter. However, if an account has only one entry, it is not necessary to label the balance separately. If an account has a zero balance after posting, draw double underlines under the posted amounts.

3. Prepare the trial balance of Flaten Delivery Service, using the current date.

Problem 2-5A   *Correcting errors in a trial balance*

The following trial balance does not balance:

Family Counseling Services
Trial Balance
June 30, 19X2

Cash...............................	$ 2,000	
Accounts receivable	10,000	
Supplies.............................	900	
Office furniture	3,600	
Land................................	26,000	
Accounts payable		$ 4,000
Note payable.........................		14,000
Lisa Vivaldi, capital..................		22,000
Lisa Vivaldi, withdrawals..............	2,000	
Counseling service revenue		6,500
Salary expense.......................	1,600	
Rent expense.........................	1,000	
Advertising expense	500	
Utilities expense	300	
Property tax expense..................	100	
Total...............................	$48,000	$46,500

The following errors were detected:

a. The cash balance is understated by $300.
b. Property tax expense of $500 is omitted from the trial balance.
c. Land should be listed in the amount of $25,000.
d. A $200 purchase of supplies on account was neither journalized nor posted.
e. A $2,800 credit to Counseling Service Revenue was not posted.
f. Rent expense of $200 was posted as a credit rather than a debit.
g. The balance of Advertising Expense is $600, but it was listed as $500 on the trial balance.
h. A $300 debit to Accounts Receivable was posted as $30.
i. The balance of Utilities Expense is overstated by $70.
j. A $400 debit to the Withdrawal account was posted as a credit to Lisa Vivaldi, Capital.

Required

Prepare the correct trial balance at June 30. Journal entries are not required.

Problem 2-6A   *Recording transactions directly in the ledger, preparing a trial balance*

Peg Howison started a consulting service and during the first month of operations completed the following selected transactions:

a. Howison began the business with an investment of $15,000 cash and a building valued at $75,000.
b. Borrowed $30,000 from the bank; signed a note payable.
c. Purchased office supplies on account, $1,300.
d. Paid $18,000 for office furniture.
e. Paid employee salary, $2,200.
f. Performed consulting service on account for client, $2,100.
g. Paid $800 of the account payable created in *c*.
h. Received a $900 bill for advertising expense that will be paid in the near future.
i. Performed consulting service for customers and received cash, $1,600.
j. Received cash on account, $1,200.
k. Paid the following cash expenses:
    (1) Rent on land, $700.
    (2) Utilities, $400.
l. Withdrew $3,500 for personal use.

Required

1. Open the following T-accounts: Cash; Accounts Receivable; Office Supplies; Office Furniture; Building; Accounts Payable; Note Payable; Peg Howison, Capital; Peg Howison, Withdrawals; Service Revenue; Salary Expense; Advertising Expense; Rent Expense; Utilities Expense.
2. Record the following transactions directly in the T-accounts without using a journal. Use the letters to identify the transactions.
3. Prepare the trial balance of Howison Consulting Service at June 30, 19X3.

(Group B)

Problem 2-1B   *Analyzing and journalizing transactions*

Roland Marks practices medicine under the business title Roland Marks, M.D. During April his medical practice engaged in the following transactions:

Apr. 1 Marks deposited $50,000 cash in the business bank account.

5 Borrowed $20,000 from the bank for business use. Marks signed a note payable to the bank in the name of the business.

9 Paid $25,000 cash to purchase land for an office site.

10 Purchased supplies on account, $1,200.

19 Paid $1,000 on account.

30 Revenues earned during the month included $6,000 cash and $5,000 on account.

30 Paid employee salaries ($2,400), office rent ($1,500), and utilities ($400).

30 Paid monthly rent on medical equipment, $700.

30 Withdrew $4,000 from the business to take his family on a trip.

Marks's business uses the following accounts: Cash; Accounts Receivable; Supplies; Land; Accounts Payable; Notes Payable; Roland Marks, Capital; Roland Marks, Withdrawals; Service Revenue; Salary Expense; Rent Expense; Utilities Expense.

Required

1. Prepare an analysis of each business transaction of Roland Marks, M.D., as shown for the April 1 transaction:

   Apr. 1 The asset Cash is increased. Increases in assets are recorded by debits; therefore, debit Cash.

   The owner's equity is increased. Increases in owner's equity are recorded by credits; therefore, credit Roland Marks, Capital.

2. Prepare the journal entry for each transaction. Explanations are not required.

Problem 2-2B *Journalizing transactions, posting to T-accounts, and preparing a trial balance*

Nancy Katz opened a law office on January 2 of the current year. During the first month of operations the business completed the following transactions:

Jan. 2 Katz deposited $45,000 cash in a business bank account entitled Nancy Katz, Attorney.

3 Purchased supplies, $300, and furniture, $2,100, on account.

4 Performed legal services for a client and received cash, $1,500.

7 Paid cash to acquire land for a future office site, $22,000.

11 Defended a client in court, billed the client, and received his promise to pay the $800 within one week.

15 Paid secretary salary, $650.

16 Paid for the furniture purchased January 3 on account.

17 Paid the telephone bill, $110.

18 Received partial payment from client on account, $400.

19 Prepared legal documents for a client on account, $600.

22 Paid the water and electricity bills, $130.

29 Received $1,800 cash for helping a client sell real estate.

31 Paid secretary salary, $650.

31 Paid rent expense, $700.

31 Withdrew $2,200 for personal use.

Required

Open the following T-accounts: Cash; Accounts Receivable; Supplies; Furniture; Land; Accounts Payable; Nancy Katz, Capital; Nancy Katz, Withdrawals; Service Revenue; Salary Expense; Rent Expense; Utilities Expense.

1. Record each transaction in the journal, using the account titles given. Key each transaction by date. Explanations are not required.

2. Post the transactions to the ledger, using transaction dates as posting references in the ledger. Label the balance of each account *Bal.* as shown in the chapter.

3. Prepare the trial balance of Nancy Katz, Attorney, at January 31 of the current year.

Problem 2-3B *Journalizing transactions, posting to accounts in four-column format and preparing a trial balance*

The trial balance of the accounting practice of Ralph Cohen, CPA, at November 15, 19X3, was

Ralph Cohen, CPA
Trial Balance
November 15, 19X3

Account Number	Account	Debit	Credit
11	Cash	$ 5,000	
12	Accounts receivable	8,000	
13	Supplies	600	
14	Land	38,000	
21	Accounts payable..............		$ 4,400
31	Ralph Cohen, capital		45,000
32	Ralph Cohen, withdrawals	2,100	
41	Service revenue		7,100
51	Salary expense	1,800	
52	Rent expense	700	
53	Utilities expense	300	
	Total	$56,500	$56,500

During the remainder of November, Cohen completed the following transactions:

Nov. 16 Collected $4,000 cash from a client on account.
17 Performed tax services for a client on account, $1,200.
19 Paid utilities, $200.
21 Paid on account, $2,600.
22 Purchased supplies on account, $200.
23 Withdrew $2,100 for personal use.
23 Paid for the renovation of private residence, $55,000.
24 Received $1,900 cash for audit work just completed.
30 Paid rent, $700.
30 Paid employees' salaries, $1,800.

Required

1. Record the transactions that occurred during November 16 through 30 in page 6 of the journal. Include an explanation for each entry.

2. Post the transactions to the ledger, using dates, account numbers, journal references, and posting references. Open the ledger accounts listed in the trial balance together with their balances at November 15. Use the four-column account format illustrated below. Enter *Bal.* (for previous balance) in the Item column, and place a check mark (✓) in the journal reference column for the November 15 balance, as illustrated for Cash:

Account   Cash   **Account No. 11**

Date	Item	Jrnl. Ref.	Debit	Credit	Balance Debit	Balance Credit
Nov. 15	Bal.	✓			5,000	

3. Prepare the trial balance of Ralph Cohen, CPA, at November 30, 19X3.

Problem 2-4B   *Journalizing, posting to T-accounts, and preparing a trial balance*

Marquardt Delivery Service began operations during May of the current year. During a short period thereafter, the entity engaged in the following transactions:

a. Rube Marquardt, the owner, deposited $3,500 cash in a bank account entitled Marquardt Delivery Service and also invested in the business a delivery truck valued at $8,000.
b. Purchased $40 fuel for the delivery truck, using a business credit card.
c. Paid $100 cash for supplies.
d. Completed a delivery job and received cash, $700.
e. Performed delivery services on account, $3,200.
f. Purchased advertising leaflets for cash, $200.
g. Paid the office manager salary, $950.
h. Received $1,000 cash for performing delivery services.
i. Received cash from customer on account, $1,800.
j. Purchased used office furniture on account, $600.
k. Paid office utility bills, $120.
l. Purchased $70 fuel on account for the truck.
m. Completed a delivery job and received the customer's promise to pay the amount due, $500, within ten days.
n. Paid cash to creditor on account, $200.
o. Paid $250 for repairs to the delivery truck.
p. Paid office manager the salary of $950 and office rent of $250.
q. Withdrew $1,700 for personal use.

Required

1. Record each transaction in the journal, using the account titles given. Key each transaction by letter. Explanations are not required.
2. Open the following T-accounts: Cash; Accounts Receivable; Supplies; Delivery Truck; Office Furniture; Accounts Payable; R. Marquardt, Capital; R. Marquardt, Withdrawals; Delivery Service Revenue; Salary Expense; Rent Expense; Repair Expense; Advertising Expense; Utilities Expense; Fuel Expense. Post the transactions to the ledger, keying transactions by letter. Label the balance of each account *Bal.* as shown in the chapter. However, if an account only has one entry, it is not necessary to label the balance separately.
3. Prepare the trial balance of Marquardt Delivery Service, using the current date.

Problem 2-5B   *Correcting errors in a trial balance.*

The trial balance on the following page does not balance.

The following errors were detected:

a. The cash balance is overstated by $400.
b. Office maintenance expense of $200 is omitted from the trial balance.

Jackson Management Consulting
Trial Balance
October 31, 19X1

Cash..................................	$ 3,800	
Accounts receivable	2,000	
Supplies...............................	500	
Office furniture	2,300	
Land..................................	46,800	
Accounts payable		$ 2,000
Note payable..........................		18,300
Pamela Jackson, capital..................		32,100
Pamela Jackson, withdrawals.............	3,700	
Consulting service revenue...............		4,900
Salary expense.........................	1,000	
Rent expense..........................	600	
Advertising expense	400	
Utilities expense	200	
Property tax...........................	100	
Total.................................	$61,400	$57,300

c.   Rent expense of $200 was posted as a credit rather than a debit.
d.   The balance of Advertising Expense is $300, but it is listed as $400 on the trial balance.
e.   A $600 debit to Accounts Receivable was posted as $60.
f.   The balance of Utilities Expense is understated by $60.
g.   A $500 debit to the withdrawal account was posted as a credit to Pamela Jackson, Capital.
h.   A $100 purchase of supplies on account was neither journalized nor posted.
i.   A $4,800 credit to Consulting Service Revenue was not posted.
j.   Office furniture should be listed in the amount of $1,300.

Required

Prepare the correct trial balance at October 31. Journal entries are not required.

Problem 2-6B   *Recording transactions directly in the ledger, preparing a trial balance*

Jack Montague started a cable television service and during the first month of operations completed the following selected transactions:

a.   Montague began the business with an investment of $30,000 cash and a building valued at $65,000.
b.   Borrowed $25,000 from the bank; signed a note payable.
c.   Paid $32,000 for transmitting equipment.
d.   Purchased office supplies on account, $400.
e.   Paid employee salary, $1,300.
f.   Received $500 for cable TV service performed for customers.
g.   Sold cable service to customers on account, $2,300.
h.   Paid $100 of the account payable created in *d*.
i.   Received a $600 bill for utility expense that will be paid in the near future.
j.   Received cash on account, $1,100.

k. Paid the following cash expenses:
    (1) Rent on land, $1,000.
    (2) Advertising, $800.
l. Withdrew $2,600 for personal use.

Required

1. Open the following T-accounts: Cash; Accounts Receivable; Office Supplies; Transmitting Equipment; Building; Accounts Payable; Note Payable; Jack Montague, Capital; Jack Montague, Withdrawals; Service Revenue; Salary Expense; Rent Expense; Advertising Expense; Utilities Expense.
2. Record the following transactions directly in the T-accounts without using a journal. Use the letters to identify the transactions.
3. Prepare the trial balance of Montague Cable TV Service at January 31, 19X7.

Decision Problem

Recording Transactions Directly in the Ledger, Preparing a Trial Balance, and Measuring Net Income or Loss

You have been requested by a friend named Milton Abel to give advice on the effects that certain business transactions will have on the entity he plans to start. Time is short, so you will not be able to do all the detailed procedures of journalizing and posting. Instead, you must analyze the transactions without the use of a journal. Abel will continue the business only if he can expect to earn monthly net income of $2,750. Assume the following transactions have occurred:

a. Abel deposited $6,000 cash in a business bank account.
b. Borrowed $4,000 cash from the bank and signed a note payable due within one year.
c. Paid $300 cash for supplies.
d. Purchased advertising in the local newspaper for cash, $800.
e. Purchased office furniture on account, $1,500.
f. Paid the following cash expenses for one month: secretary salary, $1,400; office rent, $400; utilities, $300; interest, $50.
g. Earned revenue on account for one month, $3,300.
h. Earned revenue and received $2,500 cash.
i. Collected cash from customers on account, $1,500.
j. Paid on account, $1,000.

Required

1. Open the following T-accounts: Cash; Accounts Receivable; Supplies; Furniture; Accounts Payable; Notes Payable; Milton Abel, Capital; Service Revenue; Salary Expense; Advertising Expense; Rent Expense; Utilities Expense; Interest Expense.
2. Record the transactions directly in the accounts without using a journal. Key each transaction by letter.
3. Prepare a trial balance at the current date. List expenses with the largest first, the next largest second, and so on. The business name will be Abel Apartment Locators.
4. Compute the amount of net income or net loss for this first month of operations. Would you recommend that Abel continue in business?

Financial Statement Problem

Journalizing Transactions

This problem helps to develop skill in recording transactions by using an actual company's account titles. Refer to the Gulf+Western financial statements in Appendix C. Assume Gulf+Western completed the following selected transactions during August 1987:

Aug. 5   Earned revenues on account, $40,000.

     9   Borrowed $500,000 by signing a note payable (long-term debt).

   12   Purchased equipment on account, $70,000.

   17   Paid $120,000, which represents payment of a $100,000 current maturity of long-term debt, plus interest expense of $20,000.

   19   Earned revenues and immediately received cash of $16,000.

   22   Collected the cash on account that was earned on August 5.

   24   Paid rent of $14,000 for three months in advance.

   28   Received a home-office electricity bill for $1,000, which will be paid in September (this is a general and administrative expense).

   30   Paid off half the account payable created on August 12.

Required

Journalize these transactions using the following account titles taken from the financial statements of Gulf+Western: Cash; Trade Receivables; Prepaid Expenses; Equipment; Current Maturities of Long-term Debt; Trade Accounts Payable; Long-Term Debt; Revenues; Selling, General, and Administrative Expenses; Interest Expense. Explanations are not required.

Answers to Self-Study Questions

1. a	5. c	8.	b ($6,800 = $2,500 + $4,300)
2. b	6. a	9.	b
3. c	7. a	10.	d
4. d			

3

Measuring Business Income: The Adjusting Process

LEARNING OBJECTIVES

After studying this chapter, you should be able to

1 Distinguish accrual-basis accounting from cash-basis accounting

2 Explain and apply the revenue and matching principles

3 Make the typical adjusting entries at the end of the accounting period

4 Prepare an adjusted trial balance

5 Prepare the financial statements from the adjusted trial balance

The primary goal of business is to earn a profit. By providing food and other goods at a reasonable price, a grocery store benefits its customers. The benefit to the store owner is the excess of the business's revenues over its expenses—net income. Gary Lyon, the CPA whose accounting practice we discussed in the earlier chapters, earns business income by providing accounting services for clients. Regardless of the type of activity, the profit motive increases the owner's drive to carry on the business.

At the end of each accounting period, the accountant prepares the entity's financial statements. The period may be a month, three months, six months, or a full year. Whatever the length of the period, the end accounting product is the same, the financial statements. And the most important single amount in these statements is the net income or net loss—the profit or loss—for the period. A double-entry accounting system produces not only the income statement but the other financial statements as well.

An important step in financial statement preparation is the trial balance that we discussed in Chapter 2. The trial balance includes the effects of the transactions that occurred during the period—the cash collections, purchases of assets, payments of bills, sales of assets, and so on. To measure its income properly, however, a business must do some additional accounting at the end of the period to bring the records up to date before preparing the financial statements. This process is called *adjusting the books,* and it consists of making special entries called *adjusting entries.* This chapter focuses primarily on these adjusting entries to help you better understand the nature of business income.

Accountants have devised concepts and principles to guide the measurement of business income. Chief among these are the concepts of accrual accounting, the accounting period, the revenue principle, and the matching principle. In this chapter, we apply these concepts and principles to measure the income and prepare the financial statements of Gary Lyon's business for the month of April.

Accrual-Basis Accounting versus Cash-Basis Accounting

OBJECTIVE 1

Distinguish accrual-basis accounting from cash-basis accounting

There are two widely used bases of accounting: the accrual basis and the cash basis. In **accrual-basis accounting,** an accountant recognizes the impact of a business event as it occurs. When the business performs a service, makes a sale, or incurs an expense, the accountant enters the transaction into the books, whether or not cash has been received or paid. In **cash-basis accounting,** however, the accountant does not record a transaction until cash is received or paid. GAAP requires that a business use the accrual basis. This means that the accountant records revenues as they are *earned* and expenses as they are *incurred*—not necessarily when cash changes hands.

Using accrual-basis accounting, Gary Lyon records revenue when he performs services for a client on account. Lyon has earned the revenue at that time because his efforts have generated an account receivable, a legal claim against the client for whom he did the work. By contrast, if Gary Lyon used cash-basis accounting, he would not record revenue at the time he performed the service. He would wait until he received cash.

Why does GAAP require that businesses use the accrual basis? What advantage does accrual-basis accounting offer? Suppose Gary Lyon's accounting period ends after he has earned the revenue but before he has collected the money due him. If he used the cash-basis method, his financial statements would not include this revenue or the related account receivable. As a result, the financial statements would be misleading. Revenue and the asset Accounts Receivable would be understated, and thus his business would look less successful than it actually is. If he wants to get a bank loan to expand his practice, the understated revenue and asset figures might hurt his chances.

Gary Lyon, using accrual-basis accounting, treats expenses in a like manner. For instance, salary expense includes amounts paid to employees plus any amount owed to employees but not yet paid. Lyon's use of the employee's service, not the payment of cash to the employee, brings about the expense. Under cash-basis accounting, Lyon would record the expense only when he actually paid the employee.

Suppose Gary Lyon owes his secretary a salary and the financial statements are drawn up before Lyon pays. Expenses and liabilities would be understated, so the business would look more successful than it really is. This incomplete information would not provide an accurate accounting to potential creditors.

As these examples show, accrual accounting provides more complete information than does cash-basis accounting. This is important because the more complete the data, the better equipped decision makers are to reach intelligent conclusions about the firm's financial health and future prospects. Three concepts used in accrual accounting are the accounting period, the revenue principle, and the matching principle.

The Accounting Period

The only way to know for certain how successfully a business has operated is to close its doors, sell all its assets, pay the liabilities, and return any leftover cash to the owner. This process, called liquidation, is the same as going out of business. Obviously, it is not practical for accountants to measure business income in this manner. Instead, businesses need periodic reports on their progress. Accountants slice time into small segments and prepare financial statements for specific periods. Until a business liquidates, the amounts reported in its financial statements must be regarded as estimates.

The most basic accounting period is one year, and virtually all businesses prepare annual financial statements. For about 60 percent of large companies in a recent survey, the annual accounting period runs the calendar year from January 1 through December 31. Other companies use what is called a *fiscal year*, which ends on some date other than December 31. The year-end date is usually the low point in business activity for the year. Depending on the type of business, the fiscal year may end on April 30, July 31, or some other date. Retailers are a notable example. Traditionally, they have used a fiscal year ending on January 31 because the low point in their business activity has followed the after-Christmas sales during January.

Companies cannot wait until the end of the year to gauge their progress. The manager of a business wants to know how well the business is doing each month, each quarter, and each half year. Outsiders such as lenders also demand current information about the business. So companies also prepare financial statements for *interim* periods, which are less than a year. Monthly financial statements are common, and a series of monthly statements can be combined for quarterly and semiannual periods. Most of the discussions in this book are based on an annual accounting period. However, the procedures and statements can also be applied to interim periods as well.

Revenue Principle

The **revenue principle** tells accountants (1) *when* to record revenue and (2) the *amount* of revenue to record. When we speak of "recording" something in accounting, the act of recording the item naturally leads to posting to the ledger accounts and preparing the trial balance and the financial statements. Although the financial statements are the end product of accounting and what accountants are most concerned about, our discussions often focus on recording the entry in the journal because that is where the accounting process starts.

The general principle guiding *when* to record revenue says to record revenue when, but not before, it has been earned. In most cases, revenue is earned when the business has delivered a completed good or service to the customer. The business has done everything required by the agreement, including transferring the item to the customer. Two situations that provide guidance on when to record revenue follow. The first situation illustrates when *not* to record revenue. Situation 2 illustrates when revenue should be recorded.

Situation 1—Do not record revenue. A client of another CPA expresses her intention to transfer her tax work to Gary Lyon. Should Lyon record any revenue based on this intention? The answer is no because no transaction has occurred.

Situation 2—Record revenue. Next month Gary Lyon consults with this client and tailors a business plan to her goals. After transferring the business plan to the client, Lyon should record revenue. If the client pays for this service immediately, Lyon will debit Cash. If the service is performed on account, Lyon will debit Accounts Receivable. In either case, Lyon should record revenue by crediting the Service Revenue account.

The general principle guiding the *amount* of revenue says to record revenue equal to the cash value of the goods or the service transferred to the customer. Suppose that in order to obtain a new client, Gary Lyon performs accounting

OBJECTIVE 2

Explain and apply the revenue and matching principles

service for the price of $500. Ordinarily, Lyon would have charged $600 for this service. How much revenue should Lyon record? The answer is $500 because that was the cash value of the transaction. Lyon will not receive the full value of $600, so that is not the amount of revenue to record. He will receive only $500 cash, and that pinpoints the amount of revenue earned.

Matching Principle

The **matching principle** is the basis for recording expenses. Recall that expenses, such as rent, utilities, and advertising, are the costs of operating a business. Expenses are the costs of assets that are used up in the earning of revenue. The matching principle directs accountants (1) to identify all expenses incurred during the accounting period, (2) to measure the expenses, and (3) to "match" them against the revenues earned during that same span of time. To "match" expenses against revenues means to subtract the expenses from the revenues in order to compute net income or net loss.

There is a natural link between revenues and some types of expenses. Accountants follow the matching principle by first identifying the revenues of a period and the expenses that can be linked to particular revenues. For example, a business that pays sales commissions to its sales persons will have commission expense if the employees make sales. If they make no sales, the business has no commission expense.

Other expenses are not so easy to link with particular sales. Monthly rent expense occurs, for example, regardless of the revenues earned during the period. The matching principle directs accountants to identify these types of expenses with a particular time period, such as a month or a year. If Gary Lyon employs a secretary at a monthly salary of $1,900, the business will record salary expense of $1,900 each month.

Because financial statements appear at definite intervals, there must be some cutoff date for the necessary information. Most entities engage in so many transactions that some are bound to spill over into more than a single accounting period. Gary Lyon prepares monthly statements for his business at April 30. How does he handle a transaction that begins in April but ends in May? How does he bring the accounts up to date for preparing the financial statements? To answer these questions, accountants use adjusting entries.

Adjustments to the Accounts

At the end of the period, the accountant prepares the financial statements. This end-of-the-period process begins with the trial balance that lists the accounts and their balances after the period's transaction's have been recorded in the journal and posted to the accounts in the ledger. Exhibit 3-1 is the trial balance of Gary Lyon's accounting practice at April 30, 19X1.

This *unadjusted* trial balance includes some new accounts that will be explained in this section. It lists most, but not all, of the revenue and the expenses of Lyon's accounting practice for the month of April. These trial balance amounts are incomplete because they omit certain revenue and expense transactions that affect more than one accounting period. That is why it is called an *unadjusted* trial

EXHIBIT 3-1 *Unadjusted Trial Balance*

Gary Lyon, CPA Unadjusted Trial Balance April 30, 19X1		
Cash.............................	$24,800	
Accounts receivable................	2,250	
Supplies.........................	700	
Prepaid rent......................	3,000	
Furniture	16,500	
Accounts payable..................		$13,100
Unearned service revenue...........		450
Gary Lyon, capital.................		31,250
Gary Lyon, withdrawals.............	3,200	
Service revenue		7,000
Salary expense....................	950	
Utilities expense..................	400	
Total...........................	$51,800	$51,800

balance. In most cases, however, we refer to it simply as the trial balance, without the "unadjusted" label.

Under the cash basis of accounting, there would be no need for adjustments to the accounts because all April cash transactions would have been recorded. The accrual basis requires adjusting entries at the end of the period in order to produce correct balances for the financial statements. To see why, consider the Supplies account in Exhibit 3-1.

Lyon's accounting practice uses supplies in providing accounting services for clients during the month. This reduces the quantity of supplies on hand and thus constitutes an expense, just like salary expense or rent expense. Gary Lyon does not bother to record his daily expense, and it is not worth his while to record supplies expense more than once a month. It is time consuming to make hourly, daily, or even weekly journal entries to record the expense for the use of supplies. So how does he account for supplies expense?

By the end of the month, the Supplies balance is not correct. The balance represents the amount of supplies on hand at the start of the month plus any supplies purchased during the month. This balance fails to take into account the supplies used (supplies expense) during the accounting period. It is necessary, then, to subtract the month's expenses from the amount of supplies listed on the trial balance. The resulting new adjusted balance measures the cost of supplies that are still on hand at April 30. This is the correct amount of supplies to report on the balance sheet. Adjusting entries in this way will bring the accounts up to date.

Adjusting entries assign revenues to the period in which they are earned and expenses to the period in which they are incurred. They are needed (a) to measure properly the period's income and (b) to bring related asset and liability accounts to correct balances for the financial statements. For example, an adjusting entry is needed to transfer the amount of supplies used during the period from the asset account Supplies to the expense account Supplies Expense. The adjusting entry updates both the Supplies asset account and the Supplies Expense account. This achieves accurate measures of assets and expenses. Adjusting entries, which are the key to the accrual basis of accounting, are made before preparing the financial statements.

The end-of-period process of updating the accounts is called *adjusting the accounts, making the adjusting entries,* or *adjusting the books.* Adjusting entries can be divided into five categories:

1. Prepaid expenses
2. Depreciation
3. Accrued expenses
4. Accrued revenues
5. Unearned revenues

Prepaid Expenses

Prepaid expenses is a category of miscellaneous assets that typically expire or are used up in the near future. Prepaid rent and prepaid insurance are examples of prepaid expenses. They are called prepaid expenses because they are expenses that are paid in advance. Salary expense and utilities expense, among others, are *not* prepaid expenses because they are not paid in advance.

Prepaid Rent. Landlords usually require tenants to pay rent in advance. This prepayment creates an asset for the renter because that person has purchased the future benefit of using the rented item. Suppose Gary Lyon prepays three months' rent on April 1, 19X1, after negotiating a lease for his business office. If the lease specifies monthly rental amounts of $1,000 each, the entry to record the payment for three months is a debit to the asset account, Prepaid Rent, as follows:

Apr. 1	Prepaid Rent ($1,000 × 3)............................	3,000
	Cash	3,000
	Paid three months' rent in advance.	

After posting, Prepaid Rent appears as follows:

Prepaid Rent	
Apr. 1 3,000	

The trial balance at April 30, 19X1, lists Prepaid Rent as an asset with a debit balance of $3,000. Throughout April, the Prepaid Rent account maintains this beginning balance as shown in Exhibit 3-1.

At April 30 Prepaid Rent should be adjusted to remove from its balance the amount of the asset that has *expired,* which is one month's worth of the prepayment. By definition, the amount of an asset that has expired is *expense.* The adjusting entry transfers one-third, or $1,000 ($3,000 × $\frac{1}{3}$), of the debit balance from Prepaid Rent to Rent Expense. The debit side of the entry records an increase in Rent Expense, and the credit records a decrease in the asset Prepaid Rent.

OBJECTIVE 3

Make the typical adjusting entries at the end of the accounting period

Apr. 30	Rent Expense ($3,000 × $\frac{1}{3}$)	1,000
	Prepaid Rent	1,000
	To record rent expense.	

After posting, Prepaid Rent and Rent Expense appear as follows:

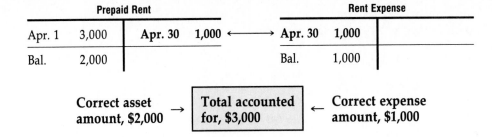

Prepaid Rent				Rent Expense		
Apr. 1	3,000	**Apr. 30**	1,000 ⟷	**Apr. 30**	1,000	
Bal.	2,000			Bal.	1,000	

Correct asset amount, $2,000 → **Total accounted for, $3,000** ← **Correct expense amount, $1,000**

The full $3,000 has been accounted for: two thirds is asset, and one-third is expense. This is correct because two thirds of the asset remains for future use, and one third of the prepayment has expired. Recording this expense illustrates the matching principle. The same analysis applies to a prepayment of three months' insurance premiums. The only difference is in the account titles, which would be Prepaid Insurance and Insurance Expense instead of Prepaid Rent and Rent Expense. This adjusting entry illustrates the matching principle.

Supplies.   Supplies are accounted for in the same way as prepaid expenses. On April 2 Gary Lyon paid cash of $700 for office supplies:

Apr. 2	Supplies	700	
	Cash		700
	Paid cash for supplies.		

Assume that Lyon purchased no additional supplies during April. The April 30 trial balance, therefore, lists Supplies with a $700 debit balance, as shown in Exhibit 3-1.

During April, Lyon used supplies in performing services for clients. The cost of the supplies used is the measure of *supplies expense* for the month.

Lyon does not keep a continuous record of supplies used each day or each week during April. To keep these detailed records would be impractical. Instead, to measure his firm's supplies expense during April, Gary Lyon counts the supplies on hand at the end of the month. This is the amount of the asset still available to the business. Assume the count indicates that supplies costing $400 remain. Subtracting the entity's $400 supplies on hand at the end of April from the cost of supplies available during April ($700) measures supplies expense during the month ($300).

Cost of asset available during the period	−	Cost of asset on hand at the end of the period	=	Cost of asset used (expense) during the period
$700	−	$400	=	$300

The April 30 adjusting entry to update the Supplies account and to record the supplies expense for the month debits the expense and credits the asset as follows:

Apr. 30	Supplies Expense ($700 − $400).	300	
	Supplies		300
	To record supplies expense.		

After posting, the Supplies and Supplies Expense accounts appear as follows:

Supplies				Supplies Expense		
Apr. 2	700	Apr. 30	300 ⟷	Apr. 30	300	
Bal.	400			Bal.	300	

Correct asset → Total accounted ← Correct expense
amount, $400   for, $700   amount, $300

The Supplies account then enters the month of May with a $400 balance, and the adjustment process is repeated each month.

Depreciation and Plant Assets

The logic of the accrual basis is probably best illustrated by how businesses account for plant assets. **Plant assets** are long-lived assets, such as land, buildings, furniture, machinery, and equipment used in the operations of the business. As one accountant said, "All assets but land are on a march to the junkyard." That is, all plant assets but land decline in usefulness as they age. This decline is an *expense* to the business. Accountants systematically spread the cost of each plant asset, except land, over the years of its useful life. This process is called the recording of **depreciation**. The concept underlying accounting for plant assets and depreciation expense is the same as for prepaid expenses. In both cases the business purchases an asset that wears out. As the asset is used, more and more of its cost is transferred from the asset account to the expense account. The only difference between prepaid expenses and plant assets is the length of time it takes for the asset to lose its usefulness. Prepaid expenses usually expire within a year. Most plant assets remain useful for a number of years.

Consider Gary Lyon's accounting practice. Suppose that on April 3 Lyon purchased furniture on account for $16,500:

Apr. 3   Furniture 16,500
               Accounts Payable 16,500
           Purchased office furniture on account.

After posting, the Furniture account appears as follows:

Furniture		
Apr. 3	16,500	

Using cash-basis accounting, Gary Lyon would enter in the ledger the entire $16,500 as an expense for April. As a result, his financial statements for that month would be extremely misleading. Income would be significantly understated. Also, the cash-basis approach fails to take into consideration that the asset will be of benefit to Lyon's business in future accounting periods.

In accrual-basis accounting, an asset is recorded when the furniture is acquired. Then, a portion of the asset's cost is transferred from the asset account to Depreciation Expense each period that the asset is used. This method matches the asset's expense to the revenue of the period, which is an application of the matching principle. We discuss how accountants determine the amount of depreciation for each accounting period in Chapter 10. For now, we need concern ourselves only with the accounts involved in recording depreciation.

Let's assume the depreciation for the month of April is $275, computed by dividing the asset's cost by its useful life. Depreciation expense for April is recorded by the following entry:

Apr. 30 Depreciation Expense   275
     Accumulated Depreciation – Furniture   275
    To record depreciation on furniture.

You may be wondering why Accumulated Depreciation is credited instead of Furniture. The reason is that the original cost of the plant asset is an objective measurement, and that figure remains in the original asset account as long as the business uses the asset. Accountants may refer to that account if they need to know how much the asset cost. This information may be useful in a decision about whether to replace the furniture and the amount to pay. The amount of depreciation, however, is an *estimate.* Accountants use the **Accumulated Depreciation** account to show the cumulative sum of all depreciation expense from the date of acquiring the asset.

Accumulated Depreciation is a **contra asset** account, which means an asset account with a credit balance. A **contra account** has two distinguishing characteristics: (1) it always has a companion account, and (2) its normal balance is opposite that of the companion account. In this case, Accumulated Depreciation accompanies Furniture. It appears in the ledger directly after Furniture. Furniture has a debit balance, and therefore Accumulated Depreciation has a credit balance. All contra asset accounts have credit balances.

A business carries an accumulated depreciation account for each depreciable asset. If a business has a building and a machine, for example, it will carry the accounts Accumulated Depreciation – Building, and Accumulated Depreciation – Machine.

After posting the depreciation entry, the Furniture, Accumulated Depreciation, and Depreciation Expense accounts are

Furniture		Accumulated Depreciation Furniture		Depreciation Expense	
Apr. 3 16,500			Apr. 30 275	Apr. 30 275	
Bal. 16,500			Bal. 275	Bal. 275	

The balance sheet shows the relationship between Furniture and Accumulated Depreciation. The balance of Accumulated Depreciation is subtracted from the balance of Furniture. The net amount of a plant asset (cost minus accumulated depreciation) is called its **book value,** as shown below for Furniture.

Plant Assets:

Furniture. $16,500
Less Accumulated depreciation.   275
Book value $16,225

Because Accumulated Depreciation is subtracted from its companion account to determine the asset's book value, Accumulated Depreciation is also called a *valuation* account.

Suppose Lyon's accounting practice owns a building that cost $48,000 and on which annual depreciation is $2,400. The amount of depreciation for one month

EXHIBIT 3-2 *Plant Assets on the Balance Sheet (April 30)*

Plant assets:			
Furniture	$16,500		
Less Accumulated depreciation....	275	$16,225	
Building	48,000		
Less Accumulated depreciation....	200	47,800	
Book value of plant assets...........		$64,025	

would be $200 ($2,400/12), and the entry to record depreciation for April is

Apr. 30	Depreciation Expense – Building	200	
	Accumulated Depreciation – Building		200
	To record depreciation on building.		

The balance sheet at April 30 would report Lyon's plant assets as shown in Exhibit 3-2. Now, however, let's return to Gary Lyon's actual situation.

Accrued Expenses

Businesses often incur expenses before they pay cash because payment is not due until later. Consider an employee's salary. The employer's salary expense and salary payable grow as the employee works, so the liability is said to *accrue*. Another example is interest expense on a note payable. Interest accrues as the clock ticks. The term **accrued expenses** refers to an expense that the business has incurred but has not yet paid.

It is time consuming to make hourly, daily, or even weekly journal entries to accrue expenses. Consequently, the accountant waits until the end of the period. Then an adjusting entry brings each expense (and related liability) up to date just before the financial statements are prepared.

Salary Expense. Most companies pay their employees at set times. Suppose Gary Lyon pays his employee a monthly salary of $1,900, half on the 15th and half on the last day of the month. Here is a calendar for April that has paydays circled:

APRIL

Sun.	Mon.	Tue.	Wed.	Thur.	Fri.	Sat.
					1	2
3	4	5	6	7	8	9
10	11	12	13	14	(15)	16
17	18	19	20	21	22	23
24	25	26	27	28	29	(30)

Assume that if either payday falls on a weekend, Lyon pays the employee on the following Monday. During April Lyon paid his employee's first half-month salary of $950 on Friday, April 15, and recorded the following entry:

Apr. 15	Salary Expense.......................................	950	
	Cash		950
	To pay salary.		

After posting, the Salary Expense account is

Salary Expense

Apr. 15 950	

The trial balance at April 30 (Exhibit 3-1) includes Salary Expense, with its debit balance of $950. Because April 30, the second payday of the month, falls on a Saturday, the second half-month amount of $950 will be paid on Monday, May 2. Without an adjusting entry, this second $950 amount is not included in the April 30 trial balance amount for Salary Expense. Therefore, at April 30 Lyon adjusts for additional *salary expense* and *salary payable* of $950 by recording an increase in each of these accounts as follows:

Apr. 30	Salary Expense....................................	950	
	Salary Payable................................		950
	To accrue salary expense.		

After posting, the Salary Expense and Salary Payable accounts appear as follows:

Salary Expense

Apr. 15	950		
Apr. 30	**950**		
Bal.	1,900		

Salary Payable

		Apr. 30	**950**
		Bal.	950

The accounts at April 30 now contain the complete salary information for the month. The expense account has a full month's salary, and the liability account shows the portion that the business still owes.

Lyon will record the payment of this liability on May 2 by debiting Salary Payable and crediting Cash for $950. This payment entry does not affect April or May expenses because the April expense was recorded on April 15 and April 30. May expense will be recorded in a like manner. All accrued expenses are recorded with similar entries—a debit to the appropriate expense account and a credit to the related liability account.

Accrued Revenues

Businesses often earn revenue before they receive the cash because payment is not due until later. A revenue that has been earned but not yet received in cash is called an **accrued revenue.** Assume Gary Lyon is hired on April 15 by Guerrero Construction Company to perform services on a monthly basis. Under this agreement, Guerrero will pay Lyon $500 monthly, with the first payment on May 15. During April, Lyon will earn half a month's fee, $250. On April 30 he makes the following adjusting entry to record an increase in Accounts Receivable and Service Revenue:

Apr. 30	Accounts Receivable ($500 × $\frac{1}{2}$)	250	
	Service Revenue................................		250
	To accrue service revenue.		

Recall that Accounts Receivable has an unadjusted balance of $2,250, and the

Service Revenue unadjusted balance is $7,000 (Exhibit 3-1). Posting this adjusting entry has the following effects on these two accounts:

Accounts Receivable			Service Revenue		
	2,250				7,000
Apr. 30	**250**		**Apr. 30**		**250**
Bal.	2,500		Bal.		7,250

This adjusting entry illustrates accrual accounting and the revenue principle in action. Without the adjustment, Lyon's financial statements would be misleading. All accrued revenues are accounted for similarly—by debiting a receivable and crediting a revenue.

Unearned Revenues

Some businesses collect cash from customers in advance of doing work for the customer. This creates a liability called **unearned revenue.** The liability arises because the business receiving cash in advance is obligated to provide a product or a service in the future. Only when the job is completed will the business have earned the revenue. Suppose Baldwin Computing Service Center engages Lyon's services, agreeing to pay him $450 monthly, beginning immediately. If Baldwin makes the first payment on April 20, Lyon records this increase in the business's liabilities by recording:

Apr. 20	Cash	450
	Unearned Service Revenue	450
	Received revenue in advance.	

After posting, the liability account appears as follows:

Unearned Service Revenue		
	Apr. 20	450

Unearned Service Revenue is a liability because it represents Lyon's obligation to perform service for the client. The April 30 unadjusted trial balance (Exhibit 3-1) lists this account with a $450 credit balance prior to the adjusting entries. During the last 10 days of the month, Lyon will have earned one third (10 days divided by April's total 30 days) of the $450, or $150. Therefore, he makes the following adjustment to decrease the liability, Unearned Service Revenue, and to record an increase in Service Revenue:

Apr. 30	Unearned Service Revenue ($450 $\times \frac{1}{3}$)...................	150
	Service Revenue................................	150
	To record unearned service revenue that has been earned.	

This adjusting entry shifts $150 of the total amount from the liability account to the revenue account. After posting, the balance of Service Revenue is increased by $150 and the balance of Unearned Service Revenue has been reduced to $300:

Unearned Service Revenue			Service Revenue	
Apr. 30 150	Apr. 21 450			7,000
	Bal. 300		Apr. 30 250	
			Apr. 30 150	
			Bal. 7,400	

Correct liability amount, $300 → **Total accounted for, $450** ← **Correct revenue amount, $150**

Accounting for all types of revenues that are collected in advance follows the same pattern.

Summary of the Adjusting Process

Because one purpose of the adjusting process is to measure business income properly, each adjusting entry affects at least one income statement account—a revenue or an expense. The other side of the entry—a debit or a credit, as the case may be—is to a balance sheet account—an asset or a liability. This step updates the accounts for preparation of the balance sheet, which is the second purpose of the adjustments. No adjusting entry debits or credits Cash because the cash transactions are recorded earlier in the period. The end-of-period adjustment process is reserved for the noncash transactions that are required by accrual accounting. Exhibit 3-3 summarizes the adjusting entries.

Appendix B at the end of the book covers the adjusting process in more detail. It also discusses and illustrates an optional category of accounting entries known as reversing entries.

Posting the Adjusting Entries

Exhibit 3-4 summarizes the adjusting entries of Lyon's business at April 30. Panel A of the exhibit briefly describes the data for each adjustment, Panel B gives the adjusting entries, and Panel C shows the accounts. The adjustments are keyed by letter.

EXHIBIT 3-3 *Summary of Adjusting Entries*

Adjusting Entry	Type of Account Debited	Type of Account Credited
Prepaid expense, supplies	Expense	Prepaid expense, supplies
Depreciation	Expense	Accumulated depreciation
Accrued expenses	Expense	Payable
Accrued revenues	Receivable	Revenue
Unearned revenues	Unearned revenue	Revenue

Adapted from Beverly Terry.

EXHIBIT 3-4　Journalizing and Posting the Adjusting Entries

Panel A—Information for Adjustments at April 30, 19X1

a. Accrued service revenue, $250.
b. Supplies on hand, $400.
c. Prepaid rent expired, $1,000.
d. Depreciation on furniture, $275.
e. Accrued salary expense, $950.
f. Amount of unearned service revenue that has been earned, $150.

Panel B—Adjusting Entries

a. Accounts Receivable... 250
　　　Service Revenue 250
　　To accrue service revenue.

b. Supplies Expense 300
　　　Supplies.. 300
　　To record supplies used.

c. Rent Expense.. 1,000
　　　Prepaid Rent 1,000
　　To record rent expense.

d. Depreciation Expense.. 275
　　　Accumulated Depreciation.. 275
　　To record depreciation on furniture.

e. Salary Expense 950
　　　Salary Payable 950
　　To accrue salary expense.

f. Unearned Service Revenue 150
　　　Service Revenue 150
　　To record unearned revenue that has been earned.

Panel C—Ledger Accounts

Assets

Cash		Accounts Receivable		Supplies	
Bal. 24,800		2,250		700	(b) 300
		(a) 250		Bal. 400	
		Bal. 2,500			

Prepaid Rent		Furniture		Accumulated Depreciation	
3,000	(c) 1,000	Bal. 16,500			(d) 275
Bal. 2,000					Bal. 275

Liabilities

Accounts Payable		Salary Payable		Unearned Service Revenue	
	Bal. 13,100		(e) 950	(f) 150	450
			Bal. 950		Bal. 300

Owner's Equity		Revenues

Gary Lyon, Capital

Bal. 31,250

Gary Lyon, Withdrawals

Bal. 3,200

Service Revenue

		7,000
(a)		250
(f)		150

Bal. 7,400

Expenses

Rent Expense

(c) 1,000

Bal. 1,000

Salary Expense

	950
(e)	950

Bal. 1,900

Supplies Expense

(b) 300

Bal. 300

Depreciation Expense

(d) 275

Bal. 275

Utilities Expense

Bal. 400

Adjusted Trial Balance

This chapter began with the trial balance before any adjusting entries—the unadjusted trial balance (Exhibit 3-1). After the adjustments are journalized and posted, the accounts appear as shown in Exhibit 3-4, Panel C. A useful step in preparing the financial statements is to list the accounts, along with their adjusted balances, on an **adjusted trial balance.** This document has the advantage of listing all the accounts and their adjusted balances in a single place. Exhibit 3-5 shows the preparation of the adjusted trial balance.

Each amount on the adjusted trial balance is computed by combining the amounts from the unadjusted trial balance and the adjustments. For example, Accounts Receivable starts with a debit balance of $2,250. Adding the $250 debit amount from adjusting entry *a* gives Accounts Receivable an adjusted balance of $2,500. Supplies begins with a debit balance of $700. After the $300 credit adjustment, its adjusted balance is $400. More than one entry may affect a single account, as is the case for Service Revenue. If accounts are unaffected by the adjustments, they show the same amount on both trial balances. This is true for Cash, Furniture, Accounts Payable, and the Owner's Equity accounts.

OBJECTIVE 4
Prepare an adjusted trial balance

Preparing the Financial Statements from the Adjusted Trial Balance

The April financial statements of Gary Lyon, CPA, can be prepared from the information on the adjusted trial balance. The income statement comes from the revenue and expense accounts. The balance sheet reports the assets, liabilities, and owner's equity. The statement of owner's equity shows the reasons for the

EXHIBIT 3-5   Preparation of Adjusted Trial Balance

Gary Lyon, CPA
Preparation of Adjusted Trial Balance
April 30, 19X1

Account Title	Trial Balance Debit	Trial Balance Credit	Adjustments Debit		Adjustments Credit		Adjusted Trial Balance Debit	Adjusted Trial Balance Credit
Cash	24,800						24,800	
Accounts receivable	2,250		(a)	250			2,500	
Supplies	700				(b)	300	400	
Prepaid rent	3,000				(c)	1,000	2,000	
Furniture	16,500						16,500	
Accumulated depreciation					(d)	275		275
Accounts payable		13,100						13,100
Salary payable					(e)	950		950
Unearned service revenue		450	(f)	150				300
Gary Lyon, capital		31,250						31,250
Gary Lyon, withdrawals	3,200						3,200	
Service revenue		7,000			(a)	250		7,400
					(f)	150		
Rent expense			(c)	1,000			1,000	
Salary expense	950		(e)	950			1,900	
Supplies expense			(b)	300			300	
Depreciation expense			(d)	275			275	
Utilities expense	400						400	
	51,800	51,800	2,925		2,925		53,275	53,275

Account Title	Adjusted Trial Balance Debit	Adjusted Trial Balance Credit	
Cash	24,800		
Accounts receivable	2,500		
Supplies	400		
Prepaid rent	2,000		
Furniture	16,500		Balance Sheet
Accumulated depreciation		275	
Accounts payable		13,100	
Salary payable		950	
Unearned service revenue		300	
Gary Lyon, capital		31,250	Statement of
Gary Lyon, withdrawals	3,200		Owner's Equity
Service revenue		7,400	
Rent expense	1,000		
Salary expense	1,900		Income Statement
Supplies expense	300		
Depreciation expense	275		
Utilities expense	400		
	53,275	53,275	

change in the owner's capital during the period. Exhibit 3-6 shows how the accounts are distributed from the adjusted trial balance to these three financial statements.

Financial Statements

The accounts and the amounts for the income statement and the balance sheet may be taken from the adjusted trial balance. The adjusted trial balance also provides the data for the statement of owner's equity. Exhibits 3-7, 3-8, and 3-9 illustrate these three financial statements, best prepared in the order shown: the income statement first, followed by the statement of owner's equity and last, the balance sheet. The essential features of all financial statements are (1) the name of the entity, (2) the title of the statement, (3) the date or the period covered by the statement, and (4) the body of the statement.

It is customary to list expenses in descending order by amount, as shown in Exhibit 3-7. However, Miscellaneous Expense, a catch-all account for expenses that do not fit another category, is usually reported last regardless of its amount.

Relationships among the Three Financial Statements _____

The arrows in Exhibits 3-7, 3-8, and 3-9 illustrate the relationship among the income statement, the statement of owner's equity, and the balance sheet.

1. The income statement reports net income or net loss, figured by subtracting expenses from revenues. Because revenues and expenses are owner's equity accounts, their net figure is then transferred to the statement of owner's equity. Note that net income in Exhibit 3-7, $3,525, increases owner's equity in Exhibit 3-8. A net loss would decrease owner's equity.

2. Capital is a balance sheet account, so the ending balance in the statement of owner's equity is transferred to the balance sheet. This amount is the final balancing element of the balance sheet. To solidify your understanding of this relationship, trace the $31,575 figure from Exhibit 3-8 to Exhibit 3-9.[1]

Microcomputers and the Accounting Process _____

Computers have been used by large businesses for years to account for their transactions. Until recently, most computers were bulky and expensive, and only large organizations could afford them. In recent years, small, more affordable microcomputers have caused a revolution in the computer industry. The term

---

[1] You may be wondering why the total assets on the balance sheet ($45,925 in Exhibit 3-9) do not equal the total debits on the adjusted trial balance ($53,275 in Exhibit 3-6). Likewise, the total liabilities and owner's equity do not equal the total credits on the adjusted trial balance. The reason for these differences is that Accumulated Depreciation and Owner Withdrawals are *subtracted* from their related accounts on the balance sheet but *added* in their respective columns on the adjusted trial balance.

OBJECTIVE 5

Prepare the financial statements from the adjusted trial balance

EXHIBIT 3-7 *Income Statement*

Gary Lyon, CPA
Income Statement
For the Month Ended April 30, 19X1

Revenue		
Service revenue....................................		$7,400
Expenses:		
Salary expense....................................	$1,900	
Rent expense.....................................	1,000	
Utilities expense	400	
Supplies expense.................................	300	
Depreciation expense	275	
Total expenses		3,875
Net income		$3,525

EXHIBIT 3-8 *Statement of Owner's Equity*

Gary Lyon, CPA
Statement of Owner's Equity
For the Month Ended April 30, 19X1

Gary Lyon, capital, April 1, 19X1	$31,250
Add: Net income..	3,525
	34,775
Less: Withdrawals..	3,200
Gary Lyon, capital, April 30, 19X1	$31,575

① ②

EXHIBIT 3-9 *Balance Sheet*

Gary Lyon, CPA
Balance Sheet
April 30, 19X1

Assets			**Liabilities**		
Cash		$24,800	Accounts payable.......		$13,100
Accounts receivable....		2,500	Salary payable		950
Supplies		400	Unearned service		
Prepaid rent..........		2,000	revenue............		300
Furniture	$16,500		Total liabilities		14,350
Less Accumulated					
depreciation	275	16,225	**Owner's Equity**		
			Gary Lyon, capital.....		31,575
			Total liabilities and		
Total assets..........		$45,925	owner's equity		$45,925

microcomputer simply means "small computer." Like the bigger computers, these machines handle electronically much of the work done by hand in the past. Their prices continue to fall, enabling more and more small businesses to own one. Names like Apple (a leading microcomputer company), IBM PC (International Business Machines Personal Computer), TRS (a line of Radio Shack microcomputers), and Epson have become almost household words.

Whether a system is manual, as we have illustrated so far, or computerized, the steps in the accounting process are essentially the same: journalize transactions, post to the ledger, prepare the trial balance, make the adjustments, and present the financial statements. Computers can perform mathematical operations fast and error free. This ability comes in handy for such routine tasks as recording cash receipts and cash payments and keeping track of accounts receivable and accounts payable. Posting, which requires no analysis, is also well suited for a computer. The computer can be programmed to print the trial balance and the financial statements. Having the machine do these routine jobs saves time and money.

What are a computer's limits? Computers are not people, so they cannot think. The adjusting entries illustrate the need for the type of analysis that requires the human touch. At the end of the period, the office manager may count the supplies on hand. The accountant then makes the necessary entry to adjust the Supplies and Supplies Expense accounts. A computer cannot perform these operations. It takes a human to count assets on hand and to enter the data for the adjustments. If the system is computerized, the machine takes over and does the posting and statement preparation. In a manual system, these steps are done by hand.

It may be economical to use a computer for some of the adjusting entries. Depreciation, for example, is often a routine computation that a computer performs well. But it takes a human to do the thinking and to program the machine to make the calculations. As we progress through the study of accounting, we will be discussing computer applications that fit the topics under discussion.

Summary Problem for Your Review

The trial balance of State Service Company at December 31, 19X1, which is the end of its year-long accounting period, is presented on the following page.

Data needed for the adjusting entries include:

a. Supplies on hand at year's end, $2,000.
b. Depreciation on furniture and fixtures, $20,000.
c. Depreciation on building, $10,000.
d. Salaries owed but not yet paid, $5,000.
e. Accrued service revenue, $12,000.
f. Of the $45,000 balance of unearned service revenue, $32,000 was earned during the year.

Required

1. Open the ledger accounts with their unadjusted balances. Show dollar amounts in thousands, as shown on the next page for Accounts Receivable:

State Service Company
Trial Balance
December 31, 19X1

Cash	$ 198,000	
Accounts receivable	370,000	
Supplies	6,000	
Furniture and fixtures	100,000	
Accumulated depreciation–furniture and fixtures		$ 40,000
Building	250,000	
Accumulated depreciation–building		130,000
Accounts payable		380,000
Salary payable		
Unearned service revenue		45,000
Capital		293,000
Owner's withdrawals	65,000	
Service revenue		286,000
Salary expense	172,000	
Supplies expense		
Depreciation expense–furniture and fixtures		
Depreciation expense–building		
Miscellaneous expense	13,000	
Total	$1,174,000	$1,174,000

Accounts Receivable

370	

2. Journalize State Service Company's adjusting entries at December 31, 19X1. Key entries by letter as in Exhibit 3-4.

3. Post the adjusting entries.

4. Write the trial balance on a sheet of paper, enter the adjusting entries, and prepare an adjusted trial balance, as shown in Exhibit 3-5.

5. Prepare the income statement, the statement of owner's equity, and the balance sheet. Draw the arrows linking the three statements together.

SOLUTION TO REVIEW PROBLEM

Requirements 1 and 3

Assets

Cash		Accounts Receivable		Supplies		Furniture and Fixtures	
Bal. 198		370		6	(a) 4	Bal. 100	
		(e) 12					
		Bal. 382		Bal. 2			

Accumulated Depreciation-Furniture and Fixtures

	40
(b)	20
Bal.	60

Building

Bal. 250	

Accumulated Depreciation-Building

	130
(c)	10
Bal.	140

Liabilities

Accounts Payable

	Bal. 380

Salary Payable

	(d) 5
	Bal. 5

Unearned Service Revenue

(f) 32	45
	Bal. 13

Owner's Equity

Capital

	Bal. 293

Owner's Withdrawals

Bal. 65	

Revenues

Service Revenue

	286
(e)	12
(f)	32
Bal.	330

Expenses

Salary Expense

172	
(d) 5	
Bal. 177	

Supplies Expense

(a) 4	
Bal. 4	

Depreciation Expense-Furniture and Fixtures

(b) 20	
Bal. 20	

Depreciation Expense-Building

(c) 10	
Bal. 10	

Miscellaneous Expense

Bal. 13	

Requirement 2

		19X1			
a.	Dec. 31	Supplies Expense ($6,000 − $2,000)............	4,000	
		Supplies.............................		4,000
		To record supplies used.		
b.	31	Depreciation Expense-Furniture and Fixtures.....	20,000	
		Accumulated Depreciation–Furniture and Fixtures.............................		20,000
		To record depreciation expense on furniture and fixtures.		

c. Dec. 31   Depreciation Expense-Building   10,000
                    Accumulated Depreciation – Building   10,000
               To record depreciation expense on building.

d.   31   Salary Expense   5,000
                    Salary Payable   5,000
               To accrue salary expense.

e.   31   Accounts Receivable.   12,000
                    Service Revenue   12,000
               To accrue service revenue.

f.   31   Unearned Service Revenue   32,000
                    Service Revenue   32,000
               To record unearned service revenue that has been
               earned.

Requirement 4

State Service Company
Preparation of Adjusted Trial Balance
December 31, 19X1
(amounts in thousands)

	Trial Balance		Adjustments		Adjusted Trial Balance	
	Debit	**Credit**	**Debit**	**Credit**	**Debit**	**Credit**
Cash	198				198	
Accounts receivable	370		(e) 12		382	
Supplies	6			(a) 4	2	
Furniture and fixtures	100				100	
Accumulated depreciation – furniture and fixtures		40		(b) 20		60
Building	250				250	
Accumulated depreciation — building		130		(c) 10		140
Accounts payable		380				380
Salary payable				(d) 5		5
Unearned service revenue		45	(f) 32			13
Capital		293				293
Owner's withdrawals	65				65	
Service revenue		286		(e) 12		330
				(f) 32		
Salary expense	172		(d) 5		177	
Supplies expense			(a) 4		4	
Depreciation expense— furniture and fixtures			(b) 20		20	
Depreciation expense— building			(c) 10		10	
Miscellaneous expense	13				13	
	1,174	1,174	83	83	1,221	1,221

Requirement 5

State Service Company
Income Statement
For the Year Ended December 31, 19X1
(amounts in thousands)

Revenues:
    Service revenue. $330
Expenses:
    Salary expense $177
    Depreciation expense–furniture & fixtures   20
    Depreciation expense–building   10
    Supplies expense.   4
    Miscellaneous expense   13
        Total expenses   224
Net income $106

State Service Company
Statement of Owner's Equity
For the Year Ended December 31, 19X1
(amounts in thousands)

Capital, January 1, 19X1 . . . . $293
Add: Net income   106
                                  399
Less: Withdrawals   65
Capital, December 31, 19X1 . . . . $334

State Service Company
Balance Sheet
December 31, 19X1
(amounts in thousands)

Assets			**Liabilities**		
Cash.		$198	Accounts payable		$380
Accounts receivable		382	Salary payable.		5
Supplies.		2	Unearned service revenue . .		13
Furniture and fixtures	$100		Total liabilities.		398
Less Accumulated depreciation . .	60	40	**Owner's Equity**		
Building	250				
Less Accumulated depreciation . .	140	110	Capital.		334
			Total liabilities and		
Total assets		$732	owner's equity.		$732

Summary

In *accrual-basis* accounting, business events are recorded as they affect the entity. In *cash-basis accounting,* only those events that affect cash are recorded. The cash basis omits important events such as purchases and sales of assets on account. It also distorts the financial statements by labeling as expenses those cash payments that have long-term effects, like the purchases of buildings and equipment. Some small organizations use cash-basis accounting, but the generally accepted method is the accrual basis.

Accountants divide time into definite periods—such as a month, a quarter, and a year—to report the entity's financial statements. The year is the basic *accounting period,* but companies prepare financial statements as often as they need the information. Accountants have developed the *revenue principle* to determine when to record revenue and the amount of revenue to record. The *matching principle* guides the accounting for expenses.

Adjusting entries are a result of the accrual basis of accounting. These entries, made at the end of the accounting period, update the accounts for preparation of the financial statements. One of the most important pieces of accounting information is net income or net loss, and the adjusting entries help to measure the *net income* of the period.

Adjusting entries can be divided into five categories: *prepaid expenses, depreciation, accrued expenses, accrued revenues,* and *unearned revenues.* To prepare the *adjusted trial balance,* enter the adjusting entries next to the *unadjusted trial balance.* This document can be used to prepare the income statement, the statement of owner's equity, and the balance sheet.

These three financial statements are related as follows: Income, shown on the *income statement,* increases owner's equity, which also appears on the *statement of owner's equity.* The ending balance of capital is the last amount reported on the *balance sheet.*

Computers can aid the accounting process in a number of ways, chiefly by performing routine operations. Many adjusting entries, however, require analysis that is best done manually, without the computer.

Self-Study Questions

Test your understanding of the chapter by marking the best answer for each of the following questions.

1. Accrual-basis accounting *(p. 86)*
   a. Results in higher income than cash-basis accounting
   b. Leads to the reporting of more complete information than does cash-basis accounting
   c. Is not acceptable under GAAP
   d. Omits adjusting entries at the end of the period
2. Under the revenue principle, revenue is recorded *(p. 87)*
   a. At the earliest acceptable time
   b. At the latest acceptable time
   c. After it has been earned, but not before
   d. At the end of the accounting period
3. The matching principle provides guidance in accounting for *(p. 88)*
   a. Expenses   c. Assets
   b. Owner's equity   d. Liabilities
4. Adjusting entries *(p. 89)*
   a. Assign revenues to the period in which they are earned
   b. Help to properly measure the period's net income or net loss
   c. Bring asset and liability accounts to correct balances
   d. All of the above
5. A law firm began November with office supplies of $160. During the month, the firm purchased supplies of $290. At November 30 supplies on hand total $210. Supplies expense for the period is *(p. 91)*

a. $210

b. $240

c. $290

d. $450

6. A building that cost $120,000 has accumulated depreciation of $50,000. The book value of the building is *(p. 93)*
   a. $50,000
   b. $70,000
   c. $120,000
   d. $170,000

7. The adjusting entry to accrue salary expense *(p. 95)*
   a. Debits Salary Expense and credits Cash
   b. Debits Salary Payable and credits Salary Expense
   c. Debits Salary Payable and credits Cash
   d. Debits Salary Expense and credits Salary Payable

8. A business received cash of $3,000 in advance for revenue that will be earned later. The cash receipt entry debited Cash and credited Unearned Revenue for $3,000. At the end of the period, $1,100 is still unearned. The adjusting entry for this situation will *(p. 96)*
   a. Debit Unearned Revenue and credit Revenue for $1,900
   b. Debit Unearned Revenue and credit Revenue for $1,100
   c. Debit Revenue and credit Unearned Revenue for $1,900
   d. Debit Revenue and credit Unearned Revenue for $1,100

9. The links between the financial statements are *(p. 102)*
   a. Net income from the income statement to the statement of owner's equity
   b. Ending capital from the statement of owner's equity to the balance sheet
   c. Both of the above
   d. None of the above

10. Accumulated Depreciation is reported on the *(p. 102)*
    a. Balance sheet
    b. Income statement
    c. Statement of owner's equity
    d. Both a and b

Answers to the self-study questions are at the end of the chapter.

Accounting Vocabulary

accrual-basis accounting *(p. 86)*,   accrued expense *(p. 94)*,   accrued revenue *(p. 95)*, accumulated depreciation *(p. 93)*,   adjusted trial balance *(p. 99)*,   adjusting entry *(p. 89)*,   book value of a plant asset *(p. 93)*,   cash-basis accounting *(p. 86)*,   contra account *(p. 93)*,   contra asset *(p. 93)*,   depreciation *(p. 92)*,   matching principle *(p. 88)*,   plant asset *(p. 92)*,   prepaid expense *(p. 90)*,   revenue principle *(p. 87)*,   unearned revenue *(p. 96)*.

Assignment Material _____

Questions

1. Distinguish the accrual basis of accounting from the cash basis.
2. How long is the basic accounting period? What is a fiscal year? What is an interim period?
3. What two questions does the revenue principle help answer?
4. Briefly explain the matching principle.
5. What is the purpose of making adjusting entries?
6. Why are adjusting entries made at the end of the accounting period, not during the period?
7. Name five categories of adjusting entries and give an example of each.
8. Do all adjusting entries affect the net income or net loss of the period? Include in your answer the definition of an adjusting entry.
9. Why does the balance of Supplies need to be adjusted at the end of the period?

10. Manning Supply Company pays $1,800 for an insurance policy that covers three years. At the end of the first year, the balance of its Prepaid Insurance account contains two elements. What are the two elements, and what is the correct amount of each?

11. The title Prepaid Expense suggests that this type of account is an expense. If so, explain why. If not, what type of account is it?

12. What is a contra account? Identify the contra account introduced in this chapter, along with the account's normal balance.

13. The manager of a Quickie-Pickie convenience store presents his entity's balance sheet to a banker to obtain a loan. The balance sheet reports that the entity's plant assets have a book value of $135,000 and accumulated depreciation of $65,000. What does *book value* of a plant asset mean? What was the cost of the plant assets?

14. Give the entry to record accrued interest revenue of $800.

15. Why is an unearned revenue a liability? Use an example in your answer.

16. Identify the types of accounts (assets, liabilities, and so on) debited and credited for the five types of adjusting entries.

17. What purposes does the adjusted trial balance serve?

18. Explain the relationship among the income statement, the statement of owner's equity, and the balance sheet.

19. Bellevue Company failed to record the following adjusting entries at December 31, the end of its fiscal year: (a) accrued expenses, $500; (b) accrued revenues, $850; and (c) depreciation, $1,000. Did these omissions cause net income for the year to be understated or overstated and by what overall amount?

20. Identify several accounting tasks for which it is efficient to use a microcomputer. What is the basic limitation on the use of a computer?

Exercises

Exercise 3-1 *Applying accounting concepts and principles*

Identify the accounting concept or principle that gives the most direction on how to account for each of the following situations:

a. The owner of a business desires monthly financial statements to measure the progress of the entity on an ongoing basis.

b. Expenses of the period total $4,900. This amount should be subtracted from revenue to compute the period's income.

c. Expenses of $650 must be accrued at the end of the period to properly measure income.

d. A customer states her intention to shift her business to a travel agency. Should the travel agency record revenue based on this intention?

Exercise 3-2 *Journalizing adjusting entries*

Journalize the entries for the following adjustments at December 31, the end of the accounting period.

a. Employee salaries owed, $3,600

b. Prepaid insurance expired, $450

c. Interest revenue accrued, $5,000

d. Unearned service revenue earned, $800

e. Depreciation, $6,200

Exercise 3-3 *Analyzing the effects of adjustments on net income.*

Suppose the adjustments required in Exercise 3-2 were not made. Compute the overall overstatement or understatement of net income as a result of the omission of these adjustments.

Exercise 3-4   *Allocating prepaid expense to the asset and the expense*

Compute the amounts indicated by question marks for each of the following Prepaid Rent situations. Consider each situation separately.

	Situation			
	1	**2**	**3**	**4**
Beginning Prepaid Rent	$ 900	$ 600	$ 300	$500
Payments for Prepaid Rent during the year	1,100	?	700	?
Total amount to account for	2,000	1,500	1,000	?
Ending Prepaid Rent	?	500	200	800
Rent Expense	1,600	1,000	?	300

Exercise 3-5   *Recording adjustments in T-accounts*

The accounting records of Manny Fernandez, Tailor, include the following unadjusted balances at May 31: Accounts Receivable, $1,200; Supplies, $600; Salary Payable, $0; Unearned Service Revenue, $400; Service Revenue, $5,100; Salary Expense, $1,200; Supplies Expense, $0.

Fernandez's accountant develops the following data for the May 31 adjusting entries:

a.   Supplies on hand, $200.

b.   Salary owed to employee, $100.

c.   Service revenue accrued, $350.

d.   Unearned service revenue that has been earned, $250.

Open the foregoing T-accounts and record the adjustments directly in the accounts, keying each adjustment amount by letter. Show each account's adjusted balance. Journal entries are not required.

Exercise 3-6   *Adjusting the accounts*

Complete the following adjusted trial balance by entering the adjustment amounts directly in the adjustment columns of the text. Service Revenue is the only account affected by more than one adjustment.

Austin Hill Travel Agency
Preparation of Adjusted Trial Balance
October 31, 19X2

Account Title	Trial Balance		Adjustments		Adjusted Trial Balance	
	Debit	**Credit**	**Debit**	**Credit**	**Debit**	**Credit**
Cash	3,000				3,000	
Accounts receivable	6,500				6,950	
Supplies	1,040				800	
Office furniture	19,300				19,300	
Accumulated depreciation		11,060				11,320
Salary payable						600
Unearned revenue		900				690
Capital		16,340				16,340
Owner's withdrawals	6,200				6,200	
Service revenue		11,830				12,490
Salary expense	2,690				3,290	
Rent expense	1,400				1,400	
Depreciation expense					260	
Supplies expense					240	
	40,130	40,130			41,440	41,440

Exercise 3-7 *Journalizing adjustments*

Make journal entries for the adjustments that would complete the preparation of the adjusted trial balance in Exercise 3-6. Include explanations.

Exercise 3-8 *Preparing the financial statements*

Refer to the adjusted trial balance in Exercise 3-6. Prepare Austin Hill Travel Agency's income statement and statement of owner's equity for the three months ended October 31, 19X2, and its balance sheet on that date. Draw the arrows linking the three statements.

Exercise 3-9 *Preparing the financial statements*

The accountant for Patrick Beckham, M.D., has posted adjusting entries *a* through *e* to the accounts at September 30, 19X2. All the revenues and expenses of the entity are listed here in T-account form.

	Accounts Receivable		
	23,000		
(e)	3,500		

	Supplies		
	4,000	(a)	2,000

Accumulated Depreciation– Furniture			
			5,000
		(b)	3,000

Accumulated Depreciation– Building			
			33,000
		(c)	6,000

	Salaries Payable		
		(d)	1,500

Service Revenue			
			135,000
		(e)	3,500

	Salary Expense		
	28,000		
(d)	1,500		

	Supplies Expense		
(a)	2,000		

Depreciation Expense– Furniture			
(b)	3,000		

Depreciation Expense– Building			
(c)	6,000		

Required

Prepare the income statement of Patrick Beckham, M.D., for the year ended September 30, 19X2. List expenses in order from the largest to the smallest.

Exercise 3-10 *Preparing the statement of owner's equity*

A. B. Leewright Company began the year with capital of $85,000. On July 9 the owner invested $12,000 cash in the business. On September 26 he transferred to the company land valued at $19,000. The income statement for the year ended September 30, 19X5, reported a net loss of $28,000. During this fiscal year, the owner withdrew $1,500 monthly for personal use. Prepare the company's statement of owner's equity for the year ended September 30, 19X5.

Problems (Group A)

Problem 3-1A *Journalizing adjusting entries*

Journalize the adjusting entry needed on December 31, end of the current account period, for each of the following independent cases affecting Willis Engineering Company.

a. Each Friday Willis pays its employees for the current week's work. The amount of the payroll is $2,500 per day for a five-day work week. The current accounting period ends on Thursday.

b. Willis has received notes receivable from some clients for professional services. During the current year, Willis has earned accrued interest revenue of $8,575, which will be received next year.

c. The beginning balance of Engineering Supplies was $3,800. During the year the entity purchased supplies costing $12,530, and at December 31 the inventory of supplies on hand is $2,970.

d. Willis is conducting tests of the strength of the steel to be used in a large building, and the client paid Willis $27,000 at the start of the project. Willis recorded this amount as Unearned Engineering Revenue. The tests will take several months to complete. Willis executives estimate that the company has earned two-thirds of the total fee during the current year.

e. Depreciation for the current year includes: Office Furniture, $4,500; Engineering Equipment, $6,360; Building, $3,790. Make a compound entry.

f. Details of Prepaid Insurance are shown in the account:

Prepaid Insurance

Jan. 1 Bal. 2,400	
Apr. 30 3,600	
Oct. 31 3,600	

Willis pays semiannual insurance premiums (the payment for insurance coverage is called a *premium*) on April 30 and October 31. At December 31, $2,400 of the last payment is still in force.

Problem 3-2A   *Preparing the financial statements from an adjusted trial balance*

The adjusted trial balance of Sommerfeld Engineering Services at December 31, 19X8 follows:

Sommerfeld Engineering Services
Adjusted Trial Balance
December 31, 19X8

Cash	$ 8,340	
Accounts receivable	41,490	
Prepaid rent	1,350	
Supplies	970	
Equipment	55,690	
Accumulated depreciation – equipment		$ 7,240
Office furniture	24,100	
Accumulated depreciation – office furniture		18,670
Accounts payable		13,600
Unearned service revenue		4,520
Interest payable		2,130
Salaries payable		930
Note payable		40,000
Lou Sommerfeld, capital		36,380
Lou Sommerfeld, withdrawals	48,000	
Service revenue		197,790
Depreciation expense – equipment	11,300	
Depreciation expense – office furniture	2,410	
Salary expense	102,800	
Rent expense	12,000	
Interest expense	4,200	
Utilities expense	3,770	
Insurance expense	3,150	
Supplies expense	1,690	
Total	$321,260	$321,260

Required

Prepare Sommerfeld's 19X8 income statement, statement of owner's equity, and balance sheet. List expenses in decreasing order on the income statement and show total liabilities on the balance sheet. Draw the arrows linking the three financial statements.

Problem 3-3A *Preparing an adjusted trial balance and the financial statements*

The unadjusted trial balance of Bette Kurtz, Consulting Psychologist, at October 31, 19X2, and the related month-end adjustment data follow:

Bette Kurtz, Consulting Psychologist
Trial Balance
October 31, 19X2

Cash	$16,300	
Accounts receivable	8,000	
Prepaid rent	4,000	
Supplies	600	
Furniture............................	12,000	
Accumulated depreciation...............		$ 3,000
Accounts payable.....................		2,800
Salary payable		
Bette Kurtz, capital....................		33,000
Bette Kurtz, withdrawals	3,600	
Consulting service revenue		7,400
Salary expense	1,400	
Rent expense		
Utilities expense......................	300	
Depreciation expense...................		
Supplies expense		
Total	$46,200	$46,200

Adjustment data:

a. Prepaid rent expired during the month, $1,000.
b. Supplies on hand at October 31, $400.
c. Depreciation on furniture for the month, $250.
d. Accrued salary expense at October 31, $300.
e. Accrued consulting service revenue at October 31, $1,000.

Required

1. Write the trial balance on a sheet of paper, using as an example Exhibit 3-5, and prepare the adjusted trial balance of Bette Kurtz, Consulting Psychologist, at October 31, 19X2. Key each adjusting entry by letter.
2. Prepare the income statement, the statement of owner's equity, and the balance sheet. Draw the arrows linking the three financial statements.

Problem 3-4A *Analyzing and journalizing adjustments*

Song Kim Sales Company's unadjusted and adjusted trial balances at December 31, 19X0, are shown on the following page.

Required

Journalize the adjusting entries that account for the differences between the two trial balances. The only account affected by more than one adjustment is Commission Revenue.

Song Kim Sales Company
Adjusted Trial Balance
December 31, 19X0

Account Title	Trial Balance		Adjusted Trial Balance	
	Debit	Credit	Debit	Credit
Cash	3,620		3,620	
Accounts receivable	11,260		12,090	
Supplies	1,090		780	
Prepaid insurance	2,200		1,330	
Office furniture	21,630		21,630	
Accumulated depreciation		8,220		10,500
Accounts payable		6,310		6,310
Salary payable				960
Interest payable				350
Note payable		12,000		12,000
Unearned commission revenue		1,440		960
Song Kim, capital		13,010		13,010
Song Kim, withdrawals	29,370		29,370	
Commission revenue		72,890		74,200
Depreciation expense			2,280	
Supplies expense			310	
Utilities expense	4,960		4,960	
Salary expense	26,660		27,620	
Rent expense	12,200		12,200	
Interest expense	880		1,230	
Insurance expense			870	
	113,870	113,870	118,290	118,290

Problem 3-5A *Journalizing and posting adjustments to T-accounts; preparing the adjusted trial balance and the financial statements*

The trial balance of Conrad Realty at August 31 of the current year and the data needed for the month-end adjustments follow.

Adjustment data:

a. Prepaid rent still in force at August 31, $900.
b. Supplies used during the month, $300.
c. Depreciation for the month, $400.
d. Accrued advertising expense at August 31, $110. (Credit Accounts Payable.)
e. Accrued salary expense at August 31, $550.
f. Unearned commission revenue still unearned at August 31, $1,670.

Conrad Realty
Trial Balance
August 31, 19XX

Cash	$ 2,200	
Accounts receivable	23,780	
Prepaid rent	2,420	
Supplies	1,180	
Furniture	19,740	
Accumulated depreciation		$ 3,630
Accounts payable		2,410
Salary payable		
Unearned commission revenue		2,790
Lou Conrad, capital		39,510
Lou Conrad, withdrawals	4,800	
Commission revenue		11,700
Salary expense	3,800	
Rent expense		
Utilities expense	550	
Depreciation expense		
Advertising expense	1,570	
Supplies expense		
Total	$60,040	$60,040

Required

1. Open T-accounts for the accounts listed in the trial balance, inserting their August 31 unadjusted balances.
2. Journalize the adjusting entries and post them to the T-accounts. Key the journal entries and the posted amounts by letter.
3. Prepare the adjusted trial balance.
4. Prepare the income statement, the statement of owner's equity, and the balance sheet. Draw the arrows linking the three financial statements.

Problem 3-6A *Journalizing and posting adjustments to four-column accounts; preparing the adjusted trial balance and the financial statements*

The trial balance of King Carpet Cleaners at May 31, 19X3, and the data needed to make the year-end adjustments follow.

Adjustment data:

a. At May 31 the business has earned $1,000 service revenue that has not yet been recorded.
b. Supplies used during the year totaled $5,650.
c. Prepaid rent still in force at May 31 is $330.
d. Depreciation for the year is $3,100.
e. King cleans the carpets of a large apartment complex that pays him in advance. At May 31 the entity has earned $3,600 of the unadjusted balance of Unearned Service Revenue.
f. At May 31 the business owes its employees accrued salaries of $1,300.

King Carpet Cleaners
Trial Balance
May 31, 19X3

Account
No.

101	Cash....................................	$ 3,260	
112	Accounts receivable	4,700	
127	Supplies..................................	7,700	
129	Prepaid rent..............................	1,430	
143	Cleaning equipment	28,300	
154	Accumulated depreciation		$ 12,550
211	Accounts payable		4,240
221	Salary payable..............................		
243	Unearned service revenue		5,810
301	Thomas King, capital		7,080
311	Thomas King, withdrawals.....................	34,800	
401	Service revenue.............................		80,610
511	Salary expense	28,800	
513	Depreciation expense		
515	Supplies expense............................		
519	Rent expense...............................		
521	Utilities expense	1,300	
	Total.....................................	$110,290	$110,290

Required

1. Open the accounts listed in the trial balance, inserting their May 31 unadjusted balances. Use four-column accounts. Date the balances of the following accounts as of May 1: Supplies, Prepaid Rent, Accumulated Depreciation, and Unearned Service Revenue.
2. Journalize the adjusting entries, using page 7 of the journal.
3. Post the adjusting entries to the ledger accounts, using all posting references.
4. Prepare the adjusted trial balance at May 31.
5. Prepare the income statement, the statement of owner's equity, and the balance sheet. Draw the arrows linking the three financial statements.

(Group B)

Problem 3-1B   *Journalizing adjusting entries*

Journalize the adjusting entry needed on December 31, end of the current accounting period, for each of the following independent cases affecting Enfield Air Conditioning Contractors.

a. Enfield pays its employees each Friday. The amount of the weekly payroll is $1,800 for a five-day work week, and the daily salary amounts are equal. The current accounting period ends on Monday.
b. Enfield has loaned money, receiving notes receivable. During the current year the entity has earned accrued interest revenue of $1,673 that it will receive next year.
c. The beginning balance of Supplies was $2,680. During the year the entity purchased supplies costing $8,180, and at December 31 the inventory of supplies on hand is $2,150.

d. Enfield is installing the air-conditioning system in a large building, and the owner of the building paid Enfield $12,900 at the start of the project. Enfield recorded this amount as Unearned Service Revenue. The installation will take several weeks to complete. Les Enfield, the owner, estimates that the company has earned one fourth of the total fee during the current year.

e. Depreciation for the current year includes: Office Furniture, $650; Equipment, $3,850; Trucks, $10,320. Make a compound entry.

f. Details of Prepaid Rent are shown in the account:

Prepaid Rent

Jan. 1 Bal.	600	
Mar. 31	1,200	
Sep. 30	1,200	

Enfield pays office rent semiannually on March 31 and September 30. At December 31 $600 of the last payment is still an asset.

Problem 3-2B *Preparing the financial statements from an adjusted trial balance*

The adjusted trial balance of Gillen Tax Service at December 31, 19X6, is as follows:

Gillen Tax Service
Adjusted Trial Balance
December 31, 19X6

Cash	$ 3,320	
Accounts receivable	11,920	
Supplies	2,300	
Prepaid rent	600	
Office equipment	23,180	
Accumulated depreciation–office equipment		$ 6,350
Office furniture	17,680	
Accumulated depreciation–office furniture		4,870
Accounts payable		3,640
Property tax payable		1,100
Interest payable		830
Unearned service revenue		620
Note payable		30,500
Monica Gillen, capital		6,090
Monica Gillen, withdrawals	44,000	
Service revenue		124,880
Depreciation expense–office equipment	6,680	
Depreciation expense–office furniture	2,370	
Salary expense	39,900	
Rent expense	14,400	
Interest expense	3,100	
Utilities expense	2,670	
Insurance expense	3,810	
Supplies expense	2,950	
Total	$178,880	$178,880

Required

Prepare Gillen's 19X6 income statement, statement of owner's equity, and balance sheet. List expenses in decreasing order on the income statement and show total liabilities on the balance sheet. Draw the arrows linking the three financial statements.

Problem 3-3B *Preparing an adjusted trial balance and the financial statements*

The unadjusted trial balance of Jack Ochs, Attorney, at July 31, 19X2, and the related month-end adjustment data are as follows:

Jack Ochs, Attorney		
Trial Balance		
July 31, 19X2		
Cash	$14,600	
Accounts receivable	11,600	
Prepaid rent	3,600	
Supplies	800	
Furniture...........................	16,000	
Accumulated depreciation...............		$ 4,000
Accounts payable......................		3,150
Salary payable		
Jack Ochs, capital.....................		38,650
Jack Ochs, withdrawals	5,000	
Legal service revenue..................		8,750
Salary expense	2,400	
Rent expense..........................		
Utilities expense	550	
Depreciation expense..................		
Supplies expense		
Total	$54,550	$54,550

Adjustment data:

a. Prepaid rent expired during the month, $900.
b. Supplies on hand at July 31, $500.
c. Depreciation on furniture for the month, $350.
d. Accrued salary expense at July 31, $200.
e. Accrued legal service revenue at July 31, $700.

Required

1. Write the trial balance on a sheet of paper similar to Exhibit 3-5 and prepare the adjusted trial balance of Jack Ochs, Attorney, at July 31, 19X2. Key each adjusting entry by letter.
2. Prepare the income statement, the statement of owner's equity, and the balance sheet. Draw the arrows linking the three financial statements.

Problem 3-4B *Analyzing and journalizing adjustments*

Maddux Service Company's unadjusted and adjusted trial balances at April 30, 19X1, are as follows:

Maddux Service Company
Adjusted Trial Balance
April 30, 19X1

Account Title	Trial Balance Debit	Trial Balance Credit	Adjusted Trial Balance Debit	Adjusted Trial Balance Credit
Cash	8,180		8,180	
Accounts receivable	6,360		6,540	
Interest receivable			50	
Note receivable	4,100		4,100	
Supplies	980		290	
Prepaid rent	1,440		720	
Building	66,450		66,450	
Accumulated depreciation		14,970		16,070
Accounts payable		6,920		6,920
Wages payable				220
Unearned service revenue		670		110
Debra Maddux, capital		60,770		60,770
Debra Maddux, withdrawals	3,600		3,600	
Service revenue		9,940		10,680
Interest revenue				50
Wage expense	1,600		1,820	
Rent expense			720	
Depreciation expense			1,100	
Insurance expense	370		370	
Supplies expense			690	
Utilities expense	190		190	
	93,270	93,270	94,820	94,820

Required

Journalize the adjusting entries that account for the differences between the two trial balances. The only account affected by more than one adjustment is Service Revenue.

Problem 3-5B   *Journalizing and posting adjustments to T-accounts; preparing the adjusted trial balance and the financial statements*

The trial balance of Impala Realty at October 31, 19X2, and the data needed for the month-end adjustments follow.

Adjustment data:

a. Prepaid rent still in force at October 31, $650.
b. Supplies used during the month, $440.
c. Depreciation for the month, $700.
d. Accrued advertising expense at October 31, $320. (Credit Accounts Payable.)
e. Accrued salary expense at October 31, $180.
f. Unearned commission revenue still unearned at October 31, $2,000.

Required

1. Open T-accounts for the accounts listed in the trial balance, inserting their October 31 unadjusted balances.

Impala Realty
Trial Balance
October 31, 19X2

Cash	$ 1,460	
Accounts receivable	14,750	
Prepaid rent	3,100	
Supplies	780	
Furniture	22,370	
Accumulated depreciation		$11,640
Accounts payable		1,940
Salary payable		
Unearned commission revenue		2,290
Ellie Taft, capital		24,140
Ellie Taft, withdrawals	2,900	
Commission revenue		8,580
Salary expense	2,160	
Rent expense		
Utilities expense	340	
Depreciation expense		
Advertising expense	730	
Supplies expense		
Total	$48,590	$48,590

2. Journalize the adjusting entries and post them to the T-accounts. Key the journal entries and the posted amounts by letter.
3. Prepare the adjusted trial balance.
4. Prepare the income statement, the statement of owner's equity, and the balance sheet. Draw the arrows linking the three financial statements.

Problem 3-6B *Journalizing and posting adjustments to four-column accounts; preparing the adjusted trial balance and the financial statements*

The trial balance of Apartment Cleaning Service at July 31, 19X3, and the data needed to make the year-end adjustments are as follows:

Adjustment data:

a. At July 31 the business has earned $1,420 of service revenue that has not yet been recorded.
b. Supplies used during the year totaled $3,060.
c. Prepaid rent still in force at July 31 is $1,040.
d. Depreciation for the year is $3,730.
e. The entity cleans the carpets of a large apartment complex that pays in advance. At July 31 the entity has earned $2,210 of the unadjusted balance of Unearned Service Revenue.
f. At July 31 the business owes its employees accrued salaries of $1,780.

Required

1. Open the accounts listed in the trial balance, inserting their July 31 unadjusted balances. Use four-column accounts. Date the balances of the following accounts as of July 1: Supplies, Prepaid Rent, Accumulated Depreciation, and Unearned Service Revenue.

Apartment Cleaning Service
Trial Balance
July 31, 19X3

Account No.			
101	Cash..	$ 2,110	
121	Accounts receivable	6,200	
131	Supplies....................................	3,400	
133	Prepaid rent................................	1,890	
141	Cleaning equipment	36,200	
151	Accumulated depreciation		$ 14,360
201	Accounts payable		6,410
211	Salary payable..............................		
221	Unearned service revenue		3,110
301	Alvin McKay, capital		14,310
302	Alvin McKay, withdrawals.....................	40,100	
401	Service revenue.............................		91,060
501	Salary expense	32,150	
504	Depreciation expense		
506	Supplies expense............................		
509	Rent expense...............................	6,000	
511	Utilities expense	1,200	
	Total......................................	$129,250	$129,250

2. Journalize the adjusting entries, using page 4 of the journal.
3. Post the adjusting entries to the ledger accounts, using all posting references.
4. Prepare the adjusted trial balance at July 31.
5. Prepare the income statement, the statement of owner's equity, and the balance sheet. Draw the arrows linking the three financial statements.

Decision Problem

Valuing a Business Based on its Net Income

Slade McQueen has owned and operated McQueen Medical Systems, a management consulting firm for physicians, since its beginning ten years ago. From all appearances the business has prospered. McQueen lives in the fast lane—flashy car, home located in an expensive suburb, frequent trips abroad, and other signs of wealth. In the past few years, you have become friends with him and his wife through weekly rounds of golf at the country club. Recently, he mentioned that he has lost his zest for the business and would consider selling it for the right price. He claims that his clientele is firmly established and that the business "runs on its own." According to McQueen, the consulting procedures are fairly simple and anyone could perform the work.

Assume you are interested in buying this business. You obtain its most recent monthly trial balance, which follows. Assume that revenues and expenses vary little from month to month and April is a typical month.

Your investigation reveals that the trial balance does not include the effects of monthly revenues of $1,100 and expenses totaling $2,100. If you were to buy McQueen Medical Systems, you would hire a manager so you could devote your time to other duties. Assume that this person would require a monthly salary of $2,000.

McQueen Medical Systems
Trial Balance
April 30, 19XX

Cash................................	$ 7,700	
Accounts receivable..................	4,900	
Prepaid expenses.....................	2,600	
Plant assets	252,300	
Accumulated depreciation		$189,600
Land................................	138,000	
Accounts payable		11,800
Salary payable.......................		
Unearned consulting revenue...........		56,700
Slade McQueen, capital		148,400
Slade McQueen, withdrawals...........	9,000	
Consulting revenue...................		12,300
Salary expense......................	3,400	
Rent expense		
Utilities expense.....................	900	
Depreciation expense		
Supplies expense.....................		
Total...............................	$418,800	$418,800

Required

1. Is this an unadjusted or an adjusted trial balance? How can you tell?
2. Assume that the most you would pay for the business is thirty times the monthly net income you could expect to earn from it. Compute this possible price.
3. McQueen states that the least he will take for the business is his ending capital. Compute this amount.
4. Under these conditions, how much should you offer McQueen? Give your reason.

Financial Statement Problem

This problem uses the notes to the financial statements in Appendix C. The notes are needed to avoid cluttering the financial statements (the balance sheet, for example) with excessive detail.

Journalizing and Posting Transactions, and Tracing Account Balances to the Financial Statements

Note J in the Gulf+Western financial statements in Appendix C gives details of these balance sheet items: prepaid expenses, and accrued expenses and other liabilities. In Note J, "Other" among the prepaid expenses includes prepaid rent, prepaid insurance, and supplies. "Accrued compensation and other employee benefit related items" is a liability similar to salary payable. "Unexpired subscriptions and advance subscription payments" are liabilities for unearned subscription revenue, which is like unearned service revenue as discussed in this chapter.

Gulf+Western's accounting year is called a *fiscal year* because it ends on a date other than December 31.

Required

1. Open T-accounts for Other Prepaid Expenses, Accrued Compensation Payable, and Unexpired Subscriptions. For each account, insert Gulf+Western's actual October 31, 1986, balance (in millions) from Note J. (Example: Other Prepaid Expenses, $150.3).

2. Journalize the following for fiscal year 1987. Key entries by letter. Explanations are not required.

    Cash transactions (amounts in millions):
    a. Paid prepaid expenses, $73.4.
    b. Paid the October 31, 1986, accrued compensation payable.
    c. Received $19.8 cash for unexpired subscriptions.

    Adjustments at October 31, 1987 (amounts in millions):
    d. Prepaid expenses expired, $40.5. (Debit General and Administrative Expense.)
    e. Accrued compensation payable, $77.7. (Debit Selling Expense.)
    f. Unexpired subscription revenue earned, $15.8. (Credit Subscription Revenue).

3. After these entries are posted, show that the balances in the three accounts opened in Requirement 1 agree with their October 31, 1987, amounts in Note J. Key posted amounts by letter.

Answers to Self-Study Questions

1. b
2. c
3. a
4. d
5. b ($160 + $290 − $210 = $240)
6. b ($120,000 − $50,000 = $70,000)

7. d
8. a ($3,000 received − $1,100 unearned = $1,900 earned)
9. c
10. a

4

Completing the Accounting Cycle

LEARNING OBJECTIVES

After studying this chapter, you should be able to

1 Give an overview of the accounting cycle

2 Prepare a work sheet

3 Use the work sheet to complete the accounting cycle

4 Close the revenue, expense, and withdrawal accounts

5 Classify assets and liabilities as current or long-term

6 Correct typical accounting errors

7 Explain how a microcomputer spreadsheet can be used in accounting

---

You have studied how accountants journalize transactions, post to the ledger accounts, prepare the trial balance and the adjusting entries, and draw up the financial statements. One major step remains to complete the accounting cycle — closing the books. This chapter illustrates the closing process for Gary Lyon's accounting practice at April 30, 19X1. It also shows how to use two additional accounting tools that are optional. One of these optional tools is the accountant's work sheet. Building upon the adjusted trial balance, the work sheet leads directly to the financial statements, which are the focal point of financial accounting. The chapter also presents an example of an actual balance sheet to show how companies classify assets and liabilities in order to provide meaningful information for decision making.

Overview of the Accounting Cycle

The **accounting cycle** is the process by which accountants produce an entity's financial statements for a specific period of time. For a new business, the cycle begins with setting up (opening) the ledger accounts. Gary Lyon started his accounting practice from scratch on April 1, 19X1, so the first step in the cycle was to open the accounts. After a business has operated for one period, however, the account balances carry over from period to period. Therefore, the accounting cycle usually starts with the account balances at the beginning of the period, as shown in Exhibit 4-1. The exhibit highlights the new steps that we will be discussing in this chapter.

EXHIBIT 4-1   *The Accounting Cycle*

During the period	1. Start with the account balances in the ledger at the beginning of the period. 2. Analyze and journalize transactions as they occur. 3. Post journal entries to the ledger accounts.

End of the period	4. Compute the unadjusted balance in each account at the end of the period.
	5. **Enter the trial balance on the work sheet, and complete the work sheet.*
	6. Using the work sheet as a guide,
	   a. Prepare the financial statements.
	   b. Journalize and post the adjusting entries.
	   c. **Journalize and post the closing entries.**
	7. **Prepare the postclosing, or afterclosing, trial balance. This trial balance becomes step 1 for the next period.**

* Optional

The accounting cycle is divided into work that is performed during the period
—journalizing transactions and posting to the ledger—and work performed at
the end of the period to prepare the financial statements. A secondary purpose of
the end-of-period work is to get the accounts ready for recording the transactions
of the next period. The greater number of individual steps at the end of the period
may imply that most of the work is done at the end. Nevertheless, the recording
and posting during the period takes far more time than the end-of-period work.
Some of the terms in Exhibit 4-1 may be unfamiliar, but they will become clear by
the end of the chapter.

The Accountant's Work Sheet

Accountants often use a **work sheet,** a columnar document that is designed to
help move data from the trial balance to the finished financial statements. The
work sheet provides an orderly way to compute net income and arrange the data
for the financial statements. By listing all the accounts and their unadjusted
balances, it helps the accountant identify the accounts needing adjustment. Although it is not essential, the work sheet is helpful because it brings together in
one place the effects of all the transactions of a particular period. The work sheet
aids the closing process by listing the adjusted balances of all the accounts. It also
helps the accountant discover potential errors.

The work sheet is not part of the ledger or the journal, nor is it a financial
statement. Therefore, it is not part of the formal accounting system. Instead, it is a
summary device that exists for the accountant's convenience.

Exhibits 4-2 through 4-6 illustrate the development of a typical work sheet for
the business of Gary Lyon, CPA. The heading at the top names the business,
identifies the document, and states the accounting period. A step-by-step description of its preparation follows. Observe that steps 1 through 4 use the adjusted trial balance that was introduced in Chapter 3. Only step 5 is entirely new.

Steps introduced in Chapter 3 to prepare the adjusted trial balance:

1. Write the account titles and their unadjusted ending balances in the Trial Balance columns of the work sheet and total the amounts.

2. Enter the adjustments in the Adjustments columns and total the amounts.

3. Compute each account's adjusted balance by combining the trial balance and adjustment figures. Enter the adjusted amounts in the Adjusted Trial Balance columns.

4. Extend the asset, liability, and owner's equity amounts from the Adjusted Trial Balance to the Balance Sheet columns. Extend the revenue and expense amounts to the Income Statement columns. Total the statement columns.

New step introduced in this chapter:

5. Compute net income or net loss as the difference between total revenues and total expenses on the income statement. Enter net income or net loss as a balancing amount on the income statement and on the balance sheet and compute the adjusted column totals.

1. Write the account titles and their unadjusted ending balances in the Trial Balance columns of the work sheet and total the amounts. Of course, total debits should equal total credits as shown in Exhibit 4-2. The account titles and balances come directly from the ledger accounts before preparing the adjusting entries. If the business uses a work sheet, there is no need for a separate trial balance. It is written directly onto the work sheet, as shown in the exhibit. Accounts are grouped on the work sheet by category and are usually listed in the order they appear in the ledger. By contrast, their order on the financial statements follows a different pattern. For example, the expenses on the work sheet in Exhibit 4-2 indicate no particular order. But on the income statement, expenses are ordered by amount with the largest first (see Exhibit 4-7).

Accounts may have zero balances (for example, Depreciation Expense). All accounts are listed on the trial balance because they appear in the ledger. Electronically prepared work sheets list all the accounts, not just those with a balance.

2. Enter the adjusting entries in the Adjustments columns and total the amounts. Exhibit 4-3 includes the April adjusting entries. These are the same adjustments that were illustrated in Chapter 3 to prepare the adjusted trial balance.

How does the accountant identify the accounts that need to be adjusted? By scanning the trial balance. Cash needs no adjustment because all cash transactions are recorded as they occur during the period. Consequently, Cash's balance is up to date.

Accounts Receivable is listed next. Has Gary Lyon earned revenue that he has not yet recorded? The answer is yes. Lyon provides professional service for a client who pays a $500 fee on the 15th of each month. At April 30 Lyon has earned half of this amount, $250, which must be accrued. To accrue this service revenue, Lyon debits Accounts Receivable and credits Service Revenue on the work sheet in Exhibit 4-3. A letter is used to link the debit and the credit of each adjusting entry. By moving down the trial balance, Lyon identifies the remaining accounts needing adjustment. Supplies is next. The business has used supplies during April, so Lyon debits Supplies Expense and credits Supplies. The other adjustments are analyzed and entered on the work sheet as shown in the exhibit.

The process of identifying accounts that need to be adjusted is aided by listing the accounts in their proper sequence. However, suppose one or more accounts is omitted from the trial balance. It can always be written below the first column

EXHIBIT 4-2

Gary Lyon, CPA
Work Sheet
For the Month Ended April 30, 19X1

Account Title	Trial Balance		Adjustments		Adjusted Trial Balance		Income Statement		Balance Sheet	
	Debit	Credit	Debit	Credit	Debit	Credit	Debit	Credit	Debit	Credit
Cash	24,800									
Accounts receivable	2,250									
Supplies	700									
Prepaid rent	3,000									
Furniture	16,500									
Accumulated depreciation										
Accounts payable		13,100								
Salary payable										
Unearned service revenue		450								
Gary Lyon, capital		31,250								
Gary Lyon, withdrawals	3,200									
Service revenue		7,000								
Rent expense										
Salary expense	950									
Supplies expense										
Depreciation expense										
Utilities expense	400									
	51,800	51,800								

EXHIBIT 4-3

Gary Lyon, CPA
Work Sheet
For the Month Ended April 30, 19X1

Account Title	Trial Balance Debit	Trial Balance Credit	Adjustments Debit	Adjustments Credit	Adjusted Trial Balance Debit	Adjusted Trial Balance Credit	Income Statement Debit	Income Statement Credit	Balance Sheet Debit	Balance Sheet Credit
Cash	24,800									
Accounts receivable	2,250		(a) 250							
Supplies	700			(b) 300						
Prepaid rent	3,000			(c) 1,000						
Furniture	16,500									
Accumulated depreciation				(d) 275						
Accounts payable		13,100								
Salary payable				(e) 950						
Unearned service revenue		450	(f) 150							
Gary Lyon, capital		31,250								
Gary Lyon, withdrawals	3,200									
Service revenue		7,000		(a) 250						
				(f) 150						
Rent expense			(c) 1,000							
Salary expense	950		(e) 950							
Supplies expense			(b) 300							
Depreciation expense			(d) 275							
Utilities expense	400									
	51,800	51,800	2,925	2,925						

totals—$51,800. Assume that Supplies Expense was accidentally omitted and thus did not appear on the trial balance. When the accountant identifies the need to update the Supplies account, he or she knows that the debit in the adjusting entry is to Supplies Expense. In this case, the accountant can write Supplies Expense on the line beneath the amount totals and enter the debit adjustment—$300—on the Supplies Expense line. Keep in mind that the work sheet is not the finished version of the financial statements, so the order of the accounts on the work sheet is not critical. When the accountant prepares the income statement, Supplies Expense can be listed in its proper sequence.

After the adjustments are entered on the work sheet, the amount columns should be totaled to see that total debits equal total credits. This provides some assurance that each debit adjustment is accompanied by an equal credit.

3. Compute each account's adjusted balance by combining the trial balance and adjustment figures. Enter the adjusted amounts in the Adjusted Trial Balance columns. Exhibit 4-4 shows the work sheet with the adjusted trial balance added.

This step is performed as it was in Chapter 3. For example, the Cash balance is up to date, so it receives no adjustment. Accounts Receivable's adjusted balance of $2,500 is computed by adding the trial balance amount of $2,250 to the $250 debit adjustment. Supplies' adjusted balance of $400 is determined by subtracting the $300 credit adjustment from the unadjusted debit balance of $700. An account may receive more than one adjustment, as does Service Revenue. The column totals should maintain the equality of debits and credits.

4. Extend the asset, liability, and owner's equity amounts from the Adjusted Trial Balance to the Balance Sheet columns. Extend the revenue and expense amounts to the Income Statement columns. Total the statement columns. Every account is either a balance sheet account or an income statement account. The asset, liability, and owner's equity accounts go to the balance sheet, and the revenues and expenses go to the income statement. Debits on the adjusted trial balance remain debits in the statement columns, and likewise for credits. Each account's adjusted balance should appear in only one statement column, as shown in Exhibit 4-5.

The income statement indicates total expenses in the debit column ($3,875) and total revenues ($7,400) in the credit column. The balance sheet shows total debits of $49,400 and total credits of $45,875. At this stage, the column totals should *not* necessarily be equal.

5. Compute net income or net loss as the difference between total revenues and total expenses on the income statement. Enter net income or net loss as a balancing amount on the income statement and on the balance sheet and compute the adjusted column totals. Exhibit 4-6 presents the completed work sheet, which shows net income of $3,525, computed as follows:

Revenue (total credits on the income statement). $7,400
Expenses (total debits on the income statement).   3,875
Net income $3,525

Net income of $3,525 is entered in the debit column of the income statement, and the income statement columns are totaled at $7,400. The net income amount is then extended to the credit column of the balance sheet. This is because an excess of revenues over expenses increases capital, and increases in capital are recorded by a credit. In the closing process, which we discuss later, net income will find its way into the capital account.

If expenses exceed revenue, the result is a net loss. In that event, the accountant writes the words *Net loss* on the work sheet. The loss amount should be entered in the credit column of the income statement and in the debit column of the balance

EXHIBIT 4-4

Gary Lyon, CPA
Work Sheet
For the Month Ended April 30, 19X1

Account Title	Trial Balance Debit	Trial Balance Credit	Adjustments Debit	Adjustments Credit	Adjusted Trial Balance Debit	Adjusted Trial Balance Credit	Income Statement Debit	Income Statement Credit	Balance Sheet Debit	Balance Sheet Credit
Cash	24,800				24,800					
Accounts receivable	2,250		(a) 250		2,500					
Supplies	700			(b) 300	400					
Prepaid rent	3,000			(c) 1,000	2,000					
Furniture	16,500				16,500					
Accumulated depreciation				(d) 275		275				
Accounts payable		13,100				13,100				
Salary payable				(e) 950		950				
Unearned service revenue		450	(f) 150			300				
Gary Lyon, capital		31,250				31,250				
Gary Lyon, withdrawals	3,200				3,200					
Service revenue		7,000		(a) 250 (f) 150		7,400				
Rent expense			(c) 1,000		1,000					
Salary expense	950		(e) 950		1,900					
Supplies expense			(b) 300		300					
Depreciation expense			(d) 275		275					
Utilities expense	400				400					
	51,800	51,800	2,925	2,925	53,275	53,275				

EXHIBIT 4-5

Gary Lyon, CPA
Work Sheet
For the Month Ended April 30, 19X1

Account Title	Trial Balance		Adjustments		Adjusted Trial Balance		Income Statement		Balance Sheet	
	Debit	Credit	Debit	Credit	Debit	Credit	Debit	Credit	Debit	Credit
Cash	24,800				24,800				24,800	
Accounts receivable	2,250		(a) 250		2,500				2,500	
Supplies	700			(b) 300	400				400	
Prepaid rent	3,000			(c) 1,000	2,000				2,000	
Furniture	16,500				16,500				16,500	
Accumulated depreciation				(d) 275		275				275
Accounts payable		13,100				13,100				13,100
Salary payable				(e) 950		950				950
Unearned service revenue		450	(f) 150			300				300
Gary Lyon, capital		31,250				31,250				31,250
Gary Lyon, withdrawals	3,200				3,200				3,200	
Service revenue		7,000		(a) 250		7,400		7,400		
				(f) 150						
Rent expense			(c) 1,000		1,000		1,000			
Salary expense	950		(e) 950		1,900		1,900			
Supplies expense			(b) 300		300		300			
Depreciation expense			(d) 275		275		275			
Utilities expense	400				400		400			
	51,800	51,800	2,925	2,925	53,275	53,275	3,875	7,400	49,400	45,875

EXHIBIT 4-6

Gary Lyon, CPA
Work Sheet
For the Month Ended April 30, 19X1

Account Title	Trial Balance Debit	Trial Balance Credit	Adjustments Debit	Adjustments Credit	Adjusted Trial Balance Debit	Adjusted Trial Balance Credit	Income Statement Debit	Income Statement Credit	Balance Sheet Debit	Balance Sheet Credit
Cash	24,800				24,800				24,800	
Accounts receivable	2,250		(a) 250		2,500				2,500	
Supplies	700			(b) 300	400				400	
Prepaid rent	3,000			(c) 1,000	2,000				2,000	
Furniture	16,500				16,500				16,500	
Accumulated depreciation				(d) 275		275				275
Accounts payable		13,100				13,100				13,100
Salary payable				(e) 950		950				950
Unearned service revenue		450	(f) 150			300				300
Gary Lyon, capital		31,250				31,250				31,250
Gary Lyon, withdrawals	3,200				3,200				3,200	
Service revenue		7,000		(a) 250 (f) 150		7,400		7,400		
Rent expense			(c) 1,000		1,000		1,000			
Salary expense	950		(e) 950		1,900		1,900			
Supplies expense			(b) 300		300		300			
Depreciation expense			(d) 275		275		275			
Utilities expense	400				400		400			
	51,800	51,800	2,925	2,925	53,275	53,275	3,875	7,400	49,400	45,875
Net income							3,525			3,525
							7,400	7,400	49,400	49,400

sheet. This is because an excess of expenses over revenue decreases capital, and decreases in capital are recorded by a debit.

The balance sheet columns are totaled at $49,400. An out-of-balance condition indicates an error in preparing the work sheet. Common mistakes include arithmetic errors and carrying an amount to the wrong column—to the incorrect statement column or extending a debit as a credit or vice versa. Columns that balance offer some, but not complete, assurance that the work sheet is correct. For example, it is possible to have offsetting errors. Fortunately, that is unlikely.

Summary Problem for Your Review

The trial balance of State Service Company at December 31, 19X1, the end of its fiscal year, is presented below:

State Service Company
Trial Balance
December 31, 19X1

Cash	$ 198,000	
Accounts receivable	370,000	
Supplies	6,000	
Furniture and fixtures	100,000	
Accumulated depreciation–furniture and fixtures		$ 40,000
Building	250,000	
Accumulated depreciation–building		130,000
Accounts payable		380,000
Salary payable		
Unearned service revenue		45,000
Capital		293,000
Withdrawals	65,000	
Service revenues		286,000
Salary expense	172,000	
Supplies expense		
Depreciation expense–furniture and fixtures		
Depreciation expense–building		
Miscellaneous expense	13,000	
Total	$1,174,000	$1,174,000

Data needed for the adjusting entries include:

a. Supplies on hand at year end, $2,000.
b. Depreciation on furniture and fixtures, $20,000.
c. Depreciation on building, $10,000.
d. Salaries owed but not yet paid, $5,000.
e. Accrued service revenue, $12,000.
f. Of the $45,000 balance of Unearned Service Revenue, $32,000 was earned during 19X1.

Required

Prepare the work sheet of State Service Company for the year ended December 31, 19X1. Key each adjusting entry by the letter corresponding to the data given.

SOLUTION TO REVIEW PROBLEM

State Service Company
Work Sheet
For the Year Ended December 31, 19X1

Account Title	Trial Balance Debit	Credit	Adjustments Debit	Credit	Adjusted Trial Balance Debit	Credit	Income Statement Debit	Credit	Balance Sheet Debit	Credit
Cash	198,000				198,000				198,000	
Accounts receivable	370,000		(e) 12,000		382,000				382,000	
Supplies	6,000			(a) 4,000	2,000				2,000	
Furniture and fixtures	100,000				100,000				100,000	
Accumulated depreciation—furniture and fixtures		40,000		(b) 20,000		60,000				60,000
Building	250,000				250,000				250,000	
Accumulated depreciation—building		130,000		(c) 10,000		140,000				140,000
Accounts payable		380,000				380,000				380,000
Salary payable				(d) 5,000		5,000				5,000
Unearned service revenue		45,000	(f) 32,000			13,000				13,000
Capital		293,000				293,000				293,000
Withdrawals	65,000				65,000				65,000	
Service revenue		286,000		(e) 12,000 (f) 32,000		330,000		330,000		
Salary expense	172,000		(d) 5,000		177,000		177,000			
Supplies expense			(a) 4,000		4,000		4,000			
Depreciation expense—furniture and fixtures			(b) 20,000		20,000		20,000			
Depreciation expense—building			(c) 10,000		10,000		10,000			
Miscellaneous expense	13,000				13,000		13,000			
	1,174,000	1,174,000	83,000	83,000	1,221,000	1,221,000	224,000	330,000	997,000	891,000
Net income							106,000			106,000
							330,000	330,000	997,000	997,000

135

Using the Work Sheet _____

OBJECTIVE 3

Use the work sheet to complete the accounting cycle

As illustrated thus far, the work sheet helps to organize accounting data and to compute the net income or net loss for the period. It also aids in preparing the financial statements, recording the adjusting entries, and closing the accounts.

Preparing the Financial Statements

Even though the work sheet shows the amount of net income or net loss for the period, it is still necessary to prepare the financial statements. The sorting of accounts to the balance sheet and the income statement eases the preparation of the statements. The work sheet also provides the data for the statement of owner's equity. Exhibit 4-7 presents the April financial statements for the accounting practice of Gary Lyon, CPA (based on data from the work sheet in Exhibit 4-6).

The financial statements can be prepared directly from the adjusted trial balance as shown in Chapter 3. That is why completion of the work sheet is optional.

Recording the Adjusting Entries

The adjusting entries are a key element of accrual-basis accounting. The work sheet helps identify the accounts that need adjustments, which may be conveniently entered directly on the work sheet as shown in Exhibits 4-2 through 4-6. However, these work sheet procedures do *not* adjust the accounts in the ledger itself. Recall that the work sheet is neither a journal nor a ledger. Actual adjustment of the accounts requires journal entries that are posted to the ledger accounts. Therefore, the adjusting entries must be recorded in the journal as shown in Panel A of Exhibit 4-8. Panel B of the exhibit shows the postings to the accounts, with ''Adj.'' denoting an amount posted from an adjusting entry. Only the revenue and expense accounts are presented here in order to focus on the closing process, which is discussed in the next section.

The adjusting entries could have been recorded in the journal as they were entered on the work sheet. However, it is not necessary to journalize them at that time. Most companies go ahead and prepare the financial statements immediately after completing the work sheet. They can wait to journalize and post the adjusting entries just before they make the closing entries.

Delaying the journalizing and posting of the adjusting entries illustrates another use of the work sheet. Many companies journalize and post the adjusting entries — as in Exhibit 4-8 — only once annually, at the end of the year. The need for monthly and quarterly financial statements, however, requires a tool like the work sheet. The entity can use the work sheet to aid in preparing interim statements without entering the adjusting entries in the journal and posting them to the ledger.

Closing the Accounts

Accountants use the term **closing the accounts** to refer to the step at the end of the period that prepares the accounts for recording the transactions of the next period. Closing the accounts consists of journalizing and posting the closing entries. Closing sets the balances of the revenue and expense accounts back to zero in order to measure the net income of the next period. Closing is a clerical procedure devoid of any new accounting theory. Recall that the income statement reports only one period's income. For example, net income for McDonald's, Inc., for 1990

EXHIBIT 4-7 *April Financial Statements of Gary Lyon, CPA*

Gary Lyon, CPA
Income Statement
For the Month Ended April 30, 19X1

Revenues:		
Service revenue......................................		$7,400
Expenses:		
Salary expense......................................	$1,900	
Rent expense.......................................	1,000	
Utilities expense	400	
Supplies expense...................................	300	
Depreciation expense	275	
Total expenses..		3,875
Net income		$3,525

Gary Lyon, CPA
Statement of Owner's Equity
For the Month Ended April 30, 19X1

Gary Lyon, capital, April 1, 19X1	$31,250
Add: Net income	3,525
	34,775
Less: Withdrawals	3,200
Gary Lyon, capital, April 30, 19X1	$31,575

Gary Lyon, CPA
Balance Sheet
April 30, 19X1

Assets			Liabilities	
Cash		$24,800	Accounts payable.....	$13,100
Accounts receivable		2,500	Salary payable	950
Supplies.....................		400	Unearned service	
Prepaid rent		2,000	revenue	300
Furniture............	$16,500		Total liabilities	14,350
Less Accumulated			**Owner's Equity**	
depreciation	275	16,225		
			Gary Lyon, capital	31,575
			Total liabilities and	
Total assets		$45,925	owner's equity	$45,925

relates exclusively to 1990. At December 31, 1990, McDonald's accountants close the company's revenue and expense accounts for that year. Because these accounts' balances relate to a particular accounting period and are therefore closed at the end of the period, the revenue and expense accounts are called **temporary (nominal) accounts.** The owner's withdrawal account—although not a revenue or an expense—is also a temporary account because it is important to measure withdrawals for a specific period. The closing process applies only to temporary accounts.

EXHIBIT 4-8 *Journalizing and Posting the Adjusting Entries*

Panel A—Journalizing:		Page 4

Adjusting Entries

Apr. 30	Accounts Receivable...............................	250	
	Service Revenue........................		250
30	Supplies Expense.................................	300	
	Supplies.....................................		300
30	Rent Expense...................................	1,000	
	Prepaid Rent................................		1,000
30	Depreciation Expense.............................	275	
	Accumulated Depreciation...................		275
30	Salary Expense..................................	950	
	Salary Payable...........................		950
30	Unearned Service Revenue........................	150	
	Service Revenue...........................		150

Panel B—Posting the Adjustments to the Revenue and Expense Accounts:

Revenue   **Expenses**

Service Revenue		Rent Expense		Salary Expense	
	7,000	Adj. 1,000		950	
	Adj. 250	Bal. 1,000		Adj. 950	
	Adj. 150			Bal. 1,900	
	Bal. 7,400				

Supplies Expense		Depreciation Expense		Utilities Expense	
Adj. 300		Adj. 275		400	
Bal. 300		Bal. 275		Bal. 400	

Adj. = Amount posted from an adjusting entry
Bal. = Balance

To better understand the closing process, contrast the nature of the temporary accounts with the nature of the **permanent (real) accounts**—the assets, liabilities, and capital. The permanent accounts are *not* closed at the end of the period because their balances are not used to measure income. Consider Cash, Accounts Receivable, Supplies, Buildings, Accounts Payable, Notes Payable, and Gary Lyon, Capital. These accounts are not increases and decreases like the revenues and expenses, which relate exclusively to only one accounting period. Instead, the permanent accounts represent assets, liabilities, and capital that are on hand at a specific time. This is why their balances at the end of one accounting period carry over to become the beginning balances of the next period. For example, the Cash balance at December 31, 19X1, is also the beginning balance for 19X2.

Briefly, **closing entries** transfer the revenue, expense, and owner withdrawal balances from their respective accounts to the capital account. As you know, revenues increase owner's equity, and expenses and owner withdrawals decrease it. It is when we post the closing entries that the capital account absorbs the impact of the balances in the temporary accounts. As an intermediate step, however, the revenues and the expenses are transferred first to an account entitled **Income Summary,** which is like a temporary "holding tank" that is used only in the closing process. Then the balance of Income Summary is transferred to capital. The steps in closing the accounts of a proprietorship like Gary Lyon, CPA, are as follows:

1. Debit each revenue account for the amount of its credit balance. Credit Income Summary for the sum of the revenues. This entry transfers the sum of the revenues to the credit side of Income Summary.

2. Credit each expense account for the amount of its debit balance. Debit Income Summary for the sum of the expenses. This entry transfers the sum of the expenses to the debit side of Income Summary.

3. Debit Income Summary for the amount of its credit balance (revenues minus expenses) and credit the Capital account. If Income Summary has a debit balance, then credit Income Summary for this amount, and debit Capital. This entry transfers the net income or loss from Income Summary to the Capital account.

4. Credit the Withdrawals account for the amount of its debit balance. Debit the Capital account of the proprietor. Withdrawals are not expenses and do not affect net income or net loss. Therefore, this account is *not* closed to the Income Summary. This entry transfers the withdrawal amount to the debit side of the Capital account.

To illustrate, suppose Gary Lyon closes the books at the end of April. Exhibit 4-9 presents the complete closing process for Lyon's business. Panel A gives the closing journal entries, and Panel B shows the accounts after the closing entries have been posted.

The amount in the debit side of each expense account is its adjusted balance. For example, Rent Expense has a $1,000 debit balance. Also note that Service Revenue has a credit balance of $7,400 before closing. These amounts come directly from the adjusted balances in Exhibit 4-8, Panel B.

EXHIBIT 4-9 *Journalizing and Posting the Closing Entries*

OBJECTIVE 4
Close the revenue, expense, and withdrawal accounts

Panel A—Journalizing:

		Closing Entries	Page 5	
1.	Apr. 30	Service Revenue	7,400	
		Income Summary		7,400
2.	30	Income Summary	3,875	
		Rent Expense		1,000
		Salary Expense		1,900
		Supplies Expense		300
		Depreciation Expense		275
		Utilities Expense		400
3.	30	Income Summary ($7,400 − $3,875)	3,525	
		Gary Lyon, Capital		3,525
4.	30	Gary Lyon, Capital	3,200	
		Gary Lyon, Withdrawals		3,200

Exhibit 4-9 continues on the following page.

Panel B—Posting:

Adj = Amount posted from an adjusting entry
Clo. = Amount posted from a closing entry
Bal. = Balance

Closing entry 1, denoted in the Service Revenue account by *Clo.*, transfers Service Revenue's balance to the Income Summary account. This entry zeroes out Service Revenue for April and places the revenue on the credit side of Income Summary. Closing entry 2 zeroes out the expenses and moves their total ($3,875) to the debit side of Income Summary. At this point, Income Summary contains the impact of April's revenues and expenses and hence Income Summary's balance is the month's net income ($3,525). Closing entry 3 closes the Income Summary account by transferring net income to the credit side of Gary Lyon, Capital.[1] The last closing entry (entry 4) moves the owner withdrawals to the debit side of Gary Lyon, Capital, leaving a zero balance in the Withdrawals account.

After all the closing entries, the revenues, the expenses, and the Withdrawals

---

[1] The Income Summary account is a convenience for combining the effects of the revenues and expenses prior to transferring their income effect to Capital. It is not necessary to use the Income Summary account in the closing process. Another way of closing the revenues and expenses makes no use of this account. In this alternative procedure, the revenues and expenses are closed directly to Capital.

account are set back to zero to make ready for the next period. The owner's Capital account includes the full effects of the April revenues, expenses, and withdrawals. These amounts, combined with the beginning Capital balance, give Capital an ending balance of $31,575. Note that this Capital balance agrees with the amount reported on the statement of owner's equity and on the balance sheet in Exhibit 4-7. Also note that the ending balance of Capital remains. We do not close it out — because it is a balance sheet account.

Closing a Net Loss.　What would the closing entries be if Lyon's business had suffered a net *loss* during April? Suppose April expenses totaled $7,700 and all other factors were unchanged. Only closing entries 2 and 3 would be altered. Closing entry 2 would transfer expenses of $7,700 to the debit side of Income Summary, which would appear as follows:

Income Summary			
Clo.	7,700	Clo.	7,400
Bal.	300		

Closing entry 3 would then credit Income Summary to close its debit balance and to transfer the net loss to Capital:

3. Apr. 30　Gary Lyon, Capital 300
　　　　　　　　Income Summary .... 　　　300

After posting, these two accounts would appear as follows:

Income Summary					Gary Lyon, Capital		
Clo.	7,700	Clo.	7,400	→ Clo.	300		31,250
Bal.	300	Clo.	300				

Finally, the Withdrawals balance would be closed to Capital, as before.

Postclosing Trial Balance

The accounting cycle ends with the **postclosing trial balance** (see Exhibit 4-10). The postclosing trial balance is the final check on the accuracy of journalizing and posting the adjusting and closing entries. Like the trial balance that begins the work sheet, the postclosing trial balance is a list of the ledger's accounts and balances. This step ensures that the ledger is in balance for the start of the next accounting period. The postclosing trial balance is dated as of the end of the accounting period for which the statements have been prepared.

Note that the postclosing trial balance resembles the balance sheet. It contains the ending balances of the permanent accounts — the balance sheet accounts: the assets, liabilities, and capital. No temporary accounts — revenues, expenses, or withdrawal accounts — are included because their balances have been closed. The ledger is up-to-date and ready for the next period's transactions.

EXHIBIT 4-10   *Postclosing Trial Balance*

Gary Lyon, CPA		
Postclosing Trial Balance		
April 30, 19X1		
Cash	$24,800	
Accounts receivable	2,500	
Supplies......................................	400	
Prepaid rent	2,000	
Furniture.....................................	16,500	
Accumulated depreciation		$ 275
Accounts payable..............................		13,100
Salary payable		950
Unearned service revenue		300
Gary Lyon, capital		31,575
Total...	$46,200	$46,200

Classification of Assets and Liabilities

OBJECTIVE 5

Classify assets and liabilities as current or long-term

On the balance sheet, assets and liabilities are classified as either *current* or *long-term* to indicate their relative *liquidity*. **Liquidity** is a measure of how quickly an item may be converted to cash. Therefore, cash is the most liquid asset. Accounts receivable is a relatively liquid asset because the business expects to collect the amount in cash in the near future. Supplies are less liquid than accounts receivable, and furniture and buildings are even less so.

Users of financial statements are interested in liquidity because business difficulties often arise owing to a shortage of cash. How quickly can the business convert an asset to cash and pay a debt? How soon must a liability be paid? These are questions of liquidity. Balance sheets list assets and liabilities in the order of their relative liquidity.

Current Assets.   **Current assets** are assets that are expected to be converted to cash, sold, or consumed during the next 12 months or within the business's normal operating cycle if longer than a year. The *operating cycle* is the time span during which (1) cash is used to acquire goods and services, and (2) these goods and services are sold to customers, who in turn pay for their purchases with cash. For most businesses, the operating cycle is a few months. A few types of business have operating cycles longer than a year. Cash, Accounts Receivable, Notes Receivable due within a year or less, and Prepaid Expenses are current assets. Merchandising entities such as Sears, Penney's and K Mart have an additional current asset, Inventory. This account shows the cost of goods that are held for sale to customers.

Long-Term Assets.   **Long-term assets** are all assets other than current assets. They are not held for sale, but rather they are used to operate the business. One category of long-term assets is plant assets, or fixed assets. Land, Buildings, Furniture and Fixtures, and Equipment are examples of plant assets.

Financial statement users such as creditors are interested in the due dates of an entity's liabilities. The sooner a liability must be paid, the more current it is.

Liabilities that must be paid on the earliest future date create the greatest strain on cash. Therefore, the balance sheet lists liabilities in the order in which they are due. Knowing how many of a business's liabilities are current and how many are long-term helps creditors assess the likelihood of collecting from the entity. Balance sheets usually have at least two liability classifications, *current liabilities* and *long-term liabilities.*

Current Liabilities. **Current liabilities** are debts that are due to be paid within one year or within the entity's operating cycles if the cycle is longer than a year. Accounts Payable, Notes Payable due within one year, Salary Payable, Unearned Revenue, and Interest Payable owed on notes payable are current liabilities.

Long-Term Liabilities. **All liabilities that are not current are classified as long-term liabilities.** Many notes payable are long-term. Other notes payable are paid in installments, with the first installment due within one year, the second installment due the second year, and so on. In this case, the first installment would be a current liability and the remainder a long-term liability.

An Actual Classified Balance Sheet

Exhibit 4-11 is a classified balance sheet of Hawaiian Airlines, Inc. Hawaiian Airlines labels its plant assets Property and Equipment. (Another common title is Property, Plant, and Equipment.) It is also common to report the *book value,* or *net* amount, of property and equipment ($121,532,000), along with the amount of accumulated depreciation ($32,398,000). The original cost of the assets included in the property and equipment category is the sum of the two amounts, $153,930,000 ($121,532,000 + $32,398,000).

As you study the balance sheet, you will be delighted at how much of it you already understand. So far, you have been exposed to every type of asset and liability reported by this actual company. Other Assets and Other Liabilities are catchall categories for items that are difficult to classify. Stockholders' equity is the owners' equity of a corporation.

Formats of Balance Sheets

The balance sheet of Hawaiian Airlines shown in Exhibit 4-11 lists the assets at the top, with the liabilities and the owners' equity below. This is the **report format.** The balance sheet of Gary Lyon, CPA, presented in Exhibit 4-7 lists the assets at the left, with the liabilities and the owner's equity at the right. That is the **account format.**

Either format is acceptable. A recent survey of 600 companies indicated that 56 percent use the account format, and 44 percent use the report format.

Detecting and Correcting Accounting Errors

You have now learned all the steps that an accountant takes from opening the books and recording a transaction in the journal through closing the books and the postclosing trial balance. Along the way, errors may occur. Accounting errors

EXHIBIT 4-11   *Classified Balance Sheet*

Hawaiian Airlines, Inc. Balance Sheet March 31, 19XX	
Assets	**(dollar amounts in thousands)**
Current assets:	
Cash	$ 25,116
Accounts receivable	10,061
Inventories	2,307
Prepaid expenses and other current assets	2,864
Total current assets.............................	40,348
Property and equipment	
Less Accumulated depreciation of $32,398	121,532
Other assets	5,285
Total	$167,165
Liabilities	
Current liabilities:	
Current portion of long-term debt	$ 6,258
Notes payable......................................	3,103
Accounts payable...................................	12,243
Accrued liabilities..................................	19,192
Other current liabilities	1,696
Total current liabilities	42,492
Long-term debt	111,156
Other liabilities and deferred credits	4,622
Owners' Equity	
Stockholders' equity	8,895
Total	$167,165

include incorrect journal entries, mistakes in posting, and transpositions and slides. This section discusses their detection and correction.

OBJECTIVE 6
Correct typical accounting errors

Incorrect Journal Entries.   When a journal entry contains an error, the entry can be erased and corrected—if the error is caught immediately. Other accountants prefer to draw a line through the incorrect entry to maintain a record of all entries to the journal. After the incorrect entry is crossed out, the accountant can make the correct entry.

If the error is detected later, the accountant makes a *correcting entry.* Suppose Gary Lyon paid $5,000 cash for furniture and erroneously debited Supplies as follows:

Incorrect Entry

May 13	Supplies	5,000	
	Cash		5,000
	Bought supplies.		

The debit to Supplies is incorrect, so it is necessary to make a correcting entry as follows:

Correcting Entry

May 15   Furniture 5,000

           Supplies 5,000

     To correct May 13 entry.

The credit to Supplies in the second entry offsets the incorrect debit of the first entry. The debit to Furniture in the correcting entry places the purchase amount in the correct account.

Incorrect posting. Sometimes an accountant posts a debit as a credit or a credit as a debit. Such an error shows up in the trial balance—total debits do not equal total credits.

Suppose a $100 debit to Cash is posted as a $100 credit. The trial balance's total debits are $100 too low. Total credits are $100 too high. The difference is $200. Whenever a debit or credit has been misplaced, the resulting difference is evenly divisible by 2, as is the $200 figure in our example. Dividing that difference by 2 yields the amount of the incorrect posting, which in this case we know is $100. The accountant may then search the journal for the $100 entry and make the corrections.

Transpositions and slides. A **transposition** occurs when digits are flip-flopped—for example, $85 is a transposition of $58. Transpositions cause errors that are evenly divisible by 9. In this particular case, the transposition causes a $27 error ($85 − $58), which is evenly divisible by 9 ($27/9 = $3).

A **slide** results from adding one or more zeroes to a number or from dropping off a zero, for example, writing $500 as $5,000 or vice versa. The difference of $4,500 ($5,000 − $500) is evenly divisible by 9 ($4,500/9 = $500). Transpositions and slides occur in the transfer of numbers, for example, from the journal to the ledger or from the ledger to the trial balance.

Incorrect postings, transpositions, and slides can be corrected by crossing out the incorrect amount and then inserting the correct amount in its appropriate place.

Microcomputer Spreadsheets

Companies offer a variety of specialized computer programs—known as *software*—that require almost no computer programming expertise. Some software programs create an electronically prepared work sheet, also called a **spreadsheet.** The spreadsheet can be programmed to complete the work sheet after the accountant has entered the trial balance and the adjustment amounts. This is a big time saver because once the spreadsheet program is set up, it can be used over and over again without having to rewrite the account titles and do the arithmetic by hand. The spreadsheet can also be programmed to journalize and post the adjusting and closing entries and prepare the financial statements directly from the data on the work sheet.

To illustrate how a spreadsheet can be programmed to complete the work sheet, let's focus on the Accounts Receivable account. Assume that the goal is to determine Accounts Receivable's balance sheet amount of $2,500. The Accounts Receivable line from Exhibit 4-5 follows:

OBJECTIVE 7
Explain how a microcomputer spreadsheet can be used in accounting

Account Title	Trial Balance		Adjustments		Adjusted Trial Balance		Income Statement		Balance Sheet	
	Debit	Credit	Debit	Credit	Debit	Credit	Debit	Credit	Debit	Credit
Cash										
Accounts receivable	2,250		250		2,500				2,500	
Supplies										

How can the accountant use a spreadsheet program to accomplish this task? The spreadsheet appears on a video screen as a matrix of columns and rows—with no amounts or labels. Assume the spreadsheet provides a work space of 500 columns and 500 rows, as follows:

Using the keyboard of a microcomputer, the accountant can program the spreadsheet to resemble a work sheet. The columns are labeled to represent the work sheet columns, and the rows represent the accounts listed on the trial balance. It is also necessary to label the spaces where the dollar amounts go. The accountant may denote Accounts Receivable's unadjusted trial balance amount as W, a debit adjustment as X, a credit adjustment as Y, and Accounts Receivable's adjusted balance as Z. Thus labeled, the partial spreadsheet appears on the video screen as follows:

A fully computerized accounting system can transfer the account balances from the ledger to the trial balance. These amounts, plus or minus the adjustments, equal the adjusted balances. The accountant can program the computer to complete the work sheet as follows:

Account Title	Trial Balance		Adjustments		Adjusted Trial Balance		Income Statement		Balance Sheet	
	Debit	Credit	Debit	Credit	Debit	Credit	Debit	Credit	Debit	Credit
Cash										
Accounts Receivable	W		X	Y	W + X −Y = Z				Z	
Supplies										

Gary Lyon can use the keyboard to enter the following values into the computer: W = \$2,250; X = \$250; and Y = \$0. The spreadsheet takes over and computes Z = \$2,500 for the adjusted trial balance and the balance sheet. The accountant gives the computer a print command, and it prints the completed work sheet as shown for Accounts Receivable at the beginning of this section. The other account balances are generated similarly.

As in a manual system, the completed work sheet yields the amounts for the adjusting entries, the closing entries, and the financial statements. The beauty of the spreadsheet is that once the computer program is written, it can perform its task as often as desired with no arithmetic errors. As the business changes and new accounts are needed, the accountant can simply insert the new account titles and adapt the spreadsheet program accordingly.

Summary Problem for Your Review

Refer to the data in the earlier Summary Problem for Your Review, presented on page 134.

Required

1. Journalize and post the adjusting entries. (Before posting to the accounts, enter their balances as shown in the trial balance. For example, enter the \$370,000 balance in the Accounts Receivable account before posting its adjusting entry.) Key adjusting entries by *letter*, as shown in the work sheet solution to the first review problem. You can take the adjusting entries straight from the work sheet on page 135.
2. Journalize and post the closing entries. (Each account should carry its balance as shown in the adjusted trial balance.) To distinguish closing entries from adjusting entries, key the closing entries by *number*. Draw the arrows to illustrate the flow of data, as shown in Exhibit 4-9, page 140. Indicate the balance of the Capital account after the closing entries are posted.

3. Prepare the income statement for the year ended December 31, 19X1. List Miscellaneous Expense last among the expenses, a common practice.

4. Prepare the statement of owner's equity for the year ended December 31, 19X1. Draw the arrow that links the income statement to the statement of owner's equity.

5. Prepare the classified balance sheet at December 31, 19X1. Use the report form. All liabilities are current. Draw the arrow that links the statement of owner's equity to the balance sheet.

SOLUTION TO REVIEW PROBLEM

Requirement 1

a.	Dec. 31	Supplies Expense		4,000	
		Supplies			4,000
b.	31	Depreciation Expense – Furniture and Fixtures		20,000	
		Accumulated Depreciation – Furniture and Fixtures			20,000
c.	31	Depreciation Expense – Building		10,000	
		Accumulated Depreciation – Building			10,000
d.	31	Salary Expense		5,000	
		Salary Payable			5,000
e.	31	Accounts Receivable		12,000	
		Service Revenue			12,000
f.	31	Unearned Service Revenue		32,000	
		Service Revenue			32,000

Accounts Receivable		Supplies		Accumulated Depreciation – Furniture and Fixtures	
370,000		6,000	(a) 4,000		40,000
(e) 12,000					(b) 20,000

Accumulated Depreciation – Building		Salary Payable		Unearned Service Revenue	
	130,000		(d) 5,000	(f) 32,000	45,000
	(c) 10,000				

Service Revenue		Salary Expense		Supplies Expense	
	286,000	172,000		(a) 4,000	
	(e) 12,000	(d) 5,000		Bal. 4,000	
	(f) 32,000	Bal. 177,000			
	Bal. 330,000				

Depreciation Expense – Building		Depreciation Expense – Furniture and Fixtures	
(c) 10,000		(b) 20,000	
Bal. 10,000		Bal. 20,000	

Requirement 2

1.	Dec. 31	Service Revenue	330,000	
		Income Summary		330,000
2.	31	Income Summary	224,000	
		Salary Expense		177,000
		Supplies Expense		4,000
		Depreciation Expense–Furniture and Fixtures		20,000
		Depreciation Expense–Building.		10,000
		Miscellaneous Expense.		13,000
3.	31	Income Summary ($330,000 − $224,000)	106,000	
		Capital.		106,000
4.	31	Capital	65,000	
		Withdrawals		65,000

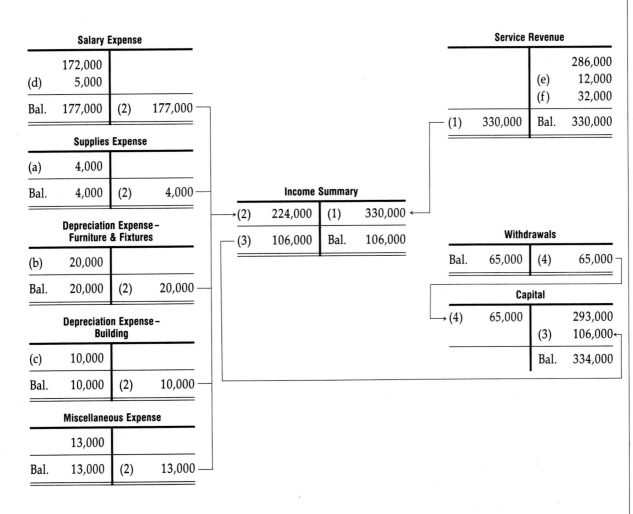

Requirement 3

State Service Company
Income Statement
For the Year Ended December 31, 19X1

Revenues:		
Service revenue		$330,000
Expenses:		
Salary expense	$177,000	
Depreciation expense – furniture and fixtures	20,000	
Depreciation expense – building	10,000	
Supplies expense	4,000	
Miscellaneous expense	13,000	
Total expenses		224,000
Net Income		$106,000

Requirement 4

State Service Company
Statement of Owner's Equity
For the Year Ended December 31, 19X1

Capital, January 1, 19X1	$293,000
Add: Net income	106,000
	399,000
Less: Withdrawals	65,000
Capital, December 31, 19X1	$334,000

Requirement 5

State Service Company
Balance Sheet
December 31, 19X1

Assets

Current assets:		
Cash		$198,000
Accounts receivable		382,000
Supplies		2,000
Total current assets		582,000
Plant assets:		
Furniture and fixtures	$100,000	
Less Accumulated depreciation	60,000	40,000
Building	250,000	
Less Accumulated depreciation	140,000	110,000
Total assets		$732,000

Liabilities

Current liabilities:	
Accounts payable	$380,000
Salary payable	5,000
Unearned service revenue	13,000
Total current liabilities	398,000

Owner's Equity

Capital	334,000
Total liabilities and owner's equity	$732,000

Summary

The *accounting cycle* is the process by which accountants produce the financial statements for a specific period of time. The cycle starts with the beginning account balances. During the period, the business journalizes transactions and posts them to the ledger accounts. At the end of the period, the trial balance is prepared, and the accounts are adjusted in order to measure the period's net income or net loss.

Completion of the accounting cycle is aided by use of a *work sheet.* This columnar document summarizes the effects of all the activity of the period. It is neither a journal nor a ledger but merely a convenient device for completing the accounting cycle.

The work sheet has columns for the trial balance, the adjustments, the adjusted trial balance, the income statement, and the balance sheet. It aids the adjusting process, and it is the place where the period's net income or net loss is first computed. The work sheet also provides the data for the financial statements and the closing entries. However, it is *not* necessary. The accounting cycle can be completed from the less elaborate adjusted trial balance.

Revenues, expenses, and withdrawals represent increases and decreases in owner's equity for a specific period. At the end of the period, their balances are closed out to zero, and, for this reason, they are called *temporary accounts.* Assets, liabilities, and owner's equity are not closed because they are the *permanent accounts.* Their balances at the end of one period become the beginning balances of the next period. The final accuracy check of the period is the *postclosing trial balance.*

Four common accounting errors are *incorrect journal entries, incorrect postings, transpositions,* and *slides.* Techniques exist for detecting and correcting these errors.

Microcomputer *spreadsheets* are extremely useful for tasks such as completing the accounting cycle. Their main advantage is that they can be programmed to print documents such as the work sheet and perform repetitious calculations without errors.

Self-Study Questions

Test your understanding of the chapter by marking the best answer to each of the following questions.

1. The focal point of the accounting cycle is the *(p. 125)*
   a. Financial statements
   b. Trial balance
   c. Adjusted trial balance
   d. Work sheet

2. Arrange the following accounting cycle steps in their proper order *(p. 126)*:
   a. Complete the work sheet
   b. Journalize and post adjusting entries
   c. Prepare the postclosing trial balance
   d. Journalize and post cash transactions
   e. Prepare the financial statements
   f. Journalize and post closing entries

3. The work sheet is a *(p. 126)*
   a. Journal
   b. Ledger
   c. Financial statement
   d. Convenient device for completing the accounting cycle

4. The usefulness of the work sheet is *(p. 126)*
   a. Identifying the accounts that need to be adjusted
   b. Summarizing the effects of all the transactions of the period
   c. Aiding the preparation of the financial statements
   d. All of the above

5. Which of the following accounts is not closed? *(pp. 137, 138)*
   a. Supplies Expense
   b. Prepaid Insurance
   c. Interest Revenue
   d. Owner Withdrawals

6. The closing entry for Salary Expense, with a balance of $322,000, is *(p. 139)*

    a. Salary Expense 322,000
       Income Summary 322,000
    b. Salary Expense 322,000
       Salary Payable............................ 322,000
    c. Income Summary 322,000
       Salary Expense 322,000
    d. Salary Payable............................ 322,000
       Salary Expense 322,000

7. The purpose of the postclosing trial balance is to *(p. 141)*
    a. Provide the account balances for preparation of the balance sheet
    b. Ensure that the ledger is in balance for the start of the next period
    c. Aid the journalizing and posting of the closing entries
    d. Ensure that the ledger is in balance for completion of the work sheet

8. Which of the following accounts will appear on the postclosing trial balance? *(p. 141)*
    a. Building
    b. Depreciation Expense–Building
    c. Service Revenue
    d. Owner Withdrawals

9. The classification of assets and liabilities as current or long-term depends on *(p. 142)*
    a. Their order of listing in the general ledger
    b. Whether they appear on the balance sheet or the income statement
    c. The relative liquidity of the item
    d. The format of the balance sheet—account format or report format

10. Posting a $300 debit as a credit causes an error *(p. 145)*
    a. That is evenly divisible by 9
    b. That is evenly divisible by 2
    c. In the journal
    d. Known as a transposition

Answers to the self-study questions are at the end of the chapter.

Accounting Vocabulary

account format of the balance sheet *(p. 143)*, accounting cycle *(p. 125)*, closing entry *(p. 138)*, closing the accounts *(p. 136)*, current assets *(p. 142)*, current liabilities *(p. 143)*, income summary *(p. 139)*, liquidity *(p. 142)*, long-term assets *(p. 142)*, long-term liabilities *(p. 143)*, nominal account *(p. 137)* permanent account *(p. 138)*, postclosing trial balance *(p. 141)*, real account *(p. 138)*, report format of the balance sheet *(p. 143)*, slide *(p. 145)*, spreadsheet *(p. 145)*, temporary account *(p. 137)*, transposition *(p. 145)*, work sheet *(p. 126)*.

ASSIGNMENT MATERIAL

Questions

1. Identify the steps in the accounting cycle, distinguishing those that occur during the period from those that are performed at the end.
2. Why is the work sheet a valuable accounting tool?
3. Name two advantages the work sheet has over the adjusted trial balance.
4. Why must the adjusting entries be journalized and posted if they have already been entered on the work sheet?

5. Why should the adjusting entries be journalized and posted before making the closing entries?

6. Which types of accounts are closed?

7. What purpose is served by closing the accounts?

8. State how the work sheet helps with recording the closing entries.

9. Distinguish between permanent accounts and temporary accounts, indicating which type is closed at the end of the period. Give five examples of each type of account.

10. Is Income Summary a permanent account or a temporary account? When and how is it used?

11. Give the closing entries for the following accounts (balances in parentheses): Service Revenue ($4,700), Salary Expense ($1,100), Income Summary (credit balance of $2,000), Rhonda McGill, Withdrawals ($2,300).

12. Why are assets classified as current or long-term? On what basis are they classified? Where do the classified amounts appear?

13. Indicate which of the following accounts are *current assets* and which are *long-term assets:* Prepaid Rent, Building, Furniture, Accounts Receivable, Merchandise Inventory, Cash, Note Receivable (due within one year), Note Receivable (due after one year).

14. In what order are assets and liabilities listed on the balance sheet?

15. Name an outside party that is interested in whether a liability is current or long-term. Why is this party interested in this information?

16. A friend tells you that the difference between a current liability and a long-term liability is that they are payable to different types of creditors. Is your friend correct? Include in your answer the definitions of these two categories of liabilities.

17. Give the name of the following accounting errors:
    a. Posted a $300 debit from the journal as a $300 credit in the ledger.
    b. Posted a $300 debit from the journal as a $3,000 debit in the ledger.
    c. Recorded a transaction by debiting one account for $3,100 and crediting the other account for $1,300.

18. How would you detect each of the errors in the preceding question?

19. Capp Company purchased supplies of $120 on account. The accountant debited Supplies and credited Cash for $120. A week later, after this entry has been posted to the ledger, the accountant discovers the error. How should he correct the error?

20. Briefly explain how a microcomputer spreadsheet can be programmed to complete the work sheet.

Exercises

Exercise 4-1 *Preparing a work sheet*

The trial balance of Alban's TV Repair Service is on the next page.

Additional information at September 30, 19X6:

a. Accrued salary expense, $600.
b. Prepaid rent expired, $900.
c. Supplies used, $2,250.
d. Accrued service revenue, $210.
e. Depreciation, $70.

Required

Complete Alban's work sheet for September 19X6.

Alban's TV Repair Service
Trial Balance
September 30, 19X6

Cash...............................	$ 1,560	
Accounts receivable	2,840	
Prepaid rent..........................	1,200	
Supplies.............................	3,390	
Equipment...........................	12,600	
Accumulated depreciation		$ 2,240
Accounts payable		1,600
Salary payable........................		
Ned Alban, capital		16,030
Ned Alban, withdrawals.................	3,000	
Service revenue.......................		7,300
Depreciation expense		
Salary expense........................	1,800	
Rent expense.........................		
Utilities expense	780	
Supplies expense......................		
Total...............................	$27,170	$27,170

Exercise 4-2   *Journalizing adjusting and closing entries*

Journalize the adjusting and closing entries in Exercise 4-1.

Exercise 4-3   *Posting adjusting and closing entries*

Set up T-accounts for those accounts affected by the adjusting and closing entries in Exercise 4-1. Post the adjusting and closing entries to the accounts, denoting adjustment amounts by Adj., closing amounts by Clo., and balances by Bal. Double rule the accounts with zero balances after closing and show the ending balance in each account.

Exercise 4-4   *Preparing a postclosing trial balance*

Prepare the postclosing trial balance in Exercise 4-1.

Exercise 4-5   *Identifying and journalizing closing entries*

From the following selected accounts that Rodriguez Sales Company reported in its June 30, 19X4, annual financial statements, prepare the entity's closing entries.

D. Rodriquez, capital	$45,600	Interest expense	$ 2,200
Service revenue	90,500	Accounts receivable	26,000
Unearned revenues	1,350	Salary payable	850
Salary expense	15,500	Depreciation expense	10,200
Accumulated depreciation	35,000	Rent expense	5,900
Supplies expense	1,400	D. Rodriguez, withdrawals	40,000
Interest revenue	700	Supplies	1,100

Exercise 4-6 *Identifying and journalizing closing entries*

The accountant for Trish Nunley, Attorney, has posted adjusting entries *a* through *e* to the accounts at December 31, 19X2. All the revenue, expense, and owner's equity accounts of the entity are listed here in T-account form.

Accounts Receivable		Supplies		Accumulated Depreciation – Furniture	
23,000		4,000	(a) 2,000		5,000
(e) 3,500					(b) 3,000

Accumulated Decpreciation – Building				Salary Payable	
	33,000				(d) 1,500
	(c) 6,000				

Trish Nunley, Capital		Trish Nunley, Withdrawals		Service Revenue	
	49,400	52,400			103,000
					(e) 3,500

Salary Expense		Supplies Expense		Depreciation Expense – Furniture		Depreciation Expense – Building	
28,000		(a) 2,000		(b) 3,000		(c) 6,000	
(d) 1,500							

Required

Journalize Nunley's closing entries at December 31, 19X2.

Exercise 4-7 *Preparing a statement of owner's equity*

From the following accounts of Kathryn Hopkins Realty Company, prepare the entity's statement of owner's equity for the year ended December 31, 19X5:

Kathryn Hopkins, Capital				Kathryn Hopkins, Withdrawals			
Dec. 31	34,000	Jan. 1	35,000	Mar. 31	8,000	Dec. 31	34,000
		Mar. 9	28,000	Jun. 30	8,000		
		Dec. 31	43,000	Sep. 30	8,000		
				Dec. 31	10,000		

Income Summary			
Dec. 31	85,000	Dec. 31	128,000
Dec. 31	43,000		

Exercise 4-8 *Identifying and recording adjusting and closing entries*

The trial balance and income statement amounts from the March work sheet of Tekell Service Company are presented on the next page.

Required

Journalize the adjusting and closing entries of Tekell Service Company at March 31.

Account Title	Trial Balance		Income Statement	
Cash	$ 3,100			
Supplies	2,400			
Prepaid rent	1,100			
Office equipment	36,800			
Accumulated depreciation.		$ 6,900		
Accounts payable.		10,600		
Salary payable				
Unearned service revenue.		4,400		
Angela Tekell, capital		14,800		
Angela Tekell, withdrawals.	1,000			
Service revenue		12,700		$16,000
Salary expense	3,000		$ 3,800	
Rent expense	1,200		1,400	
Depreciation expense.			400	
Supplies expense			1,700	
Utilities expense.	800		800	
	$49,400	$49,400	$ 8,100	$16,000
Net income.			7,900	
			$16,000	$16,000

Exercise 4-9   *Preparing a classified balance sheet*

Use the data in Exercise 4-8 to prepare Tekell Service Company's classified balance sheet at March 31 of the current year. Use the report format.

Exercise 4-10   *Correcting accounting errors*

Prepare a correcting entry for each of the following accounting errors:

a. Recorded a $400 cash purchase of supplies by debiting Supplies and crediting Accounts Payable.

b. Debited Office Furniture and credited Accounts Payable for a $2,300 credit purchase of office equipment.

c. Adjusted prepaid rent by debiting Prepaid Rent and crediting Rent Expense for $900. This adjusting entry should have debited Rent Expense and credited Prepaid Rent for $900.

d. Debited Salary Expense and credited Cash to accrue salary expense of $300.

e. Recorded the earning of $3,200 service revenue collected in advance by debiting Accounts Receivable and crediting Service Revenue.

f. Accrued interest revenue of $800 by a debit to Accounts Receivable and a credit to Interest Revenue.

(Group A)

Problem 4-1A   *Preparing financial statements from an adjusted trial balance; journalizing, adjusting, and closing entries*

The adjusted trial balance of Merced Service Company at June 30, 19X1, the end of the company's fiscal year, is on the next page.

Additional data at June 30, 19X1:

a. Supplies used during the year, $3,580.

b. Prepaid insurance expired during the year, $3,100.

Merced Service Company
Adjusted Trial Balance
June 30, 19X1

Cash..............................	$ 3,350	
Accounts receivable	11,470	
Supplies...........................	1,290	
Prepaid insurance	1,700	
Equipment.........................	55,800	
Accumulated depreciation–equipment ...		$ 16,480
Building...........................	144,900	
Accumulated depreciation–building		16,850
Accounts payable		36,900
Interest payable.....................		1,490
Wage payable		770
Unearned service revenue		2,300
Note payable, long-term..............		104,000
Ramon DeSoto, capital		37,390
Ramon DeSoto, withdrawals	52,300	
Service revenue.....................		108,360
Depreciation expense–equipment	6,300	
Depreciation expense–building	3,470	
Wage expense	18,800	
Insurance expense....................	3,100	
Interest expense.....................	11,510	
Utilities expense	4,300	
Property tax expense.................	2,670	
Supplies expense.....................	3,580	
Total..............................	$324,540	$324,540

c. Accrued interest expense, $680.

d. Accrued service revenue, $940.

e. Depreciation for the year: equipment, $6,300; building, $3,470.

f. Accrued wage expense, $770.

g. Unearned service revenue earned during the year, $6,790.

Required

1. Prepare Merced's income statement and statement of owner's equity for the year ended June 30, 19X1, and the classified balance sheet on that date. Use the account format for the balance sheet.

2. Journalize the adjusting and closing entries.

Problem 4-2A   *Preparing a work sheet*

The trial balance of Schoepplein Painting Contractors at July 31, 19X3 is on the next page.

Additional data at July 31, 19X3:

a. Accrued wage expense, $440.

b. Supplies on hand, $14,740.

Schoepplein Painting Contractors
Trial Balance
July 31, 19X3

Cash.............................	$ 4,200	
Accounts receivable	37,820	
Supplies..........................	17,660	
Prepaid insurance...................	2,300	
Equipment........................	32,690	
Accumulated depreciation–equipment ...		$ 26,240
Building..........................	36,890	
Accumulated depreciation–building.....		10,500
Land.............................	28,300	
Accounts payable		22,690
Interest payable....................		
Wage payable		
Unearned service revenue		10,560
Note payable, long-term..............		22,000
Leslie Schoepplein, capital		62,130
Leslie Schoepplein, withdrawals	4,200	
Service revenue.....................		17,190
Depreciation expense–equipment.......		
Depreciation expense–building.........		
Wage expense	5,800	
Insurance expense...................		
Interest expense....................		
Utilities expense	270	
Property tax expense.................	840	
Advertising expense	340	
Supplies expense....................		
Total.............................	$171,310	$171,310

c. Prepaid insurance expired during July, $500.
d. Accrued interest expense, $180.
e. Unearned service revenue earned during July, $4,770.
f. Accrued advertising expense, $100 (credit Accounts Payable).
g. Accrued service revenue, $1,100.
h. Depreciation: equipment, $430; building, $270.

Required

Complete Schoepplein's work sheet for July.

Problem 4-3A   *Taking the accounting cycle through the closing entries*

The unadjusted T-accounts of Julie Warner, M.D., at December 31, 19X2, and the related year-end adjustment data follow:

Cash	Accounts Receivable	Supplies
Bal. 7,000	Bal. 38,000	Bal. 9,000

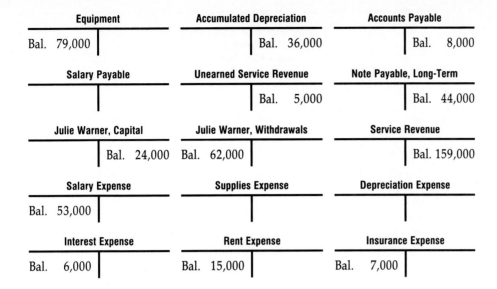

Equipment	Accumulated Depreciation	Accounts Payable
Bal. 79,000	Bal. 36,000	Bal. 8,000

Salary Payable	Unearned Service Revenue	Note Payable, Long-Term
	Bal. 5,000	Bal. 44,000

Julie Warner, Capital	Julie Warner, Withdrawals	Service Revenue
Bal. 24,000	Bal. 62,000	Bal. 159,000

Salary Expense	Supplies Expense	Depreciation Expense
Bal. 53,000		

Interest Expense	Rent Expense	Insurance Expense
Bal. 6,000	Bal. 15,000	Bal. 7,000

Adjustment data at December 31, 19X2, include:

a. Supplies on hand, $1,000.
b. Depreciation for the year, $9,000.
c. Accrued salary expense, $2,000.
d. Accrued service revenue, $1,000.
e. Unearned service revenue earned during the year, $5,000.

Required

1. Write the trial balance on a worksheet, and complete the worksheet. Key each adjusting entry by the letter corresponding to the data given.
2. Prepare the income statement, the statement of owner's equity, and the classified balance sheet in account format.
3. Journalize the adjusting and closing entries.

Problem 4-4A *Completing the accounting cycle*

This problem should be used only in conjunction with Problem 4-3A. It completes the accounting cycle by posting to T-accounts and preparing the postclosing trial balance.

Required

1. Using the Problem 4-3A data, post the adjusting and closing entries to the T-accounts, denoting adjusting amounts by Adj., closing amounts by Clo., and account balances by Bal., as shown in Exhibit 4-9. Double underline all accounts with a zero ending balance.
2. Prepare the postclosing trial balance.

Problem 4-5A *Completing the accounting cycle*

The trial balance of Moore Realty at August 31, 19X9, and the data needed for the month-end adjustments follow.

Adjustment data:

a. Prepaid insurance still in force at August 31, $1,190.
b. Supplies used during the month, $140.

Moore Realty
Trial Balance
August 31, 19X9

Account Number	Account Title	Debit	Credit
11	Cash	$ 6,800	
12	Accounts receivable	17,560	
13	Prepaid insurance	1,290	
14	Supplies	900	
15	Furniture	15,350	
16	Accumulated depreciation–furniture		$ 12,800
17	Building	89,900	
18	Accumulated depreciation–building		28,600
21	Accounts payable		6,240
22	Salary payable		
23	Unearned commission revenue		8,900
31	B. J. Moore, capital		74,920
32	B. J. Moore, withdrawals	4,800	
41	Commission revenue		7,800
51	Salary expense	1,600	
52	Insurance expense		
53	Utilities expense	410	
54	Depreciation expense–furniture		
55	Depreciation expense–building		
56	Advertising expense	650	
57	Supplies expense		
	Total	$139,260	$139,260

c. Depreciation on building for the month, $130.

d. Depreciation on furniture for the month, $370.

e. Accrued salary expense at August 31, $460.

f. Unearned commission revenue still unearned at August 31, $7,750.

Required

1. Open the accounts listed in the trial balance, inserting their August 31 unadjusted balances. Also open the Income Summary account, number 33. Use four column accounts. Date the balances of the following accounts as of August 1: Prepaid Insurance, Supplies, Building, Accumulated Depreciation–Building, Furniture, Accumulated Depreciation–Furniture, Unearned Commission Revenue, and B. J. Moore, Capital.

2. Write the trial balance on a work sheet and complete the work sheet of Moore Realty for the month ended August 31 of the current year.

3. Prepare the income statement, the statement of owner's equity, and the classified balance sheet in report format.

4. Using the work sheet data, journalize and post the adjusting and closing entries. Use dates and posting references. Use page 7 as the number of the journal page.

5. Prepare a postclosing trial balance.

Problem 4-6A *Preparing a classified balance sheet in report format*

The accounts of Matusak Sales Agency at December 31, 19X6, are listed in alphabetical order. All adjustments have been journalized and posted, but the closing entries have not yet been made. Prepare the company's classified balance sheet in report format at December 31, 19X6. Use captions for total assets, total liabilities, and total liabilities and owner's equity.

Accounts payable	$ 3,100	Interest receivable	$ 200
Accounts receivable	4,600	Inventory	6,600
Accumulated depreciation– building	37,800	Lou Matusak, capital, December 31, 19X5	50,300
Accumulated depreciation– furniture	11,600	Lou Matusak, withdrawals	47,400
Advertising expense	2,200	Note payable, long-term	7,800
Building	84,400	Note receivable, long-term	4,000
Cash	4,500	Other assets	3,600
Commission revenue	93,500	Other current assets	1,700
Current portion of note payable	2,200	Other current liabilities	4,700
Current portion of note receivable	1,000	Prepaid insurance	1,100
Depreciation expense	1,300	Salary expense	22,600
Furniture	22,700	Salary payable	1,900
Insurance expense	800	Supplies	2,500
Interest payable	600	Supplies expense	5,700
		Unearned commission revenue	3,400

Problem 4-7A *Analyzing and journalizing corrections, adjustments, and closing entries*

Accountants for Mills Service Company, a proprietorship, encountered the following situations while adjusting and closing the books at December 31. Consider each situation independently.

a. The company bookkeeper made the following entry to record a $400 credit purchase of office supplies:

Nov. 12   Office Furniture   400
                    Accounts Payable.   400

Prepare the correcting entry, dated December 31.

b. A $750 debit to Cash was posted as a credit.
    (1) At what stage of the accounting cycle will this error be detected?
    (2) Describe the technique for identifying the amount of the error.

c. The $35,000 balance of Equipment was entered as $3,500 on the trial balance.
    (1) What is the name of this type of error?
    (2) Assume this is the only error in the trial balance. Which will be greater, the total debits or the total credits, and by how much?
    (3) How can this type of error be identified?

d. The accountant failed to make the following adjusting entries at December 31:
    (1) Accrued property tax expense, $600.
    (2) Supplies expense, $1,390.
    (3) Accrued interest revenue on a note receivable, $950.
    (4) Depreciation of equipment, $4,000.
    (5) Earned service revenue that had been collected in advance, $5,300.
        Compute the overall net income effect of these omissions.

e. Record each of the adjusting entries identified in item *d*.

f. The revenue and expense accounts, after the adjusting entries had been posted were Service Revenue, $55,800; Salary Expense, $13,200; Rent Expense, $5,100; Advertising Expense, $3,550; Utilities Expense, $1,530; and Miscellaneous Expense, $1,190. Two balances prior to closing were J. E. Mills, Capital, $58,600; and J. E. Mills, Withdrawals, $30,000.

Journalize the closing entries.

(Group B)

Problem 4-1B   *Preparing financial statements from an adjusted trial balance; journalizing, adjusting, and closing entries*

The adjusted trial balance of Chun Consultants at April 30, 19X2, the end of the company's fiscal year, follows:

Chun Consultants		
Adjusted Trial Balance		
April 30, 19X2		
Cash	$ 2,370	
Accounts receivable	25,740	
Supplies	3,690	
Prepaid insurance	2,290	
Equipment	63,930	
Accumulated depreciation–equipment		$ 28,430
Building	74,330	
Accumulated depreciation–building		18,260
Accounts payable		19,550
Interest payable		2,280
Wage payable		830
Unearned service revenue		3,660
Note payable, long-term		77,900
Vivian Chun, capital		46,200
Vivian Chun, withdrawals	55,500	
Service revenue		99,550
Depreciation expense–equipment	6,700	
Depreciation expense–building	3,210	
Wage expense	29,800	
Insurance expense	5,370	
Interest expense	8,170	
Utilities expense	5,670	
Property tax expense	3,010	
Supplies expense	6,880	
Total	$296,660	$296,660

Additional data at April 30, 19X2:

a. Supplies used during the year, $6,880.
b. Prepaid insurance expired during the year, $5,370.
c. Accrued interest expense, $2,280.
d. Accrued service revenue, $2,200.
e. Depreciation for the year: equipment, $6,700; building, $3,210.
f. Accrued wage expense, $830.
g. Unearned service revenue earned during the year, $5,180.

Required

1. Prepare Chun's income statement and statement of owner's equity for the year ended April 30, 19X2, and the classified balance sheet on that date. Use the account format for the balance sheet.
2. Journalize the adjusting and closing entries.

Problem 4-2B   *Preparing a work sheet*

The trial balance of Broadmoor Realty Brokers at May 31, 19X2, follows:

Broadmoor Realty Brokers **Trial Balance** **May 31, 19X2**		
Cash...........................	$ 1,670	
Notes receivable	10,340	
Interest receivable................		
Supplies.......................	560	
Prepaid insurance	1,790	
Furniture	27,410	
Accumulated depreciation–furniture		$ 1,480
Building.......................	55,900	
Accumulated depreciation–building		33,560
Land..........................	13,700	
Accounts payable		14,730
Interest payable..................		
Salary payable...................		
Unearned commission revenue		6,800
Note payable, long-term.............		18,700
Rex Jennings, capital...............		34,290
Rex Jennings, withdrawals...........	3,800	
Commission revenue		9,970
Interest revenue		
Depreciation expense–furniture		
Depreciation expense–building........		
Salary expense...................	2,170	
Insurance expense................		
Interest expense..................		
Utilities expense	490	
Property tax expense...............	640	
Advertising expense	1,060	
Supplies expense.................		
Total.........................	$119,530	$119,530

Additional data at May 31, 19X2:

a. Accrued salary expense, $600.
b. Supplies on hand, $410.
c. Prepaid insurance expired during May, $390.
d. Accrued interest expense, $220.
e. Unearned commission revenue earned during May, $1,400.
f. Accrued advertising expense, $60 (credit Accounts Payable).

g. Accrued interest revenue, $170.

h. Depreciation: furniture, $380; building, $160.

Required

Complete Broadmoor's work sheet for May.

Problem 4-3B *Taking the accounting cycle through the closing entries*

The unadjusted T-accounts of Steve Deitmer, M.D., at December 31, 19X2, and the related year-end adjustment data follow:

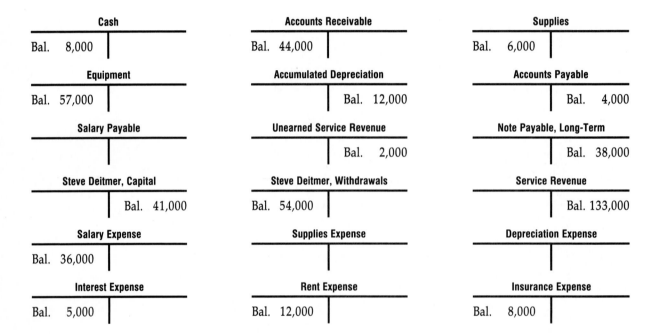

Cash		Accounts Receivable		Supplies	
Bal. 8,000		Bal. 44,000		Bal. 6,000	

Equipment		Accumulated Depreciation		Accounts Payable	
Bal. 57,000			Bal. 12,000		Bal. 4,000

Salary Payable		Unearned Service Revenue		Note Payable, Long-Term	
			Bal. 2,000		Bal. 38,000

Steve Deitmer, Capital		Steve Deitmer, Withdrawals		Service Revenue	
	Bal. 41,000	Bal. 54,000			Bal. 133,000

Salary Expense		Supplies Expense		Depreciation Expense	
Bal. 36,000					

Interest Expense		Rent Expense		Insurance Expense	
Bal. 5,000		Bal. 12,000		Bal. 8,000	

Adjustment data at December 31, 19X2, include:

a. Supplies on hand, $2,000.

b. Depreciation for the year, $6,000.

c. Accrued salary expense, $3,000.

d. Accrued service revenue, $4,000.

e. Unearned service revenue earned during the year, $2,000.

Required

1. Write the trial balance on a work sheet and complete the work sheet. Key each adjusting entry by the letter corresponding to the data given.

2. Prepare the income statement, the statement of owner's equity, and the classified balance sheet in account format.

3. Journalize the adjusting and closing entries.

Problem 4-4B *Completing the accounting cycle*

This problem should be used only in conjunction with Problem 4-3B. It completes the accounting cycle by posting to T-accounts and preparing the postclosing trial balance.

Required

1. Using the Problem 4-3B data, post the adjusting and closing entries to the T-accounts, denoting adjusting amounts by *Adj.*, closing amounts by *Clo.*, and account balances by *Bal.*, as shown in Exhibit 4-9. Double underline all accounts with a zero ending balance.

2. Prepare the postclosing trial balance.

Problem 4-5B *Completing the accounting cycle*

The trial balance of James Realty at October 31, 19X0, and the data needed for the month-end adjustments are as follows:

James Realty
Trial Balance
October 31, 19X0

Account Number	Account Title	Debit	Credit
11	Cash	$ 1,900	
12	Accounts receivable	12,310	
13	Prepaid insurance..........................	2,200	
14	Supplies	840	
15	Furniture..................................	26,830	
16	Accumulated depreciation–furniture...........		$ 3,400
17	Building	68,300	
18	Accumulated depreciation–building		9,100
21	Accounts payable..........................		7,290
22	Salary payable		
23	Unearned commission revenue.................		5,300
31	L. E. James, capital.......................		85,490
32	L. E. James, withdrawals	3,900	
41	Commission revenue		8,560
51	Salary expense	1,840	
52	Insurance expense		
53	Utilities expense	530	
54	Depreciation expense–furniture		
55	Depreciation expense–building...............		
56	Advertising expense........................	490	
57	Supplies expense		
	Total	$119,140	$119,140

Adjustment data:

a. Prepaid insurance still in force at October 31, $2,000.
b. Supplies used during the month, $570.
c. Depreciation on building for the month, $280.
d. Depreciation on furniture for the month, $250.
e. Accrued salary expense at October 31, $310.
f. Unearned commission revenue still unearned at October 31, $4,700.

Required

1. Open the accounts listed in the trial balance, inserting their October 31 unadjusted balances. Also open the Income Summary account, number 33. Use four-column accounts. Date the balances of the following accounts October 1: Prepaid Insurance, Supplies, Building, Accumulated Depreciation–Building, Furniture, Accumulated Depreciation–Furniture, Unearned Commission Revenue, and L. E. James, Capital.
2. Write the trial balance on a work sheet and complete the work sheet of James Realty for the month ended October 31 of the current year.
3. Prepare the income statement, the statement of owner's equity, and the classified balance sheet in report format.
4. Using the work sheet data, journalize and post the adjusting and closing entries. Use dates and posting references. Use 12 as the number of the journal page.
5. Prepare a postclosing trial balance.

Problem 4-6B   *Preparing a classified balance sheet in report format*

The accounts of Snyder Travel Agency at March 31, 19X3, are listed in alphabetical order. All adjustments have been journalized and posted, but the closing entries have not yet been made. Prepare the company's classified balance sheet in report format at March 31, 19X3. Use captions for total assets, total liabilities, and total liabilities and owner's equity.

Accounts payable	$ 2,700	Interest receivable	800
Accounts receivable	11,500	Inventory	$ 4,700
Accumulated depreciation–		Dot Snyder, capital,	
building	47,300	March 31, 19X2	32,800
Accumulated depreciation–		Dot Snyder, withdrawals	31,200
furniture	27,700	Note payable, long-term	3,200
Advertising expense	900	Note receivable, long-term	6,900
Building	55,900	Other assets	1,300
Cash	1,400	Other current assets	900
Commission revenue	71,100	Other current liabilities	1,100
Current portion of note payable	800	Prepaid insurance	600
Current portion of note		Salary expense	17,800
receivable	3,100	Salary payable	1,400
Depreciation expense	1,900	Supplies	3,800
Furniture	43,200	Supplies expense	4,600
Insurance expense	600	Unearned commission revenue	2,800
Interest payable	200		

Problem 4-7B   *Analyzing and journalizing corrections, adjustments, and closing entries*

The accountants of Lane Service Company, a proprietorship, encountered the following situations while adjusting and closing the books at February 28. Consider each situation independently.

a. The company bookkeeper made the following entry to record a $950 credit purchase of office supplies:

Feb. 26   Office Supplies.   950
            Cash   950

Prepare the correcting entry, dated February 28.

b. A $390 credit to Accounts Receivable was posted as $930.
   (1) At what stage of the accounting cycle will this error be detected?
   (2) Describe the technique for identifying the amount of the error.

c. The $5,630 balance of Utilities Expense was entered as $56,300 on the trial balance.
    (1) What is the name of this type of error?
    (2) Assume this is the only error in the trial balance. Which will be greater, the total debits or the total credits, and by how much?
    (3) How can this type of error be identified?
d. The accountant failed to make the following adjusting entries at February 28:
    (1) Accrued service revenue, $700
    (2) Insurance expense, $1,460
    (3) Accrued interest expense on a note payable, $520
    (4) Depreciation of building, $3,300
    (5) Earned service revenue that had been collected in advance, $2,700
    Compute the overall net income effect of these omissions.
e. Record each of the adjusting entries identified in item *d*.
f. The revenue and expense accounts after the adjusting entries had been posted, were Service Revenue, $95,330; Wage Expense, $29,340; Rent Expense, $6,180; Interest Expense, $4,590; Utilities Expense, $1,620; and Supplies Expense, $740. Two balances prior to closing were W. T. Lane, Capital, $75,150; and W. T. Lane, Drawing, $48,000. Journalize the closing entries.

Decision Problem

Completing the accounting cycle to develop the information for a bank loan

One year ago, your friend John T. Williams founded Williams Computing Service. The business has prospered. Williams, who remembers that you took an accounting course while in college, comes to you for advice. He wishes to know how much net income his business earned during the past year. He also wants to know what the entity's total assets, liabilities, and capital are. His accounting records consist of the T-accounts of his ledger, which were prepared by an accountant who moved to another city. The ledger at December 31 of the current year is

Cash		Accounts Receivable	
Dec. 31 6,830		Dec. 31 12,360	

Prepaid Rent		Supplies	
Jan. 2 2,800		Jan. 2 2,600	

Equipment		Accumulated Depreciation	
Jan. 2 23,600			

Accounts Payable		Unearned Service Revenue	
	Dec. 31 15,540		Dec. 31 4,130

Salary Payable		J. T. Williams, Capital	
			Jan. 2 25,000

J. T. Williams, Drawing		Service Revenue	
Dec. 31 39,420			Dec. 31 61,740

Salary Expense		Depreciation Expense	
Dec. 31 18,000			

Rent Expense		Utilities Expense	
		Dec. 31 800	

Supplies Expense	

Williams indicates that at the year's end customers owe him $1,600 accrued service revenue, which he expects to collect early next year. These revenues have not been recorded. During the year he collected $4,130 service revenue in advance from customers, but he earned only $1,190 of that amount. Rent expense for the year was $2,400, and he used up $2,100 in supplies. Williams estimates that depreciation on his equipment was $5,900 for the year. At December 31 he owes his employee $1,200 accrued salary.

At the conclusion of your meeting, Williams expresses concern that his withdrawals during the year might have exceeded his net income. To get a loan to expand the business, Williams must show the bank that his capital account has grown from its original $25,000 balance. Has it? You and Williams agree that you will meet again in one week. You perform the analysis and prepare the financial statements to answer his questions.

Financial Statement Problem

Using An Actual Balance Sheet

This problem, based on Gulf+Western's balance sheet in Appendix C, will familiarize you with some of the assets and liabilities of this actual company. Answer these questions, using Gulf+Western's balance sheet.

1. Which balance sheet format does Gulf+Western use?
2. Name the company's largest current asset and largest current liability at October 31, 1987.
3. How much were total current assets and total current liabilities at October 31, 1987? Which increased by the greater percentage during the year ended October 31, 1987: total current assets or total current liabilities?
4. Under what category does Gulf+Western report land, buildings, and machinery and equipment?
5. What account title does Gulf+Western use in place of Accumulated Depreciation?
6. What was the cost of the company's plant assets at October 31, 1987? What was the book value of the plant assets?

Answers to Self-Study Questions

1. a	3. d	5. b	7. b	9. c
2. d, a, e, b, f, c	4. d	6. c	8. a	10. b

Merchandising and the Accounting Cycle

In the first four chapters Gary Lyon, CPA, provided an illustration of a business that earns revenue by selling its services. Service enterprises include Holiday Inns, American Airlines, physicians, lawyers, CPAs, the Atlanta Braves baseball team, and the twelve-year-old who cuts lawns in your neighborhood. A *merchandising entity* earns its revenue by selling products, called *merchandise inventory* or simply *inventory*. A Goodyear tire store, a Safeway grocery, a Macy's department store, and an ice-cream shop are merchandising entities. Exhibit 5-1 shows the income statement for a merchandising business. You will notice that this income statement differs from those shown earlier.

The amount that a merchandiser earns from selling its inventory is called **net sales revenue,** often abbreviated as **net sales.** The income statement in Exhibit 5-1 reports net sales revenue of $680,000. The major revenue of a merchandising entity, sales revenue, represents the increase in owner's equity from delivering inventory to customers. The major expense of a merchandiser is *Cost of Goods Sold.* This expense's title is well chosen, because this account represents the entity's cost of the goods (inventory) it has sold to customers. As long as inventory is held, it is an asset. When the inventory is sold to the customer, the inventory's cost becomes an expense. The excess of Sales Revenue over Cost of Goods Sold is called **gross margin** or **gross profit.** This important business statistic is often mentioned in the business press because it helps measure a business's success. A sufficiently high gross margin is vital to success.

The following illustration will clarify the nature of gross margin. Consider a concession stand at a football game. Assume the business sells a soft drink for $1.00 and the vendor's cost is $.20. Gross margin per unit is $.80 ($1.00 − $.20), and the overall gross margin is $.80 multiplied by the number of drinks sold. If the concession stand sells 400 drinks on a Saturday afternoon, its gross margin on drink sales is $320 (400 × $.80). The gross margin on all sales, including hot dogs,

EXHIBIT 5-1 *A Merchandiser's Income Statement*

Midwest Supply Company
Income Statement
For the Year Ended December 31, 19X6

Net sales revenue		$680,000
Cost of goods sold		370,000
Gross margin		310,000
Operating expenses:		
Salary expense	$130,000	
Rent expense	60,000	
Insurance expense	18,000	
Depreciation expense	14,000	
Supplies expense	8,0000	230,000
Net income		$ 80,000

popcorn, and candy, is the sum of the gross margins on all the items sold. IBM's gross margin—and that of a Safeway store, a neighborhood drug store, and every other merchandiser—is computed in exactly the same way: Sales Revenue − Cost of Goods Sold = Gross Margin.

Margin in gross margin refers to the excess of revenue over expense. *Gross* indicates that the operating expenses (rent, depreciation, advertising, and so on) have not yet been subtracted. After subtracting all the expenses we have *net income*. Gross margin and net income are *not* accounts in the ledger, so we cannot make journal entries to them. Instead, we compute these amounts by subtracting one amount from another: Gross Margin − Operating Expenses = Net Income. Study Exhibit 5-1, focusing on the sales revenue, cost of goods sold, and gross margin. Note the separate category for operating expenses.

The Operating Cycle for a Merchandising Business _____

A merchandising entity buys inventory, sells the inventory to its customers, and uses the cash to purchase more inventory to repeat the cycle. Exhibit 5-2 diagrams the operating cycle for *cash sales* and for *sales on account.* For a cash sale—item *a* in the exhibit—the cycle is from cash to inventory, which is purchased for resale, and back to cash. For a sale on account—item *b*—the cycle is from cash to inventory to accounts receivable and back to cash.

Purchase of Merchandise Inventory _____

The cycle of a merchandising entity begins with cash, which is used to purchase inventory, as Exhibit 5-2 shows. **Purchases,** in the accounting sense, are only those items of merchandise inventory that a firm buys to resell to customers in the normal course of business. For example, a stereo center records in the Purchases account the price it pays for tape decks, turntables, and other items of inventory

EXHIBIT 5-2 *Operating Cycle of a Merchandiser*

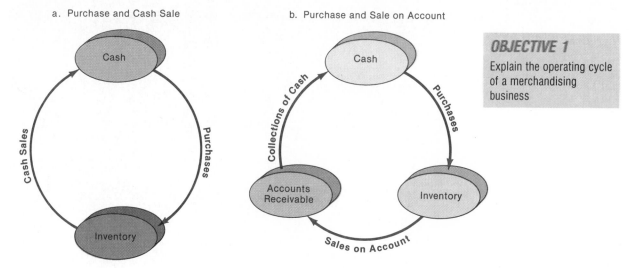

a. Purchase and Cash Sale

b. Purchase and Sale on Account

OBJECTIVE 1

Explain the operating cycle of a merchandising business

acquired for resale. A bicycle shop debits Purchases when it buys ten-speeds for its inventory. A grocery store debits Purchases when it buys canned goods, meat, frozen food, and other inventory. A $500 purchase on account is recorded as follows:

June 14   Purchases   500
                Accounts Payable   500
          Purchased inventory on account.

The Purchase Invoice: A Basic Business Document

Business documents are the tangible evidence of transactions. As we trace the steps that Austin Sound Stereo Center, an actual business, takes in ordering, receiving, and paying for inventory, we point out the roles that documents play in carrying on business.

1. Suppose Austin Sound wants to stock JVC brand turntables, cassette decks, and speakers. Austin Sound prepares a *purchase order* and mails it to JVC.
2. On receipt of the purchase order, JVC scans its warehouse for the inventory that Austin Sound ordered. JVC ships the equipment and mails the invoice to Austin on the same day. The **invoice** is the seller's request for payment from the purchaser. It is also called the *bill.*
3. Often the purchaser receives the invoice before the inventory arrives. Austin Sound does not pay immediately. Instead, Austin waits until the inventory arrives in order to ensure that it is (1) the correct type, (2) the quantity ordered, and (3) in good condition. After the inventory is inspected and approved, Austin Sound pays JVC the invoice amount.

Exhibit 5-3 is a copy of an actual invoice from JVC to Austin Sound Stereo Center. From Austin Sound's perspective, this document is a *purchase invoice,* whereas to JVC it is a *sales invoice.* The circled numbers that appear on the exhibit correspond to the following numbered explanations:

EXHIBIT 5-3   *Business Invoice*

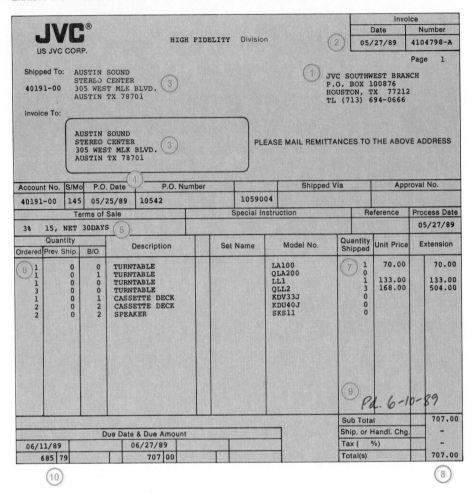

1. The seller is JVC Southwest Branch.
2. The invoice date is 05/27/89. The date is needed for determining whether the purchaser gets a discount for prompt payment (see item 5 below).
3. The purchaser is Austin Sound Stereo Center. The inventory is invoiced (billed) and shipped to the same address, 305 West Martin Luther King Blvd., Austin, Texas.
4. Austin Sound's purchase order (P.O.) date was 05/25/89.
5. Credit terms of the transaction are 3% 15, NET 30 DAYS. This means that Austin Sound may deduct 3 percent of the total amount due if Austin pays within 15 days of the invoice date. Otherwise, the full amount—net—is due in 30 days. (A full discussion of discounts appears in the next section.)
6. Austin Sound ordered six turntables, three cassettes decks, and two speakers.
7. JVC shipped five turntables, no cassette decks, and no speakers.
8. Total invoice amount is $707.
9. Austin Sound paid on 6-10-89. How much did Austin pay? (See item 10.)
10. Payment occurred 14 days after the invoice date—within the discount period. Therefore, Austin Sound paid $685.79 ($707 minus the 3 percent discount).

Discounts from Purchase Prices

There are two major types of discounts from purchase prices; cash discounts (called purchase discounts) and trade discounts.

Purchase Discounts

Many businesses offer purchase discounts to their customers. A **purchase discount** is a reward for prompt payment. JVC's credit terms of 3% 15 NET 30 DAYS can also be expressed as 3/15 n/30. Terms of simply n/30 indicate that no discount is offered and that payment is due 30 days after the invoice date. Terms of eom mean that payment is due at the end of the month.

Let's use the Exhibit 5-3 transaction to illustrate accounting for a purchase discount. Austin Sound records this purchase on account as follows:

May 27	Purchases..	707.00	
	Accounts Payable		707.00
	Purchased inventory on account.		

> **OBJECTIVE 2**
> Account for the purchase and sale of inventory

Since Austin Sound paid within the discount period, its cash payment entry is

June 10	Accounts Payable	707.00	
	Cash ($707.00 × .97)......................		685.79
	Purchase Discounts ($707.00 × .03)...........		21.21
	Paid on account within discount period.		

Purchase Discounts, which has a credit balance, is a contra account to Purchases. We show how to report Purchase Discounts on the income statement later in the chapter.

Alternatively, if Austin Sound pays this invoice after the discount period, it must pay the full invoice amount. In this case, the payment entry is

June 29	Accounts Payable	707.00	
	Cash....................................		707.00
	Paid on account after discount period.		

Trade Discounts

A second type of discount is the **trade discount,** which works this way: the larger the quantity purchased, the lower the price per item. For example, JVC may offer no trade discount for the purchase of only one or two cassette decks and charge the list price—the full price—of $200 per unit. However, JVC may offer the following trade discount terms in order to persuade customers to buy a larger number of cassette decks:

Quantity	Trade Discount	Net Price Per Unit
Buy minimum quantity, 3 cassette decks	5%	$190 [$200 − .05($200)]
Buy 4–9 decks	10%	$180 [$200 − .10($200)]
Buy more than 9 decks	20%	$160 [$200 − .20($200)]

Suppose Austin Sound purchases five cassette decks from this manufacturer. The cost of each cassette deck is, therefore, $180. Purchase of five units on account would be recorded by debiting Purchases and crediting Accounts Payable for the total price of $900 ($180 × 5).

There is no trade discount account, and there is no special accounting entry for a trade discount. Instead, all accounting entries are based on the net price of a purchase after subtracting the trade discount.

Purchase Returns and Allowances

Most businesses allow their customers to *return* merchandise that is defective, damaged in shipment, or otherwise unsuitable. Or if the buyer chooses to keep damaged goods, the seller may deduct an *allowance* from the amount the buyer owes. Because returns and allowances are closely related, they are usually recorded in a single account, **Purchase Returns and Allowances.** This account is a contra account to Purchases. Later in the chapter, we show how to report this account on the income statement.

Suppose the $70 turntable purchased by Austin Sound (in Exhibit 5-3) was not the turntable ordered. Austin returns the merchandise to the seller and records the purchase return as follows:

June 3	Accounts Payable	70.00	
	Purchase Returns and Allowances		70.00
	Returned inventory to seller.		

Now assume that one of the JVC turntables is damaged in shipment to Austin Sound. The damage is minor, and Austin decides to keep the turntable in exchange for a $10 allowance from JVC. To record this purchase allowance, Austin Sound makes this entry:

June 4	Accounts Payable	10.00	
	Purchase Returns and Allowances		10.00
	Received a purchase allowance.		

Observe that the return and the allowance had two effects. (1) They decreased Austin Sound's liability, which is why we debit Accounts Payable. (2) They decreased the net cost of the purchase, which is why we credit Purchase Returns and Allowances. It would be incorrect to credit Purchases because Austin Sound did in fact make the purchase. Changes because of returns and allowances are recorded in the contra account.

During the period, the business records the cost of all inventory bought in the Purchases account. The balance of Purchases is a *gross* amount because it does not include subtractions for purchase discounts, returns, or allowances. **Net purchases** is the remainder that is computed by subtracting the contra accounts as follows:

> **Purchases (*debit* balance account)**
> **−Purchase Discounts (*credit* balance account)**
> **−Purchase Returns and Allowances (*credit* balance account)**
> **= Net purchases (a subtotal, not a separate account)**

Transportation Costs

The transportation cost of moving inventory from seller to buyer can be significant. The purchase agreement specifies FOB terms to indicate who pays the shipping charges. The term *FOB* stands for *free on board* and governs when the legal title to the goods passes from seller to buyer. Under *FOB shipping point* terms, title passes when the inventory leaves the seller's place of business—the shipping point. The buyer owns the goods while they are in transit and therefore pays the transportation cost. Under *FOB destination* terms, title passes when the goods reach the destination, so the seller pays transportation cost.

	FOB Shipping Point	FOB Destination
When does title pass to buyer?	Shipping point	Destination
Who pays transportation cost?	Buyer	Seller

Generally, the buyer bears the shipping cost. The buyer debits Freight In (sometimes called Transportation In) and credits Cash or Accounts Payable for the amount. Suppose the buyer receives a shipping bill directly from the freight company. The payment entry is:

March 3	Freight In.	190	
	Cash		190
	Paid a freight bill.		

The seller sometimes prepays the transportation cost as a convenience and lists this cost on the invoice. The buyer would *not* debit Purchases for the combined cost of the inventory and the shipping cost. Rather, the buyer would debit Purchases for the cost of the goods and Freight In separately as follows:

March 12	Purchases	5,000	
	Freight In	400	
	Accounts Payable.		5,400
	Purchased inventory on account plus freight.		

Purchase discounts and trade discounts are computed only on the cost of the inventory, *not* on the freight charges. Suppose the $5,000 credit purchase allows a $100 discount for early payment. The cash payment within the discount period would be $5,300 [net payment of $4,900 on the inventory ($5,000, less the $100 purchase discount), plus the freight charges of $400].

Sale of Inventory

The sale of inventory may be for cash or on account, as Exhibit 5-2 shows.

Cash Sale. Sales of retailers like department stores, drug stores, gift shops, and restaurants are often for cash. A $3,000 cash sale is recorded by debiting Cash and crediting the revenue account, Sales Revenue, as follows:

Jan. 9	Cash.	3,000	
	Sales Revenue		3,000
	Cash sale.		

Sale on Account. Most sales by wholesalers, manufacturers, and retailers are made on account (on credit). A $5,000 sale on account is recorded by a debit to Accounts Receivable and a credit to Sales Revenue, as follows:

Jan. 11	Accounts Receivable..............................	5,000	
	Sales Revenue..............................		5,000
	Sale on account.		

The related cash receipt on account is journalized as follows:

Jan. 19	Cash...	5,000	
	Accounts Receivable..........................		5,000
	Collection on account.		

Sales Discounts, Sales Returns and Allowances

Sales Discounts and **Sales Returns and Allowances** are contra accounts to Sales Revenue, just as Purchase Discounts and Purchase Returns and Allowances are contra accounts to Purchases. Let's examine a sequence of the sale transactions of JVC.

On July 7, JVC sells stereo components for $7,200 on credit terms of 2/10 n/30. JVC's entry to record this credit sale follows:

July 7	Accounts Receivable	7,200	
	Sales Revenue		7,200
	Sale on account.		

Assume the buyer returns goods that cost $600. JVC records the sales return and the related decrease in Accounts Receivable as follows:

July 12	Sales Returns and Allowances..........................	600	
	Accounts Receivable...........................		600
	Received returned goods.		

JVC grants a $100 sales allowance for damaged goods. JVC journalizes this transaction by debiting Sales Returns and Allowances and crediting Accounts Receivable as follows:

July 15	Sales Returns and Allowances..........................	100	
	Accounts Receivable...........................		100
	Granted a sales allowance for damaged goods.		

After the preceding entries are posted, Accounts Receivable has a $6,500 debit balance, as follows:

Accounts Receivable

July 7	7,200	July 12	600
		15	100
Bal.	6,500		

On July 17, the last day of the discount period, JVC collects half ($3,250) of this receivable ($6,500 × ½ = $3,250). The cash receipt is $3,185 [$3,250 − ($3,250 × .02)], and the collection entry is

July 17	Cash	3,185	
	Sales Discounts ($3,250 × .02)	65	
	Accounts Receivable..........................		3,250
	Cash collection within the discount period.		

Suppose JVC collects the remainder on July 28—after the discount period—so there is no sales discount. To record this collection on account, JVC debits Cash and credits Accounts Receivable for the same amount, as follows:

July 28   Cash   3,250

            Accounts Receivable.   3,250

            Cash collection after the discount period.

Net sales is computed in a manner similar to net purchases. We subtract the contra accounts as follows:

> **Sales Revenue (*credit* balance account)**
> **− Sales Discounts (*debit* balance account)**
> **− Sales Returns and Allowances (*debit* balance account)**
> _____
> **= Net sales (a subtotal, not a separate account)**

Cost of Goods Sold

Cost of goods sold is the largest single expense of most merchandising businesses. It is the cost of the inventory that the business has sold to customers. Another name for cost of goods sold is cost of sales. How is it computed?

Recall from Chapter 3 that supplies expense is computed as follows:

> **Beginning supplies**
> **+ Supplies purchased during the period**
> _____
> **= Supplies available for use during the period**
> **− Supplies on hand at the end of the period**
> _____
> **= Supplies expense**

Cost of goods sold is computed this same way, as shown in Exhibit 5-4.

By studying the exhibit, you will see that the computation and the diagram tell the same story. That is, a company's goods available for sale during a period come from beginning inventory plus the period's net purchases and freight costs. Either the merchandise is sold during the period, or it remains on hand at the end. The merchandise that remains is an asset, Inventory, and the cost of the inventory that has been sold is an expense, Cost of Goods Sold.

Two main types of inventory accounting systems exist: the periodic system and the perpetual system. In this chapter, we illustrate the periodic inventory system because it highlights the relationship between inventory and cost of goods sold, as shown in Exhibit 5-4. This model for computing expense is used throughout accounting and is extremely useful for analytical purposes. Furthermore, the periodic system is used by many small businesses, such as the proprietorships we illustrated in the early chapters of this book. Chapter 9 discusses the perpetual system.

Under the periodic system, the business does not keep a running record of the cost of its inventory on hand. Instead, it counts the goods on hand at the end of each period to determine the inventory to be reported on the balance sheet. This ending inventory amount becomes the beginning inventory of the next period and is used to compute cost of goods sold for the income statement. *In the periodic inventory system, entries to the Inventory account are made only at the end of the period.*

EXHIBIT 5-4 *Measurement of Cost of Goods Sold*

Computation:

Beginning inventory
+ Net purchases
+ Freight in
─────────────────
= Cost of goods available for sale
− Ending inventory
─────────────────
= Cost of goods sold

Diagram:

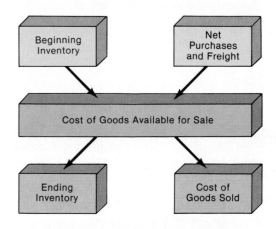

OBJECTIVE 3

Compute cost of goods sold and gross margin

In this inventory system, cost of goods sold is *not* a ledger account like Salary Expense, Rent Expense, and the other operating expenses. Instead, it is the cost left over when we subtract the cost of ending inventory from the cost of goods available for sale. Computationally, cost of goods sold is more complex than the other expenses.

Exhibit 5-5 summarizes the first half of the chapter by showing Austin Sound's net sales revenue, cost of goods sold—including net purchases—and gross margin on the income statement.

Note that arithmetic operations—addition and subtraction—move across the columns from left to right. For example, the figures for Sales Discounts and for Sales Returns and Allowances appear in a separate column. Their sum—$3,400 —appears to the right, where it is subtracted from Sales Revenue. The net sales amount of $135,900 appears in the right-most column.

Contra accounts—discounts, returns and allowances, and the like—are frequently netted against their related accounts parenthetically. Thus many accountants would report sales in our example as follows:

Net sales revenue (net of sales discounts, $1,400,
   and returns and allowances, $2,000). $135,900

EXHIBIT 5-5 *Partial Income Statement*

Austin Sound			
Income Statement			
For the Year Ended December 31, 19X6			

Sales revenue		$139,300	
Less: Sales discounts	$ 1,400		
Sales returns and allowances	2,000	3,400	
Net sales			$135,900
Cost of goods sold:			
Beginning inventory		$ 50,500	
Purchases	$89,300		
Less: Purchase discounts	$3,000		
Purchase returns and allowances	1,200	4,200	
Net purchases		85,100	
Freight in		5,200	
Cost of goods available for sale		140,800	
Less: Ending inventory		52,000	
Cost of goods sold			88,800
Gross margin			$ 47,100

Purchases can also be reported at its net amount in the following manner:

Cost of goods sold:	
Beginning inventory	$ 50,500
Net purchases (net of purchase discounts, $3,000,	
and returns and allowances, $1,200)	85,100
Freight in	5,200
Cost of goods available for sale	$140,800
Less: Ending inventory	52,000
Cost of goods sold	$ 88,800

These presentations of *net* sales and *net* purchases underscore an important fact: published financial statements usually report only *net* amounts for these items because discounts and returns and allowances are relatively small in amount. For most businesses, these contra items are details of primary interest only to managers and therefore are not highlighted in the financial statements.

Summary Problem for Your Review

Brun Sales Company engaged in the following transactions during June of the current year:

June 3 Purchased inventory on credit terms of 1/10 net eom (end of month), $1,610.

9 Returned 40 percent of the inventory purchased on June 3. It was defective.

9   Sold goods for cash, $920.
15 Purchased merchandise of $5,100, less a $100 trade discount. Credit terms were 3/15 net 30.
16 Paid a $260 freight bill on goods purchased.
18 Sold inventory on credit terms of 2/10 n/30, $2,000.
22 Received damaged merchandise from the customer to whom the June 18 sale was made, $800.
24 Borrowed money from the bank to take advantage of the discount offered on the June 15 purchase. Signed a note payable to the bank for the net amount.
24 Paid supplier for goods purchased on June 15, less all discounts.
28 Received cash in full settlement of the account from the customer who purchased inventory on June 18.
29 Paid the amount owed on account from the purchase of June 3.
30 Purchased inventory for cash, $900, less a trade discount of $35.

Required

1. Journalize the above transactions. Explanations are not required.
2. Assume the note payable signed on June 24 requires the payment of $95 interest expense. Was the decision wise or unwise to borrow funds to take advantage of the cash discount? Support your answer by comparing the discount to the interest paid.

SOLUTION TO REVIEW PROBLEM

Requirement 1

June 3	Purchases		1,610	
	Accounts Payable			1,610
9	Accounts Payable ($1,610 × .40)		644	
	Purchase Returns and Allowances			644
9	Cash		920	
	Sales Revenue			920
15	Purchases ($5,100 − $100)		5,000	
	Accounts Payable			5,000
16	Freight In		260	
	Cash			260
18	Accounts Receivable		2,000	
	Sales Revenue			2,000
22	Sales Returns and Allowances		800	
	Accounts Receivable			800
24	Cash [$5,000 − .03($5,000)]		4,850	
	Note Payable			4,850
24	Accounts Payable		5,000	
	Purchase Discounts ($5,000 × .03)			150
	Cash ($5,000 × .97)			4,850
28	Cash [($2,000 − $800) × .98]		1,176	
	Sales Discounts [($2,000 − $800) × .02]		24	
	Accounts Receivable ($2,000 − $800)			1,200
29	Accounts Payable ($1,610 − $644)		966	
	Cash			966

| 30 | Purchases ($900 − $35) .... | 865 | |
| | Cash................................ | | 865 |

Requirement 2.   The decision to borrow funds was wise because the discount ($150) exceeded the interest paid on the amount borrowed ($95). Thus the entity was $55 better off as a result of its decision.

The Adjusting and Closing Process for a Merchandising Business

A merchandising business adjusts and closes the accounts much as a service entity does. The steps of this end-of-period process are the same: If a work sheet is used, enter the trial balance, and complete the work sheet to determine net income or net loss. The work sheet provides the data for preparing the financial statements and for journalizing the adjusting and closing entries. After these entries are posted to the ledger, a post-closing trial balance can be prepared.

The Inventory account affects the adjusting and closing entries of a merchandiser. At the end of the period, before any adjusting or closing entries, the Inventory account balance is still the cost of the inventory that was on hand at the beginning date. It is necessary to remove this beginning balance and replace it with the cost of the ending inventory. Various acceptable bookkeeping techniques might be used to bring the inventory records up to date. In this chapter we illustrate the closing-entry method.

To illustrate a merchandiser's adjusting and closing process, let's use Austin Sound's December 31, 19X6, trial balance in Exhibit 5-6. All the new accounts—Inventory, Freight In, and the contra accounts—are highlighted for emphasis. However, Inventory is the only account that is affected by the new closing procedures. Note that additional-data item *g* gives the ending inventory of $52,000.

Work Sheet of a Merchandising Business

The Exhibit 5-7 work sheet is similar to the work sheets we have seen so far, but a few differences appear. Note that this work sheet does not include adjusted trial balance columns. In most accounting systems, a single operation combines trial balance amounts with the adjustments and extends the adjusted balances directly to the income statement and balance sheet columns. Therefore, to reduce clutter, the adjusted trial balance columns are omitted. A second difference is that the merchandiser's work sheet includes inventory and purchase amounts (which are highlighted). Let's examine the entire work sheet.

Account Title Columns.   The trial balance lists a number of accounts without balances. Ordinarily, these accounts are affected by the adjusting process. Examples include Interest Receivable, Interest Payable, and Depreciation Expense. The accounts are listed in the order they appear in the ledger. This eases the preparation of the work sheet. If additional accounts are needed, they can be written in at the bottom of the work sheet before net income is determined. Simply move net income down to make room for the additional accounts.

EXHIBIT 5-6 *Trial Balance*

Austin Sound		
Trial Balance		
December 31, 19X6		
Cash	$ 4,850	
Accounts receivable	17,000	
Note receivable, current....................	10,000	
Interest receivable.........................		
Inventory................................	50,500	
Supplies....................................	650	
Prepaid insurance..........................	1,200	
Furniture and fixtures......................	6,800	
Accumulated depreciation		$ 2,400
Accounts payable		7,000
Unearned sales revenue.....................		2,000
Note payable, long-term		12,600
Interest payable		
C. Ernest, capital..........................		65,900
C. Ernest, withdrawals......................	34,100	
Sales revenue		138,000
Sales discounts.........................	1,400	
Sales returns and allowances............	2,000	
Interest revenue		600
Purchases...............................	89,300	
Purchase discounts......................		3,000
Purchase returns and allowances		1,200
Freight in..............................	5,200	
Rent expense...............................	8,400	
Depreciation expense		
Insurance expense		
Supplies expense		
Interest expense	1,300	
Total	$232,700	$232,700

Additional data at December 31, 19X6:

a. Interest revenue earned but not yet collected, $400.
b. Supplies on hand, $100.
c. Prepaid insurance expired during the year, $1,000.
d. Depreciation, $600.
e. Unearned sales revenue earned during the year, $1,300.
f. Interest expense incurred but not yet paid, $200.
g. Inventory on hand, $52,000.

Trial Balance columns.   Examine the Inventory account, $50,500 in the trial balance. This $50,500 is the cost of the beginning inventory. The work sheet is designed to replace this outdated amount with the new ending balance, which in our example is $52,000 (additional-data item *g* in Exhibit 5-6). As we shall see, this task is accomplished later in the columns for the income statement and the balance sheet.

Adjustments Columns.   The adjustments are similar to those discussed in Chapters 3 and 4. They may be entered in any order desired. The debit amount of

EXHIBIT 5-7 *Work Sheet*

Austin Sound
Work Sheet
For the Year Ended December 31, 19X6

Account Title	Trial Balance Debit	Trial Balance Credit	Adjustments Debit	Adjustments Credit	Income Statement Debit	Income Statement Credit	Balance Sheet Debit	Balance Sheet Credit
Cash	4,850						4,850	
Accounts receivable	17,000						17,000	
Note receivable, current	10,000						10,000	
Interest receivable			(a) 400				400	
Inventory	50,500				50,500	52,000	52,000	
Supplies	650			(b) 550			100	
Prepaid insurance	1,200			(c) 1,000			200	
Furniture and fixtures	6,800						6,800	
Accumulated depreciation		2,400		(d) 600				3,000
Accounts payable		7,000						7,000
Unearned sales revenue		2,000	(e) 1,300					700
Interest payable				(f) 200				200
Note payable, long-term		12,600						12,600
C. Ernest, capital		65,900						65,900
C. Ernest, withdrawals	34,100						34,100	
Sales revenue		138,000		(e) 1,300		139,300		
Sales discounts	1,400				1,400			
Sales returns and allowances	2,000				2,000			
Interest revenue		600		(a) 400		1,000		
Purchases	89,300				89,300			
Purchase discounts		3,000				3,000		
Purchase returns and allowances		1,200				1,200		
Freight in	5,200				5,200			
Rent expense	8,400				8,400			
Depreciation expense			(d) 600		600			
Insurance expense			(c) 1,000		1,000			
Supplies expense			(b) 550		550			
Interest expense	1,300		(f) 200		1,500			
	232,700	232,700	4,050	4,050	160,450	196,500	125,450	89,400
Net income					36,050			36,050
					196,500	196,500	125,450	125,450

each entry should equal the credit amount, and total debits should equal total credits.

Income Statement Columns. The income statement columns contain adjusted amounts for the revenues and the expenses. Sales Revenue, for example, is $139,300, which includes the $1,300 adjustment.

You may be wondering why the two inventory amounts appear in the income statement columns. The reason is that beginning inventory and ending inventory enter the computation of cost of goods sold. Recall that beginning inventory is added to purchases and ending inventory is subtracted. Even though the resulting cost-of-goods-sold amount does not appear on the work sheet, all the components of cost of goods sold are evident there. Placement of beginning inventory ($50,500) in the work sheet's income statement debit column has the effect of adding beginning inventory in computing cost of goods sold. Placing ending inventory ($52,000) in the credit column has the opposite effect.

Purchases and Freight In appear in the debit column because they are added in computing cost of goods sold. Purchase Discounts and Purchase Returns and Allowances appear as credits because they are subtracted. Together, all these items are used to compute cost of goods sold — $88,800 on the income statement in Exhibit 5-5.

The income statement column subtotals on the work sheet indicate whether the business earned net income or incurred a net loss. If total credits are greater, the result is net income, as shown in the exhibit. Inserting the net income amount in the debit column brings total debits into agreement with total credits. If total debits are greater, a net loss has occurred. Inserting a net loss amount in the credit column would equalize total debits and total credits. Net income or net loss is then extended to the opposite column of the balance sheet.

Balance Sheet Columns. The only new item on the balance sheet is inventory. The balance listed is the ending amount of $52,000, which is determined by a physical count of inventory on hand at the end of the period.

Financial Statements of a Merchandising Business

Exhibit 5-8 presents Austin Sound's financial statements. The *income statement* through gross margin repeats Exhibit 5-5. This information is followed by the **operating expenses,** which are those expenses other than cost of goods sold that are incurred in the entity's major line of business — merchandising. Rent is the cost of obtaining store space for Austin Sound's operations. Insurance is necessary to protect the inventory. The business's store furniture and fixtures wear out, and that expense is depreciation. Supplies expense is the cost of stationery, mailing, packages, and the like, used in operations.

Many companies report their operating expenses in two categories. *Selling expenses* are those expenses related to marketing the company's products — sales salaries; sales commissions; advertising; depreciation, rent, utilities, and property taxes on store buildings; depreciation on store furniture; delivery expense, and the like. *General expenses* include *office* expenses, such as the salaries of the company president and office employees, depreciation, rent, utilities, property taxes on the home office building, and office supplies.

Gross margin minus operating expenses equals **income from operations,** or **operating income,** as it is also called. Many businesspeople view operating income as the most reliable indicator of a business's success because it measures the entity's major ongoing activities.

The last section of Austin Sound's income statement is **other revenue and expense.** This category reports revenues and expenses that are outside the main operations of the business. Examples include gains and losses on the sale of plant assets (not inventory) and gains and losses on lawsuits. Accountants have traditionally viewed Interest Revenue and Interest Expense as "other" items because they arise from loaning money and borrowing money — activities that are outside the scope of selling merchandise or, for a service entity, rendering services.

The bottom line of the income statement is net income, which includes the effects of all the revenues and gains less all the expenses and losses. We often hear the term *bottom line* used to refer to a final result. The term originated in the position of net income on the income statement.

A merchandiser's *statement of owner's equity* looks exactly like that of a service business. In fact, you cannot determine whether the entity is merchandising or service oriented from looking at the statement of owner's equity.

If the business is a merchandiser, the *balance sheet* shows inventory as a major asset. In contrast, service businesses usually have minor amounts of inventory.

EXHIBIT 5-8 *Financial Statements of Austin Sound*

Austin Sound
Income Statement
For the Year Ended December 31, 19X6

Sales revenue			$139,300
Less: Sales discounts		$ 1,400	
Sales returns and allowances		2,000	3,400
Net sales			$135,900
Cost of goods sold:			
Beginning inventory			50,500
Purchases		89,300	
Less: Purchase discounts	$3,000		
Purchase returns and allowances	1,200	4,200	
Net purchases			85,100
Freight in			5,200
Cost of goods available for sale			140,800
Less: Ending inventory			52,000
Cost of goods sold			88,800
Gross margin			47,100
Operating expenses:			
Rent expense			8,400
Insurance expense			1,000
Depreciation expense			600
Supplies expense			550	10,550
Income from operations			36,550
Other revenue and (expense):			
Interest revenue			1,000
Interest expense			(1,500)	(500)
Net income			$ 36,050

Austin Sound
Statement of Owner's Equity
For the Year Ended December 31, 19X6

C. Ernest, capital, December 31, 19X5	$ 65,900
Add: Net income	36,050
	101,950
Less: Withdrawals	34,100
C. Ernest, capital, December 31, 19X6	$ 67,850

Austin Sound
Balance Sheet
December 31, 19X6

Assets

Current:		
Cash		$ 4,850
Accounts receivable		17,000
Note receivable		10,000
Interest receivable		400
Inventory		52,000
Prepaid insurance		200
Supplies		100
Total current assets		84,550
Plant:		
Furniture and fixtures	$6,800	
Less: Accumulated depreciation	3,000	3,800
Total assets		$88,350

Liabilities

Current:	
Accounts payable	$ 7,000
Unearned sales revenue	700
Interest payable	200
Total current liabilities	7,900
Long-term:	
Note payable	12,600
Total liabilities	20,500

Owner's Equity

C. Ernest, capital	67,850
Total liabilities and owner's equity	$88,350

Adjusting and Closing Entries for a Merchandising Business

Exhibit 5-9 presents Austin Sound's adjusting entries, which are similar to those you have seen previously.

The closing entries in the exhibit include two new effects. The first closing entry debits Inventory for the ending balance of $52,000 and also debits the revenue and expense accounts that have credit balances. For Austin Sound these accounts are Sales Revenue, Interest Revenue, Purchase Discounts, and Purchase Returns and Allowances. The offsetting credit of $196,500 transfers their sum to Income Summary. This amount comes directly from the credit column of the income statement on the work sheet (Exhibit 5-7).

The second closing entry includes a credit to Inventory for its beginning balance and credits to the revenue and expense accounts with debit balances. These

OBJECTIVE 5

Adjust and close the accounts of a merchandising business

EXHIBIT 5-9A   *Journalizing and Posting the Adjusting and Closing Entries*

Journal
Adjusting Entries

a.	Dec. 31	Interest Receivable	400	
		Interest Revenue		400
b.	31	Supplies Expense ($650 − $100)	550	
		Supplies		550
c.	31	Insurance Expense	1,000	
		Prepaid Insurance		1,000
d.	31	Depreciation Expense	600	
		Accumulated Depreciation		600
e.	31	Unearned Sales Revenue	1,300	
		Sales Revenue		1,300
f.	31	Interest Expense	200	
		Interest Payable		200

Closing Entries

	Dec. 31	Inventory (ending balance)	52,000	
		Sales Revenue	139,300	
		Interest Revenue	1,000	
		Purchase Discounts	3,000	
		Purchase Returns and Allowances	1,200	
		Income Summary		196,500
	31	Income Summary	160,450	
		Inventory (beginning balance)		50,500
		Sales Discounts		1,400
		Sales Returns and Allowances		2,000
		Purchases		89,300
		Freight In		5,200
		Rent Expense		8,400
		Depreciation Expense		600
		Insurance Expense		1,000
		Supplies Expense		550
		Interest Expense		1,500
	31	Income Summary ($196,500 − $160,450)	36,050	
		C. Ernest, Capital		36,050
	31	C. Ernest, Capital	34,100	
		C. Ernest, Withdrawals		34,100

EXHIBIT 5-9B *Ledger Accounts of Austin Sound*

Assets

Cash		Accounts Receivable		Note Receivable		Interest Receivable	
4,850		17,000		10,000		(A) 400	

Inventory		Supplies		Prepaid Insurance		Furniture and Fixtures	
50,500	(C) 50,500	650	(A) 550	1,200	(A) 1,000	6,800	
(C) 52,000		100		200			

Accumulated Depreciation	
	2,400
	(A) 600
	3,000

Liabilities

Accounts Payable		Unearned Sales Revenue		Interest Payable		Note Payable	
	7,000	(A) 1,300	2,000		(A) 200		12,600
			700				

Owner's Equity

C. Ernest, Capital		C. Ernest, Withdrawals		Income Summary	
(C) 34,100	65,900	34,100	(C) 34,100	(C) 160,450	(C) 196,500
	(C) 36,050			(C) 36,050	
	67,850				

Revenues

Sales Revenue		Sales Discounts		Sales Returns and Allowances		Interest Revenue	
	138,000	1,400	(C) 1,400	2,000	(C) 2,000		600
	(A) 1,300						(A) 400
(C) 139,300	139,300					(C) 1,000	1,000

Expenses

Purchases		Purchase Discounts		Purchase Returns and Allowances		Freight In	
89,300	(C) 89,300	(C) 3,000	3,000	(C) 1,200	1,200	5,200	(C) 5,200

Rent Expense		Depreciation Expense		Insurance Expense		Supplies Expense	
8,400	(C) 8,400	(A) 600	(C) 600	(A) 1,000	(C) 1,000	(A) 550	(C) 550

Interest Expense	
1,300	
(A) 200	
1,500	(C) 1,500

A = Adjusting entry; C = Closing entry

are Sales Discounts, Sales Returns and Allowances, Purchases, Freight In, and the expense accounts. The offsetting $160,450 debit to Income Summary comes from the debit column of the income statement on the work sheet.

The last two closing entries close net income from Income Summary and also close owner Withdrawals into the Capital account.

The entries to the Inventory account deserve additional explanation. Recall that before the closing process Inventory still has the period's beginning balance. At the end of the period, this balance is one year old and must be replaced with the ending balance in order to prepare the financial statements at December 31, 19X6. The closing entries give Inventory its correct ending balance of $52,000, as shown here:

Inventory

Beginning balance (same as last period's ending balance)	50,500	Closing entry to eliminate beginning balance	50,500
Closing entry to set up ending balance	52,000		
Ending balance for the current balance sheet	52,000		

The inventory amounts for these closing entries are taken directly from the income statement columns of the work sheet. The offsetting debits and credits to Income Summary in these closing entries also serve to record the dollar amount of cost of goods sold in the accounts. Income Summary contains the cost of goods sold amount after Purchases and its related contra accounts and Freight In are closed.

Study Exhibits 5-7, 5-8, and 5-9 carefully because they illustrate the entire end-of-period process that leads to the financial statements. As you progress through this book, you may want to refer to these exhibits to refresh your understanding of the adjusting and closing process for a merchandising business.

Income Statement Format

We have seen that the balance sheet appears in two formats: the account format and the report format. There are also two basic formats for the income statement: *multiple step* and *single step.*

OBJECTIVE 6

Recognize different formats of the income statement

Multiple-Step Income Statement

The income statements presented thus far in this chapter have been multiple-step income statements. The **multiple-step format** contains subtotals to highlight significant relationships. In addition to net income, it also presents gross margin and income from operations. This format communicates a merchandiser's results of operations especially well because gross margin and income from operations are two key measures of operating performance.

Single-Step Income Statement

The **single-step format** groups all revenues together and then lists and deducts all expenses together without drawing any subtotals. The single-step format has the advantage of listing all revenues together and all expenses together, as shown in

EXHIBIT 5-10 *Single-Step Income Statement*

Austin Sound Income Statement For the Year Ended December 31, 19X6	
Revenues:	
Net sales (net of sales discounts, $1,400, and returns and allowances, $2,000)........	$135,900
Interest revenue	1,000
Total revenues	136,900
Expenses:	
Cost of goods sold	$ 88,800
Rent expense	8,400
Interest expense	1,500
Insurance expense	1,000
Depreciation expense....................	600
Supplies expense	550
Total expenses	100,850
Net income.............................	$ 36,050

Exhibit 5-10. Thus it clearly distinguishes revenues from expenses. The income statements in Chapters 1 through 4 were single step. This format works well for service entities because they have no gross margin to report. A recent survey of 600 companies indicated that 56 percent use the single-step format and 44 percent use the multiple-step format.

Most published financial statements are highly condensed. Of course, condensed statements can be supplemented with desired details. For example, in Exhibit 5-10, the single-step income statement could be accompanied by a supporting schedule that gives the detailed computation of cost of goods sold.

Summary Problem for Your Review

The trial balance of Jan King Distributing Company is on the next page.

Required:

1. Make a single summary journal entry to record King's
   a. Unadjusted sales for the year, assuming all sales were made on credit.
   b. Sales returns and allowances for the year.
   c. Sales discounts for the year, assuming the cash collected on account was $329,000 and the credit to Accounts Receivable was $339,300.
   d. Purchases of inventory for the year, assuming all purchases were made on credit.
   e. Purchase returns and allowances for the year.
   f. Purchase discounts for the year, $6,000. Cash paid on account was $188,400 and the debit to Accounts Payable was $194,400.
   g. Transportation costs for the year, assuming a cash payment in a separate entry.

2. Enter the trial balance on a work sheet and complete the work sheet.
3. Journalize the adjusting and closing entries at December 31. Post to the Income Summary account as an accuracy check on the entries affecting that account. The credit balance closed out of Income Summary should equal net income computed on the work sheet.
4. Prepare the company's multiple-step income statement, statement of owner's equity, and balance sheet in account format.

Jan King Distributing Company
Trial Balance
December 31, 19X3

Cash.	$ 5,670	
Accounts receivable	37,100	
Inventory.	190,500	
Supplies.	3,930	
Prepaid rent.	6,000	
Furniture and fixtures	26,500	
Accumulated depreciation		$ 21,200
Accounts payable		46,340
Salary payable.		
Interest payable.		
Unearned sales revenue		3,500
Note payable, long-term.		35,000
Jan King, capital		153,680
Jan King, withdrawals.	48,000	
Sales revenue		346,700
Sales discounts	10,300	
Sales returns and allowances	8,200	
Purchases.	175,900	
Purchases discounts		6,000
Purchase returns and allowances.		7,430
Freight in	9,300	
Salary expense.	82,750	
Rent expense	7,000	
Depreciation expense		
Utilities expense	5,800	
Supplies expense.		
Interest expense.	2,900	
Total.	$619,850	$619,850

Additional data at December 31, 19X3:

a. Supplies used during the year, $2,580.
b. Prepaid rent in force, $1,000.
c. Unearned sales revenue still not earned, $2,400. The company expects to earn this amount during the next few months.
d. Depreciation, $2,650.
e. Accrued salaries, $1,300.
f. Accrued interest expense, $600.
g. Inventory on hand, $195,800.

SOLUTION TO REVIEW PROBLEM

Requirement 1

Sales, purchases, and related discount and return and allowance entries:

		19X3		
a.	Accounts Receivable		346,700	
	Sales Revenue			346,700
b.	Sales Returns and Allowances		8,200	
	Accounts Receivable			8,200
c.	Cash		329,000	
	Sales Discounts		10,300	
	Accounts Receivable			339,300
d.	Purchases		175,900	
	Accounts Payable			175,900
e.	Accounts Payable		7,430	
	Purchase Returns and Allowances			7,430
f.	Accounts Payable		194,400	
	Purchase Discounts			6,000
	Cash			188,400
g.	Freight In		9,300	
	Cash			9,300

Requirement 2

Jan King Distributing Company
Work Sheet
For the Year Ended December 31, 19X3

Account Title	Trial Balance Debit	Trial Balance Credit	Adjustments Debit	Adjustments Credit	Income Statement Debit	Income Statement Credit	Balance Sheet Debit	Balance Sheet Credit
Cash	5,670						5,670	
Accounts receivable	37,100						37,100	
Inventory	190,500				190,500	195,800	195,800	
Supplies	3,930			(a) 2,580			1,350	
Prepaid rent	6,000			(b) 5,000			1,000	
Furniture and fixtures	26,500						26,500	
Accumulated depreciation		21,200		(d) 2,650				23,850
Accounts payable		46,340						46,340
Salary payable				(e) 1,300				1,300
Interest payable				(f) 600				600
Unearned sales revenue		3,500	(c) 1,100					2,400
Note payable, long-term		35,000						35,000
Jan King, capital		153,680						153,680
Jan King, withdrawals	48,000						48,000	
Sales revenue		346,700		(c) 1,100		347,800		
Sales discounts	10,300				10,300			
Sales returns and allowances	8,200				8,200			
Purchases	175,900				175,900			
Purchase discounts		6,000				6,000		
Purchase returns and allowances		7,430				7,430		
Freight in	9,300				9,300			
Salary expense	82,750		(e) 1,300		84,050			
Rent expense	7,000		(b) 5,000		12,000			
Depreciation expense			(d) 2,650		2,650			
Utilities expense	5,800				5,800			
Supplies expense			(a) 2,580		2,580			
Interest expense	2,900		(f) 600		3,500			
	619,850	619,850	13,230	13,230	504,780	557,030	315,420	263,170
Net income					52,250			52,250
					557,030	557,030	315,420	315,420

Requirement 3
Adjusting entries:

19X3

Dec. 31	Supplies Expense..............................	2,580	
	Supplies		2,580
31	Rent Expense	5,000	
	Prepaid Rent		5,000
31	Unearned Sales Revenue..........................	1,100	
	Sales Revenue		1,100
31	Depreciation Expense	2,650	
	Accumulated Depreciation		2,650
31	Salary Expense..................................	1,300	
	Salary Payable.............................		1,300
31	Interest Expense................................	600	
	Interest Payable............................		600

Closing entries:

19X3

Dec. 31	Inventory (ending balance)....................	195,800	
	Sales Revenue	347,800	
	Purchase Discounts	6,000	
	Purchase Returns............................	7,430	
	Income Summary		557,030
31	Income Summary	504,780	
	Inventory (beginning balance)		190,500
	Sales Discounts		10,300
	Sales Returns and Allowances		8,200
	Purchases..............................		175,900
	Freight In		9,300
	Salary Expense..........................		84,050
	Rent Expense		12,000
	Depreciation Expense		2,650
	Utilities Expense		5,800
	Supplies Expense.......................		2,580
	Interest Expense........................		3,500
31	Income Summary ($557,030 − $504,780)	52,250	
	Jan King, Capital		52,250
31	Jan King, Capital	48,000	
	Jan King, Withdrawals....................		48,000

Income Summary			
Clo.	504,780	Clo.	557,030
Clo.	52,250	Bal.	52,250

Requirement 4

Jan King Distributing Company
Income Statement
For the Year Ended December 31, 19X3

Sales revenue			$347,800
Less: Sales discounts		$ 10,300	
Sales returns and allowances		8,200	18,500
Net sales revenue			$329,300
Cost of goods sold:			
Beginning inventory		190,500	
Purchases		175,900	
Less: Purchase discounts	$6,000		
Purchase returns and			
allowances	7,430	13,430	
Net purchases		162,470	
Freight in		9,300	
Cost of goods available for sale		362,270	
Less: Ending inventory		195,800	
Cost of goods sold			166,470
Gross margin			162,830
Operating expenses:			
Salary expense		84,050	
Rent expense		12,000	
Utilities expense		5,800	
Depreciation expense		2,650	
Supplies expense		2,580	107,080
Income from operations			55,750
Other expense:			
Interest expense			3,500
Net income			$ 52,250

Jan King Distributing Company
Statement of Owner's Equity
For the Year Ended December 31, 19X3

Jan King, capital, December 31, 19X2	$153,680
Add: Net income	52,250
	205,930
Less: Withdrawals	48,000
Jan King, capital, December 31, 19X3	$157,930

Requirement 4 (cont.)

Jan King Distributing Company
Balance Sheet
December 31, 19X3

Assets			Liabilities		
Current:			Current:		
Cash		$ 5,670	Accounts payable		$ 46,340
Accounts receivable		37,100	Salary payable		1,300
Inventory		195,800	Interest payable		600
Supplies		1,350	Unearned sales revenue		2,400
Prepaid rent		1,000	Total current liabilities		50,640
Total current assets		240,920	Long-term:		
Plant:			Note payable		35,000
Furniture and fixtures	$26,500		Total liabilities		85,640
Less: Accumulated depreciation	23,850	2,650	**Owner's Equity**		
			Jan King, capital		157,930
			Total liabilities and		
Total assets		$243,570	owner's equity		$243,570

SUMMARY

The major revenue of a merchandising business is *sales revenue,* or *sales.* The major expense is *cost of goods sold.* Net sales minus cost of goods sold is called *gross margin,* or *gross profit.* This amount measures the business's success or failure in selling its products at a higher price than it paid for them.

The merchandiser's major asset is *inventory.* In a merchandising entity the accounting cycle is from cash to inventory as the inventory is purchased for resale, and back to cash as the inventory is sold.

Cost of goods sold is unlike the other expenses in that it is not an account in the ledger. Instead, cost of goods sold is the remainder when beginning inventory and net purchases and freight in are added and ending inventory is subtracted from that sum.

The *invoice* is the business document generated by a purchase/sale transaction. Most merchandising entities offer *discounts* to their customers and allow them to *return* unsuitable merchandise. They also grant *allowances* for damaged goods that the buyer chooses to keep. Discounts and Returns and Allowances are *contra* accounts to both Purchases and Sales.

The end-of-period adjusting and closing process of a merchandising business is similar to that of a service business. In addition, a merchandiser makes inventory entries at the end of the period. These closing entries replace the period's beginning balance with the cost of inventory on hand at the end. A by-product of these closing entries is the computation of cost of goods sold for the income statement.

The income statement may appear in the *single-step format* or the *multiple-step format.* A single-step income statement has only two sections—one for revenues and the other for expenses—and a single income amount for net income. A multiple-step income statement has subtotals for gross margin and income from operations. Both formats are widely used in practice.

Self-Study Questions

Test your understanding of the chapter by marking the best answer for each of the following questions.

1. The major expense of a merchandising business is *(p. 169)*
   a. Cost of goods sold
   b. Depreciation
   c. Rent
   d. Interest

2. Sales total $440,000, cost of goods sold is $210,000, and operating expenses are $160,000. How much is gross margin? *(pp. 169, 170)*
   a. $440,000
   b. $230,000
   c. $210,000
   d. $70,000

3. A purchase discount results from *(p. 173)*
   a. Returning goods to the seller
   b. Receiving a purchase allowance from the seller
   c. Buying a large enough quantity of merchandise to get the discount
   d. Paying within the discount period

4. Which one of the following pairs includes items that are the most similar? *(p. 177)*
   a. Purchase discounts and purchase returns
   b. Cost of goods sold and inventory
   c. Net sales and sales discounts
   d. Sales returns and sales allowances

5. Which of the following is *not* an account? *(p. 177)*
   a. Sales revenue
   b. Net sales
   c. Inventory
   d. Supplies expense

6. Cost of goods sold is computed by adding beginning inventory and net purchases and subtracting X. What is X? *(p. 178)*
   a. Net sales
   b. Sales discounts
   c. Ending inventory
   d. Net purchases

7. Which account causes the main difference between a merchandiser's adjusting and closing process and that of a service business? *(p. 181)*
   a. Advertising Expense
   b. Interest Revenue
   c. Inventory
   d. Accounts Receivable

8. The major item on a merchandiser's income statement that a service business does not have is *(p. 185)*
   a. Cost of goods sold
   b. Inventory
   c. Net purchases
   d. Net sales

9. The closing entry for Sales Discounts is *(p. 186)*
   a. Sales Discounts
        Income Summary
   b. Sales Discounts
        Sales Revenue
   c. Income Summary
        Sales Discounts
   d. Not used because Sales Discounts is a permanent account, which is not closed.

10. Which income statement format reports income from operations? *(p. 188)*
    a. Account format
    b. Report format
    c. Single-step format
    d. Multiple-step format

Answers to the self-study questions are at the end of the chapter.

Accounting Vocabulary

cost of goods sold *(p. 177)*,   gross margin *(p. 169)*,   gross profit *(p. 169)*,   income from operations *(p. 184)*,   invoice *(p. 171)*,   multiple-step income statement *(p. 188)*,   net purchases *(p. 174)*,   net sales *(p. 177)*,   operating expenses *(p. 184)*,   operating income *(p. 184)*,   other

expense *(p. 184)*,   other revenue *(p. 184)*,   purchases *(p. 170)*,   purchase discount *(p. 173)*,
purchase returns and allowances *(p. 174)*,   sales *(p. 169)*,   sales discount *(p. 176)*,   sales
returns and allowances *(p. 176)*,   sales revenue *(p. 169)*,   single-step income statement
(p. 188),   trade discount *(p. 173)*.

ASSIGNMENT MATERIAL _____

Questions

1. Gross margin is often mentioned in the business press as an important measure of success. What does gross margin measure, and why is this important?

2. Describe the operating cycle for (a) the purchase and cash sale of inventory and (b) the purchase and sale of inventory on account.

3. Identify 10 items of information on an invoice.

4. What is the similarity and what is the difference between purchase discounts and trade discounts?

5. Indicate what accounts are debited and credited for (a) a credit purchase of inventory and the subsequent cash payment and (b) a credit sale of inventory and subsequent cash collection. Assume no discounts, returns, allowances, or freight.

6. Inventory costing $1,000 is purchased and invoiced on July 28 under terms of 3/10 n/30. Compute the payment amount on August 6. How much would the payment be on August 8? What explains the difference? What is the latest acceptable payment date under the terms of sale?

7. Inventory listed at $35,000 is sold subject to a trade discount of $3,000 and under payment terms of 2/15 n/45. What is the net sales revenue on this sale if the customer pays within 15 days?

8. Name four contra accounts introduced in this chapter.

9. Briefly discuss the similarity in computing supplies expense and computing cost of goods sold.

10. Why is the title of cost of goods sold especially descriptive? What type of item is cost of goods sold?

11. Beginning inventory is $5,000, net purchases total $30,000, and freight in is $1,000. If ending inventory is $8,000, what is cost of goods sold?

12. Identify two ways that cost of goods sold differs from operating expenses such as Salary Expense and Depreciation Expense.

13. Suppose you are evaluating two companies as possible investments. One entity sells its services, and the other entity is a merchandiser. How can you identify the merchandiser by examining the two entities' balance sheets and their income statements?

14. You are beginning the adjusting and closing process at the end of your company's fiscal year. Does the trial balance carry the beginning or the ending amount of inventory? Will the balance sheet that you prepare report the beginning or the ending inventory?

15. Give the two closing entries for inventory (using no specific amount).

16. After the closing entries have been journalized and posted, what account contains the amount of cost of goods sold for the period?

17. What is the identifying characteristic of the "other" category of revenues and expenses? Give an example of each.

18. Name and describe the two income statement formats and identify the type of business to which each format best applies.

19. List eight different operating expenses.

20. Which financial statement reports sales discounts, sales returns and allowances, purchase discounts, and purchase returns and allowances? Show how they are reported, using any reasonable amounts in your illustration.

Exercises

Exercise 5-1   *Computing the elements of a merchandiser's income statement*

Supply the missing income statement amounts in each of the following situations:

Sales	Sales Discounts	Net Sales	Beginning Inventory	Net Purchases	Ending Inventory	Cost of Goods Sold	Gross Margin
$96,000	(a)	$92,800	$32,500	$66,700	$39,400	(b)	$33,000
82,400	$2,100	(c)	27,450	43,000	(d)	$44,100	36,200
91,500	1,800	89,700	(e)	54,900	22,600	59,400	(f)
(g)	3,000	(h)	40,700	(i)	48,230	62,500	36,600

Exercise 5-2   *Journalizing transactions from a purchase invoice*

As the proprietor of Davidson Tire Company, you receive the following invoice from a supplier:

ABC TIRE WHOLESALE DISTRIBUTORS, INC.
2600 Commonwealth Avenue
Boston, Massachusetts 02215

Invoice date: May 14, 19X3   **Payment terms:** 2/10 n/30

Sold to: Davidson Tire Co.
4219 Crestwood Parkway
Lexington, Mass. 02173

Quantity Ordered	Description	Quantity Shipped	Price	Amount
6	P135-X4 Radials.........	6	$37.14	$ 222.84
8	L912 Belted-bias........	8	41.32	330.56
14	R39 Truck tires	10	50.02	500.20

Total... $1,053.60

Due date:	**Amount:**
May 24, 19X3	$1,032.53
May 25 through June 13, 19X3	$1,053.60

Paid:

Required

1. Record the May 15 purchase on account.
2. The R39 truck tires were ordered by mistake and therefore were returned to ABC. Journalize the return on May 19, assuming no refund of shipping charges.
3. Record the May 22 payment of the amount owed.

Exercise 5-3   *Journalizing purchase and sale transactions*

Journalize, without explanations, the following transactions of Mattox, Inc., during July:

July 3   Purchased $1,200 of inventory under terms of 2/10 n/eom (end of month) and fob shipping point.

   7   Returned $300 of defective merchandise purchased on July 3.

   9   Paid freight bill of $90 on July 3 purchase.

   10   Sold inventory for $2,200, collecting cash of $400. Payment terms on the remainder were 2/15 n/30.

   12   Paid amount owed on credit purchase of July 3, less the discount and the return.

   16   Granted a sales allowance of $800 on the July 10 sale.

   23   Received cash from July 10 customer in full settlement of her debt, less the allowance and the discount.

Exercise 5-4   *Journalizing purchase transactions*

On April 30 Reagan Jewelers purchased inventory of $3,800 on account from a wholesale jewelry supplier. Terms were 3/15 net 45. On receiving the goods May 3, Reagan checked the order and found $800 of items that were not ordered. Therefore, Reagan returned this amount of merchandise to the supplier on May 4.

To pay the remaining amount owed, Reagan had to borrow $2,910 from the bank because of a temporary cash shortage. On May 14 Reagan signed a short-term note payable to the bank and immediately paid the borrowed funds to the wholesale jewelry supplier. On May 31 Reagan paid the bank $2,940, which included $30 interest.

Required

Record the indicated transactions in the journal of Reagan Jewelers. Explanations are not required.

Exercise 5-5   *Journalizing sale transactions*

Refer to the business situation in Exercise 5-4. Journalize the transactions of the wholesale jewelry supplier. Explanations are not required.

Exercise 5-6   *Computing cost of goods sold for an actual company*

For the year ended December 31, 19X3, General Motors Corporation, the auto maker, reported net sales of $74.6 billion and cost of goods sold of $60.7 billion. The company's balance sheet at December 31, 19X2 and 19X3, reported inventories of $6.2 billion and $6.6 billion, respectively. What were General Motors' net purchases during 19X3?

Hint: Set up the computation of cost of goods sold and ignore freight.

Exercise 5-7   *Preparing a merchandiser's multiple-step income statement*

Selected accounts of Garcia Hardware Company are listed in alphabetical order.

Accounts receivable	$48,300	Purchase discounts	$ 3,000
Accumulated depreciation	18,700	Purchase returns	2,000
Freight in	2,200	Owner's equity, May 31	126,070
General expenses	23,800	Sales revenue	186,000
Interest revenue	1,500	Sales discounts	9,000
Inventory, May 31	39,450	Sales returns	4,600
Inventory, June 30	41,870	Selling expenses	37,840
Purchases	71,300	Unearned sales revenue	6,500

Required

Prepare the business's multiple-step income statement for June of the current year.

Exercise 5-8 *Preparing a single-step income statement for a merchandising business*

Prepare Garcia Hardware Company's single-step income statement for June, using the data from the preceding exercise. In a separate schedule, show the computation of cost of goods sold.

Exercise 5-9 *Using work sheet data to prepare a merchandiser's income statement*

The trial balance and adjustments columns of the work sheet of Brownlee Supply Company include the following accounts and balances at March 31, 19X2:

Account Title	Trial Balance		Adjustments	
	Debit	Credit	Debit	Credit
Cash	2,000			
Accounts receivable	8,500		(a) 2,100	
Inventory	76,070			
Supplies	13,000			(b) 8,600
Store fixtures....................	22,500			
Accumulated depreciation...........		11,250		(c) 2,250
Accounts payable.................		9,300		
Salary payable				(d) 1,200
Note payable, long-term		27,500		
K. Brownlee, Capital		53,920		
K. Brownlee, Withdrawals...........	35,000			
Sales revenue		203,000		(a) 2,100
Sales discounts	2,000			
Purchases	94,200			
Purchase returns.................		2,600		
Selling expense..................	31,050		(b) 5,200	
			(d) 1,200	
General expense..................	20,500		(b) 3,400	
			(c) 2,250	
Interest expense	2,750			
Total	307,570	307,570	14,150	14,150

Ending inventory at March 31, 19X2, is $74,500.
Prepare the company's multiple-step income statement for the year ended March 31, 19X2.

Exercise 5-10 *Use work sheet data to prepare the closing entries of a merchandising business*

Use the data from Exercise 5-9 to journalize Brownlee Supply Company's closing entries at March 31, 19X2.

Problems   *(Group A)*

Problem 5-1A *Journalizing purchase and sale transactions*

Jastrow Distributing Company engaged in the following transactions during May of the current year:

May 3   Purchased office supplies for cash, $300.
      7   Purchased inventory on credit terms of 3/10 net eom (end of month), $2,000.

8   Returned half the inventory purchased on May 7. It was not the inventory ordered.

10   Sold goods for cash, $450.

13   Sold inventory on credit terms of 2/15 n/45, $3,900, less $600 trade discount offered to customers who purchased in large quantities.

16   Paid the amount owed on account from the purchase of May 7, less the discount and the return.

17   Received defective inventory returned from May 13 sale, $900, which is the net amount after the trade discount.

18   Purchased inventory of $4,000 on account. Payment terms were 2/10 net 30.

26   Borrowed $3,920 from the bank to take advantage of the discount offered on May 18 purchase. Signed a note payable to the bank for this amount.

26   Paid supplier for goods purchased on May 18, less the discount.

28   Received cash in full settlement of his account from the customer who purchased inventory on May 13, less the discount and the return.

29   Purchased inventory for cash, $2,000, less a trade discount of $400, plus freight charges of $160.

Required

1. Journalize the above transactions.
2. Assume the note payable signed on May 26 requires the payment of $30 interest expense. Was the decision wise or unwise to borrow funds to take advantage of the cash discount? Support your answer by comparing the discount to the interest paid.

Problem 5-2A   *Preparing a merchandiser's financial statements*

The accounts of Yosemite Trading Company are listed in alphabetical order.

Accounts receivable	$ 43,700	Office equipment	$ 33,680
Accounts payable	16,950	Purchases	364,000
Accumulated depreciation–		Purchase discounts	1,990
office equipment	22,450	Purchase returns	
Accumulated depreciation–		and allowances	3,400
store equipment	16,000	Salary payable	2,840
Capital, April 30	74,620	Sales revenue	706,000
Cash	7,890	Sales discounts	10,400
General expenses	116,700	Sales returns and allowances	18,030
Interest expense	5,400	Selling expenses	132,900
Interest payable	1,100	Store equipment	48,000
Inventory: April 30	69,350	Supplies	5,100
May 31	71,520	Unearned sales revenue	13,800
Note payable, long-term	45,000	Withdrawals	49,000

Required

1. Prepare the business's multiple-step income statement for May of the current year.
2. Prepare the income statement in single-step format.
3. Prepare the balance sheet in report format at May 31 of the current year. Show your computation of the May 31 balance of Capital.

Problem 5-3A   *Using work sheet data to prepare financial statements*

The trial balance and adjustments columns of the work sheet of Schepps Auto Supply include the following accounts and balances at November 30, 19X4:

Account Title	Trial Balance		Adjustments	
	Debit	Credit	Debit	Credit
Cash	4,000			
Accounts receivable	14,500		(a) 6,000	
Inventory	67,340			
Supplies	2,800			(b) 1,900
Furniture......................	19,600			
Accumulated depreciation		4,900		(c) 2,450
Accounts payable.................		12,600		
Salary payable				(e) 1,000
Unearned sales revenue.............		13,570	(d) 6,700	
Note payable, long-term		15,000		
A. J. Schepps, capital		60,310		
A. J. Schepps, drawing.............	42,000			
Sales revenue		164,000		(a) 6,000
				(d) 6,700
Sales returns.....................	6,300			
Purchases	73,200			
Purchase discounts................		2,040		
Selling expense...................	28,080		(e) 1,000	
General expense..................	13,100		(b) 1,900	
			(c) 2,450	
Interest expense	1,500			
Total	272,420	272,420	18,050	18,050

Required

Inventory on hand at November 30, 19X4, is $72,650. Without entering the preceding data on a formal work sheet, prepare the company's multiple-step income statement for the year ended November 30, 19X4, and its November 30, 19X4, balance sheet. Show your computation of the ending balance of A. J. Schepps, Capital. Drawing is another name for Withdrawals.

Problem 5-4A   *Preparing a merchandiser's work sheet*

Nicosia Shoe Store's trial balance at December 31 of the current year is on the next page.

Additional data at December 31, 19XX:

a. Rent expense for the year, $10,200.
b. Depreciation for the year, $3,130.
c. Accrued salaries at December 31, $900.
d. Accrued interest expense at December 31, $360.
e. Inventory on hand at December 31, $80,200.

Required

Complete Nicosia's work sheet for the year ended December 31 of the current year.

Nicosia Shoe Store
Trial Balance
December 31, 19XX

Cash............................	$ 1,270	
Accounts receivable	4,430	
Inventory........................	73,900	
Prepaid rent......................	4,400	
Store fixtures	22,100	
Accumulated depreciation		$ 8,380
Accounts payable		6,290
Salary payable....................		
Interest payable...................		
Note payable, long term..............		18,000
Angelina Nicosia, capital		55,920
Angelina Nicosia, withdrawals	39,550	
Sales revenue		170,150
Purchases........................	67,870	
Salary expense.....................	24,700	
Rent expense......................	7,700	
Advertising expense	4,510	
Utilities expense	3,880	
Depreciation expense		
Insurance expense...................	2,770	
Interest expense....................	1,660	
Total...........................	$258,740	$258,740

Problem 5-5A *Journalizing the adjusting and closing entries of a merchandising business*

Required

1. Journalize the adjusting and closing entries for the data in Problem 5-4A.
2. Determine the December 31 balance of Angelina Nicosia, Capital.

Problem 5-6A *Preparing a merchandiser's work sheet, financial statements, and adjusting and closing entries*

The year-end trial balance of McKee Sales Company at March 31 of the current year is on the next page.

Additional data at March 31, 19XX:

a. Accrued interest revenue $1,030.
b. Insurance expense for the year, $3,000.
c. Depreciation for the year, $1,000.
d. Unearned sales revenue still unearned, $8,200.
e. Accrued salaries, $1,200.
f. Accrued sales commissions, $1,700.
g. Inventory on hand, $133,200.

McKee Sales Company
Trial Balance
March 31, 19XX

Cash.	$ 7,880	
Notes receivable, current	12,400	
Interest receivable.		
Inventory.	130,050	
Prepaid insurance	3,600	
Notes receivable, long-term	62,000	
Furniture	6,000	
Accumulated depreciation		$ 4,000
Accounts payable		12,220
Sales commission payable		
Salary payable.		
Unearned sales revenue		9,610
J. R. McKee, capital.		167,380
J. R. McKee, withdrawals	66,040	
Sales revenue		440,000
Interest revenue		8,600
Purchases.	233,000	
Freight in	10,000	
Sales commission expense	78,300	
Salary expense.	24,700	
Rent expense.	6,000	
Utilities expense	1,840	
Depreciation expense		
Insurance expense.		
Total	$641,810	$641,810

Required

1. Enter the trial balance on a work sheet, and complete the work sheet for the year ended March 31 of the current year.
2. Prepare the company's multiple-step income statement and statement of owner's equity for the year ended March 31 of the current year. Also prepare its balance sheet at that date. Long-term notes receivable should be reported on the balance sheet between current assets and plant assets in a separate section labeled Investments.
3. Journalize the adjusting and closing entries at March 31.
4. Post to the J. R. McKee, Capital account and to the Income Summary account as an accuracy check on the adjusting and closing process.

Problem 5-7A *Completing a merchandiser's accounting cycle*

The end-of-month trial balance of Bucyk Trading Company at October 31 of the current year is on the next page.

Additional data at October 31, 19XX:

a. Supplies consumed during the month, $2,400. Two thirds is selling expense, and one third is general expense.
b. Depreciation for the month: building, $7,000; furniture, $1,700. Depreciation is evenly divided between selling expense and general expense.

Bucyk Trading Company
Trial Balance
October 31, 19XX

Account Number	Account Title	Balance Debit	Balance Credit
11	Cash......................................	$ 8,310	
12	Accounts receivable	14,390	
13	Inventory..................................	82,300	
14	Supplies...................................	4,100	
15	Building...................................	140,000	
16	Accumulated depreciation–building..............		$ 23,000
17	Furniture	17,500	
18	Accumulated depreciation–furniture		7,500
21	Accounts payable		16,380
22	Salary payable..............................		
23	Interest payable............................		
24	Unearned sales revenue		5,300
25	Note payable, long-term......................		79,000
31	Stu Bucyk, capital..........................		105,860
32	Stu Bucyk, withdrawals	6,000	
41	Sales revenue		143,000
42	Sales discounts	4,290	
43	Sales returns and allowances...................	4,100	
51	Purchases.................................	81,000	
52	Purchase discounts		3,750
53	Purchase returns and allowances................		1,800
54	Selling expense	14,360	
55	General expense	9,240	
56	Interest expense		
	Total.....................................	$385,590	$385,590

c. Of the unadjusted balance of Unearned Sales Revenue, $2,000 was earned during October.

d. Accrued salaries, a selling expense, $1,400.

e. Accrued interest expense, $900.

f. Inventory on hand, $86,000.

Required

1. Using four-column accounts, open the accounts listed on the trial balance, inserting their unadjusted balances. Date the balances of the following accounts October 1: Inventory; Supplies; Building; Accumulated Depreciation–Building; Furniture; Accumulated Depreciation–Furniture; Unearned Sales Revenue; and Stu Bucyk, Capital. Date all other unadjusted balances October 31.

2. Enter the trial balance on a work sheet, and complete the work sheet for the month ended October 31 of the current year. Bucyk Trading Company groups all operating expenses under two accounts, Selling Expense and General Expense. Leave three blank lines under Selling Expense and two blank lines under General Expense.

3. Prepare the company's multiple-step income statement and statement of owner's equity for the month ended October 31 of the current year. Also prepare the balance sheet at that date in report form.

4. Journalize the adjusting and closing entries, using page 6 of the journal.
5. Post the adjusting and closing entries, using dates and posting references.

(Group B)

Problem 5-1B   *Journalizing purchase and sale transactions*

Rogers Furniture Company engaged in the following transactions during July of the current year:

July   2   Purchased inventory for cash, $800, less a trade discount of $150.
    5   Purchased store supplies on credit terms of net eom (end of month), $450.
    8   Purchased inventory of $3,000 less a trade discount of 10 percent, plus freight charges of $230. Credit terms are 3/15 n/30.
    9   Sold goods for cash, $1,200.
    11   Returned $200 (net amount after the trade discount) of the inventory purchased on July 8. It was damaged in shipment.
    12   Purchased inventory on credit terms of 3/10 n/30, $3,330.
    14   Sold inventory on credit terms of 2/10 n/30, $9,600, less a $600 trade discount.
    16   Paid the electricity and water bills, $275.
    20   Received returned inventory from July 14 sale, $400 (net amount after the trade discount). Rogers shipped the wrong goods by mistake.
    21   Borrowed the amount owed on the July 8 purchase. Signed a note payable to the bank for $2,655, which takes into account the return of inventory on July 11.
    21   Paid supplier for goods purchased on July 8 less the discount and the return.
    23   Received $6,860 cash in partial settlement of his account from the customer who purchased inventory on July 14. Granted the customer a 2 percent discount and credited his account receivable for $7,000.
    30   Paid for the store supplies purchased on July 5.

Required

1. Journalize the above transactions.
2. Compute the amount of the receivable at July 31 from the customer to whom Rogers sold inventory on July 14. What amount of cash discount applies to this receivable at July 31?

Problem 5-2B   *Preparing a merchandiser's financial statements*

The accounts of Big Bend Trading Company are listed in alphabetical order.

Accounts receivable	$31,200	Office equipment	$ 49,000
Accounts payable	27,380	Purchases	273,100
Accumulated depreciation–		Purchase discounts.	4,670
office equipment.	9,500	Purchase returns	
Accumulated depreciation–		and allowances.	10,190
store equipment	6,880	Salary payable	6,120
Capital, June 30	73,720	Sales revenue	501,580
Cash	12,320	Sales discounts	8,350
General expenses	75,830	Sales returns and allowances. .	17,900
Interest expense	7,200	Selling expenses	84,600
Interest payable	3,000	Store equipment	47,500
Inventory: June 30.	60,060	Supplies	4,350
July 31	57,390	Unearned sales revenue.	9,370
Note payable, long-term	30,000	Withdrawals	11,000

Required

1. Prepare the entity's multiple-step income statement for July of the current year.
2. Prepare the income statement in single-step format.
3. Prepare the balance sheet in report format at July 31 of the current year. Show your computation of the July 31 balance of Capital.

Problem 5-3B *Using work sheet data to prepare financial statements*

The trial balance and adjustments columns of the work sheet of Francis Toy Company include the following accounts and balances at September 30, 19X5:

Account Title	Trial Balance		Adjustments	
	Debit	Credit	Debit	Credit
Cash	7,300			
Accounts receivable	4,360		(a) 1,800	
Inventory	51,530			
Supplies	10,700			(b) 7,640
Equipment	79,450			
Accumulated depreciation...........		29,800		(c) 9,900
Accounts payable.................		13,800		
Salary payable				(e) 800
Unearned sales revenue.............		3,780	(d) 2,600	
Note payable, long-term		10,000		
M. Francis, capital		78,360		
M. Francis, drawing...............	35,000			
Sales revenue		182,000		(a) 1,800
				(d) 2,600
Sales returns	3,100			
Purchases	67,400			
Purchase discounts................		3,700		
Selling expense...................	40,600		(b) 7,640	
			(e) 800	
General expense..................	21,000		(c) 9,900	
Interest expense	1,000			
Total	321,440	321,440	22,740	22,740

Required

Inventory on hand at September 30, 19X5, is $52,580. Without entering the preceding data on a formal work sheet, prepare the company's multiple-step income statement for the year ended September 30, 19X5, and its September 30, 19X5, balance sheet. Show your computation of the ending balance of M. Francis, Capital. Drawing is another name for Withdrawals.

Problem 5-4B *Preparing a merchandiser's work sheet*

Fairview Hardware's trial balance at December 31 of the current year is on the next page.

Additional data at December 31, 19XX:

a. Insurance expense for the year, $6,090.
b. Depreciation for the year, $7,240.
c. Accrued salaries at December 31, $1,260.
d. Accrued interest expense at December 31, $870.

Fairview Hardware
Trial Balance
December 31, 19XX

Cash.............................	$ 2,910	
Accounts receivable	6,560	
Inventory.........................	101,760	
Store supplies	1,990	
Prepaid insurance	3,200	
Store fixtures	63,920	
Accumulated depreciation		$ 37,640
Accounts payable		29,770
Salary payable......................		
Interest payable.....................		
Note payable, long-term..............		37,220
Ed Sanger, capital		63,120
Ed Sanger, withdrawals	36,300	
Sales revenue		286,370
Purchases.........................	161,090	
Salary expense.....................	46,580	
Rent expense......................	14,630	
Utilities expense	6,780	
Depreciation expense		
Insurance expense...................	5,300	
Store supplies expense		
Interest expense....................	3,100	
Total.............................	$454,120	$454,120

e. Store supplies on hand at December 31, $760.
f. Inventory on hand at December 31, $99,350.

Required

Complete Fairview's work sheet for the year ended December 31 of the current year.

Problem 5-5B   *Journalizing the adjusting and closing entries of a merchandising business*

Required

1. Journalize the adjusting and closing entries for the data in Problem 5-4B.
2. Determine the December 31 balance of Ed Sanger, Capital.

Problem 5-6B   *Preparing a merchandiser's work sheet, financial statements, and adjusting and closing entries*

The year-end trial balance of Port Arthur Sales Company at July 31 of the current year is on the next page.

Additional data at July 31, 19XX:

a. Accrued interest revenue, $350.
b. Prepaid insurance still in force, $310.

Port Arthur Sales Company
Trial Balance
July 31, 19XX

Cash...............................	$ 3,120	
Notes receivable, current	6,900	
Interest receivable...................		
Inventory.........................	104,000	
Prepaid insurance	2,810	
Notes receivable, long-term	19,300	
Furniture	16,000	
Accumulated depreciation		$ 12,000
Accounts payable		14,360
Salary payable......................		
Sales commission payable		
Unearned sales revenue		4,090
G. M. Blake, capital..................		97,790
G. M. Blake, withdrawals..............	59,000	
Sales revenue		337,940
Interest revenue		1,910
Purchases.........................	163,200	
Freight in.........................	11,100	
Salary expense......................	39,030	
Sales commission expense	31,500	
Rent expense.......................	10,000	
Utilities expense	2,130	
Insurance expense....................		
Depreciation expense		
Total.............................	$468,090	$468,090

c. Depreciation for the year, $2,000.
d. Unearned sales revenue still unearned, $1,900.
e. Accrued salaries, $1,640.
f. Accrued sales commissions, $1,430.
g. Inventory on hand, $102,600.

Required

1. Enter the trial balance on a work sheet, and complete the work sheet for the year ended July 31 of the current year.
2. Prepare the company's multiple-step income statement and statement of owner's equity for the year ended July 31 of the current year. Also prepare its balance sheet at that date. Long-term notes receivable should be reported on the balance sheet between current assets and plant assets in a separate section labeled Investments.
3. Journalize the adjusting and closing entries at July 31.
4. Post to the G. M. Blake, Capital account and to the Income Summary account as an accuracy check on the adjusting and closing process.

Problem 5-7B *Completing a merchandiser's accounting cycle*

The end-of-month trial balance of Lansing Building Materials at January 31 of the current year is

Lansing Building Materials
Trial Balance
January 31, 19XX

Account Number	Account Title	Balance Debit	Balance Credit
11	Cash......................................	$ 6,430	
12	Accounts receivable	19,090	
13	Inventory.................................	65,400	
14	Supplies..................................	2,700	
15	Building..................................	195,000	
16	Accumulated depreciation – building..............		$ 36,000
17	Fixtures	45,600	
18	Accumulated depreciation – fixtures...............		5,800
21	Accounts payable		28,300
22	Salary payable.............................		
23	Interest payable............................		
24	Unearned sales revenue		6,560
25	Note payable, long-term.......................		87,000
31	Ed Lansing, capital		144,980
32	Ed Lansing, withdrawals	9,200	
41	Sales revenue		177,970
42	Sales discounts	7,300	
43	Sales returns and allowances	8,140	
51	Purchases.................................	103,000	
52	Purchase discounts		4,230
53	Purchase returns and allowances.................		2,600
54	Selling expense	21,520	
55	General expense	10,060	
56	Interest expense		
	Total.....................................	$493,440	$493,440

Additional data at January 31, 19XX:

a. Supplies consumed during the month, $1,500. One half is selling expense, and the other half is general expense.

b. Depreciation for the month: building, $4,000; fixtures, $4,800. One fourth of depreciation is selling expense, and three fourths is general expense.

c. Unearned sales revenue still unearned, $1,200.

d. Accrued salaries, a general expense, $1,150.

e. Accrued interest expense, $780.

f. Inventory on hand, $60,720.

Required

1. Using four-column accounts, open the accounts listed on the trial balance, inserting their unadjusted balances. Date the balances of the following accounts January 1:

Inventory; Supplies; Building; Accumulated Depreciation–Building; Fixtures; Accumulated Depreciation–Fixtures; Unearned Sales Revenue; and Ed Lansing, Capital. Date the balance of Ed Lansing, Withdrawals, January 31.

2. Enter the trial balance on a work sheet, and complete the work sheet for the month ended January 31 of the current year. Lansing groups all operating expenses under two accounts, Selling Expense and General Expense. Leave two blank lines under Selling Expense and three blank lines under General Expense.

3. Prepare the company's multiple-step income statement and statement of owner's equity for the month ended January 31 of the current year. Also prepare the balance sheet at that date in report form.

4. Journalize the adjusting and closing entries at January 31, using page 3 of the journal.

5. Post the adjusting and closing entries, using dates and posting references.

Decision Problem

Using the Financial Statements to Decide on a Business Expansion

Lynn Kraft owns Westlake Pharmacy, which has prospered during its first year of operation. In deciding whether to open another pharmacy in the area, Lynn has prepared the current financial statements of the business.

Westlake Pharmacy
Income Statement
For the Year Ended December 31, 19X1

Sales revenue		$175,000
Interest revenue		24,600
Total revenue		199,600
Cost of goods sold		
Beginning inventory	$ 27,800	
Net purchases	87,500	
Cost of goods available for sale	115,300	
Less: Ending inventory	30,100	
Cost of goods sold		85,200
Gross margin		114,400
Operating expenses:		
Salary expense	18,690	
Rent expense	12,000	
Interest expense	6,000	
Depreciation expense	4,900	
Utilities expense	2,330	
Supplies expense	1,400	
Total operating expense		45,320
Income from operations		69,080
Other expense:		
Sales discounts ($3,600) and returns ($7,100)		10,700
Net income		$ 58,380

Westlake Pharmacy
Statement of Owner's Equity
For the Year Ended December 31, 19X1

L. Kraft, capital, January 1, 19X1	$20,000
Add increases in owner's equity:	
Net income	58,380
L. Kraft, capital, December 31, 19X1.	$78,380

Westlake Pharmacy
Balance Sheet
December 31, 19X1

Assets

Current:	
Cash	$ 5,320
Accounts receivable	9,710
Inventory	30,100
Supplies.	2,760
Store fixtures.	63,000
Total current assets.	110,890
Other:	
Withdrawals	45,000
Total assets	$155,890

Liabilities

Current:	
Accumulated depreciation–store fixtures . .	$ 6,300
Accounts payable	10,310
Salary payable	900
Total current liabilities	17,510
Other:	
Note payable due in 90 days	60,000
Total liabilities	77,510

Owner's Equity

L. Kraft, capital.	78,380
Total liabilities and owner's equity	$155,890

Lynn recently read in an industry trade magazine that a successful pharmacy meets these criteria:

(a) Gross margin is at least one half of net sales
(b) Current assets are at least two times current liabilities
(c) Owner's equity is at least as great as total liabilities

Basing her opinion on the entity's financial statement data, Lynn believes the business meets all three criteria. She plans to go ahead with her expansion plan and asks your advice on preparing the pharmacy's financial statements in accordance with generally accepted accounting principles. She assures you that all amounts are correct.

Required

1. Prepare a correct multiple-step income statement, a statement of owner's equity, and a balance sheet in report format.
2. Based on the corrected financial statements, compute correct measures of the three criteria listed in the trade journal.
3. Assuming the criteria are valid, make a recommendation about whether to undertake the expansion at this time.

Financial Statement Problem

Closing entries for a merchandising corporation

This problem uses both the income statement (statement of earnings) and the balance sheet of Gulf+Western, Inc., in Appendix C. It will aid your understanding of the closing process of a merchandising business.

Assume that the inventory and closing procedures outlined in this chapter are appropriate for Gulf+Western. Further, from the balance sheet, use only the amounts of inventories listed among current assets. Ignore freight in, and assume net purchases for the year ended October 31, 1987, totaled $1,800.5 million.

Required

1. Show the computation of Gulf+Western's cost of goods sold ($1,753.5 million) for the year ended October 31, 1987, by this formula from the chapter:

> **Beginning inventory**
> **+ Net purchases**
> ‾‾‾‾‾‾‾‾‾‾‾‾‾‾‾‾‾‾‾‾
> **= Cost of goods available for sale**
> **− Ending inventory**
> ‾‾‾‾‾‾‾‾‾‾‾‾‾‾‾‾‾‾‾‾
> **= Cost of goods sold**

2. Using Net Purchases and Net Revenues from the income statement (ignore the items above Net Revenues), journalize Gulf+Western's closing entries for the year ended October 31, 1987. Close Interest Expense and Interest Income (another name for Interest Revenue) separately—their amounts are given in Note J. Provision for Income Taxes is an expense. Corporations like Gulf+Western close Income Summary into an account called Retained Earnings (instead of Capital). Also, corporations have no Withdrawals account to close.
3. What amount was closed to Retained Earnings? How is this net income amount labeled on Gulf+Western's income statement?

Answers to Self-Study Questions

1.	a	6.	c
2.	b ($440,000 − $210,000 = $230,000)	7.	c
3.	d	8.	a
4.	d	9.	c
5.	b	10.	d

Accounting Information Systems

An **accounting information system**—often called simply an *information system*—is the combination of personnel, records, and procedures that a business uses to meet its routine needs for financial data. Because each business has different information demands, each uses a different accounting information system. For example, a jewelry store earns revenue by selling inventory, so the store's management usually wants an up-to-the-minute, accurate level of goods on hand for sale. A physician, however, earns revenue by providing service, and there is little or no inventory to control. The physician needs to keep track of the time spent on each patient. The jewelry store and the physician, then, need different information systems to answer the special sorts of questions that arise as they conduct their business. For maximum effectiveness, the information system is tailored to the business's specific needs.

A basic understanding of accounting systems is important for managing and evaluating a business. As a manager, you may be tempted to reply, "I can always hire an accountant to design the information system and do the accounting." Perhaps, but you will be better able to communicate with the members of your organization if you understand how the accounting system operates. The accounting system is the glue that holds the various parts of an organization together. It helps managers stay on top of their responsibilities. Indeed, a potential buyer of a business examines its accounting system to understand how the organization works.

Also, you do not want your employees to take advantage of you by manipulating your accounting system to cover theft. Business owners who are unfamiliar with accounting systems are victims of this practice to an alarming degree.

This chapter describes accounting information system designs and how they are implemented. It also provides a basic model of information processing and discusses what makes an information system effective. The chapter then discusses computer data processing and illustrates special journals and ledgers that accountants use to streamline information systems.

Accounting System Design and Installation _____

System Design.   An accounting information system begins with a design. The manager and the designer study the business's goals and organizational structure. They also identify management's information needs, breaking down the required information-processing tasks. The designer must consider the personnel who will operate the system, the documents and reports to be produced, and the equipment to be used. Almost every information system uses a computer for at least some tasks. Some CPA firms specialize in system design and install accounting systems for their clients.

System Installation.   Installation includes selecting and training employees to operate the system, testing the system, and modifying it as needed. For a large system, installation may take months or even years. Often installation is more difficult than planned. Even after careful consideration in the design phase, unforeseen difficulties may emerge. If the system is not debugged, it will not perform its intended tasks.

Basic Model of Information Processing _____

Processing information means collecting, organizing, and processing data, and communicating the information to statement users. In addition, accounting data are used by managers. For example, accounts receivable might be analyzed to identify the biggest customers, who will receive special privileges. Exhibit 6-1 shows how the *basic model of information processing* relates to an accounting system.

1. The *source data* for the accounting system are the *documents,* such as invoices and canceled checks, that business transactions generate.
2. *Organizing and processing* data requires transaction analysis, journalizing, posting, and preparation of the work sheet.
3. The output is *information* — the *financial statements.*

Notice that the system converts data to reports, fulfilling accounting's role of providing information.

An Effective Information System _____

Each business's accounting information system follows the basic model shown in Exhibit 6-1. Also, a well-designed information system offers control, compatibility, flexibility, and an acceptable cost/benefit relationship.

EXHIBIT 6-1 *Information-Processing Model and the Accounting System*

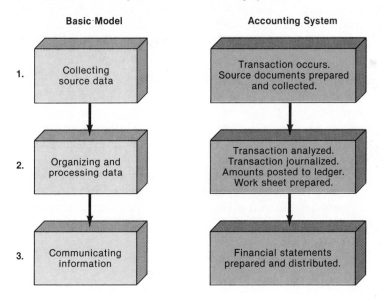

Control

A good accounting system gives management control over operations. *Internal controls* are the methods and procedures a business uses to authorize transactions, safeguard its assets, and ensure the accuracy of its accounting records. For example, most companies exert tight controls over cash disbursements to avoid theft through unauthorized payments. Also, keeping accurate records of accounts receivable is the only way to ensure that customers are billed and collections are received on time. The accounting system controls assets to different degrees. Usually control over cash is tighter than control over supplies and prepaid expenses because cash is more open to theft. Chapter 7 details internal control procedures.

OBJECTIVE 1
Describe the features of an effective information system

Compatibility

An information system meets the compatibility guideline when it works smoothly with the business's particular structure, personnel, and special features. For example, one company may be organized by geographical region, another company by product line. The accounting system for the first company would accumulate revenues and expenses by region. The second company's system would group revenues and expenses by product. Any combination of data accumulation by region and by product is possible — whatever best suits the business. The compatibility guideline means designing the information system with the human factor in mind.

Flexibility

Organizations evolve. They develop new products, sell off unprofitable operations, and adjust employee pay scales. Changes in the business often call for changes in the accounting system. A well-designed system meets the flexibility guideline if it can accommodate such changes without needing a complete overhaul. In most organizations, systems are rarely replaced in their entirety. For example, a system for control of cash might be installed one year and a system for controlling inventories a year later.

Acceptable Cost/Benefit Relationship

Control, compatibility, and flexibility can be achieved in an accounting system, but they cost money. At some point, the cost of the system outweighs its benefits. Identifying that point is the job of the accountant as systems analyst and the manager as user of the information.

Consider the growing number of businesses that have bought computers. For many companies, the computer saves time and money and results in improved decisions. The benefits usually far exceed the cost of a simple computer system. In other cases, the savings are not sufficient to justify the cost of an increasingly elaborate system.

Computer Data Processing

Much data processing in business is done by computer. Computers offer significant advantages in accuracy and in the volume of accounting work that can be performed.

EXHIBIT 6-2   *Mainframe Computer System*

Components of a Computer System

The components of a computer data processing system are *hardware, software,* and *personnel.*

Hardware.   Computer **hardware** is the equipment that makes up the system. Exhibit 6-2 shows the hardware components of a mainframe system. A **mainframe system** is characterized by a single computer that can handle a large volume of transactions very quickly. It can be used locally or by employees at various locations. Employees enter data into the mainframe through remote terminals. In large systems, the employees may be scattered all over the world yet have access to the same computer. Smaller computers, called **minicomputers,** operate like large systems but on a smaller scale.

   Exhibit 6-3 shows a microcomputer system, which is based on a different concept. In a **microcomputer** system, each work station has its own computer, often called a personal computer (PC). These small computers can be connected so that employees can work on the same project together. A group of microcomputers connected for common use is called a *network,* which achieves many of the benefits of a mainframe system. Micro systems are popular because they are more flexible and less expensive than large mainframes.

Software.   Computer **software** is the set of programs, or instructions, that cause the computer to perform the work desired. In a computer system, transactions are not entered into the accounting records by writing entries in a journal. They are entered by typing data on a keyboard similar to that of a typewriter. The keyboard is wired to the computer, which converts the typed data into instructions the computer uses to process the data. In some systems, the data are entered into the computer on punched cards.

EXHIBIT 6-3   *Microcomputer System*

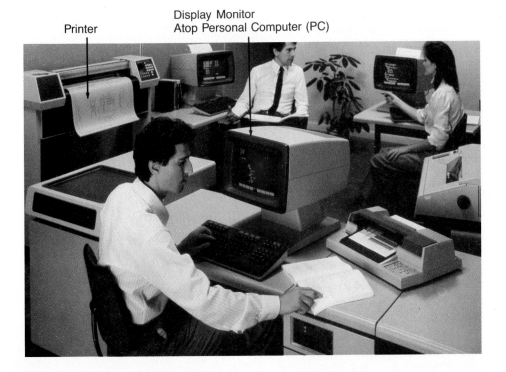

Printer

Display Monitor
Atop Personal Computer (PC)

Mainframe software includes programs written in computer languages such as FORTRAN, COBOL, and PL/1. Microcomputers use software based on computer languages such as BASIC and PASCAL. Other micro software is designed to do specialized tasks. For example, LOTUS® 1-2-3 performs financial analysis, and dBASE III organizes, stores, and retrieves large quantities of data. BPI System's© General Accounting program processes data and prints the balance sheet, income statement, and subsidiary records of accounts receivable, accounts payable, and payroll, among many other accounting tasks. Microcomputer software is popular because much of it is menu driven. This means that by following instructions—the "menu"—you can do complex tasks with little or no computer training.

Personnel.   Computer personnel in a mainframe system include a systems analyst, a programmer, and a machine operator. The *systems analyst* designs the system, based on managers' information needs and the available accounting data. It is the analyst's job to design systems that convert data into useful information—at the lowest cost. The *programmer* writes the programs (instructions) that direct the computer's actions. The computer *operator* runs the machine.

In microcomputer systems, the distinction between the programmer and the operator becomes blurry because employees may handle both responsibilities. For example, a marketing manager may use a microcomputer to identify the territory needing an advertising campaign. The company treasurer may use a micro to analyze the effects of borrowing money at various interest rates. The controller may prepare the budget on a micro. These people may program the computer to meet their specific needs and also operate the machine.

Batch versus On-line Processing

Computers process data in two main ways, in batches and on-line. **Batch processing** handles similar transactions in a group, or batch. Payroll accounting systems use batch processing. Suppose each employee fills out a weekly time sheet showing the number of hours worked. Stored in the computer are the employee's hourly pay and payroll deductions. The machine operator enters the hours worked, and the computer multiplies hours by hourly pay to determine each employee's gross pay. The computer subtracts deductions to compute net pay and prints payroll checks for the net amount. It also prints the weekly payroll report and updates the ledger accounts—all in one batch operation.

On-line processing handles transaction data continuously, often from various locations, rather than in batches at a single location. In retail stores like Sears and Penney's, the cash register does more than make change. It also doubles as a computer terminal. When you charge merchandise at a Penney's store in the United States, the transaction is recorded at Penney's dataprocessing center in Dallas, Texas, directly from the store cash register. For any one transaction the computer in Dallas may perform the following steps:

1. Accounts receivable—
   a. Compares your account number to the list of approved accounts.
      Assume your account is approved.
   b. Adds the amount of this transaction to your previous balance and determines whether the new balance, including this transaction amount, exceeds your credit limit.
      Assume it does not exceed your credit limit.
   c. Debits the Accounts Receivable account and updates your personal account balance to include the effect of this transaction.

2. Sales Revenue—Credits the Sales Revenue account.
3. Inventory—
   a. Updates inventory records for the decrease due to this transaction.
   b. Prepares an order for replacement merchandise if the updated quantity on hand is below the reorder point.

The interactive nature of on-line processing—accounting for accounts receivable, sales, and inventory simultaneously—requires a large share of the computer's capacity. On-line processing, therefore, is used more in mainframe systems than in micro systems.

Overview of an Accounting Information System _____

The purpose of an accounting information system is to produce the financial statements and other reports used by managers, creditors, and interested people to evaluate the business. Companies use computers to meet specific needs. One company's accounting system may use a computer for accounts receivable and cash receipts and a manual system for the rest of its business. Another business may computerize payroll, accounts payable, and cash disbursements, with the remainder accounted for manually. Many large companies have completely computerized systems, and many small businesses use mostly manual systems. Each entity designs its system to achieve the goals of control, compatibility, flexibility, and an acceptable cost/benefit relationship. Exhibit 6-4 diagrams a typical accounting system for a merchandising business.

Accounting procedures may be manual or computerized, mainframe or microcomputer, batch or on-line. The remainder of the chapter describes some of the more important aspects of the system described in Exhibit 6-4. Later chapters discuss the remaining system topics diagrammed in the exhibit.

EXHIBIT 6-4   *Overview of an Accounting System*

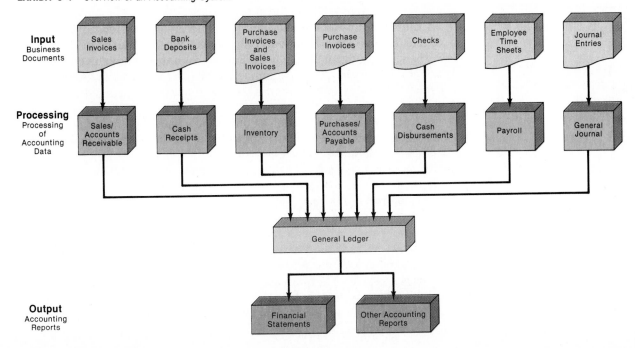

Special Accounting Journals _____

The journal entries illustrated so far in this book have been made in the *general journal.* In practice, however, it is inefficient to record all transactions there.

Think of using the general journal to debit Accounts Receivable and credit Sales Revenue for each credit sale made in a department store on a busy Saturday! Assuming you survived that, consider posting each journal entry to the ledger. Not only would the work be tedious, but it would be time consuming and expensive.

In fact, most of a business's transactions fall into one of four categories, so accountants use special journals to record these transactions. This system reduces the time and cost otherwise spent journalizing, as we will see. The four categories of transactions, the related special journal, and the posting abbreviations follow.

Transaction	Special Journal	Posting Abbreviation
1. Sale on account	Sales journal	S
2. Cash receipt	Cash receipts journal	CR
3. Purchase on account	Purchases journal	P
4. Cash disbursement	Cash disbursements journal	CD

Businesses use the **general journal** for transactions that do not fit one of the special journals. For example, adjusting and closing entries are entered in the general journal. Its posting abbreviation is J.

OBJECTIVE 2

Use the sales journal

Sales Journal

Most merchandisers sell at least some of their inventory on account. These *credit sales* are recorded in the **sales journal,** also called the *credit sales journal.* Credit sales of assets other than inventory—for example, buildings—occur infrequently and are recorded in the general journal.

Exhibit 6-5 illustrates a sales journal (Panel A) and the related posting to the ledgers (Panel B) of Austin Sound, the stereo shop introduced in Chapter 5.

The sales journal in Exhibit 6-5 (Panel A) has only one amount column, on the far right. Each entry in this column is a debit (Dr.) to Accounts Receivable and a credit (Cr.) to Sales Revenue, as the heading above this column indicates. For each transaction, the accountant enters the date, invoice number, and customer account along with the transaction amount. This streamlined way of recording sales on account saves a vast amount of time that would be spent writing account titles and dollar amounts in the general journal.

In recording credit sales in previous chapters, we did not keep a record of the names of credit sale customers. In practice the business must know the amount receivable from each customer. How else can the company keep track of who owes it money—and how much?

Consider the first transaction. On November 2 Austin Sound sold stereo equipment on account to Maria Galvez for $935. The invoice number is 422. All this information appears on a single line in the sales journal. Note that no explanation is necessary. The transaction's presence in the sales journal means that it is a credit sale—debited to Accounts Receivable—Maria Galvez and credited to Sales Revenue. To gain any additional information about the transaction, a person looks up the actual invoice.

EXHIBIT 6-5 *Sales Journal and Posting to Ledgers*

Panel A–Sales Journal:

		Sales Journal			Page 3
Date	Invoice No.	Account Debited	Post Ref.		Accounts Receivable Dr. Sales Revenue Cr.
19X6					
Nov. 2	422	Maria Galvez	✓		935
13	423	Brent Harmon	✓		694
18	424	Susan Levy	✓		907
27	425	Clay Schmidt	✓		783
30		Total			3,319
					(12/41)

Individual accounts receivable are posted daily.

Totals are posted at the end of the month.

Panel B–Posting to Ledgers:

Accounts Receivable Ledger

Maria Galvez

Date	Jrnl. Ref.	Debit	Credit	Balance
Nov. 2	S.3	935		935

Brent Harmon

Date	Jrnl. Ref.	Debit	Credit	Balance
Nov. 13	S.3	694		694

Susan Levy

Date	Jrnl. Ref.	Debit	Credit	Balance
Nov. 18	S.3	907		907

Clay Schmidt

Date	Jrnl. Ref.	Debit	Credit	Balance
Nov. 27	S.3	783		783

General Ledger

Accounts Receivable · No. 12

Date	Jrnl. Ref.	Debit	Credit	Balance
Nov. 30	S.3	3,319		3,319

Sales Revenue · No. 41

Date	Jrnl. Ref.	Debit	Credit	Balance
Nov. 30	S.3		3,319	3,319

Posting to the General Ledger.   Note the term *general ledger.* The ledger we have used so far is the **general ledger,** which holds the accounts reported in the financial statements. However, we will soon introduce other ledgers.

Posting from the sales journal to the general ledger is done monthly. First, the amounts in the journal are summed. In Exhibit 6-5, the total credit sales for November are $3,319. Recall that this column has two headings, Accounts Receivable and Sales Revenue. When the $3,319 is posted to these accounts in the general ledger, the accountant enters their account numbers beneath the total in the sales journal. Note in Panel B of Exhibit 6-5 that the account number for Accounts Receivable is 12 and the account number for Sales Revenue is 41. These account numbers are written beneath the credit sales total in the sales journal to signify that the $3,319 has been posted to the two accounts. The $3,319 is a debit to Accounts Receivable and a credit to Sales Revenue, as the heading in the sales journal states. The number of the account debited (12) appears on the left, the number of the account credited (41) on the right.

Posting to the Subsidiary Ledger.   The $3,319 sum of the November debits does not identify the amount receivable from any specific customer. Most businesses would find keeping a separate accounts receivable account in the general ledger for each customer to be unmanageable. A business may have thousands of customers. Imagine how many pages thick the general ledger for Sears would be. Locating a specific customer's account among the other accounts (Cash, Inventory, Salary Expense, and so on) would be frustrating and time consuming. To streamline operations, businesses instead place the accounts of their individual credit customers in a subsidiary ledger, called the Accounts Receivable ledger. A **subsidiary ledger** is a book of accounts that provides supporting details on individual balances, the total of which appears in a general ledger account. The customer accounts are filed alphabetically.

OBJECTIVE 3
Use control accounts and subsidiary ledgers.

Amounts in the sales journal are posted to the subsidiary ledger daily to keep a current record of the amount receivable from each customer. Note that the amounts are debits. Daily posting allows the business to answer customer inquiries promptly. Suppose Maria Galvez telephones Austin Sound on November 11 to ask how much money she owes. The subsidiary ledger readily provides that information.

When each transaction amount is posted to the subsidiary ledger, a check mark is written in the posting reference column of the sales journal.

Journal References in the Ledgers.   When amounts are posted to the ledgers, the journal page number is written in the account to identify the source of the data. All transaction data in Exhibit 6-5 originated on page 3 of the sales journal so all journal references in the ledger accounts are S.3. The S. indicates sales journal.

Trace all the postings in Exhibit 6-5. The most effective way to learn about accounting systems and special journals is to study the flow of data. The arrows indicate the direction of the information.

The arrows show the links between the individual customer accounts in the subsidiary ledger and the Accounts Receivable account. These links are summarized as follows:

Accounts Receivable debit balance		$3,319
Balances of individual customer accounts in the subsidiary ledger:		
Maria Galvez..	$935	
Brent Harmon	694	
Susan Levy	907	
Clay Schmidt..	783	
Total...		$3,319

Accounts Receivable in the general ledger is a **control account,** which is an account whose balance equals the sum of the balances of a group of related accounts in a subsidiary ledger. In this simple illustration, its balance is the total amount of credit sales. The individual customer accounts are subsidiary accounts. They are "controlled" by the Accounts Receivable account in the general ledger.

Let's look at the advantages the sales journal offers. Each transaction is entered on a single line, and the account titles do not have to be written. The accountant, then, does not have to write as much in the sales journal as in the general journal. Also, the sales journal streamlines posting. That is, fewer postings to the general ledger are necessary. Suppose that Austin Sound had 400 credit sales for the month. How many postings to the general ledger would be made from the sales journal? There are only two, one to Accounts Receivable and one to Sales Revenue. How many postings would there be from the general journal? The total would be 800 (400 debits to Accounts Receivable and 400 credits to Sales Revenue).

Additional data can be recorded in the sales journal. For example, a company may add a column to record sale terms, such as 2/10 n/30. The design of the journal depends on managers' needs for information.

Cash Receipts Journal

Cash transactions are common in most businesses because cash receipts from customers are the lifeblood of business. To streamline the recording of repetitive cash receipt transactions, accountants use the **cash receipts journal.**

Exhibit 6-6, Panel A, illustrates the cash receipts journal. The related posting to ledgers is shown in Panel B. The exhibit illustrates November transactions for Austin Sound.

Every transaction recorded in this journal is a cash receipt, so the first column is for debits to the Cash account. The next column is for debits to Sales Discounts on collections from customers. In a typical merchandising business, the main sources of cash are collections on account and cash sales. Thus the cash receipts journal has credit columns for Accounts Receivable and Sales Revenue. The journal also has a credit column for Other Accounts, which lists sources of cash other than cash sales and collections on account. This Other Accounts column is also used to record the names of customers from whom cash is received on account.

In Exhibit 6-6, cash sales occurred on November 6, 19, and 28. Observe the debits to Cash and the credits to Sales Revenue ($517, $853, and $1,802).

On November 11 Austin Sound borrowed $1,000 from First Bank. Cash is debited, and Note Payable to First Bank is credited in the Other Accounts column because no specific credit column is set up to account for borrowings. For this transaction, it is necessary to write the account title, Note Payable to First Bank, in the Other Accounts/Account Title column to record the source of cash.

On November 25 Austin Sound collected $762 of interest revenue. The account credited, Interest Revenue, must be written in the Other Accounts column. The November 11 and 25 transactions illustrate an important fact about business. Different entities have different types of transactions, and they design their special journals to meet their particular needs. In this case, the Other Accounts Credit column is the catchall that is used to record all nonroutine cash receipt transactions.

On November 14 Austin Sound collected $900 from Maria Galvez. Referring back to Exhibit 6-5, we see that on November 2 Austin Sound sold merchandise for $935 to Ms. Galvez. Assume that the terms of sale allowed a $35 discount for prompt payment and that she paid within the discount period. Austin's cash receipt is recorded by debiting Cash for $900 and Sales Discounts for $35 and by crediting Accounts Receivable for $935. Note that the customer's name appears in

OBJECTIVE 4
Use the cash receipts journal

EXHIBIT 6-6 *Cash Receipts Journal and Posting to Ledgers*

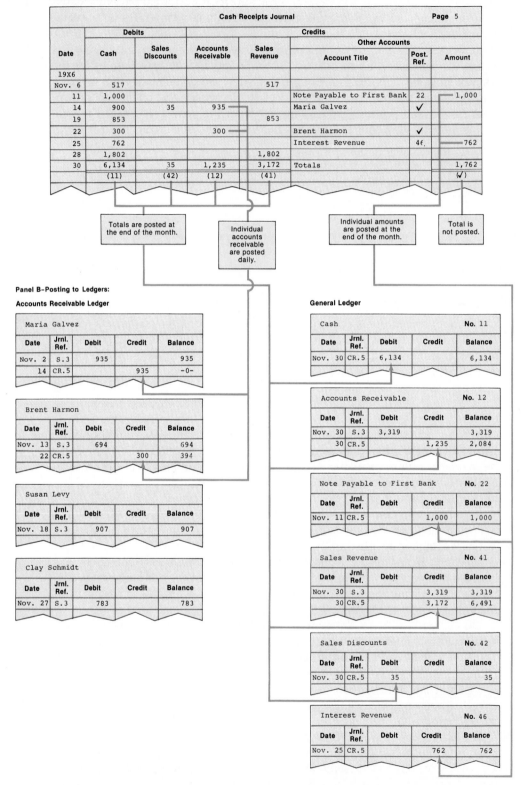

Panel A–Cash Receipts Journal:

the Other Accounts/Account Title column. This enables the business to keep exact track of each customer's account in the subsidiary ledger.

On November 22 the business collected $300 on account from Brent Harmon, who was paying for part of the November 13 purchase. Assume no discount applied to this collection.

Total debits should equal total credits in the cash receipts journal. This equality holds for each transaction and for the monthly totals. For example, the first transaction has a $517 debit and an equal credit. For the month, total debits ($6,134 + $35 = $6,169) equal total credits ($1,235 + $3,172 + $1,762 = $6,169).

Posting to the General Ledger.   The column totals are posted monthly. To indicate their posting, the account number is written below the column total in the cash receipts journal. Note the account number for Cash (11) below the column total $6,134, and trace the posting to Cash in the general ledger. Likewise, the Sales Discounts, Accounts Receivable, and Sales Revenue column totals also are posted to the general ledger.

The column total for *Other Accounts* is not posted. Instead, these credits are posted individually. In Exhibit 6-6, the November 11 transaction reads "Note Payable to First Bank." This account's number (22) in the Post. Ref. column indicates that the transaction amount was posted individually. The check mark, instead of an account number, below the column total indicates that the column total was not posted. The November 25 collection of interest revenue is also posted individually. These amounts can be posted to the general ledger at the end of the month. However, they should be dated in the ledger accounts based on their actual date in the journal. This makes it easy to trace the amounts back to the journal.

Posting to the Subsidiary Ledger.   Amounts from the cash receipts journal are posted to the subsidiary accounts receivable ledger daily to keep the individual balances up to date. The postings to the accounts receivable ledger are credits. Trace the $935 posting to Maria Galvez's account. It reduces her balance to zero. The $300 receipt from Brent Harmon reduces his accounts receivable balance to $394.

After posting, the sum of the individual balances that remain in the accounts receivable ledger equals the general ledger balance in Accounts Receivable ($2,084). Austin Sound may prepare a November 30 list of account balances from the subsidiary ledger as a check of the accuracy of journalizing and posting:

Customer Accounts Receivable

Customer	Balance
Brent Harmon............................	$ 394
Susan Levy...............................	907
Clay Schmidt.............................	783
Total accounts receivable.................	$2,084

Keeping good accounts receivable records reduces errors and helps customer relations.

The cash receipts journal offers the same advantages as the sales journal: streamlined journalizing of transactions and fewer postings to the ledgers.

Summary Problem for Your Review

A company completed the following selected transactions during March:

Mar.　4　Received $500 from a cash sale to a customer.

　　　　6　Received $60 on account from Brady Lee. The full invoice amount was $65, but Lee paid within the discount period to gain the $5 discount.

　　　　9　Received $1,080 on a note receivable from Beverly Mann. This amount includes the $1,000 note receivable plus $80 of interest revenue.

　　　15　Received $800 from a cash sale to a customer.

　　　24　Borrowed $2,200 by signing a note payable to Interstate Bank.

　　　27　Received $1,200 on account from Lance Albert. Payment was received after the discount period lapsed.

The general ledger showed the following balances at February 28: Cash, debit balance of $1,117; Accounts Receivable, debit balance of $2,790; Note Receivable–Beverly Mann, debit balance of $1,000. The accounts receivable subsidiary ledger at February 28 contained debit balances as follows: Lance Albert, $1,840; Brady Lee, $65; Melinda Fultz, $885.

Required

1. Record the transactions in the cash receipts journal, page 7.
2. Compute column totals at March 31. Show that total debits equal total credits in the cash receipts journal.
3. Post to the general ledger and the accounts receivable subsidiary ledger. Use complete posting references, including the account numbers illustrated: Cash, 11; Accounts Receivable, 12; Note Receivable–Beverly Mann, 13; Note Payable–Interstate Bank, 22; Sales Revenue, 41; Sales Discounts, 42; Interest Revenue, 46. Insert a check mark (✓) in the posting reference column for each February 28 account balance.
4. Prove the accuracy of posting by showing that the total of the balances in the subsidiary ledger equals the general ledger balance in Accounts Receivable.

SOLUTION TO REVIEW PROBLEM

Requirements 1 and 2

Cash Receipts Journal　　　　　　　　　　　　　　　　　Page 7

| | Debits | | Credits | | | | |
| | | | | | Other Accounts | | |
Date	Cash	Sales Discounts	Accounts Receivable	Sales Revenue	Account Title	Post. Ref.	Amount
Mar.　4	500			500			
6	60	5	65		Brady Lee	✓	
9	1,080				Note Receivable–		
					Beverly Mann	13	1,000
					Interest Revenue	46	80
15	800			800			
24	2,200				Note Payable–		
					Interstate Bank	22	2,200
27	1,200		1,200		Lance Albert	✓	
31	5,840	5	1,265	1,300	Total		3,280
	(11)	(42)	(12)	(41)			(✓)

　　　　　　5,845　　　　　　　　　　　　　　　　5,845

Requirement 3

Accounts Receivable Ledger

Lance Albert

Date	Jrnl. Ref.	Debit	Credit	Balance
Feb. 28	✓			1,840
Mar. 27	CR. 7		1,200	640

Brady Lee

Date	Jrnl. Ref.	Debit	Credit	Balance
Feb. 28	✓			65
Mar. 6	CR. 7		65	—

Melinda Fultz

Date	Jrnl. Ref.	Debit	Credit	Balance
Feb. 28	✓			885

General Ledger

Cash   No. 11

Date	Jrnl. Ref.	Debit	Credit	Balance
Feb. 28	✓			1,117
Mar. 31	CR.7	5,840		6,957

Accounts Receivable   No. 12

Date	Jrnl. Ref.	Debit	Credit	Balance
Feb. 28	✓			2,790
Mar. 31	CR.7		1,265	1,525

Note Receivable – Beverly Mann   No. 13

Date	Jrnl. Ref.	Debit	Credit	Balance
Feb. 28	✓			1,000
Mar. 9	CR.7		1,000	—

Note Payable – Interstate Bank   No. 22

Date	Jrnl. Ref.	Debit	Credit	Balance
Mar. 24	CR.7		2,200	2,200

Sales Revenue   No. 41

Date	Jrnl. Ref.	Debit	Credit	Balance
Mar. 31	CR. 7		1,300	1,300

Sales Discounts   No. 42

Date	Jrnl. Ref.	Debit	Credit	Balance
Mar. 31	CR. 7	5		5

Interest Revenue   No. 46

Date	Jrnl. Ref.	Debit	Credit	Balance
Mar. 9	CR. 7		80	80

Requirement 4

Lance Albert	$ 640
Melinda Fultz	885
Total	$1,525

This total agrees with the balance in Accounts Receivable.

Purchases Journal

OBJECTIVE 5
Use the purchases journal

A merchandising business purchases inventory and supplies frequently. Such purchases are usually made on account. The **purchases journal** is designed to account for all purchases of inventory, supplies, and other assets *on account*. It can also be used to record expenses incurred on account. Cash purchases are recorded in the cash disbursements journal.

Exhibit 6-7 illustrates Austin Sound's purchases journal (Panel A) and posting to ledgers (Panel B).[1]

The purchases journal in Exhibit 6-7 has amount columns for credits to Accounts Payable and debits to Purchases, Supplies, and Other Accounts. The Other Accounts columns accommodate purchases of items other than inventory and supplies. These columns make the journal flexible enough to accommodate a wide variety of transactions. Each business designs its purchases journal to meet its own needs for information and efficiency. Accounts Payable is credited for all transactions recorded in the purchases journal. Inventory purchases are debited to Purchases. Purchases of supplies are debited to Supplies.

On November 2 Austin Sound purchased from JVC Corporation stereo inventory costing $700. The creditor's name (JVC Corporation) is entered in the Account Credited column. The purchase terms of 3/15 n/30 are also entered to help identify the due date and the discount available. Accounts Payable is credited and Purchases is debited for the transaction amount. On November 19 a credit purchase of supplies is entered as a debit to Supplies and a credit to Accounts Payable.

Note the November 9 purchase of fixtures from City Office Supply. Since the purchases journal contains no column for fixtures, the Other Accounts debit column is used. Because this was a credit purchase, the accountant enters the creditor name (City Office Supply) in the Account Credited column and writes "Fixtures" in the Other Accounts/Account Title column.

The total credits in the journal ($2,876) are compared to the total debits ($1,706 + $103 + $1,067 = $2,876) to prove the accuracy of the entries in the purchases journal.

To pay debts efficiently, a company must know how much it owes particular creditors. The Accounts Payable account in the general ledger shows only a single total, however, and therefore does not indicate the amount owed to each creditor. Companies keep an accounts payable subsidiary ledger. The accounts payable ledger lists the creditors in alphabetical order, along with the amounts owed to them. Exhibit 6-7, Panel B, shows Austin Sound's accounts payable subsidiary ledger, which includes accounts for Audio Electronics, City Office Supply, and

---

[1] This is the only special journal that we illustrate with the credit column placed to the left and the debit columns to the right. This arrangement of columns focuses on Accounts Payable, which is credited for each entry to this journal—and on the individual supplier to be paid.

EXHIBIT 6-7 *Purchases Journal and Posting to Ledgers*

Panel A–Purchases Journal:

				Credit	Debits				
							Other Accounts		
Date	Account Credited	Terms	Post. Ref.	Accounts Payable	Purchases	Supplies	Account Title	Post. Ref.	Amount
19X6									
Nov. 2	JVC Corp.	3/15 n/30	✓	700	700				
5	Pioneer Sound	n/30	✓	319	319				
9	City Office Supply	2/10 n/30	✓	440			Fixtures	19	440
12	Audio Electronics, Inc.	n/30	✓	236	236				
13	JVC Corp.	3/15 n/30	✓	451	451				
19	City Office Supply Co.	2/10 n/30	✓	103		103			
23	O'Leary Furniture Co.	n/60	✓	627			Furniture	18	627
30	Totals			2,876	1,706	103			1,067
				(21)	(51)	(16)			(✓)

Purchases Journal — Page 8

Individual accounts payable are posted daily.

Totals are posted at the end of the month.

Total is not posted.

Individual amounts are posted at the end of the month.

Panel B–Posting to Ledgers:

Accounts Payable Ledger

Audio Electronics

Date	Jrnl. Ref.	Debit	Credits	Balance
Nov. 12	P.8		236	236

City Office Supply Co.

Date	Jrnl. Ref.	Debit	Credit	Balance
Nov. 9	P.8		440	440
19	P.8		103	543

JVC Corp.

Date	Jrnl. Ref.	Debit	Credit	Balance
Nov. 2	P.8		700	700
13	P.8		451	1,151

O'Leary Furniture Co.

Date	Jrnl. Ref.	Debit	Credit	Balance
Nov. 23	P.8		627	627

Pioneer Sound

Date	Jrnl. Ref.	Debit	Credit	Balance
Nov. 5	P.8		319	319

General Ledger

Supplies — No. 16

Date	Jrnl. Ref.	Debit	Credit	Balance
Nov. 30	P.8	103		103

Furniture — No. 18

Date	Jrnl. Ref.	Debit	Credit	Balance
Nov. 23	P.8	627		627

Fixtures — No. 19

Date	Jrnl. Ref.	Debit	Credit	Balance
Nov. 9	P.8	440		440

Accounts Payable — No. 21

Date	Jrnl. Ref.	Debit	Credit	Balance
Nov. 30	P.8		2,876	2,876

Purchases — No. 51

Date	Jrnl. Ref.	Debit	Credit	Balance
Nov. 30	P.8	1,706		1,706

others. After posting at the end of the period, the total of the individual balances in the subsidiary ledger equals the balance in the Accounts Payable control account in the general ledger. This system is like the accounts receivable system discussed earlier in the chapter.

Posting from the Purchases Journal.   Posting from the purchases journal is similar to posting from the sales journal and the cash receipts journal. Exhibit 6-7, Panel B illustrates the posting process.

Individual accounts payable in the *accounts payable subsidiary ledger* are posted daily, and column totals and other amounts are posted to the *general ledger* at the end of the month. In the ledger accounts, P.8 indicates the source of the posted amounts—that is, page 8 of the purchases journal.

Use of the special purchases journal offers advantages over the general journal. Each transaction is *journalized* on one line, and the general ledger accounts do not have to be written. A written explanation of each transaction is unnecessary because each transaction is a purchase on account. Posting to the general ledger is streamlined with the special journal because monthly totals can be posted to the general ledger. Contrast the number of postings from the purchases journal in Exhibit 6-7 with the number that would be required if the general journal were used to record the same seven transactions. Use of the purchases journal requires only five general ledger postings—$2,876 to Accounts Payable, $1,706 to Purchases, $103 to Supplies, $440 to Fixtures, and $627 to Furniture. Without the purchases journal, there would have been fourteen postings, two for each of the seven transactions.

OBJECTIVE 6

Use the cash disbursements journal

Cash Disbursements Journal

Businesses make most cash disbursements by check. All payments by check are recorded in the **cash disbursements journal.** Other titles of this special journal are the *check register* and the *cash payments journal.* Like the other special journals, it has multiple columns for recording cash payments that occur frequently.

Exhibit 6-8, Panel A, illustrates the cash disbursements journal, and Panel B shows the postings to the ledgers of Austin Sound.

The cash disbursements journal in the exhibit has two debit columns—for Accounts Payable and Other Accounts—and two credit columns—for Cash and Purchase Discounts. It also has columns for the date and the check number of each cash payment.

Suppose a business makes numerous cash purchases of inventory. What additional column would its cash disbursements journal need to be most useful? A column for Purchases, which would appear under the Debits heading, would streamline the accounting.

All entries in the cash disbursements journal include a credit to Cash. Payments on account are debits to Accounts Payable. On November 15 Austin Sound paid JVC on account, with credit terms of 3/15 n/30 (for details, see the first transaction in Exhibit 6-7). Therefore, Austin took the 3 percent discount and paid $679 ($700 less the $21 discount).

The Other Accounts column is used to record debits to accounts for which no special column exists. For example, on November 3 Austin Sound paid rent expense of $1,200, and on November 8 the business purchased supplies for $61.

As with all other journals, the total debits ($3,161 + $819 = $3,980) should equal the total credits ($21 + $3,959 = $3,980).

Posting from the Cash Disbursements Journal.   Posting from the cash disbursements journal is similar to posting from the cash receipts journal. Individual

EXHIBIT 6-8 *Cash Disbursements Journal and Posting to Ledgers.*

Panel A–Cash Disbursements Journal:

				Debits		Credits	
							Page 6

Cash Disbursements Journal

Date	Ck. No.	Account Debited	Post. Ref.	Other Accounts	Accounts Payable	Purchase Discounts	Cash
19X6							
Nov. 3	101	Rent Expense	54	1,200			1,200
8	102	Supplies	16	61			61
15	103	JVC Corp.	✓		700	21	679
20	104	Pioneer Sound	✓		119		119
26	105	Purchases	51	1,900			1,900
30		Totals		3,161	819	21	3,959
				(✓)	(21)	(52)	(11)

Total is not posted.

Totals are posted at the end of the month.

Individual accounts payable are posted daily

Individual amounts are posted at the end of the month.

Panel B–Posting to Ledgers:

Accounts Payable Ledger

Audio Electronics

Date	Jrnl. Ref.	Debit	Credit	Balance
Nov. 12	P.8		236	236

City Office Supply

Date	Jrnl. Ref.	Debit	Credit	Balance
Nov. 9	P.8		440	440
19	P.8		103	543

JVC Corp.

Date	Jrnl. Ref.	Debit	Credit	Balance
Nov. 2	P.8		700	700
13	P.8		451	1151
15	CD.6	700		451

O'Leary Furniture Co.

Date	Jrnl. Ref.	Debit	Credit	Balance
Nov. 23	P.8		627	627

Pioneer Sound

Date	Jrnl. Ref.	Debit	Credit	Balance
Nov. 5	P.8		319	319
20	CD.6	119		200

General Ledger

Cash   No. 11

Date	Jrnl. Ref.	Debit	Credit	Balance
Nov. 30	CR.5	6,134		6,134
30	CD.6		3,959	2,175

Supplies   No. 16

Date	Jrnl. Ref.	Debit	Credit	Balance
Nov. 30	P.8	103		103
8	CD.6	61		164

Accounts Payable   No. 21

Date	Jrnl. Ref.	Debit	Credit	Balance
Nov. 30	P.8		2,876	2,876
30	CD.6	819		2,057

Purchases   No. 51

Date	Jrnl. Ref.	Debit	Credit	Balance
Nov. 30	P.8	1,706		1,706
26	CD.6	1,900		3,606

Purchase Discounts   No. 52

Date	Jrnl. Ref.	Debit	Credit	Balance
Nov. 30	CD.6		21	21

Rent Expense   No. 54

Date	Jrnl. Ref.	Debit	Credit	Balance
Nov. 3	CD.6	1,200		1,200

creditor amounts are posted daily, and column totals and Other Accounts are posted at the end of the month. Exhibit 6-8, Panel B illustrates the posting process.

Observe the effect of posting to the Accounts Payable account in the general ledger. The first posted amount in the Accounts Payable account (credit $2,876) originated in the purchases journal, page 8 (P.8). The second posted amount (debit $819) came from the cash disbursements journal, page 6 (CD.6). The resulting credit balance in Accounts Payable is $2,057. Also, see the Cash account. After posting, its debit balance is $2,175.

Amounts in the Other Accounts column are posted individually (for example, Rent Expense—debit $1,200). When each Other Accounts amount is posted to the general ledger, the account number is written in the Post. Ref. column of the journal.

As a proof of accuracy, companies total the individual creditor balances in the accounts payable subsidiary ledger for comparison with the Accounts Payable balance in the general ledger:

Creditor Accounts Payable

Creditor	Balance
Audio Electronics	$ 236
City Office Supply.	543
JVC Corp.	451
O'Leary Furniture	627
Pioneer Sound.	200
Total accounts payable	$2,057

This total, computed at the end of the period, agrees with the Accounts Payable balance in Exhibit 6-8. Agreement of the two amounts indicates that journalizing and posting have been performed correctly and that the resulting account balances are correct.

Use of the cash disbursements journal streamlines journalizing and posting in the same way as for the other special journals.

The Credit Memorandum—A Basic Business Document

Customers sometimes bring merchandise back to the seller, and sellers grant sales allowances to customers because of product defects and for other reasons. The effect of sales returns and sales allowances is the same—both decrease net sales in the same way a sales discount does. The document issued by the seller to indicate having credited the customer's Account Receivable is called a **credit memorandum,** or **credit memo,** because the company gives the customer credit for the returned merchandise. When a company issues a credit memo, it records the transaction by debiting Sales Returns and Allowances and crediting Accounts Receivable.

Suppose Austin Sound sold two stereo speakers for $198 on account to Stephanie Baker. Later she discovered a defect and returned the speakers. Austin Sound would issue to Ms. Baker a credit memo like the one in Exhibit 6-9.

To record the *sale return,* Austin Sound would make the following entry in the general journal:

EXHIBIT 6-9 *Credit Memorandum*

Credit Memorandum		**No. 27**

Austin Sound   **Date**   November 6, 19X6
305 West Martin Luther King Blvd.
Austin, Texas 78701

Customer Name   Stephanie Baker

                                   538 Rio Grande, Apt. 236

                                   Austin, Texas 78703

Reason for Credit   Defective merchandise returned

	Description	**Amount**
2	Trailblazer JU170456 Speakers	$198

General Journal   **Page 9**

Date	Accounts	Post Ref.	Debit	Credit
Nov. 6	Sales Returns and Allowances	43	198	
	Accounts Receivable—Stephanie Baker	12/✓		198
	Credit memo no. 27			

The debit side of the entry is posted to Sales Returns and Allowances. Its account number (43) is written in the posting reference column when $198 is posted. The credit side of the entry requires two $198 postings, one to Accounts Receivable, the control account in the general ledger (account number 12), and the other to Stephanie Baker's account in the accounts receivable subsidiary ledger. These credit postings explain why the document is called a *credit memo*.

Observe that the posting references of the credit include two notations. The account number (12) denotes the posting to Accounts Receivable in the general ledger. The check mark (✓) denotes the posting to Ms. Baker's account in the subsidiary ledger. Why are two postings needed? Because this is the general journal. Without specially designed columns, it is necessary to write both posting references on the same line. Posting to the general ledger usually occurs monthly; and posting to the subsidiary ledger, daily.

Suppose Ms. Baker had paid cash. Austin Sound would either give her a credit memo or refund her cash. Austin Sound would record the cash refund in the *cash disbursements journal* as follows:

Cash Disbursements Journal   **Page 8**

Date	Ck. No.	Account Debited	Post. Ref.	Debits Other Accounts	Debits Accounts Payable	Credits Purchase Discounts	Cash
Nov. 6	106	Sales Returns and Allowances	43	198			198

A business with a high volume of sales returns, such as a department store chain, may find it efficient to use a special journal for sales returns and allowances.

The Debit Memorandum — A Basic Business Document

Purchase Returns occur when a business returns goods to the seller. The procedures for handling purchase returns are similar to those dealing with sales returns. The purchaser gives the merchandise back to the seller and receives either a cash refund or replacement goods.

When a business returns merchandise to the seller, it may also send a business document known as a **debit memorandum,** or **debit memo.** This document states that the buyer no longer owes the seller for the amount of the returned purchases. The buyer debits the Accounts Payable to the seller and credits Purchase Returns and Allowances. If the volume of purchase returns is high enough, the business may use a special journal for purchase returns.

Many businesses record their purchase returns in the general journal. Austin Sound would record its return of defective speakers to JVC as follows:

	General Journal			Page 9
Date	Accounts	Post. Ref.	Debit	Credit
Nov. 6	Accounts Payable—JVC Corp..............	21/✓	244	
	Purchase Returns and Allowances......	53		244
	Debit memo no. 16			

Sales Tax

Most states and many cities levy tax on sales (sales tax). Sellers must add the tax to the sale amount, then pay the tax to the government. In most jurisdictions, sales tax is levied only on final consumers, so retail businesses usually do not pay sales tax on the goods they purchase for resale. For example, Austin Sound would not pay tax on a purchase of equipment from JVC, a wholesaler. However, when retailers like Austin Sound make sales, they must collect sales tax from the consumer. In effect, retailers serve as collecting agents for the taxing authorities. The amount of tax depends on the total sales.

Retailers set up procedures to collect the tax, account for it, and pay it on time. Invoices may be preprinted with a place for entering the sales tax amount, and the general ledger has an account entitled Sales Tax Payable. The sales journal may include a special column for sales tax, such as the one illustrated in Exhibit 6-10.

Note that the amount debited to Accounts Receivable ($3,484.95) is the sum of the credits to Sales Tax Payable ($165.95) and Sales Revenue ($3,319.00). This is so because the customers' payments—the Accounts Receivable figures—are partly for the purchase of merchandise (Sales Revenue) and partly for tax created by the sale. Individual customer accounts are posted daily to the accounts receiv-

EXHIBIT 6-10 *Sales Journal Designed to Account for Sales Tax*

				Sales Journal		**Page 4**
Date	Invoice No.	Account Debited	Post. Ref.	Accounts Receivable Dr.	Sales Tax Payable Cr.	Sales Revenue Cr.
19X6						
Nov. 2	422	Maria Galvez	✓	981.75	46.75	935.00
13	423	Brent Harmon	✓	728.70	34.70	694.00
18	424	Susan Levy	✓	952.35	45.35	907.00
27	425	Clay Schmidt	✓	822.15	39.15	783.00
30		Totals		3,484.95	165.95	3,319.00

able subsidiary ledger, and each column total is posted at the end of the month. The check marks in the Posting Reference column show that individual amounts have been posted to the customer accounts. The absence of account numbers under the column totals shows that the total amounts have not yet been posted.

Another way to account for sales tax is to enter a single amount—which is the sum of sales revenue and sales tax—in the Sales Revenue account. This amount is what the customer pays the retailer. At the end of the period, the business computes the tax collected and transfers that amount from Sales Revenue to Sales Tax Payable through a general journal entry. This procedure eliminates the need for a special multicolumn journal.

Suppose a retailer's Sales Revenue account shows a $10,500 balance at the end of the period. This retailer chooses to enter the full amount of each sale—the actual sales revenue and the sales tax—as Sales Revenue. How does the retailer divide the total amount into its two parts?

To compute the actual sales revenue, the Sales Revenue balance is divided by 1 plus the tax rate. Assume that sales tax is 5 percent. Thus the retailer divides $10,500 by 1.05 (1 + .05), which yields $10,000. Subtracting the actual sales revenue—the $10,000—from the $10,500 total yields $500, the sales tax. The retailer records sales tax with the following entry in the general journal:

	General Journal			**Page 9**
Date	Accounts	Post. Ref.	Debit	Credit
July 31	Sales Revenue........................	41	500	
	Sales Tax Payable..................	28		500
	To transfer sales tax to the liability account.			

Balancing the Ledgers

At the end of the period, after all postings, equality should exist between:

1. Total debits and total credits in the general ledger. These amounts are used to prepare the trial balance that has been used throughout Chapters 3 through 5.

2. The balance of the Accounts Receivable control account in the general ledger and the sum of individual customer accounts in the accounts receivable subsidiary ledger.

3. The balance of the Accounts Payable control account in the general ledger and the sum of individual creditor accounts in the accounts payable subsidiary ledger.

This process is called **balancing the ledgers,** or proving the ledgers. It is an important control procedure because it helps assure the accuracy of the accounting records. Equality between Accounts Receivable control and the accounts receivable subsidiary ledger was proved as shown on page 227. A simpler and less costly procedure is to total the individual customer balances on a calculator tape for comparison to Accounts Receivable control. Balancing the accounts payable ledger follows the same pattern as illustrated on page 234.

Documents as Journals

Many small businesses streamline their accounting systems to save money by using the actual business documents as the journals. For example, Austin Sound could let its sales invoices serve as its sales journal and keep all invoices for credit sales in a looseleaf binder. At the end of the period, the accountant simply totals the sales on account and posts that amount to Accounts Receivable and Sales Revenue. Also, the accountant can post directly from invoices to customer accounts in the accounts receivable ledger. This "journal-less" system reduces accounting cost because the accountant does not have to write in journals the information already in the business documents.

Summary Problem for Your Review

Identify the journal in which each of the following transactions would be recorded. Use journal abbreviations: sales journal = S; cash receipts journal = CR; purchases journal = P; cash disbursements journal = CD; general journal = J.

Cash sale _____

Sale on account _____

Loaned cash on note receivable _____

Received cash on account _____

Purchase of building on long-term note payable _____

Paid cash on account _____

Cash purchase of inventory _____

Owner investment of cash in the business _____

Closing entries _____

Purchase of supplies on account _____

Receipt of cash on account _____

Adjusting entry for accrued salaries _____

Cash purchase of land _____

Credit purchase of inventory _____

Collection of interest revenue _____

Paid interest expense _____

Cash sale of equipment _____

Owner withdrawal of cash _____

Owner investment of land in the business _____

SOLUTION TO REVIEW PROBLEM

Cash sale	CR	Purchase of supplies on account	P
Sale on account	S	Receipt of cash on account	CR
Loaned cash on note receivable	CD	Adjusting entry for accrued salaries	J
Received cash on account	CR	Cash purchase of land	CD
Purchase of building on long-term note payable	J	Credit purchase of inventory	P
Paid cash on account	CD	Collection of interest revenue	CR
Cash purchase of inventory	CD	Paid interest expense	CD
Owner investment of cash in the business	CR	Cash sale of equipment	CR
Closing entries	J	Owner withdrawal of cash	CD
		Owner investment of land in the business	J

Summary

An efficient accounting system combines *personnel, records,* and *procedures* to meet a business's information needs. Processing accounting information means collecting data from source documents, organizing and recording the data, and communicating the information through the financial statements. Each business designs its accounting system to satisfy its particular information needs.

To be effective, the system must provide management with the information needed to *control* the organization. Also, the system must be *compatible* with the business's operations. As businesses change, the system must be *flexible* enough to handle new needs. Finally, the system must be *cost beneficial.*

Computer data processing systems include *hardware, software,* and *personnel.* Hardware may consist of a mainframe computer or microcomputers. Computer operators use software to process data *on-line* or in *batches.*

Many businesses use special journals to account for repetitive transactions such as credit sales, cash receipts, credit purchases and cash disbursements. Special journals reduce the amount of writing and posting required. Some businesses find it efficient to use source documents as journals.

Computer systems can be programmed to possess all the special journal features described in this chapter. The major goal of system design is efficient, routine handling of high volumes of transactions. Special journals were originally created to meet that objective. Similarly, computer systems can store records of sales, cash receipts, purchases, and cash disbursements and print special journals as desired.

Businesses use a subsidiary ledger to account for individual customer accounts receivable. The subsidiary ledger gives information on each customer's account. The total of the subsidiary ledger's individual account balances must match the balance in the Accounts Receivable control account in the general ledger. Companies may also keep a subsidiary ledger for accounts payable.

Self-Study Questions

Test your understanding of the chapter by marking the best answer for each of the following questions.

1. Why does a jewelry store need a different kind of accounting system than a physician uses? *(p. 215)*
   a. They have different kinds of employees.

    b. They have different kinds of journals and ledgers.

    c. They have different kinds of business transactions.

    d. They work different hours.

2. Which feature of an effective information system is most concerned with safeguarding assets? *(p. 217)*

    a. Control   c. Flexibility

    b. Compatibility   d. Acceptable cost/benefit relationship

3. Which of the following components of a computerized accounting system is more likely to be developed in-house rather than by outsiders? Why? *(pp. 218 through 220)*

    a. Hardware, because of the desire for control

    b. Hardware, because of the desire for compatibility

    c. Software, because of the desire for control

    d. Software, because of the desire for compatibility

4. Special journals help most by *(p. 222)*

    a. Limiting the number of transactions that have to be recorded

    b. Reducing the cost of operating the accounting system

    c. Improving accuracy in posting to subsidiary ledgers

    d. Easing the preparation of the financial statements

5. Galvan Company recorded 523 credit sale transactions in the sales journal. How many postings would be required if these transactions were recorded in the general journal? *(p. 225)*

    a. 523   b. 1,046   c. 1,569   d. 2,092

6. Which two dollar-amount columns in the cash receipts journal will be used the most by a department store that makes half of its sales for cash and half on credit? *(p. 226)*

    a. Cash Debit and Sales Discounts Debit

    b. Cash Debit and Accounts Receivable Credit

    c. Cash Debit and Other Accounts Credit

    d. Accounts Receivable Debit and Sales Revenue Credit

7. Entries in the purchases journal are posted to the *(p. 231)*

    a. General ledger only

    b. General ledger and the Accounts payable ledger

    c. General ledger and the Accounts receivable ledger

    d. Accounts receivable ledger and the Accounts payable ledger

8. Every entry in the cash disbursements journal includes a *(p. 233)*

    a. Debit to Accounts Payable   c. Credit to Purchase Discounts

    b. Debit to an Other Account   d. Credit to Cash

9. Mazarotti Company has issued a debit memo. The related journal entry is *(p. 236)*

    a. Accounts Payable XXX

        Purchase Returns and Allowances.   XXX

    b. Purchase Returns and Allowances XXX

        Accounts Payable   XXX

    c. Accounts Receivable. XXX

        Sales Returns and Allowances   XXX

    d. Sales Returns and Allowances. XXX

        Accounts Receivable.   XXX

10. Balancing the ledgers at the end of the period is most closely related to *(p. 238)*

    a. Control   c. Flexibility

    b. Compatibility   d. Acceptable cost/benefit relationship

Answers to the self-study questions are at the end of the chapter.

Accounting Vocabulary

accounting information system *(p. 215)*, balancing the ledgers *(p. 238)*, batch processing *(p. 220)*, cash disbursements journal *(p. 232)*, cash receipts journal *(p. 225)*, control account *(p. 224)*, credit memo *(p. 234)*, debit memo *(p. 236)*, general journal *(p. 222)*, general ledger *(p. 223)*, hardware *(p. 219)*, mainframe system *(p. 219)*, microcomputer *(p. 219)*, minicomputers *(p. 219)*, on-line processing *(p. 220)*, purchases journal *(p. 230)*, sales journal *(p. 222)*, software *(p. 219)*, subsidiary ledger *(p. 224)*.

ASSIGNMENT MATERIAL ————————————————

Questions

1. Briefly describe the two phases of implementing an accounting system.
2. Describe the basic information processing model of an accounting system.
3. What are the attributes of an effective information system? Briefly describe each attribute.
4. How does a mainframe computer system differ from a microcomputer system?
5. Identify three computer languages used with mainframes. Identify four software programs used with microcomputers.
6. Distinguish batch computer processing from on-line processing.
7. Describe an on-line computer processing operation for accounts receivable, sales, and inventory by a large retailer, such as Sears or Penney's.
8. Name four special journals used in accounting systems. For what type of transaction is each designed?
9. Describe the two advantages that special journals have over recording all transactions in the general journal.
10. What is a control account, and how is it related to a subsidiary ledger? Name two common control accounts.
11. Graff Company's sales journal has one amount column headed Accounts Receivable Dr. and Sales Revenue Cr. In this journal, 86 transactions are recorded. How many posting references appear in the journal? State what each posting reference represents.
12. Use S = Sales; CR = Cash Receipts; P = Purchases; CD = Cash Disbursements; and SRA = Sales Returns and Allowances to identify the special journal in which the following column headings appear. Some headings may appear in more than one journal.

   Sales Revenue Cr. —————————— Invoice No. ——————————
   Accounts Payable Dr. —————————— Sales Discounts Dr. ——————————
   Cash Dr. —————————— Other Accounts Cr. ——————————
   Purchase Discounts Cr. —————————— Purchases Dr. ——————————
   Accounts Receivable Cr. —————————— Cash Cr. ——————————
   Check No. —————————— Credit Memo No. ——————————
   Other Accounts Dr. —————————— Accounts Payable Cr. ——————————
   Post. Ref. —————————— Accounts Receivable Dr. ——————————

13. Identify two ways a check mark (✓) is used as a posting reference in the cash receipts journal.
14. The accountant for Bannister Company posted all amounts correctly from the cash receipts journal to the general ledger. However, she failed to post three credits to customer accounts in the accounts receivable subsidiary ledger. How would this error be detected?
15. In posting from the cash receipts journal of Enfield Homebuilders, the accountant failed to post the amount of the sales revenue credit column. Identify two ways this error can be detected.
16. At what two times is posting done from a special journal? What items are posted at each time?
17. For what purposes are a credit memo and a debit memo issued? Who issues each document, the seller or the purchaser?

18. The following entry appears in the general journal:

Nov. 25   Sales Returns and Allowances . . . .   ?   539
               Accounts Receivable–B. Goodwin . . . .   ?   539

Prepare likely posting references.

19. Describe two ways to account for sales tax collected from customers.
20. What is the purpose of balancing the ledgers?
21. Posting from the journals of McKedrick Realty is complete. However, the total of the individual balances in the accounts payable subsidiary ledger does not equal the balance in the Accounts Payable control account in the general ledger. Does this necessarily indicate that the trial balance is out of balance? Give your reason.
22. Assume that posting is completed. The trial balance shows no errors, but the sum of the individual accounts payable does not equal the Accounts Payable control balance in the general ledger. What two errors could cause this problem?
23. Describe how some businesses use their documents as journals.

Exercises

Exercise 6-1   *Using the sales and cash receipts journals*

The sales and cash receipts journals of Advanced Design Company include the following entries:

Sales Journal

Date	Account Debited	Post Ref.	Amount
Oct. 7	C. Carlson	✓	730
10	T. Muecke	✓	1,960
10	E. Lovell	✓	190
12	B. Goebel	✓	5,470
31	Total		8,350

Cash Receipts Journal

	Debits		Credits				
					Other Accounts		
Date	Cash	Sales Discounts	Accounts Receivable	Sales Revenue	Account Title	Post Ref.	Amount
Oct. 16					C. Carlson	✓	
19					E. Lovell	✓	
24	100			100			
30					T. Muecke	✓	

Advanced Design makes all sales on credit terms of 2/10 n/30. Complete the cash receipts journal for those transactions indicated. Also, total the journal and show that total debits equal total credits. Assume that each cash receipt was for the full amount of the receivable.

Exercise 6-2 *Classifying postings from the cash receipts journal*

The cash receipts journal of Cranbrook, Inc., follows.

Cash Receipts Journal   **Page 26**

	Debits			Credits			
					Other Accounts		
Date	**Cash**	**Sales Discounts**	**Accounts Receivable**	**Sales Revenue**	**Account Title**	**Post. Ref.**	**Amount**
Dec. 2	794	16	810		Johnson-McBee	(a)	
9	1,291		1,291		B. R. Blake Co.	(b)	
14	3,904			3,904		(c)	
19	4,480				Note Receivable	(d)	4,000
					Interest Revenue	(e)	480
30	314	7	321		L. M. Roose	(f)	
31	4,235			4,235		(g)	
31	15,018	23	2,422	8,139	Totals		4,480
	(h)	(i)	(j)	(k)			(l)

Required

Identify each posting reference (a) through (l) as (1) a posting to the general ledger as a column total, (2) a posting to the general ledger as an individual amount, (3) a posting to a subsidiary ledger account, or (4) an amount not posted.

Exercise 6-3 *Recording purchase transactions in the general journal and in the purchases journal*

During April, Monarch Tile Company completed the following credit purchase transactions:

April 4   Purchased inventory, $912, from McGraw Co.
7   Purchased supplies, $107, from Paine Corp.
19   Purchased equipment, $1,903, from Liston-Fry Co.
27   Purchased inventory, $2,210, from Milan, Inc.

Record these transactions first in the general journal—with explanations—and then in the purchases journal. Omit credit terms and posting references. Which procedure for recording transactions is quicker?

Exercise 6-4 *Identifying transactions from postings to the accounts receivable ledger*

An account in the accounts receivable ledger of McCray Company follows.

William H. Crocker

					Balance	
Date		**Jrnl. Ref.**	**Dr.**	**Cr.**	**Dr.**	**Cr.**
May 1	....				703	
10	....	S.5	1,180		1,883	
15	....	J.8		191	1,692	
21	....	CR.9		703	989	

Required

Describe the three posted transactions.

Exercise 6-5   *Posting from the purchases journal; balancing the ledgers*

The purchases journal of Best Merchandise Company follows.

Purchases Journal   Page 7

Date	Account Credited	Terms	Post. Ref.	Account Payable Cr.	Purchases Dr.	Supplies Dr.	Acct. Title	Post. Ref.	Amt. Dr.
							Other Accounts Dr.		
Sep. 2	Audio-Video	n/30		600	600				
5	Green Stationers	n/30		175		175			
13	Audio-Video	2/10 n/30		347	347				
26	Marks Equipment Co.	n/30		916			Equipment		916
30	Totals			2,038	947	175			916

Required

1. Open general ledger accounts for Supplies, Equipment, Accounts Payable, and Purchases. Post to these accounts from the purchase journal. Use dates and posting references in the ledger accounts.
2. Open accounts in the accounts payable subsidiary ledger for Audio-Video, Green Stationers, and Marks Equipment Company. Post from the purchase journal. Use dates and journal references in the ledger accounts.
3. Balance the Accounts Payable control account in the general ledger with the total of the balances in the accounts payable subsidiary ledger.

Exercise 6-6   *Using business documents to record transactions*

The following documents describe two business transactions:

Invoice	
Date:	August 14, 19X0
Sold to:	Zephyr Bicycle Shop
Sold by:	Schwinn Company
Terms:	2/10 n/30

Items Purchased	Bicycles	
Quantity	Price	Total
3	$90	$270
2	70	140
5	60	300
Total.		$710

Debit Memo	
Date:	August 20, 19X0
Issued to:	Schwinn Company
Issued by:	Zephyr Bicycle Shop

Items Returned	Bicycles	
Quantity	Price	Total
1	$90	$ 90
1	$70	70
Total.		$160

Reason:	Wrong sizes

Use the general journal to record these transactions and Zephyr's cash payment on August 21. Record the transactions first on the books of Zephyr Bicycle Shop and, second, on the books of Schwinn Company, which makes and sells bicycles. Explanations are not required. Set up your answer in the following format:

Date	Zephyr Journal Entries	Schwinn Journal Entries

Exercise 6-7 *Using the cash disbursements journal*

During July Mancini Company had the following transactions:

July 3 Paid $392 on account to Miller, Inc., net of an $8 discount.
   6 Purchased inventory for cash, $599.
  11 Paid $375 for supplies.
  13 Purchased inventory on credit from Monroe Corporation, $774.
  16 Paid $8,062 on account to LaGrange Associates; there was no discount.
  21 Purchased furniture for cash, $960.
  26 Paid $3,910 on account to Graff Software. The discount was $90.
  31 Made a semiannual interest payment of $800 on a long-term note payable. The entire payment was for interest.

Required

1. Draw a cash disbursements journal similar to the one illustrated in this chapter. Omit the check number (Ck. No.) and posting reference (Post. Ref.) columns.
2. Record the transactions in the journal. Note: One transaction should *not* be recorded in the cash disbursement journal. Which is it? In what journal does it belong?
3. Total the amount columns of the journal. Determine that the total debits equal the total credits.

Exercise 6-8 *Journalizing return and allowance transactions*

Greenberg Company records returns and allowances in its general journal. During April the company had the following transactions:

April 4 Issued credit memo to W. A. Wang for inventory that Wang returned to us . . . . $ 369

  10 Received debit memo from B. R. Inman, who purchased merchandise from us on April 6. We shipped the wrong items, and Inman returned them to us 1,238

  14 Issued debit memo for merchandise we purchased from Wyle Supply Company that was damaged in shipment. We returned the damaged inventory to Wyle 4,600

  22 Received credit memo from Dietrich Distributing Co., from whom we purchased inventory on April 15. Dietrich discovered that they overcharged us 900

Required

Journalize the transactions in the general journal. Explanations are not required.

Exercise 6-9 *Posting directly from sales invoices; balancing the ledgers*

Parson, Inc., uses its sales invoices as the sales journal and posts directly from them to the accounts receivable subsidiary ledger. During June the company made the following sales on account:

Date	Invoice No.	Customer Name	Amount
June 6	256	Anita Harris	$1,404
9	257	Forrest Ashworth.....	798
13	258	Paul Scott...........	550
16	259	Jan Childres	3,678
22	261	Anita Harris	1,915
30	262	Jan Childres	800
		Total	$9,145

Required

1. Open general ledger accounts for Accounts Receivable and Sales Revenue and post to those accounts. Use dates and use June Sales as the journal reference in the ledger accounts.
2. Open customer accounts in the accounts receivable subsidiary ledger and post to those accounts. Use dates and use invoice numbers as journal references.
3. Balance the ledgers.

Exercise 6-10   *Detecting errors in the special journals*

Monarch Sales Company uses special journals for credit sales, cash receipts, credit purchases, and cash disbursements, and the subsidiary ledgers illustrated in this chapter. During March the accountant made four errors. State the procedure that will detect each error described in the following:

(a) Posted a $40 debit to J. B. Carnes's account in the accounts receivable subsidiary ledger as a $400 credit.
(b) Added the Cash Credit column of the cash disbursements journal as $3,976 and posted this incorrect amount to the Cash account. The correct total was $3,796.
(c) Recorded receipt of $500 on account from Electrosystems, Inc., incorrectly as a credit to Sales Revenue in the cash receipts journal.
(d) Failed to post the total of the Accounts Receivable Dr./Sales Revenue Cr. column of the sales journal.

Problems   *(Group A)*

Problem 6-1A   *Using the sales, cash receipts, and general journals*

The general ledger of Sanchez Plaza, Inc., includes the following accounts, among others:

Cash	11	Sales Revenue....................	41
Accounts Receivable.............	12	Sales Discounts.................	42
Notes Receivable	15	Sales Returns and Allowances......	43
Supplies	16	Interest Revenue.................	47
Land	18		

All credit sales are on the company's standard terms of 2/10 n/30. Transactions in May that affected sales and cash receipts were as follows:

May 2   Sold inventory on credit to Dockery Co., $550.
       4   As an accommodation to a competitor, sold supplies at cost, $85, receiving cash.
       7   Cash sales for the week totaled $1,890.

9 Sold merchandise on account to A. L. Prince, $7,320.

10 Sold land that cost $10,000 for cash of $10,000.

11 Sold goods on account to Sloan Electric, $5,104.

12 Received cash from Dockery Co. in full settlement of its account receivable, net of the discount, from May 2.

14 Cash sales for the week were $2,106.

15 Sold inventory on credit to the partnership of Wilkie & Blinn, $3,650.

18 Issued credit memo to A. L. Prince for $600 of merchandise returned to us by Prince. The goods shipped were unsatisfactory.

20 Sold merchandise on account to Sloan Electric, $629.

21 Cash sales for the week were $990.

22 Received $4,000 cash from A. L. Prince in partial settlement of his account receivable. There was no discount.

25 Received cash from Wilkie & Blinn for the discounted amount of their account receivable from May 15.

25 Sold goods on account to Olsen Co., $720.

27 Collected $5,125 on a note receivable, of which $125 was interest.

28 Cash sales for the week totaled $3,774.

29 Sold inventory on account to R. O. Bankston, $242.

30 Issued credit memo to Olsen Co. for $40 for inventory they returned to us because it was damaged in shipment.

31 Received $2,720 cash on account from A. L. Prince. There was no discount.

Required

1. Sanchez Plaza records sales returns and allowances in the general journal. Use the appropriate journal to record the above transactions in a single-column sales journal (omit the Invoice No. column), a cash receipts journal, and a general journal.
2. Total each column of the cash receipts journal. Show that the total debits equal the total credits.
3. Show how postings would be made from the journals by writing the account numbers and check marks in the appropriate places in the journals.

Problem 6-2A *Using the purchases, cash disbursements, and general journals*

The general ledger of Dreyfuss Company includes the following accounts:

Cash	11	Purchases	51
Prepaid Insurance	16	Purchase Discounts	52
Supplies	17	Purchase Returns and Allowances	53
Furniture	19	Rent Expense	56
Accounts Payable	21	Utilities Expense	58

Transactions in August that affected purchases and cash disbursements were as follows:

Aug. 1 Purchased inventory on credit from Wood Co., $3,900. Terms were 2/10 n/30.

1 Paid monthly rent, debiting Rent Expense for $2,000.

5 Purchased supplies on credit terms of 2/10 n/30 from Ross Supply, $450.

8 Paid electricity bill, $588. Debit Utilities Expense.

9 Purchased furniture on account from A-1 Office Supply, $4,100. Payment terms were net 30.

10 Returned the furniture to A-1 Office Supply. It was the wrong color. Issued a debit memo for $4,100, and mailed a copy to A-1 Office Supply.

11 Paid Wood Co. the discounted amount owed on the purchase of August 1.

12 Purchased inventory on account from Wynne, Inc., $4,400. Terms were 3/10 n/30.

13 Purchased inventory for cash, $655.

14 Paid a semiannual insurance premium, debiting Prepaid Insurance, $1,200.

15 Paid our account payable to Ross Supply, less the discount, from August 5.

18 Paid gas and water bills, $196. Debit Utilities Expense.

21 Purchased inventory on credit terms of 1/10 n/45 from Software, Inc., $5,200.

21 Paid account payable to Wynne, Inc., less discount, from August 12.

22 Purchased supplies on account from Office Sales, Inc., $274. Terms were net 30.

25 Returned part of the inventory purchased on August 21 to Software, Inc., issuing a debit memo for $1,200.

31 Paid Software, Inc., the net amount owed from August 21, less the return, on August 25.

Required

1. Dreyfuss Company records purchase returns in the general journal. Use the appropriate journal to record the above transactions in a purchase journal, a cash disbursements journal (omit the Check No. column), and a general journal.

2. Total each column of the special journals. Show that the total debits equal the total credits in each special journal.

3. Show how postings would be made from the journals by writing the account numbers and check marks in the appropriate places in the journals.

Problem 6-3A *Using the sales, cash receipts, and general journals, posting, and balancing the ledgers*

During April, North Bay Sales Company had these transactions:

Apr. 2 Issued invoice no. 436 for credit sale to Vail Co., $5,200. All credit sales are made on the company's standard terms of 2/10 n/30.

3 Collected cash of $3,038 from H. M. Burger in payment of his account receivable, $3,100, within the discount period.

5 Cash sales for the week totaled $2,057.

7 Collected note receivable, $2,000, plus interest of $210.

10 Issued invoice no. 437 for sale on account to Van Allen Co., $1,850.

11 Sold supplies to an employee for cash of $54, which was the cost.

12 Received $5,096 cash from Vail Co. in full settlement of their account receivable, net of the discount, from the sale of April 2.

12 Cash sales for the week were $1,698.

14 Sold inventory on account to Electro, Inc., issuing invoice no. 438 for $2,000.

16 Issued credit memo to Electro, Inc., for $610 of merchandise returned to us by Electro. Part of the shipped goods were damaged.

19 Cash sales for the week were $3,130.

20 Received $1,813 from Van Allen Co. in full settlement of its account receivable, $1,850, from April 10.

25 Received cash of $7,455 from Electro, Inc., on account. There was no discount.

26 Cash sales for the week totaled $2,744.

27 Issued invoice no. 439 to Clay Co. for credit sales of inventory, $3,640.

28 Sold goods on credit to H. M. Burger, issuing invoice no. 440 for $2,689.

30 Issued credit memo to H. M. Burger for $873 for inventory he returned to us because it was unsatisfactory.

The general ledger of North Bay Sales Company includes the following accounts and balances at April 1:

Account Number	Account Title	Balance	Account Number	Account Title	Balance
111	Cash	$ 3,579	411	Sales Revenue......	
112	Accounts Receivable.	10,555	412	Sales Discounts.....	
116	Supplies...........	1,756	413	Sales Returns	
141	Notes Receivable ...	5,000		and Allowances...	
			418	Interest Revenue....	

North Bay's accounts receivable subsidiary ledger includes the following accounts and balances at April 1: H. M. Burger, $3,100; Clay Company, -0-; Electro, Inc., $7,455; Vail Company, -0-; and Van Allen Co., -0-.

Required

1. Open the general ledger and the accounts receivable subsidiary ledger accounts given, inserting their balances at April 1.
2. Record the transactions on page 4 of a single-column sales journal, page 13 of a cash receipts journal, and page 7 of a general journal, as appropriate. North Bay records sales returns and allowances in the general journal.
3. Post daily to the accounts receivable subsidiary ledger, and on April 30 post to the general ledger.
4. Show that the total debits equal the total credits in each special journal.
5. Balance the total of the customer account balances in the accounts receivable subsidiary ledger against the Accounts Receivable balance in the general ledger.

Problem 6-4A *Using the purchases, cash disbursements, and general journals; posting and balancing the ledgers*

Windsor Company's November purchases and cash disbursement transaction are as follows:

Nov. 1 Issued check no. 346 for $2,058 to pay ENTEL Corp. on account. Windsor received a $42 discount for prompt payment.

1 Issued check no. 347 to pay quarterly rent, debiting Prepaid Rent for $2,400.

2 Issued check no. 348 to pay net amount owed to Arbor Machine Co., $637. Windsor took a $13 discount.

5 Purchased supplies on credit terms of 1/10 n/30 from Chin Music Co., $264.

7 Paid delivery expense, issuing check no. 349 for $388. Debit Delivery Expense.

10 Purchased inventory on account from W. A. Mozart, Inc., $1,681. Payment terms were net 30.

11 Returned the inventory to W. A. Mozart, Inc. It was defective. We issued a debit memo for $1,681 and mailed a copy to Mozart.

15 Issued check no. 350 for a cash purchase of inventory, $2,889.

15 Paid semimonthly payroll with check no. 351, debiting Salary Expense for $1,595.

19 Issued check no. 352 to pay our account payable to Chin Music Co. from November 5. We did not earn the discount.

21 Purchased inventory on credit terms of 2/10 n/30 from Arbor Machine Co., $3,250.

24 Purchased machinery on credit terms of 2/10 n/30 from ENTEL Corp., $1,558.

26 Purchased supplies on account from W. A. Mozart, Inc., $309. Terms were net 30.

29   Issued check no. 353 to Arbor Machine Co., paying the net amount owed from November 21.

30   Paid semimonthly payroll with check no. 354, debiting Salary Expense for $1,595.

The general ledger of Windsor Company includes the following accounts and balances at November 1:

Account Number	Account Title	Balance	Account Number	Account Title	Balance
111	Cash	$17,674	511	Purchases	
115	Prepaid Rent.	800	512	Purchase Discounts	
116	Supplies	884	513	Purchase Returns	
151	Machinery.	33,600		and Allowances .	
211	Accounts Payable. .	2,750	521	Salary Expense. . . .	
			551	Delivery Expense . .	

Windsor's accounts payable subsidiary ledger includes the following balances at November 1: Arbor Machine Co., $650; Chin Music Co., -0-; ENTEL Corp., $2,100; and W. A. Mozart, Inc., -0-.

Required

1.   Open the general ledger and the accounts payable subsidiary ledger accounts given, inserting their balances at November 1.

2.   Record the above transactions on page 3 of a purchases journal, page 8 of a cash disbursements journal, and page 12 of a general journal, as appropriate. Windsor records purchase returns in the general journal.

3.   Post daily to the accounts payable subsidiary ledger. Post to the general ledger on November 30.

4.   Total each column of the special journals. Show that the total debits equal the total credits in each special journal.

5.   Balance the total of the creditor account balances in the accounts payable subsidiary ledger against the balance of the Accounts Payable control account in the general ledger.

Problem 6-5A   *Using all the journals, posting, and balancing the ledgers*

Kent Sales Company had these transactions during January:

Jan.   2   Issued invoice no. 191 for sale on account to L. E. Wooten, $2,350.

3   Purchased inventory on credit terms of 3/10 n/60 from Delwood Plaza, $1,900.

4   Sold inventory for cash, $808.

5   Issued check no. 473 to purchase furniture for cash, $1,087.

8   Collected interest revenue of $440.

9   Issued invoice no. 192 for sale on account to Cortez Co., $6,250.

10   Purchased inventory for cash, $776, issuing check no. 474.

12   Received $2,303 cash from L. E. Wooten in full settlement of her account receivable, net of the discount, from the sale of January 2.

13   Issued check no. 475 to pay Delwood Plaza net amount owed from January 3, $1,843. We received a $57 discount.

13 Purchased supplies on account from Havrilla Corp., $689. Terms were net end-of-month.

15 Sold inventory on account to J. R. Wakeland, issuing invoice no. 193 for $743.

17 Issued credit memo to J. R. Wakeland for $743 for defective merchandise returned to us by Wakeland.

18 Issued invoice no. 194 for credit sale to L. E. Wooten, $1,825.

19 Received $6,125 from Cortez Co. in full settlement of its account receivable, $6,250, from January 9.

20 Purchased inventory on credit terms of net 30 from Jasper Sales, $2,150.

22 Purchased furniture on credit terms of 3/10 n/60 from Delwood Plaza, $775.

22 Issued check no. 476 to pay for insurance coverage, debiting Prepaid Insurance for $1,345.

24 Sold supplies to an employee for cash of $86, which was their cost.

25 Issued check no. 477 to pay utilities. Debit Utilities Expense for $388.

28 Purchased inventory on credit terms of 2/10 n/30 from Havrilla Corp., $421.

29 Returned damaged inventory to Havrilla Corp., issuing a debit memo for $421.

29 Sold goods on account to Cortez Co., issuing invoice no. 195 for $567.

30 Issued check no. 478 to pay Havrilla Corp. $689 on account from January 13.

31 Received $1,825 on account from L. E. Wooten on credit sale of January 18. There was no discount.

31 Issued check no. 479 to pay monthly salaries, debiting Salary Expense for $2,600.

Required

1. Open the following general ledger accounts using the account numbers given:

Cash......................	111	Sales Returns and Allowances ...	413
Accounts Receivable...........	112	Interest Revenue	419
Supplies.....................	116	Purchases....................	511
Prepaid Insurance..............	117	Purchase Discounts............	512
Furniture	151	Purchase Returns	
Accounts Payable	211	and Allowances.............	513
Sales Revenue	411	Salary Expense	531
Sales Discounts	412	Utilities Expense	541

2. Open these accounts in the subsidiary ledgers. Accounts receivable subsidiary ledger: Cortez Co., J. R. Wakeland, and L. E. Wooten.
   Accounts payable subsidiary ledger: Delwood Plaza, Havrilla Corp., and Jasper Sales.

3. Enter the transactions in a sales journal (page 8), a cash receipts journal (page 3), a purchases journal (page 6), a cash disbursements journal (page 9), and a general journal (page 4), as appropriate.

4. Post daily to the accounts receivable subsidiary ledger and to the accounts payable subsidiary ledger. On January 31 post to the general ledger.

5. Total each column of the special journals. Show that the total debits equal the total credits in each special journal.

6. Balance the total of the customer account balances in the accounts receivable subsidiary ledger against Accounts Receivable in the general ledger. Do the same for the accounts payable subsidiary ledger and Accounts Payable in the general ledger.

Problem 6-6A   *Correcting errors in the cash receipts journal*

The cash receipts journal below contains five entries. All five entries are for legitimate cash receipt transactions, but the journal contains some errors in recording the transactions. In fact, only one entry is correct, and each of the other four entries contains one error.

Cash Receipts Journal　　　　　　　　　　　　　　　　　　　**Page 13**

Date	Debits		Credits				
	Cash	Sales Discounts	Accounts Receivable	Sales Revenue	Other Accounts		
					Account Title	P.R.	Amount
5/6		500		500			
7	429	22			Ron Bynum	✓	451
12	3170				Note Receivable	13	3000
					Interest Revenue	45	170
18				330			
24	1100		770				
	4699	522	770	830	Totals		3621
	(11)	(42)	(12)	(41)			(✓)

Total Dr. = $5,221　　　　　　　　　　Total Cr. = $5221

Required

1. Identify the correct entry.
2. Identify the error in each of the other four entries.
3. Using the following format, prepare a corrected cash receipts journal.

Cash Receipts Journal　　　　　　　　　　　　　　　　　　　**Page 13**

Date	Debits		Credits				
	Cash	Sales Discounts	Accounts Receivable	Sales Revenue	Other Accounts		
					Account Title	P.R.	Amount
5/6							
7					Ron Bynum	✓	
12					Note Receivable	13	
					Interest Revenue	45	
18							
24							
	5199	22	1221	830	Totals		3170
	(11)	(42)	(12)	(41)			(✓)

Total Dr. = $5,221　　　　　　　　　　Total Cr. = $5,221

(Group B)

Problem 6-1B　*Using the sales, cash receipts, and general journals*

The general ledger of Carmel Trading Company includes the following accounts:

Cash	111	Sales Revenue.................	411
Accounts Receivable............	112	Sales Discounts................	412
Notes Receivable	115	Sales Returns and Allowances.....	413
Equipment	141	Interest Revenue...............	417
Land	142	Gain on Sale of Land............	418

All credit sales are on the company's standard terms of 2/10 n/30. Transactions in February that affected sales and cash receipts were as follows:

Feb. 1   Sold inventory on credit to G. M. Titcher, $900.

5   As an accommodation to another company, sold new equipment for its cost of $770, receiving cash in this amount.

6   Cash sales for the week totaled $1,007.

8   Sold merchandise on account to McNair Co., $2,830.

9   Sold land that cost $22,000 for cash of $40,000, which includes a gain of $18,000.

11   Sold goods on account to Nickerson Builders, $6,099.

11   Received cash from G. M. Titcher in full settlement of her account receivable, net of the discount, from February 1.

13   Cash sales for the week were $1,995.

15   Sold inventory on credit to Montez and Montez, a partnership, $800.

18   Issued credit memo to McNair Co. for $120 of merchandise returned to us by McNair. The goods we shipped were unsatisfactory.

19   Sold merchandise on account to Nickerson Builders, $3,900.

20   Cash sales for the week were $2,330.

21   Received $1,200 cash from McNair Co. in partial settlement of their account receivable. There was no discount.

22   Received cash from Montez and Montez for the discounted amount of their account receivable from February 15.

22   Sold goods on account to Diamond Co., $2,022.

25   Collected $4,200 on a note receivable, of which $200 was interest.

27   Cash sales for the week totaled $2,970.

27   Sold inventory on account to Littleton Corporation, $2,290.

28   Issued credit memo to Diamond Co. for $680 for damaged goods they returned to us.

28   Received $1,510 cash on account from McNair Co. There was no discount.

Required

1.   Use the appropriate journal to record the above transactions in a single-column sales journal (omit the Invoice No. column), a cash receipts journal, and a general journal. Carmel records sales returns and allowances in the general journal.

2.   Total each column of the cash receipts journal. Determine that the total debits equal the total credits.

3.   Show how postings would be made from the journals by writing the account numbers and check marks in the appropriate places in the journals.

Problem 6-2B   *Using the purchases, cash disbursements, and general journals*

The general ledger of Enfield Corporation includes the following accounts:

Cash	111	Purchases	511
Prepaid Insurance	116	Purchase Discounts	512
Supplies	117	Purchase Returns and Allowances	513
Equipment	149	Rent Expense	562
Accounts Payable	211	Utilities Expense	565

Transactions in March that affected purchases and cash disbursements were as follows:

Mar. 1   Paid monthly rent, debiting Rent Expense for $1,600.

3   Purchased inventory on credit from Broussard Co., $4,600. Terms were 2/15 n/45.

6   Purchased supplies on credit terms of 2/10 n/30 from Harmon Sales, $800.

7   Paid gas and water bills, $406. Debit Utilities Expenses.

10   Purchased equipment on account from Lancer Co., $1,050. Payment terms were 2/10 n/30.

11   Returned the equipment to Lancer Co. It was defective. We issued a debit memo for $1,050 and mailed a copy to Lancer.

12   Paid Broussard Co. the discounted amount owed on the purchase of March 3.

12   Purchased inventory on account from Lancer Co., $1,100. Terms were 2/10 n/30.

14   Purchased inventory for cash, $1,585.

15   Paid an insurance premium, debiting Prepaid Insurance, $2,416.

16   Paid our account payable to Harmon Sales, less the discount, from March 6.

17   Paid electricity bill, $165. Debit Utilities Expense.

20   Paid account payable to Lancer Co., less the discount, from March 12.

21   Purchased supplies on account from Master Supply, $754. Terms were net 30.

22   Purchased inventory on credit terms of 1/10 n/30 from Linz Brothers, $3,400.

26   Returned inventory purchased on March 22, to Linz Brothers, issuing a debit memo for $500.

31   Paid Linz Brothers the net amount owed from March 22, less the return on March 26.

Required

1.   Use the appropriate journal to record the above transactions in a purchase journal, a cash disbursements journal (omit the Check No. column), and a general journal. Enfield Corporation records purchase returns in the general journal.

2.   Total each column of the special journals. Show that the total debits equal the total credits in each special journal.

3.   Show how postings would be made from the journals by writing the account numbers and check marks in the appropriate places in the journals.

Problem 6-3B   *Using the sales, cash receipts, and general journal, posting, and balancing the ledgers*

During June, Harwood Systems engaged in the following transactions:

June 1   Issued invoice no. 113 for credit sale to Aspen Co., $4,750. All credit sales are on the company's standard terms of 2/10 n/30.

3   Collected cash of $882 from Leah Burnet in payment of her account receivable, $900, within the discount period.

6   Cash sales for the week totaled $1,748.

7   Collected note receivable, $3,400, plus interest of $367.

9   Issued invoice no. 114 for sale on account to Wilder Co., $4,300.

11   Received $4,655 cash from Aspen Co. in full settlement of its account receivable, net of the discount, from the sale on June 1.

13   Cash sales for the week were $2,964.

14   Sold inventory on account to Goss Corp., issuing invoice no. 115 for $858.

15   Issued credit memo to Goss Corp. for $154 of merchandise returned to us by Goss. Part of the goods we shipped were defective.

19   Received $4,214 from Wilder Co. in full settlement of its account receivable, $4,300, from June 9.

20   Cash sales for the week were $2,175.

22   Received cash of $2,904 from Goss Corporation on account. There was no discount.

24   Sold supplies to an employee for cash of $106, which was their cost.

27 Cash Sales for the week totaled $1,650.

28 Issued invoice no. 116 to Thompson Co. for credit sale of inventory, $5,194.

29 Sold goods on credit to Leah Burnett, issuing invoice no. 117 for $3,819.

29 Issued credit memo to Leah Burnet for $1,397 of inventory she returned to us because it was unsatisfactory.

The general ledger of Harwood Systems includes the following accounts and balances at June 1:

Account Number	Account Title	Balance	Account Number	Account Title	Balance
111	Cash..............	$4,217	411	Sales Revenue......	
112	Accounts Receivable.	3,804	412	Sales Discounts.....	
116	Supplies...........	1,290	413	Sales Returns and Allowances...	
141	Notes Receivable....	7,100			
			418	Interest Revenue	

Harwood's accounts receivable subsidiary ledger includes the following accounts and balances at June 1: Aspen Company, -0-; Leah Burnet, $900; Goss Corporation, $2,904; Thompson Company, -0-; and Wilder Co., -0-.

Required

1. Open the general ledger and the accounts receivable subsidiary ledger accounts given, inserting their balances at June 1.

2. Record the above transactions on page 6 of a single-column sales journal, page 9 of a cash receipts journal, and page 5 of a general journal, as appropriate. Harwood Systems records sales returns and allowances in the general journal.

3. Post daily to the accounts receivable subsidiary ledger. On June 30 post to the general ledger.

4. Total each column of the special journals. Show that the total debits equal the total credits in each special journal.

5. Balance the total of the customer account balances in the accounts receivable subsidiary ledger against the Accounts Receivable balance in the general ledger.

Problem 6-4B *Using the purchases, cash disbursements, and general journals; posting and balancing the ledgers*

Montana Company's September transactions affecting purchases and cash disbursements were as follows:

Sep. 1 Issued check no. 406 for $1,176 to pay AmeriCorp. on account. Montana received a $24 discount for prompt payment.

1 Issued check no. 407 to pay quarterly rent, debiting Prepaid Rent for $1,800.

2 Issued check no. 408 to pay net amount owed to Lynn Co., $1,455. Montana took a $45 discount.

5 Purchased supplies on credit terms of 2/10 n/30 from Westside Supply, $121.

7 Paid delivery expense, issuing check no. 409 for $739. Debit Delivery Expense.

10 Purchased inventory on account from Hayden, Inc., $2,008. Payment terms were net 30.

11 Returned the inventory to Hayden, Inc., because it was defective. We issued a debit memo for $2,008 and mailed a copy to Hayden.

15 Issued check no. 410 for a cash purchase of inventory, $2,332.

15 Paid semimonthly payroll with check no. 411, debiting Salary Expense for $1,224.

19 Issued check no. 412 to pay our account payable to Westside Supply from September 5. We did not earn the discount.

21 Purchased inventory on credit terms of 2/10 n/30 from Lynn Co., $4,150.

24 Purchased machinery on credit terms of 2/10 n/30 from AmeriCorp., $3,195.

26 Purchased supplies on account from Hayden, Inc., $467. Terms were net 30.

29 Issued check no. 413 to Lynn Co., paying the net amount owed from September 21.

30 Paid semimonthly payroll with check no. 414, debiting Salary Expense for $1,224.

The general ledger of Montana Company includes the following accounts and balances at September 1:

Account Number	Account Title	Balance	Account Number	Account Title	Balance
111	Cash	$15,996	511	Purchases	
115	Prepaid Rent.	600	512	Purchase Discounts	
116	Supplies	703	513	Purchase Returns	
151	Machinery.	21,800		and Allowances .	
211	Accounts Payable. .	2,700	521	Salary Expense. . . .	
			551	Delivery Expense . .	

Montana's accounts payable subsidiary ledger includes the following balances at September 1: AmeriCorp., $1,200; Hayden, Inc., -0-; Lynn Company, $1,500; and Westside Supply, -0-.

Required

1. Open the general ledger and the accounts payable subsidiary ledger accounts, inserting their balances at September 1.

2. Record the above transactions on page 10 of a purchases journal, page 5 of a cash disbursements journal, and page 8 of a general journal, as appropriate. Montana records purchase returns in the general journal.

3. Post daily to the accounts payable subsidiary ledger. On September 30 post to the general ledger.

4. Total each column of the special journals. Determine that the total debits equal the total credits in each special journal.

5. Balance the total of the creditor account balances in the accounts payable subsidiary ledger against the balance of the Accounts Payable control account in the general ledger.

Problem 6-5B *Using all the journals, posting, and balancing the ledgers*

Lang Company completed the following transactions during July:

July 2 Issued invoice no. 913 for sale on account to N. J. Seiko, $4,100.

3 Purchased inventory on credit terms of 3/10 n/60 from Chicosky Co., $2,467.

5 Sold inventory for cash, $1,077.

5 Issued check no. 532 to purchase furniture for cash, $2,185.

8 Collected interest revenue of $1,775.

9 Issued invoice no. 914 for sale on account to Bell Co., $5,550.

10 Purchased inventory for cash, $1,143, issuing check no. 533.

12 Received $4,018 cash from N. J. Seiko in full settlement of her account receivable, net of the discount, from the sale on July 2.

13 Issued check no. 534 to pay Chicosky Co. the net amount owed from July 3, $2,393. We received a $74 discount.

13 Purchased supplies on account from Manley, Inc., $441. Terms were net end-of-month.

15 Sold inventory on account to M. O. Brown, issuing invoice no. 915 for $665.

17 Issued credit memo to M. O. Brown for $665 for defective merchandise returned to us by Brown.

18 Issued invoice no. 916 for credit sale to N. J. Seiko, $357.

19 Received $5,439 from Bell Co. in full settlement of its account receivable, $5,550, from July 9.

20 Purchased inventory on credit terms of net 30 from Sims Distributing, $2,047.

22 Purchased furniture on credit terms of 3/10 n/60 from Chicosky Co., $645.

22 Issued check no. 535 to pay for insurance coverage, debiting Prepaid Insurance for $1,000.

24 Sold supplies to an employee for cash of $54, which was their cost.

25 Issued check no. 536 to pay utilities, $453. Debit Utilities Expense.

28 Purchased inventory on credit terms of 2/10 n/30 from Manley, Inc., $675.

29 Returned damaged inventory to Manley, Inc., issuing a debit memo for $675.

29 Sold goods on account to Bell Co., issuing invoice no. 917 for $496.

30 Issued check no. 537 to pay Manley, Inc., $441 on account from July 13.

31 Received $357 on account from N. J. Seiko on credit sale of January 18. There was no discount.

31 Issued check no. 538 to pay monthly salaries, debiting Salary Expense for $2,347.

Required

1. Open the following general ledger accounts using the account numbers given:

Cash........................	111	Sales Returns	
Accounts Receivable...........	112	and Allowances.............	413
Supplies.....................	116	Interest Revenue..............	419
Prepaid Insurance.............	117	Purchases....................	511
Furniture....................	151	Purchase Discounts............	512
Accounts Payable.............	211	Purchase Returns	
Sales Revenue................	411	and Allowances.............	513
Sales Discounts...............	412	Salary Expense...............	531
		Utilities Expense..............	541

2. Open these accounts in the subsidiary ledgers:
   Accounts receivable subsidiary ledger: Bell Co., M. O. Brown, and N. J. Seiko.
   Accounts payable subsidiary ledger: Chicosky Co., Manley, Inc., and Sims Distributing.

3. Enter the transactions in a sales journal (page 7), a cash receipts journal (page 5), a purchases journal (page 10), a cash disbursements journal (page 8), and a general journal (page 6), as appropriate.

4. Post daily to the accounts receivable subsidiary ledger and the accounts payable subsidiary ledger. On July 31 post to the general ledger.

5. Total each column of the special journals. Show that the total debits equal the total credits in each special journal.

6. Balance the total of the customer account balances in the accounts receivable subsidiary ledger against Accounts Receivable in the general ledger. Do the same for the accounts payable subsidiary ledger and Accounts Payable in the general ledger.

Problem 6-6B *Correcting errors in the cash receipts journal*

The cash receipts journal below contains five entries. All five entries are for legitimate cash receipt transactions, but the journal contains some errors in recording the transactions. In fact, only one entry is correct, and each of the other four entries contains one error.

Cash Receipts Journal   **Page 5**

| | Debits | | Credits | | | | |
| | | | | | Other Accounts | | |
Date	Cash	Sales Discounts	Accounts Receivable	Sales Revenue	Account Title	P.R.	Amount
7/5	611	34	645		Meg Davis	✓	
9			229	229	Lou Metz	✓	
10	8000			8000	Land	19	
19	73						
31	1060			1133			
	9744	34	874	9362	Totals		
	(11)	(42)	(12)	(41)			(✓)

Total Dr. = $9,778   Total Cr. = $10,236

Required

1. Identify the correct entry.
2. Identify the error in each of the other four entries.
3. Using the following format, prepare a corrected cash receipts journal.

Cash Receipts Journal   **Page 5**

| | Debits | | Credits | | | | |
| | | | | | Other Accounts | | |
Date	Cash	Sales Discounts	Accounts Receivable	Sales Revenue	Account Title	P.R.	Amount
7/5					Meg Davis	✓	
9					Lou Metz	✓	
10					Land	19	
19							
31							
	9973	34	874	1133	Totals		8000
	(11)	(42)	(12)	(41)			(✓)

Total Dr. = $10,007   Total Cr. = $10,007

Decision Problem

Reconstructing transactions from amounts posted to the accounts receivable ledger

A fire destroyed some accounting records of Dimkoff Company. The owner, Greg Dimkoff, asks your help in reconstructing the records. *He needs to know the beginning and ending balances of Accounts Receivable and the credit sales and cash receipts on account from customers during March.* All Dimkoff Company's sales are on credit, with payment terms of 2/10 n/30. All cash receipts on account reached Dimkoff within the 10-day discount period, except as noted. The only accounting record preserved from the fire is the accounts receivable subsidiary ledger, which follows.

Grant Adams

Date	Item	Jrnl. Ref.	Debit	Credit	Balance
Mar. 8		S.6	2,178		2,178
16		S.6	903		3,081
18		CR.8		2,178	903
19		J.5		221	682
27		CR.8		682	-0-

Lou Gross

Date	Item	Jrnl. Ref.	Debit	Credit	Balance
Mar. 1	Balance				1,096
5		CR.8		1,096	-0-
11		S.6	396		396
21		CR.8		396	-0-
24		S.6	2,566		2,566

Norris Associates

Date	Item	Jrnl. Ref.	Debit	Credit	Balance
Mar. 1	Balance				883
15		S.6	2,635		3,518
29		CR.8		883*	2,635

---

* Cash receipt did not occur within the discount period.

Suzuki, Inc.

Date	Item	Jrnl. Ref.	Debit	Credit	Balance
Mar. 1	Balance				440
3		CR.8		440	-0-
25		S.6	3,655		3,655
29		S.6	1,123		4,778

Hint: Use the journal references to reconstruct the entries in the sales journal and the cash receipts journal. Then compute the amounts for total credit sales and total cash receipts on account. Round all sales discounts to the nearest dollar.

Answers to Self-Study Questions

1. c
2. a
3. d
4. b
5. c [523 × 3 (one debit, one credit, and one to the accounts receivable ledger) = 1,569]

6. b
7. b
8. d
9. a
10. a

Practice Set

DeHaviland Company closes its books and prepares financial statements at the end of each month. The company completed the following transactions during August:

Aug. 1   Issued check no. 682 for August office rent of $2,000. (Debit Rent Expense.)

2   Issued check no. 683 to pay salaries of $1,240, which includes salary payable of $930 from July 31.

2   Issued invoice no. 503 for sale on account to R. T. Loeb, $600.

3   Purchased inventory on credit terms of 1/15 n/60 from Grant Publishers, $1,400.

4   Received net amount of cash on account from Fullam Company, $2,156, within the discount period.

4   Sold inventory for cash, $330.

5   Issued credit memo no. 267 to Park-Hee, Inc., for merchandise returned to us, $550.

5   Issued check no. 684 to purchase supplies for cash, $780.

6   Collected interest revenue of $1,100.

7   Issued invoice no. 504 for sale on account to K. D. Skipper, $2,400.

8   Purchased inventory on credit terms of 3/15 n/30 from Beaver Corporation, $4,300.

8   Issued check no. 685 to pay Federal Company $2,600 of the amount owed at July 31. This payment occurred after the end of the discount period.

9   Issued invoice no. 505 for sale on account to Iba & Frazier, $5,100.

11   Issued check no. 686 to pay Grant Publishers the net amount owed from August 3.

12   Received cash from R. T. Loeb in full settlement of her account receivable from August 2.

15   Sold inventory on account to Fullam Company, issuing invoice no. 506 for $466.

16   Issued check no. 687 to pay salary expense of $1,240.

18   Received $4,998 from Iba & Frazier in full settlement of their account receivable from August 9.

19   Purchased inventory for cash, $850, issuing check no. 688.

20   Purchased inventory on credit terms of net 30 from McMinn Sales, $2,150.

22   Purchased furniture on credit terms of 3/15 n/60 from Beaver Corporation, $510.

22   Issued check no. 689 to pay Beaver Corporation the net amount owed from August 8.

24   Received half the July 31 amount receivable from K. D. Skipper — after the end of the discount period.

25   Issued check no. 690 to pay utilities, $432.

26 Purchased supplies on credit terms of 2/10 n/30 from Federal Company, $180.

27 Returned damaged inventory to company from whom we made the cash purchase on August 19, receiving cash of $850.

28 Paid the amount payable to McMinn Sales at July 31, issuing check no. 691. There was no discount.

29 Sold goods on account to Iba & Frazier, issuing invoice no. 507 for $3,970.

30 Granted a sales allowance of $175 to K. D. Skipper, issuing credit memo no. 268.

31 Received $7,000 on account from Park-Hee, Inc. There was no discount.

31 Purchased inventory on credit terms of 1/10 n/30 from Suncrest Supply, $1,330.

31 Issued check no. 692 to J. M. DeHaviland, owner of the business, for personal withdrawal, $1,700.

Required:

1. Open these accounts with their account numbers and July 31 balances in the various ledgers.

General Ledger:

101	Cash	$ 4,490
102	Accounts Receivable	22,560
104	Interest Receivable	
105	Inventory	41,800
109	Supplies	1,340
117	Prepaid Insurance	2,200
140	Note Receivable, Long-term	11,000
160	Furniture	37,270
161	Accumulated Depreciation	10,550
201	Accounts Payable	19,050
204	Salary Payable	930
207	Interest Payable	320
208	Unearned Sales Revenue	
220	Note Payable, Long-term	42,000
301	J. M. DeHaviland, Capital	47,810
302	J. M. DeHaviland, Withdrawals	
400	Income Summary	
401	Sales Revenue	
402	Sales Discounts	
403	Sales Returns and Allowances	
410	Interest Revenue	
501	Purchases	
502	Purchase Discounts	
503	Purchase Returns and Allowances	
510	Salary Expense	
513	Rent Expense	
514	Depreciation Expense	

516   Insurance Expense . . . .

517   Utilities Expense . . . .

519   Supplies Expense . . . .

523   Interest Expense . . . .

Accounts Receivable Subsidiary Ledger: Fullam Company, $2,200; Iba & Frazier; R. T. Loeb; Park-Hee, Inc., $11,590; K. D. Skipper, $8,770.

Accounts Payable Subsidiary Ledger: Beaver Corporation; Federal Company, $12,600; Grant Publishers; McMinn Sales, $6,450; Suncrest Supply.

2. Journalize the August transactions in a sales journal (page 4), a cash receipts journal (page 11), a purchases journal (page 8), a cash disbursements journal (page 5), and a general journal (page 9). Use the journals as illustrated in Chapter 6. DeHaviland makes all credit sales on terms of 2/10 n/30.

3. Post daily to the accounts receivable subsidiary ledger and the accounts payable subsidiary ledger. On August 31, post to the general ledger.

4. Prepare a trial balance in the Trial Balance columns of a work sheet, and use the following information to complete the work sheet for the month ended August 31:
    a. Accrued interest revenue, $100
    b. Supplies on hand, $990.
    c. Prepaid insurance expired, $550.
    d. Depreciation expense, $230.
    e. Accrued salary expense, $1,030.
    f. Accrued interest expense, $320.
    g. Unearned sales revenue, $450.*
    h. Inventory on hand, $47,700.
    * Sales Revenue was credited when collected in advance. At August 31, $450 of unearned sales revenue needs to be recorded.

5. Prepare DeHaviland's multiple-step income statement and statement of owner's equity for August. Prepare the balance sheet at August 31.

6. Journalize and post the adjusting and closing entries.

7. Prepare a post-closing trial balance at August 31. Also, balance the total of the customer accounts in the accounts receivable subsidiary ledger against the Accounts Receivable balance in the general ledger. Do the same for the accounts payable subsidiary ledger and Accounts Payable in the general ledger.

Internal Control and Cash Transactions

You learned in Chapter 6 that a well-designed accounting system helps managers control the business. Chapter 7 looks in more detail at **internal control,** which is the organizational plan and all the related measures adopted by an entity to

1. Safeguard assets
2. Ensure accurate and reliable accounting records
3. Promote operational efficiency
4. Encourage adherence to company policies

OBJECTIVE 1
Define internal control

Internal controls include *administrative controls* and *accounting controls.*

Administrative controls include the plan of organization, the methods, and the procedures that help managers achieve operational efficiency and adherence to company policies. The goal of administrative controls is to eliminate waste.

Accounting controls include the methods and procedures that safeguard assets, authorize transactions, and ensure the accuracy of the financial records. Of these elements, safeguarding assets is most important. This chapter focuses on internal accounting controls, with emphasis on cash transactions.

The need for laws requiring internal control has received increased attention in the 1970s and 1980s. During this time many illegal payments, embezzlements, and other criminal business practices came to light. Concerned citizens wanted to know why the companies' internal controls had failed to alert management that these illegalities had occurred. To answer these growing worries, the U.S. Congress passed the Foreign Corrupt Practices Act. This act requires companies under SEC jurisdiction to maintain an appropriate system of internal control whether or not they have foreign operations.[1] Thus its title is a bit misleading.

---

[1] The Foreign Corrupt Practices Act contains specific prohibitions against bribery and other corrupt practices in addition to requiring the maintenance of accounting records in reasonable detail and accuracy.

EXHIBIT 7-1   *Management Statement about Internal Controls*
General Motors Corporation

Responsibilities for Financial Statements

The following financial statements of General Motors Corporation . . . were prepared by the management which is responsible for their integrity and objectivity.

Management is further responsible for maintaining a system of *internal accounting controls* designed to provide reasonable assurance that the books and records reflect the transactions of the companies and that the established policies and procedures are carefully followed. Perhaps the most important feature in the *system of control* is that it is continually reviewed for its effectiveness and is augmented by written policies and guidelines, the careful selection and training of qualified personnel, and a strong program of *internal audit.*

Deloitte Haskins & Sells, independent certified public accountants, are engaged to examine the financial statements of General Motors Corporation.

The Board of Directors, through the Audit Committee . . . is responsible for assuring that management fulfills its responsibilities in the preparation of the financial statements. . . . To assure complete independence, Deloitte Haskins & Sells have full and free access to meet with the Committee . . . to discuss . . . the adequacy of *internal controls.* . . .

Signed by the *Chairman of the Board of Directors* and the *Chief Financial Officer*

Wise management has always kept a system of strong internal control, so before the law was enacted many businesses had already met the requirements for internal control policies. However, the Foreign Corrupt Practices Act has affected companies' approaches to internal control. Formerly, internal control was viewed as an auditing consideration. The act shifted responsibility for internal control to company managers. Furthermore, boards of directors, to comply with the act and with other SEC requirements, compile written evidence of management's evaluations and ongoing reviews of the internal control system.

Exhibit 7-1 presents excerpts from General Motors Management's Statement, included in its annual report. Note the frequent references to internal controls and audits and observe that the chairman of the board of directors, who heads the entire organization, and the chief financial officer, who is one of the top five officers of the company, sign the statement. Likewise, management teams in other businesses state their responsibility for internal control in their annual reports.

Effective Systems of Internal Control _____

Whether the business is General Motors or a local department store, its system of internal controls, if effective, has the following noteworthy characteristics.

Competent and Reliable Personnel

OBJECTIVE 2

Identify the characteristics of an effective system of internal control

Employees should be *competent* and *reliable.* Paying top salaries to attract top-quality employees, training them to do their job well, and supervising their work all help to build a competent staff. A business adds flexibility to its staffing by rotating employees through various jobs. If one employee is sick or on vacation, a second employee is already trained to step in and do the job.

Rotating employees through various jobs also promotes reliability. An employee is less likely to handle her job improperly if she knows that her misconduct may come to light when a second employee takes over the job. This same reasoning leads businesses to require that employees take an annual vacation. A second employee, stepping in to handle the position, may uncover any wrongdoing.

Assignment of Responsibilities

In a business with an effective internal control system, no important duty is overlooked. A model of such assignment of responsibilities appears in the corporate organizational chart in Exhibit 7-2.

Notice that the corporation has a vice-president of finance and accounting.

EXHIBIT 7-2   *Organization Chart of a Corporation*

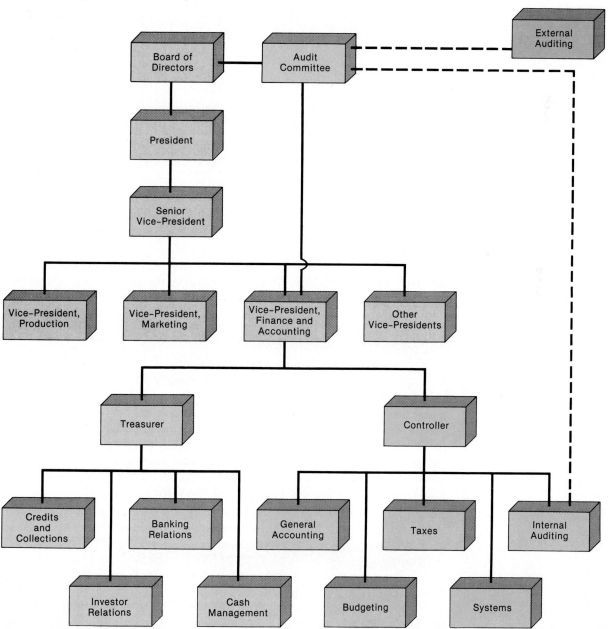

Two other officers, the treasurer and the controller, report to the vice-president. The treasurer is responsible for cash management. The controller performs accounting duties.

Within this organization, the controller may be responsible for approving invoices for payment, and the treasurer may actually sign the checks. Working under the controller, one accountant may be responsible for property taxes, another accountant for income taxes. In sum, all duties are clearly defined and assigned to individuals who bear responsibility for carrying them out.

Proper Authorization

An organization generally has a written set of rules that outlines approved procedures. Any deviation from standard policy requires *proper authorization*. For example, managers or assistant managers of retail stores must approve customer checks for amounts above the store's usual limit. Likewise, deans or department chairpersons of colleges and universities must give the authorization for a freshman, sophomore, or junior to enroll in courses otherwise restricted to seniors.

Separation of Duties

Smart management divides the responsibilities for transactions between two or more people or departments. Separation of duties limits the chances for fraud and also promotes the accuracy of the accounting records. This crucial and often neglected component of the internal control system may be subdivided into four parts.

1. *Separation of operations from accounting.* The entire accounting function should be completely separate from operating departments so that objective records may be kept. For example, product inspectors, not machine operators, should count units produced by a manufacturing process. Accountants, not salespersons, should keep inventory records. Observe the separation of accounting from production and marketing in Exhibit 7-2.

2. *Separation of the custody of assets from accounting.* To reduce temptation and fraud, the accountant should not handle cash, and the cashier should not have access to the accounting records. If one employee had both cash-handling and accounting duties, this person could steal cash and conceal the theft by making a bogus entry on the books. We see this component of internal control in the organization chart in Exhibit 7-2. Note that the treasurer has custody of the cash and the controller accounts for the cash. Neither person has both responsibilities.

Warehouse employees with no accounting duties should handle inventory. If they were allowed to account for the inventory, they could steal it and write it off as obsolete. In a computerized accounting system, a person with custody of assets should not have access to the computer programs. Similarly, the programmer should not have access to tempting assets like cash.

3. *Separation of the authorization of transactions from the custody of related assets.* If possible, persons who authorize transactions should not handle the related asset. For example, the same individual should not authorize the payment of a supplier's invoice and also sign the check to pay the bill. With both duties, the person can authorize payments to himself and then sign the checks. By separating these duties, only legitimate bills are paid.

For another example, an individual who handles cash receipts should not have the authority to write off accounts receivable. (Businesses that sell on credit declare certain of their accounts receivable as uncollectible, realizing that these receivables will never be collected. Chapter 8 looks at uncollectible accounts receivable in detail.) Suppose the company shown in Exhibit 7-2 employs V. Saucier. He works in Credits and Collections (under the treasurer) and handles cash receipts from customers.

Among the business's accounts receivable in the subsidiary ledger is Gina Kowalski's $500 balance. Saucier could label Kowalski's account as uncollectible, and the business might cease trying to collect from her. When Kowalski mails a $500 check to pay off her balance, Saucier forges the endorsement and pockets the money. Kowalski, of course, has no reason to notify anyone else at the business that she has mailed a check, so Saucier's crime goes undetected. This theft would have been avoided by denying Saucier either the access to cash receipts or the authority to declare accounts uncollectible.

4. Separation of duties within the accounting function. Independent performance of various phases of accounting helps to minimize errors and the opportunities for fraud. For example, different accountants in a manual system keep the cash receipts journal and the cash disbursements journal. In a computer system, the employees who enter data into the computer do not also operate the machines.

Internal and External Audits

It is not economically feasible for auditors to examine all the transactions during a period, so they must rely to some degree on the accounting system to produce accurate accounting records. To gauge the reliability of the company's accounting system, auditors evaluate its system of internal controls. Auditors also spot the weaknesses in the system and recommend corrections. Auditors offer *objectivity* in their reports, while managers immersed in operations may overlook weaknesses.

Audits are internal or external. Exhibit 7-2 shows *internal auditors* as employees of the business, under the controller. Some organizations have the internal auditors report directly to the audit committee. Throughout the year, they audit various segments of the organization. *External auditors* are entirely independent of the business. These people, employed by an accounting firm, are hired by an entity as outsiders to audit the entity as a whole. Both groups of auditors are independent of the operations they examine, and their reviews of internal controls often are similar.

An auditor may find that an employee has both cash-handling and cash-accounting duties or may learn that a cash shortage has resulted from lax efforts to collect accounts receivable. In such cases, the auditor suggests improvements. Auditors' recommendations assist the business in running smoothly and economically.

Documents and Records

Business *documents and records* vary considerably, from source documents like sales invoices and purchase orders to special journals and subsidiary ledgers. Specially designed records—for example, the special journals discussed in the last chapter—speed the flow of paper work and enhance efficiency.

Documents should be prenumbered. A gap in the numbered sequence calls attention to a missing document.

Prenumbering cash sale receipts discourages theft by the cashier because the copy retained by the cashier, which lists the amount of the sale, can be checked against the actual amount of cash received. If the receipts are not prenumbered, the cashier can destroy the copy and pocket the cash sale amount. However, if the receipts are prenumbered, the missing copy can easily be identified.

Limitations of Internal Control

Most internal control measures can be overcome. Systems designed to thwart an *individual* employee's fraud can be beaten by two or more employees working as a team—colluding—to defraud the firm. Consider a movie theater. The ticket seller takes in the cash, and the ticket taker tears the tickets in half so they cannot be reused, retaining the torn ticket stub. But suppose they put a scheme together in which the ticket seller pockets the cash for ten tickets and the ticket taker pockets ten stubs. Who would catch them? The manager could take the additional control measure of counting the people in the theater and matching that figure against the number of ticket stubs retained. But that takes time away from other duties. As you see, the stricter the internal control system, the more expensive it becomes.

A system of internal control that is too complex may strangle people in red tape. Efficiency and control are hurt rather than helped. The more complicated the system, the more time and money it takes to maintain. Just how tight should an internal control system be? Managers must make sensible judgments. Investments in internal control must be judged in the light of the costs and benefits.

The Bank Account as a Control Device

Keeping cash in a *bank account* is part of internal control because banks have established practices for safeguarding cash. Banks also provide depositors with detailed records of cash transactions. To take full advantage of these control features, the business should deposit all cash receipts in the bank account and make all cash payments through it (except petty cash disbursements, which we look at later). We now discuss banking records and documents.

For many businesses, cash is the most important asset. After all, cash is the most common means of exchange, and most transactions ultimately affect cash.

Cash is the most tempting asset for theft. Consequently, internal controls for cash are more elaborate than for most other assets. The rest of this chapter describes internal control over cash. We consider cash to be not just paper money and coins but also checks, money orders, and money kept in bank accounts. Cash includes neither stamps, because they are supplies, nor IOUs payable to the business, because these are receivables.

The documents used to control a bank account include the signature card, the deposit ticket, the check, and the bank reconciliation.

Signature Card.   Banks require each person authorized to transact business through an account in that bank to sign a *signature card.* The bank compares the signatures on documents against the signature card to protect the bank and the depositor against forgery.

Deposit Ticket.   Banks supply standard forms as *deposit tickets.* The customer fills in the dollar amount and the date of deposit. The customer retains either (1) a duplicate copy of the deposit ticket or (2) a deposit receipt, depending on the bank's practice, as proof of the transaction.

Check.   To draw money from an account, the depositor writes a **check,** which is the document that instructs the bank to pay the designated person or business the specified amount of money. There are three parties to a check: the *maker,* who signs the check; the *payee,* to whose order the check is drawn; and the *bank* on which the check is drawn.

Most checks are serially numbered and preprinted with the name and address of the depositor and the bank. The checks have places for the date, the name of the payee, the signature of the maker, and the amount. The bank name and bank identification number and the depositor account number are usually imprinted in magnetic ink for machine processing.

Exhibit 7-3 shows a check drawn on the bank account of Business Research, Inc. The check has two parts, the check itself and the remittance advice. The *remittance advice,* an optional attachment, tells the payee the reason for the payment. The maker (Business Research) retains a carbon copy of the check for its recording in the check register (cash disbursements journal). Note that internal controls at Business Research require two signatures on checks.

Bank Statement.   Most banks send monthly **bank statements** to their depositors. The statement shows the account's beginning and ending balance for the period and lists the month's transactions. Included with the statement are the maker's *canceled checks,* those checks that have been paid by the bank on behalf of the depositor. The bank statement also lists any other deposits and changes in the account. Deposits appear in chronological order, checks in a logical order, along with the date each check cleared the bank.

EXHIBIT 7-3   *Check with Remittance Advice*

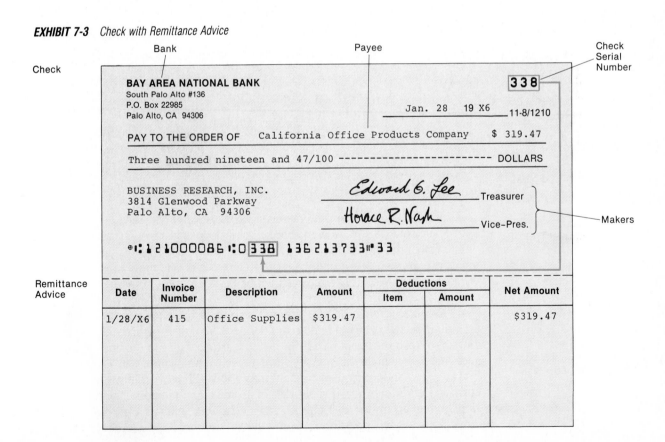

EXHIBIT 7-4 *Bank Statement*

BAY AREA NATIONAL BANK
South Palo Alto #136
P.O. Box 22985
Palo Alto, CA   94306

ACCOUNT STATEMENT

Business Research, Inc.
3814 Glenwood Parkway
Palo Alto, CA 94306

CHECKING ACCOUNT 136-213733

CHECKING ACCOUNT SUMMARY AS OF 01-31-X6

BEGINNING BALANCE	TOTAL DEPOSITS	TOTAL WITHDRAWALS	SERVICE CHARGES	ENDING BALANCE
6556.12	3448.61	4602.00	14.25	5388.48

——————————— CHECKING ACCOUNT TRANSACTIONS ———————————

DEPOSITS

DEPOSIT	01-04	1000.00
DEPOSIT	01-04	112.00
DEPOSIT	01-08	194.60
BANK COLLECTION	01-26	2114.00
INTEREST	01-31	28.01

CHARGES

SERVICE CHARGE	01-31	14.25

CHECKS:

CHECKS			CHECKS			BALANCES	
NUMBER	DATE	AMOUNT	NUMBER	DATE	AMOUNT	DATE	BALANCE
332	01-12	3000.00	334	01-12	100.00	12-31	6556.12
656	01-06	100.00	335	01-06	100.00	01-04	7616.12
333	01-12	150.00	336	01-31	1100.00	01-06	7416.12
						01-08	7610.72
						01-12	4360.72
						01-26	6474.72
						01-31	5388.48

OTHER CHARGES		DATE	AMOUNT
NSF		01-04	52.00

——————————— MONTHLY SUMMARY ———————————

7 WITHDRAWALS	4360 MINIMUM BALANCE	5812 AVERAGE BALANCE

Exhibit 7-4 is the bank statement of Business Research, Inc., for the month ended January 31, 19X6. At many banks, some depositors receive their statements on the first of the month, some on the second, and so on. This spacing eliminates the clerical burden of supplying all the statements at one time. Most businesses —like Business Research—receive their bank statement for the calendar month.

Bank Reconciliation. There are two records of the business's cash: its Cash account in its own general ledger and the bank statement, which tells the actual amount of cash the business has in the bank. The balance in the business's Cash account rarely equals the balance shown on the bank statement.

The books and the bank statement may show different amounts but both are correct. The difference arises because of a time lag in recording certain transactions. When a firm writes a check, it immediately credits its Cash account. The bank, however, will not subtract the amount of the check until the check reaches it for payment. This may take days, even weeks if the payee waits to cash the check. Likewise, the business debits Cash for all cash receipts, and it may take a day or so for the bank to add this amount to the business's bank balance.

Good internal control means knowing where a company's money comes from, how it is spent, and the current cash balance. How else can the accountant keep the accurate records management needs to make informed decisions? The accountant must explain the reasons for the difference between the firm's records and the bank statement figures and determine the actual amount of cash in the bank on a certain date. This process is called the **bank reconciliation.** Properly done, the bank reconciliation assures that all cash transactions have been accounted for and that the bank and book records of cash are correct.

Common items that cause differences between the bank balance and the book balance are

1. Items recorded by the *company* but not yet recorded by the *bank:*
   a. **Deposits in transit** (outstanding deposits). The company has recorded these deposits but the bank has not.
   b. **Outstanding checks.** These checks have been issued by the company and recorded on its books but have not yet been paid by its bank.
2. Items recorded by the *bank* but not yet recorded by the *company:*
   a. **Bank collections.** The bank sometimes collects money on behalf of depositors. Many businesses have their customers pay directly to the company bank account. This practice, called a lock-box system, reduces the possibility of theft and also places the business's cash in circulation faster than if the cash had to be collected and deposited by company personnel. An example is a bank's collecting cash on a note receivable and the related interest revenue for the depositor. The bank may notify the depositor of these bank collections on the bank statement.
   b. **Service charge.** This amount is the bank's fee for processing the depositor's transactions. Banks commonly base the service charge on the balance in the account. The depositor learns the amount of the service charge from the bank statement.
   c. *Interest revenue on checking account.* Many banks pay interest to depositors who keep a large enough balance of cash in the account. This is generally the case with business checking accounts. The bank notifies the depositor of this interest on the bank statement.
   d. **NSF (nonsufficient funds) checks** received from customers. To understand how to handle NSF checks, also called hot checks, you first need to know the route a check takes. The maker writes the check, credits Cash to record the payment on the books, and gives the check to the payee. On receiving the check, the payee debits Cash on his or her books and deposits the check in the bank. The payee's bank immediately adds the receipt amount to the payee's bank balance on the assumption that the check is good. The check is returned to the maker's bank, which then deducts the check amount from the maker's bank balance. If the maker's bank balance is insufficient to pay the check, the maker's bank refuses to pay the check, reverses this deduction, and sends an NSF notice back to the payee's bank. The payee bank subtracts the receipt amount from the payee's bank balance and notifies the payee of this action. This process may take from three to seven days. The company may learn of NSF checks through the bank statement, which lists the NSF check as a charge (subtraction), as shown near the bottom of Exhibit 7-4.
   e. *Checks collected, deposited, and returned to payee by the bank for reasons other than NSF.* Banks return checks to the payee if (1) the maker's account has closed, (2) the date is stale (some checks state "void after 30 days"), (3) the

signature is not authorized, (4) the check has been altered, or (5) the check form is improper. Accounting for all returned checks is the same as for NSF checks.

    f. *The cost of printed checks.* This charge against the company's bank account balance is handled like a service charge.

3. Errors by either the company or the bank. For example, a bank may improperly charge (decrease) the bank balance of Business Research, Inc., for a check drawn by another company, perhaps Business Research Associates. Or a company may miscompute its bank balance on its own books. Computational errors are becoming less frequent with widespread use of computers. Nevertheless, all errors must be corrected, and the corrections will be a part of the bank reconciliation.

Steps in Preparing the Bank Reconciliation

The steps in preparing the bank reconciliation are

1. Start with two figures, the balance shown on the bank statement *(balance per bank)* and the balance in the company's Cash account *(balance per books)*. These two amounts will probably disagree because of the timing differences discussed earlier.

2. Add to, or subtract from, the *bank* balance those items that appear on the books but not on the bank statement:

    a. Add *deposits in transit* to the bank balance. Deposits in transit are identified by comparing the deposits listed on the bank statement to the company list of cash receipts. They show up as cash receipts on the books but not as deposits on the bank statement. As a control measure, the accountant should also ensure that deposits in transit from the preceding month appear on the current month's bank statement. If they do not, the deposits may be lost.

    b. Subtract *outstanding checks* from the bank balance. Outstanding checks are identified by comparing the canceled checks returned with the bank statement to the company list of checks in the cash disbursements journal. They show up as cash payments on the books but not as paid checks on the bank statement. This comparison also verifies that all checks paid by the bank were valid company checks and were correctly recorded by the bank and by the company. Outstanding checks are usually the most numerous items on a bank reconciliation.

3. Add to, or subtract from, the *book* balance those items that appear on the bank statement but not on the company books:

    a. Add to the book balance (a) *bank collections* and (b) any *interest revenue* earned on the money in the bank. These items are identified by comparing the deposits listed on the bank statement to the company list of cash receipts. They show up as cash receipts on the bank statement but not on the books.

    b. Subtract from the book balance (a) *service charges,* (b) *cost of printed checks,* and (c) *other bank charges* (for example, charges for NSF or stale date checks). These items are identified by comparing the other charges listed on the bank statement to the cash disbursements recorded on the company books. They show up as subtractions on the bank statement but not as cash payments on the books.

4. Compute the *adjusted bank balance* and the *adjusted book balance.* The two adjusted balances should be equal.

5. Journalize each item in 3, that is, each item listed on the book portion of the bank reconciliation. These items must be recorded on the company books because they affect cash.
6. Correct all book errors and notify the bank of any errors it has made.

Bank Reconciliation Illustrated

The bank statement in Exhibit 7-4 indicates that the January 31 bank balance of Business Research, Inc., is $5,388.48. However, the company's Cash account has a balance of $3,294.21. In following the steps outlined above, the accountant finds these reconciling items:

1. The January 30 deposit of $1,591.63 does not appear on the bank statement.
2. The bank erroneously charged a $100 check—number 656—written by Business Research Associates against the Business Research, Inc., account.
3. Five company checks issued late in January and recorded in the cash disbursements journal have not been paid by the bank:

OBJECTIVE 3

Prepare a bank reconciliation and related journal entries

Check No.	Date	Amount
337	Jan. 27	$286.00
338	28	319.47
339	28	83.00
340	29	203.14
341	30	458.53

4. The bank collected on behalf of the company a note receivable, $2,114 (including interest revenue of $214). This cash receipt has not been recorded in the cash receipts journal.
5. The bank statement shows interest revenue of $28.01 that the bank has paid the company on its cash balance.
6. Check number 333 for $150 paid to Brown Company on account was recorded in the cash disbursements journal as a $510 amount, creating a $360 understatement of the Cash balance per books.
7. The bank service charge for the month was $14.25.
8. The bank statement shows an NSF check for $52 that was received from customer L. Ross.

Exhibit 7-5 is the bank reconciliation based on the above data. Panel A lists the reconciling items, which are keyed by number to the actual reconciliation in Panel B. Note that after the reconciliation, the adjusted bank balance equals the adjusted book balance. This equality is the accuracy check for the reconciliation.

Recording Entries from the Reconciliation

The bank reconciliation does not directly affect the journals or the ledgers. Like the work sheet, the reconciliation is an accountant's tool, separate from the company's books.

The bank reconciliation acts as a control device by signaling the company to record the transactions listed as reconciling items in the Books section because the company has not yet done so. For example, the bank collected the note receivable on behalf of the company, but the company has not yet recorded this cash receipt. In fact, the company learned of the cash receipt only when it received the bank statement.

EXHIBIT 7-5 *Bank Reconciliation*

Panel A—Reconciling Items:

1. Deposit in transit, $1,591.63.
2. Bank error; add $100 to bank balance.
3. Outstanding checks: no. 337, $286; no. 338, $319.47; no. 339, $83; no. 340, $203.14; no. 341, $458.53.

4. Bank collection, $2,114, including interest revenue of $214.
5. Interest earned on bank balance, $28.01.
6. Book error; add $360 to book balance.
7. Bank service charge, $14.25.
8. NSF check from L. Ross, $52.

Panel B—Bank Reconciliation:

Business Research, Inc.
Bank Reconciliation
January 31, 19X6

Bank:			Books:		
Balance, January 31...................		$5,388.48	Balance, January 31.................		$3,294.21
Add:			Add:		
1. Deposit of January 30 in transit......		1,591.63	4. Bank collection of note receivable, including interest revenue of $214 ..		2,114.00
2. Correction of bank error – Business Research Associates check erroneously charged against company account		100.00	5. Interest revenue earned on bank balance		28.01
		7,080.11	6. Correction of book error – Overstated amount of check no. 333		360.00
3. Less outstanding checks:					5,796.22
No. 337	$286.00		Less:		
No. 338	319.47		7. Service charge...........	$14.25	
No. 339	83.00		8. NSF check..............	52.00	(66.25)
No. 340	203.14				
No. 341	458.53	(1,350.14)			
Adjusted bank balance		$5,729.97	Adjusted book balance		$5,729.97

Why does the company *not* need to record the reconciling items on the Bank side of the reconciliation? Those items have already been recorded on the company books.

Based on the reconciliation in Exhibit 7-5, Business Research, Inc., makes these entries. They are dated January 31 to bring the Cash account to the correct balance on that date:

Jan. 31	Cash	2,114.00	
	Notes Receivable		1,900.00
	Interest Revenue........................		214.00
	Note receivable collected by bank.		
31	Cash	28.01	
	Interest Revenue........................		28.01
	Interest earned on bank balance.		
31	Cash	360.00	
	Accounts Payable – Brown Co..............		360.00
	Correction of check register, check no. 333.		
31	Miscellaneous Expense......................	14.25	
	Cash		14.25
	Bank service charge.		

Note: Miscellaneous Expense is debited for the bank service charge because the service charge pertains to no particular expense category.

31	Accounts Receivable–L. Ross	52.00
	Cash	52.00
	NSF check returned by bank.	

These entries bring the business's books up to date.

The entry for the NSF check needs explanation. Upon learning that L. Ross's $52 check was not good, Business Research credits Cash to bring the Cash account up to date. Since Business Research still has a receivable from Ross, it debits Accounts Receivable—L. Ross and pursues collection from him.

Summary Problem for Your Review

1. The Cash account of Bain Company at February 28, 19X3, follows.

Cash

Feb. 1	Balance	4,195	Feb. 3		400
6		800	12		3,100
15		1,800	19		1,100
23		900	25		500
28		2,400	27		900
Feb. 28	Balance	4,095			

2. Bain Company receives this bank statement on February 28, 19X3 (negative amounts appear in parentheses):

Bank Statement for February 19X3

Beginning balance...		$4,195
Deposits:		
Feb. 7......................................	$ 800	
15......................................	1,800	
24......................................	900	3,500
Checks (total per day):		
Feb. 8......................................	$ 400	
16......................................	3,100	
23......................................	1,100	(4,600)
Other items:		
Service charge		(10)
NSF check from M. E. Crown		(700)
Bank collection of note receivable for the company		1,000*
Interest on account balance		15
Ending balance		$3,400

* Includes interest of $119.

Additional data:

Bain Company deposits all cash receipts in the bank and makes all cash disbursements by check.

Required:

1. Prepare the bank reconciliation of Bain Company at February 28, 19X3.
2. Record the entries based on the bank reconciliation.

SOLUTION TO REVIEW PROBLEM

Requirement 1

Bain Company
Bank Reconciliation
February 28, 19X3

Bank:

Balance, February 28, 19X3	$3,400
Add: Deposit of February 28 in transit	2,400
	5,800
Less: Outstanding checks issued on Feb. 25 ($500) and Feb. 27 ($900)	(1,400)
Adjusted bank balance, February 28, 19X3	$4,400

Books:

Balance, February 28, 19X3		$4,095
Add: Bank collection of note receivable, including interest of $119		1,000
Interest earned on bank balance....................		15
		5,110
Less: Service charge	$ 10	
NSF check.....................................	700	(710)
Adjusted book balance, February 28, 19X3		$4,400

Requirement 2

Feb. 28	Cash..		1,000	
		Note Receivable ($1,000 − $119)................		881
		Interest Revenue		119
	Note receivable collected by bank.			
28	Cash..		15	
		Interest Revenue		15
	Interest earned on bank balance.			
28	Miscellaneous Expense		10	
		Cash.......................................		10
	Bank service charge.			
28	Accounts receivable — M. E. Crown		700	
		Cash.......................................		700
	NSF check returned by bank.			

Reporting of Cash _____

Cash is the first current asset listed on the balance sheet of most companies. Even small businesses have several bank accounts and one or more petty cash funds that are kept on hand for making small disbursements. However, companies usually combine all cash amounts into a single total for reporting on the balance sheet. They also include liquid assets like time deposits and certificates of deposit. These are interest-bearing accounts that can be withdrawn with no penalty after a short period of time. Although they are slightly less liquid than cash, they are sufficiently similar to be reported along with cash. For example, the balance sheet of Kraft, Inc., maker of Miracle Whip, Philadelphia Cream Cheese, Duracell batteries, and other well-known products, recently reported (in millions of dollars):

Assets:

Cash, time deposits, and certificates of deposit......	$ 194.1
Temporary investments.........................	127.6
Accounts and notes receivable	941.7
Inventories	1,211.3
Total current assets	$2,474.7

It is important to perform the bank reconciliation on the balance sheet date in order to be assured of reporting the correct amount of cash.

Internal Control over Cash Receipts _____

Internal control over cash receipts ensures that all cash receipts are deposited in the bank and the company's accounting record is correct. Many businesses receive cash over the counter and through the mail. Each source of cash receipts calls for specific controls.

OBJECTIVE 4
Apply internal controls to cash receipts

The cash register offers management control over cash received in a store. First, the machine should be positioned so that customers can see the amounts the cashier enters into the register. No person willingly pays more than the marked price for an item, so the customer helps prevent the sales clerk from overcharging and pocketing the excess over actual prices. Also, company policy should require issuance of a receipt to make sure each sale is recorded in the register.

Second, the register's cash drawer opens only when the sales clerk enters an amount on the keys, and a roll of tape locked inside the machine records each amount. At the end of the day, a manager proves the cash by comparing the total amount in the cash drawer against the tape's total. This step helps prevent outright theft by the clerk. For security reasons, the clerk should not have access to the tape.

Third, pricing merchandise at ''uneven'' amounts—say, $3.95 instead of $4.00—means that the clerk generally must make change, which in turn means having to get into the cash drawer. This requires entering the amount of the sale on the keys and so onto the register tape.

At the end of the day, the cashier or other employee with cash-handling duties deposits the cash in the bank. The tape goes to the accounting department as the basis for an entry in the cash receipts journal. These security measures, coupled with periodic on-site inspection by a manager, discourage fraud.

All incoming mail should be opened by a mail-room employee. This person should compare the actual enclosed amount of cash or check with the attached remittance advice. If no advice was sent, the mail-room employee should prepare one and enter the amount of each receipt on a control tape. At the end of the day, this control tape is given to a responsible official, such as the controller, for verification. Cash receipts should be given to the cashier, who combines them with any cash received over the counter and prepares the bank deposit.

Having a mail-room employee be the first to handle postal cash receipts is just another application of a good internal control procedure — in this case, separation of duties. If the accountants opened postal cash receipts, they could easily hide a theft.

The mail-room employee forwards the remittance advices to the accounting department. They provide the data for entries in the cash receipts journal and postings to customers' accounts in the accounts receivable ledger. As a final step, the controller compares the three records of the day's cash receipts: (1) the control tape total from the mail room, (2) the bank deposit amount from the cashier, and (3) the debit to Cash from the accounting department.

An added measure used to control cash receipts is a *fidelity bond*, which is an insurance policy that the business buys to guard against theft. The fidelity bond helps in two ways. First, the insurance company that issues the policy investigates the backgrounds of the workers whose activities will be covered, such as the mail-room employees who handle incoming cash and the employees who handle inventory. Second, if the company suffers a loss due to the misconduct of a covered employee, the insurance company reimburses the business.

Cash Short and Over.   A difference often exists between actual cash receipts and the day's record of cash received. Usually the difference is small and results from honest errors. Suppose the cash register tapes of a large department store indicate sales revenue of $25,000, but the cash received is $24,980. To record the day's sales, the store would make this entry:

Cash.	24,980	
Cash Short and Over	20	
Sales Revenue		25,000
Daily cash sales.		

As the entry shows, Cash Short and Over is debited when sales revenue exceeds cash receipts. This account is credited when cash receipts exceed sales. A debit balance appears on the income statement as Miscellaneous Expense, a credit balance as Other Revenue.

This account's balance should be small. The debits and credits for cash over and short collected over an accounting period tend to cancel each other out. A large balance signals the accountant to investigate. For example, too large a debit balance may mean an employee is stealing. Cash Short and Over, then, acts as an internal control device.

Internal Control Over Cash Disbursements _____

Payment by *check* is an important control over cash disbursements. First, the check acts as a source document. Second, to be valid the check must be signed by an authorized official, so each payment by check draws the attention of management. Before signing the check, the manager should study the invoice, the receiving report, the purchase order, and other supporting documents. (A discussion of these documents follows.) As further security and control over cash disbursements, many firms require two signatures on a check, as we saw in Exhibit 7-3. To avoid document alteration, some firms also use machines that indelibly stamp the amount on the check.

OBJECTIVE 5
Apply internal controls to cash disbursements

In very small businesses, the proprietor or partners may control cash disbursements by reviewing the supporting documents themselves and personally writing all checks. However, in larger businesses this is impractical, so the duties of approving invoices for payment and writing checks are performed by authorized employees. Strong internal control is achieved through clear-cut assignment of responsibility, proper authorization, and separation of duties.

Controlling the Cost of Inventory

Cost of goods sold is the major expense of most merchandising businesses. Therefore, it is important to control the cost of inventory purchases. Overall control is achieved by the same measures used to control all other cash disbursements—assignment of responsibility, authorization for payment, separation of duties, and so on.

A measure that is designed specifically to control the cost of inventory concerns the manner of recording purchases. There are two ways to record purchases: (1) at the *gross* cost, as illustrated thus far; and (2) at the *net* cost, which takes into account any discount on the purchase. For example, a $2,000 invoice subject to credit terms of 2/10 n/30 could be recorded at gross ($2,000) or net ($1,960). The discount terms of 2/10 n/30 (that is, a 2 percent discount for payment within 10 days, or the full $2,000 within 30 days) indicate a very high rate of interest when expressed as an annual rate. Paying after the discount period costs 2 percent for the extra 20 days of credit, an annual rate of 36 percent (.02 $\times$ 360 days/20 days = .36). For this reason, companies adopt the policy of taking all such discounts.

Recording the purchase at its net amount has a control advantage because it highlights the inefficiency of paying late. Recorded at net cost, the purchase entry is

Purchases ($2,000 − $40)	1,960	
Accounts Payable		1,960

Purchase on account.

The actual cost of the inventory is $1,960 because this is the cash cost of the goods if they are paid for immediately. The gross cost of $2,000 includes a $40 charge for payment beyond the discount period. Therefore, the net cost method is helpful. To see the control advantage of the net cost approach, suppose the invoice is *not* paid within the discount period. This inefficiency costs an extra $40, debited to Purchase Discounts Lost as follows:

Accounts Payable	1,960	
Purchase Discounts Lost	40	
Cash in Bank		2,000

Payment after discount period.

Purchase Discounts Lost is an expense account reported as Other Expense on the income statement:

Grant Company
Income Statement
Year Ended December 31, 19X8

Sales revenue......................	$700,000
Cost of goods sold.................	380,000
Gross margin......................	320,000
Operating expenses.................	230,000
Income from operations.............	90,000
Other revenue (expense):	
Purchase discounts lost...........	**(2,000)**
Net income........................	$ 88,000

Reporting Purchase Discounts Lost on the income statement draws attention to the inefficiency of losing the discounts. The net method thus captures the information needed to evaluate employee performance. Managers can then correct those actions that led to payment of the full amount. Contrast this accounting treatment with recording the purchases at gross cost. If the invoice is paid late, there is no record of the discount because the purchase and the related payment are both recorded at $2,000. Managers lose the notification provided by the Purchase Discounts Lost account.

Petty Cash Disbursements

It would be uneconomical for a business to write a separate check for an executive's taxi fare, a box of pencils needed right away, or the delivery of a special message across town. Therefore, companies keep a small amount of cash on hand to pay for such minor amounts. This fund is called **petty cash.**

Even though the individual amounts paid through the petty cash fund may be small, such expenses occur so often that the total amount over an accounting period may grow quite large. Thus the business needs to set up these controls over petty cash: (1) designate an employee to administer the fund as its custodian, (2) keep a specific amount of cash on hand, (3) support all fund disbursements with a petty cash ticket, and (4) replenish the fund through normal cash disbursement procedures.

OBJECTIVE 6

Account for petty cash transactions

To open the petty cash fund, a payment is approved for a predetermined amount and a check for this amount is issued to Petty Cash. Assume that on February 28 the business decides to establish a petty cash fund of $200. The custodian cashes the check and places the currency and coin in the fund, which may be a cash box, safe, or other device. The petty cash custodian is assigned the responsibility for controlling the fund. Starting the fund is recorded as follows:

Feb. 28 Petty Cash 200
            Cash in Bank   200
        To open the petty cash fund.

For each petty cash disbursement, the custodian prepares a *petty cash ticket* like the one illustrated in Exhibit 7-6.

Observe the signatures (or initials, for the custodian) that identify the recipient of petty cash and the fund custodian. Requiring both signatures reduces unauthorized cash disbursements. The custodian keeps all the petty cash tickets in the

EXHIBIT 7-6 *Petty Cash Ticket*

Petty Cash
Ticket

```
                    PETTY CASH TICKET

  Date   Mar. 25, 19X4                    No.  45

  Amount   $23.00

  For   Box of floppy diskettes

  Debit   Office Supplies, Acct. No. 145

  Received by  Lewis Wright    Fund Custodian  WAR
```

fund. The sum of the cash plus the total of the ticket amounts should equal the opening balance at all times—in this case, $200. Also, the Petty Cash account keeps its prescribed $200 balance at all times. Maintaining the Petty Cash account at this balance, supported by the fund (cash plus tickets totaling the same amount) is a characteristic of an *imprest system.* The control feature of an imprest system is that it clearly identifies the amount that the custodian is responsible for.

Disbursements reduce the amount of cash in the fund, so periodically the fund must be replenished. Suppose that on March 31 the fund has $118 in cash and $82 in tickets. A check for $82 is issued, made payable to Petty Cash. The fund custodian cashes this check for currency and coins and puts the money in the fund to return its actual cash to $200. The petty cash tickets identify the accounts to be debited: Office Supplies for $23, Delivery Expense for $17, and Miscellaneous Selling Expense for $42. The entry to record replenishment of the fund is

Mar. 31	Office Supplies	23	
	Delivery Expense	17	
	Miscellaneous Selling Expense	42	
	Cash in Bank		82
	To replenish the petty cash fund.		

If this cash payment exceeds the sum of the tickets—that is, if the fund comes up short, Cash Short and Over is debited for the missing amount. If the sum of the tickets exceeds the payment, Cash Short and Over is credited. Note that replenishing the fund does *not* affect the Petty Cash account. Petty Cash keeps its $200 balance at all times.

Whenever petty cash runs low, the fund is replenished. It *must* be replenished on the balance sheet date. Otherwise, the reported balance for Petty Cash will be overstated by the amount of the tickets in the fund. The income statement will understate the expenses listed on these tickets.

Petty Cash is debited only when starting the fund (see the February 28 entry) or changing its amount. In our illustration, suppose the business decides to raise the fund amount from $200 to $250 because of increased demand for petty cash. This step would require a $50 debit to Petty Cash.

The Voucher System

As we saw in Chapter 6, some businesses use the purchases journal and the cash disbursements journal to record cash payments. Other businesses use a voucher system. The **voucher system** for recording cash payments offers the business greater internal control by formalizing the process of approving and recording invoices for payment. We will examine the voucher system as it is used by a merchandising business.

OBJECTIVE 7

Use the voucher system

The voucher system uses (1) vouchers, (2) a voucher register, (3) an unpaid voucher file, (4) a check register, and (5) a paid voucher file. The merchandising business we discuss has separate departments for purchasing goods, receiving goods, disbursing cash, and accounting.

Vouchers.   A **voucher** is a document authorizing a cash disbursement. The accounting department prepares vouchers. Exhibit 7-7 illustrates the voucher of Bliss Wholesale Company. In addition to places for writing in the *payee, due date, terms, description,* and *invoice amount,* the voucher includes a section for designated officers to sign their *approval* for payment. The back of the voucher has places for recording the *account debited, date paid,* and *check number.* You should locate these nine items in Exhibit 7-7.

To better understand the voucher system, let's take an in-depth look at the purchasing process. Exhibit 7-8 lists the various business documents used to ensure that the company receives the goods it ordered and pays only for the goods it has actually received.

EXHIBIT 7-7   *Voucher*

Front of Voucher

BLISS WHOLESALE COMPANY

Voucher No. 326

Payee	Van Heusen, Inc.
Address	4619 Shotwell Avenue
	Brooklyn, NY 10564

| Due Date | March 7 |
| Terms | 2/10, n/30 |

Date	Invoice No.	Description	Amount
Mar. 1	6380	144 men's shirts stock no. X14	$1,800

Approved *Jane Trent* Controller   Approved *Bob Kraft* Treasurer

Back of Voucher

Voucher No. 326
Payee Van Heusen, Inc.

Invoice Amount $1,800

Discount   36

Net Amount $1,764

Due Date   Mar. 7

Date Paid   Mar. 6

Check No.   694

Account Distribution

Account Debited	Acct. No.	Amount
Purchases	501	$1,800
Store Supplies	145	
Salary Expense	538	
Advertising Expense	542	
Utilities Expense	548	
Delivery Expense	544	
Total		$1,800

EXHIBIT 7-8 *Purchasing Process*

Business Document	Prepared by	Sent to
Purchase request	Sales department	Purchasing department
Purchase order	Purchasing department	Outside company that sells the needed merchandise (supplier, or vendor)
Invoice	Outside company that sells the needed merchandise (supplier, or vendor)	Accounting department
Receiving report	Receiving department	Accounting department
Voucher	Accounting department	Officer who signs the check

The purchasing process starts when the sales department identifies the need for merchandise and prepares a *purchase request* (or requisition). A separate purchasing department specializes in locating the best buys and mails a *purchase order* to the supplier, the outside company that sells the needed goods. When the supplier ships the goods to the requesting business, the supplier also mails the *invoice* (or bill), which is a notification of the need to pay. As the goods arrive, the receiving department checks them for any damage and lists the merchandise received on a document called the *receiving report.* The accounting department prepares a *voucher* and attaches all the foregoing documents, checks them for accuracy and agreement, and forwards this voucher packet to designated officers for approval and payment. Exhibit 7-9 shows how a voucher packet looks.

Before approving the voucher, the controller and the treasurer should examine a sample of vouchers to determine that the following control steps have been performed by the accounting department:

1. The invoice is compared to a copy of the purchase order and purchase request to ensure that the business pays cash only for the goods that it ordered.
2. The invoice is compared to the receiving report to ensure that cash is paid only for the goods that are actually received.
3. The mathematical accuracy of the invoice is proved.

The voucher packet includes the voucher, invoice, receiving report, purchase order, and purchase request, as shown in Exhibit 7-9.

EXHIBIT 7-9 *Voucher Packet*

Purchase Request
Purchase Order
Receiving Report
Invoice
Voucher

EXHIBIT 7-10 Voucher Register

Voucher Register

Page 16

			Payment		Credit	Debit						Other Accounts		
Date	Voucher No.	Payee	Date	Check No.	Vouchers Payable	Purchases	Store Supplies	Salary Expense	Advertising Expense	Utilities Expense	Delivery Expense	Title	No.	Amount
Mar. 1	326	Van Heusen, Inc.	3/6	694	1,800	1,800								
1	327	Howell Properties	3/2	693	1,500							Rent Expense	547	1,500
4	328	Bell Telephone	3/10	696	128					128				
5	329	Schick Supplies	3/11	697	85		85							
8	330	Daily Journal			369				369					
9	331	Ace Delivery Service	3/9	695	37						37			
26	348	Carr Products			1,638	1,638								
28	349	Petty Cash	3/31	717	82		23				17	Miscellaneous Selling Expense	563	42
29	350	Consumers Gas Co.	3/31	718	195					195				
30	351	City National Bank	3/31	719	360							Interest Expense	546	360
31	352	Ralph Grant	3/31		864			864						
31		Totals			12,580	6,209	137	1,781	753	602	185			2,913
					(201)	(501)	(145)	(538)	(542)	(548)	(544)			(✓)

Account numbers in parentheses indicate the accounts to which these amounts have been posted.

Voucher Register.   After approval by the designated officers, the voucher goes to the accounting department where it is recorded in the **voucher register.** This journal is similar to the purchases journal (discussed in Chapter 6), but the voucher register is more comprehensive. In a voucher system, *all* expenditures are recorded first in the voucher register. This is a fundamental control feature of the voucher system because it centralizes the initial recording of all expenditures in this one journal. That is, all cash payments must be vouchered and approved prior to payment. For each transaction, the debit is to the account for which payment is being made, and the credit is to Vouchers Payable, the account that replaces Accounts Payable if a voucher system is used. Exhibit 7-10 illustrates the voucher register of Bliss Wholesale Company.

The voucher register has columns to record payment date and check number, which are entered when the voucher is paid. The absence of a payment date and check number means that the voucher is unpaid. In Exhibit 7-10, for example, Bliss Wholesale has a $2,202 liability at March 31 for vouchers 330 ($369 payable to the *Daily Journal*), 348 ($1,638 payable to Carr Products), and 350 ($195 payable to Consumers Gas Company). If these were the company's only unpaid vouchers at March 31, the balance sheet would report:

Current liabilities:
    Vouchers payable* $2,202
* Usually reported as Accounts Payable, even by companies that use a voucher system.

Unpaid Voucher File.   After recording a voucher in the voucher register, the accountant places the voucher packet in the unpaid voucher file, where it stays until the voucher is paid. The unpaid voucher file acts as the accounts payable subsidiary ledger because each voucher serves as an individual account payable. There is no need for a separate accounts payable ledger.

The unpaid voucher file has 31 slots, one for each day of the month. Each voucher is filed according to its due date. For example, voucher no. 326, in Exhibit 7-7, was due March 7, so it was filed in the slot marked 7.

Check Register.   The **check register** is the journal in which are recorded all checks issued in a voucher system. It replaces the cash disbursements journal. All entries in the check register debit Vouchers Payable and credit Cash (and Purchase Discounts, as appropriate).

Exhibit 7-11 shows a check register. Notice that all the transactions include a credit to the Cash in Bank account.

On or before the due date, the accountant removes the voucher packet from the unpaid voucher file and sends it to the officers for signing. After the checks are signed, the check number and payment date are entered on the back of the voucher, in the check register, and in the voucher register.

Paid Voucher File.   After payment, the voucher packet is canceled to avoid paying the bill twice. Typically, a hole is punched through the voucher packet. It is then filed alphabetically by payee name. Most businesses also file a copy in numerical sequence by voucher number as a cross reference. With this dual filing system, a voucher can be located using either classification scheme.

In summary, the voucher system works as follows:

1. The accounting department prepares a *voucher* for each invoice to be paid.
2. Supporting documents (invoice, receiving report, purchase order, and purchase request) are compared in the accounting department for accuracy and attached to the voucher. These documents make up the *voucher packet.*

EXHIBIT 7-11   *Check Register*

				Debit	Credit	
Date	Check No.	Payee	Voucher No.	Vouchers Payable	Purchase Discounts	Cash in Bank
Mar. 1	692	Trent Co.	322	600	18	582
2	693	Howell Properties	327	1,500		1,500
6	694	Van Heusen, Inc.	326	1,800	36	1,764
9	695	Ace Delivery Service	331	37		37
10	696	Bell Telephone	328	128		128
11	697	Schick Supplies	329	85		85
31	717	Petty Cash	349	82		82
31	718	City National Bank	351	360		360
31	719	Ralph Grant	352	864		864
31	720	Krasner Supply Co.	336	92		92
31		Totals		11,406	317	11,089
				(201)	(503)	(103)

Check Register   Page 9

Account numbers in parentheses indicate the accounts to which these amounts have been posted.

3. Designated officials examine the supporting documents and approve the voucher for payment.
4. The accounting department enters the voucher payable in the *voucher register*. The entry is a debit to the account of the item purchased (for example, Purchases) and a credit to Vouchers Payable. The voucher remains in the *unpaid voucher file* until payment.
5. Prior to the invoice due date, a check is issued to pay the voucher. The official reviews the supporting documents and signs the check.
6. The accounting department enters the check in the *check register* and updates the voucher and the voucher register to record payment. All checks are debits to Vouchers Payable and credits to Cash.
7. Paid vouchers are canceled and filed by payee name and by voucher number.

To gain a complete understanding of the voucher system, trace voucher no. 326 from Exhibit 7-7 through the voucher register in Exhibit 7-10 to the check register in Exhibit 7-11. Also, trace the check register entries from Exhibit 7-11 back to Exhibit 7-10.

Computers and Internal Control

Computers have had both positive and negative effects on internal control. On the positive side, their speed of operation and high reliability increase efficiency. On the negative side, computer systems are less flexible than manual systems.

Computers can take data in only one programmed format, whereas humans can process data if it is merely legible.

Effective internal control is as important to computer systems as it is to manual systems. For example, consider the separation of duties. Programmers should not be allowed to physically operate the computers. A computer consultant commented that he had opportunities to steal when he ran computer operations for a large bank. "I alone designed the dividend-payment operation, wrote the program for it, and ran the job on the machine. The operation was so big that it had a mistake tolerance of nearly $100,000. I could have paid at least half that much to myself, in small checks, and the money wouldn't even have been missed." To avoid theft, no one person should have complete control over system design, programming, and machine operation.

The computer has brought about an important development in cash payments. **Electronic funds transfer (EFT)** is a system that relies on electronic impulses — not paper documents — to account for cash transactions. To manage payroll, an employer enters the employee's name, pay rate, and any other needed data on a magnetic tape, which is transferred to a bank. The bank runs the tape, which automatically decreases the business's cash account and increases the employee's cash account. Some retailers use EFT to handle sales. Customers pay with a card that activates a computer. The computer automatically decreases the customer's bank account balance and increases the store's account balance.

EFT systems reduce the cost of processing cash transactions. However, this savings is achieved by reducing the documentary evidence of transactions. Traditional approaches to internal control have relied on documents, so EFT and other computer systems pose a significant challenge to managers and accountants who design and enforce internal control systems. Computer systems also create problems in protecting private information. For example, a group of students in Milwaukee gained access to highly confidential national defense data by computer! Such situations point to the need for computer security measures.

Summary Problem for Your Review

Grudnitski Company established a $300 petty cash fund. James C. Brown is the fund custodian. At the end of the first week, the petty cash fund contains the following:

1. Cash: $171
2. Petty cash tickets:

No.	Amount	Issued to	Signed by	Account Debited
44	$14	B. Jarvis	B. Jarvis and JCB	Office Supplies
45	9	S. Bell	S. Bell	Miscellaneous Expense
47	43	R. Tate	R. Tate and JCB	—
48	33	L. Blair	L. Blair and JCB	Travel Expense

Required

1. Identify the four internal control weaknesses revealed in the above data.
2. Prepare the general journal entries to record:
    a. Establishment of the petty cash fund.

b. Replenishment of the fund. Assume petty cash ticket no. 47 was issued for the purchase of office supplies.

3. What is the balance in the Petty Cash account immediately before replenishment? Immediately after replenishment?

SOLUTION TO REVIEW PROBLEM

Requirement 1.   The four internal control weaknesses are

a. Petty cash ticket no. 46 is missing. Coupled with weakness b, this omission raises questions about the administration of the petty cash fund and about how the petty cash funds were used.

b. The $171 cash balance means that $129 has been disbursed ($300 − $171 = $129). However, the total amount of the petty cash tickets is only $99 ($14 + $9 + $43 + $33). The fund, then, is $30 short of cash ($129 − $99 = $30). Was petty cash ticket no. 46 issued for $30? The data in the problem offer no hint that helps answer this question. In a real-world setting, management would investigate the problem.

c. The petty cash custodian (JCB) did not sign petty cash ticket no. 45. This omission may have been an oversight on his part. However, it raises the question of whether he authorized the disbursement. Both the fund custodian and the recipient of cash should sign the ticket.

d. Petty cash ticket no. 47 does not indicate which account to debit. This omission raises two internal control questions. What did Tate do with the money, and what account should be debited? At worst, the funds have been stolen. At best, asking the custodian to reconstruct the transaction from memory is a haphazard way to identify the account to debit.

Requirement 2.   Petty cash journal entries:

a. Entry to establish the petty cash fund:

Petty Cash	300	
Cash in Bank		300

b. Entry to replenish the fund:

Office Supplies	14	
Miscellaneous Expense ($9 + $43)	52	
Travel Expense	33	
Cash Short and Over	30	
Cash in Bank		129

Requirement 3.   The balance in Petty cash is *always* its specified balance, in this case $300, as shown by posting the above entries to the account:

Petty Cash

(a)   300

Note that the entry to establish the fund (entry a) debits Petty Cash. The entry to replenish the fund (entry b) neither debits nor credits Petty Cash.

Summary

Internal controls should safeguard assets, ensure accurate accounting records, promote operational efficiency, and encourage adherence to company policies. An effective internal control system includes these features: *reliable personnel, clear-cut assignment of responsibility, proper authorization,* and *separation of duties,* which is the primary element of internal control. Many businesses use security devices, audits, and specially designed documents and records in their internal control systems.

The *bank account* helps to control and safeguard cash. Businesses use the *bank statement* and the *bank reconciliation* to account for banking transactions. An *imprest system* is used to control petty cash disbursements. Many companies record purchases at *net cost* in order to highlight the inefficiency of paying invoices late and thus losing purchase discounts.

Businesses often control cash disbursements by using a *voucher system,* which features the voucher, the unpaid voucher file, the voucher register, and the check register.

Businesses may handle their payroll by computer and through *electronic funds transfers.* Effective computerized internal control systems must meet the same basic standards that good manual systems do.

Self-Study Questions

Test your understanding of the chapter by marking the best answer for each of the following questions.

1. Which of the following is an element of internal control? *(p. 265)*
    a. Safeguarding assets
    b. Ensuring accurate and reliable accounting records
    c. Promoting operational efficiency
    d. Encouraging adherence to company policies
    e. All the above are elements of internal control
2. Which of the characteristics of an effective system of internal control is violated by allowing the employee who handles inventory to also account for inventory? *(p. 268)*
    a. Competent and reliable personnel   c. Proper authorization
    b. Assignment of responsibilities   d. Separation of duties
3. What control function is performed by auditors? *(p. 269)*
    a. Objective opinion of the effectiveness of the internal control system
    b. Assurance that all transactions are accounted for correctly
    c. Communication of the results of the audit to regulatory agencies
    d. Guarantee that a proper separation of duties exists within the business
4. The bank account serves as a control device over *(pp. 270, 279, 280, 281)*
    a. Cash receipts   c. Both of the above
    b. Cash disbursements   d. None of the above
5. Which of the following items appears on the bank side of a bank reconciliation? *(p. 276)*
    a. Book error   c. NSF check
    b. Outstanding check   d. Interest revenue earned on bank balance
6. Which of the following reconciling items requires a journal entry on the books of the company? *(pp. 276, 277)*
    a. Book error   d. Interest revenue earned on bank balance
    b. Outstanding check   e. All but b
    c. NSF check   f. None of the above
7. What is the major internal control measure over the cash receipts of a K-Mart store? *(p. 279)*
    a. Reporting the day's cash receipts to the controller
    b. Preparing a petty cash ticket for all disbursements from the fund
    c. Pricing merchandise at uneven amounts, coupled with use of a cash register

   d. Channeling all cash receipts through the mail room, whose employees have no cash-accounting responsibilities

8. What is the control advantage of the net method of accounting for inventory purchases? *(pp. 281, 282)*
   a. It highlights the inefficiency of losing purchase discounts
   b. It guarantees that all purchase discounts will be taken
   c. It automatically increases the business's cash balance
   d. It results in a higher quality of inventory on hand for customers

9. The internal control feature that is specific to petty cash is *(p. 283)*
   a. Separation of duties
   b. Assignment of responsibility
   c. Proper authorization
   d. The imprest system

10. The most fundamental control feature provided by a voucher system is *(p. 287)*
   a. Assuring that only approved invoices are paid
   b. Centralizing the recording of all expenditures in one place — the voucher register
   c. Using the check register along with the voucher register
   d. Placing all incoming invoices in the unpaid voucher file

Answers to the self-study questions are at the end of the chapter.

Accounting Vocabulary

accounting controls *(p. 265)*,   administrative controls *(p. 265)*,   bank collections *(p. 273)*, bank reconciliation *(p. 273)*,   bank statement *(p. 271)*,   check *(p. 271)*,   check register *(p. 287)*,   deposit in transit *(p. 273)*,   electronic fund transfer *(p. 289)*,   internal control *(p. 265)*,   nonsufficient fund (NSF) check *(p. 273)*,   outstanding check *(p. 273)*,   petty cash *(p. 282)*,   service charge *(p. 273)*,   voucher *(p. 284)*,   voucher register *(p. 287)*,   voucher system *(p. 283)*.

ASSIGNMENT MATERIAL _____

Questions

1. Which of the features of effective internal control is the most fundamental? Why?
2. What is the title of the federal act that affects internal control? What requirement does it place on management?
3. Which company employees bear primary responsibility for a company's financial statements and for maintaining the company's system of internal control? How do these persons carry out this responsibility?
4. Identify features of an effective system of internal control.
5. Separation of duties may be divided into four parts. What are they?
6. How can internal control systems be circumvented?
7. Are internal control systems designed to be foolproof and perfect? What is a fundamental constraint in planning and maintaining systems?
8. Briefly state how each of the following serves as an internal control measure over cash: bank account, signature card, deposit ticket, and bank statement.
9. What is the remittance advice of a check? What use does it serve?
10. Each of the items in the following list must be accounted for in the bank reconciliation. Next to each item, enter the appropriate letter from the following possible treatments: (a) bank side of reconciliation — add the item; (b) bank side of reconciliation — subtract the item; (c) book side of reconciliation — add the item; (d) book side of reconciliation — subtract the item.

   _____ Outstanding check   _____ Deposit in transit
   _____ NSF check   _____ Bank collection

_____ Bank service charge	_____ Customer check returned be-
_____ Cost of printed checks	cause of unauthorized signa-
_____ Bank error that decreased	ture
bank balance	_____ Book error that increased bal-
	ance of Cash account

11. What purpose does a bank reconciliation serve?

12. Suppose a company has six bank accounts, two petty cash funds, and three certificates of deposit that can be withdrawn on demand. How many cash amounts would this company likely report on its balance sheet?

13. What role does a cash register play in an internal control system?

14. Describe internal control procedures for cash received by mail.

15. Large businesses often have elaborate internal control systems that may be uneconomical for small businesses. Where does the internal control rest in small proprietorships, and how do they control cash disbursements?

16. What is the internal control advantage of recording purchases at net cost?

17. What balance does the Petty Cash account have at all times? Does this balance always equal the amount of cash in the fund? When are the two amounts equal? When are they unequal?

18. List the five elements of a voucher system, and briefly describe the purpose of each.

19. Describe how a voucher system works.

20. What documents make up the voucher packet? Describe three procedures that use the voucher packet to ensure that each payment is appropriate.

21. Why should the same employee not write the computer programs for cash disbursements, sign checks, and mail the checks to payees?

Exercises

Exercise 7-1   *Identifying internal control strengths and weaknesses*

The following situations suggest either a strength or weakness in internal control. Identify each as *strength* or *weakness,* and give the reason for your answer.

a. Cash received over the counter is controlled by the sales clerk, who rings up the sale and places the cash in the register. The sales clerk has access to the control tape stored in the register.

b. Cash received by mail goes straight to the accountant, who debits Cash and credits Accounts Receivable from the customer.

c. The vice-president who signs checks assumes the accounting department has matched the invoice with other supporting documents and therefore does not examine the voucher packet.

d. Purchase invoices are recorded at net amount to highlight purchase discounts lost because of late payment.

e. The accounting department orders merchandise and approves vouchers for payment.

f. The operator of the computer has no other accounting or cash-handling duties.

Exercise 7-2   *Identifying internal controls*

Identify the missing internal control characteristic in the following situations:

1. Business is slow at Westwood Movie Theater on Tuesday, Wednesday, and Thursday nights. To reduce expenses the owner decides not to use a ticket taker on those nights. The ticket seller (cashier) is told to keep the tickets as a record of the number sold.

2. The manager of a discount store wants to speed the flow of customers through checkout. She decides to reduce the time spent by cashiers making change, so she prices merchandise at round dollar amounts—such as $8.00 and $15.00—instead of the customary amounts—$7.95 and $14.95.

3. Grocery stores such as Safeway and A&P purchase large quantities of their merchandise from a few suppliers. At another grocery store the manager decides to reduce

paper work. He eliminates the requirement that a receiving department employee prepare a receiving report, which lists the quantities of items received from the supplier.

4. When business is brisk, Seven-Eleven and many other retail stores deposit cash in the bank several times during the day. The manager at another convenience store wants to reduce the time spent by employees delivering cash to the bank, so he starts a new policy. Cash will build up over Saturdays and Sundays, and the total two-day amount will be deposited on Sunday evening.

5. In the course of auditing the records of a company, you find that the same employee orders merchandise and approves invoices for payment.

Exercise 7-3   *Classifying bank reconciliation items*

The following seven items may appear on a bank reconciliation:

1. Outstanding checks.
2. Bank error: the bank charged our account for a check written by another customer.
3. Service charge.
4. Deposits in transit.
5. NSF check.
6. Bank collection of a note receivable on our behalf.
7. Book error: we debited Cash for $1,000. The correct debit was $100.

Classify each item as (a) an addition to the bank balance, (b) a subtraction from the bank balance, (c) an addition to the book balance, or (d) a subtraction from the book balance.

Exercise 7-4   *Bank reconciliation*

Rachel Lazimy's checkbook lists the following:

Date	Check No.	Item	Check	Deposit	Balance
9/1					$525
4	622	Apple Tree Gift Shop	$19		506
9		Dividends		$ 116	622
13	623	Bell Telephone Co.	43		579
14	624	Gulf Oil Co.	58		521
18	625	Cash	50		471
26	626	St. Alban's Episcopal Church	25		446
28	627	Bent Tree Apartments	275		171
30		Paycheck		1,000	1,171

The September bank statement shows:

Balance		$525
Add: Deposits		116
Deduct checks: No.	Amount	
622	$19	
623	43	
624	68*	
625	50	(180)
Other charges:		
Printed checks	$8	
Service charge	6	(14)
Balance		$447

* This is the correct amount of check number 624.

Required:

Prepare Rachel's bank reconciliation at September 30.

Exercise 7-5   *Bank reconciliation*

Gary Walters operates four EXXON stations. He has just received the monthly bank statement at October 31 from First National Bank, and the statement shows an ending balance of $3,968. Listed on the statement are a service charge of $12, two NSF checks totaling $46, and a $9 charge for printed checks. In reviewing his cash records, Walters identifies outstanding checks totaling $467 and an October 31 deposit of $788, which does not appear on the bank statement. During October he recorded a $190 check for the salary of a part-time employee by debiting Salary Expense and crediting Cash for $19. Walters's cash account shows an October 31 cash balance of $4,527. Prepare the bank reconciliation at October 31.

Exercise 7-6   *Journal entries from a bank reconciliation*

Using the data from Exercise 7-5, record the entries that Walters should make in the general journal on October 31. Include an explanation for each entry.

Exercise 7-7   *Income statements with purchases at gross and at net*

Motorex, Inc., began July with inventory of $470,000 and ended the month with inventory of $510,000. During July the company purchased $800,000 of inventory and took the 2 percent discount on $700,000 of the purchases. The remaining $100,000 in inventory cost was paid after the discount period. Sales during July were $1,600,000, and operating expenses (including income tax) were $490,000.

Required:

1. Prepare the company's income statement for July assuming Motorex records inventory purchases at gross cost.
2. Prepare the company's income statement for July assuming the company records inventory purchases at net cost.
3. Which method provides the internal control advantage? Describe how this internal control feature works.

Exercise 7-8   *Accounting for petty cash*

United Way of Altoona, Pennsylvania, created a $100 imprest petty cash fund. During the first month of use, the fund custodian authorized and signed petty cash tickets as follows:

Ticket No.	Item	Account Debited	Amount
1	Delivery of pledge cards to donors	Delivery Expense	$19.22
2	Mail package	Postage Expense	2.80
3	Newsletter	Supplies Expense	4.14
4	Key to closet	Miscellaneous Expense	.85
5	Waste basket	Miscellaneous Expense	3.78
6	Staples	Supplies Expense	5.37

Required:

1. Make general journal entries for creation of the petty cash fund and its replenishment. Include explanations.
2. Immediately prior to replenishment, describe the items in the fund.
3. Immediately after replenishment, describe the items in the fund.

Exercise 7-9   *Purchases at gross and at net*

McCabe Hardware Company uses a voucher system. Prepare its general journal entries for the following transactions under two assumptions (explanations are not required):

Assumption 1—Inventory purchases recorded at gross cost
Assumption 2—Inventory purchases recorded at net cost

May   3   Purchased inventory costing $3,600 on account, subject to terms of 2/10 n/30
  11   Paid the liability created on May 3.
  14   Purchased inventory costing $2,200 on account, subject to terms of 2/10 n/30.
  27   Paid the liability created on May 14.

Which method provides the hardware store with a measure of discounts lost? Describe how this internal control feature works.

Exercise 7-10   *Petty cash; cash short and over*

Record the following selected transactions in general journal format (explanations are not required):

April   1   Issued voucher no. 637 to establish a petty cash fund with a $250 balance.
  1   Issued check no. 344 to pay voucher no. 637.
  2   Journalized the day's cash sales. Cash register tapes show a $2,859 total, but the cash in the register is only $2,853.
  10   The petty cash fund has $119 in cash and $131 in petty cash tickets issued to pay for Office Supplies ($61), Delivery Expense ($23), and Entertainment Expense ($47). Issued voucher no. 669 to replenish the fund.
  10   Issued check no. 402 to pay voucher no. 669.

Problems   *(Group A)*

Problem 7-1A   *Identifying internal control weaknesses*

Each of the following situations has an internal control weakness:

a. Myra Jones, a widow with no known sources of outside income, has been a trusted employee of Stone Products Company for 15 years. She performs all cash handling and accounting duties, including opening the mail, preparing the bank deposit, accounting for all aspects of cash and accounts receivable, and preparing the bank reconciliation. She has just purchased a new Cadillac and a new home in an expensive suburb. Lou Stone, the owner of the company, wonders how she can afford these luxuries on her salary.

b. Linda Cyert employs three professional interior designers in her design studio. She is located in an area with a lot of new construction, and her business is booming. Ordinarily, Linda does all the purchasing of furniture, draperies, carpets, fabrics, sewing services, and other materials and labor needed to complete jobs. During the summer she takes a long vacation, and in her absence she allows each designer to purchase materials and labor. At her return, Cyert reviews operations and notes that expenses are much higher and net income much lower than in the past.

c. Discount stores such as Target, Solo-Serve, and Medallion receive a large portion of their sales revenue in cash, with the remainder in credit card sales. To reduce expenses, a store manager ceases purchasing fidelity bonds on the cashiers.

d. The office supply company from which Dysan Stereo Center purchases cash receipt forms recently notified Dysan that the last shipped receipts were not prenumbered. Stan

Dysan, the owner, replied that he did not use the receipt numbers, so the omission is not important.

e. Lancer Computer Programs is a software company that specializes in computer programs with accounting applications. Their most popular program prepares the general journal, cash receipts journal, voucher register, check register, accounts receivable subsidiary ledger, and general ledger. In the company's early days, the owner and eight employees wrote the computer programs, lined up manufacturers to produce the diskettes, sold the products to stores such as ComputerLand and ComputerCraft, and performed the general management and accounting of the company. As the company has grown, the number of employees has increased dramatically. Recently, the development of a new software program stopped while the programmers redesigned Lancer's accounting system. Lancer's own accountants could have performed this task.

Required

1. Identify the missing internal control characteristic in each situation.
2. Identify the business's possible problem.
3. Propose a solution to the problem.

Problem 7-2A   *Bank reconciliation and related journal entries*

The May 31 bank statement of Malcolm & Fisk, a partnership, has just arrived from Lake Star Bank. To prepare the Malcolm & Fisk bank reconciliation, you gather the following data:

1. The May 31 bank balance is $4,119.82.
2. The bank statement includes two charges for returned checks from customers. One is an NSF check in the amount of $67.50 received from Harley Doherty, a customer, recorded on the books by a debit to Cash, and deposited on May 19. The other is a $195.03 check received from Maria Gucci and deposited on May 21. It was returned by Ms. Gucci's bank with the imprint "Unauthorized Signature."
3. The following Malcolm & Fisk checks are outstanding at May 31:

Check No.	Amount
616	$403.00
802	74.25
806	36.60
809	161.38
810	229.05
811	48.91

4. The bank statement includes two special deposits: $688.14, which is the amount of dividend revenue the bank collected from General Electric Company on behalf of Malcolm & Fisk; and $16.86, the interest revenue Malcolm & Fisk earned on its bank balance during May.
5. The bank statement lists a $6.25 subtraction for the bank service charge.
6. On May 31 the Malcolm & Fisk treasurer deposited $381.14, but this deposit does not appear on the bank statement.
7. The bank statement includes a $410.00 deduction for a check drawn by Marimont Freight Company. Malcolm & Fisk promptly notified the bank of its error.
8. Malcolm & Fisk's Cash account shows a balance of $3,521.55 on May 31.

Required

1. Prepare the bank reconciliation for Malcolm & Fisk at May 31.
2. Record in general journal form the entries necessary to bring the book balance of Cash into agreement with the adjusted book balance on the reconciliation. Include an explanation for each entry.

Problem 7-3A *Bank reconciliation and related journal entries*

Assume selected columns of the cash receipts journal and the check register of Radio Shack Store No. 147 appear as follows at March 31, 19X5:

Cash Receipts Journal (Posting reference is CR)		Check Register (Posting reference is CD)	
Date	Cash Debit	Check No.	Cash Credit
Mar. 4	$2,716	1413	$ 1,465
9	544	1414	1,004
11	1,655	1415	450
14	896	1416	8
17	367	1417	775
25	890	1418	88
31	2,038	1419	4,126
Total	$9,106	1420	760
		1421	200
		1422	2,267
		Total	$11,143

Assume the Cash account of the Radio Shack store shows the following information on March 31, 19X5.

Cash

Date	Item	Jrnl. Ref.	Debit	Credit	Balance
Mar. 1	Balance				14,188
31		CR. 10	9,106		23,294
31		CD. 16		11,143	12,151

Radio Shack Store No. 147 received the following bank statement on March 31, 19X5.

Bank Statement for March 19X5

Beginning balance		$14,188
Deposits and other Credits:		
Mar. 5..........................	$2,716	
10........................	544	
11........................	1,655	
15........................	896	
18........................	367	
25........................	890	
31........................	1,000 BC	8,068
Checks and other Debits:		
Mar. 8..........................	441 NSF	
9..........................	1,465	
13........................	1,004	
14........................	450	
15........................	8	
22........................	775	
29........................	88	
31........................	4,216	
31........................	25 SC	8,472
Ending balance		$13,784

Explanation: BC-Bank Collection   NSF-Nonsufficient Fund Check   SC-Service Charge

Additional data for the bank reconciliation include:

1. The NSF check was received late in February from L. M. Arnett.
2. The $1,000 bank collection of a note receivable on March 31 included $122 interest revenue.
3. The correct amount of check number 1419, a payment on account, is $4,216. (The Radio Shack accountant mistakenly recorded the check for $4,126.)

Required

1. Prepare the bank reconciliation of Radio Shack Store No. 147 at March 31, 19X5.
2. Record the entries based on the bank reconciliation. Include explanations.

Problem 7-4A *Recording and reporting purchases at gross and at net*

Superior Products Company does not use a voucher system. On May 1 of the current year the company had inventory of $58,000. On May 31 the company had inventory of $53,700. Net sales for May were $212,800, and operating expenses were $65,100. During May Superior completed the following transactions:

May 3 Purchased inventory costing $38,500 under terms of 2/10 n/30.

  7 Returned $2,000 of the inventory purchased on May 3.

  10 Purchased inventory costing $28,500 on credit terms of 2/10 n/45.

  12 Paid the amount owed from the May 3 invoice, net of the return on May 7 and also net of the discount.

  18 Purchased inventory costing $31,900 on credit terms of 2/10 n/30.

  19 Paid for the inventory purchased on May 10, less the discount.

  29 Paid the gross amount of the purchase on May 18, missing the discount because payment occurred after the discount period.

Required

1. Assuming Superior records inventory purchases at gross cost:
   a. Record the transactions in a general journal. Explanations are not required.
   b. Prepare the company's income statement for May of the current year.
2. Assuming Superior records inventory purchases at net cost:
   a. Record the transactions in a general journal. Explanations are not required.
   b. Prepare the company's income statement for May of the current year.
3. Which method of recording purchases offers the internal control advantage? Give your reason.

Problem 7-5A *Accounting for petty cash transactions*

Suppose that on April 1 Texaco opens a regional office in Oklahoma City and creates a petty cash fund with an imprest balance of $200. During April, Eleanor McGillicuddy, the fund custodian, signs the following petty cash tickets:

Ticket Number	Item	Amount
101	Pencils	$ 6.89
102	Cab fare for executive	14.50
103	Delivery of package across town	7.75
104	Dinner money for executives entertaining a customer	80.00
105	Postage for package received	10.00
106	Christmas decorations for office party	18.22
107	Two boxes of floppy disks	14.37

On April 30, prior to replenishment, the fund contains these tickets plus $45.27. The accounts affected by petty cash disbursements are Office Supplies Expense, Travel Expense, Delivery Expense, Entertainment Expense, and Postage Expense.

Required

1. Discuss the characteristics and the internal control features of an imprest fund.
2. Make the general journal entries to create the fund and to replenish it. Include explanations. Also, briefly describe what the custodian does on these dates.
3. Make the entry on May 1 to increase the fund balance to $300. Include an explanation, and briefly describe what the custodian does.

Problem 7-6A *Voucher system entries*

Assume R. H. Macy & Company, Inc., the department-store chain, uses a voucher system and records purchases at *gross* cost. Assume further that a Macy store completed the following transactions during July:

July 2 Issued voucher no. 614 payable to Hathaway Shirt Company for the purchase of inventory costing $16,000, with payment terms of 2/10 n/30.
  3 Issued voucher no. 615 payable to Edison Electric for electricity usage of $2,589.
  5 Issued check no. 344 to pay voucher no. 614, less the discount.
  6 Issued voucher no. 616 payable to Baylor Supply Company for inventory costing $850, with payment terms of 2/10 n/45.
  7 Issued check no. 345 to pay voucher no. 615.
  13 Issued voucher no. 617 payable to replenish the petty cash fund. The payee is Petty Cash, the amount is $203, and the petty cash tickets list store supplies ($119), delivery expense ($48), and miscellaneous expense ($36). Also issued check no. 346 to pay the voucher.
  14 Issued check no. 347 to pay voucher no. 616, less the discount.
  18 Issued voucher no. 618 payable to the *New York Times* for advertising, $2,800.
  19 Issued voucher no. 619 payable to Levi Strauss & Company for inventory costing $65,800, with payment terms of 3/10 n/30.
  28 Issued voucher no. 620 payable to city of New York for property tax of $9,165.
  30 Issued check no. 348 to pay voucher no. 619. Because of a filing error, we failed to earn the discount.
  31 Issued voucher no. 621 payable to Maine Bank for interest expense of $7,000.
  31 Issued voucher no. 622 to pay executive salary of $4,644 to Sharon Kratzman. Also issued check no. 349 to pay the voucher.

Required

1. Record Macy's transactions in a voucher register and a check register like those illustrated in the chapter. Posting references are unnecessary.
2. Open the Vouchers Payable account with a zero beginning balance, and post amounts to that account.
3. Prepare the list of unpaid vouchers at July 31 and show that the total matches the balance of Vouchers Payable.

Problem 7-7A *Voucher system; purchases at net*

Assume that the Macy store in Problem 7-6A records its purchases of inventory and supplies at *net* cost.

Required

1. Record the transactions of Problem 7-6A in a voucher register and a check register. To

account for purchase discounts lost, it is necessary to use a check register designed as follows:

Check Register

| Date | Check No. | Payee | Voucher No. | Debit | | Credit |
				Vouchers Payable	Purchase Discounts Lost	Cash in Bank

2. Post to the Vouchers Payable account.
3. Prepare the list of unpaid vouchers at July 31 and show that the total matches the balance of Vouchers Payable.

(Group B)

Problem 7-1B   *Identifying internal control weaknesses*

Each of the following situations has an internal control weakness.

a. Most large companies have internal audit staffs that continuously evaluate the business's internal control. Part of the auditor's job is to evaluate how efficiently the company is running. For example, is the company purchasing inventory from the least expensive wholesaler? After a particularly bad year, Mason Tile Company eliminates its internal audit department to reduce expenses.

b. CPA firms, law firms, and other professional organizations use paraprofessional employees to do some of their routine tasks. For example, an accounting paraprofessional might examine documents to assist a CPA in conducting an audit. In the CPA firm of Grosso & Howe, Lou Grosso, the senior partner, turns over a significant portion of his high-level audit work to his paraprofessional staff.

c. In evaluating the internal control over cash disbursements, an auditor learns that the purchasing agent is responsible for purchasing diamonds for use in the company's manufacturing process, approving the invoices for payment, and signing the checks. No supervisor reviews the purchasing agent's work.

d. Grant Kowalzyak owns a firm that performs engineering services. His staff consists of twelve professional engineers, and he manages the office. Often his work requires him to travel to meet with clients. During the past six months he has observed that when he returns from a business trip, the engineering jobs in the office have not progressed satisfactorily. He learns that when he is away several of his senior employees take over office management and neglect their engineering duties. One employee could manage the office.

e. Lew Jackson has been an employee of Brazleton Lumber Company for many years. Because the business is relatively small, Lew performs all accounting duties, including opening the mail, preparing the bank deposit, and preparing the bank reconciliation.

Required

1. Identify the missing internal control characteristic in each situation.
2. Identify the business's possible problem.
3. Propose a solution to the problem.

Problem 7-2B   *Bank reconciliation and related journal entries*

The August 31 bank statement of Spinnaker Software has just arrived from United Bank. To prepare the Spinnaker bank reconciliation, you gather the following data:

1. Spinnaker's Cash account shows a balance of $5,503.77 on August 31.
2. The bank statement includes two charges for returned checks from customers. One is a $395.00 check received from Shoreline Express and deposited on August 20, returned by Shoreline's bank with the imprint "Unauthorized Signature." The other is an NSF check in the amount of $146.67 received from Lipsey, Inc. This check had been deposited on August 17.
3. The following Spinnaker checks are outstanding at August 31:

Check No.	Amount
237	$ 46.10
288	141.00
291	578.05
293	11.87
294	609.51
295	8.88
296	101.63

4. The bank statement includes a deposit of $1,191.17, collected by the bank on behalf of Spinnaker. Of the total, $1,011.81 is collection of a note receivable, and the remainder is interest revenue.
5. The bank statement shows that Spinnaker earned $38.19 on its bank balance during August. This amount was added to Spinnaker's account by the bank.
6. The bank statement lists a $10.50 subtraction for the bank service charge.
7. On August 31 the Spinnaker treasurer deposited $193.78, but this deposit does not appear on the bank statement.
8. The bank statement includes a $300.00 deposit that Spinnaker did not make. The bank erroneously had credited the Spinnaker account for another bank customer's deposit.
9. The August 31 bank balance is $7,784.22.

Required

1. Prepare the bank reconciliation for Spinnaker Software at August 31.
2. Record in general journal form the entries necessary to bring the book balance of Cash into agreement with the adjusted book balance on the reconciliation. Include an explanation for each entry.

Problem 7-3B *Bank reconciliation and related journal entries*

Assume selected columns of the cash receipts journal and the check register of Computer-Land Store No. 89 appear as follows at April 30, 19X4:

Cash Receipts Journal (Posting reference is CR)		Check Register (Posting reference is CD)	
Date	Cash Debit	Check No.	Cash Credit
Apr. 2	$ 4,174	3113	$ 991
8	407	3114	147
10	559	3115	1,930
16	2,187	3116	664
22	1,854	3117	1,472
29	1,060	3118	1,000
30	337	3119	632
		3120	1,675
Total	$10,578	3121	100
		3122	2,413
		Total	$11,024

Assume the Cash account of the ComputerLand store shows the following information at April 30, 19X4.

Cash

Date	Item	Jrnl. Ref.	Debit	Credit	Balance
Apr. 1	Balance				7,911
30		CR.6	10,578		18,489
30		CD.11		11,024	7,465

ComputerLand Store No. 89 received the following bank statement on April 30, 19X4.

Bank Statement for April 19X4

Beginning balance		$ 7,911
Deposits and other Credits:		
Apr. 4	$4,174	
9	407	
12	559	
17	2,187	
22	1,185 BC	
23	1,854	10,366
Checks and other Debits:		
Apr. 7	$ 991	
13	1,390	
14	903 US	
15	147	
18	664	
26	1,472	
30	1,000	
30	20 SC	6,587
Ending Balance		$11,690

Explanation: BC-Bank Collection US-Unauthorized Signature SC-Service Charge

Additional data for the bank reconciliation include:

1. The unauthorized signature check was received from S. M. Holt.
2. The $1,185 bank collection of a note receivable on April 22 included $185 interest revenue.
3. The correct amount of check number 3115, a payment on account, is $1,390. (The ComputerLand accountant mistakenly recorded the check for $1,930.)

Required

1. Prepare the bank reconciliation of ComputerLand Store No. 89 at April 30, 19X4.
2. Record the entries based on the bank reconciliation. Include explanations.

Problem 7-4B   *Recording and reporting purchases at gross and at net*

Randolph Distributing Company does not use a voucher system. On June 1 of the current year, the company had inventory of $71,300. On June 30 the company had inventory of $74,100. Net sales for June were $263,700, and operating expenses were $106,200. During June Randolph completed the following transactions:

June 2 Purchased inventory costing $41,800 under terms of 2/10 n/30.

8 Returned $5,800 of the inventory purchased on June 2.

11 Purchased inventory costing $39,000 on credit terms of 2/10 n/45.

11 Paid the amount owed from the June 2 invoice, net of the return on June 8 and also net of the discount.

17 Purchased inventory costing $52,300 on credit terms of 2/10 n/30.

20 Paid for the inventory purchased on June 11, less the discount.

30 Paid the gross amount of the purchase on June 17, missing the discount because payment occurred after the discount period.

Required

1. Assuming Randolph records inventory purchases at gross cost:
    a. Record the transactions in a general journal. Explanations are not required.
    b. Prepare the company's income statement for June of the current year.
2. Assuming Randolph records inventory purchases at net cost:
    a. Record the transactions in a general journal. Explanations are not required.
    b. Prepare the company's income statement for June of the current year.
3. Which method of recording purchases offers the internal control advantage? Give your reason.

Problem 7-5B *Accounting for petty cash transactions*

Suppose that on June 1 Goodyear Tire and Rubber Company opens a district office in Salt Lake City and creates a petty cash fund with an imprest balance of $350. During June Mordecai Klever, the fund custodian, signs the following petty cash tickets:

Ticket Number	Item	Amount
1	Postage for package received	$26.20
2	Decorations and refreshments for office party	13.19
3	Two boxes of floppy disks	16.82
4	Typewriter ribbons	27.13
5	Dinner money for sales manager entertaining a customer	50.00
6	Plane ticket for executive business trip to Cody, Wyoming	69.00
7	Delivery of package across town	6.30

On June 30, prior to replenishment, the fund contains these tickets plus $155.51. The accounts affected by petty cash disbursements are Office Supplies Expense, Travel Expense, Delivery Expense, Entertainment Expense, and Postage Expense.

Required

1. Discuss the characteristics and the internal control features of an imprest fund.
2. Make the general journal entries to create the fund and to replenish it. Include explanations. Also, briefly describe what the custodian does on these dates.
3. Make the entry on July 1 to increase the fund balance to $500. Include an explanation, and briefly describe what the custodian does.

Problem 7-6B *Voucher system entries*

Assume a ComputerLand store in Phoenix, Arizona, uses a voucher system and records purchases at *gross* cost. Assume further that the store completed the following transactions during January:

Jan 3 Issued voucher no. 135 payable to Western Telephone for telephone service of $1,007.

  5 Issued voucher no. 136 payable to IBM for the purchase of inventory costing $21,500, with payment terms of 3/10 n/30.

  6 Issued voucher no. 137 payable to City Supply Company for inventory costing $250, with payment terms of 2/10 n/45.

  7 Issued check no. 404 to pay voucher no. 136, less the discount.

  10 Issued check no. 405 to pay voucher no. 135.

  14 Issued check no. 406 to pay voucher no. 137, less the discount.

  15 Issued voucher no. 138 payable to the *Phoenix Sun* for advertising of $1,990.

  17 Issued voucher no. 139 payable to replenish the petty cash fund. The payee is Petty Cash, the amount is $176, and the petty cash tickets list Store Supplies ($16), Delivery Expense ($96), and Miscellaneous Expense ($64). Also issued check no. 407 to pay the voucher.

  18 Issued voucher no. 140 payable to Apple Computer Company for inventory costing $27,600, with payment terms of 2/10 n/30.

  24 Issued voucher no. 141 payable to city of Phoenix for property tax of $4,235. Debit Property Tax Expenses.

  27 Issued voucher no. 142 payable to First State Bank for payment of a note payable ($10,000) and interest expense ($1,200).

  30 Issued check no. 408 to pay voucher no. 140. Because of a filing error, we paid after the discount period and failed to earn the discount.

  31 Issued voucher no. 143 to pay salesperson salary of $2,309 to Lester Gibbs. Also issued check no. 409 to pay the voucher.

Required

1. Record ComputerLand's transactions in a voucher register and a check register like those illustrated in the chapter. Posting references are unnecessary.
2. Open the Vouchers Payable account and post amounts to that account.
3. Prepare the list of unpaid vouchers at January 31 and show that the total matches the balance of Vouchers Payable.

Problem 7-7B   *Voucher system; purchases at net*

Assume that the ComputerLand store in Problem 7-6B records its purchases of inventory and supplies at *net* cost.

Required

1. Record the transactions of Problem 7-6B in a voucher register and a check register. To account for purchase discounts lost, it is necessary to use a check register designed as follows:

Check Register   **Page 4**

Date	Check No.	Payee	Voucher No.	Vouchers Payable	Purchase Discounts Lost	Cash in Bank
				Debit		Credit

2. Post to the Vouchers Payable account.
3. Prepare the list of unpaid vouchers at July 31, and show that the total matches the balance of Vouchers Payable.

Decision Problem

Using the Bank Reconciliation to Detect a Theft

Schaeffer Art Supply has poor internal control over its cash transactions. Recently G. M. Schaeffer, the owner, has suspected the cashier of stealing. Details of the business's cash position at September 30 follow.

1. The Cash account shows a balance of $19,502. This amount includes a September 30 deposit of $3,794 that does not appear on the September 30 bank statement.
2. The September 30 bank statement shows a balance of $15,924. The bank statement lists a $200 credit for a bank collection, an $8 debit for the service charge, and a $36 debit for an NSF check. The Schaeffer accountant has not recorded any of these items on the books.
3. At September 30 the following checks are outstanding:

Check No.	Amount
154	$116
256	150
278	253
291	190
292	206
293	145

4. The cashier handles all incoming cash and makes bank deposits. He also reconciles the monthly bank statement. His September 30 reconciliation follows.

Balance per books, September 30....................			$19,502
Add:	Outstanding checks........................		60
	Bank collection		200
			19,762
Less:	Deposits in transit.................	$3,794	
	Service charge....................	8	
	NSF check.......................	36	3,838
Balance per bank, September 30			$15,924

Schaeffer has requested that you determine whether the cashier has stolen cash from the business and, if so, how much. Schaeffer also asks you to identify how the cashier has attempted to conceal the theft. To make this determination, you perform your own bank reconciliation using the format illustrated in the chapter. There are no bank or book errors. Schaeffer also asks you to evaluate the internal controls and to recommend any changes needed to improve them.

Financial Statement Problem

Internal Controls and Cash

Study the audit opinion of Gulf+Western's financial statements, given at the beginning of Appendix C. Answer the following questions about Gulf+Western's internal controls and cash position.

1. What is the name of Gulf+Western's outside auditing firm? What office of this firm signed the audit? How long after Gulf+Western's fiscal year end did the auditors issue their opinion?
2. Does it appear that Gulf+Western's internal controls are adequate? How can you tell?

3. What standard of auditing did the outside auditors use in examining the Gulf+Western financial statements? By what accounting standards were the Gulf+Western statements evaluated?

4. By how much did Gulf+Western's cash position increase during fiscal 1987? The statement of cash flows (discussed in detail in a later chapter) tells why this increase occurred. Which type of activity—operating, investment, or financing—contributed most to this increase?

Answers to Self-Study Questions

1. e	3. a	5. b	7. c	9. d
2. d	4. c	6. e	8. a	10. b

Accounts and Notes Receivable

From automobiles to houses to bicycles to dinners, people buy on credit every day. As high as annual credit sales for retailers are, credit sales are even higher for manufacturers and wholesalers. Clearly, credit sales lie at the heart of the United States economy, as they do in other developed countries.

Each credit transaction involves at least two parties — the **creditor,** who sells a service or merchandise and obtains a receivable, and the **debtor,** who makes the purchase and creates a payable. This chapter focuses on the creditor's accounting. The accounts that generally appear on a creditor's balance sheet are highlighted in Exhibit 8-1. We will discuss these accounts in our study of receivables.

Different Types of Receivables

A receivable arises when a business (or person) sells goods or services to a second business (or person) on credit. A receivable is the seller's claim against the buyer for the amount of the transaction.

Receivables are monetary claims against businesses and individuals. They are acquired mainly by selling goods and services and by lending money.

The two major types of receivables are accounts receivable and notes receivable. A business's *accounts receivable* are the amounts that its customers owe it. These accounts receivable are sometimes called *trade receivables.* They are *current assets.*

Accounts receivable should be distinguished from accruals, notes and other assets not arising from everyday sales because accounts receivable pertain to the main thrust of the business's operations. Moreover, amounts included as accounts receivable should be collectible according to the business's normal sale terms (such as net 30, or 2/10 n/30).

OBJECTIVE 1
Define different types of receivables

EXHIBIT 8-1 *Balance Sheet*

Example Company		
Balance Sheet		
Date		

Assets

Current:

Cash		$X,XXX
Accounts receivable	$X,XXX	
Less Allowance for uncollectible		
accounts	(XXX)	X,XXX
Notes receivable, short-term		X,XXX
Inventories.		X,XXX
Prepaid expenses.		X,XXX
Total		X,XXX

Investments and long-term receivables:

Investments in other companies	X,XXX
Notes receivable, long-term	X,XXX
Other receivables	X,XXX
Total	X,XXX

Plant assets:

Property, plant, and equipment	X,XXX
Total assets	$X,XXX

Liabilities

Current:

Accounts payable	$X,XXX
Notes payable, short-term	X,XXX
Accrued current liabilities	X,XXX
Total current liabilities	X,XXX

Long-term:

Notes payable, long-term.	X,XXX
Total liabilities	X,XXX

Owner's Equity

Capital	X,XXX
Total liabilities and owner's equity	$X,XXX

Notes receivable are more formal than accounts receivable. The debtor in a note receivable arrangement promises in writing to pay the creditor a definite sum at a definite future date. The terms of these notes usually extend for at least 60 days. A written document known as a *promissory note*, serves as evidence of the receivable. A note may require the debtor to pledge *security* for the loan. This means that the borrower promises that the lender may claim certain assets if the borrower fails to pay the amount due at maturity.

Notes receivable due within one year or less are *current assets*. Those notes due beyond one year are *long-term receivables*. Some notes receivable are collected in periodic installments. The portion due within one year is a current asset, with the remaining amount a long-term asset. GM may hold a $6,000 note receivable from you, but only the $1,500 you owe on it this year is a current asset to GM.

Other receivables is a miscellaneous category that includes loans to employees and branch companies. Usually these are long-term assets but they are current if receivable within one year or less. Long-term notes receivable, and other receivables are often reported on the balance sheet after current assets and before plant assets as shown in Exhibit 8-1.

Each type of receivable is a separate account in the general ledger and may be supported by a subsidiary ledger if needed.

The Credit Department _____

A customer who buys goods using a credit card is buying on account. This transaction creates a receivable for the store. Most companies with a high proportion of sales on account have a separate credit department. This department evaluates customers who apply for credit cards by using standard formulas—which include the applicant's income and credit history, among other factors—for deciding which customers the store will sell to on account. After approving a customer, the credit department monitors customer payment records. Customers with a history of paying on time may receive higher credit limits. Those who fail to pay on time have their limits reduced or eliminated. The credit department also assists the accounting department in measuring collection losses on customers who do not pay.

Uncollectible Accounts (Bad Debts)

Selling on credit creates both a benefit and a cost. Customers unwilling or unable to pay cash immediately may make a purchase on credit. Revenue and profit rise as sales increase. The cost to the seller of extending credit arises from the failure to collect from some credit customers. Accountants label this cost **uncollectible account expense, doubtful account expense,** or **bad debt expense.**

The extent of uncollectible account expense varies from company to company. It depends on the credit risks that managers are willing to accept. Many small retail businesses accept a higher level of risk than do large stores like Sears. Why? Small businesses often have personal ties to customers, which increases the likelihood that customers will pay their accounts.

Measuring Uncollectible Accounts

For a firm that sells on credit, uncollectible account expense is as much a part of doing business as salary expense and depreciation expense. Uncollectible Account Expense—an operating expense—must be measured, recorded, and reported. To do so, accountants use the direct write-off method or the allowance method.

Direct Write-off Method. Under the **direct write-off method** of accounting for bad debts, the company waits until the credit department decides that a customer's account receivable is uncollectible. Then the accountant debits Uncollectible Account Expense and credits the customer's account receivable to write off the account.

Assume it is 19X2 and most credit customers have paid for their 19X1 purchases. At this point, the credit department believes that two customers—Garcia and Smith—will never pay. The department directs the accountant to write off Garcia and Smith as bad debts.

The following entries show the business's accounting for 19X1 credit sales and 19X2 collections and uncollectible accounts.

19X1	Accounts Receivable–Garcia	800	
	Accounts Receivable–Smith	1,200	
	Accounts Receivable–Various Customers	98,000	
	Sales Revenue		100,000
	To record credit sales of $100,000.		
19X2	Cash	97,000	
	Accounts Receivable–Various Customers		97,000
	To record cash collections of $97,000.		

19X2 Uncollectible Account Expense..................... 2,000
           Accounts Receivable–Garcia 800
           Accounts Receivable–Smith................. 1,200
       To write off uncollectible accounts and record bad debt
       expense of $2,000.

Of course, this company would continue making credit sales as an important part of doing business. But what we want to know right now is how the direct write-off method affects financial statements. To see its impact most clearly, let's assume that the company stopped making credit sales altogether in 19X2. Consider the following partial financial statements for 19X1 and 19X2, based on the above journal entries.

Income Statement:	19X1	19X2
Revenue		
Sales revenue.....................................	$100,000	$ -0-
Expense		
Uncollectible account expense	-0-	2,000

	December 31,	
Balance Sheet:	19X1	19X2
Accounts receivable................................	$100,000	$1,000

Let's ask two important questions about this approach to accounting for bad debts.

1. How accurately does the direct write-off method measure income? As we have seen, following generally accepted accounting principles means matching an accounting period's expenses against its revenues. This provides the most accurate picture of operating income, which measures how well a business's operations are running. But the direct write-off method does not match a period's bad debt expense against the same period's sales revenues. In our example, the full amount of sales revenue appears for 19X1, but the expenses incurred to generate this revenue — the bad debts — appear in 19X2. This gives misleading income figures for both years, as would failing to report any other expense — salary, depreciation, and so on — in the correct period. The $2,000 bad debt expense should be matched against the $100,000 sales revenue.

2. How accurately does the direct write-off method value accounts receivable? The 19X1 balance sheet shows accounts receivable at the full $100,000 figure. But any businessperson knows that bad debts are unavoidable when selling on credit. No intelligent manager expects to collect the entire amount. Is the $100,000 figure, then, the expected realizable value of the account? No, showing the full $100,000 in the balance sheet falsely implies that these accounts receivable are worth their face value.

The direct write-off method is simple to use, and it causes no great error if collection losses are insignificant in amount. However, you see that the resulting accounting records are not as accurate as they could be. The allowance method is a better way to account for uncollectible account expense.

Allowance Method.   To present the most accurate financial statements possible, accountants in firms with large credit sales use the **allowance method** of measuring bad debts. This method records collection losses based on estimates prior to determining that the business will not collect from specific customers.

Smart managers know that not every customer will pay in full. But they should not simply credit Accounts Receivable for the amount they believe will not be collected. That would cause the balance of Accounts Receivable to be less than the total of the individual accounts, and managers do not simply write off a customer's account on a hunch.

Rather than try to guess which accounts will go bad, managers, based on collection experience, estimate the total bad debt expense for the period. The business debits Uncollectible Account Expense (or Doubtful Account Expense) for the estimated amount and credits **Allowance for Uncollectible Accounts** (or **Allowance for Doubtful Accounts**), a contra account related to Accounts Receivable. This account shows the estimated amount of collection losses.

To properly match expense against revenue, the uncollectible account expense is estimated—based on past collection experience—and recorded when the sales are made. This expense entry has two effects: (1) it decreases net income by debiting an expense account, and (2) it decreases *net* accounts receivable by crediting the allowance account. (Allowance for Uncollectible Accounts, the contra account, is subtracted from Accounts Receivable to measure *net* accounts receivable.)

Assume the company's sales for 19X1 are $240,000 and that past collection experience suggests estimated bad debts of $3,100. The 19X1 journal entries are as follows, with accounts receivable from customers Rolf and Anderson separated for emphasis:

19X1	Accounts Receivable–Rolf	1,300	
	Accounts Receivable–Anderson...................	1,700	
	Accounts Receivable–Various Customers	237,000	
	Sales Revenue		240,000
	To record credit sales.		
19X1	Uncollectible Account Expense...................	3,100	
	Allowance for Uncollectible Accounts		3,100
	To record estimated bad debt expense, based on past collection experience.		

OBJECTIVE 2
Use the allowance method of accounting for uncollectibles

The account balances at December 31, 19X1, are as follows:

Accounts Receivable	Allowance for Uncollectible Accounts	Sales Revenue	Uncollectible Account Expense
240,000	3,100	240,000	3,100

Net accounts receivable
= $236,900

The 19X1 financial statements will report:

Income Statement:	**19X1**
Revenue:	
Sales revenue..	$240,000
Expense:	
Uncollectible account expense	3,100

Balance Sheet:	December 31, 19X1
Current assets:	
Accounts receivable...................................	$240,000
Less: Allowance for uncollectible accounts...................	3,100
Net accounts receivable	$236,900

Writing off Uncollectible Accounts

During 19X2 the company collects on most of the accounts receivable. However, the credit department determines that customers Rolf and Anderson cannot pay the amounts they owe. The accountant writes off their receivables and makes the following entries:

19X2	Cash	235,000	
	Accounts Receivable—Various Customers		235,000
	To record collections on account.		

19X2	Allowance for Uncollectible Accounts	3,000	
	Accounts Receivable—Rolf		1,300
	Accounts Receivable—Anderson.............		1,700
	To write off uncollectible accounts.		

The write-off entry has no effect on net income because it includes no debit to an expense account. The entry also has no effect on *net* accounts receivable because both the Allowance account debited and the Accounts Receivable account credited are part of *net* accounts receivable. The account balances at December 31, 19X2, are as follows:

Accounts Receivable		Allowance for Uncollectible Accounts	
240,000	235,000		
	1,300	3,000	3,100
	1,700		100
2,000			

The financial statements for 19X1 and 19X2 will report the following. In order to highlight the matching of expense and revenue, we are assuming no sales are made in 19X2.

Income Statement:	19X1	19X2
Revenue:		
Sales revenue..................................	$240,000	$ 0
Expense:		
Uncollectible account expense	3,100	0

	December 31,	
Balance Sheet:	19X1	19X2
Current assets:		
Accounts receivable...........................	$240,000	$ 2,000
Less: Allowance for uncollectible accounts.........	3,100	100
Net accounts receivable	$236,900	$ 1,900

Compare these income statement and balance sheet effects with those for the direct write-off method on page 312. Which method, direct write-off or allowance, better matches bad debt expense with sales revenue? The allowance method ties this expense of 19X1 to 19X1 revenue and so provides a better matching of expense to revenue—a key objective of accounting. The allowance method also reports accounts receivable at their expected realizable value.

Bad Debt Write-Offs Rarely Equal the Allowance for Uncollectibles

Bad debt write-offs of customer accounts are actual amounts due from customers, but the allowance amount is based on estimates. Write-offs equal the allowance only if the estimate of bad debts is perfect—a rare occurrence. Usually the difference between write-offs and the allowance is small, as shown in the preceding example. If the allowance is too large for one period, the estimate of bad debts for the next period can be cut back. If the allowance is too low, an adjusting entry debiting Uncollectible Account Expense and crediting Allowance for Uncollectible Accounts can be made at the end of the period. This credit brings the Allowance account to a realistic balance. Estimating uncollectibles will be discussed shortly.

Recoveries of Uncollectible Accounts

When an account receivable is written off as uncollectible, the receivable does not die. The customer still has an obligation to pay. However, the likelihood of receiving cash is so low that the company ceases its collection effort and writes off the account. Such accounts are filed for use in future credit decisions. Some companies turn them over to an attorney for collection in the hope of recovering part of the receivable. To record a recovery, the accountant reverses the write-off and records the collection in the regular manner. The reversal of the write-off is needed to give the customer account receivable a debit balance.

Assume that the write-off of Rolf's account ($1,300) occurs in February 19X2. In August Rolf pays the account in full. The journal entries for this situation follow:

Feb. 19X2	To write off Rolf's account as uncollectible (same as above):		
	Allowance for Uncollectible Accounts...............	1,300	
	Accounts Receivable—Rolf.................		1,300
Aug. 19X2	To reinstate Rolf's account:		
	Accounts Receivable—Rolf......................	1,300	
	Allowance for Uncollectible Accounts.........		1,300
	To record collection from Rolf:		
	Cash...	1,300	
	Accounts Receivable—Rolf.................		1,300

Estimating Uncollectibles

We have seen that the allowance method results in more realistic financial statements. The more accurate the estimate, the more reliable the information in the statements. How are bad debt estimates made?

The most logical way to estimate bad debts is to look at the business's past records. Both the *percentage of sales* method and the *aging of accounts receivable* method use the company's collection experience.

OBJECTIVE 3

Estimate uncollectibles by the percentage of sales and the aging approaches

Percentage of Sales.　A business may compute uncollectible account expense as a percentage of total credit sales (or total sales). Uncollectible account expense is recorded as an adjusting entry at the end of the period.

Basing its decision on figures from the last four periods, a business estimates that bad debt expense will be 2.5 percent of credit sales. If credit sales for 19X3 total $500,000, the adjusting entry to record bad debt expense for the year is

Adjusting Entries

Dec. 31	Uncollectible Account Expense ($500,000 × .025)	12,500
	Allowance for Uncollectible Accounts	12,500

Under the percentage of sales method, the amount of this entry ignores the prior balance in Allowance for Uncollectible Accounts.

A business may change the percentage rate from year to year, depending on its collection experience. Suppose collections of accounts receivable in 19X4 are greater, and write-offs are less, than expected. The credit balance in Allowance for Doubtful Accounts would be too large in relation to the debit balance of Accounts Receivable. How would the business change its bad debt percentage rate in this case? *Decreasing* the percentage rate would reduce the credit entry to the allowance account, and the allowance account balance would not grow too large.

New businesses, with no credit history on which to base their rates, may obtain estimated bad debt percentages from industry trade journals, government publications, and other sources of collection data.

Aging the Accounts.　The second popular method of estimating bad debts is called **aging the accounts.** In this approach, individual accounts receivable are analyzed according to the length of time that they have been due. Performed manually, this is time consuming. Computers greatly ease the burden. Schmidt Home Builders groups its accounts receivable into 30-day periods, as the following table shows.

	Age of Account				
Customer Name	1–30 Days	31–60 Days	61–90 Days	Over 90 Days	Total Balance
Oxwall Tools Co.	$20,000				$ 20,000
Chicago Pneumatic Parts	10,000				10,000
Sarasota Pipe Corp.		$13,000	$10,000		23,000
Seal Coatings, Inc.			3,000	$1,000	4,000
Other accounts*	39,000	12,000	2,000	2,000	55,000
Totals	$69,000	$25,000	$15,000	$3,000	$112,000
Estimated percentage uncollectible	0.1%	1%	5%	90%	
Allowance for Uncollectible Accounts	$69	$250	$750	$2,700	$3,769

* Each of the "Other accounts" would appear individually.

Schmidt bases the percentage figures on the company's collection experience. In the past, the business has collected all but 0.1 percent of accounts aged from 1 to 30 days, all but 1 percent of accounts aged 31 to 60 days, and so on.

The total amount receivable in each age group is multiplied by the appropriate percentage figure. For example, the $69,000 in accounts aged 1 to 30 days is multiplied by 0.1 percent (.001), which comes to $69. The total balance needed in the Allowance for Uncollectible Accounts — $3,769 — is the sum of the amounts computed for the various groups ($69 + $250 + $750 + $2,700).

Suppose the Allowance account has a $2,100 *credit* balance from the previous period:

Allowance for Uncollectible Accounts	
	Unadjusted balance 2,100

Under the aging method, the adjusting entry is designed to adjust this account balance from $2,100 to $3,769, the needed amount determined by the aging schedule. To bring the Allowance balance up to date, Schmidt makes this entry:

Adjusting Entries

Dec. 31	Uncollectible Account Expense......................	1,669	
	Allowance for Uncollectible Accounts		
	($3,769 − $2,100)		1,669

Observe that under the aging method, the adjusting entry takes into account the prior balance in Allowance for Uncollectibles. Now the Allowance account has the correct balance:

Allowance for Uncollectible Accounts	
	Unadjusted balance 2,100
	Adjustment amount 1,669
	Adjusted balance 3,769

It is possible that the allowance account might have a *debit* balance at year end prior to the adjusting entry. How can this occur? Bad debt write-offs during the year could have exceeded the allowance amount. Suppose the unadjusted Allowance for Uncollectible Accounts balance is a *debit* amount of $1,500:

Allowance for Uncollectible Accounts	
Unadjusted balance 1,500	

In this situation, the adjusting entry is

Adjusting Entries

Dec. 31	Uncollectible Account Expense ($3,769 + $1,500)	5,269	
	Allowance for Uncollectible Accounts		5,269

After posting, the allowance account is up to date:

Allowance for Uncollectible Accounts

Unadjusted balance	1,500	Adjustment amount	5,269
		Adjusted balance	3,769

On the balance sheet, the $3,769 is subtracted from the Accounts Receivable figure—which the table at the bottom of page 316 shows is $112,000—to report the expected realizable value of the accounts receivable—$108,231 ($112,000 − $3,769).

In addition to supplying the information needed for sound financial reporting, the aging method directs management's attention to the accounts that need to be pursued for payment.

Comparing the Two Methods. In practice, many companies use both the percentage of sales and the aging of accounts methods. For interim statements (monthly or quarterly), companies use the percent of sales method because it is easier to apply. At the end of the year, these companies use the aging method to ensure that they report Accounts Receivable at their expected realizable value. For this reason auditors usually require an aging of the accounts on the year-end date. The two methods work well together because the percent of sales approach focuses on measuring bad debt expense on the income statement whereas the aging approach is designed to measure net accounts receivable on the balance sheet.

Credit Balances in Accounts Receivable _____

Occasionally, customers overpay their accounts or return merchandise for which they have already paid. The result is a credit balance in the customer's account receivable. Assume the company's subsidiary ledger contains 213 accounts, with balances as shown:

210 accounts with *debit* balances totaling..............................	$185,000
3 accounts with *credit* balances totaling	2,800
Net total of debit balances..	$182,200

The company should not report the asset Accounts Receivable at the net amount—$182,200. Why not? The credit balance—the $2,800—is a liability. Like any other liability, customer credit balances are debts of the business. A balance sheet that did not indicate to management or to other financial statement users that the company had this liability amount would be misleading if the $2,800 is material in relation to net income or total current assets. Therefore, the company would report on its balance sheet:

Assets		**Liabilities**	
Current:		Current:	
Accounts receivable.....	$185,000	Credit balances in customer accounts.......	$ 2,800

Credit Card Sales _____

Credit card sales are common in the retail industry. American Express, Diners Club, Carte Blanche, VISA, and MasterCard are popular.

The customer presents the credit card as payment for a purchase. The seller prepares a sales invoice in triplicate. The customer and the seller keep copies as receipts. The third copy goes to the credit card company, which then pays the seller the transaction amount and bills the customer.

Credit cards offer consumers the convenience of buying without having to pay the cash immediately. Also, consumers receive a monthly statement from the credit card company, detailing each credit card transaction. They can write a single check to cover the entire month's credit card purchases.

Retailers also benefit from credit card sales. They do not have to check a customer's credit rating. The company that issues the card has already done so. Retailers do not have to keep an accounts receivable subsidiary ledger account for each customer, and they do not have to collect cash from customers. The copy of the sale invoice that retailers send to the credit card company signals the card issuer to pursue payment. Further, retailers receive cash more quickly from the credit card companies than they would from the customers themselves. Of course, these services to the seller do not come free.

The seller receives less than 100 percent of the face value of the invoice. The credit card company takes a 5 percent[1] discount on the sale to cover its services. The seller's entry to record a $100 Diners Club sale is

Accounts Receivable–Diners Club............................	100	
Sales Revenue		100

On collection of the discounted value, the seller records:

Cash..	95	
Credit Card Discount Expense	5	
Accounts Receivable–Diners Club........................		100

Internal Control over Collections of Accounts Receivable _____

Businesses that sell on credit receive most of their cash receipts by mail. Internal control over collections on account is an important part of the overall internal control system. Chapter 7 detailed control procedures over cash receipts, but a critical element of internal control deserves emphasis here: the separation of cash-handling and cash-accounting duties. Consider the following case.

Butler Supply Co. is a small, family-owned business that takes pride in the loyalty of its workers. Most company employees have been with the Butlers for at least five years. The company makes 90 percent of its sales on account.

The office staff consists of a bookkeeper and a supervisor. The bookkeeper maintains the general ledger and the accounts receivable subsidiary ledger. He

---

[1] The rate varies among companies and over time.

also makes the daily bank deposit. The supervisor prepares monthly financial statements and any special reports the Butlers require. She also takes sales orders from customers and serves as office manager.

OBJECTIVE 4
Identify internal control weaknesses in accounts receivable

Can you identify the internal control weakness? The bookkeeper has access to the general ledger, the accounts receivable subsidiary ledger, and the cash. The bookkeeper could take a customer check and write off the customer's account as uncollectible.[2] Unless the supervisor or some other manager reviews the bookkeeper's work regularly, the theft may go undetected. In small businesses like Butler Supply Co., such a review may not be routinely performed.

How can this control weakness be corrected? The supervisor could open incoming mail and make the daily bank deposit. The bookkeeper should not be allowed to handle cash. Only the remittance slips would be forwarded to the bookkeeper to indicate which customer accounts to credit. Removing cash-handling duties from the bookkeeper, and keeping the accounts receivable subsidiary ledger away from the supervisor, separates duties and strengthens internal control. It reduces an employee's opportunity to steal cash and then cover it up with a false credit to a customer account. Also, the owner should prepare the bank reconciliation.

---

[2] The bookkeeper would need to forge the endorsements of the checks and deposit them in a bank account he controls. This is easier to do than you might imagine.

Summary Problem for Your Review

CPC International, Inc., is the food-products company that produces Skippy peanut butter, Hellman's mayonnaise, and Mazola corn oil. The company balance sheet at December 31, 19X7, reported:

	Millions
Notes and accounts receivable [total].	$549.9
Allowances for doubtful accounts	(12.5)

Required

a. How much of the December 31, 19X7, balance of notes and accounts receivable did CPC expect to collect? Stated differently, what was the expected realizable value of these receivables?

b. Journalize, without explanations, 19X8 entries for CPC International, assuming:
   1) Estimated Doubtful Account Expense of $19.2 million, based on the percentage of sales method.
   2) Write-offs of accounts receivable totaling $23.6 million.
   3) December 31, 19X8, aging of receivables, which indicates that $15.3 million of the total receivables of $582.7 million is uncollectible.

c. Show how CPC International's receivables and related allowance will appear on the December 31, 19X8, balance sheet.

d. What is the expected realizable value of receivables at December 31, 19X8? How much is doubtful account expense for 19X8?

SOLUTION TO REVIEW PROBLEM

		Millions
a.	Expected realizable value of receivables ($549.9 − $12.5)	$537.4

			Millions
b.	1) Doubtful Account Expense	19.2	
	Allowance for Doubtful Accounts.		19.2
	2) Allowance for Doubtful Accounts.	23.6	
	Accounts Receivable.		23.6

Allowance for Doubtful Accounts

19X8	23.6	Dec. 31, 19X7	12.5
		19X8	19.2
		19X8 balance prior to December 31, 19X8	8.1

			Millions
	3) Doubtful Account Expense ($15.3 − $8.1)	7.2	
	Allowance for Doubtful Accounts.		7.2

		Millions
c.	Notes and accounts receivable	$582.7
	Allowance for doubtful accounts	(15.3)

		Millions
d.	Expected realizable value of receivables at December 31, 19X8 ($582.7 − $15.3)	$567.4
	Doubtful Account Expense for 19X8 ($19.2 + $7.2)	26.4

Notes Receivable

As we pointed out earlier in this chapter, notes receivable are more formal arrangements than accounts receivable. Often the debtor signs a promissory note, which serves as evidence of the debt. Let's take a moment to define the special terms used to discuss notes receivable.

OBJECTIVE 5

Use notes receivable terminology

Promissory note. A written promise to pay a specified amount of money at a particular future date.

Maker of a note. The person or business that signs the note and promises to pay the amount required by the note agreement. The maker is the debtor.

Payee of the note. The person or business to whom the maker promises future payment. The payee is the creditor.

Principal amount, or **principal.** The amount loaned out by the payee and borrowed by the maker of the note.

EXHIBIT 8-2   *A Promissory Note*

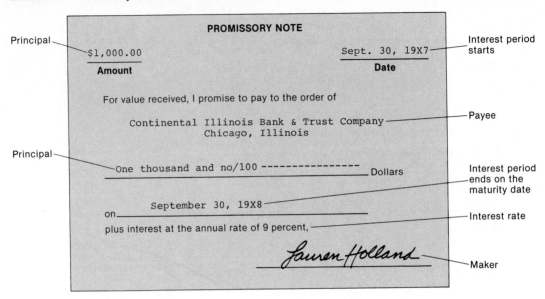

Principal

$1,000.00

Amount

Sept. 30, 19X7

Date

Interest period starts

For value received, I promise to pay to the order of

Continental Illinois Bank & Trust Company
Chicago, Illinois

Payee

Principal

One thousand and no/100 ---------------- Dollars

Interest period ends on the maturity date

September 30, 19X8

on_____

plus interest at the annual rate of 9 percent, _____

Interest rate

Lauren Holland

Maker

Interest. The revenue to the payee for loaning out the principal and the expense to the maker for borrowing the principal.

Interest period. The period of time during which interest is to be computed. It extends from the original date of the note to the maturity date.

Interest rate. The percentage rate that is multiplied by the principal amount to compute the amount of interest on the note.

Maturity date, or **due date.** The date on which final payment of the note is due.

Maturity value. The sum of principal and interest due at the maturity date of a note.

Note period or **note term.** Synonyms for the interest period.

Exhibit 8-2 illustrates a promissory note. Study it carefully, and identify each of the above items for the note agreement.

Identifying the Maturity Date of a Note

Some notes specify the maturity date of a note, as shown in Exhibit 8-2. Other notes state the period of the note, in days or months. When the period is given in months, the note's maturity date falls on the same day of the month as the date the note was issued. For example, a 6-month note dated February 16 matures on August 16.

When the period is given in days, the maturity date is determined by counting the days from date of issue. A 120-day note dated September 14, 19X2, matures on January 12, 19X3, as shown below:

Month	Number of Days	Cumulative Total
Sept. 19X2	16*	16
Oct. 19X2	31	47
Nov. 19X2	30	77
Dec. 19X2	31	108
Jan. 19X3	12	120

———————
* 30 − 14 = 16.

Computing Interest on a Note

The formula for computing interest is

Principal × Rate × Time = Amount of Interest

Using the data in Exhibit 8-2, Continental Bank computes its interest revenue for one year on its note receivable as:

Principal   Rate   Time   Interest
$1,000   × .09   × 1 (yr.) = $90

The *maturity value* of the note is $1,090 ($1,000 principal + $90 interest). Note that the time element is one (1) because interest is computed over a 1-year period.

When the interest period of a note is stated in months, we compute the interest based on the 12-month year. Interest on a $2,000 note at 15 percent for 3 months is computed as:

Principal   Rate   Time   Interest
$2,000   × .15   × 3/12 = $75

When the interest period of a note is stated in days, we sometimes compute interest based on a 360-day year rather than a 365-day year. The interest on a $5,000 note at 12 percent for 60 days is computed as:

Principal   Rate   Time   Interest
$5,000   × .12   × 60/360 = $100

Recording Notes Receivable

Consider the loan agreement shown in Exhibit 8-2. After Holland signs the note and presents it to the bank, Continental Bank gives her $1,000 cash. At maturity, Holland pays the bank $1,090 ($1,000 principal plus $90 interest). The bank's entries are

Sept. 30, 19X7	Note Receivable–L. Holland	1,000	
	Cash		1,000
	To record the loan.		
Sept. 30, 19X8	Cash	1,090	
	Note Receivable–L. Holland		1,000
	Interest Revenue ($1,000 × .09 × 1)		90
	To record collection at maturity.		

OBJECTIVE 6
Account for notes receivable

Some companies sell merchandise in exchange for notes receivable. This arrangement occurs often when the payment term extends beyond the customary accounts receivable period, which generally ranges from 30 to 60 days.

Suppose that on October 20, 19X3, General Electric sells equipment for $15,000 to Dorman Builders. Dorman signs a 90-day promissory note at 10 percent annual interest. General Electric's entries to record the sale and collection from Dorman are

Oct. 20, 19X3	Note Receivable–Dorman Builders	15,000	
	Sales Revenue		15,000
	To record sale.		
Jan. 18, 19X4	Cash	15,375	
	Note Receivable–Dorman Builders		15,000
	Interest Revenue ($15,000 × .10 ×		
	90/360)		375
	To record collection at maturity.		

A company may accept a note receivable from a trade customer who fails to pay an account receivable within the customary 30 to 60 days. The customer signs a promissory note — that is, becomes the maker of the note — and gives it to the creditor, who becomes the payee.

Suppose Casa de Sanchez, Inc., sees that it will not be able to pay off its account payable to Hoffman Supply that is due in 15 days. Hoffman may accept a note receivable from Casa de Sanchez. Hoffman's entry is

May 3	Note Receivable–Casa de Sanchez, Inc.	2,400	
	Accounts Receivable–Casa de Sanchez, Inc..		2,400
	To receive a note on account from a customer.		

Hoffman later records interest and collection as illustrated in the preceding examples.

Why does a company accept a note receivable instead of pressing its demand for payment of the account receivable? The company may pursue receipt but learn that its customer does not have the money. A note receivable gives the company written evidence of the maker's debt, which may aid any legal action for collection. Also, the note receivable may carry a pledge by the maker that gives the payee certain assets if cash is not received by the due date. The company's reward for its patience is the interest revenue that it earns on the note receivable.

Discounting a Note Receivable

A note receivable is a *negotiable instrument,* which means it is readily transferrable from one business or person to another and may be sold for cash. To get cash quickly, payees sometimes sell a note receivable to another party before the note matures. The payee endorses the note and hands it over to the note purchaser — often a bank — who collects the maturity value of the note at the maturity date. Selling a note receivable before maturity is called **discounting a note receivable** because the payee of the note receives less than its maturity value. This lower price decreases the amount of interest revenue the payee earns on the note. Giving up some of this interest is the price the payee is willing to pay for the convenience of receiving cash early.

Return to the preceding example with General Electric and Dorman Builders. Recall that the maturity date of the Dorman note is January 18, 19X4. Let's assume General Electric discounts the Dorman note at First City National Bank on December 9, 19X3. The discount period — which is the number of days from the date of discounting to the date of maturity (this is the period the bank will hold the note) — is 40 days; 22 days in December, and 18 days in January. Assume the bank applies a 12 percent annual interest rate in computing the discounted value of the note. The bank will want to use a discount rate that is higher than the interest rate on the note in order to increase its earnings. GE may be willing to accept this higher rate in order to get cash quickly. The discounted value, called the *proceeds,* is the amount that GE receives from the bank. The proceeds are computed as follows:

Principal amount..................	$15,000
+ Interest ($15,000 × .10 × 90/360)....	375
= Maturity value....................	$15,375
− Discount ($15,375 × .12 × 40/360)...	(205)
= Proceeds........................	$15,170

$170 $170

At maturity the bank collects $15,375 from the maker of the note, earning $205 of interest revenue.

Observe two points in the above computation: (1) The discount is computed on the *maturity value* of the note (principal plus interest) rather than on the original principal amount, and (2) the discount period extends *backward* from the maturity date (January 18, 19X4) to the date of discounting (December 9, 19X3). Follow this diagram:

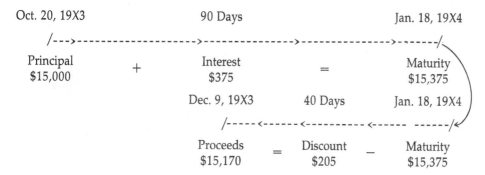

General Electric's entry to record discounting the note is

Dec. 9, 19X3	Cash....................................	15,170	
	Note Receivable—Dorman Builders		15,000
	Interest Revenue ($15,170 − $15,000).....		170
	To record discounting a note receivable.		

When the proceeds from discounting a note receivable are less than the principal amount of the note, the payee records a debit to Interest Expense for the amount of the difference. The term *discount* has been used here to distinguish the interest earned by the payee of the note from the interest to be earned by the purchaser of the note. Fundamentally, the discount is interest.

Contingent Liabilities on Discounted Notes Receivable

Discounting a note receivable creates a **contingent**—that is, a potential—**liability** for the endorser. The contingent liability is this: If the maker of the note (Dorman, in our example) fails to pay the maturity value to the new payee (the bank), then the original payee (General Electric, the note's endorser) legally must pay the bank the amount due.[3] Now we see why the liability is "potential." If

---

[3] The discounting agreement between the endorser and the purchaser may specify that the endorser has no liability if the note is dishonored at maturity.

Dorman pays the bank, then General Electric can forget the note. But if Dorman dishonors the note—fails to pay it—General Electric has an actual liability.

This contingent liability of General Electric exists from the time of endorsement to the maturity date of the note. In our example, the contingent liability exists from December 9, 19X3—when General Electric endorsed the note—to the January 18, 19X4, maturity date.

Contingent liabilities are not reported with actual liabilities on the balance sheet. After all, they are not real debts. However, financial-statement users should be alerted that the business has *potential* debts. Many businesses report contingent liabilities in a footnote to the financial statements. General Electric's end-of-period balance sheet might carry this note:

> As of December 31, 19X3, the Company is contingently liable on notes receivable discounted in the amount of $15,000.

Dishonored Notes Receivable

If the maker of a note does not pay a note receivable at maturity, the maker is said to **dishonor,** or **default on,** the note. Because the term of the note has expired, the note agreement is no longer in force, nor is it negotiable. However, the payee still has a claim against the maker of the note and usually transfers the claim from the note receivable account to Accounts Receivable. The payee records interest revenue earned on the note and debits Accounts Receivable for the full maturity value of the note.

Suppose Rubinstein Jewelers has a six-month, 10 percent note receivable for $1,200 from D. Hatachi. On the February 3 maturity date, Hatachi defaults. Rubinstein Jewelers would record the default as follows:

Feb. 3	Accounts Receivable–D. Hatachi [$1,200 + ($1,200 × .10 × 6/12)] 1,260	
	Note Receivable–D. Hatachi. . . . . :	1,200
	Interest Revenue ($1,200 × .10 × 6/12).	60
	To record dishonor of note receivable.	

Rubinstein would pursue collection from Hatachi as a promissory note default. The company may treat accounts receivable such as this as a special category to highlight them for added collection efforts. If the account receivable later proves uncollectible, the account is written off against Allowance for Uncollectible Accounts in the manner previously discussed.

The maker may dishonor a note after it has been discounted by the original payee. For example, suppose Dorman Builders dishonors its note (maturity value, $15,375) to General Electric (GE) after GE has discounted the note to the bank. On dishonor, the bank adds a *protest fee* to cover the cost of a statement about the facts of the dishonor and requests payment from General Electric, which then becomes the holder of the dishonored note. Assume GE pays the maturity value of the note, plus the $25 protest fee, to the bank. This creates an obligation for Dorman to pay GE. GE then presents the statement to Dorman and makes the following entry on the maturity date of the note:

Jan. 18, 19X4	Accounts Receivable–Dorman Builders ($15,375 + $25) 15,400	
	Cash	15,400
	To record payment of dishonored note receivable that has been discounted.	

GE's collection of cash, or write off of the uncollectible account receivable, would be recorded in the normal manner, depending on the ultimate outcome. If GE charges Dorman additional interest, GE's collection entry debits Cash and credits Accounts Receivable and Interest Revenue.

Accruing Interest Revenue

Notes receivable may be outstanding at the end of the accounting period. The interest revenue that was accrued on the note up to that point should be recorded as part of that period's earnings. Recall that interest revenue is earned over time, not just when cash is received.

Suppose First City Bank receives a one-year $1,000 note receivable, with 9 percent interest, on October 1, 19X7. The bank's accounting period ends December 31. How much of the total interest revenue does First City Bank earn in 19X7? How much in 19X8?

The bank will earn three months' interest in 19X7 — for October, November, and December. In 19X8, the bank will earn nine months' interest — for January through September. Therefore, at December 31, 19X7, First City will make the following adjusting entry to accrue interest revenue:

Dec. 31, 19X7	Interest Receivable ($1,000 × .09 × 3/12)	22.50	
	Interest Revenue		22.50
	To accrue interest revenue earned in 19X7 but not yet received.		

Then, on the maturity date First City Bank may record collection of principal and interest as follows:

Sept. 30, 19X8	Cash [$1,000 + ($1,000 × .09)]	1,090.00	
	Note Receivable		1,000.00
	Interest Receivable ($1,000 × .09 × 3/12).		22.50
	Interest Revenue ($1,000 × .09 × 9/12) ..		67.50
	To record collection of note receivable on which interest has been previously accrued.		

The entries to accrue interest revenue earned in 19X7 and to record collection in 19X8 assign the correct amount of interest to each year.

Reporting Receivables and Allowances: Actual Reports

Let's take a look at how some well-known companies report their receivables and related allowances for uncollectibles on the balance sheet. The terminology and setup vary, but you can understand these actual presentations based on what you have learned in this chapter.

Bobbie Brooks, a manufacturer of women's clothing, reports under Current Assets (in thousands):

Accounts receivable, less allowance for doubtful accounts of $602	$35,873

OBJECTIVE 7

Report receivables on the balance sheet

To figure the total accounts receivable amount, add the allowance to the net accounts receivable amount: $602 + $35,873 = $36,475.

Premark International, Inc., which makes Tupperware plastic food-storage containers, combines accounts and notes receivable (amounts in millions):

> Accounts and notes receivable, less
> allowances of $19.5 . . . . $309.9

General Electric Company reports a single amount for its current receivables in the body of the balance sheet and supplements it with a detailed note (amounts in millions):

> Current receivables (note 8) $4,872
>
> Note 8:   Current Receivables
> Customers' accounts and notes $3,989
> Associated companies   49
> Nonconsolidated affiliates   21
> Other   927
> 4,986
> Less allowance for losses . . . .   (114)
> $4,872

Deere & Company, maker of farm machinery, lists more detail in the body of the balance sheet (amounts in thousands of dollars):

> Trade receivables:
> Dealer accounts and notes $2,373,018
> Retail notes   40,558
> Total   2,413,576
> Less allowances   39,183
> Trade receivables, net $2,374,393

Nashua Corporation, manufacturer of copying machines and paper products, reported approximately $70,000,000 in net accounts and notes receivable. In addition, the company disclosed a contingent liability for discounted accounts and notes receivable in its Notes to Financial Statements:

ACCOUNTS RECEIVABLE:

At December 31, 19X1 and 19X0, the company was contingently liable to third parties as a result of the sale of certain accounts and notes receivable of approximately $19,000,000 and $16,000,000, respectively.

The companies we have featured so far list receivables as *current assets.* National Can Corporation, however, had some long-term receivables that it reported as other assets (amounts in thousands of dollars).

OTHER ASSETS:

Notes and accounts receivable, less allowances . . . $36,970

National Can also disclosed in a note entitled Notes and Accounts Receivable that:

> Notes and accounts receivable included in other assets are net of allowances for doubtful accounts of $16,772.

Using Computers to Account for Receivables

A computer greatly eases accounting for receivables. Painstaking work—like posting credit sales and collections, aging accounts receivable, and computing interest—can be performed with a computer in far less time than it takes to do them manually, and with fewer errors. Once the program is written and the data are entered, the machine can perform the calculations again and again. Commercial software is available to perform these tasks on a microcomputer, so even small businesses use them.

Suppose a homebuilder uses an Apple micro and commercial software to handle routine accounting work. Assume the business accepts notes receivable for its work and, rather than hold the notes for several years, sells them to a local bank. The owner can use a program to compute a range of cash proceeds amounts that depend on different discount rates the bank is likely to propose. With this knowledge, the business person can probably strike a better deal with the bank. Instead of having to perform a half dozen such calculations by hand, the business owner or accountant can program the micro to do the arithmetic.

Suppose the homebuilder's accountant "roughs out" the calculations for discounting prior to writing the program in BASIC programming language. In computer programming, symbols are less cumbersome to work with than full terms because each term may be lengthy and may have to be written several times. For each note receivable,

Let: M = Maturity value
 P = Principal value
 R = Interest rate
 T = Time period
 D = Dollar amount of the discount
 BR = Bank's interest rate used to discount the note (the discount rate)
 BT = Time period the bank will hold the note (the discount period)
 C = Cash proceeds from discounting the note

Then the cash proceeds (C) can be computed as follows:

$$M = P + (P \times R \times T)$$
$$D = M \times BR \times BT$$
$$C = M - D$$

Prior to discounting a note, the builder or his accountant can simply enter the value of each variable into the computer, and it will determine the cash proceeds. The program and all the data on notes receivable can be stored on a floppy disk for future use. The information can be retrieved when needed—for example, for preparation of the financial statements, including the note for contingent liabilities.

Summary Problem for Your Review

Suppose Exxon, Inc., engaged in the following transactions:

19X4

Apr. 1   Loaned $8,000 to Bland Co., a service station. Received a one-year, 10 percent note.

June 1   Discounted the Bland note at the bank at a discount rate of 12 percent.

Nov. 30   Loaned $6,000 to Flores, Inc., a regional distributor of Exxon products, on a three-month, 11 percent note.

19X5

Feb. 28   Collected the Flores note at maturity.

Exxon's accounting period ends on December 31.

Required

Explanations are not needed.

1.   Record the 19X4 transactions on April 1, June 1, and November 30 on Exxon's books.
2.   Make any adjusting entries needed on December 31, 19X4.
3.   Record the February 28, 19X5, collection of the Flores note.
4.   Which transaction creates a contingent liability for Exxon? When does the contingency begin? When does it end?
5.   Write a footnote that Exxon could use in its 19X4 financial statements to report the contingent liability.

SOLUTION TO REVIEW PROBLEM

1.   19X4

Apr. 1   Note Receivable–Bland Co.   8,000

        Cash   8,000

June 1   Cash 7,920*

      Interest Expense.   80

        Note Receivable–Bland Co.   8,000

      * Computation of proceeds:

        Principal. $8,000

        + Interest ($8,000 × .10 × 12/12).   800

        = Maturity value   8,800

        − Discount ($8,800 × .12 × 10/12)   880

        = Proceeds $7,920

Nov. 30   Note Receivable–Flores, Inc.   6,000

        Cash   6,000

2.   Adjusting Entry

19X4

Dec. 31   Interest Receivable ($6,000 × .11 × 1/12)   55

        Interest Revenue   55

19X5

3. Feb. 28   Cash [$6,000 + ($6,000 × .11 × 3/12)]   6,165

           Note Receivable – Flores, Inc.   6,000

           Interest Receivable.   55

           Interest Revenue ($6,000 × .11 × 2/12) . .   110

4. Discounting the Bland note receivable creates a contingent liability for Exxon. The contingency exists from the date of discounting the note receivable (June 1) to the maturity date of the note (April 1, 19X5).

5. Note XX—Contingent liabilities: At December 31, 19X4, the Company is contingently liable on notes receivable discounted in the amount of $8,000.

Summary

Credit sales create receivables. Accounts receivable are usually current assets, and notes receivable may be current or long term.

Uncollectible receivables are accounted for by the direct write-off method or the allowance method. The *direct write-off method* is easy to apply, but it fails to match the uncollectible account expense to the corresponding sales revenue. Also, Accounts Receivable are reported at their full amount, which misleadingly suggests that the company expects to collect all its accounts receivable. The *allowance method* matches expenses to sales revenue and also results in a more realistic measure of net accounts receivable. The *percent of sales method* and the *aging of accounts receivable method* are the two main approaches to estimating bad debts under the allowance method.

In *credit card* sales, the seller receives cash from the credit card company (American Express, for example), which bills the customer. For the convenience of receiving cash immediately, the seller pays a fee, which is a percentage of the sale.

Companies that sell on credit receive most customer collections in the mail. Good *internal control* over mailed-in cash receipts means separating cash-handling duties from cash-accounting duties.

Notes receivable are formal credit agreements. Interest earned by the creditor is computed by multiplying the note's principal amount by the interest rate times the length of the interest period.

Because notes receivable are negotiable, they may be sold. Selling a note receivable—called *discounting a note*—creates a *contingent (possible) liability* for the note's payee.

All accounts receivable, notes receivable, and allowance accounts appear in the balance sheet. However, companies use various formats and terms to report these assets.

Self-Study Questions

Test your understanding of the chapter by marking the best answer for each of the following questions.

1. The party that holds a receivable is called the *(p. 309)*
   - a. Creditor
   - b. Debtor
   - c. Maker
   - d. Security holder
2. The function of the credit department is to *(p. 311)*
   - a. Collect accounts receivable from customers
   - b. Report bad credit risks to other companies
   - c. Evaluate customers who apply for credit
   - d. Write off uncollectible accounts receivable

3. Longview, Inc., made the following entry related to uncollectibles:

Uncollectible Account Expense 1,900
      Allowance for Uncollectible Accounts   1,900

The purpose of this entry is to *(p. 313)*
a. Write off uncollectibles   c. Age the accounts receivable
b. Close the expense account   d. Record bad debt expense

4. Longview, Inc., also made this entry:

Allowance for Uncollectible Accounts 2,110
      Accounts Receivable (detailed)   2,110

The purpose of this entry is to *(p. 314)*
a. Write off uncollectibles   c. Age the accounts receivable
b. Close the expense account   d. Record bad debt expense

5. The credit balance in Allowance for Uncollectibles is $14,300 prior to the adjusting entries at the end of the period. The aging of accounts indicates that an allowance of $78,900 is needed. The amount of expense to record is *(p. 317)*
  a. $14,300   c. $78,900
  b. $64,600   d. $93,200

6. The most important internal control over cash receipts is *(p. 319)*
  a. Assigning an honest employee the responsibility for handling cash
  b. Separating the cash-handling and cash-accounting duties
  c. Ensuring that cash is deposited in the bank daily
  d. Centralizing the opening of incoming mail in a single location

7. A six-month, $30,000 note specifies interest of 9 percent. The full amount of interest on this note will be *(p. 323)*
  a. $450   c. $1,350
  b. $900   d. $2,700

8. The note in the preceding question was issued on August 31, and the company's accounting year ends on December 31. The year-end balance sheet will report interest receivable of *(p. 327)*
  a. $450   c. $1,350
  b. $900   d. $2,700

9. Discounting a note receivable is a way to *(p. 324)*
  a. Collect on a note   c. Both of the above
  b. Increase interest revenue   d. None of the above

10. Discounting a note receivable creates a (an) *(p. 325)*
  a. Cash disbursement   c. Protest fee
  b. Interest expense   d. Contingent liability

Answers to the self-study questions are at the end of the chapter.

Accounting Vocabulary

aging of accounts receivable *(p. 316)*, allowance for doubtful accounts *(p. 313)*, allowance for uncollectible accounts *(p. 313)*, allowance method *(p. 312)*, bad debt expense *(p. 311)*, contingent liability *(p. 325)*, creditor *(p. 309)*, debtor *(p. 309)*, default on a note *(p. 326)*, direct write-off method *(p. 311)*, discounting a note receivable *(p. 324)*, dishonor of a note *(p. 326)*, doubtful account expense *(p. 311)*, interest *(p. 322)*, interest period *(p. 322)*, interest rate *(p. 322)*, maker of a note *(p. 321)*, maturity date *(p. 322)*, maturity value *(p. 322)*, other receivables *(p. 310)*, payee of a note *(p. 321)*, principal amount *(p. 321)*, promissory note *(p. 321)*, receivable *(309)*, uncollectible account expense *(p. 311)*.

ASSIGNMENT MATERIAL _____

Questions

1. Name the two parties to a receivable/payable transaction. Which party has the receivable? Which party has the payable? Which party has the asset? Which party has the liability?

2. List three categories of receivables. State how each category is classified for reporting on the balance sheet.

3. Name the two methods of accounting for uncollectible receivables. Which method is easier to apply? Which method is consistent with generally accepted accounting principles?

4. Which of the two methods of accounting for uncollectible accounts is preferable? Why?

5. Identify the accounts debited and credited to account for uncollectibles under (a) the direct write-off method and (b) the allowance method.

6. What is another term for Allowance for Uncollectible Accounts? What are two other terms for Uncollectible Account Expense?

7. Which entry decreases net income under the allowance method of accounting for uncollectibles: the entry to record uncollectible account expense or the entry to write off an uncollectible account receivable?

8. May a customer pay his or her account receivable after it has been written off ? If not, why not? If so, what entries are made to account for reinstating the customer's account and collecting cash from the customer?

9. Identify and briefly describe the two ways to estimate bad debt expense and uncollectible accounts.

10. Briefly describe how a company may use both the percentage of sales method and the aging method to estimate uncollectibles.

11. How does a credit balance arise in a customer's account receivable? How does the company report this credit balance on its balance sheet?

12. Many businesses receive most of their cash on credit sales through the mail. Suppose you own a business so large that you must hire employees to handle cash receipts and perform the related accounting duties. What internal control feature should you use to ensure that the cash received from customers is not taken by a dishonest employee?

13. Use the terms *maker, payee, principal amount, maturity date, promissory note,* and *interest* in an appropriate sentence or two.

14. For each of the following notes receivable, compute the amount of interest revenue earned during 19X6:

	Principal	Interest Rate	Interest Period	Maturity Date
a. Note 1	$ 10,000	9%	90 days	11/30/19X6
b. Note 2	$ 50,000	10%	6 months	9/30/19X6
c. Note 3	$100,000	8%	5 years	12/31/19X7
d. Note 4	$ 15,000	12%	60 days	1/15/19X7

15. Name three situations in which a company might receive a note receivable. For each situation, show the account debited and the account credited to record receipt of the note.

16. Suppose you hold a 180-day, $5,000 note receivable that specifies 10 percent interest. After 60 days you discount the note at 12 percent. How much cash do you receive?

17. How does a contingent liability differ from an ordinary liability? How does discounting a note receivable create a contingent liability? When does the contingency cease to exist?

18. When the maker of a note dishonors the note at maturity, what accounts does the payee debit and credit?

19. Why does the payee of a note receivable usually need to make adjusting entries for interest at the end of the accounting period?

20. Recall the real-world disclosures of receivables the chapter presents. Show three ways to report Accounts Receivable of $100,000 and Allowance for Uncollectible Accounts of $2,800 on the balance sheet or in the related notes.

Exercises

Exercise 8-1 *Using the direct write-off method for bad debts*

On September 30, Maxwell Co. had a $32,000 debit balance in Accounts Receivable. During October the company had sales revenue of $135,000, which included $88,000 in credit sales. Other data for October include:

Collections on accounts receivable, $91,000
Write-offs of uncollectible receivables, $1,520

Required

1. Record uncollectible account expense for October by the *direct write-off* method.
2. What amount of *net* accounts receivable would Maxwell report on its October 31 balance sheet under the direct write-off method? Does Maxwell expect to collect this much of the receivable? Give your reason.

Exercise 8-2 *Using the allowance method for bad debts*

Refer to the situation in Exercise 8-1, and add these facts:

September 30 credit balance in Allowance for Uncollectible Accounts, $2,100
Uncollectible account expense, estimated as 2 percent of credit sales

Required

1. Prepare journal entries to record sales, collections, uncollectible account expense by the allowance method, and write-offs of uncollectibles during October.
2. Show the ending balances in Accounts Receivable, Allowance for Uncollectible Accounts, and *net* accounts receivable at October 31. Does Maxwell expect to collect the net amount of the receivable?

Exercise 8-3 *Recording bad debts by the allowance method*

Prepare general journal entries to record the following transactions under the allowance method of accounting for uncollectibles:

Apr. 2   Sold merchandise for $4,650 on credit terms of 2/10 n/30 to McBee Sales Company.

May 28   Received legal notification that McBee Sales Company was bankrupt. Wrote off McBee's accounts receivable balance.

Aug. 11   Received $2,000 from McBee Sales Company, together with a letter indicating that the company intended to pay its account within the next month.

    30   Received the remaining amount due from McBee.

Exercise 8-4 *Recording bad debts by the allowance method*

At December 31, 19X5, Knudsen Company has an accounts receivable balance of $129,000. Sales revenue for 19X5 is $950,000, including credit sales of $600,000. For each of the following situations, prepare the year-end adjusting entry to record doubtful account expense. Show how the accounts receivable and the allowance for doubtful accounts are reported on the balance sheet.

a. Allowance for Doubtful Accounts has a credit balance before adjustment of $1,600. Knudsen Company estimates that doubtful account expense for the year is 3/4 of 1 percent of credit sales.
b. Allowance for Doubtful Accounts has a debit balance before adjustment of $1,100. Knudsen Company estimates that $6,100 of the accounts receivable will prove uncollectible.

Exercise 8-5 *Using the aging approach to estimate bad debts*

At December 31, 19X7, the accounts receivable balance of Granite Shoals Co. is $266,000. The allowance for doubtful accounts has a $3,910 credit balance. Accountants for Granite Shoals Company prepare the following aging schedule for its accounts receivable:

Total Balance	Age of Accounts			
	1–30 Days	31–60 Days	61–90 Days	Over 90 Days
$266,000	$104,000	$78,000	$69,000	$15,000
Estimated percentage uncollectible	.3%	1.2%	4.0%	50%

Journalize the adjusting entry for doubtful accounts based on the aging schedule. Show the T-account for the allowance.

Exercise 8-6 *Reporting receivables with credit balances*

The accounts receivable subsidiary ledger includes the following summarized data:

83 accounts with debit balances totaling	$63,240
9 accounts with credit balances totaling	2,690
Net total of balances	$60,550

Show how these data should be reported on the balance sheet.

Exercise 8-7 *Recording a note receivable and accruing interest revenue*

Record the following transactions in the general journal.

Nov. 1 Loaned $10,000 cash to E. Gomez on a 1-year, 9% note.
Dec. 3 Sold goods to Lofland, Inc., receiving a 90-day, 12% note for $3,750.
     16 Received a $2,000, 6-month, 12% note on account from J. Baker.
     31 Accrued interest revenue on all notes receivable.

Exercise 8-8 *Recording notes receivable, discounting a note, and reporting the contingent liability in a note*

Prepare general journal entries to record the following transactions:

Aug. 14 Sold goods on account to Bert Lewis, $4,000.
Dec. 2 Received a $4,000, 90-day, 10% note from Bert Lewis in satisfaction of his past-due account receivable.
     30 Sold the Lewis note by discounting it to a bank at 15%. (Use a 360-day year, and round amounts to the nearest dollar.)

Write the note to disclose the contingent liability at December 31.

Exercise 8-9   *Accounting for a dishonored note receivable*

Record the following transactions in the general journal, assuming the company uses the allowance method to account for uncollectibles:

May 18   Sold goods to Computer Specialties, receiving a 120-day, 10% note for $2,700.

Sep. 15   The note is dishonored.

Nov. 30   After pursuing collection from Computer Specialties, wrote off their account as uncollectible.

Exercise 8-10   *Recording a note receivable and accruing interest revenue*

Record the following transactions in the general journal:

Apr.   1, 19X2   Loaned $4,800 to Linda Rutishauser on a 1-year, 9% note.

Dec. 31, 19X2   Accrued interest revenue on the Rutishauser note.

Dec. 31, 19X2   Closed the interest revenue account.

Apr.   1, 19X3   Received the maturity value of the note from Linda Rutishauser.

Problems   *(Group A)*

Problem 8-1A   *Accounting for uncollectibles by the direct write-off and allowance methods*

On February 28 Contessa Gallery had a $61,800 debit balance in Accounts Receivable. During March the company had sales revenue of $509,000, which includes $443,000 in credit sales. Other data for March include:

Collections on accounts receivable, $451,600

Write-offs of uncollectible receivables, $4,990

February 28 unadjusted balance in Allowance for Uncollectible Accounts, $800 (debit)

Uncollectible account expense, estimated as 2 percent of credit sales

Required

1. Record uncollectible account expense for March by the *direct write-off* method. Show all March activity in Accounts Receivable and Uncollectible Account Expense.
2. Record uncollectible account expense and write-offs of customer accounts for March by the *allowance* method. Show all March activity in Accounts Receivable, Allowance for Uncollectible Accounts, and Uncollectible Account Expense.
3. What amount of uncollectible account expense would Contessa Gallery report on its March income statement under the two methods? Which amount better matches expense with revenue? Give your reason.
4. What amount of *net* accounts receivable would Contessa Gallery report on its March 31 balance sheet under the two methods? Which amount is more realistic? Give your reason.

Problem 8-2A   *Using the percent of sales and aging approaches for uncollectibles*

Masters Company completed the following transactions during 19X1 and 19X2:

19X1

Dec. 31   Estimated that uncollectible account expense for the year was 3/4 of 1 percent on credit sales of $300,000, and recorded that amount as expense.

   31   Made the appropriate closing entry.

19X2

Jan. 17   Sold inventory to Mary Lee, $652, on credit terms of 2/10 n/30.

June 29 Wrote off the Mary Lee account as uncollectible after repeated efforts to collect from her.

Aug. 6 Received $250 from Mary Lee, along with a letter stating her intention to pay her debt in full within 30 days. Reinstated her account in full.

Sept. 4 Received the balance due from Mary Lee.

Dec. 31 Made a compound entry to write off the following accounts as uncollectible: Bernard Klaus, $737, Louis Mann, $348, and Millie Burnett, $622.

   31 Estimated that uncollectible account expense for the year was 2/3 of 1 percent on credit sales of $420,000, and recorded that amount as expense.

   31 Made the appropriate closing entry.

Required

1. Open general ledger accounts for Allowance for Uncollectible Accounts and Uncollectible Account Expense. Keep running balances.
2. Record the transactions in the general journal, and post to the two ledger accounts.
3. The December 31, 19X2, balance of Accounts Receivable is $139,000. Show how Accounts Receivable would be reported at that date.
4. Assume that Masters Company begins aging accounts receivable on December 31, 19X2. The balance in Accounts Receivable is $139,000, the credit balance in Allowance for Uncollectible Accounts is $543, and the company estimates that $2,600 of its accounts receivable will prove uncollectible.
   a. Make the adjusting entry for uncollectibles.
   b. Show how Accounts Receivable will be reported on the December 31, 19X2, balance sheet.

Problem 8-3A *Using the percent of sales and aging approaches for uncollectibles*

The December 31, 19X6, balance sheet of Marlin Products Co. reports the following:

Accounts Receivable $256,000
Allowance for Doubtful Accounts (credit balance) 7,100

At the end of each quarter, Marlin Products Company estimates doubtful account expense to be 2 percent of credit sales. At the end of the year, the company ages its accounts receivable and adjusts the balance in Allowance for Doubtful Accounts to correspond to the aging schedule. During 19X7 Marlin completes the following selected transactions:

Jan. 31 Wrote off as uncollectible the $855 account receivable from Spinelli Company and the $3,287 account receivable from J. M. Bartlett.

Mar. 31 Recorded doubtful account expense based on credit sales of $120,000.

May 2 Received $1,000 from J. M. Bartlett after prolonged negotiations with Bartlett's attorney. Marlin has no hope of collecting the remainder.

June 15 Wrote off as uncollectible the $1,120 account receivable from Lisa Brown.

June 30 Recorded doubtful account expense based on credit sales of $166,000.

July 14 Made a compound entry to write off the following uncollectible accounts: C. H. Harris, $766; Graphics Unlimited, $2,413; and Ben McQueen, $134.

Sept. 30 Recorded doubtful account expense based on credit sales of $141,400.

Nov. 22 Wrote off the following accounts receivable as uncollectible: Monet Corp., $1,345; Blocker, Inc., $2,109; and Main Street Plaza, $755.

Dec. 31 Recorded doubtful account expense based on the following summary of the aging of accounts receivable:

Total	Age of Accounts			
Balance	1–30 Days	31–60 Days	61–90 Days	Over 90 Days
$287,600	$154,500	$86,000	$32,000	$15,100
Estimated percentage uncollectible	0.2%	0.5%	3.0%	40.0%

Dec. 31   Made the closing entry for Doubtful Account Expense for the entire year.

Required

1. Record the transactions in the general journal.
2. Open the Allowance for Doubtful Accounts, and post entries affecting that account. Keep a running balance.
3. Most companies report two-year comparative financial statements. If Marlin's Accounts Receivable balance is $287,600 at December 31, 19X7, show how the company would report its accounts receivable in a comparative balance sheet for 19X7 and 19X6, as follows:

	19X7	**19X6**
Accounts receivable.................................	————	————
Less: Allowance for doubtful accounts.............	————	————
Net accounts receivable..........................	————	————

Problem 8-4A   *Accounting for notes receivable, including discounting notes and accruing interest revenue*

A company received the following notes during 19X3. Notes (1), (2), and (3) were discounted on the dates and at the rates indicated.

Note	Date	Principal Amount	Interest Rate	Term	Date Discounted	Discount Rate
(1)	July 12	$10,000	10%	3 months	Aug. 12	15%
(2)	Aug. 4	6,000	11%	90 days	Aug. 30	13%
(3)	Oct. 21	8,000	15%	60 days	Nov. 3	18%
(4)	Nov. 30	12,000	12%	6 months	—	—
(5)	Dec. 7	9,000	10%	30 days	—	—
(6)	Dec. 23	15,000	9%	1 year	—	—

Required

As necessary in requirements 1 through 5, identify each note by number, compute interest using a 360-day year for those notes with terms specified in days or years, round all interest amounts to the nearest dollar, and present entries in general journal form. Explanations are not required.

1. Determine the due date and maturity value of each note.
2. For each discounted note, determine the discount and proceeds from sale of the note.
3. Journalize the discounting of notes (1) and (2).
4. Journalize a single adjusting entry at December 31, 19X3, to record accrued interest revenue on notes (4), (5), and (6).
5. Journalize the collection of principal and interest on note (5).

Problem 8-5A   *Notes receivable, discounted notes, dishonored notes, and accrued interest revenue*

Record the following selected transactions in the general journal. Explanations are not required.

19X6

Dec. 19   Received a $2,000, 60-day, 12 percent note on account from Claude Bernard.

    31   Made an adjusting entry to accrue interest on the Bernard note.

    31   Made an adjusting entry to record doubtful account expense in the amount of 1 percent of credit sales of $474,500.

    31   Made a compound closing entry for interest revenue and doubtful account expense.

19X7

Feb. 17   Collected the maturity value of the Bernard note.

Mar. 22   Sold merchandise to Idaho Power Co., receiving $1,400 cash and a 90-day, 10 percent note for $6,000.

May 3   Discounted the Idaho Power Co. note to First National Bank at 15 percent.

June 1   Loaned $10,000 cash to Linz Brothers, receiving a 6-month, 11 percent note.

Oct. 31   Received a $1,500, 60-day, 12 percent note from Ned Pierce on his past-due account receivable.

Dec. 1   Collected the maturity value of the Linz Brothers note.

    30   Ned Pierce dishonored his note at maturity; wrote off the note receivable as uncollectible, debiting Allowance for Doubtful Accounts.

    31   Wrote off as uncollectible the accounts receivable of Al Bynum, $435, and Ray Sharp, $276.

Problem 8-6A   *Uncollectibles, notes receivable, discounting notes, dishonored notes, and accrued interest revenue*

Assume Chesapeake Corp. of Virginia, a major manufacturer of paper products, completed the following selected transactions:

19X4

Dec. 1   Sold goods to McNamara Company, receiving a $24,000, 3-month, 10 percent note.

    31   Made an adjusting entry to accrue interest on the McNamara note.

    31   Made an adjusting entry to record doubtful account expense based on an aging of accounts receivable. The aging analysis indicates that $355,800 of accounts receivable will not be collected. Prior to this adjustment, the credit balance in Allowance for Uncollectible Accounts is $341,900.

19X5

Feb. 18   Received a 90-day, 10 percent, $5,000 note from Dilley, Inc., on account. (This year February has 28 days.)

Mar. 1   Collected the maturity value of the McNamara Company note.

     8   Discounted the Dilley note to First State Bank at 16 percent.

Apr. 21   Sold merchandise to Brown Group, receiving a 60-day, 9 percent note for $4,000.

June 20   Brown Group dishonored its note at maturity and converted the maturity value of the note to an account receivable.

July 12   Loaned $60,000 cash to Consolidated Investments, receiving a 90-day, 13 percent note.

    13   Sold merchandise to Scott Corp., receiving a 4-month, 12 percent, $2,500 note.

Aug. 2   Collected $4,060 on account from Brown Group.

Sept. 13   Discounted the Scott Corp. note to First State Bank at 18 percent.

Oct. 10   Collected the maturity value of the Consolidated Investments note.

Nov. 13   Scott Corp. dishonored its note at maturity; paid First State Bank the maturity value of the note plus a protest fee of $35 and debited an account receivable from Scott Corp.

Dec. 31   Wrote off as uncollectible the account receivable from Scott Corp.

Required

Record the transactions in the general journal. Explanations are not required.

(Group B)

Problem 8-1B *Accounting for uncollectibles by the direct write-off and allowance methods*

On May 31, Krakow Tool Company had a $104,300 debit balance in Accounts Receivable. During June the company had sales revenue of $788,000, which includes $640,000 in credit sales. Other data for June include:

Collections on accounts receivable, $599,400

Write-offs of uncollectible receivables, $6,100

May 31 unadjusted balance in Allowance for Uncollectible Accounts, $2,200 (credit)

Uncollectible account expense, estimated as 2 percent of credit sales

Required

1. Record uncollectible account expense for June by the *direct write-off* method. Show all June activity in Accounts Receivable and Uncollectible Account Expense.
2. Record uncollectible account expense and write-offs of customer accounts for June by the *allowance* method. Show all June activity in Accounts Receivable, Allowance for Uncollectible Accounts, and Uncollectible Account Expense.
3. What amount of uncollectible account expense would Krakow Tool Company report on its June income statement under the two methods? Which amount better matches expense with revenue? Give your reason.
4. What amount of *net* accounts receivable would Krakow Tool Company report on its June 30 balance sheet under the two methods? Which amount is more realistic? Give your reason.

Problem 8-2B *Using the percent of sales and aging approaches for uncollectibles*

Reynaldo Company completed the following selected transactions during 19X1 and 19X2:

19X1
Dec. 31 Estimated that uncollectible account expense for the year was 2/3 of 1 percent on credit sales of $450,000 and recorded that amount as expense.
    31 Made the appropriate closing entry.
19X2
Feb. 4 Sold inventory to Gary Carter, $1,521, on credit terms of 2/10 n/30.
July 1 Wrote off Gary Carter's account as uncollectible after repeated efforts to collect from him.
Oct. 19 Received $521 from Gary Carter, along with a letter stating his intention to pay his debt in full within 30 days. Reinstated his account in full.
Nov.15 Received the balance due from Gary Carter.
Dec. 31 Made a compound entry to write off the following accounts as uncollectible: Kris Moore, $899; Marie Mandue, $530; and Grant Frycer, $1,272.
    31 Estimated that uncollectible account expense for the year was 2/3 of 1 percent on credit sales of $540,000 and recorded the expense.
    31 Made the appropriate closing entry.

Required

1. Open general ledger accounts for Allowance for Uncollectible Accounts and Uncollectible Account Expense. Keep running balances.
2. Record the transactions in the general journal, and post to the two ledger accounts.
3. The December 31, 19X2, balance of Accounts Receivable is $164,500. Show how Accounts Receivable would be reported at that date.

4. Assume that Reynaldo Company begins aging its accounts receivable on December 31, 19X2. The balance in Accounts Receivable is $164,500, the credit balance in Allowance for Uncollectible Accounts is $299, and the company estimates that $3,545 of its accounts receivable will prove uncollectible.
   a. Make the adjusting entry for uncollectibles.
   b. Show how Accounts Receivable will be reported on the December 31, 19X2, balance sheet.

Problem 8-3B *Using the percent of sales and aging approaches for uncollectibles*

The December 31, 19X4, balance sheet of Bonini Corporation reports the following:

Accounts Receivable $141,000
Allowance for Doubtful Accounts (credit balance) 3,200

At the end of each quarter, Bonini estimates doubtful account expense to be 1½ percent of credit sales. At the end of the year, the company ages its accounts receivable and adjusts the balance in Allowance for Doubtful Accounts to correspond to the aging schedule. During 19X5 Bonini completes the following selected transactions:

Jan. 16   Wrote off as uncollectible the $403 account receivable from Platt Co. and the $1,719 account receivable from Wise Corp.
Mar. 31   Recorded doubtful account expense based on credit sales of $100,000.
Apr. 15   Received $300 from Wise Corp. after prolonged negotiations with Wise's attorney. Bonini has no hope of collecting the remainder.
May 13   Wrote off as uncollectible the $2,980 account receivable from M. E. Cate.
June 30   Recorded doubtful account expense based on credit sales of $114,000.
Aug. 9   Made a compound entry to write off the following uncollectible accounts: Clifford, Inc., $235; Matz Co., $188; and Lew Norris, $1,006.
Sept. 30   Recorded doubtful account expense based on credit sales of $130,000.
Oct. 18   Wrote off as uncollectible the $767 account receivable from Bliss Co. and the $430 account receivable from Micro Data.
Dec. 31   Recorded doubtful account expense based on the following summary of the aging of accounts receivable.

Total Balance	Age of Accounts			
	1–30 Days	31–60 Days	61–90 Days	Over 90 Days
$167,400	$114,600	$31,100	$12,000	$9,700
Estimated percentage uncollectible	0.1%	.4%	5.0%	30.0%

Dec. 31   Made the closing entry for Doubtful Account Expense for the entire year.

Required

1. Record the transactions in the general journal.
2. Open the Allowance for Doubtful Accounts and post entries affecting that account. Keep a running balance.
3. Most companies report two-year comparative financial statements. If Bonini's Accounts Receivable balance is $167,400 at December 31, 19X5, show how the company would report its accounts receivable on a comparative balance sheet for 19X5 and 19X4, as follows:

	19X5	19X4
Accounts receivable...........................	_____	_____
Less: Allowance for doubtful accounts.............	_____	_____
Net accounts receivable.......................	_____	_____

Problem 8-4B *Accounting for notes receivable, including discounting notes and accruing interest revenue*

A company received the following notes during 19X5. Notes (1), (2), and (3) were discounted on the dates and at the rates indicated.

Note	Date	Principal Amount	Interest Rate	Term	Date Discounted	Discount Rate
(1)	July 15	$ 6,000	10%	6 months	Oct. 15	12%
(2)	Aug. 19	9,000	12%	90 days	Aug. 30	15%
(3)	Sept. 1	8,000	15%	120 days	Nov. 2	20%
(4)	Oct. 30	7,000	12%	3 months	—	—
(5)	Nov. 19	15,000	10%	60 days	—	—
(6)	Dec. 1	12,000	9%	1 year	—	—

Required

As necessary in requirements 1 through 5, identify each note by number, compute interest using a 360-day year for those notes with terms specified in days or years, round all interest amounts to the nearest dollar, and present entries in general journal form. Explanations are not required.

1. Determine the due date and maturity value of each note.
2. For each discounted note, determine the discount and proceeds from sale of the note.
3. Journalize the discounting of notes (1) and (2).
4. Journalize a single adjusting entry at December 31, 19X5, to record accrued interest revenue on notes (4), (5), and (6).
5. Journalize the collection of principal and interest on note (4).

Problem 8-5B *Notes receivable, discounted notes, dishonored notes, and accrued interest revenue*

Record the following selected transactions in the general journal. Explanations are not required.

19X2

Dec. 21   Received a $3,600, 30-day, 10 percent note on account from Myron Blake.

   31   Made an adjusting entry to accrue interest on the Blake note.

   31   Made an adjusting entry to record doubtful account expense in the amount of ¾ of 1 percent on credit sales of $604,800.

   31   Made a compound closing entry for interest revenue and doubtful account expense.

19X3

Jan. 20   Collected the maturity value of the Blake note.

Apr. 19   Sold merchandise to city of Akron, receiving $500 cash and a 120-day, 12 percent note for $5,000.

May 1   Discounted the city of Akron note to First National Bank at 15 percent.

Sept. 14   Loaned $6,000 cash to Allstate Investors, receiving a 3-month, 13 percent note.

   30   Received a $1,675, 60-day, 16 percent note from Matt Kurtz on his past-due account receivable.

Nov. 29 Matt Kurtz dishonored his note at maturity; wrote off the note as uncollectible, debiting Allowance for Doubtful Accounts.

Dec. 14 Collected the maturity value of the Allstate Investors note.

   31 Wrote off as uncollectible the accounts receivable of Ty Larson, $1,005; and Terry Gee, $140.

Problem 8-6B   *Uncollectibles, notes receivable, discounting notes, dishonored notes, and accrued interest revenue*

Assume Chesebrough-Ponds, manufacturer of cosmetic and other products, completed the following selected transactions:

19X5

Nov. 1 Sold goods to Eckerd Drug Co., receiving a $15,000, 3-month, 12 percent note.

Dec. 31 Made an adjusting entry to accrue interest on the Eckerd Drug note.

   31 Made an adjusting entry to record doubtful account expense based on an aging of accounts receivable. The aging analysis indicates that $202,670 of accounts receivable will not be collected. Prior to this adjustment, the credit balance in Allowance for Uncollectible Accounts is $189,900.

19X6

Feb. 1 Collected the maturity value of the Eckerd Drug note.

   23 Received a 90-day, 15 percent, $4,000 note from Bliss Company on account. (This year February has 28 days.)

Mar. 31 Discounted the Bliss Co. note to Lakewood Bank at 20 percent.

Apr. 23 Sold merchandise to K Lynn Corporation, receiving a 60-day, 10 percent note for $9,000.

June 22 K Lynn Corp. dishonored its note at maturity; converted the maturity value of the note to an account receivable.

July 15 Loaned $8,500 cash to McNeil, Inc., receiving a 30-day, 12 percent note.

   17 Sold merchandise to Grant Corp., receiving a 3-month, 10 percent, $8,000 note.

Aug. 5 Collected $9,150 on account from K Lynn Corporation.

   14 Collected the maturity value of the McNeil, Inc., note.

   17 Discounted the Grant Corp. note to Lakewood Bank at 15 percent.

Oct. 17 Grant Corp. dishonored its note at maturity; paid Lakewood Bank the maturity value of the note plus a protest fee of $50 and debited an account receivable from Grant Corp.

Dec. 15 Wrote off as uncollectible the account receivable from Grant Corp.

Required

Record the transactions in the general journal. Explanations are not required.

Decision Problem

Uncollectible Accounts and Evaluating a Business

Bentwood Appliances sells its products either for cash or on notes receivable that earn interest. The business uses the direct write-off method to account for bad debts. Mark Moore, the owner, has prepared the financial statements of the store. The most recent comparative income statements, for 19X3 and 19X2, are as follows:

	19X3	19X2
Total revenue	$210,000	$195,000
Total expenses	157,000	153,000
Net income	$ 53,000	$ 42,000

Based on the increase in net income, Moore seeks to expand his operations. He asks you to invest $50,000 in the business. You and Moore have several meetings, at which you learn that notes receivable from customers were $100,000 at the end of 19X1 and $300,000 at the end of 19X2. Also, total revenues for 19X3 and 19X2 include interest at 15 percent on the year's beginning notes receivable balance. Total expenses include doubtful account expense of $5,000 each year, based on the direct write-off basis. Moore estimates that doubtful account expense would be 4 percent of sales revenue if the allowance method were used.

Required

1. Prepare for the Bentwood Appliances a comparative single-step income statement that identifies sales revenue, interest revenue, doubtful account expense, and other expenses.
2. Is Bentwood's future as promising as Moore's income statement makes it appear? Give the reason for your answer.

Financial Statement Problem

Accounts Receivable and Related Uncollectibles

Use data from the Gulf+Western balance sheet, in Appendix C, to answer these questions. Show all amounts in millions, rounded to the nearest $100,000. For example, show $8,600,000 as $8.6 million.

1. How much did Gulf+Western's customers owe the company at October 31, 1987? Of this amount, how much did Gulf+Western expect to collect?
2. Journalize the following for the fiscal year ended October 31, 1988, using Gulf+Western account titles. Explanations are not required.
   a. Net revenues of $3,117.1 million. Give one entry for the year's total, assuming all net revenues are earned on account.
   b. Cash collections on account, $3,040.5 million.
   c. Doubtful account expense, estimated to equal 1½ percent of net revenues.
   d. Write-offs of uncollectibles totaling $44.9 million.
3. Post to Trade Receivable and Allowance for Doubtful Accounts, inserting these accounts' October 31, 1987, balances.
4. Show trade receivables as Gulf+Western would report this asset on the October 31, 1988, balance sheet.

Answers to Self-Study Questions

1. a
2. c
3. d
4. a
5. b ($78,900 − $14,300 = $64,600)
6. b
7. c ($30,000 × .09 × 6/12 = $1,350)
8. b ($30,000 × .09 × 4/12 = $ 900)
9. a
10. d

Merchandise Inventory

Merchandise inventory is the largest *current asset* on the balance sheet of most businesses that manufacture or buy inventory for resale. Polaroid Corporation reported inventories of $412.7 million, compared to receivables of $289.5 million and cash of $187.0 million. Inventories are important to merchandisers of all sizes. Buying and selling inventory is the heart of wholesaling and retailing, whether the business is Sears, Safeway, or the corner hardware store.

Inventory is the major current asset of most merchandisers. What is their major expense? It is *cost of sales*, or *cost of goods sold*. For example, Westinghouse Electric Corporation reported its cost of sales at $7.1 billion compared to distribution, administrative, and general expenses of $1.5 billion. For Westinghouse and many other companies, cost of goods sold is greater than all other expenses combined.

Exhibit 9-1 traces the flow of inventory costs during the accounting period. The model presented in Exhibit 9-1 is fundamental to accounting for inventory.

The business starts each period with **beginning inventory,** the goods that are left over from the preceding period. During the period, the business purchases additional goods for resale. Together, beginning inventory and net purchases make up **goods available for sale.** Over the course of the period, the business sells some of the available goods. The cost of the inventory sold to customers is called the **cost of goods sold.** This cost is an expense because the inventory is no longer of use to the company. The goods still on hand at the end of the period are called **ending inventory.** Its cost is an asset because these goods are still available for sale.

Exhibit 9-2 uses data from the financial statements of Revco D. S., Inc., a chain of discount drug stores concentrated in Ohio, Texas, and the Southeast, to present

EXHIBIT 9-1 *Flow of Inventory Costs*

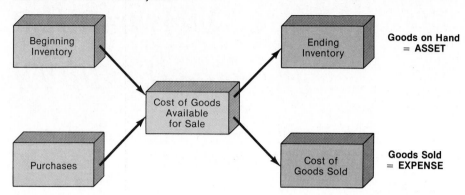

the flow of inventory costs in a different format from that shown in Exhibit 9-1. Notice that ending inventory is subtracted from cost of goods available for sale to figure the cost of goods sold. Throughout this chapter we ignore freight-in to avoid clutter.

The rest of this chapter fills in the details of our inventory cost flow model.

Figuring the Cost of Inventory

A necessary step in accounting for inventory is determining the cost of *ending inventory*. At the end of each period the *quantity* of inventory is multiplied by the *unit cost* of inventory to compute the cost of ending inventory.

Determining the Quantity of Inventory. Most businesses physically count their inventory at least once each year, often on the last day of the fiscal year. Inventory, an asset, must be reported accurately on the balance sheet.

You may have worked at a grocery store or some other type of retail business. If so, you will recall the process of "taking the inventory." Some entities shut the business down to get a good count of inventory on hand. Others count the goods on a weekend. Still others inventory the merchandise while business is being conducted. How is it done in a large organization?

Assume Revco Drug takes a complete physical inventory on its year-end date. Teams of counters in the company's approximately 1,700 stores record the quantities of each inventory item on hand. Each store forwards its total count to corporate headquarters, where home office employees determine the inventory grand total.

Complications may arise in determining the inventory quantity. Suppose the

EXHIBIT 9-2 *Inventory and Cost of Goods Sold for Revco D.S., Inc.*

	(amounts in millions)
Beginning inventory	$ 276
+ Net purchases	1,348
= Cost of goods available for sale	1,624
− Ending inventory.................................	317
= Cost of goods sold................................	$1,307

business has purchased some goods that are in transit when the inventory is counted. Even though these items are not physically present, they should be included in the inventory count if title to the goods has passed to the purchaser. When title passes from seller to purchaser, the purchaser becomes the legal owner of the goods.

The FOB—free on board—terms of the transaction govern when title passes from the seller to the purchaser. **FOB shipping point** indicates that title passes when the goods leave the seller's place of business. **FOB destination** means that title passes when the goods arrive at the purchaser's location. Therefore, goods in transit that are purchased FOB shipping point should be included in the purchaser's inventory. Goods in transit that are bought FOB destination should not be included.

Usually, the business has a purchase invoice, which lists the quantity of goods in transit and shows the FOB terms. Similarly, the business may have sold inventory that has not yet been shipped to the customer. If title has passed, these goods should be excluded from the seller's inventory, even though they may still be at the seller's place of business.

Another complication in counting inventory arises from consigned goods. In a **consignment** arrangement, the owner of the inventory (the consignor) transfers the goods to another business (the consignee). For a fee, the consignee sells the inventory on the owner's behalf. The consignee does *not* take title to the consigned goods and, therefore, should not include them in its own inventory. Consignments are common in retailing. Suppose Revco Drug is the consignee for some L'Eggs hosiery in its stores. Should Revco include this consigned merchandise in its inventory count? No, because Revco does not own the goods. Instead, the L'Eggs wholesaler—the consignor—includes the consigned goods in his or her inventory. A rule of thumb is to include in inventory only what the business owns.

Determining the Unit Cost of Inventory. Inventories are normally accounted for at historical cost, as the *cost principle* requires. **Inventory cost** is the price the business pays to acquire the inventory—not the selling price of the goods. Suppose a business purchases inventory for $10 and offers it for sale at $15. The inventory cost is reported at $10, not $15. Inventory cost includes its invoice price, less any purchase discount, plus sales tax, tariffs, transportation charges, insurance while in transit, and all other costs incurred to make the goods ready for sale.

The inventory quantity multiplied by the unit cost equals the cost of inventory. Thirty tape recorders at a cost of $100 each results in an inventory cost of $3,000.

Inventory Costing Methods

Determining the unit cost of inventory is easy when the unit cost remains constant during the period. However, the unit cost often changes. For example, during times of inflation, prices rise. The tape recorder model that cost the retailer $100 in January may cost $115 in June and $122 in October. Suppose the retailer sells 15 tape recorders in November. How many of them cost $100, how many cost $115, and how many cost $122? To compute the cost of goods sold and ending inventory amounts, the accountant must have some means of assigning the business's cost to each item sold. The four costing methods that GAAP allows are

1. Specific unit cost
2. Average cost

OBJECTIVE 1

Apply four inventory costing methods

3. First-in, first-out (FIFO) cost
4. Last-in, first-out (LIFO) cost

A company can use any of these methods.

Specific Unit Cost

Some businesses deal in inventory items that may be identified individually, like automobiles, jewels, and real estate. These businesses usually cost their inventory at the **specific cost** of the particular unit. For instance, a Chevrolet dealer may have two vehicles in the showroom—a "stripped-down" model that cost $12,000 and a "loaded" model that cost $15,000. If the dealer sells the loaded model for $16,700, cost of goods sold is $15,000, the cost of the specific unit. The gross margin on this sale is $1,700 ($16,700 − $15,000). If the stripped-down auto is the only unit left in inventory at the end of the period, ending inventory is $12,000, the cost to the retailer of the specific unit on hand.

The specific unit cost method is also called the *specific identification* or *specific invoice cost* method. This method is not practical for inventory items that have common characteristics, such as bushels of wheat, gallons of paint, or boxes of laundry detergent.

Average Cost, FIFO Cost, and LIFO Cost

The average cost, first-in, first-out (FIFO), and last-in, first-out (LIFO) methods are fundamentally different from the specific unit cost method. These methods do not assign to inventory the specific cost of particular units. Instead, they assume different flows of costs into and out of inventory.

Average Cost.   The **average cost method** is based on the average cost of inventory during the period. Average cost is determined by dividing the cost of goods available for sale (beginning inventory plus purchases) by the number of units available. Ending inventory and cost of goods sold are computed by multiplying the number of units by average cost per unit. Assume that cost of goods available for sale is $90, and 60 units are available. Average cost is $1.50 per unit ($90/60 = $1.50). Ending inventory of 20 units has an average cost of $30 (20 × $1.50 = $30). Cost of goods sold (40 units) is $60 (40 × $1.50). Panel A of Exhibit 9-3 gives the data in more detail. Panel B of the exhibit shows the average cost computations.

First-in, First-out (FIFO) Cost.   Under the **first-in, first-out (FIFO) method,** the company must keep a record of the cost of each inventory unit purchased. The unit costs used in computing the ending inventory may be different from the unit costs used in computing the cost of goods sold. Under FIFO, the first costs into inventory are the first costs out to cost of goods sold—hence the name *first-in, first-out.* Ending inventory is based on the costs of the most recent purchases. In our example, the FIFO cost of ending inventory is $36. Cost of goods sold is $54. Panel A of Exhibit 9-3 gives the data, and Panel B shows the FIFO computations.

Last-in, First-out (LIFO) Cost.   The **last-in, first-out (LIFO) method** also depends on the costs of particular inventory purchases. LIFO is the opposite of

EXHIBIT 9-3   *Inventory and Cost of Goods Sold under Average, FIFO, and LIFO Inventory Costing Methods*

Panel A—Illustrative Data:

Beginning inventory (10 units @ $1 per unit)........		$ 10
Purchases:		
No. 1 (25 units @ $1.40 per unit)	$ 35	
No. 2 (25 units @ $1.80 per unit)	45	
Total....................................		80
Cost of goods available for sale (60 units)...........		$ 90
Ending inventory (20 units @ $? per unit)		?
Cost of goods sold (40 units @ $? per unit		$?

Panel B—Ending Inventory and Cost of Goods Sold:

Average Cost Method:

Cost of goods available for sale—see Panel A (60 units @ average cost of $1.50* per unit)		$ 90
Ending inventory (20 units @ $1.50 per unit)		30
Cost of goods sold (40 units @ $1.50 per unit)		$ 60

* Cost of goods available for sale..............	$ 90
Number of units available for sale	÷ 60
Average cost per unit	$1.50

FIFO Cost Method:

Cost of goods available for sale (60 units—see Panel A)..............		$ 90
Ending inventory (cost of the *last* 20 units available):		
20 units @ $1.80 per unit		36
Cost of goods sold (cost of the *first* 40 units available):		
10 units @ $1.00 per unit	$ 10	
25 units @ $1.40 per unit	35	
5 units @ $1.80 per unit	9	
Total		$ 54

LIFO Cost Method:

Cost of goods available for sale (60 units—see Panel A)..............		$ 90
Ending inventory (cost of the *first* 20 units available):		
10 units @ $1.00 per unit	$ 10	
10 units @ $1.40 per unit	14	
Total		24
Cost of goods sold (cost of the *last* 40 units available):		
25 units @ $1.80 per unit	45	
15 units @ $1.40 per unit	21	
Total		$ 66

FIFO. Under LIFO, the last costs into inventory are the first costs out to cost of goods sold. This leaves the oldest costs—those of beginning inventory and the earliest purchases of the period—in ending inventory. In our example, the LIFO cost of ending inventory is $24. Cost of goods sold is $66. Panel A of Exhibit 9-3 gives the data, and Panel B shows the LIFO computations.

Income Effects of FIFO, LIFO, and Average Cost _____

In our discussion and examples, the cost of inventory rose during the accounting period. When prices change, different costing methods produce different cost of goods sold and ending inventory figures, as Exhibit 9-3 shows. When inventory costs are increasing, FIFO ending inventory is *highest* because it is priced at the most recent costs, which are the highest. LIFO ending inventory is *lowest* because it is priced at the oldest costs, which are the lowest. *Average* cost avoids the extremes of FIFO and LIFO. When inventory costs are decreasing, FIFO ending inventory is lowest, and LIFO is highest.

Exhibit 9-4 summarizes the income effects of the three inventory methods. Study the exhibit carefully, focusing on ending inventory, cost of goods sold, and gross margin.

The Income Tax Advantage of LIFO _____

OBJECTIVE 2

Distinguish between the income effects and the tax effects of the inventory costing methods

When prices are rising, applying the LIFO method results in the *lowest taxable income* and thus the *lowest income taxes.* Let's use the gross margin data of Exhibit 9-4.

	FIFO	LIFO	Average
Gross margin	$46,000	$34,000	$40,000
Operating expenses (assumed)	26,000	26,000	26,000
Income before income tax	$20,000	$ 8,000	$14,000
Income tax expense (40%)........................	$ 8,000	$ 3,200	$ 5,600

Income tax expense is lowest under LIFO ($3,200) and highest under FIFO ($8,000). The most attractive feature of LIFO is reduced income tax payments.

The Internal Revenue Service allows companies to use LIFO for tax purposes only if they use LIFO for financial reporting purposes. Therefore, businesses that use LIFO for tax purposes must report inventory and income on the LIFO basis for

EXHIBIT 9-4 *Income Effects of FIFO, LIFO, and Average Cost Inventory Methods*

	FIFO		LIFO		Average	
Sales revenue (assumed)............		$100,000		$100,000		$100,000
Cost of goods sold:						
Goods available for sale (assumed) .	$ 90,000		$ 90,000		$ 90,000	
Ending inventory...............	36,000		24,000		30,000	
Cost of goods sold		54,000		66,000		60,000
Gross margin		$ 46,000		$ 34,000		$ 40,000

Summary of Income Effects — When Inventory Costs Are Increasing:

FIFO—Highest ending inventory	LIFO—Lowest ending inventory	Average—Results fall between
Lowest cost of goods sold	Highest cost of goods sold	the extremes of FIFO
Highest gross margin	Lowest gross margin	and LIFO

their financial statements. However, they may also report an alternative inventory amount in the notes to their financial statements. Federal-Mogul Corporation, a maker of industrial products, reported inventories at LIFO cost but also disclosed the FIFO cost of inventory in Note D, as follows. Observe that FIFO cost is higher than LIFO cost (amounts in millions).

	19X6	19X5
Inventories—Note D	$189	$148

Note D: *Inventories*
Inventories are stated at . . . last-in, first-out (LIFO) cost. . . . Use of the first-in, first-out (FIFO) cost method would have increased inventories by $95 million in 19X6 and $89 million in 19X5. . . .

Of what use is Federal-Mogul's disclosure of the alternate amounts under FIFO? An investor may be comparing Federal-Mogul with another retail company that uses FIFO. Federal-Mogul's inventory and cost of goods sold amounts under LIFO are not comparable to the other company's FIFO figures. To compare the two companies, the investor can convert Federal-Mogul's LIFO amounts to the FIFO basis. Simply substitute the FIFO amounts in place of those reported under LIFO. Here are the cost of goods figures (amounts in millions):

	LIFO Amounts as Reported in the Income Statement	FIFO Amounts Based on Information in the Notes
Beginning inventory................	$ 148	$ 237
Net purchases	765	765
Cost of goods available for sale	913	1,002
Less: Ending inventory..............	189	284
Cost of goods sold..................	$ 724	$ 718

Cost of goods sold under FIFO ($718 million) can now be used to compare the two companies. In the computation, notice that purchases is the same under FIFO and LIFO. Beginning FIFO inventory is the LIFO amount ($148 million) plus the increase to FIFO ($89 million), a total of $237 million. Ending FIFO inventory is the LIFO amount ($189 million) plus the increase ($95 million), a total of $284 million. These changes cause FIFO cost of goods sold to be less than the LIFO amount, which would cause income to be higher under FIFO. This is valuable information for an investor.

The 1970s were marked by high inflation, so many companies changed to LIFO for its tax advantage. Figure 9-1, based on an American Institute of Certified Public Accountants (AICPA) survey of 600 companies, indicates that LIFO is the most popular inventory costing method.

Comparison of the Inventory Methods _____

We may ask three questions to judge the inventory costing methods. (1) How well does each method match inventory expense—the cost of goods sold—to sales revenue on the income statement? (2) Which method reports the most up-to-date

Figure 9-1   *Use of the Various Inventory Methods*

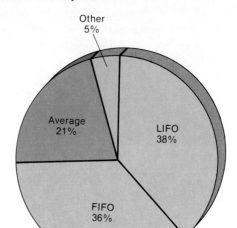

inventory amount on the balance sheet? (3) What effect do the methods have on income taxes? The average cost method produces amounts between the extremes of LIFO and FIFO. The specific unit cost method is used only for inventory made up of individually identifiable units. Therefore, we focus these questions on the differences between LIFO and FIFO.

LIFO better matches the current value of cost of goods sold with current revenue by assigning to this expense the most recent inventory costs. By contrast, FIFO matches the oldest inventory costs against the period's revenue—a poor matching of current expense with current revenue.

FIFO reports the most current inventory costs on the balance sheet. LIFO can result in absurd balance sheet valuations of inventories because the oldest prices are left in ending inventory.

As shown in the preceding section, LIFO results in the lowest income tax payments when prices are rising. Tax payments are highest under FIFO. When inventory prices are decreasing, tax payments are highest under LIFO and lowest under FIFO.

FIFO is criticized because it overstates income by so-called inventory profit during periods of inflation. Briefly, **inventory profit** is the difference between gross margin figured on the FIFO basis and gross margin figured on the LIFO basis. Exhibit 9-4 illustrates inventory profit. The $12,000 difference between FIFO and LIFO gross margins ($46,000 − $34,000 = $12,000) results from the difference in cost of goods sold and in ending inventory. This $12,000 amount is called FIFO inventory profit, phantom profit, or illusory profit. Why? Because to stay in business the company must replace the inventory it has sold. The replacement cost of the merchandise is essentially the same as the cost of goods sold under LIFO ($66,000) not the FIFO amount ($54,000).

LIFO is criticized because it allows managers to manipulate net income. Assume inventory prices are rising rapidly, and a company wants to show less income for the year (in order to pay less taxes). Managers can buy a large amount of inventory near the end of the year. Under LIFO these high inventory costs immediately become expense—as cost of goods sold. As a result, the income statement reports a lower net income. Conversely, if the business is having a bad year, management may wish to increase reported income. To do so, managers can delay a large purchase of high-cost inventory until the next period. This inventory is not expensed as cost of good sold in the current year. Thus management avoids decreasing the current year's reported income.

A company may want to report the highest income, and FIFO meets this need when prices are rising. But the company must pay the highest income taxes under FIFO. When prices are falling, LIFO reports the highest income.

Which inventory method is best? There is no single answer to this question. Different companies have different motives for the inventory method they choose. Polaroid Corporation uses FIFO, J. C. Penny uses LIFO, and Motorola, Inc., uses average cost. Still other companies use more than one method. The Black and Decker Manufacturing Company uses both LIFO and FIFO, as they stated in an annual report (amounts in millions):

OBJECTIVE 3
Read and understand actual company inventory disclosures

Inventories $390

NOTES TO CONSOLIDATED FINANCIAL STATEMENTS
Note 1: Summary of Accounting Policies
Inventories: The cost of United States inventories is based on the last-in, first-out (LIFO) method; all other inventories are based on the first-in, first-out (FIFO) method. The cost of . . . inventories stated under the LIFO method represents approximately 40% of the value of total inventories.

Consistency Principle

The **consistency principle** states that businesses should use the same accounting methods and procedures from period to period. Consistency makes it possible to compare a company's financial statements from one period to the next.

Suppose you are analyzing a company's net income pattern. The company has switched from LIFO to FIFO. Its net income has increased dramatically but only as a result of the change in inventory method. If you did not know of the change, you might believe that the company's increased income arose from improved operations, which is not the case.

The consistency principle does not require that all companies within an industry use the same accounting method. Nor does it mean that a company may *never* change its own accounting method. However, a company making an accounting change must disclose the effect of the change on net income, as shown below for Midland-Ross Corporation, a large company that makes electrical products, mechanical controls, foundry products, and thermal systems:

EXCERPT FROM NOTE A OF THE MIDLAND-ROSS FINANCIAL STATEMENT
Inventories: The LIFO method of valuing inventories was extended to substantially all of the electrical and mechanical controls inventories. . . . The effect of the change was to reduce net income . . . by $4,638,000. . . .

Summary Problem for Your Review

Suppose an IBM division that handles computer components has these inventory records for January 19X6:

Date	Item	Quantity	Unit Cost	Sale Price
Jan. 1	Beginning inventory	100 units	$ 8	$ —
6	Purchase	60 units	9	—
13	Sale	70 units	—	20
21	Purchase	150 units	9	—
24	Sale	210 units	—	22
27	Purchase	90 units	10	—
30	Sale	30 units	—	25

Company accounting records reveal that related operating expense for January was $1,900.

Required

1. Prepare the January income statement, using the following format. (Round figures to whole dollar amounts.)

IBM Corporation
Income Statement
Month Ended January 31, 19X6

	LIFO	FIFO	Average
Sales revenue.	6770	6770	6770
Cost of goods sold:			
Beginning inventory	800	800	800
Net purchases	2790	2790	2790
Cost of goods available for sale	3590	3590	3590
Ending inventory.	720	900	808
Cost of goods sold.	—	—	—
Gross margin.	—	—	—
Operating expenses.	—	—	—
Operating income	—	—	—

2. Suppose you are the financial vice-president of IBM Corporation. Which inventory method would you use if your motive is to
   a. Minimize income taxes?
   b. Report the highest operating income?
   c. Report operating income between the extremes of FIFO and LIFO?
   d. Report inventory at the most current cost?
   e. Attain the best matching of current expense with current revenue?

State the reason for each of your answers.

SOLUTION TO REVIEW PROBLEM

Requirement 1

IBM Corporation
Income Statement for Component
Month Ended January 31, 19X6

	LIFO		FIFO		Average	
Sales revenue..........		$6,770		$6,770		$6,770
Cost of goods sold:						
Beginning inventory	$ 800		$ 800		$ 800	
Net purchases	2,790		2,790		2,790	
Cost of goods available for sale	3,590		3,590		3,590	
Ending inventory........	720		900		808	
Cost of goods sold		2,870		2,690		2,782
Gross margin		3,900		4,080		3,988
Operating expenses.......		1,900		1,900		1,900
Operating income		$2,000		$2,180		$2,088

Computations:

Sales revenue:	$(70 \times \$20) + (210 \times \$22) + (30 \times \$25) = \$6,770$
Beginning inventory:	$100 \times \$8 = \$800$
Purchases:	$(60 \times \$9) + (150 \times \$9) + (90 \times \$10) = \$2,790$
Ending inventory – LIFO:	$90^* \times \$8 = \$720$
FIFO:	$90 \times \$10 = \$900$
Average:	$90 \times \$8.975^{**} = \$808$ (rounded from 807.75)

* Number of units in ending inventory $= 100 + 60 - 70 + 150 - 210 + 90 - 30 = 90$
** $\$3,590/400$ units $= \$8.975$ per unit
  Number of units available $= 100 + 60 + 150 + 90 = 400$

Requirement 2

a. Use LIFO to minimize income taxes. Operating income under LIFO is lowest when inventory unit costs are increasing, as they are in this case (from $8 to $10). (If inventory costs were decreasing, income under FIFO would be lowest.)

b. Use FIFO to report the highest operating income. Income under FIFO is highest when inventory unit costs are increasing, as in this situation.

c. Use *average cost* to report an operating income amount between the FIFO and LIFO extremes. This is true in this problem situation and in others whether inventory unit costs are increasing or decreasing.

d. Use FIFO to report inventory at the most current cost. The oldest inventory costs are expensed as cost of goods sold, leaving in ending inventory the most recent (most current) costs of the period.

e. Use LIFO to attain the best matching of current expense with current revenue. The most recent (most current) inventory costs are expensed as cost of goods sold.

Accounting Conservatism _____

Conservatism in accounting means to present the gloomiest possible figures in the financial statements. What advantage does conservatism give a business? Management often looks on the brighter side of operations and may overstate a company's income and asset values. Many accountants regard conservatism as a counterbalance to management's optimistic tendencies. The goal is for financial statements to present realistic figures.

Conservatism appears in accounting guidelines like "anticipate no gains, but provide for all probable losses" and "if in doubt, record an asset at the lowest reasonable amount and a liability at the highest reasonable amount."

Accountants generally regard the historical cost of acquiring an asset as its maximum value. Even if the current market value of the asset increases above its cost, businesses do *not* write up (that is, increase) the asset's accounting value. Assume that a company purchased land for $100,000, and its value increased to $300,000. Accounting conservatism dictates that the historical cost $100,000 be maintained as the accounting value of the land.

Conservatism also directs accountants to decrease the accounting value of an asset if it appears unrealistically high — even if no transaction occurs. Assume that a company paid $35,000 for inventory that has become obsolete, and its current value is only $12,000. Conservatism dictates that the inventory be written down (that is, decreased) to $12,000.

Lower-of-Cost-or-Market Rule

The **lower-of-cost-or-market rule** (abbreviated as *LCM*) shows accounting conservatism in action. LCM requires that an asset be reported in the financial statements at the lower of its historical cost or its market value. Applied to inventories, *market value* means *current replacement cost* (that is, how much the business would have to pay in the market on that day to purchase the same amount of inventory that it has on hand). If the replacement cost of inventory falls below its historical cost, the business must write down the value of its goods. The business reports ending inventory at its LCM value on the balance sheet.

Suppose a business paid $3,000 for inventory on September 26. By December 31, its value has fallen. The inventory can now be replaced for $2,200. Market value is below cost, and the December 31 balance sheet reports this inventory at its LCM value of $2,200. Usually, the market value of inventory is higher than historical cost, so inventory's LCM value is cost for most companies. Exhibit 9-5 presents the effects of LCM on the income statement and the balance sheet. The point of the exhibit is to show that the lower of (a) cost or (b) market value — replacement cost — is the relevant amount for valuing inventory on the income statement and the balance sheet. Companies are not required to show both cost and market value amounts. However, they may report the higher amount in parentheses, as shown on the balance sheet in the exhibit.

LCM states that of the $3,000 cost of ending inventory in Exhibit 9-5, $800 is considered to have expired even though the inventory was not sold during the period. Its replacement cost is only $2,200, and that amount is carried forward to the next period as the cost of beginning inventory. Suppose during the next period the replacement cost of this inventory increases to $2,500. Accounting conservatism states that it would not be appropriate to write up the book value of inven-

EXHIBIT 9-5   *Lower-of-Cost-or-Market (LCM) Effects*

Income Statement:

Sales revenue.		$20,000
Cost of goods sold:		
Beginning inventory (LCM = Cost).	$ 2,800	
Net purchases	11,000	
Cost of goods available for sale	13,800	
Ending inventory-		
Cost = $3,000		
Replacement cost (market value) = $2,200		
LCM = Market	2,200	
Cost of goods sold.		11,600
Gross margin		$ 8,400

Balance Sheet:

Current assets:		
Cash	$	XXX
Short-term investments.		XXX
Accounts receivable.		XXX
Inventories, at LCM (Cost, $3,000)		2,200
Prepaid investments		XXX
Total current assets	$	X,XXX

> **OBJECTIVE 4**
>
> Apply the lower-of-cost-or-market rule to inventory

tory. The LCM value of inventory ($2,200 in this case) is used as its cost in future LCM determinations.

Examine the following income statement effect of LCM summarized from Exhibit 9-5. What expense absorbs the impact of the $800 inventory write down? *Cost of goods sold* is increased by $800 because ending inventory is $800 less at LCM ($2,200) than it would have been at cost ($3,000).

	Ending Inventory at	
	Cost	**LCM**
Cost of goods available for sale	$13,800	$13,800
Ending inventory:		
Cost	3,000	
Replacement cost (market value)		2,200
Cost of goods sold.	$10,800	$11,600

$800 Lower at LCM

$800 Higher at LCM

Exhibit 9-5 also reports the application of LCM for inventories in the body of the balance sheet. Companies often disclose LCM in notes to their financial statements, as shown below for CBS, Inc.:

NOTE 1: STATEMENT OF SIGNIFICANT ACCOUNTING POLICIES

Inventories. Inventories are stated at the *lower of cost* (principally based on average cost) *or market value.* [emphasis added]

Effect of Inventory Errors

Businesses determine inventory amounts at the end of the period. In the process of counting the items, applying unit costs, and computing amounts, errors may arise. As the period 1 segment of Exhibit 9-6 shows, an error in the ending inventory amount creates errors in the cost of goods sold and gross margin amounts. Compare periods 1 and 3.

OBJECTIVE 5

Explain why inventory errors counterbalance

Recall that one period's ending inventory is the next period's beginning inventory. Thus the error in ending inventory carries over into the next period: note the highlighted amounts in Exhibit 9-6.

Because the same ending inventory figure that is *subtracted* in computing cost of goods sold in one period is *added* to compute cost of goods sold in the next period, the error's effect cancels out. The overstatement of cost of goods sold in period 2 counterbalances the understatement in cost of goods sold in period 1. Thus the total gross margin amount for the two periods is the correct $100,000 figure whether or not an error entered into the computation.

However, inventory errors should not be dismissed lightly. Suppose you are analyzing trends in the business's operations. Exhibit 9-6 reports a drop in gross margin from period 1 to period 2, followed by an increase in period 3. But that picture of operations is untrue because of the inventory error. Correct gross margin is $50,000 each period. To provide accurate information for decision making, all inventory errors should be corrected.

Methods of Estimating Inventory

Often a business must *estimate* the value of its inventory. Because of cost and inconvenience, few companies physically count their inventories at the end of each month, yet they may need monthly financial statements. A fire or a flood may destroy inventory, and to file an insurance claim, the business must estimate the value of its loss. In both cases, the business needs to know the value of ending inventory without being able to count it. Two methods for estimating ending

OBJECTIVE 6

Estimate inventory by two methods

EXHIBIT 9-6   *Effects of Inventory Errors*

	Period 1 Ending Inventory Overstated By $5,000		Period 2 Beginning Inventory Overstated By $5,000		Period 3 Correct	
Sales revenue		$100,000		$100,000		$100,000
Cost of goods sold:						
Beginning inventory.	$10,000		$15,000		$10,000	
Net purchases.	50,000		50,000		50,000	
Cost of goods available for sale.	60,000		65,000		60,000	
Ending inventory	15,000		10,000		10,000	
Cost of goods sold		45,000		55,000		50,000
Gross margin		$55,000		$45,000		$50,000
			$100,000			

The authors thank Carl High for this example.

inventory are the *gross margin method* (or *gross profit method*) and the *retail method.* These methods are widely used in actual practice.

Gross Margin (Gross Profit) Method

The **gross margin method** is a way of estimating inventory based on the familiar cost of goods sold model:

> **Beginning inventory**
> **+ Net purchases**
> **= Cost of goods available for sale**
> **− Ending inventory**
> **= Cost of goods sold**

Rearranging *ending inventory* and *cost of goods sold,* the model becomes useful for estimating ending inventory:

> **Beginning inventory**
> **+ Net purchases**
> **= Cost of goods available for sale**
> **− Cost of goods sold**
> **= Ending inventory**

Suppose a fire destroys your business's inventory. To collect insurance, you must estimate the cost of the ending inventory. If the fire did not also destroy your accounting records, beginning inventory and net purchases amounts may be taken directly from the accounting records. The Sales Revenue, Sales Returns, and Sales Discounts accounts indicate net sales up to the date of the fire. Using the entity's normal *gross margin rate* (that is, gross margin divided by net sales revenue), you can estimate cost of goods sold. The last step is to subtract cost of goods sold from goods available to estimate ending inventory. Exhibit 9-7 illustrates the gross margin method.

Accountants, managers, and auditors use the gross margin method to test the overall reasonableness of an ending inventory amount that has been determined by a physical count for all types of businesses. This method helps to detect large errors.

Retail Method

Retail establishments (department stores, drug stores, hardware stores, and so on) use the **retail method** to estimate their inventory cost. The retail method, like the gross margin method, is based on the cost of goods sold model. However, the

EXHIBIT 9-7 *Gross Margin Method of Estimating Inventory (amounts assumed)*

Beginning inventory		$14,000
Net purchases		66,000
Cost of goods available for sale		80,000
Cost of goods sold:		
Net sales revenue	$100,000	
Less estimated gross margin of 40%	40,000	
Estimated cost of goods sold		60,000
Estimated cost of *ending inventory*		$20,000

EXHIBIT 9-8 *Retail Method of Estimating Inventory (amounts assumed)*

	Cost	Retail
Beginning inventory..............................	$ 24,000	$ 40,000
Net purchases....................................	144,000	240,000
Goods available for sale.........................	$168,000	280,000
Cost ratio: $168,000/$280,000 = .60		
Less: Net sales revenue (which is stated at retail)		(230,000)
Ending inventory, at retail........................		$ 50,000
Ending inventory, at cost ($50,000 × .60)	$ 30,000	

retail method requires that the business record inventory purchases both at *cost* —as shown in the purchase records—and at *retail* (selling) price—as shown on the price tags. This is not a burden because price tags show the retail price of inventory, and most retailers set their retail prices by adding standard markups to their cost. For example, a department store may pay $6 for a man's belt, mark it up $4, and price the belt at $10 retail. In the retail method, the seller's inventory cost is determined by working backward from its retail value. Exhibit 9-8 illustrates the process.

In Exhibit 9-8 the accounting records show the goods available for sale at cost ($168,000) and at retail ($280,000). The cost ratio is .60 ($168,000/$280,000). For simplicity, we round all such percentages to two decimal places in this chapter. Subtracting *net sales revenue* (a retail amount) from *goods available for sale at retail* yields *ending inventory at retail* ($50,000). The business multiplies *ending inventory at retail* by the cost ratio to figure *ending inventory at cost* ($30,000).

Suppose the retailer has four categories of inventory, each with a different cost ratio. How would the business use the retail method to estimate the overall cost of the ending inventory? Apply the retail method separately to each category of inventory, using its specific cost ratio, then add the costs of the four categories to determine the overall cost of inventory.

Even though the retail method is an estimation technique, some retailers use it to compute the inventory value for their financial statements. They make physical counts of inventory throughout the year to validate the retail-method amounts. For example, Marshall Field & Company, a department store chain headquartered in Chicago, uses the retail method, as disclosed in its annual report:

Merchandise inventories (note 1C) $179,007,250

Note 1C: Inventory Pricing
    Substantially all merchandise inventories are valued by use of the *retail method.* [emphasis added]

Periodic and Perpetual Inventory Systems _____

Different businesses have different inventory information needs. We now look at the two main inventory systems: the *periodic system* and the *perpetual system.*

Periodic Inventory System.   In the **periodic inventory system,** the business does not keep a continuous record of the inventory on hand. Instead, at the end of the period, the business makes a physical count of the on-hand inventory and applies the appropriate unit costs to determine the cost of ending inventory. The business makes the standard end-of-period inventory entries, as discussed in Chapter 5 and shown in the example that follows. This system is also called the *physical system* because it relies on the actual physical count of inventory. The periodic system is used to account for inventory items that have a low unit cost. Low-cost items may not be valuable enough to warrant the cost of keeping a running record of the inventory on hand.

Entries Under the Periodic System.   In the periodic system, the business records purchases of inventory in the Purchases account (an expense account). At the end of the period, the business removes the beginning balance from the Inventory account and enters the ending balance, as determined by the physical count. Assume the following data for a K-Mart store's April transactions.

Beginning inventory	$ 80,000
Ending inventory	102,000
Credit purchases (net of discounts and returns)	600,000
Credit sales (net of discounts and returns)	900,000

> **OBJECTIVE 7**
>
> Account for inventory by the periodic and perpetual systems

Summary entries for April:

To record credit purchases:

Purchases	600,000	
Accounts Payable		600,000

To record credit sales:

Accounts Receivable	900,000	
Sales Revenue		900,000

Inventory entries at the end of the period:

Income Summary	80,000	
Inventory (beginning balance)		80,000
Inventory (ending balance)	102,000	
Income Summary		102,000

Reporting on the financial statements:

Balance sheet at April 30:

Inventory	$102,000

Income statement for April:

Sales revenue		$900,000
Cost of goods sold:		
Beginning inventory	$ 80,000	
Net purchases	600,000	
Cost of goods available	680,000	
Ending inventory	102,000	
Cost of goods sold		578,000
Gross margin		$322,000

Perpetual Inventory System.   In the **perpetual inventory system,** the business keeps a continuous record for each inventory item. The records thus show the inventory on hand at all times. Perpetual records are useful in preparing monthly, quarterly, or other interim financial statements. The business can determine the cost of ending inventory and the cost of goods sold directly from the accounts without having to physically count the merchandise.

The perpetual system offers a higher degree of control than the periodic system

EXHIBIT 9-9 *Perpetual Inventory Record*

Item   Home Computer Model RK-42

Date	Received Qty.	Received Unit Cost	Received Total	Sold Qty.	Sold Unit Cost	Sold Total	Balance Qty.	Balance Unit Cost	Balance Total
Nov. 1							14	$300	$4,200
5				4	$300	$1,200	10	300	3,000
7				9	300	2,700	1	300	300
12	5	$320	$1,600				1	300	300
							5	320	1,600
26	7	330	2,310				1	300	300
							5	320	1,600
							7	330	2,310
30				1	300	300	1	320	320
				4	320	1,280	7	330	2,310
Totals	12	—	$3,910	18	—	$5,480	8	—	$2,630

does because the inventory information is always up to date. Consequently businesses use the perpetual system for high-unit-cost inventories, such as gemstones and automobiles. Nevertheless, companies physically count their inventory at least once each year to check the accuracy of their perpetual records.

Perpetual inventory records can be computer listings of inventory items or inventory cards like the Computerworld record shown in Exhibit 9-9. The accountant adds information to the computer list or the card on a daily basis. A running balance conveniently shows the latest inventory value. The perpetual record serves as a subsidiary record to the inventory account in the general ledger.

The perpetual inventory record indicates that the business uses the FIFO basis, as shown by the November 30 sale. The cost of the first unit sold is the oldest unit cost on hand. Perpetual records may also be kept on the LIFO basis or the average basis. Perpetual inventory records provide information such as the following:

1. When customers inquire about how soon they can get a home computer, the salesperson can answer the question after referring to the perpetual inventory record. On November 7 the salesperson would reply that the company's stock is low, and the customer may have to wait a few days. On November 26 the salesperson could offer immediate delivery.

2. The perpetual records alert the business to reorder when inventory becomes low. On November 7 the company would be wise to purchase inventory. Sales may be lost if the business cannot promise immediate delivery.

3. At November 30 the company prepares monthly financial statements. The perpetual inventory records show the company's ending inventory of home computers at $2,630, and its cost of goods sold for this product at $5,480. No physical count is necessary at this time. However, a physical inventory is needed once a year to verify the accuracy of the records.

Entries under the Perpetual System. In the perpetual system, the business records purchases of inventory by debiting the Inventory account. When the business makes a sale, two entries are necessary. The company records the sale in the usual manner—debits Cash or Accounts Receivable and credits Sales Revenue for the sale price of the goods. The company also debits Cost of Goods Sold and credits Inventory for cost. The debit to Inventory (for purchases) and the credit to Inventory (for sales) serve to keep an up-to-date record of inventory on hand. Therefore, no end-of-period adjusting entries are needed. The Inventory account already carries the correct ending balance.

In the perpetual system, Cost of Goods Sold is an account in the general ledger. By contrast, in the periodic system, cost of goods sold is simply a total on the income statement.

To illustrate the entries under the perpetual system, let's use the same data we used in discussing the periodic system, which follow.

Ending inventory..	$102,000
Credit purchases (net of discounts and returns)	600,000
Credit sales (net of discounts and returns).....................	900,000
Cost of goods sold..	578,000

Summary entries for April:

To record credit purchases:

Inventory	600,000	
Accounts Payable.................................		600,000

To record credit sales:

Accounts Receivable................................	900,000	
Sales Revenue......................................		900,000
Cost of Goods Sold	578,000	
Inventory...		578,000

Reporting on the financial statements:

Balance sheet at April 30:

Inventory..	$102,000

Income statement for April:

Sales revenue	$900,000
Cost of goods sold	578,000
Gross margin....................................	$322,000

You should compare the entries and financial statement presentations under the *periodic* and the *perpetual* systems. Note that the entries to record purchases and sales differ under the two systems but that the financial statement amounts are the same.

Internal Control over Inventory

Internal control over inventory is important because inventory is the lifeblood of a merchandiser. Successful companies take great care to protect their inventory. Elements of good internal control over inventory include:

1. Physically counting inventory at least once each year no matter which system is used
2. Maintaining efficient purchasing, receiving, and shipping procedures
3. Storing inventory to protect it against theft, damage, and decay

4. Limiting access to inventory to personnel who do *not* have access to the accounting records
5. Keeping perpetual inventory records for high-unit-cost merchandise
6. Purchasing inventory in economical quantities
7. Keeping enough inventory on hand to prevent shortage situations, which lead to lost sales
8. Not keeping too large an inventory stockpiled, thus avoiding the expense of tying up money in unneeded items

The annual physical count of inventory (item 1) is necessary because the only way to be certain of the amount of inventory on hand is to count it. Errors arise in the best accounting systems, and the count is needed to establish the correct value of the inventory. When an error is detected, the records are brought into agreement with the physical count.

Keeping inventory handlers away from the accounting records (item 4) is an essential separation of duties, discussed in Chapter 7. An employee with access to inventory and the accounting records can steal the goods and make an entry to conceal the theft. For example, he could increase the amount of an inventory write-down to make it appear that goods decreased in value when in fact they were stolen.

Computerized Inventory Records

Computer systems have revolutionized accounting for inventory. They can provide up-to-the-minute inventory data useful for managing the business. They help cut accounting cost by processing large numbers of transactions without computational error. Computer systems also enhance internal control. They increase efficiency because managers always know the quantity and cost of inventory on hand. Managers can make better decisions about quantities to buy, prices to pay for the inventory, prices to charge customers, and sale terms to offer. Knowing the quantity on hand helps to safeguard the inventory.

Computer inventory systems vary considerably. At one extreme are complex systems used by huge retailers like Sears, Penney's, and K-Mart. Purchases of inventory are recorded in perpetual records stored in a central computer. The inventory tags are coded electronically for updating the perpetual records when a sale is recorded on the cash register. Have you noticed sales clerks passing the inventory ticket over a particular area of the checkout counter? A sensing device in the counter reads the stock number, quantity, cost, and sale price of the item sold. In other systems, the sales clerk passes an electronic device over the inventory tag. The computer records the sale and updates the inventory records. In effect, a journal entry is recorded for each sale, a procedure that is not economical without a computer.

Small companies also use minicomputers and microcomputers to keep perpetual inventory records. These systems may be similar to the systems used by large companies. In less sophisticated systems, a company may have sales clerks write inventory stock numbers on sales slips. The stock number identifies the particular item of inventory, such as men's shirts or children's shoes. The business may accumulate all sales slips for the week. If the company has its own computer system, an employee may type the sales information into the computer and store the perpetual records on a magnetic disk. To learn the quantity, cost, or other characteristic of a particular item of inventory, a manager can view the inventory record on the computer monitor. For broader-based decisions affecting the entire inventory, managers use printouts of all items in stock. Many small businesses hire outside computer service centers to do much of the accounting for inventory. Regardless of the arrangement, managers get periodic printouts showing inventory data needed for managing the business. Manual reporting of this information is more time consuming and expensive.

Summary Problems for Your Review

Problem 1

Centronics Data Computer Corporation reported a net loss for the year. In its financial statements, the company noted:

Balance Sheet:

Current assets:
Inventories (notes 1C and 2)............................... $48,051,000

> Note 1C: Inventories are stated at the lower of cost or market. Cost is determined on a first-in, first-out (FIFO) basis.
> Note 2: Declining . . . market conditions during [the] fiscal [year] adversely affected anticipated sales of the Company's older printer products; . . . Accordingly, the statement of loss . . . includes a [debit] of $9,600,000.

Required

1. At which amount did Centronics report its inventory, cost or market value? How can you tell?
2. If the reported inventory of $48,051,000 represents market value, what was the cost of the inventory?

Problem 2

American Hospital Supply Corporation reported using the LIFO inventory method. Its inventory amount was $490.5 million.

Required

1. Suppose that during the period covered by this report, the company made an error that understated its inventory by $15 million. What effect would this error have on *cost of goods sold* and *gross margin* of the period? On *cost of goods sold* and *gross margin* of the following period? On *total gross margin* of both periods combined?
2. When American Hospital Supply reported the above amount for inventory, prices were rising. Would FIFO or LIFO have shown a higher gross margin? Why?

SOLUTIONS TO REVIEW PROBLEMS

Problem 1

1. Centronics reported its inventory at *market value,* as indicated by (a) their valuing inventories at LCM and (b) the declining market conditions that caused the company to "include a [debit] of $9,600,000" in "the statement of

loss." The company debited the $9,600,000 to a loss account or to cost of goods sold. The credit side of the entry was to Inventory — for a write-down to market value.

2. The cost of inventory before the write-down was $57,651,000 ($48,051,000 + $9,600,000). The $48,051,000 market value is what is left of the original cost. Thus the amount to be carried forward to future periods is $48,051,000.

Problem 2

1. Understating ending inventory by $15 million has the following effects on *cost of goods sold* and *gross margin*:

	Cost of Goods Sold	Gross Margin
Period during which error was made	OVERSTATED by $15 million	UNDERSTATED by $15 million
Following period	UNDERSTATED by $15 million	OVERSTATED by $15 million
Combined total	CORRECTLY STATED	CORRECTLY STATED

2. When prices are rising, FIFO results in higher gross margin than LIFO. FIFO matches against sales revenue the lower inventory costs of beginning inventory and purchases made during the early part of the period.

Summary

Accounting for inventory plays an important part in merchandisers' accounting systems because selling inventory is the heart of their business. Inventory is generally the largest current asset on their balance sheet, and inventory expense — called cost of goods sold — is usually the largest expense on the income statement.

Businesses multiply the quantity of inventory items by their unit cost to determine inventory cost. Inventory costing methods are *specific unit cost; average cost; first-in, first-out (FIFO) cost; and last-in, first-out (LIFO) cost.* Businesses that sell individually identifiable items, like automobiles and jewels, use the specific unit cost method. Most other companies use the other methods.

FIFO reports ending inventory at the most current cost. LIFO reports cost of goods sold at the most current cost. When inventory costs increase, LIFO produces the highest cost of goods sold and the lowest income, thus minimizing income taxes. FIFO results in the highest income. The average cost method avoids the extremes of FIFO and LIFO.

The *consistency principle* demands that a business stick with the inventory method it chooses. If a change in inventory method is warranted, the company must report the effect of the change on income. The *lower-of-cost-or-market rule* — an example of accounting *conservatism* — requires that businesses report inventory on the balance sheet at the lower of its cost or current replacement value.

The *gross profit method* and the *retail method* are two techniques for estimating the cost of inventory. These methods come in handy for preparing interim financial statements and for estimating the cost of inventory destroyed by fire and other casualties.

Merchandisers with high-price-tag items generally use the *perpetual inventory system,* which features a running inventory balance. Merchandisers handling low-price-tag items usually use the *periodic system.* A physical count of inventory is needed in both systems for control purposes.

Self-Study Questions

Test your understanding of the chapter by marking the best answer to each of the following questions.

1. Which of the following items is the greatest in dollar amount? *(p. 346)*
   a. Beginning inventory
   b. Purchases
   c. Cost of goods available for sale
   d. Ending inventory
   e. Cost of goods sold

2. Sound Warehouse counts 15,000 stereo albums, including 1,000 albums held on consignment, in its Waco, Texas, store. The business has purchased an additional 2,000 units on FOB destination terms. These goods are still in transit. Each album cost $3.40. The cost of the inventory to report on the balance sheet is *(p. 347)*
   a. $47,600
   b. $51,000
   c. $54,400
   d. $57,800

3. The inventory costing method that best matches current expense with current revenue is *(p. 352)*
   a. Specific unit cost
   b. Average cost
   c. FIFO
   d. LIFO
   e. FIFO or LIFO, depending on whether inventory costs are increasing or decreasing

4. The consistency principle has the most direct impact on *(p. 353)*
   a. Whether to include or exclude an item in inventory
   b. Whether to change from one inventory method to another
   c. Whether to write inventory down to a market value below cost
   d. Whether to use the periodic or the perpetual inventory system

5. Application of the lower-of-cost-or-market rule often results in *(p. 357)*
   a. Higher ending inventory
   b. Lower ending inventory
   c. A counterbalancing error
   d. A change from one inventory method to another

6. An error understated ending inventory of 19X7. This error will *(p. 358)*
   a. Overstate 19X7 cost of sales
   b. Understate 19X8 cost of sales
   c. Not affect owner's equity at the end of 19X8
   d. All of the above

7. Beginning inventory was $35,000, purchases were $146,000, and sales totaled $240,000. With a normal gross margin rate of 35 percent, how much is ending inventory? *(p. 359)*
   a. $25,000
   b. $35,000
   c. $97,000
   d. $181,000

8. Beginning inventory was $20,000 at cost and $40,000 at retail. Purchases were $120,000 at cost and $210,000 at retail. Sales were $200,000. How much is ending inventory at cost? *(p. 360)*
   a. $22,000
   b. $26,000
   c. $28,000
   d. $50,000

9. The year-end entry to close beginning inventory in a perpetual inventory system is *(p. 363)*
   a. Income Summary XXX
          Inventory. XXX
   b. Inventory. XXX
          Income Summary XXX
   c. Either of the above, depending on whether inventory increased or decreased during the period
   d. Not needed

10. Which of the following statements is true? *(pp. 363, 364)*
    a. Separation of duties is not an important element of internal control for inventories.

b. The perpetual system is used primarily for low-unit-cost inventory.

c. An annual physical count of inventory is needed regardless of the type of inventory system used.

d. All the above are true.

Answers to the self-study questions are at the end of the chapter.

Accounting Vocabulary

average cost method *(p. 348)*, beginning inventory *(p. 345)*, conservatism *(p. 356)*, consignment *(p. 347)*, consistency principle *(p. 353)*, ending inventory *(p. 345)*, first-in, first-out (FIFO) method *(p. 348)*, FOB destination *(p. 347)*, FOB shipping point *(p. 347)*, goods available for sale *(p. 345)*, gross margin (gross profit) method *(p. 359)*, inventory cost *(p. 347)*, inventory profit *(p. 352)*, last-in, first-out (LIFO) method *(p. 348)*, lower-of-cost-or-market (LCM) rule *(p. 356)*, periodic inventory system *(p. 360)*, perpetual inventory system *(p. 361)*, retail method *(p. 359)*, specific cost method *(p. 348)*.

ASSIGNMENT MATERIAL

Questions

1. Why is merchandise inventory so important to a retailer or wholesaler?

2. If beginning inventory is $10,000, purchases total $85,000, and ending inventory is $12,700, how much is cost of goods sold?

3. If beginning inventory is $32,000, purchases total $119,000, and cost of goods sold is $127,000, how much is ending inventory?

4. What role does the cost principle play in accounting for inventory?

5. What two items determine the cost of ending inventory?

6. Briefly describe the four generally accepted inventory cost methods. During a period of rising prices, which method produces the highest reported income? Which produces the lowest reported income?

7. Which inventory costing method produces the ending inventory valued at the most current cost? Which method produces the cost-of-goods-sold amount valued at the most current cost?

8. What is the most attractive feature of LIFO? Does LIFO have this advantage during periods of increasing prices or during periods of decreasing prices? Why has LIFO had this advantage recently?

9. Which inventory costing method is used the most in practice? Which method is used second most? third most?

10. What is inventory profit? Which method produces it?

11. Identify the chief criticism of LIFO.

12. How does the consistency principle affect accounting for inventory?

13. Briefly describe the influence that the concept of conservatism has on accounting for inventory.

14. Manley Company's inventory has a cost of $48,000 at the end of the year, and the current replacement cost of the inventory is $51,000. At which amount should the company report the inventory on its balance sheet? Suppose the current replacement cost of the inventory is $45,000 instead of $51,000. At which amount should Manley report the inventory? What rule governs your answers to these questions?

15. Gabriel Company accidentally overstated its ending inventory by $10,000 at the end of period 1. Is gross margin of period 1 overstated or understated? Is gross margin of period 2 overstated, understated, or unaffected by the period 1 error? Is total gross

margin for the two periods overstated, understated, or correct? Give the reason for your answer.

16. Identify two methods of estimating inventory amounts. What familiar model underlies both estimation methods?

17. A fire destroyed the inventory of Olivera Company, but the accounting records were saved. The beginning inventory was $22,000, purchases for the period were $71,000, and sales were $140,000. Olivera's customary gross margin is 45 percent of sales. Use the gross margin method to estimate the cost of the inventory destroyed by the fire.

18. Suppose your company deals in expensive jewelry. Which inventory system should you use to achieve good internal control over the inventory? If your business is a hardware store that sells low-cost goods, what inventory system would you be likely to use? Why would you choose this system?

19. Identify the accounts debited and credited in the standard purchase and sale entries under (a) the periodic inventory system and (b) the perpetual inventory system.

20. What is the role of the physical count of inventory in (a) the periodic inventory system and (b) the perpetual inventory system?

21. True or false? A company that sells inventory of low unit cost needs no internal controls over the goods. Any inventory loss would probably be small.

Exercises

Exercise 9-1   *Computing ending inventory by four methods*

The inventory records for stereo tuner/amplifiers indicate the following at October 31:

Oct.	1	Beginning inventory	10 units @ $130
	8	Purchase	4 units @ 140
	15	Purchase	11 units @ 150
	26	Purchase	5 units @ 156

The physical count of inventory at October 31 indicates that seven units are on hand, and the company owns them. Compute ending inventory and cost of goods sold using each of the following methods:

1. Specific unit cost, assuming five $150 units and two $130 units are on hand
2. Average cost
3. First in, first out
4. Last in, first out

Exercise 9-2   *Recording periodic inventory transactions*

Assume the data in Exercise 9-1 pertain to Ching Company. Prepare the general journal entries under the periodic inventory system to record:

1. Total October purchases in one summary entry. All purchases were on credit.
2. Total October sales in one summary entry. Assume the selling price was $300 per unit, and all sales were on credit.
3. October 31 entries for inventory. Ching uses FIFO.

Exercise 9-3   *Computing the tax advantage of LIFO over FIFO*

Use the data in Exercise 9-1 to illustrate the income tax advantage of LIFO over FIFO, assuming sales revenue is $6,500, operating expenses are $1,100, and the income tax rate is 40 percent.

Exercise 9-4   *Converting LIFO financial statements to the FIFO basis*

Maxus Corporation reported:

Balance sheet:	19X5	19X4
Inventories—note 4	$ 65,800	$ 59,300
Income statement:		
Net purchases	404,100	372,700
Cost of sales....................	397,600	381,400

Note 4. The company determines inventory cost by the last-in, first-out method. If the first-in, first-out method were used, inventories would be $8,200 higher at year end 19X5 and $7,500 higher at year end 19X4.

Required

Show the cost of goods sold computations for 19X5 under LIFO and FIFO. Which method would result in higher reported income? Show the amount of the difference.

Exercise 9-5   *Note disclosure of a change in inventory method*

A company has used the first-in, first-out inventory method for many years. At the start of the current year the company switched to the last-in, first-out method. This change decreased net income by $263,000. Write the note to disclose this accounting change in the company's financial statements.

Exercise 9-6   *The effect of lower-of-cost-or-market on the income statement*

From the following inventory records of Barnet, Inc., for 19X7, prepare the company's income statement through gross margin. Apply the lower-of-cost-or-market rule.

Beginning inventory (average cost).................	300 @ $41.33 =	$ 12,399
(replacement cost)..............	300 @ 41.91 =	12,573
Purchases during the year........................	2,600 @ 45.50 =	118,300
Ending inventory (average cost)....................	400 @ 45.07 =	18,028
(replacement cost)	400 @ 42.10 =	16,840
Sales during the year............................	2,500 @ 91.00* =	227,500

---

* Selling price per unit.

Exercise 9-7   *Applying the lower-of-cost-or-market rule*

Danos Company's income statement for March reported the following data:

Income Statement:

Sales revenue		$83,000
Cost of goods sold:		
Beginning inventory	$17,200	
Net purchases	51,700	
Cost of goods available for sale	68,900	
Ending inventory	22,800	
Cost of goods sold		46,100
Gross margin		$36,900

Prior to releasing the financial statements, it was discovered that the current replacement cost of ending inventory was $19,600. Correct the above data to include the lower-of-cost-or-market value of ending inventory. Also, show how inventory would be reported on the balance sheet.

Exercise 9-8 *Correcting an inventory error*

Lee Corporation reported the following comparative income statement for the years ended September 30, 19X5 and 19X4:

<table>
<tr><td colspan="5" align="center">**Lee Corporation**
Income Statements
For the Years Ended September 30,</td></tr>
<tr><td></td><td colspan="2" align="center">**19X5**</td><td colspan="2" align="center">**19X4**</td></tr>
<tr><td>Sales revenue</td><td></td><td>$132,300</td><td></td><td>$121,700</td></tr>
<tr><td>Cost of goods sold:</td><td></td><td></td><td></td><td></td></tr>
<tr><td> Beginning inventory</td><td>$14,000</td><td></td><td>$12,800</td><td></td></tr>
<tr><td> Net purchases</td><td>72,000</td><td></td><td>66,000</td><td></td></tr>
<tr><td> Cost of goods available</td><td>86,000</td><td></td><td>78,800</td><td></td></tr>
<tr><td> Ending inventory</td><td>16,600</td><td></td><td>14,000</td><td></td></tr>
<tr><td> Cost of goods sold</td><td></td><td>69,400</td><td></td><td>64,800</td></tr>
<tr><td>Gross margin</td><td></td><td>62,900</td><td></td><td>56,900</td></tr>
<tr><td>Operating expenses</td><td></td><td>30,300</td><td></td><td>26,100</td></tr>
<tr><td>Net income</td><td></td><td>$ 32,600</td><td></td><td>$ 30,800</td></tr>
</table>

During 19X5 accountants for the company discovered that ending 19X4 inventory was overstated by $1,500. Prepare the corrected comparative income statement for the two-year period. What was the effect of the error on net income for the two years combined? Explain your answer.

Exercise 9-9 *Estimating inventory by the gross margin method*

McIntosh Company began April with inventory of $41,000. The business made net purchases of $37,600 and had net sales of $51,000 before a fire destroyed the company's inventory. For the past several years, McIntosh's gross margin on sales has been 30 percent. Estimate the cost of the inventory destroyed by the fire.

Exercise 9-10 *Estimating inventory by the retail method*

Assume the inventory records of a small department of Macy's, a large chain of department stores, revealed the following:

	At Cost	At Retail
Beginning inventory	$ 26,000	$ 48,000
Net purchases	103,000	191,000
Net sales.		201,000

Use the retail inventory method to estimate the ending inventory of the department. Round the cost ratio to two decimal places.

Exercise 9-11 *Recording perpetual inventory transactions*

King Chevrolet Company keeps perpetual inventory records for its automobile inventory. During May the company made credit purchases of inventory costing $111,300. Cash sales came to $26,800, credit sales totaled $130,400, and cost of goods sold reached $119,550. Record these summary transactions in the general journal.

Problems

(Group A)

Problem 9-1A   *Computing inventory by three methods*

Hernandez Imports began the year with 230 units of inventory that cost $80 each. During the year Hernandez made the following purchases:

Feb. 3	217 @ $81
Apr. 12	95 @ 82
Aug. 8	210 @ 84
Oct. 24	248 @ 88

The company uses the periodic inventory system, and the physical count at December 31 indicates that ending inventory consists of 319 units.

Required

Compute the ending inventory and cost of goods sold amounts under (1) average cost, (2) FIFO cost, and (3) LIFO cost. Round average cost per unit to the nearest cent, and round all other amounts to the nearest dollar.

Problem 9-2A   *Computing inventory, cost of goods sold, and FIFO inventory profits*

Campus Sportswear specializes in men's shirts. The store began operations on January 1, 19X1, with an inventory of 200 shirts that cost $13 each, a $2,600 total. During the year the store purchased inventory as follows:

Purchase no. 1	110 @ $14
Purchase no. 2	80 @ 15
Purchase no. 3	320 @ 15
Purchase no. 4	100 @ 18

The ending inventory consists of 250 shirts.

Required

1. Complete the following tabulation, rounding average cost to the nearest cent and all other amounts to the nearest dollar:

	Ending Inventory	Cost of Goods Sold
a. Average cost	_____	_____
b. FIFO cost.......................................	_____	_____
c. LIFO cost.......................................	_____	_____

2. Compute the amount of inventory profit under FIFO.
3. Which method produces the most current ending inventory cost? Which method produces the most current cost-of-goods-sold amount? Give the reason for your answers.

Problem 9-3A   *Preparing an income statement directly from the accounts*

The records of Janeway Retailers include the following accounts for one of its products at December 31 of the current year:

Inventory

Jan. 1	Balance	{ 300 units @ $3.00	1,210	
		100 units @ 3.10 }		

Purchases

Feb. 6	800 units @ $3.15	2,520	
May 19	600 units @ 3.35	2,010	
Aug. 12	460 units @ 3.50	1,610	
Oct. 4	800 units @ 3.75	3,000	
Dec. 31	Balance	9,140	

Sales Revenue

		Mar. 12	500 units @ $4.00	2,000
		June 9	1,100 units @ 4.20	4,620
		Aug. 21	300 units @ 4.50	1,350
		Nov. 2	400 units @ 4.50	1,800
		Dec. 18	100 units @ 4.75	475
		Dec. 31	Balance	10,245

Required

1. Compute the quantities of goods in (a) ending inventory and (b) cost of goods sold during the year.
2. Prepare the following partial income statement under the average cost, FIFO cost, and LIFO cost methods. Round average cost to the nearest cent and all other amounts to the nearest dollar.

Janeway Retailers
Income Statement
For the year ended December 31, 19XX

	Average Cost	FIFO Cost	LIFO Cost
Sales revenue	$ _____	$ _____	$ _____
Cost of goods sold:			
Beginning inventory	$ _____	$ _____	$ _____
Purchases	_____	_____	_____
Cost of goods available	_____	_____	_____
Ending inventory	_____	_____	_____
Cost of goods sold			
Gross margin	$ _____	$ _____	$ _____

Problem 9-4A *Recording periodic and perpetual inventory transactions*

Using the data in Problem 9-3A, make summary entries in the general journal to record:

1. Purchases, sales, and end-of-period inventory entries, assuming Janeway Retailers uses the periodic inventory system and the average cost method. All purchases are on credit. Cash sales are $4,000, with the remaining sales on account.
2. Purchases, sales, and cost of goods sold, assuming Janeway Retailers uses the perpetual inventory system and the average cost method. All purchases are on credit. Cash sales total $4,000, with the remainder on account.

Problem 9-5A   *Applying the lower-of-cost-or-market rule*

Assume that accountants prepared the financial statements of Dysan Company on the cost basis without considering whether the replacement value of ending inventory was less than cost. Following are selected data from those statements:

From the income statement:

Sales revenue......................		$832,000
Cost of goods sold:		
Beginning inventory	$104,000	
Net purchases	587,000	
Cost of goods available for sale	691,000	
Ending inventory................	143,000	
Cost of goods sold		548,000
Gross margin		$284,000

From the balance sheet:

Current assets:		
Inventory		$143,000

The replacement costs were $122,000 for beginning inventory and $138,000 for ending inventory.

Required

1. Revise the data to include the appropriate lower-of-cost-or-market value of inventory.
2. How is the lower-of-cost-or-market rule conservative?

Problem 9-6A   *Correcting inventory errors over a three-year period*

The Power & Masters Company books show these data (in millions):

	19X3		19X2		19X1	
Net sales revenue..................		$200		$160		$175
Cost of goods sold:						
Beginning inventory.............	$ 15		$ 25		$ 40	
Net purchases.................	135		100		90	
Cost of goods available	150		125		130	
Less ending inventory	30		15		25	
Cost of goods sold		120		110		105
Gross margin		80		50		70
Operating expenses		74		38		46
Net income.......................		$ 6		$ 12		$ 24

In early 19X4, a team of internal auditors discovered that the ending inventory of 19X1 had been overstated by $20 million. Also, the ending inventory for 19X3 had been understated by $5 million. The ending inventory at December 31, 19X2, was correct.

Required

1. Prepare corrected income statements for the three years.
2. State whether each year's net income and owner's equity amounts are understated or overstated. For each incorrect figure, indicate the amount of the understatement or overstatement.

Problem 9-7A *Estimating inventory by the gross margin method; preparing a multiple-step income statement*

Assume Kentucky Fried Chicken, Inc., estimates its inventory by the gross margin method when preparing monthly financial statements. For the past two years, gross margin has averaged 35 percent of net sales. Assume further that the company's inventory records for stores in the southeastern region reveal the following data:

Inventory, March 1	$ 398,000
Transactions during March:	
Purchases	5,685,000
Purchase discounts.	49,000
Purchase returns.	8,000
Sales	8,667,000
Sales returns	17,000

Required

1. Estimate the March 31 inventory using the gross margin method.
2. Prepare the March income statement through gross margin, for the Kentucky Fried Chicken, Inc., stores in the southeastern region. Use the multiple-step format.

Problem 9-8A *Estimating inventory by the retail method; recording periodic inventory transactions*

The fiscal year of J. C. Penney Company, Inc., (and many other retailers) ends on January 31. Assume the following inventory data for the women's sportswear department of a J. C. Penney store:

	Cost	Retail
Inventory, Jan. 31, 19X5	$ 84,500	$153,636
Transactions during the year ended January 31, 19X6:		
Purchases	419,220	762,500
Purchase returns.	18,090	33,172
Sales		783,740
Sales returns		9,676

Required

1. Use the retail method to estimate the cost of the store's ending inventory of women's sportswear at January 31, 19X6. Round off the ratio to two decimal places.
2. Assuming J. C. Penney uses the periodic inventory system, prepare general journal entries to record:
   a. Inventory purchases and sales during fiscal year 19X6. Assume all purchases and one-half of company sales were on credit. All other sales were for cash.
   b. Inventory entries at January 31, 19X6. Closing entries for Purchases and Purchase Returns are not required.

Problem 9-9A *Using the perpetual inventory system; applying the lower-of-cost-or-market rule*

Rockwell International Corporation manufactures high-technology products used in the aviation and automotive industries. Perhaps its most famous product is the United States space shuttle. Assume the following data for Rockwell's product TU477:

	Purchased	Sold	Balance
Dec. 31, 19X1			110 @ $5 = $550
Feb. 10, 19X2	80 @ $6 = $480		
Apr. 7		60	
May 29	110 @ 7 = 770		
July 13		120	
Oct. 4	100 @ 8 = 800		
Nov. 22		80	

Required

1. Prepare a perpetual inventory record for product TU477, using the FIFO method.
2. Assume Rockwell sold the 60 units on April 7 on account for $13 each. Record the sale and related cost of goods sold in the general journal under the FIFO method.
3. Suppose the current replacement cost of the ending inventory of product TU477 is $970 at December 31, 19X2. Use the answer to Requirement 1 to compute the lower-of-cost-or-market (LCM) value of the ending inventory.

(Group B)

Problem 9-1B   *Computing inventory by three methods*

Microdot Software began the year with 73 units of inventory that cost $26 each. During the year Microdot made the following purchases:

Mar. 11	113 @ $27
May 2	81 @ 29
July 19	167 @ 32
Nov. 18	44 @ 36

The company uses the periodic inventory system, and the physical count at December 31 indicates that ending inventory consists of 131 units.

Required

Compute the ending inventory and cost of goods sold amounts under (1) average cost, (2) FIFO cost, and (3) LIFO cost. Round average cost per unit to the nearest cent, and round all other amounts to the nearest dollar.

Problem 9-2B   *Computing inventory, cost of goods sold, and FIFO inventory profit*

University Paperbacks specializes in softcover books. The store began operations on January 1, 19X1, with an inventory of 500 books that cost $2.01 each, a $1,005 total. During the first month of operations the store purchased inventory as follows:

Purchase no. 1.......................	60 @ $2.10
Purchase no. 2.......................	120 @ 2.35
Purchase no. 3.......................	600 @ 2.50
Purchase no. 4.......................	40 @ 2.75

The ending inventory consists of 600 books.

Required

1. Complete the following tabulation, rounding average cost to the nearest cent and all other amounts to the nearest dollar.

	Ending Inventory	Cost of Goods Sold
a. Average cost	_____	_____
b. FIFO cost	_____	_____
c. LIFO cost	_____	_____

2. Compute the amount of inventory profit under FIFO.
3. Which method produces the most current ending inventory cost? Which method produces the most current cost-of-goods-sold amount? Give the reason for your answers.

Problem 9-3B *Preparing an income statement directly from the accounts*

The records of Blaine Wholesale Company include the following accounts for one of its products at December 31 of the current year:

Inventory

Jan. 1	Balance	700 units @ $7.00	4,900	

Purchases

Jan. 6	300 units @ $7.05	2,115	
Mar. 19	1,100 units @ 7.35	8,085	
June 22	8,400 units @ 7.50	63,000	
Oct. 4	500 units @ 8.80	4,400	
Dec. 31	Balance	77,600	

Sales Revenue

	Feb. 5	1,000 units @ $12.00	12,000
	Apr. 10	700 units @ 12.10	8,470
	July 31	1,800 units @ 13.25	23,850
	Sept. 4	2,200 units @ 13.50	29,700
	Nov. 27	3,100 units @ 15.00	46,500
	Dec. 31	Balance	120,520

Required

1. Compute the quantities of goods in (a) ending inventory and (b) cost of goods sold during the year.
2. Prepare the following partial income statement under the average cost, FIFO cost, and LIFO cost methods.

Blaine Wholesale Company
Income Statement
For the year ended December 31, 19XX

	Average Cost	FIFO Cost	LIFO Cost
Sales revenue	$ _____	$ _____	$ _____
Cost of goods sold:			
Beginning inventory	$ _____	$ _____	$ _____
Purchases	_____	_____	_____
Cost of goods available	_____	_____	_____
Ending inventory	_____	_____	_____
Cost of goods sold	_____	_____	_____
Gross margin	$ _____	$ _____	$ _____

Problem 9-4B *Recording periodic and perpetual inventory transactions*

Using the data in Problem 9-3B, make summary journal entries in the general journal to record:

1. Purchases, sales, and end-of-period inventory entries, assuming Blaine Wholesale Company uses the periodic inventory system and the FIFO cost method. All purchases are on credit. Cash sales are $50,000, with the remaining sales on account.
2. Purchases, sales, and cost of goods sold, assuming Blaine Wholesale Company uses the perpetual inventory system and the FIFO cost method. All purchases are on credit. Cash sales are $50,000, with the remaining sales on account.

Problem 9-5B *Applying the lower-of-cost-or-market rule*

The financial statements of LaValle Company were prepared on the cost basis without considering whether the replacement value of ending inventory was less than cost. Following are selected data from those statements:

From the income statement:

Sales revenue		$278,000
Cost of goods sold:		
Beginning inventory	$ 54,000	
Net purchases	119,000	
Cost of goods available for sale	173,000	
Ending inventory	53,000	
Cost of goods sold		120,000
Gross margin		$158,000

From the balance sheet:

Current assets:	
Inventory	$ 53,000

The replacement costs were $57,000 for beginning inventory and $49,000 for ending inventory.

Required

1. Revise the data to include the appropriate lower-of-cost-or-market value of inventory.
2. How is the lower-of-cost-or-market rule conservative? How is conservatism shown in LaValle's situation?

Problem 9-6B *Correcting inventory errors over a three-year period*

The Balcones Company books show these data (in millions):

	19X6		19X5		19X4	
Net sales revenue		$350		$280		$240
Cost of goods sold:						
Beginning inventory	$ 65		$ 55		$ 70	
Net purchases	195		135		130	
Cost of goods available	260		190		200	
Less Ending inventory	70		65		55	
Cost of goods sold		190		125		145
Gross margin		160		155		95
Operating expenses		113		109		76
Net income		$ 47		$ 46		$ 19

In early 19X7, a team of internal auditors discovered that the ending inventory of 19X4 had been understated by $12 million. Also, the ending inventory for 19X6 had been overstated by $8 million. The ending inventory at December 31, 19X5, was correct.

Required

1. Prepare corrected income statements for the three years.
2. State whether each year's net income and owner's equity amount are understated or overstated. For each incorrect figure, indicate the amount of the understatement or overstatement.

Problem 9-7B *Estimating inventory by the gross margin method; preparing a multiple-step income statement*

Assume Burger King, Inc., estimates its inventory by the gross margin method when preparing monthly financial statements. For the past two years, the gross margin has averaged 40 percent of net sales. Assume further that the company's inventory records for stores in the southwestern region reveal the following data:

Inventory, July 1	$ 267,000
Transactions during July:	
Purchases	3,589,000
Purchase discounts.................	26,000
Purchase returns...................	12,000
Sales	5,773,000
Sales returns	22,000

Required

1. Estimate the July 31 inventory using the gross margin method.
2. Prepare the July income statement through gross margin for the Burger King, Inc., stores in the southwestern region. Use the multiple-step format.

Problem 9-8B *Estimating inventory by the retail method; recording periodic inventory transactions*

The fiscal year of K-Mart Corporation ends on January 31. Assume the following inventory data for the hardware department of a K-Mart Store:

	Cost	Retail
Inventory, Jan. 31, 19X3	$ 31,200	$ 63,300
Transactions during the year ended January 31, 19X4:		
Purchases	154,732	301,190
Purchase returns.................................	5,800	11,290
Sales		283,420
Sales returns		3,320

Required

1. Use the retail method to estimate the cost of the store's ending inventory of hardware at January 31, 19X4.
2. Assuming K-Mart uses the periodic inventory system, prepare general journal entries to record:
   a. Inventory purchases and sales during fiscal year 19X4. Assume all purchases and one-half of company sales were on credit. All other sales were for cash.
   b. Inventory entries at January 31, 19X4. Closing entries for Purchases and Purchase Returns are not required.

Problem 9-9B *Using the perpetual inventory system; applying the lower-of-cost-or-market rule*

Coachman Industries, Inc., manufactures recreational vehicles and products. Assume the following data for Coachman's product EK-133:

	Purchased	Sold	Balance
Dec. 31, 19X3			120 @ $6 = $720
Mar. 15, 19X4	50 @ $7 = $350		
Apr. 10		80	
May 29	100 @ 8 = 800		
Aug. 3		110	
Nov. 16	90 @ 9 = 810		
Dec. 12		70	

Required

1. Prepare a perpetual inventory card for product EK-133, using the FIFO method.
2. Assume Coachman sold the 110 units on August 3 on account for $16 each. Record the sale and related cost of goods sold in the general journal under the FIFO method.
3. Suppose the current replacement cost of the ending inventory of product EK-133 is $750 at December 31, 19X4. Use the answer to requirement 1 to compute the lower-of-cost-or-market (LCM) value of the ending inventory.

Decision Problem

Assessing the impact of a year-end purchase of inventory

Yakima Paper Corporation is nearing the end of its first year of operations. The company made the following inventory purchases:

January	1,000	$10	$10,000
March	1,000	10	10,000
May	1,000	11	11,000
July	1,000	13	13,000
September	1,000	14	14,000
November	1,000	15	15,000
Totals	6,000		$73,000

Sales for the year will be 5,000 units for $120,000 revenue. Expenses other than cost of goods sold and income taxes will be $20,000. The president of the company is undecided about whether to adopt FIFO or LIFO.

The company has storage capacity for 5,000 additional units of inventory. Inventory prices are expected to stay at $15 per unit for the next few months. The president is considering purchasing 4,000 additional units of inventory at $15 each before the end of the year. He wishes to know how the purchase would affect net income under both FIFO and LIFO. The income tax rate is 40 percent, and income tax is an expense.

Required

1. To aid company decision making, prepare income statements under FIFO and under LIFO, both without and with the year-end purchase of 4,000 units of inventory at $15 per unit.
2. Compare net income under FIFO without and with the year-end purchase. Make the same comparison under LIFO. Under which method does the year-end purchase have the greater effect on net income?

3. Under which method can a year-end purchase be made in order to manipulate net income?

Financial Statement Problem

Inventories

The notes are an important part of a company's financial statements, giving valuable details that would clutter the tabular data presented in the statements. This problem will help you learn to use a company's inventory notes. Refer to the Gulf+Western statements and related notes in Appendix C. Answer the following questions.

1. How much were Gulf+Western's total inventories at October 31, 1987? Of this amount, how much were current assets? How much were long-term assets? Describe the difference between these current assets and long-term assets?
2. How does Gulf+Western value its inventories? Which cost method does the company use?
3. Note D lists four categories of inventories that are classified as current assets. Name these, and briefly explain what you think each category means.
4. The financial statement problem in Chapter 5 required the computation of cost of goods sold. By rearranging the cost-of-goods-sold formula, you can solve for purchases, which are not disclosed in Gulf+Western's statements. Using only the inventories classified as current assets, show how to compute Gulf+Western's purchases during fiscal 1987.

Answers to the Self-Study Questions

1. c
2. a (15,000 − 1,000) × $3.40 = $47,600
3. d
4. b
5. b
6. d
7. a $35,000 + $146,000 = $181,000
   $240,000 − (.35 × $240,000) = $156,000
   $181,000 − $156,000 = $25,000

	Cost	Retail	
8. c Beginning inventory	$ 20,000	$ 40,000	
Purchases	120,000	210,000	**Cost Ratio**
Goods available.	140,000 ÷	250,000	= .56
Sales.		200,000	
Ending inventory – at retail		$ 50,000	
at cost ($50,000 × .56)	$ 28,000		

9. d
10. c

Plant Assets,
Intangible Assets,
and Related Expenses

LEARNING OBJECTIVES
After studying this chapter, you should be able to

1 Identify the elements of a plant asset's cost

2 Explain the concept of depreciation

3 Account for depreciation by four methods

4 Identify the best depreciation method for income tax purposes

5 Account for disposal of plant assets

6 Account for natural resource assets and depletion

7 Account for intangible assets and amortization

8 Distinguish capital expenditures from revenue expenditures

Business assets are separated into current assets—those useful for one year or less—and long-lived assets—those useful for longer than a year. Long-lived assets used in the operation of the business and not held for sale as investments are further divided into plant assets and intangible assets.

Plant assets are those long-lived assets that are tangible. Their physical form provides their usefulness, for instance, land, buildings, equipment, and coal and other minerals. Of the plant assets, land is unique. Its cost is *not* depreciated—expensed over time—because its usefulness does not decrease like that of other assets. Most companies report plant assets under the heading Property, Plant, and Equipment.

Intangible assets are useful not because of their physical characteristics but because of the special rights they carry. Patents, copyrights, and trademarks are intangible assets. Examples of famous patents are the recipe for Coca-Cola and the Dolby noise-reduction process. Accounting for intangibles is similar to accounting for plant assets.

This area has its own terminology. Different names apply to the expense for the cost of the various assets, as shown in Exhibit 10-1.

The first half of the chapter discusses and illustrates how to identify the cost of a plant asset and how to expense its cost. The second half considers disposing of plant assets and how to account for natural resources and intangible assets. Unless stated otherwise, we describe accounting in accordance with generally accepted accounting principles, as distinguished from reporting to the IRS for income tax purposes.

EXHIBIT 10-1   *Terminology Used in Accounting for Plant Assets and Intangible Assets*

Asset Account on the Balance Sheet	Related Expense Account on the Income Statement
Land	None
Buildings, Machinery and Equipment, Furniture and Fixtures, and Land Improvements	Depreciation
Natural Resources	Depletion
Intangibles	Amortization

The Cost of a Plant Asset

The cost principle directs a business to carry an asset on the balance sheet at the amount paid for it. The **cost of a plant asset** is the purchase price, applicable taxes, purchase commissions, and all other amounts paid to acquire the asset and to ready it for its intended use. Because the types of cost differ for various categories of plant assets, we discuss the major groups individually.

Land

The cost of land includes its purchase price (cash plus any note payable given), brokerage commission, survey fees, legal fees, and any back property taxes that the purchaser pays. Land cost also includes any expenditures for grading and clearing the land and for demolishing or removing any unwanted buildings.

The cost of land does *not* include the cost of fencing, paving, sprinkler systems, and lighting. These separate plant assets—called land improvements—are subject to depreciation.

Suppose you are a real estate developer, and you sign a $300,000 note payable to purchase 100 acres of land for subdivision into 5-acre lots. You also pay $10,000 in back property tax, $8,000 in transfer taxes, $5,000 for removal of an old building, a $1,000 survey fee, and $260,000 for the construction of roads, all in cash. What is the cost of this land?

Purchase price of land		$300,000
Add related costs:		
Back property tax	$10,000	
Transfer taxes	8,000	
Removal of building	5,000	
Survey fee	1,000	
Total incidental costs		24,000
Total cost of land		$324,000

The entry to record purchase of the land is

Land	324,000	
Note Payable		300,000
Cash		24,000

Buildings

OBJECTIVE 1
Identify the elements of a plant asset's cost

The cost of constructing a building includes architectural fees, building permits, contractors' charges, and payments for materials, labor, and overhead. When an existing building (new or old) is purchased, its cost includes the purchase price, brokerage commission, sales and other taxes, and expenditures for repairing and renovating the building for its intended purpose.

Machinery and Equipment

The cost of machinery and equipment includes its purchase price (less any discounts), transportation charges, insurance while in transit, sales and other taxes, purchase commission, installation costs, and any expenditures to test the asset before placing it in service.

Land Improvements

In the land example, the cost of the roads ($260,000) is not part of the cost of the land. Instead, the $260,000 would be recorded in a separate account entitled Land Improvements. This account includes costs for such other items as fences, driveways, parking lots, and sprinkler systems. Although these assets are located on the land, they are subject to decay, and therefore their cost should be depreciated, as we discuss later in this chapter. Also, the cost of a new building constructed on the land is a debit to the asset account Building.

Group (or Basket) Purchases of Assets

Businesses often purchase several assets (as a group, or in a "basket") for a single amount. For example, a company may pay one price for land and an office building. The company must identify the cost of each asset. The total cost is divided between the assets according to their relative sales (or market) values. This allocation technique is called the **relative-sales-value method.**

Suppose Xerox Corporation purchases land and a building in Kansas City for a midwestern sales office. The building sits on two acres of land, and the combined purchase price of land and building is $2,800,000. An appraisal indicates that the land's market (sales) value is $300,000 and the building's market (sales) value is $2,700,000.

An accountant first figures the ratio of each asset's market price to the total market price. Total appraised value is $3,000,000. Thus land, valued at $300,000, is 10 percent of the total market value. Building's appraised value is 90 percent of the total.

Asset	Market (Sales) Value		Total Market Value		Percentage
Land	$ 300,000	÷	$3,000,000	=	10%
Building	2,700,000	÷	$3,000,000	=	90%
Total	$3,000,000				100%

The percentage for each asset is multiplied by the total purchase price to give its cost in the purchase.

Asset	Total Purchase Price		Percentage		Allocated Cost
Land	$2,800,000	×	.10	=	$ 280,000
Building	$2,800,000	×	.90	=	2,520,000
Total			1.00		$2,800,000

Assuming Xerox pays cash, the entry to record the purchase of the land and building is

Land	280,000	
Building	2,520,000	
Cash		2,800,000

Depreciation of Plant Assets

OBJECTIVE 2

Explain the concept of depreciation

The process of allocating a plant asset's cost to expense over the period the asset is used is called *depreciation.* It is designed to match this expense against revenue over the asset's life, as the matching principle directs.

Suppose a company buys a computer. The business believes the computer offers four years of service after which obsolescence will make it worthless. Using straight-line depreciation (which we discuss later in this chapter), the business expenses one quarter of the asset's cost in each of its four years of use.

Let's contrast what depreciation accounting is with what it is *not.* (1) *Depreciation is not a process of valuation.* Businesses do not record depreciation based on appraisals of their plant assets made at the end of each period. Instead, businesses allocate the asset's cost to the periods of its useful life based on a specific depreciation method. (We discuss these methods in this chapter.) (2) *Depreciation does not mean that the business sets aside cash to replace assets as they become fully depreciated.* Establishing such a cash fund is a decision entirely separate from depreciation. *Accumulated depreciation* is that portion of the plant asset's cost that has already been recorded as expense. Accumulated depreciation does not represent a growing amount of cash.

Determining the Useful Life of a Plant Asset

No asset (other than land) offers an unlimited useful life. For some plant assets physical *wear and tear* from operations and the elements may be the important cause of depreciation. For example, physical deterioration takes its toll on the usefulness of trucks and furniture.

Assets like computers, other electronic equipment, and airplanes may become *obsolete* before they physically deteriorate. An asset is obsolete when another asset can do the job better or more efficiently. Thus an asset's useful life may be much shorter than its physical life. Accountants usually depreciate computers over a short period of time—perhaps four years—even though they know the computers will remain in working condition much longer. Whether wear and tear or obsolescence causes depreciation, the asset's cost is depreciated over its expected useful life.

Measuring Depreciation _____

To measure depreciation for a plant asset, we must know its *cost*, its *estimated useful life,* and its *estimated residual value.*

Cost is the purchase price of the asset. We discussed cost under the heading The Cost of a Plant Asset, beginning on page 384.

Estimated useful life is the length of the service the business expects to get from the asset. Useful life may be expressed in years (as we have seen so far), units of output, miles, or other measures. For example, the useful life of a building is stated in years. The useful life of a bookbinding machine may be stated as the number of books the machine is expected to bind — that is, its expected units of output. A reasonable measure of a delivery truck's useful life is the total number of miles the truck is expected to travel. Companies base such estimates on past experience and information from industry trade magazines and government publications.

Estimated residual value — also called *scrap value* and *salvage value* — is the expected cash value of the asset at the end of its useful life. For example, a business may believe that a machine's useful life will be seven years. After that time, the company expects to sell the machine as scrap metal. The amount the business believes it can get for the machine is the estimated residual value. In computing depreciation, estimated residual value is *not* depreciated because the business expects to receive this amount from disposing of the asset. The full cost of a plant asset is depreciated if the asset is expected to have no residual value. The plant asset's cost minus its estimated residual value is called the *depreciable cost.*

Of the factors entering the computation of depreciation, only one factor is known — cost. The other two factors — residual value and useful life — must be estimated. Depreciation, then, is an estimated amount.

The basic equation for computing depreciation is

$$\text{Depreciation} = \frac{\text{cost} - \text{estimated residual value}}{\text{expected useful life}} = \frac{\text{depreciable cost}}{\text{expected useful life}}$$

The equation shows that depreciable cost is depreciated over the useful life of the asset.

Depreciation Methods _____

OBJECTIVE 3
Account for depreciation by four methods

Four basic methods exist for computing depreciation: straight-line, units-of-production, declining-balance, and sum-of-years-digits. These four methods allocate different amounts of depreciation expense to different periods. However, they all result in the same total amount of depreciation, the asset's depreciable cost over the life of the asset. Exhibit 10-2 presents the data used to illustrate depreciation computations by the four methods.

Straight-Line (SL) Method

In the **straight-line (SL)** method, an equal amount of depreciation expense is assigned to each year (or period) of asset use. Depreciable cost is divided by useful life in years to determine the annual depreciation expense. The equation for SL

EXHIBIT 10-2 *Data for Depreciation Computations*

Data Item	Amount
Cost of limousine.	$41,000
Estimated residual value	1,000
Depreciable cost.	$40,000
Estimated useful life:	
Years.	5 years
Units of production	400,000 units

depreciation, applied to the limo data from Exhibit 10-2, is

$$\text{Straight-line depreciation per year} = \frac{\text{cost} - \text{residual value}}{\text{useful life in years}}$$

$$= \frac{\$41,000 - \$1,000}{5}$$

$$= \$8,000$$

The entry to record this depreciation is

Depreciation Expense	8,000	
Accumulated Depreciation		8,000

Assume that the limo was purchased on January 1, 19X1, and the business's fiscal year ends on December 31. A *straight-line depreciation schedule* is presented in Exhibit 10-3.

The final column of Exhibit 10-3 shows the asset's *book value,* which is its cost less accumulated depreciation. Book value is also called carrying value.

As an asset is used, accumulated depreciation increases, and the book value decreases. (Note the Accumulated Depreciation column and the Book Value column.) An asset's final book value is its *residual value* ($1,000 in the exhibit). At the end of its useful life, the asset is said to be fully depreciated.

EXHIBIT 10-3 *Straight-Line Depreciation Schedule*

		Depreciation for the Year					Asset
Date	Asset Cost	Depreciation Rate		Depreciable Cost		Depreciation Amount	Accumulated Depreciation	Asset Book Value
1- 1-X1	$41,000							$41,000
12-31-X1		.20	×	$40,000	=	$8,000	$ 8,000	33,000
12-31-X2		.20	×	40,000	=	8,000	16,000	25,000
12-31-X3		.20	×	40,000	=	8,000	24,000	17,000
12-31-X4		.20	×	40,000	=	8,000	32,000	9,000
12-31-X5		.20	×	40,000	=	8,000	40,000	1,000

EXHIBIT 10-4   *Units-of-Production Depreciation Schedule*

Date	Asset Cost	Depreciation for the Year			Accumulated Depreciation	Asset Book Value
		Depreciation Per Unit	Number of Units	Depreciation Amount		
1-1-19X1	$41,000					$41,000
12-31-19X1		$.10 ×	90,000 =	$ 9,000	$ 9,000	32,000
12-31-19X2		.10 ×	120,000 =	12,000	21,000	20,000
12-31-19X3		.10 ×	100,000 =	10,000	31,000	10,000
12-31-19X4		.10 ×	60,000 =	6,000	37,000	4,000
12-31-19X5		.10 ×	30,000 =	3,000	40,000	1,000

Units-of-Production (UOP) Method

In the **units-of-production (UOP)** method, a fixed amount of depreciation is assigned to each unit of output produced by the plant asset. Depreciable cost is divided by useful life in units to determine this amount. This per-unit depreciation expense is multiplied by the number of units produced each period to compute depreciation for the period. The UOP depreciation equation for the limo data in Exhibit 10-2 is

$$\text{Units-of-production depreciation per unit of output} = \frac{\text{cost} - \text{residual value}}{\text{useful life in units}}$$

$$= \frac{\$41,000 - \$1,000}{400,000 \text{ miles}}$$

$$= \$.10$$

Assume the limo is expected to be driven 90,000 miles (*miles* are the *units* in our example) during the first year, 120,000 during the second, 100,000 during the third, 60,000 during the fourth, and 30,000 during the fifth. The UOP depreciation schedule for this asset is shown in Exhibit 10-4.

The amount of UOP depreciation per period varies with the number of units the asset produces. Note that the total number of units produced is 400,000, the measure of this asset's useful life. Therefore, UOP depreciation does not depend directly on time as the other methods do.

Double-Declining-Balance (DDB) Method

Double-declining-balance (DDB) is one of the accelerated-depreciation methods. An **accelerated-depreciation** method writes off a relatively larger amount of the asset's cost nearer the start of its useful life than does straight-line. **DDB depreciation** computes annual depreciation by multiplying the asset's book value by a constant percentage, which is two times the straight-line depreciation rate. DDB amounts are computed as follows:

First, the straight-line depreciation rate per year is computed. For example, a 5-year limousine has a straight-line depreciation rate of 1/5, or 20 percent. A 10-year asset has a straight-line rate of 1/10, or 10 percent, and so on.

Second, the straight-line rate is multiplied by 2 to compute the DDB rate. The DDB rate for a 5-year asset is 40 percent (20% $\times$ 2 = 40%). For a 10-year asset the DDB rate is 20 percent (10% $\times$ 2 = 20%).

Third, The DDB rate is multiplied by the period's beginning asset book value (cost less accumulated depreciation). Residual value of the asset is ignored in computing depreciation by the DDB method, except during the last year.

The DDB rate for the limousine in Exhibit 10-2 is

$$\text{DDB rate per year} = \left(\frac{1}{\text{useful life in years}} \times 2 \right) = \left(\frac{1}{5 \text{ years}} \times 2 \right) = (20\% \times 2) = 40\%$$

Fourth, the final year's depreciation amount is the amount needed to reduce the asset's book value to its residual value. In the following schedule, the fifth and final year's depreciation is $4,314—the $5,314 book value less the $1,000 residual value. The DDB depreciation schedule for the asset is illustrated in Exhibit 10-5.

The DDB method differs from the other methods in two ways. (1) The asset's residual value is ignored initially. Depreciation is computed on the asset's full cost. (2) The final year's calculation is changed in order to bring the asset's book value to the residual value.

Sum-of-Years-Digits (SYD) Method

In the **sum-of-years-digits** (SYD) method—another accelerated method—depreciation is figured by multiplying the depreciable cost of the asset by a fraction. The *denominator* of the SYD fraction is the sum of the years' digits. For a 5-year asset, the years' digits are 1, 2, 3, 4, and 5, and their sum is 15 (1 + 2 + 3 + 4 + 5 = 15). For a 10-year asset, the denominator is 55. Adding the years for a very long-lived asset is tedious. Chances arise for error in the mathematics. Thus we have an easy formula for computing the sum of the years' digits:

$$\textbf{Sum of the years' digits} = \textbf{N(N + 1)/2}$$

where N is the useful life of the asset expressed in years. For example, when N equals 5, we have:

$$\frac{5(5 + 1)}{2} = \frac{30}{2} = 15$$

EXHIBIT 10-5   *Double-Declining-Balance Depreciation Schedule*

Date	Asset Cost	DDB Rate		Asset Book Value		Depreciation Amount	Accumulated Depreciation	Asset Book Value
				Depreciation for the Year				
1-1-19X1	$41,000							$41,000
12-31-19X1		.40	$\times$	$41,000	=	$16,400	$16,400	24,600
12-31-19X2		.40	$\times$	24,600	=	9,840	26,240	14,760
12-31-19X3		.40	$\times$	14,760	=	5,904	32,144	8,856
12-31-19X4		.40	$\times$	8,856	=	3,542	35,686	5,314
12-31-19X5						4,314*	40,000	1,000

* Last-year depreciation is the amount needed to reduce asset book value to the residual value ($5,314 − $1,000 = $4,314).

The *numerator* of the SYD fraction for the first year of a 5-year asset is 5. The numerator is 4 for the second year, 3 for the third year, 2 for the fourth year, and 1 for the fifth year.

The SYD depreciation equation for the limo in Exhibit 10-2 is

$$\frac{\text{SYD depreciation}}{\text{per year}} = (\text{cost} - \text{residual value}) \times \frac{\text{years' digits, largest first}}{\text{sum of years' digits}}$$

$$= (\$41{,}000 - \$1{,}000) \times \frac{5^*}{1 + 2 + 3 + 4 + 5}$$

$$= \$40{,}000 \times \frac{5}{15} = \$13{,}333$$

Exhibit 10-6 is the SYD depreciation schedule based on our example data. Note that each year's fraction is multiplied by the depreciable cost ($40,000).

Comparison of the Depreciation Methods _____

Compare the four methods in terms of the yearly amount of depreciation:

Amount of Depreciation Per Year

			Accelerated Methods	
Year	Straight-Line	Units-of-Production	Double-Declining-Balance	Sum-of-Years-Digits
1	$ 8,000	$ 9,000	$16,400	$13,333
2	8,000	12,000	9,840	10,667
3	8,000	10,000	5,904	8,000
4	8,000	6,000	3,542	5,333
5	8,000	3,000	4,314	2,667
Total	$40,000	$40,000	$40,000	$40,000

EXHIBIT 10-6   *Sum-of-Years-Digits Depreciation Schedule*

Date	Asset Cost	SYD Fraction	Depreciable Cost		Depreciation Amount	Accumulated Depreciation	Asset Book Value
1-1-19X1	$41,000						$41,000
12-31-19X1		5/15 ×	$40,000	=	$13,333	$13,333	27,667
12-31-19X2		4/15 ×	40,000	=	10,667	24,000	17,000
12-31-19X3		3/15 ×	40,000	=	8,000	32,000	9,000
12-31-19X4		2/15 ×	40,000	=	5,333	37,333	3,667
12-31-19X5		1/15 ×	40,000	=	2,667	40,000	1,000

The header "Depreciation for the Year" spans the SYD Fraction, Depreciable Cost, and Depreciation Amount columns.

---

* 5 for first year; 4 for second year; 3 for third year; 2 for fourth year; 1 for fifth year.

EXHIBIT 10-7 *Depreciation Patterns*

The yearly amount of depreciation varies by method, but the total $40,000 depreciable cost systematically becomes expense under all four methods.

Generally accepted accounting principles (GAAP) direct a business to match the expense of an asset against the revenue that the asset produces. For a plant asset that generates revenue evenly over time, the straight-line method best meets the matching principle. During each period the asset is used, an equal amount of depreciation is recorded.

The units-of-production method best fits those assets that wear out because of physical use, not obsolescence. Depreciation is recorded only when the asset is used, and the more units the asset generates in a given year, the greater the depreciation expense.

The accelerated methods (DDB and SYD) apply best to those assets that generate greater revenue earlier in their useful lives. The greater expense recorded under the accelerated methods in the early periods is matched against those periods' greater revenue.

Exhibit 10-7 graphs the relationship between annual depreciation amounts for straight-line, units-of-production, and the accelerated depreciation methods.

The graph of straight-line depreciation is flat because annual depreciation is the same amount in each period. Units-of-production depreciation follows no particular pattern because annual depreciation depends on the use of the asset. The greater the use, the greater is the amount of depreciation. Accelerated depreciation is greatest in the asset's first year and less in the later years.

A recent survey indicated that over 70 percent of companies use the straight-line method, approximately 20 percent use an accelerated method, and the remainder use the units-of-production method. For example, Sears uses straight-line, Motorola uses double-declining-balance, Eastman Kodak uses sum-of-years-digits, and Gulf Oil uses units-of-production.

Summary Problem for Your Review

Hubbard Company purchased equipment on January 1, 19X5, for $44,000. The expected life of the equipment is 10 years, and its residual value is $4,000. Under three depreciation methods, the annual depreciation expense and the balance of accumulated depreciation at the end of 19X5 and 19X6 are

	Method A		Method B		Method C	
Year	Annual Depreciation Expense	Accumulated Depreciation	Annual Depreciation Expense	Accumulated Depreciation	Annual Depreciation Expense	Accumulated Depreciation
19X5	$4,000	$4,000	$7,273	$ 7,273	$8,800	$ 8,800
19X6	4,000	8,000	6,545	13,818	7,040	15,840

Required

1. Identify the depreciation method used in each instance, and show the equation and computation for each. (Round off to the nearest dollar.)
2. Assume continued use of the same method through year 19X7. Determine the annual depreciation expense, accumulated depreciation, and book value of the equipment for 19X5 through 19X7 under each method.

SOLUTION TO REVIEW PROBLEM

Requirement 1

Method A: Straight-line

$$\text{Depreciable cost} = \$40,000 \; (\$44,000 - \$4,000)$$
$$\text{Each year: } \$40,000/10 \text{ years} = \$4,000$$

Method B: Sum-of-years-digits

$$\text{SYD} = N(N + 1)/2 = 10(10 + 1)/2 = 55$$
$$\text{Depreciable cost} = \$40,000 \; (\$44,000 - \$4,000)$$
$$\text{19X5: } 10/55 \times \$40,000 = \$7,273$$
$$\text{19X6: } 9/55 \times \$40,000 = \$6,545$$

Method C: Double-declining-balance

$$\text{Rate} = \left(\frac{1}{10 \text{ years}} \times 2 \right) = (10\% \times 2) = 20\%$$
$$\text{19X5: } \quad .20 \times \$44,000 = \$8,800$$
$$\text{19X6: } \quad .20 \times (\$44,000 - \$8,800) = \$7,040$$

Requirement 2

	Method A Straight-Line			Method B Sum-of-Years-Digits			Method C Double-Declining-Balance		
Year	Annual Depreciation Expense	Accumulated Depreciation	Book Value	Annual Depreciation Expense	Accumulated Depreciation	Book Value	Annual Depreciation Expense	Accumulated Depreciation	Book Value
Start			$44,000			$44,000			$44,000
19X5	$4,000	$4,000	40,000	$7,273	$ 7,273	36,727	$8,800	$ 8,800	35,200
19X6	4,000	8,000	36,000	6,545	13,818	30,182	7,040	15,840	28,160
19X7	4,000	12,000	32,000	5,818	19,636	24,364	5,632	21,472	22,528

Computations for 19X7:

Straight-line:	**$40,000/10 years = $4,000**
Sum-of-years-digits:	**8/55 × $40,000 = $5,818**
Double-declining-balance:	**.20 × $28,160 = $5,632**

Depreciation and Income Taxes

The majority of companies use the straight-line depreciation method for reporting to their stockholders and creditors on their financial statements. Companies keep a separate set of depreciation records for computing their income taxes. For income tax purposes, most companies use an accelerated depreciation method.

Suppose you are a business manager. The IRS allows an accelerated depreciation method, which most managers choose in preference to straight-line depreciation. Why? Because it provides the most depreciation expense as quickly as possible, thus decreasing your immediate tax payments. The cash you save may be applied to best fit your business needs. This is the strategy most businesses follow.

To understand the relationships among cash flow (cash provided by operations), depreciation, and income tax, recall our earlier depreciation example: First-year depreciation under straight-line is $8,000, and under double-declining-balance it is $16,400. For illustrative purposes here, assume that DDB is permitted for reporting to the income tax authorities. Assume that the business has $400,000 in cash sales and $300,000 in cash operating expenses during the asset's first year, and the income tax rate is 40 percent. The cash flow analysis appears in Exhibit 10-8.

Exhibit 10-8 highlights several important business relationships. Compare the amount of cash provided by operations before income tax. Both columns show $100,000. If there were no income taxes, the total cash provided by operations would be the same regardless of the depreciation method used. Depreciation is a noncash expense and so does not affect cash from operations.

However, depreciation is a tax-deductible expense. The higher the depreciation expense, the lower the income before tax and thus the lower the income tax payment. Therefore, accelerated depreciation helps conserve cash for use in the business. Exhibit 10-8 indicates that the business will have $3,360 more cash at the end of the first year if it uses accelerated depreciation instead of SL ($66,560 against $63,200). Suppose the company invests this money to earn a return of 10 percent during the second year. Then the company will be better off by $336 ($3,360 × 10% = $336). The cash advantage of using the accelerated method is the $336 of additional revenue.

The Tax Reform Act of 1986 created a special depreciation method—used only for income tax purposes—called the Modified Accelerated Cost Recovery System (MACRS). Under this method, assets are grouped into one of eight classes: 3-year, 5-year, 7-year, 10-year, 15-year, and 20-year assets. Real estate assets, such as buildings, are depreciated over 27½ years or 31½ years. Cars and light trucks belong in the 5-year class. Many types of equipment are classified as 7-year assets or 10-year assets. Depreciation for the first four classes is computed by the double-declining-balance method. Depreciation for 15-year assets and 20-year

OBJECTIVE 4

Identify the best depreciation method for income tax purposes

EXHIBIT 10-8 *Cash Flow Advantage of Accelerated Depreciation over Straight-Line (SL) Depreciation for Income Tax Purposes*

	Income Tax Rate 40 Percent	
	SL	Accelerated
Revenues	$400,000	$400,000
Cash operating expenses.	300,000	300,000
Cash provided by operations before income tax	100,000	100,000
Depreciation expense (a noncash expense)	8,000	16,400
Income before income tax.	92,000	83,600
Income tax expense (40%).	36,800	33,440
Net income.	$ 55,200	$ 50,160
Supplementary cash flow analysis:		
Cash provided by operations before income tax	$100,000	$100,000
Income tax expense	36,800	33,440
Cash provided by operations.	$ 63,200	$ 66,560
Extra cash available for investment if DDB is used		
($66,560 − $63,200).		$3,360
Assumed earnings rate on investment of extra cash .		× .10
Cash advantage of using DDB over SL.		$ 336

assets is computed by the 150-percent-declining-balance method. Under this method, the annual depreciation rate is computed by multiplying the straight-line rate by 1.50. For a 20-year asset, the straight-line rate is .05 ($1/20$ = .05), so the annual depreciation rate is .075 (.05 × 1.50 = .075). Real estate is depreciated by the straight-line method.

Special Issues in Depreciation Accounting _____

Two special issues in depreciation accounting are (1) depreciation for partial periods and (2) change in the useful life of a depreciable asset.

Depreciation for Partial Years

Companies purchase plant assets as needed. They do not wait until the beginning of a year or a month. Therefore, companies must develop policies to compute *depreciation for partial years.* Suppose a company purchases a building on April 1 for $500,000. The building's estimated life is 20 years, and its estimated residual value is $20,000. The company's fiscal year ends on December 31. Consider how the company computes depreciation for the year ended December 31.

Many companies compute partial-year depreciation by first computing a full year's depreciation. They then multiply this amount by the fraction of the year they held the asset. Assuming the straight-line method, the year's depreciation is $18,000, computed as follows:

$$\frac{(\$500,000 - \$20,000)}{20} = \$24,000 \text{ per year} \times \frac{9}{12} = \$18,000$$

What if the company bought the asset on April 18? A widely used policy directs businesses to record no depreciation on assets purchased after the fifteenth of the month and to record a full month's depreciation on an asset bought on or before the fifteenth. Thus the company would record no depreciation for April on an April 18 purchase. In this case, the year's depreciation would be $16,000 ($24,000 × 8/12).

How is partial-year depreciation computed under the other depreciation methods? Suppose this building is acquired on October 4 and the company uses the double-declining-balance method. For a 20-year asset, the DDB rate is 10 percent (1/20 = 5% × 2 = 10%). First-year depreciation is $50,000 ($500,000 × .10), and the DDB amount for October, November, and December is $12,500 ($50,000 × 3/12). For the second calendar year, DDB depreciation is $48,750 [($500,000 – $12,500) × .10]. For year three, DDB depreciation is $43,875 [($500,000 – $12,500 – $48,750) × .10], and so on.

Partial-year depreciation under the sum-of-years-digits method is computed similarly, by taking the appropriate fraction of a full year's amount. No special computation is needed for partial-year depreciation under the units-of-production method. Simply use the number of units produced, regardless of the time period the asset is held.

Change in the Useful Life of a Depreciable Asset

As previously discussed, a business must estimate the useful life of a plant asset to compute depreciation. This prediction is the most difficult part of accounting for depreciation. After the asset is put into use, the business is able to refine its estimate based on experience and new information. Such a change is called a *change in accounting estimate.* In an actual example, Walt Disney Productions included the following note in its financial statements:

Note 5

. . . the Company extended the estimated useful lives of certain theme park ride and attraction assets based upon historical data and engineering studies. The effect of this change was to decrease depreciation by approximately $8 million (an increase in net income of approximately $4.2 million . . .).

Such accounting changes are common because no business has perfect foresight. Generally accepted accounting principles require the business to report the nature, reason, and effect of the change on net income, as the Disney example shows. To *record* a change in accounting estimate, the remaining book value of the asset is spread over its adjusted remaining useful life. The adjusted useful life may be longer or shorter than the original useful life.

Assume that a Disney hot dog stand cost $40,000 and the company originally believed the asset had an 8-year useful life with no residual value. Using the straight-line method, the company would record $5,000 depreciation each year ($40,000/8 years = $5,000). Suppose Disney used the asset for 2 years. Accumulated depreciation reached $10,000, leaving a book value of $30,000 ($40,000 – $10,000). From its experience with the asset during the first 2 years, management believes the asset will remain useful for an additional 10 years. The company would compute a revised annual depreciation amount and record it as follows:

Asset's Remaining Book Value	÷	(New) Estimated Useful Life Remaining	=	(New) Annual Depreciation Amount
$30,000	÷	10 years	=	$3,000

Yearly depreciation entry based on new estimated useful life:

Depreciation Expense—Hot Dog Stand   3,000
        Accumulated Depreciation—Hot Dog Stand   3,000

Using Fully Depreciated Assets _____

A fully depreciated asset is one that has reached the end of its *estimated* useful life. No more depreciation is recorded for the asset. If the asset is no longer suitable for its purpose, the asset is disposed of, as discussed in the next section. However, the company may be in a cash bind and unable to replace the asset. Or the asset's useful life may have been underestimated at the outset. Foresight is not perfect. In any event, companies sometimes continue using fully depreciated assets. The asset account and its related accumulated depreciation account remain in the ledger even though no additional depreciation is recorded for the asset.

Disposal of Plant Assets _____

Eventually, a plant asset ceases to serve a company's needs. The asset may have become worn out, obsolete, or for some other reason no longer useful to the business. Generally, a company disposes of a plant asset by selling or exchanging it. If the asset cannot be sold or exchanged, then disposal takes the form of junking the asset. Whatever the method of disposal, the business should bring depreciation up to date to measure the asset's final book value properly.

To account for disposal, credit the asset account and debit its related accumulated depreciation account. Suppose the final year's depreciation expense has just been recorded for a machine that cost $6,000 and was estimated to have zero residual value. The machine's accumulated depreciation thus totals $6,000. Assuming this asset cannot be sold or exchanged, the entry to record its disposal is

Accumulated Depreciation—Machinery.   6,000
        Machinery   6,000
To dispose of fully depreciated machine.

> **OBJECTIVE 5**
> Account for disposal of plant assets

If assets are junked prior to being fully depreciated, the company records a loss equal to the asset's book value. Suppose store fixtures that cost $4,000 are disposed of in this manner. Accumulated depreciation is $3,000, and book value is therefore $1,000. Disposal of these store fixtures is recorded as follows:

Accumulated Depreciation—Store Fixtures   3,000
Loss on Disposal of Store Fixtures   1,000
        Store Fixtures.   4,000
To dispose of store fixtures.

Loss accounts such as Loss on Disposal of Store Fixtures decrease net income. Losses are reported on the income statement and closed to Income Summary along with expenses.

Selling a Plant Asset

Suppose the business sells furniture on September 30, 19X4, for $5,000 cash. The furniture cost $10,000 when purchased on January 1, 19X1, and has been depreciated on a straight-line basis. Managers estimated a 10-year useful life and no residual value. Prior to recording the sale of the furniture, accountants must update depreciation. Since the business uses the calendar year as its accounting period, partial depreciation must be recorded for the asset's expense from January 1, 19X4, to the sale date. The straight-line depreciation entry at September 30, 19X4, is

Sep. 30   Depreciation Expense ($10,000/10 years $\times$ $^9/_{12}$)   750
            Accumulated Depreciation–Furniture   750
      To update depreciation.

After this entry is posted, the Furniture account and the Accumulated Depreciation–Furniture account appear as follows. The furniture book value is $6,250 ($10,000 − $3,750).

Furniture		Accumulated Depreciation–Furniture	
Jan. 1, 19X1 10,000		Dec. 31, 19X1 1,000	
		Dec. 31, 19X2 1,000	
		Dec. 31, 19X3 1,000	
		Sept. 30, 19X4 750	
		Balance 3,750	

The entry to record sale of the furniture for $5,000 cash is

Sept. 30   Cash   5,000
        Accumulated Depreciation–Furniture.   3,750
        Loss on Sale of Furniture   1,250
            Furniture   10,000
      To sell furniture.

When recording the sale of a plant asset the business must remove the balances in the asset account (Furniture, in this case) and its related accumulated depreciation account and also record a gain or a loss if the amount of cash received differs from the asset's book value. In our example, cash of $5,000 is less than the book value of the furniture, $6,250. The result is a loss of $1,250.

Suppose the sale price had been $7,000. The business would have had a gain of $750 (Cash, $7,000 − asset book value, $6,250).

The entry to record this transaction would be

Sept. 30.   Cash   7,000
        Accumulated Depreciation–Furniture.   3,750
            Furniture   10,000
            Gain on Sale of Furniture.   750
      To sell furniture.

A gain is recorded when an asset is sold for a price greater than the asset's book value. A loss is recorded when the sale price is less than book value. Gains increase net income. Gains are reported on the income statement and closed to Income Summary along with the revenues.

Exchanging Plant Assets

Businesses often exchange (trade in) their old plant assets for similar assets that are newer and more efficient. For example, a pizzeria may decide to trade in its five-year-old Nissan delivery car for a newer model. To record the exchange, the business must remove from the books the balances for the asset being exchanged and its related accumulated depreciation account.

Assume that the pizzeria's old delivery car cost $7,000 and has accumulated depreciation totaling $6,000. The book value, then, is $1,000. The cash price for a new delivery car is $9,000, and the auto dealer offers a $1,000 trade-in allowance. The pizzeria pays cash for the remaining $8,000. The trade-in is recorded with this entry:

Delivery Auto (new)	9,000	
Accumulated Depreciation (old)	6,000	
Delivery Auto (old)		7,000
Cash ($9,000 − $1,000)		8,000

In this example, the book value and the trade-in allowance are both $1,000, and so no gain or loss occurs on the exchange. Usually, however, an exchange results in a gain or a loss. If the trade-in allowance received is greater than the book value of the asset being given, the business has a gain. If the trade-in allowance received is less than the book value of the asset given, the business has a loss. Generally accepted accounting principles allow losses, but not gains, to be recognized on the exchange of similar assets. We now turn to the entries for gains and losses on exchanges, continuing our delivery-car example and its data.[1]

Situation 1.   Loss recognized on asset exchange:

Assume that the new Nissan has a cash price of $9,000 and the dealer gives a trade-in allowance of $600 on the old vehicle. The pizzeria pays the balance, $8,400, in cash. The loss on the exchange is $400 (book value of old asset given, $1,000, minus trade-in allowance received, $600). The account Loss on Exchange of Delivery Auto is debited for $400. The entry to record this exchange is

Delivery Auto (new)	9,000	
Accumulated Depreciation – Delivery Auto (old)	6,000	
Loss on Exchange of Delivery Auto	400	
Delivery Auto (old)		7,000
Cash ($9,000 − $600)		8,400

Situation 2.   Gain *not* recognized on asset exchange:

Assume that the new Nissan's cash price is $9,000 and the dealer gives a $1,300 trade-in allowance. The pizzeria pays the balance, $7,700, in cash. The gain is $300 (trade-in allowance received, $1,300, minus book value of old asset given, $1,000). However, the pizzeria does not recognize the gain. Instead, it reduces the cost of the new asset by the amount of the unrecognized gain.

Delivery Auto (new) ($9,000 – gain of $300)	8,700	
Accumulated Depreciation – Delivery Auto (old)	6,000	
Delivery Auto (old)		7,000
Cash ($9,000 − $1,300)		7,700

---

[1] GAAP rules for exchanges may differ from income tax rules. In this discussion, we are concerned with the accounting rules.

Why are losses, and not gains, recognized? The Accounting Principles Board reasons a company should not record a gain merely because it has substituted one plant asset for a similar plant asset. However, losses are recorded because conservatism favors the recognition of losses rather than gains.

Control of Plant Assets

Control of plant assets includes safeguarding them and having an adequate accounting system. To see the need for controlling plant assets, consider the following actual situation. The home office and top managers of the company are in New Jersey. The company manufactures gas pumps in Canada, which are sold in Europe. Top managers and owners of the company rarely see the manufacturing plant and therefore cannot control plant assets by on-the-spot management. What features does their internal control system need?

Safeguarding plant assets includes:

1. Assigning responsibility for custody of the assets.
2. Separating custody of assets from accounting for the assets. (This is a cornerstone of internal control in almost every area.)
3. Setting up security measures, for instance, armed guards and restricted access to plant assets, to prevent theft.
4. Protecting assets from the elements (rain, snow, and so on).
5. Having adequate insurance against fire, storm, and other casualty losses.
6. Training operating personnel in the proper use of the asset.
7. Keeping a regular maintenance schedule.

Plant assets are controlled in much the same way that high-priced inventory is controlled — with subsidiary records. For plant assets, companies use a plant asset ledger. Each plant asset is represented by a card describing the asset and listing its location and the employee responsible for it. These details aid in safeguarding the asset. The ledger card also shows the asset's cost, useful life, and other accounting data. Exhibit 10-9 is an example.

EXHIBIT 10-9   *Plant Asset Ledger Card*

Asset Clothing racks				Location Ladies better dresses			
Employee responsible for the asset Department manager							
Cost $190,000				**Purchased From** Boone Supply Co.			
Depreciation Method SL							
Useful Life 10 years				**Residual Value** $10,000			
General Ledger Account Store fixtures							

Date	Explanation	Asset			Accumulated Depreciation		
		Dr	Cr	Bal	Dr	Cr	Bal
Jul. 3, 19X4	Purchase	190,000		190,000			
Dec. 31, 19X4	Deprec.					9,000	9,000
Dec. 31, 19X5	Deprec.					18,000	27,000
Dec. 31, 19X6	Deprec.					18,000	45,000

The ledger card provides the data for computing depreciation on the asset. It serves as a subsidiary record of accumulated depreciation. The asset balance ($190,000) and accumulated depreciation amount ($45,000) agree with the balances in the respective general ledger accounts (Store Fixtures and Accumulated Depreciation–Store Fixtures).

Accounting for Natural Resources and Depletion

OBJECTIVE 6
Account for natural resource assets and depletion

Natural resources such as iron ore, coal, oil, gas, and timber are plant assets of a special type. An investment in natural resources could be described as an investment in inventories in the ground (coal) or on top of the ground (timber). As plant assets (such as machines) are expensed through depreciation, so natural resource assets are expensed through depletion. **Depletion expense** is that portion of the cost of natural resources that is used up in a particular period. Depletion expense is computed in the same way as *units-of-production* depreciation.

An oil well may cost $100,000 and contain an estimated 10,000 barrels of oil. The depletion rate would be $10 per barrel ($100,000/10,000 barrels). If 3,000 barrels are extracted during the first year, depletion expense is $30,000 (3,000 barrels × $10 per barrel). If 4,500 barrels are removed the second year, that period's depletion is $45,000 (4,500 barrels × $10 per barrel). The depletion entry for the first year is

Depletion Expense (3,000 barrels × $10)...................	30,000	
Accumulated Depletion–Oil		30,000

Accumulated Depletion is a contra account similar to Accumulated Depreciation.

Natural resource assets can be reported as follows:

Property, Plant, and Equipment:		
Land		$120,000
Buildings.......................................	$800,000	
Equipment	160,000	
	960,000	
Less: Accumulated depreciation	410,000	550,000
Coal....	**$340,000**	
Less: Accumulated depletion....................	**90,000**	**250,000**
Total property, plant, and equipment...............		$920,000

Accounting for Intangible Assets and Amortization ————

Intangible assets are a class of long-lived assets that are not physical in nature. Instead, these assets are special rights to current and expected future benefits from patents, copyrights, trademarks, franchises, leaseholds, and goodwill.

The acquisition cost of an intangible asset is debited to an asset account. The intangible is expensed through **amortization,** which applies to intangible assets in the same way depreciation applies to plant assets and depletion applies to natural resources. All three methods of expensing assets are conceptually the same.

Amortization is generally computed on a straight-line basis over the asset's estimated useful life—up to a maximum of 40 years, according to GAAP. However, obsolescence often cuts an intangible asset's useful life shorter than its legal life. Amortization expense is written off directly against the asset account rather than held in an accumulated amortization account. The residual value of most intangible assets is zero.

Assume that a business purchases a patent on a special manufacturing process. Legally, the patent may run for 17 years. However, the business realizes that new technologies will limit the patented process's life to 4 years. If the patent cost $80,000, each year's amortization expense is $20,000 ($80,000/4). The balance sheet reports the patent at its acquisition cost less amortization expense to date. After 1 year, the patent has a $60,000 balance ($80,000 − $20,000), after 2 years a $40,000 balance, and so on.

Patents are federal government grants giving a holder the exclusive right for 17 years to produce and sell an invention. Patented products include IBM computers and the recipe for Coca-Cola. Like any other asset, a patent may be purchased. Suppose a company pays $170,000 to acquire a patent and the business believes the expected useful life of the patent is only 5 years. Amortization expense is $34,000 per year ($170,000/5 years). The company's acquisition and amortization entries for this patent are

<table>
<tr><td>**OBJECTIVE 7**</td><td>Jan. 1</td><td>Patents . . . .</td><td>170,000</td><td></td></tr>
</table>

Jan. 1	Patents	170,000	
	Cash		170,000
	To acquire a patent.		
Dec. 31	Amortization Expense–Patents ($170,000/5)	34,000	
	Patents		34,000
	To amortize the cost of a patent.		

OBJECTIVE 7

Account for intangible assets and amortization

Copyrights are exclusive rights to reproduce and sell a book, musical composition, film, or other work of art. Issued by the federal government, copyrights extend 50 years beyond the author's (composer's, artist's) life. The cost of obtaining a copyright from the government is low, but a company may pay a large sum to purchase an existing copyright from the owner. For example, a publisher may pay the author of a popular novel $1 million or more for the book's copyright. The useful life of a copyright is usually no longer than 2 or 3 years, so each period's amortization amount is a high proportion of the copyright's cost.

Trademarks and **trade names** are distinctive identifications of products or services. The "eye" symbol that flashes across the television screen is a trademark that identifies the CBS television network. NBC uses the peacock as its trademark. Seven-Up, Pepsi, Egg McMuffin, and Rice-a-Roni are everyday trade names. Advertising slogans that are legally protected include United Airlines' "Fly the friendly skies" and Avis Rental Car's "We try harder."

The cost of a trademark or trade name is amortized over its useful life, not to exceed 40 years. The cost of advertising and promotions that use the trademark or trade name is not a part of the asset's cost but a debit to the advertising expense account.

Franchises and **licenses** are privileges granted by a private business or a government to sell a product or service in accordance with specified conditions. The Dallas Cowboys football organization is a franchise granted to its owner by the National Football League. McDonald's restaurants and Holiday Inns are popular franchises. Consolidated Edison Company (ConEd) holds a New York City franchise right to provide electricity to residents. The acquisition costs of franchises and licenses are amortized over their useful lives rather than over legal lives, subject to the 40-year maximum.

A **leasehold** is a prepayment that a lessee (renter) makes to secure the use of an asset from a lessor (landlord). Often leases require the lessee to make this prepayment in addition to monthly rental payments. The lessee debits the monthly lease payments to the Rent Expense account. The prepayment, however, is a debit to an intangible asset account entitled Leaseholds. This amount is amortized over the life of the lease by debiting Rent Expense and crediting Leaseholds. Some leases stipulate that the last year's rent must be paid in advance when the lease is signed. This prepayment is debited to Leaseholds and transferred to Rent Expense during the last year of the lease.

Sometimes lessees modify or improve the leased asset. For example, a lessee may construct a fence on leased land. The lessee debits the cost of the fence to a separate intangible asset account, Leasehold Improvements, and amortizes its cost over the term of the lease or the life of the asset, if shorter.

Goodwill in accounting is a more limited term than in everyday use, as in "goodwill among men." In accounting, *goodwill* is defined as the excess of the cost of an acquired company over the sum of the market values of its net assets (assets minus liabilities). Suppose Company A acquires Company B at a cost of $10 million. The market value of Company B's assets is $9 million, and its liabilities total $1 million. In this case, Company A paid $2 million for goodwill, computed as follows:

Purchase price paid for Company B		$10 million
Market value of Company B's assets	$9 million	
Less: Company B's liabilities	1 million	
Market value of Company B's net assets		8 million
Excess is called *goodwill*		$ 2 million

Company A's entry to record the acquisition of Company B, including its goodwill, would be

Assets (Cash, Receivables, Inventories, Plant Assets, all at market value)	9,000,000	
Goodwill	2,000,000	
Liabilities		1,000,000
Cash		10,000,000

Goodwill has special features, which include the following points:

1. Goodwill is recorded, at its cost, only when it is purchased in the acquisition of another company. Even though a favorable location, a superior product, or an outstanding reputation may create goodwill for a company, it is never recorded by that entity. Instead, goodwill is recorded only by another company that purchases the entity with goodwill. A purchase transaction provides objective evidence of the value of the goodwill.

2. According to generally accepted accounting principles, goodwill is amortized over a period not to exceed 40 years. In reality, the goodwill of many entities increases in value. Nevertheless, the Accounting Principles Board specified in *Opinion No. 17* that the cost of all intangible assets must be amortized as expense. The *Opinion* prohibits a lump-sum write-off of the cost of goodwill upon acquisition.

Capital Expenditures versus Revenue Expenditures (Expenses)

When a company makes a plant asset expenditure, it must decide whether to debit an asset account or an expense account. In this context, *expenditure* refers to either a cash or credit purchase of goods or services related to the asset. Examples of these expenditures range from replacing the windshield wipers on an automobile to adding a wing to a building.

Expenditures that increase the capacity or efficiency of the asset or extend its useful life are called **capital expenditures.** For example, the cost of a major overhaul that extends a taxi's useful life is a capital expenditure. Repair work that generates a capital expenditure is called an **extraordinary repair.** The amount of the capital expenditure, said to be capitalized, is a debit to an asset account. For an extraordinary repair on a taxi, we would debit the asset account Automobile.

Other expenditures do not extend the asset's capacity or efficiency. Expenditures that merely maintain the asset in its existing condition or restore the asset to good working order are called **revenue expenditures** because these costs are matched against revenue. Examples include the costs of repainting a taxi, repairing a dented fender, and replacing tires. The work that creates the revenue expenditure, said to be expensed, is a debit to an expense account. For the **ordinary repairs** on the taxi, we would debit Repair Expense.

The distinction between capital and revenue expenditures is often a matter of opinion. Does the work extend the life of the asset, or does it only maintain the asset in good order? When doubt exists as to whether to debit an asset or an expense, companies tend to debit an expense for two reasons. First, many expenditures are minor in amount, and most companies have a policy of debiting expense for all expenditures below a specified minimum, such as $1,000. Second, the income tax motive favors debiting all borderline expenditures to expense in order to create an immediate tax deduction. Capital expenditures are not immediate tax deductions.

Exhibit 10-10 illustrates the distinction between capital expenditures and revenue expenditures (expense) for several delivery truck expenditures. Note also the difference between extraordinary and ordinary repairs.

Treating a capital expenditure as a revenue expenditure, or vice versa, creates errors in the financial statements. Suppose a company makes an extraordinary repair to equipment and erroneously expenses this cost. It is a capital expenditure that should have been debited to an asset account. This accounting error overstates expenses and understates net income on the income statement. On the balance sheet, the equipment account is understated, and so is owner's equity. Capitalizing the cost of an ordinary repair creates the opposite error. Expenses are understated and net income is overstated on the income statement. The balance sheet reports overstated amounts for assets and owners' equity.

EXHIBIT 10-10   *Delivery Truck Expenditures*

Debit an Asset Account for Capital Expenditures	Debit Repair and Maintenance Expense for Revenue Expenditures
Extraordinary repairs:	Ordinary repairs:
Major engine overhaul	Repair of transmission or other mechanism
Modification of body for new use of truck	Oil change, lubrication, and so on
Addition to storage capacity of truck	Replacement tires, windshield, and the like
	Paint job

Summary Problems for Your Review

Problem 1. The figures that follow appear in the Solution to the Summary Problem, Requirement 2, on page 393.

Year	Method A Straight-Line			Method C Double-Declining-Balance		
	Annual Depreciation Expense	Accumulated Depreciation	Book Value	Annual Depreciation Expense	Accumulated Depreciation	Book Value
Start			$44,000			$44,000
19X5	$4,000	$4,000	40,000	$8,800	$ 8,800	35,200
19X6	4,000	8,000	36,000	7,040	15,840	28,160
19X7	4,000	12,000	32,000	5,632	21,472	22,528

Required

Suppose the income tax authorities permitted a choice between these two depreciation methods. Which method would you select for income tax purposes? Why?

Problem 2. A corporation purchased a building at a cost of $500,000 on January 1, 19X3. Management has depreciated the building by using the straight-line method, a 35-year life, and a residual value of $150,000. On July 1, 19X7, the company sold the building for $575,000 cash. The fiscal year of the corporation ends on December 31.

Required

Record depreciation for 19X7 and record the sale of the building on July 1, 19X7.

SOLUTIONS TO REVIEW PROBLEMS

1. For tax purposes, most companies select the accelerated method because it results in the most depreciation in the earliest years of the equipment's life. Accelerated depreciation minimizes taxable income and income tax payments in the early years of the asset's life, thereby maximizing the business's cash at the earliest possible time.

2. To record depreciation to date of sale and related sale of building:

19X7			
July 1	Depreciation Expense–Building		
	[($500,000 − $150,000)/35 years × ½ year]	5,000	
	Accumulated Depreciation–Building		5,000
	To update depreciation.		
July 1	Cash	575,000	
	Accumulated Depreciation–Building		
	[($500,000 − $150,000)/35 years × 4½ years] . . .	45,000	
	Building		500,000
	Gain on Sale of Building		120,000
	To record sale of building.		

Summary

Plant assets are long-lived assets that the business uses in its operation. These assets are not held for sale as inventory. The cost of all plant assets but land is expensed through *depreciation.* The cost of natural resources, a special category of long-lived assets, is expensed through *depletion.* Long-lived assets called *intangibles* are rights that have no physical form. The cost of intangibles is expensed through *amortization.* Depreciation, depletion, and amortization are identical in concept.

Businesses may compute the depreciation of plant assets by four methods: *straight-line, units-of-production,* and the *accelerated* methods: *double-declining-balance* and *sum-of-years-digits.* To measure depreciation, the accountant subtracts the asset's estimated residual value from its cost and divides that amount by the asset's estimated useful life. Most companies use the straight-line method for financial reporting purposes, and almost all companies use an accelerated method for income tax purposes. Accelerated depreciation results in greater tax deductions early in the asset's life. These deductions decrease income tax payments and conserve cash that the company can use in its business.

Before disposing of a plant asset, the business updates the asset's depreciation. Disposal is recorded by removing the book balances from both the asset account and its related accumulated depreciation account. Disposal often results in recognition of a gain or a loss.

Depletion of natural resources is computed on a units-of-production basis. *Amortization* of intangibles is computed on a straight-line basis over a maximum of 40 years. However, the useful lives of most intangibles are shorter than their legal lives.

Capital expenditures increase the capacity or the efficiency of an asset or extend its useful life. Accordingly, they are debited to an asset account. *Revenue expenditures,* on the other hand, merely maintain the asset's usefulness and are debited to an expense account.

Self-Study Questions

Test your understanding of the chapter by marking the best answer for each of the following questions.

1. Which of the following payments is *not* included in the cost of land? *(p. 384)*
   a. Removal of old building   c. Back property taxes paid at acquisition
   b. Legal fees   d. Cost of fencing and lighting

2. A business paid $120,000 for two machines valued at $90,000 and $60,000. The business will record these machines at *(p. 385)*
   a. $90,000 and $60,000   c. $72,000 and $48,000
   b. $60,000 each   d. $70,000 and $50,000

3. Which of the following definitions fits depreciation? *(pp. 385, 386)*
   a. Allocation of the asset's market value to expense over its useful life
   b. Allocation of the asset's cost to expense over its useful life
   c. Decreases in the asset's market value over its useful life
   d. Increases in the fund set aside to replace the asset when it is worn out

4. Which depreciation method's amounts are not computed based on time? *(p. 389)*
   a. Straight-line   c. Double-declining-balance
   b. Units-of-production   d. Sum-of-years-digits

5. Which depreciation method gives the largest amount of expense in the early years of using the asset and therefore is best for income tax purposes? *(p. 394)*
   a. Straight-line   c. Accelerated
   b. Units-of-production   d. All are equal.

6. A company paid $450,000 for a building and was depreciating it by the straight-line method over a 40-year life with estimated residual value of $50,000. After 10 years, it became evident that the building's remaining useful life would be 40 years. Depreciation for the eleventh year is *(p. 396)*
   a. $7,500   c. $10,000
   b. $8,750   d. $12,500

7. Labrador, Inc., scrapped an automobile that cost $14,000 and had book value of $1,100. The entry to record this disposal is *(p. 397)*

    a. Loss on Disposal of Automobile..................... 1,100

        Automobile 1,100

    b. Accumulated Depreciation 14,000

        Automobile 14,000

    c. Accumulated Depreciation 12,900

        Automobile 12,900

    d. Accumulated Depreciation 12,900

        Loss of Disposal of Automobile 1,100

        Automobile 14,000

8. Depletion is computed in the same manner as which depreciation method? *(p. 401)*

    a. Straight-line   c. Double-declining-balance

    b. Units-of-production   d. Sum-of-years-digits

9. Lacy Corporation paid $550,000 to acquire Gentsch, Inc. Gentsch's assets had a market value of $900,000, and its liabilities were $400,000. In recording the acquisition, Lacy will record goodwill of *(p. 403)*

    a. $50,000   c. $550,000

    b. $100,000   d. $0

10. Which of the following items is a revenue expenditure? *(p. 404)*

    a. Property tax paid on land one year after it is acquired

    b. Survey fee paid during the acquisition of land

    c. Legal fee paid to acquire land

    d. Building permit paid to construct a warehouse on the land

Answers to the self-study questions are at the end of the chapter.

Accounting Vocabulary

accelerated depreciation *(p. 389)*, amortization *(p. 401)*, capital expenditure *(p. 404)*, copyright *(p. 402)*, cost of a plant asset *(p. 384)*, double-declining-balance (DDB) method *(p. 389)*, depletion *(p. 401)*, estimated residual value *(p. 387)*, estimated useful life *(p. 387)*, extraordinary repair *(p. 404)*, franchises and licenses *(p. 402)*, goodwill *(p. 403)*, intangible assets *(p. 383)*, leasehold *(p. 402)*, ordinary repair *(p. 404)*, patent *(p. 402)*, plant asset *(p. 383)*, relative-sales-value method *(p. 385)*, revenue expenditure *(p. 404)*, straight-line (SL) method *(p. 387)*, sum-of-years-digits (SYD) method *(p. 390)*, trademarks and trade names *(p. 402)*, units-of-production (UOP) method *(p. 389)*.

ASSIGNMENT MATERIAL _____

Questions

1. To what types of long-lived assets do the following expenses apply: depreciation, depletion, and amortization?

2. Describe how to measure the cost of a plant asset. Would an ordinary cost of repairing the asset after it is placed in service be included in the asset's cost?

3. Suppose land is purchased for $100,000. How do you account for the $8,000 cost of removing an unwanted building?

4. When assets are purchased as a group for a single price and no individual asset cost is given, how is each asset's cost determined?

5. Define depreciation. Present the common misconceptions about depreciation.

6. Which depreciation method does each of the graphs on the next page characterize—straight-line, units-of-production, or accelerated?

7. Which of the four depreciation methods results in the most depreciation in the first year of the asset's life?

8. Explain the concept of accelerated depreciation. Which other depreciation method is used in the definition of accelerated depreciation?

9. The level of business activity fluctuates widely for Harwood Delivery Service, reaching its peak around Christmas each year. At other times, business is slow. What depreciation method is most appropriate for the company's fleet of Chevy Luv trucks?

10. Oswalt Computer Service Center uses the most advanced computers available to keep a competitive edge over other service centers. To maintain this advantage, Oswalt usually replaces its computers before they are worn out. Describe the major factors affecting the useful life of a plant asset and indicate which seems more relevant to Oswalt's computers.

11. Estimated residual value is not considered in computing depreciation during the early years of the asset's life by one of the methods. Which method is it?

12. Which type of depreciation method is best from an income tax standpoint? Why?

13. How does depreciation affect income taxes? How does depreciation affect cash provided by operations?

14. Describe how to compute depreciation for less than a full year and how to account for depreciation for less than a full month.

15. Ragland Company paid $10,000 for office furniture. The company expected it to remain in service for 6 years and to have a $1,000 residual value. After 2 years' use, company accountants believe the furniture will last an additional 6 years. How much depreciation will Ragland record for each of these 6 years, assuming straight-line depreciation and no change in the estimated residual value?

16. What three pieces of information should a company disclose about a change in accounting estimate, such as extending the useful life of a depreciable asset?

17. When a company sells a plant asset before the year's end, what must it record before accounting for the sale?

18. Describe how to determine whether a company experiences a gain or a loss when an old plant asset is exchanged for a new one. Does generally accepted accounting favor the recognition of gains or losses? Which accounting concept underlies your answer?

19. Identify seven elements of internal control designed to safeguard plant assets.

20. What expense applies to natural resources? By which depreciation method is this expense computed?

21. How do intangible assets differ from most other assets? Why are they assets at all? What expense applies to intangible assets?

22. Why is the cost of patents and other intangible assets often expensed over a shorter period than the legal life of the asset?

23. Your company has just purchased another company for $400,000. The market value of the other company's net assets is $325,000. What is the $75,000 excess called? What type of asset is it? What is the maximum period over which its cost is amortized under generally accepted accounting principles?

24. IBM Corporation is recognized as a world leader in the manufacture and sale of computers. The company's success has created vast amounts of business goodwill.

Would you expect to see *this* goodwill reported on IBM's financial statements? Why or why not?

25. Distinguish a capital expenditure from a revenue expenditure. The title "revenue expenditure" is curious in that a revenue expenditure is a debit to an expense account. Explain why revenue expenditures are so named.

26. Are ordinary repairs capital expenditures or revenue expenditures? Which type of expenditures are extraordinary repairs?

Exercises

Exercise 10-1 *Identifying the elements of a plant asset's cost*

A company purchased land, paying $30,000 cash as a down payment and signing a $120,000 note payable for the balance. In addition, the company paid back property tax of $6,000, a title fee of $500, and a $3,100 charge for leveling the land and removing an unwanted building. The company constructed an office building on the land at a cost of $640,000. It also paid $12,000 for a fence around the boundary of the property, $2,400 for the company sign near the entrance to the property, and $6,000 for special lighting of the grounds. Determine the cost of the company's land, land improvements, and building.

Exercise 10-2 *Allocating cost to assets acquired in a basket purchase*

Balcones Research Center bought three used machines in a $21,000 purchase. An independent appraisal of the machines produced the following figures:

Machine No.	Appraised Value
1	$ 4,000
2	12,000
3	8,000

Assuming Balcones paid cash for the machines, record the purchase in the general journal, identifying each machine's individual cost in a separate Machine account.

Exercise 10-3 *Computing depreciation by four methods*

A company delivery truck was acquired on January 2, 19X1, for $12,000. The truck was expected to remain in service for 4 years and last 88,000 miles. At the end of its useful life, company officials estimated that the truck's residual value would be $1,000. The truck traveled 24,000 miles in the first year, 28,000 in the second year, 21,000 in the third year, and 15,000 in the fourth year. Prepare a schedule of *depreciation expense* per year for the truck under the four depreciation methods. Show your computations.

			Depreciation Expense per Year		
Year	Straight-line	Units-of-Production	Double-Declining-Balance	Sum-of-Years-Digits
19X1				
19X2				
19X3				
19X4				

Exercise 10-4 *Identifying depreciation methods for income tax and financial reporting purposes*

Using the data in Exercise 10-3, identify the depreciation method that would be most advantageous from an income tax perspective. Which depreciation method do most companies use for reporting to their stockholders and creditors on their financial statements?

Exercise 10-5 *Recording partial-year depreciation computed by two methods*

Situation 1. Hunt Corporation purchased office furniture on March 3, 19X4, for $2,600 cash. Donna Hunt expects it to remain useful for 8 years and to have a residual value of $200. Hunt uses the straight-line depreciation method. Record Hunt's depreciation on the furniture for the year ended December 31, 19X4.

Situation 2. Chen Company purchased equipment on May 19, 19X2, for $19,500, signing a note payable for that amount. Chen estimated that this equipment will be useful for 3 years and have a residual value of $1,500. Assuming Chen uses sum-of-years-digits depreciation, record Chen's depreciation on the machine for the year ended December 31, 19X2.

Exercise 10-6 *Journalizing a change in a plant asset's useful life*

A company purchased a building for $680,000 and depreciated it on a straight-line basis over a 30-year period. The estimated residual value was $80,000. After using the building for 10 years, the company realized that wear and tear on the building would force the company to replace it before 30 years. Starting with the 11th year, the company began depreciating the building over a revised total life of 20 years, retaining the $80,000 estimate of residual value. Record depreciation expense on the building for years 10 and 11.

Exercise 10-7 *Recording the sale of a plant asset*

On January 2, 19X1, Oakwood Sales Company purchased store fixtures for $7,700 cash, expecting the fixtures to remain in service for 10 years. Oakwood has depreciated the fixtures on a sum-of-years-digits basis, assuming no estimated residual value. On June 30, 19X8, Oakwood sold the fixtures for $1,600 cash. Record depreciation expense on the fixtures for the 6 months ended June 30, 19X8, and also record the sale of the fixtures.

Exercise 10-8 *Exchanging plant assets*

A machine cost $10,000. At the end of 4 years, its accumulated depreciation was $4,500. For each of the following situations, record the trade-in of this old machine for a new, similar machine.

Situation 1. The new machine had a cash price of $12,400; the dealer allowed a trade-in allowance of $5,200 on the old machine, and you paid the $7,200 balance in cash.

Situation 2. The new machine had a cash price of $13,000; the dealer allowed a trade-in allowance of $6,300 on the old machine; and you signed a note payable for the $6,700 balance.

Exercise 10-9 *Preparing a plant ledger card*

McBee Delivery Service uses a plant ledger card to account for its delivery vehicles, which are located at the company's service garage. The fleet of vehicles cost $96,000 when purchased from Ericksen Ford Company on September 1, 19X2. This cost is the debit balance in the Delivery Vehicles account in the general ledger. McBee uses the straight-line depreciation method and estimates a four-year useful life and a $6,000 residual value for the trucks. The garage foreman is responsible for the vehicles. The company's fiscal year ends on December 31. Complete a plant ledger card for these vehicles through December 31, 19X4, using a format similar to Exhibit 10-9.

Exercise 10-10 *Recording natural resource assets and depletion*

Sasquatch Mining Company paid $178,500 for the right to extract ore from a 200,000-ton mineral deposit. In addition to the purchase price, Sasquatch also paid a $500 filing fee and a $1,000 license fee to the state of Wyoming. Because Sasquatch purchased the rights to the minerals only, the company expected the asset to have zero residual value when fully depleted. During the first year of production, Sasquatch removed 35,000 tons of ore. Make general journal entries to record (a) purchase of the mineral rights (debit Mineral Asset), (b) payment of fees, and (c) depletion for first-year production.

Exercise 10-11 *Recording intangibles, amortization, and a change in the asset's useful life*

Part 1. Lutz Corporation manufactures high-speed printers and has recently purchased for $4 million a patent for the design for a new laser printer. Although it gives legal protection for 17 years, the patent is expected to provide Lutz with a competitive advantage for only 8 years. Assuming the straight-line method of amortization, use general journal entries to record (a) the purchase of the patent and (b) amortization for 1 year.

Part 2. After using the patent for 3 years, Lutz learns at an industry trade show that another company is designing a more efficient printer. Based on this new information, Lutz decides, starting with year 4, to amortize the remaining cost of the patent over 2 additional years, giving the patent a total useful life of 5 years. Record amortization for year 4.

Exercise 10-12 *Computing and recording goodwill*

Company P purchased Company S, paying $1 million cash. The market value of Company S assets was $1.7 million, and Company S had liabilities of $.9 million.

(a) Compute the cost of the goodwill purchased by Company P.
(b) Record the purchase by Company P.
(c) Record amortization of goodwill for year 1, assuming the straight-line method and a useful life of 20 years.

Exercise 10-13 *Distinguishing capital expenditures from revenue expenditures*

Classify each of the following expenditures as a capital expenditure or a revenue expenditure (expense) related to machinery: (a) purchase price, (b) sales tax paid on the purchase price, (c) transportation and insurance while machinery is in transport from seller to buyer, (d) installation, (e) training of personnel for initial operation of the machinery, (f) special reinforcement to the machinery platform, (g) income tax paid on income earned from the sale of products manufactured by the machinery, (h) major overhaul to extend useful life by three years, (i) ordinary recurring repairs to keep the machinery in good working order, (j) lubrication of the machinery before it is placed in service, (k) periodic lubrication after the machinery is placed in service.

Problems (Group A)

Problem 10-1A *Identifying the elements of a plant asset's cost*

Mazzoti Company incurred the following costs in acquiring land and a garage, making land improvements, and constructing and furnishing a home office building.

(a)	Purchase price of 3½ acres of land, including an old building that will be used as a garage for company vehicles (land market value is $600,000; building market value is $60,000)	$605,000
(b)	Delinquent real estate taxes on the land to be paid by Mazzoti	14,600
(c)	Landscaping (additional dirt and earth moving).	3,550
(d)	Title insurance on the land acquisition	1,000
(e)	Fence around the boundary of the land	12,500
(f)	Building permit for the home office building	200
(g)	Architect fee for the design of the home office building	25,000

(h)	Company signs near front and rear approaches to the company property..	23,550
(i)	Renovation of the garage......................................	23,800
(j)	Concrete, wood, steel girders, and other materials used in the construction of the home office building...............................	385,000
(k)	Masonry, carpentry, roofing, and other labor to construct home office building...	734,000
(l)	Repair of vandalism damage to home office building during construction..	4,100
(m)	Parking lots and concrete walks on the property.................	17,450
(n)	Lights for the parking lot, walkways, and company signs...........	8,900
(o)	Supervisory salary of construction supervisor (90 percent to home office building, 6 percent to fencing, parking lot, and concrete walks, and 4 percent to garage renovation)	55,000
(p)	Office furniture for the home office building	267,500
(q)	Transportation of furniture from seller to the home office building ...	700
(r)	Landscaping (trees and shrubs)	9,100

Mazotti depreciates buildings over 40 years, land improvements over 20 years, and furniture over 8 years, all on a straight-line basis with zero residual value.

Required

1. Using the following format, account for each cost by listing it as a debit to Land, Land Improvements, Home Office Building, Garage, or Furniture:

Item	Land	Land Improvements	Home Office Building	Garage	Furniture
(a)	$	$	$	$	$
⋮					
(r)					
Totals	$	$	$	$	$

2. Assuming that all construction was complete and the assets were placed in service on March 19, record depreciation for the year ended December 31. Round figures to the nearest dollar.

Problem 10-2A   *Computing depreciation by four methods and the cash flow advantage of accelerated depreciation for tax purposes*

On January 2, 19X1, Morse, Inc., purchased 3 used delivery trucks at a total cost of $41,000. Before placing the trucks in service, the company spent $1,200 painting them, $1,800 replacing their tires, and $4,000 overhauling their engines and reconditioning their bodies. Morse management estimates that the trucks will remain in service for 6 years and have a residual value of $6,000. The trucks' combined annual mileage is expected to be 16,000 miles in each of the first 4 years and 18,000 miles in each of the next 2 years. In trying to decide which depreciation method to use, Ted Morse requests a depreciation schedule for each of the four generally accepted depreciation methods (straight-line, units-of-production, double-declining-balance, and sum-of-years-digits).

Required

1. Assuming Morse depreciates its delivery trucks as a unit, prepare a depreciation schedule for each of the four generally accepted depreciation methods, showing asset cost, depreciation expense, accumulated depreciation, and asset book value. Use the formats of Exhibits 10-3 through 10-6. (Note: Double-declining-balance depreciation for

year 6 is the amount needed to reduce asset book value to the residual value.)

2. Morse reports to stockholders and creditors in the financial statements using the depreciation method that maximizes reported income in the early years of asset use. For income tax purposes, however, the company uses the depreciation method that minimizes income tax payments in those early years. Consider the first year that Morse uses the delivery trucks. Identify the depreciation methods that meet Morse's objectives, assuming the income tax authorities would permit the use of any of the methods.

3. Assume cash provided by operations before income tax is $80,000 for the delivery trucks' first year. The income tax rate is 40 percent. For the two depreciation methods identified in Requirement 2, compare the net income and cash provided by operations (cash flow). Use the following outline for your answer.

	Depreciation Method That in the Early Years	
	A **Maximizes** **Reported** **Income**	**B** **Minimizes** **Income Tax** **Payments**
Comparison of net income for first year:		
Cash provided by operations before income tax	$	$
Depreciation expense		
Income before income tax		
Income tax expense (40%)		
Net income	$	$
Advantage of Method A over Method B.	$	
Cash flow analysis for first year:		
Cash provided by operations before income tax	$	$
Income tax expense		
Cash provided by operations (called cash flow).	$	$
Advantage of Method B over Method A.	$	

Problem 10-3A *Journalizing and posting plant asset transactions; capital expenditures versus revenue expenditures*

Pennsylvania Power & Light Company provides electrical power to part of eastern Pennsylvania. Assume that the company completed the following transactions:

19X4

Jan. 3 Paid $16,000 cash for a used service truck.

　　 5 Paid $1,200 to have the truck engine overhauled.

　　 7 Paid $300 to have the truck modified for business use.

Oct. 3 Paid $855 for transmission repair and oil change.

Dec. 31 Used the double-declining-balance method to record depreciation on the truck. (Assume a 4-year life.)

　　 31 Closed the appropriate accounts.

19X5

Mar. 13 Replaced the truck's broken windshield for $275 cash.

June 26 Traded in the service truck for a new truck costing $22,000. The dealer granted a $6,000 allowance on the old truck, and Pennsylvania Power paid the balance in cash. Recorded 19X5 depreciation for the year to date and then recorded the exchange of trucks.

Dec. 31 Used the double-declining-balance method to record depreciation on the new truck. (Assume a 4-year life.)

31 Closed the appropriate accounts.

Required

1. Open the following accounts in the general ledger: Service Trucks; Accumulated Depreciation – Service Trucks; Truck Repair Expense; Depreciation Expense – Service Trucks; and Loss on Exchange of Service Trucks.
2. Record the transactions in the general journal and post to the ledger accounts opened.

Problem 10-4A   *Recording plant asset transactions; exchanges; changes in useful life.*

A. C. Nielsen Company surveys American viewing trends. Nielsen's balance sheet reports the following assets under Property and Equipment: Land, Buildings, Office Furniture, Communication Equipment, Televideo Equipment, and Leasehold Improvements. The company has a separate accumulated depreciation account for each of these assets except land and leasehold improvements. Amortization on leasehold improvements is credited directly to the Leasehold Improvements account rather than to Accumulated Depreciation – Leasehold Improvements.

Assume that Nielsen completed the following transactions:

Jan. 4 Traded in communication equipment with book value of $22,000 (cost of $51,000) for similar new equipment with a cash cost of $78,000. The seller gave Nielsen a trade-in allowance of $15,000 on the old equipment, and Nielsen paid the remainder in cash.

19 Purchased office furniture for $45,000 plus 6 percent sales tax and $300 shipping charge. The company gave a 90-day, 10 percent note in payment.

Apr. 19 Paid the furniture note and related interest.

Aug. 29 Sold a building that had cost $475,000 and had accumulated depreciation of $353,500 through December 31 of the preceding year. Depreciation is computed on a straight-line basis. The building has a 30-year useful life and a residual value of $47,500. Nielsen received $250,000 cash and a $750,000 note receivable.

Sep. 6 Paid cash to improve leased assets at a cost of $39,000.

Nov. 10 Purchased used communication and televideo equipment from the Gallup polling organization. Total cost was $90,000 paid in cash. An independent appraisal valued the communication equipment at $65,000 and the televideo equipment at $35,000.

Dec. 31 Recorded depreciation as follows:

Equipment is depreciated by the double-declining-balance method over a 6-year life with zero residual value. Record depreciation on the equipment purchased on January 4 and on November 10 separately.

Office furniture has an expected useful life of 8 years with an estimated residual value of $5,000. Depreciation is computed by the sum-of-years-digits method.

Amortization on leasehold improvements is computed on a straight-line basis over the life of the lease, which is 6 years, with zero residual value.

Depreciation on buildings is computed by the straight-line method. The company had assigned buildings an estimated useful life of 30 years and a residual value that is 10 percent of cost. After using the buildings for 20 years, the company has come to believe that their total useful life will be 35 years. Residual value remains unchanged. The buildings cost $96,000,000.

Required

Record the transactions in the general journal.

Problem 10-5A *Distinguishing capital expenditures from revenue expenditures; preparing a plant ledger card*

Suppose Public Service Company of Colorado uses plant ledger cards to control its service trucks, purchased from Wallen Motor Company. The supervisor is responsible for the trucks, which are located at the company's service garage. The following transactions were completed during 19X6 and 19X7:

19X6

Jan. 10	Paid $14,000 cash for a used service truck (truck no. 214).
11	Paid $1,500 to have the truck engine overhauled.
12	Paid $250 to have the truck modified for business use.
Aug. 3	Paid $603 for transmission repair and oil change.
Dec. 31	Recorded depreciation on the truck by the double-declining-balance method, based on a 4-year life and a $1,500 residual value.

19X7

Mar. 13	Replaced a damaged bumper on truck no. 214 at a cash cost of $295.
Aug. 12	Traded in service truck no. 214 for a new one (truck no. 267) with a cash cost of $20,000. The dealer granted a $7,000 allowance on the old truck, and Public Service Company paid the balance in cash. Recorded 19X7 depreciation for year to date and then recorded exchange of the trucks.
Dec. 31	Recorded depreciation on truck no. 267 by the double-declining-balance method, based on a 4-year life and a $2,000 residual value.

Required

1. Identify the capital expenditures and the revenue expenditures in the transactions. Which expenditures are debited to an asset account? Which expenditures are debited to an expense account?
2. Prepare a separate plant ledger card for each of the trucks.

Problem 10-6A *Recording intangibles, natural resources, and the related expenses*

Part 1. United Telecommunications, Inc., (United Telecom) provides communication services in Florida, North Carolina, New Jersey, Texas, and other states. The company's balance sheet reports the asset Cost of Acquisitions in Excess of the Fair Market Value of the Net Assets of Subsidiaries. Assume that United Telecom purchased this asset as part of the acquisition of another company, which carried these figures:

Book value of assets....................	$215,000
Market value of assets..................	300,000
Liabilities............................	135,000

Required

1. What is another title for the asset Cost of Acquisitions in Excess of the Fair Market Value of the Net Assets of Subsidiaries?
2. Make the general journal entry to record United Telecom's purchase of the other company for $220,000 cash.
3. Assuming United Telecom amortizes Cost of Acquisitions in Excess of the Fair Market Value of the Net Assets of Subsidiaries over 20 years, record the straight-line amortization for 1 year.

Part 2. Suppose United Telecom purchased a patent for $455,000. Before using the patent, United incurred an additional cost of $25,000 for a lawsuit to defend the company's right to purchase it. Even though the patent gives United legal protection for 17 years, company management has decided to amortize its cost over an 8-year period because of the industry's fast-changing technologies.

Required

Make general journal entries to record the patent transactions, including straight-line amortization for 1 year.

Part 3.   Transco Energy Company operates a pipeline that provides natural gas to Atlanta, Washington, D.C., Philadelphia, and New York City. The company's balance sheet includes the asset Oil Properties.

Suppose Transco paid $2,800,000 cash for an oil lease that contained an estimated reserve of 300,000 barrels of oil. Assume that the company paid $350,000 for additional geological tests of the property and $50,000 to prepare the surface for drilling. Prior to production, the company signed a $40,000 note payable to have a building constructed on the property. Because the building provides on-site headquarters for the drilling effort and will be abandoned when the oil is depleted, its cost is debited to the Oil properties account and included in depletion charges. During the first year of production, Transco removed 26,000 barrels of oil, which it sold on credit for $19 per barrel.

Required

Make general journal entries to record all transactions related to the oil and gas property, including depletion and sale of the first-year production.

(Group B)

Problem 10-1B   *Identifying the elements of a plant asset's cost*

Anotelli Company incurred the following costs in acquiring land, making land improvements, and constructing and furnishing an office building.

(a)	Purchase price of four acres of land, including an old building that will be used for storage (land market value is $380,000; building market value is $20,000)	$350,000
(b)	Landscaping (additional dirt and earth moving)	8,100
(c)	Fence around the boundary of the land	23,650
(d)	Attorney fee for title search on the land	600
(e)	Delinquent real estate taxes on the land to be paid by Anotelli	5,900
(f)	Company signs at front of the company property	7,600
(g)	Building permit for the office building	350
(h)	Architect fee for the design of the office building	19,800
(i)	Masonry, carpentry, roofing, and other labor to construct office building	509,000
(j)	Concrete, wood, steel girders, and other materials used in the construction of the office building	453,000
(k)	Renovation of the storage building	41,800
(l)	Repair of storm damage to storage building during construction	2,200
(m)	Landscaping (trees and shrubs)	6,400
(n)	Parking lot and concrete walks on the property	19,750
(o)	Lights for the parking lot, walkways, and company signs	7,300
(p)	Supervisory salary of construction supervisor (85 percent to office building, 9 percent to fencing, parking lot, and concrete walks, and 6 percent to storage building renovation)	40,000
(q)	Office furniture for the office building	174,400
(r)	Transportation and installation of furniture	1,100

Anotelli depreciates buildings over 40 years, land improvements over 20 years, and furniture over 8 years, all on a straight-line basis with zero residual value.

Required

1. Using the following format, account for each cost by listing it as a debit to Land, Land Improvements, Office Building, Storage Building, or Furniture:

Item	Land	Land Improvements	Office Building	Storage Building	Furniture
(a)	$	$	$	$	$
⋮					
(r)					
Totals	$	$	$	$	$

2. Assuming that all construction was complete and the assets were placed in service on May 4, record depreciation for the year ended December 31. Round off figures to the nearest dollar.

Problem 10-2B *Computing depreciation by four methods and the cash flow advantage of accelerated depreciation for tax purposes*

On January 9, 19X1, Lynch, Inc., paid $82,000 for equipment that manufactures stereo cassette tapes. In addition to the basic purchase price, the company paid $700 transportation charges, $100 insurance for the goods in transit, $4,100 sales tax, and $3,100 for a special platform on which to place the equipment in the plant. Lynch management estimates that the equipment will remain in service for 5 years and have a residual value of $11,250. The equipment will produce 45,000 units in the first year, with annual production decreasing by 5,000 units during each of the next 4 years (that is, 40,000 units in year 2, 35,000 units in year 3, and so on). In trying to decide which depreciation method to use, Charlene Lynch has requested a depreciation schedule for each of the four generally accepted depreciation methods (straight-line, units-of-production, double-declining-balance and sum-of-years-digits).

Required

1. For each of the four generally accepted depreciation methods, prepare a depreciation schedule showing asset cost, depreciation expense, accumulated depreciation, and asset book value. Use the format of Exhibits 10-3 through 10-6.
2. Lynch reports to stockholders and creditors in the financial statements using the depreciation method that maximizes reported income in the early years of asset use. For income tax purposes, however, the company uses the depreciation method that minimizes income tax payments in those early years. Consider the first year Lynch uses the equipment. Identify the depreciation methods that meet Lynch's objectives, assuming the income tax authorities would permit the use of any of the methods.
3. Assume cash provided by operations before income tax is $110,000 for the equipment's first year. The income tax rate is 40 percent. For the two depreciation methods identified in Requirement 2, compare the net income and cash provided by operations (cash flow). Use the following outline for your answer.

	Depreciation Method That in the Early Years	
	A Maximizes Reported Income	**B** Minimizes Income Tax Payments
Comparison of net income for first year:		
Cash provided by operations before income tax	$	$
Depreciation expense.		
Income before income tax		
Income tax expense (40%).		
Net income	$	$
Advantage of Method A over Method B.	$	

	Depreciation Method That in the Early Years	
Cash flow analysis for first year:	A Maximizes Reported Income	B Minimizes Income Tax Payments
Cash provided by operations before income tax	$	$
Income tax expense		
Cash provided by operations (called cash flow)......	$	$
Advantage of Method B over Method A............	$	

Problem 10-3B *Journalizing and posting plant asset transactions; capital expenditures versus revenue expenditures*

Assume that a Revco drugstore completed the following transactions:

19X2

Jan. 6 Paid $6,000 cash for a used delivery truck.

7 Paid $800 to have the truck engine overhauled.

8 Paid $200 to have the truck modified for business use.

Aug. 21 Paid $127 for a minor tuneup.

Dec. 31 Recorded depreciation on the truck by the sum-of-years-digits method (assume a 4-year life and a $1,500 residual value).

31 Closed the appropriate accounts.

19X3

May 8 Traded in the delivery truck for a new truck costing $10,000. The dealer granted a $4,000 allowance on the old truck, and the store paid the balance in cash. Recorded 19X3 depreciation for the year to date and then recorded the exchange of trucks.

July 8 Repaired the new truck's damaged fender for $625 cash.

Dec. 31 Recorded depreciation on the new truck by the sum-of-years-digits method. (Assume a 4-year life and a residual value of $2,000).

31 Closed the appropriate accounts.

Required

1. Open the following accounts in the general ledger: Delivery Trucks; Accumulated Depreciation–Delivery Trucks; Truck Repair Expense; Depreciation Expense–Delivery Trucks; and Loss on Exchange of Delivery Trucks.
2. Record the transactions in the general journal, and post to the ledger accounts opened.

Problem 10-4B *Recording plant asset transactions; exchanges; changes in useful life*

Consolidated Freightways, Inc., provides nationwide general freight service. The company's balance sheet includes the following assets under Property, Plant, and Equipment: Land, Buildings, Motor Carrier Equipment, and Leasehold Improvements. Assume the company has a separate accumulated depreciation account for each of these assets except land and leasehold improvements. Amortization on leasehold improvements is credited directly to the Leasehold Improvements account rather than to Accumulated Amortization–Leasehold Improvements.

Assume that Consolidated Freightways completed the following transactions:

Jan. 5 Traded in motor-carrier equipment with book value of $34,000 (cost of $90,000) for similar new equipment with a cash cost of $128,000. Consolidated received a trade-in allowance of $40,000 on the old equipment and paid the remainder in cash.

Feb. 22   Purchased motor-carrier equipment for $136,000 plus 5 percent sales tax and $200 title fee. The company gave a 60-day, 12 percent note in payment.

Apr. 23   Paid the equipment note and related interest.

July   9   Sold a building that had cost $550,000 and had accumulated depreciation of $247,500 through December 31 of the preceding year. Depreciation is computed on a straight-line basis. The building has a 30-year useful life and a residual value of $55,000. Consolidated received $100,000 cash and a $600,000 note receivable.

Aug. 16   Paid cash to improve leased assets at a cost of $21,600.

Oct. 26   Purchased land and a building for a single price of $300,000. An independent appraisal valued the land at $115,000 and the building at $230,000.

Dec. 31   Recorded depreciation as follows:

   Motor-carrier equipment has an expected useful life of 6 years and an estimated residual value of 5 percent of cost. Depreciation is computed on the sum-of-years-digits method. Make separate depreciation entries for equipment acquired on January 5 and February 22.

   Amortization on leasehold improvements is computed on a straight-line basis over the life of the lease, which is 5 years, with zero residual value.

   Depreciation on buildings is computed by the straight-line method. The company had assigned to its older buildings, which cost $200,000,000, an estimated useful life of 30 years with a residual value equal to 10 percent of the asset cost. However, management has come to believe that the buildings will remain useful for a total of 40 years. Residual value remains unchanged. The company has used all its buildings, except for the one purchased on October 26, for 10 years. The new building carries a 40-year useful life and a residual value equal to 10 percent of its cost. Make separate entries for depreciation on the building acquired on October 26 and the other buildings purchased in earlier years.

Required

Record the transactions in the general journal.

Problem 10-5B   *Distinguishing capital expenditures from revenue expenditures; preparing a plant ledger card*

Suppose Pacific Power & Light Company uses plant ledger cards to control its service trucks, purchased from Grant Motor Co. The supervisor is responsible for the trucks, which are located at the company's service garage. The following transactions were completed during 19X3 and 19X4:

19X3

Jan.   6   Paid $13,800 cash for a used service truck (truck no. 501).

   7   Paid $2,500 to have the truck engine overhauled.

   8   Paid $180 to have the truck modified for business use.

Nov.   5   Paid $107 for replacement of one tire.

Dec. 31   Recorded depreciation on the truck by the double-declining-balance method, based on a 4-year useful life and a $2,000 residual value.

19X4

Apr. 19   Repaired a damaged fender on truck no. 501 at a cash cost of $877.

Nov.   6   Traded in service truck no. 501 for a new one (truck no. 633) with a cash cost of $18,000. The dealer granted a $6,000 allowance on the old truck, and Pacific Power paid the balance in cash. Recorded 19X4 depreciation for year to date and then recorded exchange of the trucks.

Dec. 31   Recorded depreciation on truck no. 633 by the double-declining-balance method, on a 4-year life and a $2,500 residual value.

Required

1. Identify the capital expenditures and the revenue expenditures in the transactions. Which expenditures are debited to an asset account? Which expenditures are debited to an expense account?
2. Prepare a separate plant ledger card for each of the trucks.

Problem 10-6B   *Recording intangibles, natural resources, and the related expenses*

Part 1.   Collins Foods International, Inc., is the largest of the companies that operate Kentucky Fried Chicken franchised restaurants and is also the majority owner of Sizzler Restaurants. The company's balance sheet reports the asset Cost in Excess of Net Assets of Purchased Businesses. Assume that Collins purchased this asset as part of the acquisition of another company, which carried these figures:

Book value of assets....................	$275,000
Market value of assets	420,000
Liabilities............................	167,500

Required

1. What is another title for the asset Cost in Excess of Net Assets of Purchased Businesses?
2. Make the general journal entry to record Collins's purchase of the other company for $292,500 cash.
3. Assuming Collins amortizes Cost in Excess of Net Assets of Purchased Businesses over 10 years, record the straight-line amortization for 1 year.

Part 2.   Suppose Collins purchased a Kentucky Fried Chicken franchise license for $162,000. In addition to the basic purchase price, Collins also paid a lawyer $8,000 for assistance with the negotiations. Collins management believes the appropriate amortization period for its cost of the franchise license is 8 years.

Required

Make general journal entries to record the franchise transactions, including straight-line amortization for one year.

Part 3.   Georgia-Pacific Corporation is one of the world's largest forest products companies. The company's balance sheet includes the assets Natural Gas, Oil, and Coal.

   Suppose Georgia-Pacific paid $800,000 cash for a lease giving the firm the right to work a mine that contained an estimated 80,000 tons of coal. Assume that the company paid $5,000 to remove unwanted buildings from the land and $15,000 to prepare the surface for mining. Further assume that Georgia-Pacific signed a $20,000 note payable for a landscaping company to return the land surface to its original condition after the lease ends. During the first year, Georgia-Pacific removed 15,000 tons of coal, which it sold on account for $17 per ton.

Required

Make general journal entries to record all transactions related to the coal, including depletion and sale of the first-year production.

Decision Problem

Measuring Profitability Based on Different Inventory and Depreciation Methods

Suppose you are considering investing in two businesses, Frycer Company and Bergdahl Company. The two companies are virtually identical, and both began operations at the beginning of the current year. During the year, each company purchased inventory as follows:

Jan.	4	12,000 units at $4 =	$ 48,000
Apr.	6	5,000 units at 5 =	25,000
Aug.	9	7,000 units at 6 =	42,000
Nov.	27	10,000 units at 7 =	70,000
Totals		34,000	$185,000

Over the first year, both companies sold 25,000 units of inventory.

In early January both companies purchased equipment costing $100,000 that had a 10-year estimated useful life and a $10,000 residual value. Frycer Company uses the first-in, first-out (FIFO) method for its inventory and straight-line depreciation for its equipment. Bergdahl Company uses last-in, first-out (LIFO) and double-declining-balance depreciation. Both companies' trial balances at December 31 included the following:

Sales revenue	$250,000
Purchases	185,000
Operating expenses	80,000

Required

1. Prepare both companies' income statements.
2. Prepare a schedule that shows why one company appears to be more profitable than the other. Explain the schedule and amounts in your own words. What accounts for the different amounts?
3. Is one company more profitable than the other? Give your reason.

Financial Statement Problem

Plant Assets and Intangible Assets
Refer to the Gulf+Western financial statements in Appendix C, and answer the following questions.

1. Which depreciation method does Gulf+Western use for the purpose of reporting to stockholders and creditors in the financial statements? Although Gulf+Western does not disclose it in the statements, what type of depreciation method does the company probably use for income tax purposes?
2. Depreciation and amortization expenses are embedded in the expense amounts listed on the income statement (statement of earnings). The statement of cash flows gives the amounts of depreciation and amortization. What were their amounts for fiscal 1987?
3. The statement of cash flows also reports purchases of plant assets and the proceeds (sale prices) on disposal of plant assets. How much were Gulf+Western's plant asset expenditures during fiscal 1987? Were these capital expenditures or revenue expenditures? How much did Gulf+Western receive on the sale of plant assets this year?
4. In what category on the income statement are revenue expenditures most likely included?
5. What is Gulf+Western's major intangible asset? As of October 31, 1987, what was the company's cost of intangible assets? Identify the nature of the transactions in which Gulf+Western acquired this asset. What is the maximum period over which the cost of an intangible asset can be expensed under GAAP?

Answers to Self-Study Questions

1. d
2. c $90,000/($90,000 + $60,000) × $120,000 = $72,000;
   $60,000/($90,000 + $60,000) × $120,000 = $48,000
3. b
4. b
5. c
6. a Depreciable cost = $450,000 − $50,000 = $400,000
   $400,000/40 years = $10,000 per year
   $400,000 − ($10,000 × 10 years) = $300,000/40 years = $7,500 per year
7. d
8. b
9. a $550,000 − ($900,000 − $400,000) = $50,000
10. a

11

Current Liabilities
and Payroll Accounting

LEARNING OBJECTIVES
After studying this chapter, you should be able to

1 Classify liabilities as current or long-term

2 Account for current liabilities

3 Account for contingent liabilities

4 Make basic payroll entries

5 Use a payroll-accounting system

6 Report current liabilities

A *liability* is an obligation to transfer assets or to provide services in the future. The obligation may arise from a transaction with an outside party. For example, a business incurs a liability when it issues a note payable to buy equipment or to borrow money. Also, the obligation may arise in the absence of individual transactions. For example, interest expense accrues with the passage of time. Until this interest is paid it is a liability. Income tax, a liability of corporations, accrues as income is earned. Proper accounting for liabilities is as important as proper accounting for assets. The failure to record an accrued liability causes the balance sheet to understate the related expense and thus overstates owner's equity. An overly positive view of the business is the result.

All liabilities are classified as current—those due within one year or the company's operating cycle if longer than a year, or long-term—those liabilities not classified as current. We now turn to accounting for current liabilities, including those arising from payroll expenses.

OBJECTIVE 1
Classify liabilities as current or long-term

Current Liabilities of Known Amount _____

Current liabilities fall into one of two categories: those of a known amount and those whose amount must be estimated. We look first at current liabilities of known amount.

Trade Accounts Payable

Amounts owed to suppliers for products or services that are purchased on open account are accounts payable. We have seen many accounts payable examples in previous chapters. For example, a business may purchase inventories and office supplies on an account payable.

Short-Term Notes Payable

Short-term notes payable, a common form of financing, are notes payable that are due within one year. Companies often issue short-term notes payable to borrow cash or to purchase inventory or plant assets. In addition to recording the note payable and its eventual payment, the business must also accrue interest expense and interest payable at the end of the period. The following entries are typical of this liability:

19X1			
Sep. 30	Purchases	8,000	
	Note Payable, Short-Term		8,000
	Purchase of inventory by issuing a one-year 10 percent note payable.		

OBJECTIVE 2
Account for current liabilities

Dec. 31	Interest Expense ($8,000 × .10 × 3/12)	200	
	Interest Payable		200
	Adjusting entry to accrue interest expense at year end.		

The balance sheet at December 31, 19X1, will report the Note Payable of $8,000 and the related Interest Payable of $200 as current liabilities. The 19X1 income statement will report interest expense of $200.

The following entry records the note's payment:

19X2			
Sep. 30	Note Payable, Short-Term.	8,000	
	Interest Payable	200	
	Interest Expense ($8,000 × .10 × 9/12)	600	
	Cash [$8,000 + ($8,000 × .10)]		8,800
	Payment of a note payable and interest at maturity.		

The cash payment entry must split the total interest on the note between the portion accrued at the end of the previous period ($200) and the current period's expense ($600).

Short-Term Notes Payable Issued at a Discount

In another common borrowing arrangement, a company may **discount a note payable** at the bank. Discounting means that the bank subtracts the interest amount from the note's face value. The borrower receives the net amount. In effect, the borrower prepays the interest, which is computed on the principal of the note.

Suppose Procter & Gamble discounts a $100,000, 60-day note payable to their bank at 12 percent. The company will receive $98,000 — that is, the $100,000 face value less interest of $2,000 ($100,000 × .12 × 60/360). Assume this transaction occurs on November 25, 19X1. Procter & Gamble's entries to record discounting the note would be

19X1			
Nov. 25	Cash ($100,000 − $2,000)	98,000	
	Discount on Note Payable ($100,000 ×		
	.12 × 60/360)	2,000	
	Note Payable, Short-Term		100,000
	Discounted a $100,000, 60-day, 12-percent note payable to borrow cash.		

Discount on Note Payable is a contra account to the liability Note Payable, Short-Term. A balance sheet prepared immediately after this transaction would report the note payable at its net amount of $98,000, as follows:

Current liabilities:
Note payable, short-term. $100,000
  Less: Discount on note payable . . . . (2,000)
Note payable, short-term, net . . . . $ 98,000

The accrued interest at year end must still be recorded, as it would for any note payable. The adjusting entry at December 31 records interest for 36 days as follows:

19X1

Dec. 31 Interest Expense ($100,000 × .12 × 36/360). 1,200
    Discount on Note Payable   1,200
  Adjusting entry to accrue interest expense at year end.

This entry credits the Discount account instead of Interest Payable. Why? Because the Discount balance is like prepaid interest, and the accrual of interest uses up part of the prepayment. Furthermore, crediting the Discount reduces this contra account's balance and increases the net amount of the Note Payable. After the adjusting entry, only $800 of the Discount remains, and the carrying value of the Note Payable increases to $99,200, as follows:

Current liabilities:
Note payable, short-term $100,000
  Less: Discount on note payable ($2,000 − $1,200) . . . . (800)
Note payable, short-term, net . . . . $ 99,200

Finally, the business records the note's payment:

19X2

Jan. 24 Interest Expense ($100,000 × .12 × 24/360) 800
    Discount on Note Payable   800
  To record interest expense.
  Note Payable, Short-Term 100,000
    Cash   100,000
  To pay note payable at maturity.

After these entries, the balances in the note payable account and the discount account are zero. Each period's income statement reports the appropriate amount of interest expense.

Sales Tax Payable

Most states levy a sales tax on retail sales. Retailers charge their customers the sales tax in addition to the price of the item sold. Because the retailers owe the state the sales tax collected, the account Sales Tax Payable is a current liability. For example, Pizza Time Theatre, Inc., (home of Chuck E. Cheese) reported sales tax payable of $737,712 as a current liability. States do not levy sales tax on the sales of manufacturers like Procter & Gamble and General Motors. Such companies sell their products to wholesalers and retailers rather than to final consumers. Therefore, they have no sales tax liability.

Suppose one Saturday's sales at a Pizza Time Theatre totaled $2,000. The business would have collected an additional 5 percent in sales tax, which would equal $100 ($2,000 × .05). The business would record that day's sales as follows:

Cash ($2,000 × 1.05)	2,100	
Sales Revenue		2,000
Sales Tax Payable ($2,000 × .05).....................		100

To record cash sales of $2,000 subject to 5 percent sales tax.

Companies forward the collected sales tax to the taxing authority at regular intervals, at which time they debit Sales Tax Payable and credit Cash. Observe that Sales Tax Payable does *not* correspond to any sales tax expense that the business is incurring. Nor does this liability arise from the purchase of any asset. Rather, it is the cash that the business is collecting for the government.

Many companies consider it inefficient to credit Sales Tax Payable when recording sales. They record the sale in an amount that includes the tax. Then prior to paying tax to the state, they make a single entry for the entire period's transactions to bring Sales Revenue and Sales Tax Payable to their correct balances.

Suppose a company made July sales of $100,000, subject to a tax of 6 percent. Its summary entry to record the month's sales could be

July 31	Cash ($100,000 × 1.06)	106,000	
	Sales Revenue............................		106,000
	To record sales for the month.		

The entry to adjust Sales Revenue and Sales Tax Payable to their correct balances is

July 31	Sales Revenue [$106,000 − ($106,000 ÷ 1.06)]	6,000	
	Sales Tax Payable..........................		6,000
	To record sales tax.		

Companies that follow this procedure need to make an adjusting entry at the end of the period in order to report the correct amounts of revenue and sales tax liability on their financial statements.

Current Portion of Long-Term Debt

Some long-term notes payable and long-term bonds payable must be paid in installments. The **current portion of long-term debt,** or *current maturity,* is the amount of the principal that is payable within one year. This amount does not include the interest due. Of course, any liability for accrued interest payable must also be reported, but a separate account, Interest Payable, is used for that purpose.

H. J. Heinz Company, probably best known for its ketchup, owed almost $200 million on long-term debt at April 30, the end of its fiscal year. Nearly $14 million was a current liability because it was due within one year. The remaining $186 million was a long-term liability. Suppose the interest rate on the debt was 6 percent and that interest was last paid the preceding November 30. Heinz Company's April 30 balance sheet would report:

Current Liabilities (in part)	Millions
Portion of long-term debt due within one year	$ 14
Interest payable ($200 × .06 × 5/12).	5

Long-Term Debt and Other Liabilities (in part)	
Long-term debt	$186

Accrued Expenses

As shown in the Heinz Company presentation, *accrued expenses,* such as interest expense, create current liabilities because the interest is due within the year. Therefore, the interest payable (accrued interest) is reported as a current liability. Other important liabilities for accrued expenses are payroll and the related payroll taxes, which we discuss in the second part of this chapter.

Unearned Revenues

Unearned revenues are also called *deferred revenues, revenues collected in advance,* and *customer prepayments.* Each account title indicates that the business has received cash from its customers before earning the revenue. The company has an obligation to provide goods or services to the customer.

The Dun & Bradstreet (D&B) Corporation provides credit evaluation services on a subscription basis. When finance companies pay in advance to have D&B investigate the credit histories of potential customers, D&B incurs a liability to provide future service. The liability account is called Unearned Subscription Revenue (which could also be titled Unearned Subscription Income).

Assume that Dun & Bradstreet charges $150 for a finance company's three-year subscription. Dun & Bradstreet's entries would be

```
19X1
Jan.  1  Cash............................................  150
                Unearned Subscription Revenue.................          150
         To record receipt of cash at start of the three-year
         subscription agreement.


19X1, 19X2, 19X3
Dec. 31  Unearned Subscription Revenue.......................   50
                Subscription Revenue ($150/3) .................           50
         To record subscription revenue earned at the
         end of each of three years.
```

Dun & Bradstreet's financial statements would report this sequence:

	December 31		
Balance Sheet	Year 1	Year 2	Year 3
Current liabilities			
Unearned subscription revenue	$100	$50	$-0-
Income Statement	Year 1	Year 2	Year 3
Revenues			
Subscription revenue	$50	$50	$50

Customer Deposits Payable

Some companies require cash deposits from customers as security on borrowed assets. These amounts are called Customer Deposits Payable because the company must refund the cash to the customer under certain conditions.

For example, telephone companies demand a cash deposit from a customer before installing a telephone. Utility companies and businesses that lend tools and appliances commonly demand a deposit as protection against damage and theft. When the customer ends service or returns the borrowed asset, the company refunds the cash deposit—if the customer has paid all the bills and has not damaged the company's property. Because the company generally must return the deposit, that obligation is a liability. The uncertainty of when the deposits will be refunded and their relatively small amounts cause many companies to classify Customer Deposits Payable as current liabilities. This is consistent with the concept of conservatism.

Certain manufacturers demand security deposits from the merchandisers who sell their products. Stanley Home Products, Inc., for example, demands a deposit from its dealers. The security deposits, called Dealers' Security Deposits, recently came to $4 million on Stanley's balance sheet, a small amount compared to its total current liabilities of over $62 million.

Current Liabilities That Must Be Estimated

A business may know that a liability exists but not know the exact amount. The liability may not simply be ignored. The unknown amount of a liability must be estimated for reporting on the balance sheet.

Estimated current liabilities vary among companies. As an example, let's look at Estimated Warranty Payable, a liability account common among merchandisers.

Estimated Warranty Payable

Many merchandising companies guarantee their products against defects under *warranty* agreements. The warranty period may extend for any length of time. Ninety-day warranties and one-year warranties are common.

Whatever the warranty's lifetime, the matching principle demands that the company record the *warranty expense* in the same period that the business recognizes sales revenue. After all, offering the warranty—and incurring any possible expense through the warranty agreement—is a part of generating revenue through sales. At the time of the sale, however, the company does not know which products are defective. The exact amount of warranty expense cannot be known with certainty, so the business must estimate its warranty expense and open the related liability account—Estimated Warranty Payable (also called Accrued Warranty Costs and Product Warranty Liability). Even though the warranty liability is a contingency, it is accounted for as an actual liability because it is probable that warranty expense has occurred and its amount can be estimated.

Companies may make a reliable estimate of their warranty expense based on their experience. Assume a company made sales of $200,000, subject to product warranties. Company management, noting that in past years between 2 percent and 4 percent of products proved defective, estimates that 3 percent of the products will require repair or replacement during the one-year warranty period.

The company records warranty expense of $6,000 ($200,000 × .03) for the period:

Warranty Expense.   6,000
    Estimated Warranty Payable   6,000
To accrue warranty expense.

Assume that defective merchandise totals $5,800. The company may either repair or replace it. Corresponding entries follow.

Estimated Warranty Payable   5,800
    Cash.   5,800
To repair defective products sold under warranty.

Estimated Warranty Payable   5,800
    Inventory.   5,800
To replace defective products sold under warranty.

Note that the expense is $6,000 on the income statement no matter what the cash payment or the cost of the replacement inventory. In future periods, the company may come to debit the liability Estimated Warranty Payable for the remaining $200. However, *when* the company repairs or replaces defective merchandise has no bearing on when the company records warranty expense. The business records warranty expense in the same period as the sale.

Contingent Liabilities

A *contingent liability* is not an actual liability. Instead, it is a potential liability that depends on a *future* event arising out of a past transaction. For example, a town government may sue the company that installed new street lights, claiming that the electrical wiring is faulty. The past transaction is the street-light installation. The future event is the court case that will decide the suit. The lighting company thus faces a contingent liability, which may or may not become an actual obligation.

Sometimes the contingent liability has a definite amount. From Chapter 8 recall that the payee of a discounted note has a contingent liability. If the maker of the note pays at maturity, the contingent liability ceases to exist. However, if the maker defaults, the payee, who sold the note, must pay its maturity value to the purchaser. In this case, the payee knows the note's maturity value, which is the amount of the contingent liability.

Another contingent liability of known amount arises from guaranteeing that another company will pay a note payable that the other company owes a third party. This practice, called cosigning a note, obligates the guarantor to pay the note and interest if, and only if, the primary debtor fails to pay. Thus the guarantor has a contingent liability until the note becomes due. If the primary debtor pays off, the contingent liability ceases to exist. If the primary debtor fails to pay, the guarantor's liability becomes actual.

The amount of a contingent liability may be hard to determine. For example, companies face lawsuits, which may cause possible obligations of amounts to be determined by the courts.

Contingent liabilities may be reported in two ways. In what is called a **short**

presentation, the contingent liability appears in the body of the balance sheet, after total liabilities, but with no amount given. Generally an explanatory note accompanies a short presentation. Sears, Roebuck and Company reported contingent liabilities this way:

	Millions
Total liabilities	$27,830.7
Contingent liabilities (note 10)	—

Note 10: Various legal actions and governmental proceedings are pending against Sears, Roebuck and Co. and its subsidiaries. . . . The consequences of these matters are not presently determinable but, in the opinion of management, the ultimate liability resulting, if any, will not have a material effect on the company.

OBJECTIVE 3

Account for contingent liabilities

Contingent liabilities do not have to be mentioned in the body of the balance sheet. Many companies use a second method of reporting, presenting the footnote only. International Business Machines Corporation (IBM) mentions its contingent liabilities in a half-page supplementary note labeled *litigation.*

The line between a contingent liability and a real liability may be hard to draw. As a practical guide, the FASB says to record an actual liability if (1) it is probable that the business has suffered a loss and (2) its amount can be reasonably estimated. If both of these conditions are met, the FASB reasons that the obligation has passed from contingent to real, even if its amount must be estimated. Suppose that at the balance sheet date, a hospital expects to lose a court case for uninsured malpractice but the amount of damages is uncertain. The hospital estimates that the liability will fall between $1.0 and $2.5 million. In this case, the hospital must record a loss or expense and a liability for $1.0 million. The income statement will report the loss and the balance sheet the liability. Also, the hospital must disclose in a note the possibility of an additional $1.5 million loss.

Summary Problem for Your Review

This problem consists of three independent parts.

1. A Wendy's hamburger restaurant made cash sales of $4,000 subject to a 5 percent sales tax. Record the sales and the related sales tax. Also record Wendy's payment of the tax to the state government.

2. At April 30, 19X2, H. J. Heinz Company reported its 6 percent long-term debt:

Current Liabilities (in part)	Millions
Portion of long-term debt due within one year. . . .	$ 14
Interest payable ($200 × .06 × 5/12)	5
Long-Term Debt and Other Liabilities (in part)	
Long-term debt	$186

The company pays interest on its long-term debt on November 30 each year.

Show how Heinz Company would report its liabilities on the year-end balance sheet at April 30, 19X3. Assume the current maturity of its long-term debt is $16 million, and the long-term portion is $170 million.

3. What distinguishes a contingent liability from an actual liability?

SOLUTION TO REVIEW PROBLEM

1.

Cash ($4,000 × 1.05)	4,200	
Sales Revenue.......................................		4,000
Sales Tax Payable ($4,000 × .05).....................		200
To record cash sales and related sales tax.		
Sales Tax Payable......................................	200	
Cash		200
To pay sales tax to the state government.		

2.   H. J. Heinz Company balance sheet at April 30, 19X3:

Current Liabilities (in part)	Millions
Portion of long-term debt due within one year . . .	$ 16.00
Interest payable ($186 × .06 × 5/12)...........	4.65
Long-Term Debt and Other Liabilities (in part)	
Long-term debt............................	$170.00

3. A contingent liability is a *potential* liability, which may or may not become an actual liability.

Accounting for Payroll ———————————————

Payroll, also called *employee compensation,* is a major expense of many businesses. For service organizations, such as CPA firms, real estate brokers, and travel agents, payroll is *the* major expense of conducting business. Service organizations sell their employees' service, so employee compensation is their primary cost of doing business, just as cost of goods sold is the largest expense in merchandising.

Employee compensation takes different forms. Some employees collect a **salary,** which is income stated at a yearly, monthly, or weekly rate. Other employees work for **wages,** which is employee pay stated at an hourly figure. Sales employees often receive a **commission,** which is a percentage of the sales the employee has made. Some companies reward excellent performance with a **bonus,** an amount over and above regular compensation.

Businesses often pay employees at a base rate for a set number of hours — called straight time. For working any additional hours — called overtime — the employee receives a higher rate.

Assume that Lucy Childres is an accountant for an electronics company. Lucy earns $600 per week straight time. The company work week runs 40 hours, so Lucy's hourly straight-time pay is $15 ($600/40). Her company pays her **time and a half** for overtime. That rate is 150 percent (1.5 times) the straight-time rate. Thus Lucy earns $22.50 for each hour of overtime she works ($15.00 × 1.5 = $22.50). For working 42 hours during a week, she earns $645, computed as follows:

Straight-time pay for 40 hours	$600
Overtime pay for 2 overtime hours:	
2 × $22.50	45
Total pay	$645

Gross Pay and Net Pay

Many years ago, employees brought home all that they had earned. For example, Lucy Childres would have taken home the full $645 total that she made. Payroll accounting was straightforward. Those days are long past.

The federal government, most state governments, and even some city governments demand that employers act as collection agents for employee taxes, which are deducted from employee checks. Insurance companies, labor unions, and other organizations may also receive pieces of employees' pay. Amounts withheld from an employee's check are called deductions.

Gross pay is the total amount of salary, wages, commissions, or any other employee compensation before taxes and other deductions are taken out. **Net pay** —the gross pay minus all deductions—is the amount that the employee actually takes home.

Many companies also pay employee **fringe benefits,** which are a form of employee compensation like health and life insurance and retirement pay, which the employee does not receive immediately in cash. Payroll accounting has become quite complex. Let's turn now to a discussion of payroll deductions.

Payroll Deductions

Payroll deductions that are *withheld* from employees' *pay* fall into two categories: (1) *required deductions,* which include employee income tax and social security tax; and (2) *optional deductions,* which include union dues, insurance premiums, charitable contributions, and other amounts that are withheld at the employee's request. After they are withheld, payroll deductions become the liability of the employer who assumes responsibility for paying the outside party. For example, the employer pays the government the employee income tax withheld and pays the union the employee union dues withheld.

Required Payroll Deductions

Employee Income Tax. The law requires most employers to withhold income tax from their employees' salaries and wages. The amount of income tax deducted from gross pay is called **withheld income tax.** For many employees, this deduc-

EXHIBIT 11-1 *W-4 Form*

```
------------------  Cut here and give the certificate to your employer. Keep the top portion for your records.  ------------------

Form  W-4          Employee's Withholding Allowance Certificate          OMB No. 1545-0010
Department of the Treasury    ▶ For Privacy Act and Paperwork Reduction Act Notice, see reverse.        1988
Internal Revenue Service
1 Type or print your first name and middle initial    Last name                2 Your social security number
  R.C.                                                 Dean                       344-86-4529
  Home address (number and street or rural route)           ☐ Single   [X] Married
  4376 Palm Drive                                   3 Marital  ☐ Married, but withhold at higher Single rate.
                                                      Status   Note: If married, but legally separated, or spouse is a
  City or town, state, and ZIP code                          nonresident alien, check the Single box.
  Fort Lauderdale, FL 33317

4 Total number of allowances you are claiming (from line G above or from the Worksheets on back if they apply) .  4 | 4
5 Additional amount, if any, you want deducted from each pay  .  .  .  .  .  .  .  .  .  .  .  .  .  .  5 | $
6 I claim exemption from withholding because (check boxes below that apply):
  a  ☐ Last year I did not owe any Federal income tax and had a right to a full refund of ALL income tax withheld, AND
  b  ☐ This year I do not expect to owe any Federal income tax and expect to have a right to a full refund of
        ALL income tax withheld.
  c   If both a and b apply and you satisfy the additional conditions outlined above under "Exemption From      Year
      Withholding," enter the year effective and "EXEMPT" here. Do not complete lines 4 and 5 above .  .  .  .  ▶  19
7 Are you a full-time student? ( Note: Full-time students are not automatically exempt.)                        ☐ Yes  [X] No
Under penalties of perjury, I certify that I am entitled to the number of withholding allowances claimed on this certificate or, if claiming exemption from withholding, that I am
entitled to claim the exempt status.
Employee's signature ▶   R.C. Dean                        Date ▶  7-22        , 1988
8 Employer's name and address (Employer: Complete 8, 9, and 10 only if sending to IRS)  9 Office  10 Employer identification number
  Blumenthal's                                                                          code
  Crescent Square Shopping Center                                                        14       83-19475
  Fort Lauderdale, FL 33310
```

tion is the largest. The amount withheld depends on the employee's gross pay and on the number of withholding allowances the employee claims.

Each employee may claim himself or herself, his or her spouse, and each dependent as a withholding allowance. An unmarried taxpayer has one allowance, a married couple two allowances, a married couple with one child three allowances, and so on. Each allowance lowers the amount of tax withheld from the employee's paycheck. The employee files a Form W-4 with the employer to indicate the number of allowances claimed for withholding purposes. Exhibit 11-1 shows a W-4 for R. C. Dean, who claims four.

The employer sends its employees' withheld income tax to the government. The amount of the income tax withheld determines how often the employer submits tax payments. The employer must remit the taxes to the government at least quarterly. Every business must account for payroll taxes on a calendar-year basis regardless of its fiscal year.

The employer accumulates taxes in the Employee Income Tax Payable account. The word *payable* indicates that the account is the employer's liability to the government, even though the employees are the people taxed.

Employee Social Security (FICA) Tax.   The *Federal Insurance Contributions Act (FICA)*, also known as the Social Security Act, created the Social Security Tax. The Social Security program provides retirement, disability, and medical benefits. The law requires employers to withhold Social Security (FICA) tax from employees' pay.

The amount of tax withheld from employees' pay varies from year to year as Congress adjusts tax rates and the level of employee pay subject to the tax. In recent years, both of these factors have risen dramatically, as shown in Exhibit 11-2.

Because the FICA tax rate has hovered near 7 percent for the first $40,000 that the employee earns in a year, we use these figures in our examples and in the assignment materials at the end of the chapter. For each employee who earns $40,000 or more, the employer withholds $2,800 ($40,000 × .07) from the employee's pay and sends that amount to the federal government. The employer records this employee tax in the account, FICA Tax Payable.

Assume that Rex Jennings, an employee, earned $38,500 prior to December.

EXHIBIT 11-2 *Social Security Taxes*

Year	Employee Earnings Subject to the Tax	Social Security (FICA) Tax Rate	Maximum Amount of Social Security (FICA) Tax Withheld from Employee Pay during the Year
1980	$25,900	.0613	$1,588
1985	39,600	.0705	2,792
1987	43,800	.0715	3,132
1989	48,000	.0751	3,605
1990 and beyond	*	.0765	?

* Adjusted for the increase in the cost of living.

Jennings's salary for December is $3,500. How much FICA tax will be withheld from his December paycheck? The computation follows.

Employee earnings subject to the tax in one year	$40,000
Employee earnings prior to the current pay period	38,500
Current pay subject to FICA tax	$ 1,500
FICA tax rate	× .07
FICA tax to be withheld from current pay	$105.00

Optional Payroll Deductions

As a convenience to its employees, many companies make payroll deductions and disburse cash according to employee instructions. Union dues, insurance payments, payroll savings plans, and gifts to charities are examples. The account Employees' Union Dues Payable holds employee deductions for union membership.

Employer Payroll Taxes

Employers must bear the expense of at least three payroll taxes: (1) Social Security (FICA) tax, (2) state unemployment compensation tax, and (3) federal unemployment compensation tax.

Employer FICA Tax. In addition to the responsibility of handling the employee contribution to Social Security, the employer also must pay into the program. The employer's Social Security tax is the same as the amount withheld from employee pay. Thus the Social Security system is funded by equal contributions from employees and employers. Using our 7 percent and $40,000 annual pay figures, the maximum annual employer tax on each employee is $2,800 ($40,000 × .07). The liability account the employer uses for this payroll tax is the same FICA Tax Payable account used for the amount withheld from employee pay. The tax rate and the amount of earnings subject to the tax both change as Congress passes new legislation.

State and Federal Unemployment Compensation Taxes.   These two payroll taxes are products of the Federal Unemployment Tax Act (FUTA). In recent years, employers have paid a combined tax of 6.2 percent on the first $7,000 of each employee's annual earnings. The proportion paid to the state is 5.4 percent, and .8 percent is paid to the federal government. The government then uses the money to pay unemployment benefits to people who are out of work. The employer uses the accounts Federal Unemployment Tax Payable and State Unemployment Tax Payable.

Payroll Entries

Exhibit 11-3 summarizes an employer's entries to record a monthly payroll of $10,000 (all amounts are assumed for illustration only).

Entry A in Exhibit 11-3 records the employer's *salary expense.* The *gross salary* of all employees, $10,000, is their monthly pay before any deductions. The federal government imposes the two taxes. Most states and some cities also levy income taxes, which are accounted for in like manner. The union dues are optional. Employees' take-home (net) pay is $7,960. The important point about this payroll transaction is that the employees pay their own income and FICA taxes and union dues. The employer serves merely as a collecting agent and sends these amounts to the government and the union.

Entry B records the employer's *payroll taxes.* In addition to the employees' FICA tax ($700 in entry A), the employer must also pay the $700 FICA tax shown in entry B. The other two employer payroll taxes are state and federal unemployment taxes. *Employees* make no payments for unemployment taxes.

Entry C records employee *fringe benefits* paid by the employer. The company in

EXHIBIT 11-3   *Payroll Accounting by the Employer*

OBJECTIVE 4
Make basic payroll entries

A.	Salary Expense (or Wage Expense or Commission Expense)	10,000	
	Employee Income Tax Payable		1,200
	FICA Tax Payable ($10,000 × .07)		700
	Employee Union Dues Payable		140
	Salary Payable to Employees (take-home pay)		7,960
	To record *salary expense.*		
B.	Payroll Tax Expense	1,320	
	FICA Tax Payable ($10,000 × .07)		700
	State Unemployment Tax Payable ($10,000 × .054)		540
	Federal Unemployment Tax Payable ($10,000 × .008)		80
	To record employer's *payroll taxes.*		
C.	Health Insurance Expense for Employees	800	
	Life Insurance Expense for Employees	200	
	Pension Expense	500	
	Employee Benefits Payable		1,500
	To record employee *fringe benefits* payable by employer.		

the exhibit pays health and life insurance for its employees, a common practice. Also, the employer funds pensions (that is, pays cash into a pension plan) for the benefit of employees when they retire. In the exhibit, the employer's pension expense for the month is $500, and the total employer expense for fringe benefits is $1,500. The total payroll expense of the employer in Exhibit 11-3 is $12,820 (gross salary of $10,000 + employer payroll taxes of $1,320 + fringe benefits of $1,500).

A company's payments to people who are not employees — outsiders called independent contractors — are *not* company payroll expenses. Consider two CPAs, Fermi and Scott. Fermi is a corporation's chief financial officer. Scott is the corporation's outside auditor. Fermi is an employee of the corporation and his compensation is a debit to Salary Expense. Scott, on the other hand, performs auditing service for many clients, and the corporation debits Auditing Expense when it pays her. Any payment for services performed by a person outside the company is a debit to an expense account other than payroll.

The Payroll System

Good business means paying employees all that they have earned — and paying them on time. Also, companies face the legal responsibility of handling employees' and their own payroll taxes, as we have seen. These demands require companies to process a great deal of payroll data. Efficient accounting is important. To make payroll accounting accurate and effective, accountants have developed the payroll system.

The components of the payroll system are a *payroll register*, a special *payroll bank account, payroll checks,* and an *earnings record* for each employee.

Payroll Register

OBJECTIVE 5

Use a payroll-accounting system

Each pay period, the company organizes the payroll data in a special journal called the *payroll register*, or *payroll journal*. This register lists each employee and the figures the business needs to record payroll amounts. The payroll register, which resembles the cash disbursement register, or check register, also serves as a check register by providing a column for recording each payroll check number.

The payroll register in Exhibit 11-4 includes sections for recording Gross Pay, Deductions, Net Pay, and Account Debited. *Gross Pay* has columns for straight-time pay, overtime pay, and total gross pay for each employee. Columns under the *Deductions* heading vary from company to company. Of course the employer must deduct federal income tax and FICA tax. (State tax is left out for convenience.) Additional column headings depend on which optional deductions the business handles. In the exhibit, the employer deducts employee payroll taxes, union dues, and gifts to United Way and then sends the amounts to the proper parties. The business may add deduction columns as needed. The *Net Pay* section lists each employee's net (take-home) pay and the number of the check issued to him or her. The last two columns indicate the *Account Debited* for the employee's gross pay. (The company has office workers and sales people.)

In the exhibit, W. L. Chen earned gross pay of $500. His net pay was $386.45, paid with check number 1621. Chen is an office worker, so his salary is debited to Office Salary Expense.

Note that the business deducted no FICA tax from E. A. Trimble. She has

EXHIBIT 11-4 *Payroll Register*

Week ended December 27, 19X3

Employee Name	Hours	Gross Pay a Straight-time	b Overtime	c Total	Deductions d Federal Income Tax	e FICA Tax	f Union Dues	g United Way Charities	h Total	Net Pay i (c−h) Amount	j Check No.	Account Debited k Office Salary Expense	l Sales Salary Expense
Chen, W. L.	40	500.00		500.00	71.05	35.00	5.00	2.50	113.55	386.45	1621	500.00	
Dean, R. C.	46	400.00	90.00	490.00	59.94	34.30		2.00	96.24	393.76	1622		490.00
Ellis, M.	41	560.00	21.00	581.00	86.14	40.67	5.00		131.81	449.19	1623	581.00	
Trimble, E. A.	40	1,360.00		1,360.00	463.22		85.00	15.00	478.22	881.78	1641		1,360.00
Total		12,940.00	714.00	13,654.00	3,167.76	801.36	85.00	155.00	4,209.12	9,444.88		4,464.00	9,190.00

already earned more than $40,000. Any employee whose earnings exceed this annual maximum pays no additional FICA tax during that year.

The payroll register in Exhibit 11-4 gives the employer the information needed to record salary expense for the pay period. Using the total amounts for columns d through l, the employer records total salary expense as follows:

Dec. 27	Office Salary Expense	4,464.00	
	Sales Salary Expense	9,190.00	
	Employee Income Tax Payable		3,167.76
	FICA Tax Payable		801.36
	Employee Union Dues Payable		85.00
	Employee United Way Payable		155.00
	Salary Payable to Employees		9,444.88

Payroll Bank Account

After recording the payroll, the company books include a credit balance in Salary Payable to Employees for net pay of $9,444.88. (See Column i in Exhibit 11-4.) How the business pays this liability depends on its payroll system. Many companies disburse paychecks to employees from a special payroll bank account. The employer draws a check for net pay ($9,444.88 in our illustration) on its regular bank account and deposits this check in the special payroll bank account. Then the company writes paychecks to employees out of the payroll account. When the paychecks clear the bank, the payroll account has a zero balance, ready for the activity of the next pay period. Disbursing paychecks from a separate bank account isolates net pay for analysis and control, as discussed later in the chapter.

Other payroll disbursements—for withheld taxes, union dues, and so on—are neither as numerous nor as frequent as weekly or monthly paychecks. The employer pays taxes, union dues, and charities from its regular bank account.

Payroll Checks

Most companies pay employees by check. A *payroll check* is like any other check except that its perforated attachment lists the employee's gross pay, payroll deductions, and net pay. These amounts are taken from the payroll register. Exhibit 11-5 shows payroll check number 1622, issued to R. C. Dean for net pay of $393.76 earned during the week ended December 27, 19X3. To enhance your ability to use payroll data, trace all amounts on the check attachment to the payroll register in Exhibit 11-4.

Recording Cash Disbursements for Payroll _____

Most employers must make at least three entries to record payroll cash disbursements: net pay to employees, payroll taxes to the government and payroll deductions, and employee fringe benefits.

Net Pay to Employees.   When the employer issues payroll checks to employees, the company debits Salary Payable to Employees and credits Cash.

EXHIBIT 11-5 *Payroll Check*

| Blumenthal's Payroll Account Fort Lauderdale, FL | | | | | | 1622 |

```
Blumenthal's                                                    1622
Payroll Account
Fort Lauderdale, FL
                                              12-27  19 X3

Pay to the     R. C. Dean                              $   393.76
Order of

Three hundred ninety-three & 76/100 ---------------------- Dollars

Republic Bank
Fort Lauderdale,
Florida  33310
                                              Anna Figaro
                                                        Treasurer

  ⑈ ⑆111900031⑈  0787⑈500004654⑈
```

Pay			Deductions					Net Pay	Check No.
Straight-time	Over-time	Gross	Income Tax	FICA	Union Dues	United Way	Total		
400.00	90.00	490.00	59.94	34.30		2.00	96.24	393.76	1622

Using the data in Exhibit 11-4, the company would make the following entry to record the cash payment (column i) for the December 27 weekly payroll:

Dec. 27	Salary Payable to Employees	9,444.88	
	Cash		9,444.88

Payroll Taxes to the Government and Payroll Deductions. The employer must send to the government two sets of payroll taxes: those withheld from employees' pay and those paid by the employer. Based on Exhibit 11-4, columns d through g, the business would record a series of cash payment entries summarized as follows (employer tax amounts are assumed):

Dec. 27	Employee Income Tax Payable	3,167.76	
	FICA Tax Payable ($801.36 × 2)	1,602.72	
	Employee Union Dues Payable	85.00	
	Employee United Way Payable	155.00	
	State Unemployment Tax Payable	104.62	
	Federal Unemployment Tax Payable	15.50	
	Cash		5,130.60

Fringe Benefits. The employer might pay for employees' insurance coverage and pension plan. Assuming the total cash payment for these benefits is $1,927.14, this entry for payments to third parties would be

Dec. 27	Employee Benefits Payable	1,927.14	
	Cash		1,927.14

Earnings Record

The employer must file payroll tax returns with the federal and state governments and must provide the employee with a wage and tax statement, Form W-2, at the end of the year. Therefore, employers maintain an earnings record for each

EXHIBIT 11-6 *Employee Earnings Record for 19X3*

Employee Name and Address:

Dean, R. C.
4376 Palm Drive
Fort Lauderdale, FL 33317

Social Security No.: 344-86-4529
Marital Status: Married
Withholding Exemptions: 4
Pay Rate: $400 per week
Job Title: Salesperson

Week Ended	Hours	Gross Pay				Deductions					Net Pay	
		Straight-time	Overtime	Total	To Date	Federal Income Tax	FICA Tax	Union Dues	United Way Charities	Total	Amount	Check No.
Nov. 29	40	400.00		400.00	21,340.00	42.19	28.00		2.00	72.19	327.81	1525
Dec. 6	40	400.00		400.00	21,740.00	42.19	28.00		2.00	72.19	327.81	1548
Dec. 13	44	400.00	60.00	460.00	22,200.00	54.76	32.20		2.00	88.96	371.04	1574
Dec. 20	48	400.00	120.00	520.00	22,720.00	66.75	36.40		2.00	105.15	414.85	1598
Dec. 27	46	400.00	90.00	490.00	23,210.00	59.94	34.30		2.00	96.24	393.76	1622
Total		20,800.00	2,410.00	23,210.00		2,346.72	1,555.07		104.00	4,005.79	19,204.21	

employee. Exhibit 11-6 is a five-week excerpt from the earnings record of employee R. C. Dean.

The employee earnings record is not a journal or a ledger, and it is not required by law. It is an accounting tool—like the worksheet—that the employer uses to prepare payroll tax reports. Year-to-date earnings also indicate when an employee has earned $40,000, the point at which the employer can stop deducting FICA tax.

Exhibit 11-7 is the Wage and Tax Statement, Form W-2, for employee R. C. Dean. The employer prepares this statement and gives copies to the employee and to the Internal Revenue Service (IRS). Dean uses the W-2 to prepare his personal income tax return. The IRS uses the W-2 to ensure that Dean is paying income tax on all his income from that job. The IRS matches Dean's income as reported on his tax return with his earnings as reported on the W-2.

Internal Control over Payrolls

The internal controls over cash disbursements discussed in Chapter 7 apply to payroll. In addition, companies adopt special controls in payroll accounting. The large number of transactions and the many different parties involved increase the risk of a control failure. Accounting systems feature two types of special controls over payroll: controls for efficiency and controls for safeguarding cash.

Controls for Efficiency

For companies with many employees, reconciling the bank account can be time consuming because of the large number of outstanding payroll checks. For example, a March 30 payroll check would probably not have time to clear the bank before a bank statement on March 31. This check and others in a March 30 payroll would be outstanding. Identifying a large number of outstanding checks for the bank reconciliation increases accounting expense. To limit the number of outstanding checks, many companies use two payroll bank accounts. They make payroll disbursements from one payroll account one month and from the other

EXHIBIT 11-7 *Employee Wage and Tax Statement, Form W-2*

payroll account the next month. By reconciling each account every other month, a March 30 paycheck has until April 30 to clear the bank before the account is reconciled. This essentially eliminates outstanding checks, cuts down the time it takes to prepare the bank reconciliation, and decreases accounting expense. Also, many companies' checks become void if not cashed within a certain period of time. This too limits the number of outstanding checks.

Other payroll controls for efficiency include following established policies for hiring and firing employees and complying with government regulations. Hiring and firing policies provide guidelines for keeping a qualified, diligent work force dedicated to achieving the business's goals. Complying with government regulations avoids paying fines and penalties.

Controls for Safeguarding of Cash

Owners and managers of small businesses can monitor their payroll disbursements by personal contact with their employees. Large corporations cannot do so. These businesses must establish controls to assure that payroll disbursements are made only to legitimate employees and for the correct amounts. A particular danger is that payroll checks may be written to a fictitious employee and cashed by a dishonest employee. To guard against this crime and other possible breakdowns in internal control, large businesses adopt strict internal control policies.

The duties of hiring and firing employees should be separated from the duties of distributing paychecks. Otherwise, a dishonest supervisor, for example, could add a fictitious employee to the payroll. When paychecks are issued, the supervisor could simply pocket the nonexistent person's paycheck for his or her own use.

Requiring an identification badge bearing an employee's photograph helps internal control. Issuing pay checks only to employees with badges ensures that only actual employees receive pay.

On occasion management should instruct an employee from the home office, perhaps an internal auditor, to distribute checks in the branch office personally rather than have the payroll department mail the checks. No one will claim a paycheck that has been issued to a fictitious employee. Any check left over after the distribution signals that payroll fraud has been attempted. Management would pursue an investigation.

A time-keeping system helps ensure that employees have actually worked the number of hours claimed. Having employees punch time cards at the start and end of the work day proves their attendance—as long as management makes sure that no employee punches in and out for others too. Some companies have their workers fill in weekly or monthly time sheets.

Again we see that the key to good internal control is separation of duties. The responsibilities of the personnel department, the payroll department, the accounting department, time-card management, and paycheck distribution should be kept separate.

Reporting Payroll Expense and Liabilities _____

At the end of its fiscal year, the company reports the amount of *payroll liability* owed to all parties—employees, state and federal governments, unions, and so forth. Payroll liability is *not* the payroll expense for the year. The liability at year end is the amount of the expense that is still unpaid. Payroll expense appears on the income statement, payroll liability on the balance sheet.

Exhibit 11-8   *Partial Burroughs Corporation Balance Sheet*

OBJECTIVE 6
Report current liabilities

Current Liabilities	Millions
Notes payable within one year	$ 397
Current maturities of long-term debt	31
Accounts payable	397
Accrued payrolls and commissions	**164**
Accrued taxes other than income taxes	69
Customers' deposits and prepayments	155
Dividends payable to shareholders	28
Estimated income taxes	111
Total current liabilities	$1,352

Burroughs Corporation reported accrued payrolls and commissions of approximately $164 million as a current liability on its year-end balance sheet (see Exhibit 11-8). However, Burroughs's payroll expense for the year far exceeded $164 million. (Exhibit 11-8 also presents the other current liabilities that we have discussed in this chapter.)

Exhibit 11-9 summarizes all the current liabilities that we have discussed in this chapter.

Computer Accounting Systems for Current Liabilities

Current liabilities arising from a high volume of similar transactions are well suited for computerized accounting. One of the most common transactions of a merchandiser is the credit purchase of inventory. It is efficient to integrate the

EXHIBIT 11-9   *Categories of Current Liabilities*

Amount of Liability Known When Recorded	Amount of Liability Must Be Estimated When Recorded
Trade accounts payable	Warranty payable
Short-term notes payable	Income tax payable
Sales tax payable	
Current portion of long-term debt	
Accrued expenses payable:	
Interest payable	
Payroll liabilities (salary payable, wages payable, and commissions payable)	
Payroll taxes payable (employee and employer)	
Unearned revenues (revenues collected in advance of being earned)	
Customer deposits payable	

accounts payable and perpetual inventory systems. When merchandise dips below a predetermined level, the system automatically prepares a purchase request. After the order is placed and the goods are received, inventory and accounts payable data are entered on magnetic tape. The computer reads the tape, then debits Inventory and credits Accounts Payable to account for the purchase. For payments, the computer debits Accounts Payable and credits Cash. The program may also update account balances and print journals, ledger accounts, and the financial statements.

The face amount of notes payable and their interest rates and payment dates can be stored for electronic data processing. Computer programs calculate interest, print the interest checks, journalize the transactions, and update account balances.

Payroll transactions are also ideally suited for computer processing. Employee pay rates and withholding data are stored on magnetic tape. Each payroll period, computer operators enter the number of hours worked by each employee. The machine performs the calculations, prints the payroll register and pay checks, and updates the employee earnings records. The program also computes payroll taxes and prepares quarterly reports to government agencies. Expense and liability accounts are automatically updated for the payroll transactions.

The estimated amounts of current liabilities for warranties and income taxes may require personal attention. However, once accountants estimate these liabilities, their amounts can be entered into accounts that are maintained in computerized form.

Summary Problem for Your Review

Beth Denius, Limited, a clothing store, employs one salesperson, Alan Kingsley. His straight-time pay is $360 per week. He earns time and a half for hours worked in excess of 40 per week. Denius withholds income tax (11.0 percent) and FICA tax (7.0 percent) from Kingsley's pay. She also pays the following employer payroll taxes: FICA (7.0 percent) and state and federal unemployment (5.4 percent and 0.8 percent, respectively). In addition, Denius contributes to a pension plan an amount equal to 10 percent of Kingsley's gross pay.

During the week ended December 26, 19X4, Kingsley worked 48 hours. Prior to this week Kingsley has earned $5,470.

Required

1. Compute Kingsley's gross pay and net pay for the week.
2. Record the following payroll entries that Denius would make:
   a. Expense for Kingsley's salary, including overtime pay
   b. Employer payroll taxes
   c. Expense for fringe benefits
   d. Payment of cash to Kingsley
   e. Payment of all payroll taxes
   f. Payment for fringe benefits
3. How much total payroll expense did Denius incur for the week? How much cash did the business spend on its payroll?

SOLUTION TO REVIEW PROBLEM

Requirement 1

Gross Pay:	Straight-time pay for 40 hours.................		$360.00	
	Overtime pay:			
	Rate per hour ($360/40 × 1.5)........	$13.50		
	Hours (48 − 40)...................	X 8	108.00	
	Total gross pay		$468.00	
Net Pay:	Gross pay................................			$468.00
	Less: Withheld income tax ($468 × .11)		$ 51.48	
	Withheld FICA tax ($468 × .07)		32.76	84.24
	Net pay			$383.76

Requirement 2

a.	Sales Salary Expense	468.00	
	Employee Income Tax Payable		51.48
	FICA Tax Payable....................................		32.76
	Salary Payable to Employee...........................		383.76
b.	Payroll Tax Expense..................................	61.77	
	FICA Tax Payable ($468 × .07).........................		32.76
	State Unemployment Tax Payable ($468 × .054)...........		25.27
	Federal Unemployment Tax Payable ($468 × .008).........		3.74
c.	Pension Expense ($468 × .10)...........................	46.80	
	Employee Benefits Payable		46.80
d.	Salary Payable to Employee	383.76	
	Cash		383.76
e.	Employee Income Tax Payable	51.48	
	FICA Tax Payable ($32.76 × 2).........................	65.52	
	State Unemployment Tax Payable	25.27	
	Federal Unemployment Tax Payable	3.74	
	Cash		146.01
f.	Employee Benefits Payable	46.80	
	Cash		46.80

Requirement 3

Denius incurred *total payroll expense* of $576.57 (gross salary of $468.00 + payroll taxes of $61.77 + fringe benefits of $46.80). See entries a–c.

Denius *paid cash* of $576.57 on payroll (Kingsley's net pay of $383.76 + payroll taxes of $146.01 + fringe benefits of $46.80). See entries d–f.

Summary _____

Current liabilities may be divided into those of *known amount* and those that must be *estimated.* Trade accounts payable, short-term notes payable, and the related liability for accrued expenses are among current liabilities of known amount. Current liabilities that must be estimated are warranties payable and corporations' income tax payable.

Contingent liabilities are not actual liabilities but potential liabilities that may arise in the future. Contingent liabilities, like current libilities, may be of known amount or an indefinite amount. A business that faces a lawsuit not yet decided in court has a contingent liability of indefinite amount.

Payroll accounting handles the expenses and liabilities arising from compensating employees. Employers must withhold income and FICA taxes from employees' pay and send these *employee payroll taxes* to the government. In addition, many employers allow their employees to pay for insurance and union dues and to make gifts to charities through payroll deductions. An employee's net pay is the gross pay less all payroll taxes and optional deductions.

An *employer's* payroll expenses include FICA and unemployment taxes, which are separate from the payroll taxes borne by the employees. Also, most employers provide their employees with fringe benefits, like insurance coverage and retirement pensions.

A *payroll system* consists of a payroll register, a payroll bank account, payroll checks, and an earnings record for each employee. Good *internal controls* over payroll disbursements help the business to conduct payroll accounting efficiently and to safeguard the company's cash. The cornerstone of internal controls is the separation of duties.

Current liabilities arising from a high volume of repetitive transactions are well suited for computer processing. Trade accounts payable, notes payable and the related interest, and payrolls are three examples.

Self-Study Questions

Test your understanding of the chapter by marking the best answer for each of the following questions.

1. A $10,000, 9 percent, one-year note payable was issued on July 31. The balance sheet at December 31 will report interest payable of *(p. 424)*
   a. $0 because the interest is not due yet
   b. $300
   c. $375
   d. $900

2. If the note payable in the preceding question had been discounted, the cash proceeds from issuance would have been *(p. 424)*
   a. $9,100
   b. $9,625
   c. $9,700
   d. $10,000

3. Which of the following liabilities creates *no* expense for the company? *(p. 426)*
   a. Interest
   b. Sales tax
   c. FICA tax
   d. Warranty

4. Suppose Unitex Tire Company estimates that warranty costs will equal 1 percent of tire sales. Assume that November sales totaled $900,000, and the company's outlay in tires and cash to satisfy warranty claims was $7,400. How much warranty expense should the November income statement report? *(p. 428, 429)*
   a. $1,600
   b. $7,400
   c. $9,000
   d. $16,400

5. XYZ Company is a defendant in a lawsuit that claims damages of $55,000. On the balance sheet date, it appears likely that the court will render a judgment against the company. How should XYZ report this event in its financial statements? *(p. 430)*
   a. Omit mention because no judgment has been rendered
   b. Disclose the contingent liability in a note
   c. Use a short presentation only
   d. Report the loss on the income statement and the liability on the balance sheet

6. Emilie Frontenac's weekly pay is $320, plus time and half for overtime. The tax rates applicable to her earnings are 8 percent for income tax and 7 percent for FICA. What is Emilie's take-home pay for a week in which she works 50 hours? *(pp. 432, 435)*
   a. $374.00
   b. $392.00
   c. $404.80
   d. $440.00

7. Which payroll tax applies (or taxes apply) only to the employer? *(pp. 434, 435)*
   a. Withheld income tax
   b. FICA tax
   c. Unemployment compensation tax
   d. Both b and c

8. The main reason for using a separate payroll bank account is to *(p. 438)*
   a. Safegurd cash by avoiding writing payroll checks to fictitious employees
   b. Safeguard cash by limiting paychecks to amounts based on time cards
   c. Increase efficiency by isolating payroll disbursements for analysis and control
   d. All of the above

9. The key to good internal controls in the payroll area is *(p. 442)*
   a. Using a payroll bank account
   b. Separating payroll duties
   c. Using a payroll register
   d. Using time cards

10. Which of the following items is reported as a current liability on the balance sheet? *(p. 443)*
    a. Short-term notes payable
    b. Estimated warranties
    c. Accrued payroll taxes
    d. All of the above

Answers to the self-study questions are at the end of the chapter.

Accounting Vocabulary

bonus *(p. 431)*, commission *(p. 431)*, current portion of long-term debt *(p. 426)*, discounting a note payable *(p. 424)*, FICA tax *(p. 433)*, fringe benefits *(p. 432)*, gross pay *(p. 432)*, net pay *(p. 432)*, payroll *(p. 431)*, salary *(p. 431)*, short presentation *(pp. 429, 430)*, short-term note payable *(p. 424)*, Social Security tax *(p. 433)*, time and a half *(p. 432)*, unemployment compensation tax *(p. 435)*, wages *(p. 431)*, withheld income tax *(p. 432)*.

ASSIGNMENT MATERIAL _____

Questions

1. Give a more descriptive account title for each of the following current liabilities: Accrued Interest, Accrued Salaries, Accrued Income Tax.

2. What distinguishes a current liability from a long-term liability? What distinguishes a contingent liability from an actual liability?

3. A company purchases a machine by signing a $21,000, 10 percent, one-year note payable on July 31. Interest is to be paid at maturity. What two current liabilities related to this purchase does the company report on its December 31 balance sheet? What is the amount of each liability?

4. A company borrowed cash by discounting a $15,000, 8 percent, six-month note payable to the bank, receiving cash of $14,400. (a) Show how the amount of cash was computed. Also, identify (b) the total amount of interest expense to be recognized on this note and (c) the amount of the borrower's cash payment at maturity.

5. Explain how sales tax that is paid by consumers is a liability of the store that sold the merchandise.

6. What is meant by the term *current portion of long-term debt,* and how is this item reported in the financial statements?

7. At the beginning of the school term, what type of account is the tuition that your college or university collects from students? What type of account is the tuition at the end of the school term?

8. Why is a customer deposit a liability? Give an example.

9. Patton Company warrants its products against defects for three years from date of sale. During the current year, the company made sales of $300,000. Store manage-

ment estimates warranty costs on those sales will total $18,000 over the three-year warranty period. Ultimately, the company paid $22,000 cash on warranties. What is the company's warranty expense for the year? What accounting principle governs this answer?

10. Identify two contingent liabilities of a definite amount and two contingent liabilities of an indefinite amount.

11. Describe two ways to report contingent liabilities.

12. Why is payroll expense relatively more important to a service business such as a CPA firm, than it is to a merchandising company?

13. Two persons are studying Allen Company's manufacturing process. One person is Allen's factory supervisor, and the other person is an outside consultant who is an expert in the industry. Which person's salary is the payroll expense of Allen Company? Identify the expense account that Allen would debit to record the pay of each person.

14. What are two elements of an employer's payroll expense in addition to salaries, wages, commissions, and overtime pay?

15. What determines the amount of income tax that is withheld from employee paychecks?

16. What are FICA taxes? Who pays them? What are the funds used for?

17. Identify two required deductions and four optional deductions from employee paychecks.

18. Identify three employer payroll taxes.

19. Who pays state and federal unemployment taxes? What are these funds used for?

20. Briefly describe a payroll accounting system's components and their functions.

21. How much Social Security tax has been withheld from the pay of an employee who has earned $42,000 during the current year? How much Social Security tax must the employer pay for this employee?

22. Briefly describe the two principal categories of internal controls over payroll.

23. Why do some companies use two special payroll bank accounts?

24. Identify three internal controls designed to safeguard payroll cash.

Exercises

Exercise 11-1 *Recording note payable transactions*

Record the following note payable transactions of McBee Company in the company's general journal. Explanations are not required.

19X2

May 1 Purchased equipment costing $4,500 by issuing a one-year, 10 percent note payable.

Dec. 31 Accrued interest on the note payable.

19X3

May 1 Paid the note payable at maturity.

Exercise 11-2 *Discounting a note payable*

On November 1, 19X4, Maxwell Company discounted a six-month, $8,000 note payable to the bank at 12 percent.

Required

1. Prepare general journal entries to record (a) issuance of the note, (b) accrual of interest at December 31, and (c) payment of the note at maturity in 19X5. Explanations are not required.

2. Show how Maxwell would report the note on the December 31, 19X4, balance sheet.

Exercise 11-3 *Recording sales tax two ways*

Make general journal entries to record the following transactions of Ransom Distributors, Inc., for a two-month period. Explanations are not required.

March 31 Recorded cash sales of $68,100 for the month, plus sales tax of 7 percent collected on behalf of the state of California. Record sales tax in a separate account.

April 6 Sent March sales tax to the state.

Journalize these transactions a second time. Record the sales tax initially in the Sales Revenue account.

Exercise 11-4 *Reporting current and long-term liabilities*

Suppose Taco Bell borrowed $400,000 on December 31, 19X0, by issuing 9 percent long-term debt that must be paid in annual installments of $100,000 plus interest each January 2. By inserting appropriate amounts in the following excerpts from the company's partial balance sheet, show how Taco Bell would report its long-term debt.

	December 31,			
	19X1	**19X2**	**19X3**	**19X4**
Current liabilities:				
Current portion of long-term debt	$____	$____	$____	$____
Interest payable	____	____	____	____
Long-term liabilities:				
Long-term debt	____	____	____	____

Exercise 11-5 *Accounting for warranty expense and the related liability*

The accounting records of Shotwell, Inc., included the following balances at the end of the period:

Estimated Warranty Payable	Sales Revenue	Warranty Expense
Beg. bal 3,800	141,000	

In the past, Shotwell's warranty expense has been 8 percent of sales. During the current period, Shotwell paid $11,790 to satisfy the warranty claims of customers.

Required

1. Record Shotwell's warranty expense for the period and the company's cash payments during the period to satisfy warranty claims. Explanations are not required.
2. What ending balance of Estimated Warranty Payable will Shotwell report on its balance sheet?

Exercise 11-6 *Reporting a contingent liability*

Falcon Lamp Company is a defendant in lawsuits brought against the marketing and distribution of its products. Damages of $2 million are claimed against Falcon, but the company denies the charges and is vigorously defending itself. In a recent talk-show interview, the president of the company stated that he could not predict the outcome of the lawsuits. Nevertheless, he said, management does not believe that any actual liabilities resulting from the lawsuits will significantly affect the company's financial position.

Required

Prepare a partial balance sheet to show how Falcon Lamp Company would report this contingent liability in a short presentation. Total actual liabilities are $3 million. Also, write the disclosure note to describe the contingency.

Exercise 11-7 *Accruing a contingency*

Refer to the Falcon Lamp Company situation in the preceding exercise. Suppose that Falcon Lamp's attorneys believe it is probable that a judgment of $350,000 will be rendered against the company.

Required

Describe how to report this situation in the Falcon Lamp Company financial statements. Journalize any entry required under GAAP. Explanations are not required.

Exercise 11-8 *Computing net pay*

Chil Pilsbury is a salesman in the men's department of Rich's Department Store in Atlanta. He earns a base monthly salary of $550 plus an 8 percent commission on his sales. Through payroll deductions, Chil donates $5 per month to a charitable organization, and he authorizes Rich's to deduct $16.25 monthly for health insurance on his family. Tax rates on Chil's earnings are 9 percent for income tax and 7 percent for FICA, subject to the maximum. During the first 11 months of the year, he earned $37,140. Compute Chil's gross pay and net pay for December, assuming his sales for the month are $61,300.

Exercise 11-9 *Computing and recording gross pay and net pay*

Melanie Baker works for a Seven-Eleven store for straight-time earnings of $6 per hour, with time-and-a-half compensation for hours in excess of 40 per week. Melanie's payroll deductions include withheld income tax of 12 percent of total earnings, FICA tax of 7 percent of total earnings, and a weekly deduction of $5 for a charitable contribution to United Fund. Assuming Melanie worked 43 hours during the week, (a) compute her gross pay and net pay for the week, and (b) make a general journal entry to record the store's wage expense for Melanie's work, including her payroll deductions. Explanations are not required. Round all amounts to the nearest cent.

Exercise 11-10 *Recording a payroll*

Filene's Department Store incurred salary expense of $42,000 for December. The store's payroll expense includes employer FICA tax of 7 percent in addition to state unemployment tax of 5.4 percent and federal unemployment tax of .8 percent. Of the total salaries, $38,400 is subject to FICA tax, and $9,100 is subject to unemployment tax. Also, the store provides the following fringe benefits for employees: health insurance (cost to the store, $1,134.68); life insurance (cost to the store, $351.07); and pension benefits (cost to the store, $707.60). Record Filene's payroll taxes and its expenses for employee fringe benefits. Explanations are not required.

Problems   *(Group A)*

Problem 11-1A *Reporting current liabilities*

Following are six pertinent facts about events during the current year at Woodhaven Sales.

1. On September 30, Woodhaven signed a six-month, 9 percent note payable to purchase inventory costing $22,000. The note requires payment of principal and interest at maturity.

2. On October 31, Woodhaven discounted a $50,000 note payable to Lake Air National Bank and received cash of $44,000. The interest rate on the one-year note is 12 percent.

3. On November 30, Woodhaven received rent of $4,200 in advance for a lease on a building. This rent will be earned evenly over three months.

4. December sales totaled $38,000 and Woodhaven collected an additional state sales tax of 7 percent. This amount will be sent to the State of Arizona early in January.

5. Woodhaven owes $100,000 on a long-term note payable. At December 31, $20,000 of this principal plus $2,100 of accrued interest are payable within one year.

6. Sales of $430,000 were covered by Woodhaven's product warranty. At December 31 estimated warranty payable is $8,100.

Required

For each item, indicate the account and the related amount to be reported as a current liability on Woodhaven's December 31 balance sheet.

Problem 11-2A *Journalizing liability-related transactions*

The following transactions of Ortega, Inc., occurred during 19X4 and 19X5. Record the transactions in the company's general journal. Explanations are not required.

19X4

Jan.   9   Purchased inventory for $3,100, signing a six-month, 8 percent note payable.

      29   Recorded the week's sales of $10,240, three fourths on credit, and one fourth for cash. Sales amounts are subject to an additional 5 percent state sales tax.

Feb.   5   Sent the last week's sales tax to the state.

      28   Borrowed $300,000 on a 10 percent, long-term note payable that calls for annual installment payments of $50,000 principal plus interest.

Apr.   8   Received $778 in deposits from distributors of company products. Ortega refunds the deposits after six months.

July   9   Paid the six-month, 8 percent note at maturity.

Oct.   8   Refunded security deposits of $778 to distributors.

      22   Discounted a $5,000, 10 percent, 90-day note payable to the bank, receiving cash for the net amount after interest was deducted from the note's maturity value.

Nov. 30   Purchased a machine at a cost of $3,000, signing a 12 percent, six-month note payable for that amount.

Dec. 31   Accrued warranty expense, which is estimated at 2 1/2 percent of sales of $650,000.

      31   Accrued interest on all outstanding notes payable. Make a separate interest accrual entry for each note payable.

19X5

Jan. 20   Paid off the 10 percent discounted note payable. Made a separate entry for the interest.

Feb. 28   Paid the first installment and interest for one year on the long-term note payable.

May   31   Paid off the 12 percent machine note plus interest at maturity.

Problem 11-3A *Journalizing, posting, and reporting liabilities*

The general ledger of Mayes Company at June 30, 19X3, end of the company's fiscal year, includes the following account balances before adjusting entries. Parentheses indicate a debit balance.

Notes Payable, Short-Term ..	$ 21,000	Employer Payroll	
Discount on Notes Payable ..	(900)	Taxes Payable	$ —
Accounts Payable	105,520	Employee Benefits Payable ..	—
Current Portion of Long-		Sales Tax Payable	738
Term Debt Payable	—	Customer Deposits Payable ..	6,950
Interest Payable	—	Estimated Warranty Payable .	—
Salary Payable	—	Unearned Rent Revenue	4,800
Employee Payroll		Long-Term Debt Payable	120,000
Taxes Payable	—	Contingent Liabilities	—

The additional data needed to develop the adjusting entries at June 30 are as follows:

a. The $21,000 balance in Notes Payable, Short-Term consists of two notes. The first note, with a principal amount of $15,000, was issued on January 31. It matures six months from date of issuance and was discounted at 12 percent. The second note, with a principal amount of $6,000, was issued on April 22 for a term of 90 days. It bears interest at 10 percent. It was not discounted. Interest on this note will be paid at maturity.

b. The long-term debt is payable in annual installments of $20,000 with the next installment due on July 31. On that date, Mayes will also pay one year's interest at 9 percent. Interest was last paid on July 31 of the preceding year. To shift the current installment of the long-term debt to a current liability, debit Long-Term Debt Payable and credit Current Portion of Long-Term Debt Payable.

c. Gross salaries for the last payroll of the fiscal year were $5,044. Of this amount, employee payroll taxes payable were $1,088, and salary payable was $3,956.

d. Employer payroll taxes payable were $876, and Mayes's liability for employee health insurance was $1,253.

e. Mayes estimates that warranty expense is 2 percent of sales, which were $494,000. The company has not yet recorded warranty expense for the year.

f. On February 1 the company collected one year's rent of $4,800 in advance.

g. At June 30 Mayes is the defendant in a $200,000 lawsuit, which the company expects to win. However, the outcome is uncertain. Mayes reports contingent liabilities short, with an explanatory note.

Required

1. Open the listed accounts, inserting their unadjusted June 30 balances.
2. Journalize and post the June 30 adjusting entries to the accounts opened. Key adjusting entries by letter.
3. Prepare the liability section of the balance sheet at June 30.

Problem 11-4A   *Computing and recording payroll amounts*

The partial monthly records of Wilcox Company show the following figures:

Employee Earnings:

(1) Straight-time employee		(7) Medical insurance	$ 668
earnings	$16,246	(8) Total deductions	3,884
(2) Overtime pay	?	(9) Net pay	15,936
(3) Total employee earnings . . .	?		

Accounts Debited:

Deductions and Net Pay:

		(10) Salary Expense	?
(4) Withheld income tax	1,903	(11) Wage Expense	4,573
(5) FICA tax	?	(12) Sales Commission	
(6) Charitable contributions . . .	340	Expense	5,077

Required

1. Determine the missing amounts on lines (2), (3), (5), and (10).
2. Prepare the general journal entry to record Wilcox's payroll for the month. Credit Payrolls Payable for net pay. No explanation is required.

Problem 11-5A *Computing and recording payroll amounts*

Assume that Joyce Stankov is a vice-president of Bank of America's leasing operations in San Francisco. During 19X6 she worked for the company all year at a $3,625 monthly salary. She also earned a year-end bonus equal to 10 percent of her salary.

Stankov's federal income tax withheld during 19X6 was $537 per month. Also, she paid a one-time federal withholding tax of $1,007 on her bonus check. State income tax withheld came to $43 per month, and she paid a one-time state withholding tax of $27 on the bonus. The FICA tax withheld was 7.0 percent of the first $40,000 in annual earnings. Stankov authorized the following payroll deductions: United Fund contribution of 1 percent of total earnings, and life insurance of $19 per month.

Bank of America incurred payroll tax expense on Stankov for FICA tax of 7 percent of the first $40,000 in annual earnings. The bank also paid state unemployment tax of 5.4 percent and federal unemployment tax of .8 percent on the first $7,000 in annual earnings. In addition, the bank provides Stankov with health insurance at a cost of $35 per month and pension benefits. During 19X6 Bank of America paid $7,178 into Stankov's pension program.

Required

1. Compute Stankov's gross pay, payroll deductions, and net pay for the full year 19X6. Round all amounts to the nearest dollar.
2. Compute Bank of America's total 19X6 payroll cost for Stankov.
3. Prepare Bank of America's summary general journal entries to record its expense for
   a. Stankov's total earnings for the year, her payroll deductions, and her net pay. Debit Salary Expense and Executive Bonus Compensation as appropriate. Credit liability accounts for the payroll deductions and Cash for net pay.
   b. Employer payroll taxes on Stankov. Credit liability accounts.
   c. Fringe benefit provided to Stankov. Credit a liability account.
   Explanations are not required.

Problem 11-6A *Selecting the correct data to record a payroll*

Assume that the payroll information on the following page appeared in the records of the *Bristol Globe* newspaper.

Required

1. Prepare the general journal entries to record the payroll for the week ended March 31, including payroll taxes and fringe benefits.
2. Prepare the general journal entry to record the payment of the week's salaries to employees on March 31.
3. Assume that the *Globe* pays all its liabilities to the federal government in a single monthly amount. Prepare the general journal entry to record the April 1, 19X9, payment of federal taxes. (Liabilities to the federal government include FICA taxes and those items with *federal* and *U.S.* in the account title.)
4. Assume that the *Globe* pays all other payroll liabilities shortly after the end of the month. Prepare a single general journal entry to record the April 4 payment for these March liabilities.

Explanations are not required for journal entries.

	Payroll for Week Ended Friday, March 31, 19X9	Payroll for Month of March 19X9
Salaries:		
Editorial salaries.	$6,455	$27,178
Warehousing salaries.	3,118	13,128
Deductions:		
Employee federal income tax	1,415	5,958
FICA tax.	641	2,699
Employee health insurance	481	2,025
Employee contributions to United Fund.	367	1,545
Employee U.S. savings bonds	288	1,213
Net pay.	6,381	26,866
Employer payroll taxes:		
FICA tax.	641	2,699
State unemployment tax	520	2,160
Federal unemployment tax	77	320
Employer cost of fringe benefits for employees:		
Health insurance	663	2,791
Life insurance.	324	1,368
Pensions	451	1,899

Note: One challenge of this problem is to use only the relevant data. Not all the information given is necessary for making the required journal entries.

Problem 11-7A *Using payroll register; recording a payroll*

Assume that the payroll records of a district sales office of Carolina Freight Corporation provided the following information for the weekly pay period ended December 21, 19X5:

Employee	Hours Worked	Hourly Earnings Rate	Federal Income Tax	Union Dues	United Way Contributions	Earnings through Previous Week
Maria Burnett	42	$18	$153	$6	$5	$42,474
James English	47	8	56	4	4	23,154
Louise French	40	11	72	-	4	4,880
Roberto Garza	41	16	137	6	8	39,600

James English and Louise French work in the office, and Maria Burnett and Roberto Garza work in sales. All employees are paid time and a half for hours worked in excess of 40 per week. For convenience, round all amounts to the nearest dollar. Show computations. Explanations are not required for journal entries.

Required

1. Enter the appropriate information in a payroll register similar to Exhibit 11-4. In addition to the deductions listed, the employer also takes out FICA tax: 7 percent of the first $40,000 of each employee's annual earnings.
2. Record the payroll information in the general journal.
3. Assume that the first payroll check is number 319, paid to Maria Burnett. Record the check numbers in the payroll register. Also, prepare the general journal entry to record payment of net pay to the employees.
4. The employer's payroll taxes include FICA tax of 7 percent of the first $40,000 of each employee's earnings. The employer also pays unemployment taxes of 6.2 percent (5.4

percent for the state and .8 percent for the federal government on the first $7,000 of each employee's annual earnings). Record the employer's payroll taxes in the general journal.

(Group B)

Problem 11-1B *Reporting current liabilities*

Following are six pertinent facts about events during the current year at Brookview Products.

1. On August 31, Brookview signed a six-month, 12 percent note payable to purchase a machine costing $14,000. The note requires payment of principal and interest at maturity.
2. On September 30, Brookview discounted a $10,000 note payable to InterBank Savings and received cash of $9,000. The interest rate on the one-year note is 10 percent.
3. On October 31, Brookview received rent of $2,000 in advance for a lease on a building. This rent will be earned evenly over four months.
4. December sales totaled $63,000 and Brookview collected sales tax of 9 percent. This amount will be sent to the State of Tennessee early in January.
5. Brookview owes $75,000 on a long-term note payable. At December 31, $25,000 of this principal plus $900 of accrued interest are payable within one year.
6. Sales of $509,000 were covered by Brookview's product warranty. At December 31 estimated warranty payable is $11,300.

Required

For each item, indicate the account and the related amount to be reported as a current liability on Brookview's December 31 balance sheet.

Problem 11-2B *Journalizing liability-related transactions*

The following transactions of Lancaster Company occurred during 19X2 and 19X3. Record the transactions in the company's general journal. Explanations are not required.

19X2

Feb.	3	Purchased a machine for $2,200, signing a six-month, 11 percent note payable.
	28	Recorded the week's sales of $9,000, one third for cash, and two thirds on credit. All sales amounts are subject to a 5 percent state sales tax.
Mar.	7	Sent the last week's sales tax to the state.
Apr.	30	Borrowed $500,000 on a 9 percent, long-term note payable that calls for annual installment payments of $100,000 principal plus interest.
May	10	Received $1,125 in security deposits from customers. Lancaster refunds most deposits within three months.
Aug.	3	Paid the six-month, 11 percent note at maturity.
	10	Refunded security deposits of $1,125 to customers.
Sep.	14	Discounted a $6,000, 12 percent, 60-day note payable to the bank, receiving cash for the net amount after interest was deducted from the note's maturity value.
Nov.	13	Recognized interest on the 12 percent discounted note and paid off the note at maturity.
	30	Purchased inventory at a cost of $7,200, signing a 10 percent, three-month note payable for that amount.
Dec.	31	Accrued warranty expense, which is estimated at 3 percent of sales of $145,000.
	31	Accrued interest on all outstanding notes payable. Make a separate interest accrual entry for each note payable.

19X3

Feb. 28   Paid off the 10 percent inventory note, plus interest, at maturity.

Apr. 30   Paid the first installment and interest for one year on the long-term note payable.

Problem 11-3B   *Journalizing, posting, and reporting liabilities*

The Loflin Company general ledger at September 30, 19X7, the end of the company's fiscal year, includes the following account balances before adjusting entries. Parentheses indicate a debit balance.

Notes Payable, Short-Term . .	$ 32,000	Employer Payroll	
Discount on Notes Payable . .	(2,100)	Taxes Payable	$ —
Accounts Payable	88,240	Employee Benefits Payable . .	—
Current Portion of Long-		Sales Tax Payable	372
Term Debt Payable	—	Property Tax Payable	1,433
Interest Payable	—	Estimated Warranty Payable .	—
Salary Payable	—	Unearned Rent Revenue	3,900
Employee Payroll		Long-Term Debt Payable . . .	165,000
Taxes Payable	—	Contingent Liabilities	—

The additional data needed to develop the adjusting entries at September 30 are as follows:

a.   The $32,000 balance in Notes Payable, Short-Term consists of two notes. The first note, with a principal amount of $21,000, was issued on August 31, matures one year from data of issuance, and was discounted at 10 percent. The second note, with a principal amount of $11,000, was issued on September 2 for a term of 90 days and bears interest at 9 percent. It was not discounted.

b.   The long-term debt is payable in annual installments of $55,000, with the next installment due on January 31, 19X8. On that date, Loflin will also pay one year's interest at 10.5 percent. Interest was last paid on January 31. To shift the current installment of the long-term debt to a current liability, debit Long-Term Debt Payable and credit Current Portion of Long-Term Debt Payable.

c.   Gross salaries for the last payroll of the fiscal year were $4,319. Of this amount, employee payroll taxes payable were $958, and salary payable was $3,361.

d.   Employer payroll taxes payable were $755, and Loflin's liability for employee life insurance was $1,004.

e.   Loflin estimates that warranty expense is 3 percent of sales, which were $387,000. The company has not yet recorded warranty expense for the year.

f.   On August 1 the company collected six months' rent of $3,900 in advance.

g.   At June 30 Loflin is the defendant in a $50,000 lawsuit, which the company expects to win. However, the outcome is uncertain. Loflin reports contingent liabilities "short," with an explanatory note.

Required

1.   Open the listed accounts, inserting their unadjusted September 30 balances.

2.   Journalize and post the September 30 adjusting entries to the accounts opened. Key adjusting entries by letter.

3.   Prepare the liability section of Loflin's balance sheet at September 30.

Problem 11-4B   *Computing and recording payroll amounts*

The partial monthly records of Friedrich Company show the following figures.

Employee Earnings:

(1) Straight-time earnings	$?		(7) Medical insurance.......	$ 1,373
(2) Overtime pay	5,109		(8) Total deductions	?
(3) Total employee earnings...	?		(9) Net pay	58,813

Deductions and Net Pay: **Accounts Debited:**

(4) Withheld income tax......	8,993		(10) Salary Expense	31,278
(5) FICA tax	4,784		(11) Wage Expense..........	?
(6) Charitable contributions...	885		(12) Sales Commission Expense	27,931

Required

1. Determine the missing amounts on lines (1), (3), (8), and (11).
2. Prepare the general journal entry to record Friedrich's payroll for the month. Credit Payrolls Payable for net pay. No explanation is required.

Problem 11-5B   *Computing and recording payroll amounts*

Assume that Leslie Walker is a commercial lender in Chase Manhattan Bank's mortgage banking department in New York City. During 19X2 she worked for the bank all year at a $4,195 monthly salary. She also earned a year-end bonus equal to 12 percent of her salary.

Walker's federal income tax withheld during 19X2 was $822 per month. Also, she paid a one-time withholding of $2,487 on her bonus check. State income tax withheld came to $61 per month, and the city of New York withheld income tax of $21 per month. In addition, Walker paid one-time withholdings of $64 (state) and $19 (city) on the bonus. The FICA tax withheld was 7 percent of the first $40,000 in annual earnings. Walker authorized the following payroll deductions: United Fund contribution of 1 percent of total earnings, and life insurance of $17 per month.

Chase Manhattan Bank incurred payroll tax expense on Walker for FICA tax of 7 percent of the first $40,000 in annual earnings. The bank also paid state unemployment tax of 5.4 percent, and federal unemployment tax of .8 percent on the first $7,000 in annual earnings. The bank also provided Walker with the following fringe benefits: health insurance at a cost of $48 per month, and pension benefits to be paid to Walker during her retirement. During 19X2 Chase Manhattan's cost of Walker's pension program was $8,083.

Required

1. Compute Walker's gross pay, payroll deductions, and net pay for the full year of 19X2. Round all amounts to the nearest dollar.
2. Compute Chase Manhattan Bank's total 19X2 payroll cost for Walker.
3. Prepare Chase Manhattan Bank's summary general journal entries to record its expense for
   a. Walker's total earnings for the year, her payroll deductions, and her net pay. Debit Salary Expense and Executive Bonus Compensation as appropriate. Credit liability accounts for the payroll deductions and Cash for net pay.
   b. Employer payroll taxes for Walker. Credit liability accounts.
   c. Fringe benefits provided to Walker. Credit a liability account.
   Explanations are not required.

Problem 11-6B   *Selecting the correct data to record a payroll*

Assume the following payroll information appeared in the records of a small plant operated by Ford Motor Company:

	Payroll for Week Ended Friday July 31, 19X4	Payroll for Month of July 19X4
Salaries:		
Supervisor salaries	$39,668	$162,639
Office salaries	9,088	37,261
Deductions:		
Employee federal income tax	5,960	24,435
FICA tax	3,266	13,392
Employee health insurance	922	3,780
Employee union dues	708	2,903
Employee U.S. savings bonds	665	2,727
Net Pay.	37,235	152,663
Employer payroll taxes:		
FICA tax	3,266	13,392
State unemployment tax	2,633	10,793
Federal unemployment tax	390	1,599
Employer cost of fringe benefits for employees:		
Health insurance	2,034	8,339
Life insurance.	1,857	7,614
Pension.	1,667	6,835

Note: One challenge of this problem is to use only the relevant data. Not all the information given is necessary for making the required journal entries.

Required

1. Prepare the general journal entry to record the payroll for the week ended July 31, including payroll taxes and fringe benefits.
2. Prepare the general journal entry to record the payment of the week's salaries to employees on July 31.
3. Assume that Ford pays all its liabilities to the federal government in a single monthly amount. Prepare the general journal entry to record the August 1, 19X4, payment of federal taxes. (Liabilities to the federal government include FICA taxes and those items with *federal* and *U.S.* in the account title.)
4. Assume that Ford pays all other payroll liabilities shortly after the end of the month. Prepare a single general journal entry to record the August 3 payment for these July liabilities.

Explanations are not required for journal entries.

Problem 11-7B   *Using a payroll register; recording a payroll*

Assume that payroll records of a district sales office of Emery Air Freight Corporation provided the following information for the weekly pay period ended December 18, 19X3:

Employee	Hours Worked	Weekly Earnings Rate	Federal Income Tax	Health Insurance	United Way Contribution	Earnings through Previous Week
Tina Cruz	43	$400	$ 94	$9	$7	$17,060
Leroy Dixon	46	480	121	5	5	22,365
Karol Stastny	41	800	196	6	—	39,247
David Trent	40	240	32	4	2	3,413

Tina Cruz and David Trent work in the office, and Leroy Dixon and Karol Stastny work in sales. All employees are paid time and a half for hours worked in excess of 40 per week. For convenience, round all amounts to the nearest dollar. Show computations. Explanations are not required for journal entries.

Required

1. Enter the appropriate information in a payroll register similar to Exhibit 11-4. In addition to the deductions listed, the employer also takes out FICA tax: 7 percent of the first $40,000 of each employee's annual earnings.
2. Record the payroll information in the general journal.
3. Assume that the first payroll check is number 178, paid to Tina Cruz. Record the check numbers in the payroll register. Also, prepare the general journal entry to record payment of net pay to the employees.
4. The employer's payroll taxes include FICA of 7 percent of the first $40,000 of each employee's annual earnings. The employer also pays unemployment taxes of 6.2 percent (5.4 percent for the state and .8 percent for the federal government) on the first $7,000 of each employee's annual earnings. Record the employer's payroll taxes in the general journal.

Decision Problem

Identifying Internal Control Weaknesses and their Solution

Hall Custom Homes is a large home-building business in Phoenix, Arizona. The owner and manager is Lawrence Hall, who oversees all company operations. He employs 15 work crews, each made up of 6 to 10 members. Construction supervisors, who report directly to Hall, lead the crews. Most supervisors are long-time employees, so Hall trusts them greatly. Hall's office staff consists of an accountant and an office manager.

Because employee turnover is rapid in the construction industry, supervisors hire and terminate their own crew members. Supervisors notify the office of all personnel changes. Also, supervisors forward to the office the employee W-4 forms, which the crew members fill out to claim tax-withholding exemptions. Each Thursday the supervisors submit weekly time sheets for their crews, and the accountant prepares the payroll. At noon on Friday the supervisors come to the office to get paychecks for distribution to the workers at 5 P.M.

Hall's accountant prepares the payroll, including the payroll checks, which are written on a single payroll bank account. Hall signs all payroll checks after matching the employee name to the time sheets submitted by the foremen. Often the construction workers wait several days to cash their pay checks. To verify that each construction worker is a bona fide employee, the accountant matches the employee's endorsement signature on the back of the canceled payroll check with the signature on that employee's W-4 form.

Required

1. List one *efficiency* weakness in Hall's payroll accounting system. How can Hall correct this weakness?
2. Identify one way that a supervisor can defraud Hall under the present system.
3. Discuss a control feature Hall can use to *safeguard* against the fraud you identified in Requirement 2.

Financial Statement Problem

Current and Contingent Liabilities and Payroll

Details about a company's current and contingent liabilities and payroll costs appear in a number of places in the annual report. Use the Gulf+Western financial statements to answer these questions.

1. How much were the current maturities of Gulf+Western's long-term debt at October 31, 1987? In Note F, what interest rates applied to the current maturities payable in 1988?
2. Give the breakdown of accrued expenses and other liabilities. Identify the two un-earned revenues in this group. Give the fiscal 1988 entries to record the earning of these revenues.
3. Does Gulf+Western use a short presentation for contingent liabilities? Where does the company report contingencies? What is the attorney's opinion as to the ultimate effect of lawsuits pending against the company?
4. What employee fringe benefit is mentioned in Note I? How much expense did Gulf+Western incur for this item during fiscal 1987? Which liability in Note J includes any year-end accrual for this item?
5. Note J lists a $77.7 million liability for "Accrued compensation and other employee benefit related items." Was compensation expense for the year equal to, less than, or greater than this amount? Give your reason.

Answers to Self-Study Questions

1. c $10,000 \times .09 \times 5/12 = $375
2. a $10,000 − ($10,000 \times .09) = $9,100
3. b
4. c $900,000 \times .01 = $9,000
5. d
6. a Overtime pay: $320/40 = $8 \times 1.5 = $12 per hour \times 10 hours = $120
   Gross pay = $320 + $120 = $440
   Deductions = $440 \times (.08 + .07) = $66
   Take-home pay = $440 − $66 = $374

7. c
8. c
9. b
10. d

12

The Foundation for Generally Accepted Accounting Principles

Every technical area seems to have professional associations and regulatory bodies that govern the practice of the profession. Accounting is no exception. During the 1970s and 1980s generally accepted accounting principles in the United States have been influenced most by the Financial Accounting Standards Board (FASB) and its predecessor, the Accounting Principles Board (APB). The FASB consists of seven full-time members. A large staff and an annual budget of $10 million support the FASB. Its financial support comes from various professional associations, such as the American Institute of Certified Public Accountants.

From 1962 to 1973 the APB issued accounting pronouncements called *Opinions,* many of which are still part of generally accepted accounting principles (GAAP). In 1973 the FASB was established to replace the APB. The FASB is an independent organization with no government or professional affiliation. The FASB's pronouncements, called *Statements of Financial Accounting Standards,* currently specify how to account for certain business transactions. Each new *Standard* becomes part of GAAP, the "accounting law of the land." In the same way that our laws draw authority from their acceptance by the people, GAAP depends upon the general acceptance by the business community. Throughout this book, we refer to GAAP as the proper way to do accounting.

The United States Congress has given the Securities and Exchange Commission (SEC) ultimate responsibility for establishing accounting rules for companies that are owned by the general investing public. However, the SEC has delegated much of its rule-making power to the FASB. Exhibit 12-1 outlines the flow of authority for developing GAAP.

EXHIBIT 12-1 *Flow of Authority for Developing GAAP*

Setting accounting standards is a complex process involving the FASB, the SEC, and occasionally Congress. Also, individuals and companies often exert pressure on all three bodies in their efforts to shape accounting decisions to their advantage. Accountants also try to influence accounting decisions. Although any overruling is rare, the SEC has the authority to override an FASB decision, and Congress itself can override an SEC or an FASB decision, as the authority structure in Exhibit 12-1 shows. In most cases, however, the FASB plays the key role.

We have seen that GAAP guides companies in their financial statement preparation. Independent auditing firms of certified public accountants (CPAs) hold the responsibility for making sure companies do indeed follow GAAP.

The Conceptual Framework

Throughout the first 11 chapters, we have introduced key concepts and principles as they have applied to the topics under discussion. For example, Chapter 1 introduced the entity concept so that we could account for the transactions of a particular business. In Chapter 2, we discussed the revenue and matching principles as the guidelines for measuring income. Now that you have an overview of the accounting process, we consider the full range of accounting concepts and principles. Collectively, they form the foundation for accounting practice — GAAP.

Shortly after its formation in 1973, the Financial Accounting Standards Board (FASB) began the Conceptual Framework Project. The FASB's goal is to develop a constitution that will define the nature and function of financial accounting. This project provides a framework for the various accounting concepts and principles that are used to prepare the financial statements.

Accounting principles differ from natural laws like the law of gravity. Accounting principles draw their authority from their acceptance in the business community rather than from their ability to explain physical phenomena. Thus they really are *generally accepted* by those people and organizations who need guidelines in accounting for their financial undertakings. Exhibit 12-2 diagrams how we move from the conceptual framework to the financial statements.

EXHIBIT 12-2   *Overview of Generally Accepted Accounting Principles*

We now look at the objective of financial reporting. This objective tells what financial accounting is intended to accomplish. Thus it provides the goal for accounting information. Next, we examine particular accounting concepts and principles used to implement the objective. What is the difference between a concept and a principle? The concepts are broader in their application, and the principles are more specific. Last, we discuss the financial statements—the end product of financial accounting—and their elements—assets, liabilities, owner's equity, revenues, expenses, and so on.

Objective of Financial Reporting

The basic *objective of financial reporting* is to provide information that is useful in making investment and lending decisions. To be useful in decision making, the FASB believes accounting information should be *relevant, reliable,* and *comparable.*

Relevant information is useful for making predictions and for evaluating past performance. *Reliable* information is free from significant error and free from the bias of a particular viewpoint. *Comparable* information can be compared from period to period to help investors and creditors track the business's progress through time. These characteristics combine to shape the concepts and principles that make up GAAP.

OBJECTIVE 1
Identify the basic objective of financial reporting

Underlying Concepts

Entity Concept

The **entity concept** is the most basic concept in accounting because it draws a boundary around the organization being accounted for. That is, the transactions of each entity are accounted for separately from transactions of all other organiza-

OBJECTIVE 2
Identify and apply the underlying concepts of accounting

tions and persons, including the owners of the entity. This separation allows us to measure the performance and the financial position of each entity independent of all other entities.

A business entity may be a sole proprietorship (owned and operated by a single individual), a partnership of two or more persons, or a large corporation like EXXON. The entity concept applies with equal force to all types and sizes of organizations. The proprietor of a travel agency, for example, accounts for her personal transactions separately from those of her business. This division allows her to evaluate the success or failure of the travel agency. If she were to mix her personal and business accounting records, she would lose sight of the information needed to evaluate the business alone.

At the other end of the spectrum, EXXON is a giant company with oil-refining, retail gasoline sales, and chemical operations. EXXON accounts for each of these divisions separately in order to know which part of the business is earning a profit, which needs to borrow money, and so on.

The entity concept also applies to nonprofit organizations such as churches, synagogues, and government agencies. A hospital, for example, may be organized as a nonprofit entity, and it may have an emergency room, a pediatrics unit, and a surgery unit. The accounting system of the hospital should account for each separately to allow the managers to evaluate the progress of each unit.

The entity concept also provides the basis for consolidating subentities into a single set of financial statements. For example, the directors want to know the overall result of operating the entire hospital. Accountants, therefore, summarize the results of the various subentities into a consolidated set of financial statements. This is also done for profit-oriented businesses like EXXON, which has a single set of consolidated financial statements.

Going-Concern Concept

Under the **going-concern concept,** accountants assume the business will continue operating for the foreseeable future. The logic behind the going-concern concept is best illustrated by considering the alternative assumption: going out of business.

When a business stops, it sells its assets, converting them to cash. This process is called liquidation. With the cash, the business pays off its liabilities, and the owners keep any remaining cash. In liquidation, the amount of cash for which the assets are sold measures their current value. Likewise, the liabilities are paid off at their current value. However, if the business does not halt operations—if it remains a going concern—how are its assets and liabilities reported on the balance sheet?

For a going concern, the balance sheet reports assets and liabilities based on historical cost. For example, in a normal buyer-seller transaction, cost is an objective measure of the asset's worth. To consider what the asset may be worth on the current market requires making an estimate. This may or may not be objective. Under the going-concern concept, it is assumed that the entity will continue long enough for it to recover the cost of its assets.

The going-concern concept allows for the reporting of assets and liabilities as current or long-term, a distinction that investors and creditors find useful in evaluating a company. For example, a creditor wants to know the portion of a company's liabilities that are scheduled to come due within the next year and the portion payable beyond the year. The assumption is that the entity will continue in business and honor its commitments.

Time-Period Concept

The **time-period concept** ensures that accounting information is reported at regular intervals. This timely presentation of accounting data aids the comparison of business operations over time; from year to year, quarter to quarter, and so on. Managers, owners, lenders, and other people and businesses need regular reports to assess the business's success—or failure. These persons are making decisions daily. Although the ultimate success of a company cannot be known for sure until the business liquidates, decision makers cannot wait until liquidation to learn whether operations yielded a profit.

Nearly all companies use the year as their basic time period. *Annual* reports are common in business. Companies also prepare quarterly and monthly reports—called interim reports—to meet managers', investors', and creditors' need for timely information.

The time-period concept underlies the use of accruals. Suppose the business's accounting year ends at December 31 and the business has accrued—but will not pay until the next accounting period—$900 in salary expense. To tie this expense to the appropriate period, the accountant enters this adjusting entry, as we have seen:

Dec. 31	Salary Expense............	900	
	Salary Payable........		900

Accrual entries assign revenue and expense amounts to the correct accounting period and thus help produce meaningful financial statements.

Approximately 70 percent of all companies report their financial statements on a calendar-year basis, January through December. The remaining 30 percent use a fiscal year that ends at the business's annual low point in operations. For example, K-Mart and most large retailers use a fiscal year ending January 31. Their operations reach their most active point during December and then taper off at the end of January when the after-Christmas sales have finished.

Stable-Monetary-Unit Concept

Accounting information is expressed primarily in monetary terms. The monetary unit is the prime means of measuring assets. This measure is not surprising given that money is the common denominator in business transactions. In the United States, the monetary unit is the dollar; in Great Britain, the pound sterling; in Japan, the yen. The stable-monetary-unit concept provides an orderly basis for handling account balances to produce the financial statements.

Unlike a liter, a foot, and many other measurements, the value of the monetary unit may change over time. Most of us are familiar with inflation. Groceries that cost $50 three years ago may cost $60 today. The value of the dollar changes. In view of the fact that the dollar does not maintain a constant value, how does a business measure the worth of assets and liabilities acquired over a long span of time? The business records all assets and liabilities at cost. Each asset and each liability on the balance sheet is the sum of all the individual dollar amounts added over time. For example, if a company bought 100 acres of land in 1975 for $60,000 and another 100 acres of land in 1990 for $300,000, the asset Land on the balance sheet carries a $360,000 balance, and the change in the purchasing power of the dollar is ignored. The **stable-monetary-unit concept** is the accountant's basis for ignoring the effect of inflation and making no adjustments for the changing value of the dollar. Let's look at the shortcomings of this concept.

The December 26, 1987, balance sheet of Kraft, Inc., reported Land at $47.6 million. Assume that Kraft purchased land in 1971 for $4 million and land in 1987 for $43.6 million. The period from 1971 to 1987 witnessed high inflation. We know, therefore, that the dollar had significantly higher value in 1971. Kraft may have bought more land in 1971 for $4 million than it did in 1987 for so much more money. Now suppose that a second company spent a full $47.6 million on land in 1987. The acreage would be far less than the acreage purchased with mixed 1971 and 1987 dollars. How do we compare the two companies' balance sheets? The comparison based on the stable monetary unit concept may not be valid because mixing dollar values at different times is like mixing apples and oranges.

Many businesspeople believe that accounting information must be adjusted for changes in the dollar's purchasing power. The FASB encourages large companies to present supplementary inflation-adjusted information in their financial reports. Generally, however, accounting is based on historical costs.

Accounting Principles

Reliability (Objectivity) Principle

OBJECTIVE 3

Identify and apply the principles of accounting

The **reliability principle** requires that accounting information be dependable. Reliable information is free from significant error and bias. Users of this accounting information may rely on its truthfulness. To be reliable, information must be verifiable by people outside the business. Financial statement users may consider information reliable if independent experts would agree that the information is based on objective and honest measurement.

Consider the error in a company's failure to accrue interest revenue at the end of an accounting period. This error results in understated interest revenue and understated net income. Clearly, this company's accounting information is unreliable.

Biased information—data prepared from a particular viewpoint and not based on objective facts—is also unreliable. Suppose a company purchased inventory for $25,000. At the end of the accounting period, the inventory has declined in value and can be replaced for $20,000. Under the lower-of-cost-or-market rule, the company must record a $5,000 loss for the decrease in the inventory's value. Company management may believe that the appropriate value for the inventory is $22,000, but that amount is only an opinion. If management reports the $22,000 figure, total assets and owner's equity will be overstated on the balance sheet. Income will be overstated on the income statement.

To establish a *reliable* figure for the inventory's value, management could get a current price list from the inventory supplier or call in an outside professional appraiser to revalue the inventory. Evidence obtained from outside the company leads to reliable, verifiable information. The reliability principle applies to all financial accounting information—from assets to owner's equity on the balance sheet and from revenue to net income on the income statement.

Comparability Principle

The **comparability principle** has two requirements. First, accounting information must be comparable from business to business. Second, a single business's financial statements must be comparable from one period to the next. The FASB encourages comparability in order to make possible useful analysis from business to business, from period to period.

Standard formats for financial statements promote comparability among different companies. Using the same terms to describe the statement elements—assets, liabilities, revenues, and so on—also aids the comparison process.

Even among companies that adhere to standard formats and standard terms, comparability may be less than perfect. Comparisons of companies that use different inventory methods—LIFO and FIFO, for example—are difficult. Likewise, comparisons of companies that use different depreciation methods—straight-line and double-declining-balance, for example—are also quite complex. When GAAP allows a choice among acceptable accounting methods—in inventory, depreciation, and other areas—comparability may be harder to achieve.

Recall that the comparability principle directs each individual company to produce accounting information that is comparable over time. To achieve this quality—which accountants call *consistency*—companies must follow the same accounting practices from period to period. The business that uses FIFO for inventory and straight-line for depreciation in one period ought to use those same methods in the next period. Otherwise, a financial statement user could not tell whether changes in income and asset values result from operations or from the way the business accounts for operations.

Companies may change accounting methods in response to a change in business operations. A company may open up a new product line that calls for a different inventory method. GAAP allows the company to make a change in accounting method, but the business must disclose the change, the reason for making the change, and the effect of the change on net income. This disclosure is made in a note to the financial statements.

Cost Principle

The **cost principle** states that assets and services are recorded at their purchase cost and that the accounting record of the asset continues to be based on cost rather than current market value. By specifying that assets be recorded at cost, this principle also governs the recording of liabilities and owner's equity. Suppose that a land developer purchased 20 acres of land for $50,000. Additional costs included fees paid to the county ($1,500), removal of an unwanted building ($10,000), and landscaping ($20,000), a total cost of $81,500. The Land account carries this balance because it is the cost of bringing the land to its intended use. Assume that the developer holds the land for one year, then offers it for sale at a price of $200,000. The cost principle requires the accounting value of the land to remain at $81,500.

The developer may wish to lure buyers by showing them a balance sheet that reports the land at $200,000. However, this would be inappropriate under GAAP because $200,000 is merely the developer's opinion of what the land is worth.

The underlying basis for the cost principle is the reliability principle. Cost is a reliable value for assets and services because cost is supported by completed transactions between parties with opposing interests. Buyers try to pay the lowest price possible, and sellers try to sell for the highest price. The actual cost of an asset or service is objective evidence of its value.

Revenue Principle

The **revenue principle** provides guidance on the *timing* of the recording of revenue and the *amount* of revenue to record. The general rule is that revenue should be recorded when it is earned and not before.

Some revenues, such as interest and rent, accrue with the passage of time. Their timing and amount are easy to figure. The accountant records the amount of revenue earned over each period of time.

Other revenues are earned by selling goods or rendering services. Identifying *when* these revenues are earned depends on more factors than the passage of time. Under the revenue principle, three conditions must be met before revenue is recorded: (1) the seller has done everything necessary to expect to collect from the buyer; (2) the amount of revenue can be objectively measured; and (3) collectibility is reasonably assured. In most cases, these conditions are met at the point of sale or when services are performed.

The *amount* of revenue to record is the value of the assets received—usually cash or a receivable. However, situations may arise in which the amount of revenue or the timing of earning the revenue is not easily determined. We turn now to four methods that guide the accountant in applying the revenue principle in different circumstances.

OBJECTIVE 4

Allocate revenue to the appropriate period by four methods

Sales Method.   Under the **sales method,** revenue is recorded at the point of sale. Consider a retail sale in a hardware store. At the point of sale, the customer pays the store and takes the merchandise. The store records the sale by debiting Cash and crediting Sales Revenue. In other situations, the point of sale occurs when the seller ships the goods to the buyer. Suppose a mining company sells iron ore to Bethlehem Steel Corporation. By shipping the ore to Bethlehem Steel, the mining company has completed its duty and may expect to collect revenue. If the amount of revenue can be objectively measured and collection is reasonably certain, the mining company can then record revenue. The sale entry is a debit to Accounts Receivable and a credit to Sales Revenue. The sales method is used for most sales of goods and services.

Collection Method.   The **collection method** is used only if the receipt of cash is uncertain. Under this method, the seller waits until cash is received to record the sale. Professionals such as physicians and attorneys use the collection method because they often find it difficult to collect their receivables. They may not reasonably assume that they can collect the revenue, so they wait until actual receipt of the cash before recording it. The collection method is conservative in that revenue is not recorded in advance of its receipt.

Installment Method.   The **installment method** is a type of collection method that is used for installment sales. In a typical installment sale, the buyer makes a down payment when the contract is signed and pays the remainder in installments. Department stores, such as Sears and J. C. Penney, auto dealers, and real estate companies sell on the installment plan. Under the installment method, gross profit (sales revenue minus cost of goods sold) is recorded as cash is collected.

Suppose a real estate developer sells land for a down payment of $80,000 plus three annual installments of $120,000, $140,000, and $160,000 (a total of $500,000). The developer's cost of the land is $300,000, so the gross profit is $200,000, computed as follows:

Installment sale	$500,000
Cost of the land sold	300,000
Gross profit	$200,000

To determine the gross profit associated with each collection under the installment method, we must compute the gross profit percentage, as follows:

$$\text{Gross profit percentage} = \frac{\text{Gross profit}}{\text{Installment sale}} = \frac{\$200,000}{\$500,000} = 40\%$$

We next apply the gross profit percentage to each collection. The result is the amount of gross profit recorded as revenue at the time of cash receipt.

Year	Collections	×	Gross Profit Percentage	=	Gross Profit
1	$ 80,000	×	40%	=	$ 32,000
2	120,000	×	40%	=	48,000
3	140,000	×	40%	=	56,000
4	160,000	×	40%	=	64,000
Total	$500,000	×	40%	=	$200,000

Accountants would record gross profit of $32,000 in year 1, $48,000 in year 2, and so on. The total gross profit ($200,000) is the same as under the sales method. However, under the sales method, the full $200,000 of gross profit would be recorded at the beginning of the contract.

Of course, companies make installment sales year after year. Each year's sales may have a different gross profit percentage. In the preceding example, year 1 installment sales earned gross profit of 40 percent. Suppose year 2 sales earn gross profit of 45 percent, year 3 sales earn 42 percent, and year 4 sales earn 35 percent. The total gross profit for a year is the sum of all the gross profit amounts recorded on cash collections made that year.

Using assumed cash receipts on installment sales made in years 2, 3, and 4, the gross profit computations for years 1 through 4 follow. All year 1 amounts are taken from our computations above.

	Year 1 Sales	Year 2 Sales	Year 3 Sales	Year 4 Sales
Gross profit percentage	40%	45%	42%	35%

Gross profit by year:

	Year 1	Year 2	Year 3	Year 4
Year 1 sales:	$80,000 × .40 = $32,000	$120,000 × .40 = $48,000	$140,000 × .40 = $56,000	$160,000 × .40 = $64,000
Year 2 sales:		90,000 × .45 = 40,500	100,000 × .45 = 45,000	20,000 × .45 = 9,000
Year 3 sales:			75,000 × .42 = 31,500	65,000 × .42 = 27,300
Year 4 sales:				30,000 × .35 = 10,500
Total gross profit	$32,000	$88,500	$132,500	$110,800

The installment method is attractive for income tax purposes because it postpones the recording of revenue and thus the payment of taxes. However, it can be used only under limited circumstances. Under generally accepted accounting principles, this method is permissible only when no reasonable basis exists for estimating collections.

Percentage-of-Completion Method.   Construction of office buildings, bridges, dams, and other large assets often extends over several years. The accounting issue for the construction company is *when* to record the revenue. The most conservative approach is to record all the revenue earned on the project in the period when the project is completed. This procedure, called the **completed-contract method,** is acceptable under limited circumstances.

Under the preferred method, called the **percentage-of-completion method,** the construction company recognizes revenue as work is performed. Each year the company estimates the percentage of project completion as construction progresses. One way to make this estimate is to compare the cost incurred for the year to the total estimated project cost. This percentage is then multiplied by the total project revenue to compute the construction revenue for the year. Construction income for the year is revenue minus cost.

Assume Combustion Engineering Company receives a contract to build a power plant for a price of $42 million. Combustion estimates total costs of $36 million over the three-year construction period: $6 million in year 1, $18 million in year 2, and $12 million in year 3. Construction revenue and income during the three years are as follows (amounts in millions):

Year	Cost for Year	Total Project Cost	Percentage of Project Completion for Year	Total Project Revenue	Construction Revenue for Year	Construction Income for Year
1	$ 6	$36	$ 6/$36 = $1/6$	$42	$42 \times 1/6 =$ $ 7	$ 7 − $ 6 = $1
2	18	36	$18/36 = 1/2$	42	$42 \times 1/2 =$ 21	21 − 18 = 3
3	12	36	$12/36 = 1/3$	42	$42 \times 1/3 =$ 14	14 − 12 = 2
	$36	$36		$42	$42	$42 $36 $6

The percentage-of-completion method is appropriate when the company can estimate the degree of completion during the construction period, which most construction companies can do. When estimates are not possible, the completed-contract method is required. If Combustion Engineering had used the completed-contract method, its income statement for year 3 would report total project revenue of $42 million, total project expenses of $36 million, and income of $6 million. The income statements of years 1 and 2 would report nothing concerning this project. Most accountants believe the results under the percentage-of-completion method are more realistic.

Matching Principle

The **matching principle** governs the recording and reporting of expenses. This principle goes hand in hand with the revenue principle to govern income recognition in accounting. Recall that income is revenue minus expense. During any period, the company first measures its revenues by the revenue principle. The company then identifies and measures all the expenses it incurred during the period to earn the revenues. To *match* the expenses against the revenues means to subtract the expenses from the revenues. The result is the income for the period.

Some expenses are easy to match against particular revenues. For example, cost of goods sold relates directly to sales revenue, because without the sales, there would be no cost of goods sold. Commissions and fees paid for selling the goods, delivery expense, and sales supplies expense relate to sales revenue for the same reason.

Other expenses are not so easily linked to particular sales because they occur whether or not any revenues arise. Depreciation, salaries, and all types of home-office expense are in this category. Accountants usually match these expenses against revenue on a time basis. For example, the company's home-office building may be used for general management, manufacturing, and marketing. Straight-line depreciation of a 40-year building assigns one fortieth of the building's cost to expense each year, whatever the level of revenue. The annual salary expense for an employee is the person's total salary for the year, regardless of revenue.

Losses, like expenses, are matched against revenue on a time basis. For example, if an asset like inventory loses value, the loss is recorded when it occurs, without regard for the revenues earned during the period.

Disclosure Principle

The **disclosure principle** holds that a company's financial statements should report enough information for outsiders to make knowledgeable decisions about the company. In short, the company should report *relevant, reliable,* and *comparable* information about its economic affairs. This section of the chapter discusses and illustrates different types of disclosures.

Summary of Significant Accounting Policies.   To evaluate a company, investors and creditors need to know how its financial statements were prepared. This consideration is especially important when the company can choose from several acceptable methods. Companies summarize their accounting policies in the first note to their financial statements. The note may include both monetary amounts and written descriptions. Companies commonly disclose revenue-recognition method, inventory method, and depreciation method.

OBJECTIVE 5
Report information that satisfies the disclosure principle

Dresser Industries, Inc., reported the following:

NOTE A—SUMMARY OF SIGNIFICANT ACCOUNTING POLICIES (IN PART)

Long-Term Contracts

Revenues and earnings related to products requiring long-term construction periods, principally draglines and electrostatic precipitators, are recognized for financial reporting purposes on the percentage of completion basis.

Inventories

Substantially all the U.S. inventories of the Company are recorded on a last-in, first-out (LIFO) cost basis. Inventories not on LIFO cost valuation, principally foreign inventories, are recorded at the "lower of cost (principally average cost) or market."

Fixed Assets

Fixed assets are depreciated over the estimated service life. Accelerated depreciation methods are used for financial statement purposes, except for U.S. fixed assets with a service life of 10 years or less which are depreciated on a straight-line basis. Accelerated depreciation methods are also used for tax purposes wherever permitted.

Probable Losses.   The disclosure principle directs a business to record and report a probable loss *before* it occurs if the loss is likely and its amount can be estimated. Phillips Petroleum Company reported such a loss in its 1985 financial statements. Observe that the disposal of assets has not occurred yet, but the company does *expect* the disposal to result in a loss.

NOTE 1—DISCONTINUED OPERATION [IN PART]

During 1985, the company announced plans to discontinue its minerals operation. Assets associated with these operations were sold, abandoned, or written down . . . in anticipation of their future sale or abandonment, resulting in an estimated net loss on disposal in 1985 of $171 million, net of income tax. . . .

The $171 million loss on disposal appeared on Phillips's 1985 income statement as follows:

	Millions
Income from Continuing Operations	$ 596
Discontinued operations (net of income taxes)	
Loss from operations	(7)
Loss on disposal.	(171)
Net Income	$ 418

Accounting Changes. Consistent use of accounting methods and procedures is important, as we saw in discussing comparability. When a company does change from one accounting method or procedure to another, it must disclose the change, the reason for making the change, and the effect of the change on net income. Two common accounting changes are *changes in accounting principles* and *changes in accounting estimates.*

A **change in accounting principle** is a change in accounting method. A switch from the LIFO method to the FIFO method for inventories and a switch from the sum-of-years-digits depreciation method to the straight-line method are examples of accounting changes. Special rules that apply to changes in accounting principles are discussed in later accounting courses. Whatever the change in principle, the notes to the financial statements must inform the reader that the change has occurred.

A **change in accounting estimate** occurs in the normal course of business as the company alters earlier expectations. A company may record uncollectible account expense based on the estimate that bad debts will equal 2 percent of sales. If actual collections exceed this estimate, the company may lower its estimated expense to 1½ percent of sales in the future.

A company may originally estimate that a new delivery truck will provide four years' service. After two years of using the truck, the company sees that the truck's full useful life will stretch to six years. The company must recompute depreciation based on this new information at the start of the truck's third year of service. Assume that this truck cost $14,000, has an estimated residual value of $2,000, and is depreciated by the straight-line method.

Annual depreciation for each of the first two years of the asset's life is $3,000, computed as follows:

$$\text{Depreciation per year} = \frac{\$14,000 - \$2,000}{4 \text{ years}} = \$3,000$$

Changes in estimate are accounted for by spreading the asset's remaining depreciable cost over its remaining life. Annual depreciation after the accounting change is $1,500, computed in the following manner:

$$\frac{\text{Depreciation}}{\text{per year}} = \frac{\text{Asset depreciable cost}}{\text{Remaining life}} = \frac{\$14,000 - \$2,000 - (\$3,000 \times 2)}{6 \text{ total years} - 2 \text{ years used}}$$

$$= \frac{\$6,000}{4 \text{ years}} = \$1,500$$

This revised amount of depreciation is recorded in the usual manner.

Walt Disney Productions disclosed a similar change in accounting estimate. Observe that Disney reported the nature of the change, the reason for making the change, and its effect on income.

> **NOTE 5 [IN PART]:**
>
> Effective [at the beginning of the year], the Company extended the estimated useful lives of certain theme park ride and attraction assets based upon historical data and engineering studies. The effect of this change was to decrease depreciation by approximately $8 million (an increase in net income of approximately $4.2 million . . .).

Subsequent Events. A company usually takes several weeks after the end of the year to close its books and to publish its financial statements. Occasionally, events occur during this period that affect the interpretation of the information in those financial statements. Such an occurrence is called a **subsequent event** and should be disclosed in the prior period's statements. The most common examples of subsequent events are borrowing money, paying debts, making investments, selling assets, and becoming a defendant in a lawsuit.

United Merchants and Manufacturers, Inc., operates principally in the apparel, textiles, and home furnishings industries. The company reported the following subsequent event in its financial statements for the year ended June 30, 19X6:

> **NOTE 17—SUBSEQUENT EVENTS**
>
> On September 11, 19X6, the Company sold 17 percent of [its investment in] Victoria Creations, Inc., which is in the costume jewelry business. The sale resulted in cash proceeds to the Company of $13,910,000, which has been used to reduce indebtedness. The sale also resulted in a gain . . . of approximately $6,400,000, which will be reflected in the Company's results of operations for . . . 19X7.

Business Segments. Most large companies operate in more than one area. Each area is called a *business segment.* Sears, Roebuck, and Company, best known for its retail stores, also has real estate, investment banking, and other financial service operations. Union Pacific Corporation, the railroad company, is also active in the oil and gas business. The Coca-Cola Company not only sells soft drinks and food, but it also operates in the entertainment business. Diversification like this is not limited to large international companies. A realtor may also own a restaurant. A farmer may sell farm implements. An automobile dealer may also own a furniture store.

Suppose you are considering investing in a company that is active in the steel industry but also owns a meat packer and several leisure resorts. Assume the American steel industry is in retreat because of intense foreign competition. With income and asset data broken down by business segments, you can determine how much of the company's assets are committed to each segment and which lines of business are most (and least) profitable. Companies disclose segment data in notes to their financial statements.

The Scott Paper Company data at the top of the next page meet the GAAP requirement for adequate disclosure.

To satisfy the disclosure principle, Scott Paper breaks down sales, income before taxes, and assets two ways: by business segments and by geographic area. GAAP also requires companies to disclose capital expenditures and depreciation by business segment, as shown in the last two columns.

Disclosure Techniques. Companies use parenthetical notes in the financial statements. An example is the allowance for uncollectibles, reported as follows by

Year 19X6	(Millions)	Sales	Income before Taxes	Identifiable Assets	Capital Expenditures	Depreciation and Cost of Timber Harvested
Business Segment	Personal Care and Cleaning	$2,349.5	$252.7	$2,105.4	$220.0	$124.1
	Printing and Publishing Papers	921.2	149.2	1,217.4	178.3	62.4
	Pulp, Forest Products and Minerals	166.3	17.6	188.4	16.7	11.6
	Total business segments	3,437.0	419.5	3,511.2	415.0	198.1
	Corporate	—	(51.1)	428.2	5.7	4.7
	Interest expense	—	(122.0)	—	—	—
	Other income and (expense)	—	28.7	—	—	—
	Consolidated total	$3,437.0	$275.1	$3,939.4	$420.7	$202.8
Geographic Area	United States	$2,786.6	$342.4	$2,870.4		
	Europe	580.1	66.4	575.5		
	Pacific	73.6	10.7	65.2		
		3,440.3	419.5	3,511.1		
	Intergeographic sales	(3.3)	—	—		
	Corporate	—	(51.1)	428.3		
	Interest expense	—	(122.0)	—		
	Other income and (expense)	—	28.7	—		
	Consolidated total	$3,437.0	$275.1	$3,939.4		

RJR Nabisco, Inc. (in millions):

	December 31, 19X7	19X6
Accounts and notes receivable (less allowances of $61 and $67, respectively)	$1,745	$1,675

Other companies, including CPC International, Inc., list the allowance on a separate line of the balance sheet, as follows (in millions):

	December 31, 19X7	19X6
Notes and accounts receivable [summarized]	$549.9	$592.5
Allowances for doubtful accounts	(12.5)	(14.2)

Both disclosure techniques provide adequate information on the total amount receivable and the net amount expected to be collected.

Constraints on Accounting

Do financial statements report every detail, no matter how small, to meet the need for relevant, reliable, and comparable information? The result would be an avalanche of data. To address this problem, accountants use the *materiality concept*. Also, a company's top managers are responsible for its financial statements. To add balance to managers' optimism—which could bias the statements and so present too favorable a picture of company operations—accountants follow the *conservatism concept.* This section discusses these constraints on accounting information.

Materiality Concept

The **materiality concept** states that a company must perform strictly proper accounting only for items and transactions that are significant to the business's financial statements. Information is significant—what accountants call *material*—when its inclusion and correct presentation in the financial statement would cause a statement user to change a decision because of that information. Immaterial—insignificant—items justify less than perfect accounting. The inclusion and proper presentation of *immaterial* items would not affect a statement user's decision. The materiality concept frees accountants from having to compute and report every last item in strict accordance with GAAP. Thus the materiality concept reduces the cost of recording accounting information.

> **OBJECTIVE 6**
> Apply two constraints to accounting

How does a business decide where to draw the line between what is material and what is immaterial? This decision rests to a great degree on how large the business is. Wendy's, for example, has close to $500 million in assets. Management would likely treat as immaterial a $100 purchase of wastebaskets. These wastebaskets may well remain useful for ten years, and strictly speaking, Wendy's should capitalize their cost and depreciate the wastebaskets. However, this treatment is not practical. The accounting cost of computing, recording, and properly reporting this asset outweighs the information provided. No statement user—a potential investor or lender, for example—would change a decision based on so insignificant (immaterial) an amount. The cost of accounting in this case outweighs the benefit of the resulting information.

Large companies may draw the materiality line at as high a figure as $10,000 and expense any smaller amount. Smaller firms may choose to expense only those items less than $50. Materiality varies from company to company. An amount that is material to the local service station may not be material to General Motors.

The materiality concept does not free a business from having to account for every item. Wendy's, for example, must still account for the wastebaskets. Wendy's would credit Cash (or Accounts Payable) to record their purchase, of course, but what account would the company debit? Because the amount is immaterial, management may decide to debit Supplies, which is an asset account, or Supplies Expense. No matter what account receives the debit, no statement user's decision would be changed by the information.

Conservatism Concept

Business managers are often optimists. Asked how well the company is doing, its president will likely answer, "Great, we're having our best year ever." Without constraints this optimism could find its way into the company's reported assets and profits. Managers may try to present too favorable a view of the company. For example, they may pressure accountants to capitalize costs associated with fixed assets that should be expensed. This would result in less immediate expense and higher current income on the income statement. The balance sheet would report unduly high fixed asset values and owner's equity. The overall result would be that the managers' performance would appear to be better than it actually was. Traditionally, accountants have been conservative, to counter management's optimism.

Conservatism has been interpreted as "Anticipate no profits, but anticipate all losses." A clear-cut example is the lower-of-cost-or-market (LCM) method for inventories. Under LCM, inventory is reported at the *lower* of its cost or market value, which results in higher cost of goods sold and lower net income. Thus profits and assets are reported at their lowest reasonable amount. Other conservative accounting practices include the LIFO method for inventories when inventory costs are increasing, accelerated depreciation, and the completed-contract method for construction revenues. These methods result in earlier recording of expenses or later recording of revenues. Both effects postpone the reporting of net income and therefore are conservative.

In recent years, conservatism's effect on accounting has decreased. The FASB has stated that conservatism should not mean deliberate understatement of assets, profits, and owner's equity. However, if two different values can be used for an asset or a liability, the concept suggests using the less optimistic value. Conservatism is a secondary consideration in accounting. Relevant, reliable, and comparable information is the goal, and conservatism is a factor only after these primary goals are met.

Financial Statements and Their Elements

We have examined the concepts and principles that shape accounting practice. The FASB aims for financial statements that best meet user needs for business information.

This accounting information appears in four statements: the balance sheet, the income statement, the statement of owner's equity, and the statement of cash flows. The FASB provides definitions for the elements that make up these statements. Financial information presentation, to be most useful to the greatest number of statements users, must be presented in a standard format with well-defined terms, as we learned in our discussion of the comparability concept.

FASB Concepts Statement No. 3 provides authoritative definitions of the elements of financial statements.[1]

Balance Sheet Elements

Assets are future economic benefits obtained or controlled by a particular entity as a result of past transactions.

Liabilities are the obligations of an entity to transfer assets or provide services to other entities as a result of past transactions.

Equity (Owner's Equity) is the interest in the assets of an entity that remains after subtracting its liabilities. It is the ownership interest in the entity.

OBJECTIVE 7

Name and define the elements of financial statements

Income Statement Elements

Revenues are inflows of assets that arise from delivering or producing goods, rendering services, or performing other activities that constitute the entity's ongoing central operations.

Expenses are outflows of assets or the incurrences of liabilities that arise from delivering or producing goods, rendering services, or carrying out activities that constitute the entity's ongoing central operations.

Gains are increases in owner's equity that do not result from revenues or investments by owners.

---

[1] The definitions here are paraphrased from FASB, *Concepts Statement No. 3*, "Elements of Financial Statements of Business Enterprises" (Stamford, CT: December 1980), highlights.

EXHIBIT 12-3   *Reporting Revenues, Expenses, Gains, and Losses*

Multiple-Step Income Statement			Single-Step Income Statement		
Sales revenue		$XXX	Revenues and gains:		
Cost of goods sold................		XXX	Sales revenue..................		$XXX
Gross profit		XXX	Gain on sale of land		XXX
Operating expenses..............		XXX	Total revenues and gains.......		XXX
Income from operations		XXX	Expenses and losses:		
Other items:			Cost of goods sold..............	$XXX	
Gain on sale of land	$XXX		Operating expenses	XXX	
Loss due to fire.................	XXX	XXX	Loss due to fire.................	XXX	
			Total expenses and losses......		XXX
Net income....................		$XXX	Net income		$XXX

Losses are decreases in owner's equity that do not result from expenses or distributions to owners.

Note that *revenues* and *expenses* arise from the business's ongoing central operations, but *gains* and *losses* do not. Sales are revenues because most companies make sales and earn interest as part of their central operations. Selling cars and trucks lies at the heart of an automobile dealership. To this business, a gain on the sale of a truck is revenue, and a loss on the sale is expense. However, a gain on the sale of a truck is not revenue for a trucking company because that entity buys trucks for use rather than for sale. Selling a truck is not a part of central operations. Exhibit 12-3 shows how to report revenues, expenses, gains, and losses on a multiple-step and a single-step income statement.

Statement of Owner's Equity Elements

Investments by owners are increases in owner's equity that result from the owner's transferring to the entity something of value. The most common investment is cash, but owners sometimes invest land, buildings, legal services, or other assets. In some cases, an owner's investment in the business may consist of paying off its liabilities.

Distributions to owners are decreases in owner's equity that result from the owner's transferring assets or services from the business to himself or herself, or from the business taking on the owner's liabilities. When the business is a corporation, owner withdrawals are called dividends. The most commonly distributed asset is cash, but businesses sometimes distribute other assets, such as stock investments they hold in other companies, to their owners.

Summary Problem for Your Review

This chapter has discussed the following principles and concepts:

Entity concept	Cost principle
Going-concern concept	Revenue principle
Time-period concept	Matching principle
Reliability principle	Disclosure principle
Comparability principle	Materiality concept

Indicate which of these concepts is being violated in each of the following situations:

1. A construction company signs a two-year contract to build a bridge for the state of Montana. The president of the company immediately records the full contract price as revenue.

2. Competition has taken away much of the business of a small airline. The airline is unwilling to report its plans to sell half its fleet of planes.

3. After starting the business in February 19X2, a coal-mining company keeps no accounting records for 19X2, 19X3, and 19X4. The owner is waiting until the mine is exhausted to determine the success or failure of the business.

4. Assets recorded at cost by a drug store chain are written up to their fair market value at the end of each year.

5. The accountant for a manufacturing company keeps detailed depreciation records on every asset no matter how small its value.

6. A physician mixes her personal accounting records with those of the medical practice.

7. Expenses are reported whenever the bookkeeper records them rather than when related revenues are earned.

8. The damaged inventory of a discount store is being written down. The store manager bases the write-down entry on his own subjective opinion in order to minimize income taxes.

9. A quick-copy center changes accounting methods every year in order to report the maximum amount of net income possible under generally accepted accounting principles.

10. The owners of a private hospital base its accounting records on the assumption that the hospital might have to close at any time. The hospital has a long record of service to the community.

SOLUTION TO REVIEW PROBLEM

1. Revenue principle
2. Disclosure principle
3. Time-period concept
4. Cost principle
5. Materiality concept
6. Entity concept
7. Matching principle
8. Reliability principle
9. Comparability principle
10. Going-concern concept

Summary

The Financial Accounting Standards Board (FASB) formulates generally accepted accounting principles (GAAP) to provide relevant, reliable, and comparable accounting information. *Relevant* information allows users to make business predictions and to evaluate past decisions. *Reliable* data are free from material error and bias. Accounting information is also intended to be *comparable* from company to company and from period to period.

Four concepts underlie accounting. The most basic, the *entity concept,* draws clear boundaries around the accounting entity. The entity, based on the *going-concern concept* is assumed to remain in business for the foreseeable future. The *time-period concept* is the basis for reporting accounting information for particular time periods such as months, quarters, and years. Under the *stable-monetary-unit concept,* no adjustment is made for the changing value of the dollar.

Accounting principles provide detailed guidelines for recording transactions and preparing the financial statements. The *reliability* and *comparability principles* require that accounting information be based on objective data and be useful for comparing companies across different time periods. The *cost principle* governs accounting for assets and liabilities, and the *revenue principle* governs accounting for revenues. *Matching* is the basis for recording expenses. The *disclosure* principle requires companies to report their accounting policies, probable future losses, accounting changes, subsequent events, and business-segment data. They use different disclosure techniques.

Two constraints on accounting are materiality and conservatism. The *materiality concept* allows companies to avoid excessive cost in accounting for immaterial items. *Conservatism* constrains the optimism of managers by anticipating no profits, but anticipating all losses.

Financial statements and their elements include:

Balance sheet: assets, liabilities, and *equity (owner's equity)*

Income statement: revenues, expenses, gains, and *losses*

Statement of owner's equity: investments by owners and *distributions to owners.*

Self-Study Questions

Test your understanding of the chapter by marking the best answer for each of the following questions.

1. The organization that issues accounting pronouncements that make up GAAP is the *(p. 461, 462)*
    a. U.S. Congress
    b. Accounting Principles Board
    c. Financial Accounting Standards Board
    d. Securities and Exchange Commission

2. Which of the following characteristics of accounting information does the objective of financial reporting omit? *(p. 463)*
    a. Timeliness
    b. Relevance
    c. Reliability
    d. Comparability

3. A new business is starting. The president wishes to wait until significant contracts have been fulfilled before reporting the results of the business's operations. Which underlying concept serves as the basis for preparing financial statements at regular intervals? *(p. 465)*
    a. Entity
    b. Going concern
    c. Time period
    d. Stable monetary unit

4. Which of these revenue methods is the most conservative? *(pp. 468, 475, 476)*
    a. Sales method
    b. Collection method
    c. Percentage-of-completion method
    d. All the above are equally conservative

5. Suppose a Montgomery Ward store sells $10,000 worth of kitchen appliances on the installment plan and collects a down payment of $1,500. Ward's cost of the appliances is $7,000. How much gross profit will the company report this period under the installment revenue method *(pp. 468, 469)*
    a. $450
    b. $1,500
    c. $3,000
    d. $10,000

6. A construction company spent $180,000 during the current year on a building with a contract price of $900,000. The company estimated total construction cost at $720,000. How much construction *income* will the company report under the percentage-of-completion method? *(p. 470)*
    a. $45,000
    b. $144,000
    c. $180,000
    d. $225,000

7. Which of the following items should be disclosed to satisfy the disclosure principle? *(pp. 471, 472, 473)*
   a. Business segment data
   b. Probable losses
   c. Accounting changes
   d. All of the above

8. Important subsequent events should be disclosed because they *(p. 473)*
   a. Occur immediately after the current period
   b. Describe changes in accounting methods
   c. Reveal losses that have a high probability of occuring in the future
   d. May affect the interpretation of the current-period financial statements

9. Which of the following statements is most in keeping with the materiality concept? *(p. 475)*
   a. Accountants record material losses but are reluctant to record material gains
   b. Different companies have different materiality limits, depending on their size
   c. Business-segment data are disclosed to fulfill the materiality concept
   d. Companies report all the information needed to communicate a material view of the entity

10. Gains and losses are most similar to *(pp. 476, 477)*
    a. Assets and liabilities
    b. Revenues and expenses
    c. Investments by owners and distributions to owners

Answers to the self-study questions are at the end of the chapter.

Accounting Vocabulary

change in accounting estimate *(p. 472)*, change in accounting principle *(p. 472)*, collection method *(p. 468)*, comparability principle *(p. 466)*, completed-contract method *(p. 470)*, cost principle *(p. 467)*, disclosure principle *(p. 471)*, gains *(p. 476)*, going-concern concept *(p. 464)*, installment method *(p. 468)*, losses *(p. 477)*, materiality concept *(p. 475)*, percentage-of-completion method *(p. 470)*, reliability principle *(p. 466)*, sales method *(p. 468)*, stable-monetary-unit concept *(p. 465)*, subsequent event (p. 473), time-period concept *(p. 465)*.

ASSIGNMENT MATERIAL

Questions

1. How do accounting principles differ from natural laws?
2. State the basic objective of financial reporting.
3. What three characteristics make accounting information useful for decision making? Briefly discuss each characteristic.
4. What is the entity concept?
5. How does the going-concern concept affect accounting? What is liquidation?
6. Identify two practical results of the time-period concept.
7. What is the shortcoming of the stable-monetary-unit concept?
8. What are the two requirements of the comparability principle?
9. Why is consistency important in accounting?
10. Discuss the relationship between the cost principle and the reliability principle.
11. What three conditions must be met before revenue is recorded? What determines the amount of the revenue?
12. Which revenue recognition method is more conservative, the sales method or the collection method? Give your reason.
13. Suppose Montgomery Ward sold a lawn mower on an installment basis, receiving a down payment of $50 to be followed by 12 monthly installments of $12.50 each. If

Ward's cost of the mower was $120, how much gross profit would Ward record under the installment method (a) when the down payment is received and (b) when each installment is received?

14. Briefly discuss two methods of recognizing revenue on long-term construction contracts.

15. Give two examples of expenses that are easy to relate to sales revenue and two examples of expenses that are not so easy to relate to particular sales. On what basis are the latter expenses matched against revenue?

16. ABC Company agreed on November 22, 19X7, to sell an unprofitable manufacturing plant. ABC estimates on December 31 that the company is likely to incur a $4 million loss on the sale when it is finalized in 19X8. In which year should ABC report the loss? What accounting principle governs this situation?

17. Identify three items commonly disclosed in a company's summary of significant accounting policies.

18. What is a subsequent event? Why should companies disclose important subsequent events in their financial statements?

19. How does information on business segments help an investor?

20. Classify each of the following as a change in accounting principle or a change in accounting estimate:
    a. Change from straight-line to sum-of-years-digits depreciation.
    b. Change in the uncollectibility of accounts receivable.
    c. Change from LIFO to FIFO for inventory.
    d. Change from the percentage-of-completion method to the completed-contract method for revenue on long-term construction contracts.
    e. Change from an 8-year life to a 10-year life for a machine.
    f. Change in estimated warranty expense rate stated as a percent of sales.

21. Sloan Sales Company expenses the cost of plant assets below $500 at the time of purchase. What accounting concept allows this departure from strictly proper accounting? Why would Sloan Sales follow such a policy?

22. Give three examples of conservative accounting methods, stating why the methods are conservative.

23. Identify two balance sheet elements that are defined independently and give the definition of the third balance sheet element.

24. The four income statement elements may be divided into two pairs of similar elements. What elements make up these two pairs?

Exercises

Exercise 12-1 *Reporting assets under GAAP*

Identify the amount at which each of the following assets should be reported in the financial statements of Monroe Company. Cite the principle or concept that is most applicable to each answer.

a. Monroe purchased land for $100,000 and paid $2,500 to have the land surveyed, $15,400 to have old buildings removed, and $40,300 for landscaping. Monroe is offering the land for sale at $225,000 and has received a $200,000 offer.

b. Inventory has a cost of $45,000, but its current market value is $39,600.

c. Monroe purchased a machine for $25,000 less a $2,100 cash discount. To ship the machine to the office, Monroe paid transportation charges of $500 and insurance of $200 while in transit. After using the machine for one month, Monroe purchases lubricating oil costing $150 for use in operating the machine.

Exercise 12-2 *Reporting assets as a going concern and as a liquidating entity*

Lincoln Company has the following assets:

Cash, $15,000

Accounts Receivable, $25,600; allowance for uncollectible accounts, $4,300

Office supplies, cost $280; scrap value $70

Office machinery, cost $72,000; accumulated depreciation, $54,000; current sales value, $8,400

Land, cost $85,000; current sales value, $135,000

Required

1. Assume Lincoln continues as a going concern. Compute the amount of its assets for reporting on the balance sheet.
2. Assume Lincoln is going out of business by liquidating its assets. Compute the amount of its assets at liquidation value.

Use the following format for your answers.

	Assets of a Going Concern	Assets at Liquidation Value
Cash..........................	$ _____	$ _____
Accounts receivable	$ _____	
Less: Allowance for uncollectible accounts..........................	_____	_____
Office supplies.....................	_____	_____
Office machinery...................	_____	
Less: Accumulated depreciation.......	_____	
Land..........................	_____	_____
Total..........................	$ _____	$ _____

Exercise 12-3   *Reporting revenues under GAAP*

For each of the following situations, indicate the amount of revenue to report for the current year ended December 31 and for the following year:

a. On July 1 collected one year's rent of $12,000 in advance on a building leased to another company.
b. Sold gift certificates, collecting $4,000 in advance. At December 31, $2,200 of the gifts have been claimed. The remainder were claimed during the next year.
c. Sold merchandise for $5,900, receiving a down payment of $1,100 and the customer's receivable for the balance. The company accounts for these sales by the sales method.
d. On April 1 loaned $25,000 at 12 percent on a three-year note.
e. Performed $900 of services for a high-risk customer on August 18, accounting for the revenue by the collection method. At December 31 the company had received $200 of the total; $550 was received the following year.

Exercise 12-4   *Reporting income under GAAP*

Lotus Management Company failed to record the following items at December 31, 19X4, the end of its fiscal year:

Accrued salary expense, $2,800	Prepaid insurance, $400
Accrued interest expense, $600	Depreciation expense, $500

Instead of recording the accrued expenses at December 31, 19X4, Lotus recorded the expenses when it paid them in 19X5. The company recorded the insurance as expense when it was prepaid for one year, early in 19X4. Depreciation expense for 19X5 was correctly recorded.

Lotus incorrectly reported net income of $9,000 in 19X4 and $5,300 in 19X5 because of the above errors.

Required

Compute Lotus's correct net income for 19X4 and 19X5.

Exercise 12-5 *Computing gross profit under the sales method and the installment method*

Allied Appliance Store sells on the installment plan. The store's installment sales figures for 19X7 follow.

Sales	$420,000
Down payments received on the sales	80,000
Collections on installments	170,000
Inventory at beginning of 19X7............	60,000
Inventory at end of 19X7.................	45,000
Purchases	216,000

Required

Compute the store's gross profit if it uses (a) the sales method of revenue recognition and (b) the installment method.

Exercise 12-6 *Computing construction revenue under the completed-contract method and the percentage-of-completion method*

McMinn Construction Company builds bridges for the state of Florida. The construction period typically extends for several years. During 19X5 McMinn completed a small bridge with a contract price of $400,000. McMinn's $320,000 cost of the bridge was incurred as follows: $20,000 in 19X3, $180,000 in 19X4, and $120,000 in 19X5. Compute McMinn's revenue for each year 19X3 through 19X5 if the company uses (a) the completed-contract method and (b) the percentage-of-completion method.

Exercise 12-7 *Changing the useful life of a depreciable asset*

McMinn Construction Company uses a crane on its construction projects. The company purchased the crane early in January 19X3 for $500,000. For 19X3 and 19X4 depreciation was taken by the straight-line method based on a six-year life and an estimated residual value of $80,000. In early 19X5 it became evident that the crane would be useful beyond the original life of six years. Therefore, beginning in 19X5, McMinn changed the depreciable life of the crane to a total life of nine years. The company retained the straight-line method and did not alter the residual value.

Required

Prepare McMinn's depreciation entries for 19X4 and 19X5.

Exercise 12-8 *Identifying subsequent events for the financial statements*

Bush, Inc., experienced the following events after May 31, 19X8, the end of the company's fiscal year, but before publication of its financial statements on July 12:

a. Bush collected $126,000 of the $480,000 accounts receivable reported on the May 31 balance sheet. Bush expects to collect the remainder in the course of business during the next fiscal year.

b. A major customer, who owed Bush $220,000 at May 31, declared bankruptcy on June 21.

c. Bush sales personnel received a contract to supply Bronson Company with laser equipment.

d.   Increased demand for Bush products suggests that the next fiscal year will be the best in the company's history.

e.   On July 6 Bush is sued for $3 million. Loss of the lawsuit could lead to Bush's bankruptcy.

Required

Identify the subsequent events that Bush should disclose in its May 31, 19X8, financial statements.

Exercise 12-9   *Using accounting concepts and principles*

Identify the accounting concept or principle, if any, that is violated in each of the following situations. You may choose from among *disclosure, conservatism, cost, entity,* and *matching.*

a.   The owner of a travel agency used the business bank account to pay her family's household expenses, making no note that the expenses were personal.

b.   A manufacturing company changed from the FIFO inventory method to the LIFO method and failed to report the accounting change in the financial statements.

c.   A paper company that purchased 5,000 acres of timberland at $150 per acre in 1953 reports the land at its current market value of $3,000 per acre.

d.   A railroad records depreciation during years when net income is high but fails to record depreciation when net income is low. Revenues are relatively constant.

e.   The inventory of a clothing store has a current market value of $80,000. The store reports the inventory at its cost of $124,000.

Exercise 12-10   *Using accounting concepts and principles*

Indicate the accounting concept or principle that applies to the following situations. Choose from among *comparability, materiality, reliability, revenue,* and *time period.*

a.   New Wave Distributors expenses the cost of plant assets that cost less than $300.

b.   Although Bracken Company could increase its reported income by changing depreciation methods, Bracken management has decided not to make the change.

c.   Lim Ting Restaurant was recently sued for $200,000, but the plaintiff has indicated a willingness to settle for less than that amount. Lim Ting hopes to settle for $50,000, but their attorneys believe the settlement will be between $90,000 and $100,000. Lim Ting's auditor reports it as a real liability on the balance sheet. The only remaining issue is whether to report the liability at $50,000 or at $95,000.

d.   Northern Union Company is considering publishing quarterly financial statements to provide more current information about its affairs.

e.   POA, Inc., is negotiating the sale of $500,000 of inventory. POA has been in financial difficulty and desperately needs to report this sale on its income statement of the current year. At December 31, the end of the company's accounting year, the sale has not been closed.

Problems   *(Group A)*

Problem 12-1A   *Identifying the basis for good accounting practices*

The following accounting practices are in accord with generally accepted accounting principles. Identify all the accounting concepts and principles that form the basis for each accounting practice. More than one concept or principle may apply.

a.   The personal residence of the owner of a freight company is not disclosed in the financial statements of the business.

b. A manufacturing company's plant assets are carried on the books at cost under the assumption that the company will remain in operation for the foreseeable future.

c. A clothing store discloses in notes to its financial statements that it uses the FIFO inventory method.

d. A real estate developer paid $450,000 for land and held it for three years before selling it for $800,000. There was significant inflation during this period, but the developer reports the $350,000 gain on sale with no adjustment for the change in the value of the dollar.

e. Liabilities are reported in two categories, current and long-term.

f. A travel agent's payments for fire insurance are so small that the company expenses them and makes no year-end adjustment for prepaid insurance.

g. The inventory of a personal computer store declined substantially in value because of changing technology, and the store wrote its computer inventory down to the lower of cost or market.

h. A construction company changed from the completed-contract method to the percentage-of-completion method of recording revenue on its long-term construction contracts. The company disclosed this accounting change in the notes to its financial statements.

i. A mining company recorded an intangible asset at the cost of the mineral lease and all other cost necessary to bring the mine to the point of production. After the mine was in operation, the company amortized the asset's cost as expense in proportion to the revenues from sale of the minerals.

j. Because of a downturn in the economy, a jeweler increased his business's allowance for doubtful accounts.

Problem 12-2A   *Identifying the concepts and principles violated by bad accounting practices*

The following accounting practices are *not* in accord with generally accepted accounting principles. Identify the single accounting concept or principle that is most clearly violated by each accounting practice.

a. Royal Iron Works regularly changes accounting methods in order to report a target amount of net income each year.

b. Texas Land Company reports land at its market value of $820,000, which is greater than the cost of $400,000.

c. A flood on July 2 caused $150,000 in damage to Tyler Construction property. The company did not report the flood as a subsequent event in the June 30 financial statements.

d. Hernandez, Inc., overstates depreciation expense in order to report low amounts of net income.

e. The balance sheet of Rhonda Green's medical practice includes receivables that she will probably never collect. Nevertheless, Green's accountant refuses to use the collection method to account for revenue.

f. The current market value of Miska Electronics's inventory is $65,000, but the company reports its inventory at cost of $91,000. The decline in value is permanent.

g. The liabilities of Waco Jet Company exceed the company's assets. In order to get a loan from the bank, Waco Jet's owner, Slade McQueen, includes his personal investments as assets on the balance sheet of the business.

h. Lancer Corporation increases the carrying value of its land based on recent sales of adjacent property.

i. Mission Ford Sales records expenses on an irregular basis without regard to the pattern of the company's revenues.

j. Frisco Software Company omits the significant accounting policies note from its financial statements because the company uses the same accounting methods that its competitors use.

Problem 12-3A *Recording and reporting transactions according to GAAP*

The accounting records of San Felipe Wholesale Distributors reveal the following information prior to closing the books at September 30, the end of the current fiscal year:

a. Accounts receivable include $42,000 from Glenwood Drug Company, which has declared bankruptcy. San Felipe, which uses the allowance method to account for bad debts, expects to receive one third of the amount receivable from Glenwood.

b. No interest has been accrued on a $50,000, 12 percent, six-month note receivable that was received on May 31.

c. The merchandise inventory, with a cost of $69,000, has a current market value of only $31,000. San Felipe uses a periodic inventory system and has not made the September 30 entry to record ending inventory.

d. Accrued salaries of $21,800 have been earned by San Felipe employees but have not been recorded at September 30 because the company plans to record the salaries when it pays them in October.

e. The company's office building has been valued recently by independent appraisers at $400,000. This valuation is $180,000 more than San Felipe paid for the building and is $270,000 more than its cost less accumulated depreciation.

f. Two years ago on October 1, San Felipe paid $120,000 for its delivery trucks. During the prior year the company has depreciated the trucks by the straight-line method over an expected useful life of 4 years, using a residual value of $20,000. After using the trucks for the first year, San Felipe decided at the beginning of the current year that the trucks will remain in service for a total of 5 years. The company will continue to use the straight-line method and the $20,000 residual value for accounting purposes.

g. On October 19, before San Felipe issued its financial statements for the year ended September 30, a competitor sued the company for damages of $500,000. Attorneys for San Felipe believe San Felipe will win the case. However, a $500,000 loss would make it difficult for the company to continue in business.

Required

Make all journal entries needed at September 30 to record this information. Explanations are not required. Identify those items *not* requiring a journal entry, giving the reason why an entry is not needed. If a note to the financial statements is needed, write the note.

Problem 12-4A *Using the installment-revenue method*

Fountain City Appliances sells on the installment plan. Collections of installment receivables have deteriorated. The store's accountants are considering the different methods of recording revenues. Revenue, expense, and collection data for the current year are as follows:

	19X6
Installment sales	$90,000
Cost of goods sold	54,000
Collections of installment receivables from sales of 19X5	20,000
19X6	24,000

The gross profit percentage on 19X5 installment sales was 42 percent.

Required

1. Which method should be used to account for revenues if collections are reasonably assured? If collections are extremely doubtful? Which method is more advantageous for income tax purposes? Why?

2. Compute gross profit for 19X6 under the sales method, the collection method, and the installment method.

Problem 12-5A   *Using the installment-revenue method*

Pine Valley Appliance Store makes all sales on the installment basis but uses the sales method to record revenue. The company's income statements for the most recent three years follow.

	Year 1	Year 2	Year 3
Sales	$240,000	$210,000	$290,000
Cost of goods sold	144,000	121,800	179,800
Gross profit.	96,000	88,200	110,200
Operating expenses	51,400	49,300	61,300
Net income.	$ 44,600	$ 38,900	$ 48,900
Collections from sales of year 1	$ 80,000	$105,000	$ 40,000
Collections from sales of year 2		68,000	120,000
Collections from sales of year 3			145,000

Required

Compute the amount of net income Pine Valley would have reported if the company had used the installment method for revenue. Ignore the effect of uncollectible accounts and present your answer in the following format:

Installment-method net income:	Year 1	Year 2	Year 3
Gross profit	$	$	$
Operating expenses.	51,400	49,300	61,300
Net income	$	$	$

Problem 12-6A   *Accounting for construction income*

Newport Shipbuilding Company participates in the construction of small ships under long-term contracts. During 19X7 Newport began three projects that progressed according to the following schedule during 19X7, 19X8, and 19X9:

Project	Contract Price	Total Project Cost	19X7		19X8		19X9	
			Cost for Year	% Completed During Year	Cost for Year	% Completed During Year	Cost for Year	% Completed During Year
1	$3,500,000	$2,800,000	$ 924,000	33%	$1,876,000	67%	—	—
2	1,200,000	880,000	880,000	100	—	—	—	—
3	7,400,000	6,300,000	1,260,000	20	2,205,000	35	$2,835,000	45%

Required

1. Assume Newport uses the completed-contract method for construction revenue. Compute the company's construction revenue and income to be reported in 19X7, 19X8, and 19X9.
2. Compute Newport's construction revenue and income to be reported in the three years if the company uses the percentage-of-completion method.

Problem 12-7A   *Accounting for revenues and expenses according to GAAP*

Nathan Nielsen established Nielsen Furniture Importers in January 19X4 to import furniture from Denmark. During 19X4 and 19X5 Nielsen kept the company's books and prepared the financial statements, although he had no training or experience in accounting. As a result, the accounts contain numerous errors. Nielsen recorded revenue from sales on the collection method, which is not appropriate for the company. Nielsen should have been using the sales method for revenues. He also recorded inventory purchases as the cost of goods sold.

When the value of the company warehouse increased by $35,000 in 19X6, Nielsen recorded an increase in the Warehouse Building account and credited Revenue. On January 2, 19X4, he borrowed $100,000 on a 9 percent, three-year note. He intended to wait until 19X7, when the note was due, to record the full amount of interest expense for three years. The company's records reveal the following amounts:

	19X4	19X5	19X6
Reported net income (net loss)................	$ (24,200)	$ 41,600	$ 44,100
Sales	256,700	303,500	366,800
Cash collections from customers	210,400	309,000	317,800
Purchases of inventory.....................	141,000	187,400	202,300
Ending inventory	35,800	59,900	73,400
Accrued expenses not recorded at year end; these expenses were recorded during the next year, when paid	13,500	22,600	30,100
Interest expense recorded....................	-0-	-0-	-0-
Revenue recorded for increase in the value of the warehouse building			35,000

Required

In early 19X7 Nielsen employed you as an accountant. Apply the concepts and principles of GAAP to compute the correct net income of Nielsen Furniture Importers for 19X4, 19X5, and 19X6.

(Group B)

Problem 12-1B *Identifying the basis for good accounting practices*

The following accounting practices are in accord with generally accepted accounting principles. Identify all the accounting concepts and principles that form the basis for each accounting practice. More than one concept or principle may apply.

a. The cost of office equipment such as staplers and wastebaskets is not capitalized and depreciated because of their relative insignificance.

b. A fire destroyed the company warehouse after December 31, 19X7, and before the financial statements were published in early February 19X8. Although the fire loss is insured, reconstruction of the warehouse will disrupt the company's operations. This subsequent event will be reported in the 19X7 financial statements.

c. A chemical company accounts for its operations by dividing the business into four separate units. This division enables the company to evaluate each unit apart from the others.

d. A building-materials company accrues employee salaries at year end even though the salaries will be paid during the first few days of the new year.

e. Assets are reported at liquidation value on the financial statements of a company that is going out of business.

f. The cost of machinery is being depreciated over a 5-year life because independent engineers believe the machinery will become obsolete after that time. (The company had hoped to depreciate the machinery over 10 years to report lower depreciation and higher net income in the early years of the asset's life.)

g. A manufacturing firm built some specialized equipment for its own use. The equipment would have cost $75,000 if purchased from an outside company, but the cost of constructing the equipment was only $48,000. The firm recorded the equipment at cost of $48,000.

h. Depreciation of the home-office building is difficult to relate to particular sales. Therefore, the company records depreciation expense on a time basis.

i. A company wishes to change its method of accounting for revenue. However, the company does not switch because it wants to use the same accounting method that other companies in the industry use.

j. Because it is often difficult to collect installment receivables, a retailer uses the installment method of revenue recognition rather than the sales method.

Problem 12-2B *Identifying the concepts and principles violated by bad accounting practices*

The following accounting practices are *not* in accord with generally accepted accounting principles. A few of the practices violate more than one concept or principle. Identify all the accounting concepts and principles not followed in each situation.

a. Butler Manufacturing does not report a lawsuit in which it is the defendant. Alvin Butler, the president, argues that the outcome of the case is uncertain and that to report the lawsuit would introduce subjective data into the financial statements.

b. Todd Department Store records cost of goods sold in a predetermined amount each month regardless of the level of sales.

c. Tim Ihnacek is having difficulty evaluating the success of his advertising firm because he fails to separate business assets from personal assets.

d. Tapes Unlimited is continuing in business, but its owner accounts for assets as though the store were liquidating.

e. Major Construction Company recognizes all revenue on long-term construction projects at the start of construction.

f. All amounts on the balance sheet and income statement of Business Products Company have been adjusted for changes in the value of the dollar during the period.

g. Rizzuto Grain Company records one half of the depreciation of its grain silos when it purchases them and the other half over their estimated useful lives.

h. Day's Boutique sells high-fashion clothing to customers on credit. Thus far, collection losses on receivables have been very small. Nevertheless, Bonnie Day, the owner, uses the collection method to recognize revenue. The entity's revenue is understated because credit sales are not accounted for properly.

i. Alvarez Importers changed from the FIFO method to the LIFO method for inventory but did not report the accounting change in the financial statements.

j. Martin Supply Company applied the lower-of-cost-or-market method to account for its inventory. Martin used an estimate of the inventory value developed by its management. This estimate differed widely from estimates supplied by two independent appraisers. The estimates of the two appraisers were close together.

Problem 12-3B *Recording and reporting transactions according to GAAP*

The accounting records of Mortensen Publishing Company reveal the following information prior to closing the books at April 30, the end of the current fiscal year:

a. Accounts receivable include $29,800 from Miller Bookstore, which has declared bankruptcy. Mortensen, which uses the allowance method to account for bad debts, expects to receive only one fourth of the amount receivable from Miller.

b. No interest has been accrued on a $60,000, 11 percent, 90-day note payable issued on March 31.

c. The merchandise inventory, with a cost of $54,000, has a current market value of only $40,700. Mortensen uses a periodic inventory system and has not made the April 30 entry to record ending inventory.

d. Property tax is due each April 30, and Mortensen has received the city/county property tax bill of $3,650. However, the company has not recorded property tax at April 30 because Mortensen plans to record the tax when it is paid in May.

e. The company's office building was recently valued by independent appraisers at

$640,000. This valuation is $290,000 more than Mortensen paid for the building and is $410,000 more than its cost less accumulated depreciation.

f. Three years ago on May 1, Mortensen paid $440,000 for its printing equipment. The company has depreciated the equipment by the straight-line method over an expected useful life of 10 years using a residual value of $40,000. Having used the equipment for 2 years, Mortensen determined at the beginning of the current year that it will remain in service for a total of only 8 years. The company will continue to use the straight-line method and $40,000 residual value for accounting purposes.

g. On May 13, before Mortensen issued its financial statements for the year ended April 30, the company's principal customer, Mears, Rareback and Co., declared its intention to cease doing business with Mortensen. This event is significant because for the past 10 years Mears has accounted for approximately 65 percent of Mortensen's sales. Consequently, Mortensen's ability to sustain its recent level of sales in future years is seriously in doubt.

Required

Make all journal entries needed at April 30 to record this information. Explanations are not required. Identify those items *not* requiring a journal entry, giving the reason why an entry is not needed. If a note to the financial statements is needed, write the note.

Problem 12-4B   *Using the installment-revenue method*

Bayview Resorts sells land on the installment plan. Collections of installment receivables have deteriorated. The company's accountants are considering the different methods of recording revenues. Revenue, expense, and collection data for the current year are as follows:

	19X3
Installment sales	$1,200,000
Cost of land sold	660,000
Collections of installment receivables from sales of 19X2	240,000
19X3	210,000

The gross profit percentage on 19X2 installment sales was 46 percent.

Required

1. Which method should be used to account for revenues if collections are extremely doubtful? If collections are reasonably assured? Which method is more advantageous for income tax purposes? Why?

2. Compute gross profit for 19X3 under the sales method, the collection method, and the installment method.

Problem 12-5B   *Using the installment-revenue method*

Meridian Electrical makes all sales on the installment basis but uses the sales method to record revenue. The company's income statements for the most recent three years are as follows:

	Year 1	Year 2	Year 3
Sales	$380,000	$404,000	$370,000
Cost of goods sold	190,000	181,800	199,800
Gross profit	190,000	222,200	170,200
Operating expenses	110,600	130,700	125,100
Net income	$ 79,400	$ 91,500	$ 45,100
Collections from sales of year 1	$108,000	$181,000	$ 82,000
Collections from sales of year 2		143,000	209,000
Collections from sales of year 3			163,000

Required

Compute the amount of net income Meridian would have reported if the company had used the installment method for revenue. Ignore the effect of uncollectible accounts and present your answer in the following format:

Installment-method net income:	Year 1	Year 2	Year 3
Gross profit	$	$	$
Operating expenses.	110,600	130,700	125,100
Net income	$	$	$

Problem 12-6B *Accounting for construction income*

Diamond Bridge Company constructs bridges under long-term contracts. During 19X5, Diamond began three projects that progressed according to the following schedule during 19X5, 19X6, and 19X7:

			19X5		19X6		19X7	
Project	Contract Price	Total Project Cost	Cost for Year	% Completed During Year	Cost for Year	% Completed During Year	Cost for Year	% Completed During Year
1	$2,100,000	$1,600,000	$1,600,000	100%	—	—	—	—
2	3,100,000	2,200,000	484,000	22	$1,716,000	78%	—	—
3	1,800,000	1,400,000	140,000	10	840,000	60	$420,000	30%

Required

1. Assume Diamond uses the completed-contract method for construction revenue. Compute the company's construction revenue and income to be reported in 19X5, 19X6, and 19X7.

2. Compute Diamond's construction revenue and income to be reported in the three years if the company uses the percentage-of-completion method.

Problem 12-7B *Accounting for revenues and expenses according to GAAP*

Roberta Katz established Katz Home Furnishings in January 19X7. During 19X7, 19X8, and most of 19X9 Katz kept the company's books and prepared its financial statements, although she had no training or experience in accounting. As a result, the accounts and statements contain numerous errors. For example, Katz recorded only cash receipts from customers as revenue. The sales method is appropriate for the business. She recorded inventory purchases as the cost of goods sold. When the current market value of her company's inventory increased by $15,600 in 19X7 and by $3,900 in 19X9, Katz debited the Inventory account and credited Revenue. She recorded no depreciation during 19X7, 19X8, and 19X9.

Late in 19X9 Katz employed an accountant, who determined that depreciable assets of the firm cost $170,000 on June 30, 19X7, had an expected residual value of $10,000, and a total useful life of eight years. The accountant believes the straight-line depreciation method is appropriate for Katz's plant assets. The company's fiscal year ends December 31. At the end of 19X9 the company's records reveal the amounts on the following page.

Required

Apply the concepts and principles of GAAP to compute the correct net income of Katz Home Furnishings for 19X7, 19X8, and 19X9.

	19X7	19X8	19X9
Reported net income (net loss)...............	$ 9,300	$ (11,200)	$ 52,900
Sales	131,800	164,700	226,100
Cash collections from customers..............	106,500	151,300	239,600
Purchases of inventory.....................	100,600	136,000	191,700
Ending inventory	20,800	47,400	83,700
Accrued expenses not recorded at year end; these expenses were recorded during the next year, when paid..............................	3,800	2,700	6,800
Depreciation expense recorded	-0-	-0-	-0-
Revenue recorded for increase in the value of inventory	15,600		3,900

Decision Problem

Measuring Income According to GAAP

O'Hara Furniture Company was founded in January 19X5 by Bernard and Virginia O'Hara, who share the management of the business. Virginia does the purchasing and manages the sales staff. Bernard keeps the books and handles financial matters. The O'Haras believe the store has prospered, but they are uncertain about precisely how well it has done. It is now December 31, 19X5, and they are trying to decide whether to borrow a substantial sum in order to expand the business.

They have asked your help because of your accounting knowledge. You learn that the O'Haras opened the store with an initial investment of $45,000 cash and a building valued at $100,000. The cash receipts totaled $180,000, which included collections, $15,000 invested by the O'Haras, $50,000 borrowed from the bank in the name of the furniture store, and $7,500 of earnings from a family inheritance. The store made credit sales of $95,000 that have not been collected at December 31. The O'Haras purchased furniture inventory on credit for $160,000, and inventory at December 31, 19X5, was $75,000. The store paid $90,000 on account.

The 19X5 cash expenses were $92,000. Additional miscellaneous expenses totaled $2,700 at year's end. These expenses included the O'Haras' household costs of $10,000 and interest on the business debt. The $5,000 of depreciation on the store building was omitted.

Bernard and Virginia have decided to proceed with the expansion plan only if net income for the first year was $40,000 or more. Bernard's analysis of the cash account leads him to believe that net income was $43,000, so he is ready to expand. You are less certain than Bernard of the wisdom of this decision primarily because the O'Haras have mixed personal and business assets.

Required

1. Use a Cash T-account to show how Bernard arrived at the $43,000 amount for net income.
2. Prepare the income statement of the furniture store for 19X5.
3. Should the O'Haras borrow to expand their business?
4. Which accounting concept or principle is most fundamental to this problem situation?

Financial Statement Problem

Disclosure in action

The most fundamental note in a company's financial statement is the summary of significant policies. Examine Gulf+Western's statements in Appendix C, and answer these questions.

1. The section headed "Theatrical and Television Inventories, Revenues and Costs" in Note A—Significant Accounting Policies tells how Gulf+Western accounts for its theatrical and television revenues. When does the company record theatrical revenues? Revenues from television license agreements? Revenues from the sale of videocassettes?
2. The last paragraph in the "theatrical" section in Note A refers to *unamortized film costs.* What does this term mean? What was this item's remaining life at October 31, 1987?
3. Do the notes indicate any important subsequent events? If so, describe them.
4. Page 26—immediately after the income statement—reports revenues and operating income by business segment. Which segment produced the most revenue in fiscal 1987? Which segment generated the highest operating income?
5. Explain how the concept of materiality is clearly evident in the financial statements.

Answers to Self-Study Questions

1.	c	7.	d
2.	a	8.	d
3.	c	9.	b
4.	b	10.	b

5. a ($10,000 − $7,000)/$10,000 = .30 × $1,500 = $450
6. a $180,000/$720,000 = .25 × $900,000 = $225,000;
    $225,000 − $180,000 = $45,000

Accounting for Partnerships

Forming a partnership is easy. It requires no permission from government authorities and involves no legal procedures. When two persons decide to go into business together, a partnership is automatically formed.

A **partnership** is an association of two or more persons who co-own a business for profit. This definition stems from the Uniform Partnership Act, which nearly every state has adopted to regulate partnership practice.

A partnership brings together the capital, talents, and experience of the partners. Business opportunities closed to an individual may open up to a partnership. Suppose neither Pedigo nor Lee has enough capital individually to buy a $300,000 parcel of land. They may be able to afford it together in a partnership. Or VanAllen, a tax accountant, and Kahn, an investment counselor, may pool their talents and know-how. Their partnership may offer a fuller range of money management services than either person could offer alone. Combining their experience may increase income for each of them.

Partnerships come in all sizes. Many partnerships have fewer then 10 partners. Some physician and law firms may have 20 or more partners. The largest CPA firms have 1,000 or more partners.

Characteristics of a Partnership _____

Starting a partnership is voluntary. A person cannot be forced to join a partnership, and partners cannot be forced to accept another person as a partner. Although the partnership agreement may be oral, a written agreement between the partners reduces the chance of a misunderstanding. Several features are unique to the partnership form of business. The following characteristics distinguish partnerships from sole proprietorships and corporations, which we examine in later chapters.

The Written Partnership Agreement

OBJECTIVE 1

Identify the characteristics, including advantages and disadvantages, of a partnership

A business partnership is like a marriage. To be successful, the partners must cooperate. However, business partners do not vow to remain together for life. Business partnerships come and go. To make certain that each partner fully understands how a particular partnership operates, and to cut down on the chances that any partner might misunderstand how the business is run, partners may draw up a **partnership agreement,** also called the **articles of partnership.** This agreement is a contract between the partners, so transactions involving the agreement are governed by contract law. The articles of partnership should make the following points clear:

1. Name, location, and nature of the business
2. Name, capital investment, and duties of each partner
3. Method of sharing profits and losses by the partners
4. Withdrawals allowed to the partners
5. Procedures for settling disputes between the partners
6. Procedures for admitting new partners
7. Procedures for settling up with a partner who withdraws from the business
8. Procedures for liquidating the partnership—selling the assets, paying the liabilities, and disbursing any remaining cash to the partners

As partners enter and leave the business, the old partnership is dissolved and a new partnership is formed. Drawing up a separate agreement for each new partnership may be expensive and time consuming.

Limited Life

A partnership has a life limited by the length of time that all partners continue to own the business. When a partner withdraws from the business, that partnership ceases to exist. A new partnership may emerge to continue the same business, but the old partnership has been *dissolved.* **Dissolution** is the ending of a partnership. Likewise, the addition of a new partner dissolves the old partnership and creates a new partnership. Partnerships are sometimes formed for a particular business venture, like a mining operation or a real estate investment. When the mine is depleted or the real estate is sold, the partnership may be dissolved.

Mutual Agency

Mutual agency in a partnership means that every partner can bind the business to a contract within the scope of the partnership's regular business operations. If an individual partner in a CPA firm enters into a contract with a person or another business to provide accounting service, then the firm—not the individual who signs the contract—is bound to provide that service. However, if that same CPA signs a contract to purchase home lawn services for the summer months, the partnership would not be bound to pay. Contracting for lawn services does not fall within the partnership's regular business operations.

Unlimited Liability

Each partner has an **unlimited personal liability** for the debts of the partnership. When a partnership cannot pay its debts with business assets, the partners must use their personal assets to meet the debt.

Avilla and Davis are the two partners in AD Company. The business has had an unsuccessful year, and the partnership's liabilities exceed its assets by $120,000. Davis and Avilla must pay this amount with their personal assets.

Recall that each partner has *unlimited* liability. If a partner is unable to pay his or her part of the debt, the other partner (or partners) must make payment. If Davis can pay only $50,000 of the liability, Avilla must pay $70,000 ($120,000 − $50,000).

Unlimited liability and mutual agency are closely related. A dishonest partner or a partner with poor judgment may commit the partnership to a contract under which the business loses money. In turn, creditors may force *all* the partners to pay the debt from their personal assets. Hence, a business partner should be chosen with great care.

Co-ownership of Property

Any asset—cash, inventory, machinery, and so on—that a partner invests in the partnership becomes the joint property of all the partners. Also, each partner has a claim to the business's profits.

No Partnership Income Taxes

A partnership pays no income tax on its business income. Instead, the net income of the partnership is divided and becomes the taxable income of the partners. Suppose AD Company earned net income of $80,000, shared equally by partners Avilla and Davis. AD Company would pay no income tax *as a business entity*. However, Avilla and Davis would pay income tax as individuals on their $40,000 shares of partnership income.

Accounting for a partnership is much like accounting for a proprietorship. We record buying and selling, collecting and paying in a partnership just as we do for a business with only one owner. However, because a partnership has more than one owner, the partnership must have more than one owner's equity account. Every partner in the business—whether the firm has two or two thousand partners—has an individual owner's equity account. Often these accounts carry the name of the particular partner and the word *capital*. For example, the owner's equity account for Larry Insdorf would read "Insdorf, Capital." Similarly, each partner has a withdrawal account. If the number of partners is large, the general ledger may contain the single account Partners' Capital, or Owners' Equity. A subsidiary ledger can be used for individual partner accounts.

Let's see how to account for the multiple owner's equity accounts—and learn how they appear on the balance sheet—by taking a look at how to account for starting up a partnership.

Initial Investments by Partners _____

Partners in a new partnership may invest assets and liabilities in the business. These contributions are entered in the books in the same way that a proprietor's assets and liabilities are recorded. Subtracting each person's liabilities from his or her assets yields the amount to be credited to the capital account for that person. Often the partners hire an independent firm to appraise their assets and liabilities at current market value at the time a partnership is formed. This outside evaluation assures an objective accounting for what each partner brings into the business.

Assume Benz and Hanna form a partnership to manufacture and sell computer software. Benz brings to the partnership cash of $10,000, accounts receivable of $30,000, inventory of $70,000, computer equipment with a cost of $400,000, and accounts payable of $85,000. Hanna contributes cash of $5,000 and a software program. The development of this program cost Hanna $18,000, but its current market value is much greater. Suppose the partners agree on the following values based on an independent appraisal:

Benz's contributions:

Cash, $10,000; inventory, $70,000; and accounts payable, $85,000 (the appraiser believes the current market values for these items equal Benz's values)
Accounts receivable, $30,000, less allowance for doubtful accounts of $5,000
Computer equipment, $500,000, less accumulated depreciation of $50,000

Hanna's contributions:

Cash, $5,000
Computer software, $100,000

Note that current market value differs only slightly from book value for Benz's computer equipment. However, the appraiser valued Hanna's $18,000 computer software at the much higher $100,000 figure. The partners record their initial investments at the current market values. The title of each owner's equity account includes the owner's name and *Capital*—exactly as for a proprietorship.

Benz's investment:

June 1	Cash	10,000	
	Accounts Receivable	30,000	
	Inventory	70,000	
	Computer Equipment	500,000	
	Allowance for Doubtful Accounts		5,000
	Accumulated Depreciation		50,000
	Accounts Payable		85,000
	Benz, Capital		470,000
	To record Benz's investment in the partnership.		

OBJECTIVE 2

Account for partners' initial investments in a partnership

Hanna's investment:

June 1	Cash	5,000	
	Computer Software	100,000	
	Hanna, Capital.		105,000
	To record Hanna's investment in the partnership.		

The initial partnership balance sheet reports these amounts as follows:

Benz and Hanna **Balance Sheet** **June 1, 19X5**					
Assets			**Liabilities**		
Cash.		$ 15,000	Accounts payable . . .		$ 85,000
Accounts receivable .	$ 30,000				
Less allowance for doubtful accounts	(5,000)	25,000			
Inventory.		70,000	**Capital**		
Computer equipment	500,000				
Less accumulated depreciation.	50,000	450,000	Benz, capital . . . . Hanna, capital.		470,000 105,000
Computer software. .		100,000	Total liabilities and		
Total assets		$660,000	capital		$660,000

Each owner's capital account appears under the heading Capital. Having more than one capital account distinguishes a partnership balance sheet from a proprietorship balance sheet.

Sharing Partnership Profits and Losses _____

How to distribute profits and losses among partners is one of the most challenging aspects of managing a partnership. If the partners have not drawn up an agreement, or if the agreement does not state how the partners will divide profits and losses, then, according to law, the partners must share profits and losses equally. If the agreement specifies a method for sharing profits but not losses, then losses are shared in the same proportion as profits. For example, a partner receiving 75 percent of the profits would likewise absorb 75 percent of any losses.

In some cases, an equal division is not fair. One partner may perform more work for the business than the other partner, or one partner may make a larger capital contribution. In the preceding example, Hanna might agree to work longer hours for the partnership than Benz in order to earn a greater share of profits. Benz could argue that he should receive more of the profits because he contributed more net assets ($470,000) than Hanna did ($105,000). Hanna might contend that her computer software program is the partnership's most important asset and that her share of the profits should be greater than Benz's share. Arriving at fair sharing of profits and losses in a partnership may be difficult. We now discuss the options available in determining partners' shares.

Sharing Based on a Stated Fraction

Partners may agree to any profit-and-loss-sharing method they desire. Suppose the partnership agreement of Cagle and Dean allocates two thirds of the business profits and losses to Cagle and one third to Dean. If net income for the year is $90,000 and all revenue and expense accounts have been closed, the Income Summary account has a credit balance of $90,000, as follows:

Income Summary

	Bal.	90,000

The entry to close this account and allocate the profit to the partners' capital accounts is

Dec. 31	Income Summary..............................	90,000	
	Cagle, Capital ($90,000 × ⅔)		60,000
	Dean, Capital ($90,000 × ⅓)		30,000
	To allocate net income to partners.		

Consider the effect of this entry. Does Cagle get cash of $60,000 and Dean cash of $30,000? No. The increase in the capital accounts of the partners cannot be linked to any particular asset, including cash. Instead, the entry indicates that Cagle's ownership in *all* the assets of the business increased by $60,000 and Dean's by $30,000.

If the year's operations resulted in a net loss of $66,000, the Income Summary account would have a debit balance of $66,000. In that case, the closing entry to allocate the loss to the partners' capital accounts would be

Dec. 31	Cagle, Capital ($66,000 × ⅔)	44,000	
	Dean, Capital ($66,000 × ⅓)	22,000	
	Income Summary.........................		66,000
	To allocate net loss to partners.		

Sharing Based on Partners' Capital Contributions

Profits and losses are often allocated in proportion to the partners' capital contributions in the business. Suppose Antoine, Barber, and Cabañas are partners in ABC Company. Their capital accounts have the following balances at the end of the year, before the closing entries:

Antoine, Capital.........................	$ 40,000
Barber, Capital	60,000
Cabañas, Capital	50,000
Total capital balances...................	$150,000

Assume that the partnership earned a profit of $120,000 for the year. To allocate this amount based on capital contributions, each partner's percentage share of the partnership's total capital balance must be computed. We simply divide each partner's contribution by the total capital amount. These figures, multiplied by the $120,000 profit amount, yield each partner's share of the year's profits:

Antoine:	$40,000/$150,000 × $120,000	= $ 32,000
Barber:	$60,000/$150,000 × $120,000	= 48,000
Cabañas:	$50,000/$150,000 × $120,000	= 40,000
	Net income allocated to partners	= **$120,000**

The closing entry to allocate the profit to the partners' capital accounts is

Dec. 31 Income Summary..............................	120,000	
Antoine, Capital.........................		32,000
Barber, Capital...........................		48,000
Cabañas, Capital		40,000
To allocate net income to partners.		

After this closing entry, the partners' capital balances are

Antoine, Capital ($40,000 + $32,000)	$ 72,000
Barber, Capital ($60,000 + $48,000).................	108,000
Cabañas, Capital ($50,000 + $40,000)..............	90,000
Total capital balances after allocation of net income....	$270,000

Sharing Based on Capital Contributions and Service to the Partnership

One partner, regardless of his or her capital contribution, may put more work into the business than the other partners. Even among partners who log equal service time, one person's superior experience and knowledge may command a greater share of income. To reward the harder-working or more valuable person, the profit-and-loss-sharing method may be based on a combination of contributed capital *and* service to the business.

Assume Randolph and Scott formed a partnership in which Randolph invested $60,000 and Scott invested $40,000, a total of $100,000. Scott devotes more time to the partnership and earns the larger salary. Accordingly, the two partners have agreed to share profits as follows:

1. The first $50,000 of partnership profits is to be allocated based on partners' capital contributions to the business.
2. The next $60,000 of profits is to be allocated based on service, with Randolph receiving $24,000 and Scott receiving $36,000.
3. Any remaining amount is allocated equally.

If net income for the first year is $125,000, the partners' shares of this profit are computed as follows:

	Randolph	Scott	Total
Total net income............................			$125,000
Sharing of first $50,000 of net income, based on capital contributions:			
Randolph ($60,000/$100,000 × $50,000)........	$30,000		
Scott ($40,000/$100,000 × $50,000)........		$20,000	
Total.................................			50,000
Net income remaining for allocation.............			75,000
Sharing of next $60,000, based on service:			
Randolph.................................	24,000		
Scott....................................		36,000	
Total.................................			60,000
Net income remaining for allocation.............			15,000
Remainder shared equally:			
Randolph ($15,000 × ½)	7,500		
Scott ($15,000 × ½)		7,500	
Total.................................			15,000
Net income remaining for allocation.............			$ -0-
Net income allocated to the partners.............	$61,500	$63,500	$125,000

Based on this allocation, the closing entry is

Dec. 31	Income Summary.............................	125,000	
	Randolph, Capital		61,500
	Scott, Capital		63,500
	To allocate net income to partners.		

Sharing Based on Salaries and Interest

Partners may be rewarded for their service and their capital contributions to the business in other ways. In one sharing plan, the partners are allocated salaries plus interest on their capital balances. Assume Lewis and Clark form an oil-exploration partnership. At the beginning of the year, their capital balances are $80,000 and $100,000, respectively. The partnership agreement allocates annual salary of $43,000 to Lewis and $35,000 to Clark. After salaries are allocated, each partner earns 8 percent interest on his beginning capital balance. Any remaining net income is divided equally. Partnership profit of $96,000 would be allocated as follows:

	Lewis	Clark	Total
Total net income................................			$96,000
First, salaries:			
Lewis.....................................	$43,000		
Clark		$35,000	
Total.....................................			78,000
Net income remaining for allocation...............			18,000
Second, interest on beginning capital balances:			
Lewis ($80,000 × .08)........................	6,400		
Clark ($100,000 × .08)........................		8,000	
Total.....................................			14,400
Net income remaining for allocation...............			3,600
Third, remainder shared equally:			
Lewis ($3,600 × ½).........................	1,800		
Clark ($3,600 × ½).........................		1,800	
Total.....................................			3,600
Net income remaining for allocation..............			$ -0-
Net income allocated to the partners	$51,200	$44,800	$96,000

Based on this allocation, the closing entry is

Dec. 31	Income Summary.............................	96,000	
	Lewis, Capital		51,200
	Clark, Capital...........................		44,800
	To allocate net income to partners.		

These salaries and interest amounts are *not* business expenses in the usual sense. Partners do not work for their own business to earn a salary, as an employee does. They do not loan money to their own business to earn interest. Their goal is for the partnership to earn a profit. Therefore, salaries and interest in partnership agreements are simply ways of expressing the allocation of profits and losses to the partners. For example, the salary component of partner income rewards service to the partnership. The interest component rewards a partner's investment of cash or other assets in the business.

In the preceding illustration, net income exceeded the sum of salary and interest. If the partnership profit is less than the allocated sum of salary and interest, a negative remainder will occur at some stage in the allocation process. Even so, the partners use the same method for allocation purposes. For example, assume that Lewis and Clark Partnership earned only $82,000.

	Lewis	Clark	Total
Total net income			$ 82,000
First, salaries:			
Lewis	$43,000		
Clark....................................		$35,000	
Total			78,000
Net income remaining for allocation			4,000
Second, interest on beginning capital balances:			
Lewis ($80,000 × .08)	6,400		
Clark ($100,000 × .08)		8,000	
Total			14,400
Net income remaining for allocation			(10,400)
Third, remainder shared equally:			
Lewis ($10,400 × ½)	(5,200)		
Clark ($10,400 × ½)		(5,200)	
Total			(10,400)
Net income remaining for allocation			$ -0-
Net income allocated to the partners	$44,200	$37,800	$ 82,000

A net loss would be allocated to Lewis and Clark in the same manner outlined for net income. The sharing procedure would begin with the net loss and then allocate salary, interest, and any other specified amounts to the partners.

We see that partners may allocate profits and losses based on a stated fraction, contributed capital, service, interest on capital, or any combination of these factors. Each partnership shapes its profit-and-loss-sharing ratio to fit its own needs.

Partner Drawings

Partners, like anyone else, need cash for personal living expenses. Partnership agreements usually allow partners to withdraw cash or other assets from the business. Drawings from a partnership are recorded exactly as illustrated in previous chapters for drawings from a proprietorship. Assume Lewis and Clark are each allowed a monthly withdrawal of $3,500. The partnership records the March withdrawal with this entry:

Mar. 31	Lewis, Drawing.................................	3,500	
	Clark, Drawing	3,500	
	Cash.....................................		7,000
	Monthly partner withdrawals.		

During the year, each partner drawing account accumulates 12 such amounts, a total of $42,000 ($3,500 × 12). At the end of the period, the general ledger shows the following account balances immediately after net income has been closed to the partners' capital accounts. Assume these beginning balances for Lewis and Clark at the start of the year and that $82,000 of profit has been allocated based on the preceding illustration.

Lewis, Capital				Clark, Capital		
	Jan. 1	Bal.	80,000		Jan. 1	Bal.	100,000
	Dec. 31	Net inc.	44,200		Dec. 31	Net inc.	37,800

Lewis, Drawing				Clark, Drawing		
Dec. 31 Bal.	42,000			Dec. 31 Bal.	42,000	

The withdrawal accounts must be closed at the end of the period. The final closing entries transfer their balances to the partner's capital account as follows:

Dec. 31	Lewis, Capital	42,000	
	Lewis, Drawing		42,000
	Clark, Capital.................................	42,000	
	Clark, Drawing		42,000
	To close partner drawing accounts.		

After closing, the accounts appear as follows:

Lewis, Capital						Clark, Capital					
Dec. 31 Clo.	42,000	Jan. 1	Bal.	80,000		Dec. 31 Clo.	42,000	Jan. 1	Bal.	100,000
		Dec. 31	Net inc.	44,200				Dec. 31	Net inc.	37,800
		Dec. 31	Bal.	82,200				Dec. 31	Bal.	95,800

Lewis, Drawing					Clark, Drawing			
Dec. 31 Bal.	42,000	Dec. 31 Clo.	42,000		Dec. 31 Bal.	42,000	Dec. 31 Clo.	42,000

In this case, Lewis withdrew less than his share of the partnership net income. Consequently, his capital account grew during the period. Clark, however, withdrew more than his share of net income. His capital account decreased.

Partnerships, as we have mentioned, do not last forever. We turn now to a discussion of how partnerships dissolve—and how new partnerships arise.

Dissolution of a Partnership

A partnership lasts only as long as its partners remain in the business. The addition of a new member or the withdrawal of an existing member dissolves the partnership.

Often a new partnership is formed to carry on the former partnership's business. In fact, the new partnership may choose to retain the dissolved partnership's name. Price Waterhouse & Company, for example, is an accounting firm that retires and hires partners during the year. Thus the former partnership dissolves and a new partnership begins many times. The business, however, retains the name and continues operations. Other partnerships may dissolve and then re-form under a new name. Let's look now at the ways that a new member may gain admission into an existing partnership.

Admission by Purchasing a Partner's Interest

A person may become a member of a partnership by gaining the approval of the other partner (or partners) for entrance into the firm *and* by purchasing a present partner's interest in the business. Let's assume that Fisher and Garcia have a partnership that carries these figures:

Cash.....................	$ 40,000	Total liabilities.............	$120,000
Other assets..............	360,000	Fisher, capital	110,000
		Garcia, capital	170,000
Total assets	$400,000	Total liabilities and capital ...	$400,000

Business is going so well that Fisher receives an offer from Dynak, an outside party, to buy her $110,000 interest in the business for $150,000. Fisher agrees to sell out to Dynak, and Garcia approves Dynak as a new partner. The firm records the transfer of capital interest in the business with this entry:

Apr. 16	Fisher, Capital	110,000	
	Dynak, Capital........................		110,000
	To transfer Fisher's equity in the business to Dynak.		

OBJECTIVE 4

Account for the admission of a new partner to the business

The debit side of the entry closes Fisher's capital account because she is no longer a partner in the firm. The credit side opens Dynak's capital account because Fisher's equity has been transferred to Dynak. Notice that the entry amount is Fisher's capital balance ($110,000) and not the $150,000 price that Dynak paid Fisher to buy into the business. The full $150,000 goes to Fisher, including the $40,000 difference between her capital balance and the price received from Dynak. In this example, the partnership receives no cash because the transaction was between Dynak and Fisher, not between Dynak and the partnership. Suppose Dynak pays Fisher less than Fisher's capital balance. That does not affect the entry on the partnership books. Fisher's equity is transferred to Dynak at book value ($110,000).

The old partnership has dissolved. Garcia and Dynak draw up a new partnership agreement, with a new profit-and-loss-sharing ratio, and continue business operations. If Garcia does not accept Dynak as a partner, Dynak gets no voice in management of the firm. However, under the Uniform Partnership Act, the purchaser shares in the profits and losses of the firm and in its assets at liquidation.

Admission by Investing in the Partnership

A person may also be admitted as a partner by investing directly in the partnership rather than by purchasing an existing partner's interest. The new partner contributes assets—for example, cash, inventory, or equipment—to the business. Assume that the partnership of Ingel and Jay has the following assets, liabilities, and capital:

Cash.....................	$ 20,000	Total liabilities.............	$100,000
Other assets...............	240,000	Ingel, capital	70,000
		Jay, capital................	90,000
Total assets	$260,000	Total liabilities and capital ...	$260,000

Kahn offers to invest equipment and land (Other assets) with a market value of $80,000 to persuade the existing partners to take her into the business. Ingel and Jay agree to dissolve the existing partnership and to start up a new business, giving Kahn one-third interest in exchange for the contributed assets. The entry to record Kahn's investment is

July 18	Other Assets................................	80,000	
	Kahn, Capital		80,000
	To admit L. Kahn as a partner with a one-third interest in the business.		

After this entry, the partnership books show:

Cash....................	$ 20,000	Total liabilities.............	$100,000
Other assets ($240,000 +		Ingel, capital	70,000
$80,000)...............	320,000	Jay, capital................	90,000
		Kahn, capital	80,000
Total assets	$340,000	Total liabilities and capital ...	$340,000

Kahn's one-third interest in the partnership [$80,000/($70,000 + $90,000 + $80,000) = 1/3] does not necessarily entitle her to one third of the profits. The sharing of profits and losses is a separate consideration in the partnership agreement.

In the previous example, Dynak paid an individual member (Fisher), not the partnership. Note that Kahn's payment (the other assets) goes into the partnership.

Admission by Investing in the Partnership — Bonus to the Old Partners. The more successful a partnership, the higher the payment the partners may demand from a person entering the business. Partners in a business that is doing quite well might require an incoming person to pay them a bonus. The bonus increases the current partners' capital accounts.

Suppose that Nagasawa and Osburn's partnership has earned above-average profits for 10 years. The two partners share profits and losses equally. The balance sheet carries these figures:

Cash....................	$ 40,000	Total liabilities.............	$100,000
Other assets...............	210,000	Nagasawa, capital..........	70,000
		Osburn, capital	80,000
Total assets	$250,000	Total liabilities and capital ...	$250,000

The partners agree to admit Parker to a one-fourth interest with his cash investment of $90,000. Parker's capital balance on the partnership books is $60,000, computed as follows:

Partnership capital before Parker is admitted ($70,000 + $80,000)	$150,000
Parker's investment in the partnership.	90,000
Partnership capital after Parker is admitted	$240,000
Parker's capital in the partnership ($240,000 × ¼)	$ 60,000

The entry on the partnership books to record Parker's investment is

Mar. 11	Cash.	90,000	
	Parker, Capital.		60,000
	Nagasawa, Capital ($30,000 × ½)		15,000
	Osburn, Capital ($30,000 × ½)		15,000
	To admit G. Parker as a partner with a one-fourth interest in the business.		

Parker's capital account is credited for his one-fourth interest in the partnership. The other partners share the $30,000 difference between Parker's investment ($90,000) and his equity in the business ($60,000). This difference is accounted for as income to the old partners and is, therefore, allocated to them based on their profit-and-loss ratio.

The new partnership's balance sheet reports these amounts:

Cash ($40,000 + $90,000) . . .	$130,000	Total liabilities	$100,000
Other assets	210,000	Nagasawa, capital ($70,000 + $15,000)	85,000
		Osburn, capital ($80,000 + $15,000)	95,000
		Parker, capital	60,000
Total assets	$340,000	Total liabilities and capital . . .	$340,000

Admission by Investing in the Partnership — Bonus to the New Partner. A potential new partner may be so important that the existing partners offer him or her a partnership share that includes a bonus. A law firm may strongly desire a former governor or other official as a partner because of the person's reputation. A restaurant owner may want to go into partnership with a famous sports personality like Jack Nicklaus or Magic Johnson.

Suppose Page and Osuka is a law partnership. The firm's balance sheet appears as follows:

Cash.	$140,000	Total liabilities	$120,000
Other assets	360,000	Page, capital	230,000
		Osuka, capital	150,000
Total assets	$500,000	Total liabilities and capital . . .	$500,000

The partners admit Schiller, a former attorney general, as a partner with a one-third interest in exchange for his cash investment of $100,000. At the time of Schiller's admission, the firm's capital is $380,000 — Page, $230,000, and Osuka, $150,000. Page and Osuka share profits and losses in the ratio of two thirds to Page and one third to Osuka. The computation of Schiller's equity in the partnership is

Partnership capital before Schiller is admitted ($230,000 + $150,000)	$380,000
Schiller's investment in the partnership	100,000
Partnership capital after Schiller is admitted	$480,000
Schiller's capital in the partnership ($480,000 × ⅓)	$160,000

The capital accounts of Page and Osuka are debited for the $60,000 difference between the new partner's equity ($160,000) and his investment ($100,000). The existing partners share this decrease in capital, which is accounted for as though it were a loss, based on their profit-and-loss ratio.

The entry to record Schiller's investment is

Aug. 24	Cash....................................	100,000	
	Page, Capital ($60,000 × ⅔)..................	40,000	
	Osuka, Capital ($60,000 × ⅓).................	20,000	
	Schiller, Capital.......................		160,000
	To admit M. Schiller as a partner with a one-third interest in the business.		

The new partnership's balance sheet reports these amounts:

Cash ($140,000 + $100,000)...............	$240,000	Total liabilities.............		$120,000
Other assets..............	360,000	Page, capital ($230,000 − $40,000)...............		190,000
		Osuka, capital ($150,000 − $20,000)...............		130,000
		Schiller, capital............		160,000
Total assets	$600,000	Total liabilities and capital ...		$600,000

Summary Problem for Your Review

The partnership of Taylor and Uvalde is considering admitting Vaughn as a partner on January 1, 19X8. The partnership general ledger includes the following balances on that date:

Cash......................	$ 9,000	Total liabilities.............	$ 50,000
Other assets..............	110,000	Taylor, capital	45,000
		Uvalde, capital.............	24,000
Total assets	$119,000	Total liabilities and capital ...	$119,000

Taylor's share of profits and losses is 60 percent, and Uvalde's share is 40 percent.

Required

1. Suppose Vaughn pays Uvalde $31,000 to acquire Uvalde's interest in the business. Taylor approves Vaughn as a partner.
   a. Record the transfer of owner's equity on the partnership books.
   b. Prepare the partnership balance sheet immediately after Vaughn is admitted as a partner.
2. Suppose Vaughn becomes a partner by investing $31,000 cash to acquire a one-fourth interest in the business.
   a. Compute Vaughn's capital balance, and record Vaughn's investment in the business.

b. Prepare the partnership balance sheet immediately after Vaughn is admitted as a partner. Include the heading.

3. Which way of admitting Vaughn to the partnership increases its total assets? Give your reason.

SOLUTION TO REVIEW PROBLEM

Requirement 1

a. Jan. 1 Uvalde, Capital 24,000

   Vaughn, Capital 24,000

   To transfer Uvalde's equity in the partnership to Vaughn.

b. The balance sheet for the partnership of Taylor and Vaughn is identical to the balance sheet given for Taylor and Uvalde in the problem, except that Vaughn's name replaces Uvalde's name in the title and in the listing of capital accounts.

Requirement 2

a. Computation of Vaughn's capital balance:

Partnership capital before Vaughn is admitted ($45,000 + $24,000) .	$ 69,000
Vaughn's investment in the partnership	31,000
Partnership capital after Vaughn is admitted	$100,000
Vaughn's capital in the partnership ($100,000 × ¼)	$ 25,000

Jan. 1. Cash 31,000

   Vaughn, Capital 25,000

   Taylor, Capital [($31,000 − $25,000) × .60]. . 3,600

   Uvalde, Capital [($31,000 − $25,000) × .40] . 2,400

   To admit Vaughn as a partner with a one-fourth interest in the business.

b.

Taylor, Uvalde, and Vaughn
Balance Sheet
January 1, 19X8

Cash ($9,000 +		Total liabilities	$ 50,000
$31,000)	$ 40,000	Taylor, capital ($45,000 +	
Other assets	110,000	$3,600)	48,600
		Uvalde, capital ($24,000 +	
		$2,400)	26,400
		Vaughn, capital	25,000
Total assets.	$150,000	Total liabilities and capital	$150,000

Requirement 3

Vaughn's investment in the partnership increases its total assets by the amount of his contribution. Total assets of the business are $150,000 after his investment, compared to $119,000 before. By contrast, Vaughn's purchase of Uvalde's interest in the business is a personal transaction between the two individuals. It does not affect the assets of the partnership regardless of the amount Vaughn pays Uvalde.

Withdrawal of a Partner

A partner may withdraw from the business for many reasons, including retirement or a dispute with the other partners. The partnership agreement should contain a provision to govern how to settle with a withdrawing partner. In the simplest case, as illustrated on page 505, a partner may withdraw and sell his or her interest to another partner in a personal transaction. The only entry needed to record this transfer of equity debits the withdrawing partner's capital account and credits the purchaser's capital account. The dollar amount of the entry is the capital balance of the withdrawing partner, regardless of the price paid by the purchaser. The accounting when one current partner buys a second partner's interest is the same as when an outside party buys a current partner's interest.

If the partner withdraws in the middle of the accounting period, it is necessary to update the partnership books to determine the withdrawing partner's capital balance. The business must measure net income or net loss for the fraction of the year up to the withdrawal date and allocate profit or loss according to the existing ratio. After closing the books, the business then accounts for the change in partnership capital.

The withdrawing partner may receive his or her share of the business in partnership assets other than cash. The question arises as to what value to assign the partnership assets: book value or current market value. The settlement procedure may specify an independent appraisal of assets to determine their current market value. If market values have changed, the appraisal will result in revaluing the partnership assets. This way the partners share in any market value changes that their efforts caused.

Suppose Isaac is retiring in midyear from the partnership of Green, Henry, and Isaac. After the books have been adjusted for partial-period income but before the asset appraisal, revaluation, and closing entries, the balance sheet reports:

Cash	$ 39,000	Total liabilities		$ 80,000
Inventory	44,000	Green, capital		54,000
Land	55,000	Henry, capital		43,000
Building	$95,000		Issac, capital	21,000
Less accum. depr.	35,000	60,000	Total liabilities and	
Total assets		$198,000	capital	$198,000

Assume an independent appraiser revalues the inventory at $38,000 (down from $44,000) and the land at $101,000 (up from $55,000). The partners share the differences between these assets' market values and their prior book values based on their profit-and-loss ratio. The partnership agreement has allocated one fourth of the profits to Green, one half to Henry, and one fourth to Isaac. (This ratio may be written 1 : 2 : 1 for one part to Green, two parts to Henry, and one part to Isaac.) For each share that Green or Isaac has, Henry has two. The entries to record the revaluation of the inventory and land are

July 31	Green, Capital ($6,000 × ¼)	1,500	
	Henry, Capital ($6,000 × ½)	3,000	
	Isaac, Capital ($6,000 × ¼)	1,500	
	Inventory ($44,000 − $38,000)		6,000
	To revalue the inventory and allocate the loss in value to the partners.		

31	Land ($101,000 − $55,000)	46,000	
	Green, Capital ($46,000 × ¼)		11,500
	Henry, Capital ($46,000 × ½)		23,000
	Isaac, Capital ($46,000 × ¼)		11,500

To revalue the land and allocate the gain in value to the partners.

After the revaluations, the partnership balance sheet reports:

Cash		$ 39,000	Total liabilities	$ 80,000
Inventory		38,000	Green, capital	
Land		101,000	($54,000 − $1,500 +	
Building	$95,000		$11,500)	64,000
Less accum. depr.	35,000	60,000	Henry, capital	
			($43,000 − $3,000 +	
			$23,000)	63,000
			Isaac, capital ($21,000 −	
			$1,500 + $11,500) . . .	31,000
			Total liabilities and	
Total assets		$238,000	capital	$238,000

The books now carry the assets at current market value, which becomes the new book value, and the capital accounts have been adjusted accordingly. Isaac has a claim to $31,000 in partnership assets. How is his withdrawal from the business accounted for?

Withdrawal at Book Value

If Isaac withdraws by taking cash equal to the book value of his owner's equity, the entry would be

July 31	Isaac, Capital.	31,000	
	Cash		31,000

To record withdrawal of K. Isaac from the partnership.

This entry records the payment of partnership cash to Isaac and the closing of his capital account upon withdrawal from the business.

Withdrawal at Less Than Book Value

The withdrawing partner may be so eager to leave the business that he is willing to take less than his equity. This situation has occurred in real estate and oil-drilling partnerships. Assume Isaac withdraws from the business and agrees to take partnership cash of $10,000 and the new partnership's note for $15,000. This $25,000 settlement is $6,000 less than Isaac's $31,000 equity in the business. The remaining partners share this $6,000 difference—which is a gain to them—according to their profit-and-loss ratio. However, since Isaac has withdrawn from the partnership, a new agreement—and a new profit-and-loss ratio—must be drawn up. Henry and Green, in forming a new partnership, may decide on any ratio that they see fit. Let's assume they agree that Henry will earn two thirds of partnership profits and losses and Green one third. The entry to record Isaac's withdrawal at less than book value is

July 31	Isaac, Capital.	31,000	
	Cash		10,000
	Note Payable to K. Isaac		15,000
	Green, Capital ($6,000 × ⅓)		2,000
	Henry, Capital ($6,000 × ⅔)		4,000
	To record withdrawal of K. Isaac from the partnership.		

Isaac's account is closed, and Henry and Green may or may not continue the business.

Withdrawal at More Than Book Value

The settlement with a withdrawing partner may allow him to take assets of greater value than the book value of his capital. Also, the remaining partners may be so eager for the withdrawing partner to leave the firm that they pay him a bonus to withdraw from the business. In either case, the partner's withdrawal causes a decrease in the book equity of the remaining partners. This decrease is allocated to the partners based on their profit-and-loss ratio.

Assume Chang, Daley, and Evans share profits in a ratio of $3:2:1$. Their partnership accounts include the following balances:

Cash.	$ 50,000	Total liabilities.	$110,000
Other assets.	220,000	Chang, capital	80,000
		Daley, capital.	50,000
		Evans, capital.	30,000
Total assets	$270,000	Total liabilities and capital . . .	$270,000

Assume Evans withdraws, taking cash of $15,000 and the new partnership's note for $25,000. This $40,000 settlement exceeds Evans's capital balance by $10,000. Chang and Daley share this loss in equity based on their profit-and-loss ratio ($3:2$). The withdrawal entry is

Nov. 30	Evans, Capital.	30,000	
	Chang, Capital ($10,000 × ⅗).	6,000	
	Daley, Capital ($10,000 × ⅖)	4,000	
	Cash.		15,000
	Note Payable to R. Evans.		25,000
	To record withdrawal of R. Evans from the partnership.		

The withdrawal entry closes Evans's capital account and updates those of Chang and Daley.

Death of a Partner _____

Death of a partner, like any other form of partnership withdrawal, dissolves a partnership. The partnership accounts are adjusted to measure net income or loss for the fraction of the year up to the date of death, then closed to determine the partners' capital balances on that date. Settlement with the deceased partner's estate is based on the partnership agreement, with the estate commonly receiving partnership assets equal to the partner's capital balance. The partnership closes the deceased partner's capital account with a debit. This entry credits a payable to the estate.

Alternatively, a remaining partner may purchase the deceased partner's equity. The deceased partner's equity is debited and the purchaser's equity is credited. The amount of this entry is the ending credit balance in the deceased partner's capital account.

Liquidation of a Partnership

Admission of a new partner or withdrawal or death of an existing partner dissolves the partnership. However, the business may continue operating with no apparent change to outsiders such as customers and creditors.

Business **liquidation,** however, is the process of going out of business by selling the entity's assets and paying its liabilities. The final step in liquidation of a business is the *distribution of the remaining cash to the owners.* Before liquidating the business, the books should be adjusted and closed. After closing, only asset, liability, and partners' capital accounts remain open.

Liquidation of a partnership includes three basic steps:

1. Sell the assets. Allocate the gain or loss to the partners' capital accounts based on the profit-and-loss ratio.
2. Pay the partnership liabilities.
3. Disburse the remaining cash to the partners based on their capital balances.

In actual practice, the liquidation of a business can stretch over weeks or months. Selling every asset and paying every liability of the entity may take a long time. To avoid excessive detail in our illustrations, we include only two asset categories—Cash and Noncash Assets—and a single liability category—Liabilities. Our examples also assume that the business sells the noncash assets in a single transaction and pays the liabilities in a single transaction.

Assume that Aviron, Bloch, and Crane have shared profits and losses in the ratio of 3:1:1. (This ratio is equal to ⅗, ⅕, ⅕, or a 60-percent, 20-percent, 20-percent sharing ratio.) They decide to liquidate their partnership. After the books are adjusted and closed, the general ledger contains the following balances:

Cash.....................	$ 10,000	Liabilities	$ 30,000
Noncash assets	90,000	Aviron, capital.............	40,000
		Bloch, capital..............	20,000
		Crane, capital	10,000
Total assets	$100,000	Total liabilities and capital ...	$100,000

We will use the Aviron, Bloch, and Crane partnership data to illustrate accounting for liquidation in three different situations.

Sale of Noncash Assets at a Gain

Assume the partnership sells its noncash assets (shown on the balance sheet at $90,000) for cash of $150,000. The partnership realizes a gain of $60,000, which is allocated to the partners based on their profit-and-loss-sharing ratio. The entry to record this sale and allocation of the gain is

> **OBJECTIVE 6**
> Account for the liquidation of a partnership

Oct. 31	Cash 150,000	
	Noncash Assets	90,000
	Aviron, Capital ($60,000 × .60)	36,000
	Bloch, Capital ($60,000 × .20)	12,000
	Crane, Capital ($60,000 × .20)	12,000
	To sell noncash assets in liquidation and allocate gain to partners.	

The partnership must next pay off its liabilities:

Oct. 31	Liabilities 30,000	
	Cash	30,000
	To pay liabilities in liquidation.	

In the final liquidation transaction, the remaining cash is disbursed to the partners. *The partners share in the cash according to their capital balances.* (By contrast, *gains and losses* on the sale of assets are shared by the partners based on their profit-and-loss-sharing ratio.) The amount of cash left in the partnership is $130,000—the $10,000 beginning balance plus the $150,000 cash sale of assets minus the $30,000 cash payment of liabilities. The partners divide the remaining cash according to their capital balances:

Oct. 31	Aviron, Capital ($40,000 + $36,000) 76,000	
	Bloch, Capital ($20,000 + $12,000) 32,000	
	Crane, Capital ($10,000 + $12,000) 22,000	
	Cash	130,000
	To disburse cash to partners in liquidation.	

A convenient way to summarize the transactions in a partnership liquidation is given in Exhibit 13-1.

After the disbursement of cash to the partners, the business has no assets, liabilities, or owners' equity. The balances are all zero. At all times, partnership

EXHIBIT 13-1 *Partnership Liquidation—Sale of Assets at a Gain*

	Cash	+ Noncash Assets	= Liabilities +	Aviron (60%) +	Bloch (20%) +	Crane (20%)
					Capital	
Balances before sale of assets .	$ 10,000	$ 90,000	$ 30,000	$ 40,000	$ 20,000	$ 10,000
Sale of assets and sharing of gain	150,000	(90,000)		36,000	12,000	12,000
Balances	160,000	-0-	30,000	76,000	32,000	22,000
Payment of liabilities	(30,000)		(30,000)			
Balances	130,000	-0-	-0-	76,000	32,000	22,000
Disbursement of cash to partners.................	(130,000)			(76,000)	(32,000)	(22,000)
Balances	$ -0-	$ -0-	$ -0-	$ -0-	$ -0-	$ -0-

assets must equal partnership liabilities plus partnership capital, by the accounting equation:

	Total assets	=	Total liabilities	+	Total capital
Before liquidation	$100,000	=	$30,000	+	$ 70,000
After sale of assets	160,000	=	30,000	+	130,000
After payment of liabilities.	130,000	=	0	+	130,000
After final disbursement to the partners	0	=	0	+	0

Sale of Noncash Assets at a Loss

Assume that Aviron, Bloch, and Crane sell the noncash assets for $75,000, realizing a loss of $15,000. The summary of transactions appears in Exhibit 13-2. The journal entries to record the liquidation transactions are

Oct. 31	Cash	75,000	
	Aviron, Capital ($15,000 × .60)	9,000	
	Bloch, Capital ($15,000 × .20)	3,000	
	Crane, Capital ($15,000 × .20)	3,000	
	Noncash Assets		90,000
	To sell noncash assets in liquidation and allocate loss to partners.		
31	Liabilities	30,000	
	Cash		30,000
	To pay liabilities in liquidation.		
31	Aviron, Capital ($40,000 − $9,000)	31,000	
	Bloch, Capital ($20,000 − $3,000)	17,000	
	Crane, Capital ($10,000 − $3,000)	7,000	
	Cash		55,000
	To disburse cash to partners in liquidation.		

EXHIBIT 13-2 *Partnership Liquidation — Sale of Assets at a Loss*

				Capital		
				Aviron	Bloch	Crane
	Cash	+ Noncash Assets	= Liabilities +	(60%) +	(20%) +	(20%)
Balances before sale of assets. . .	$ 10,000	$ 90,000	$ 30,000	$ 40,000	$ 20,000	$ 10,000
Sale of assets and sharing of loss.	75,000	(90,000)		(9,000)	(3,000)	(3,000)
Balances	85,000	-0-	30,000	31,000	17,000	7,000
Payment of liabilities	(30,000)		(30,000)			
Balances	55,000	-0-	-0-	31,000	17,000	7,000
Disbursement of cash to partners	(55,000)			(31,000)	(17,000)	(7,000)
Balances	$ -0-	$ -0-	$ -0-	$ -0-	$ -0-	$ -0-

Sale of Noncash Assets at a Loss—Deficiency in a Partner's Capital Account. The sale of noncash assets at a loss may result in a debit balance in a partner's capital account. This situation is called a *capital deficiency* because the partner's capital balance is insufficient to cover his share of the partnership's loss. The unlimited liability of partners forces the other partners to absorb this deficiency through debits to their own capital accounts if the deficient partner does not erase his deficiency. The deficiency is a loss to the other partners, and they share it based on their profit-and-loss ratio.

DEFICIENT PARTNER UNABLE TO ERASE DEFICIENCY. Assume that Aviron, Bloch, and Crane's partnership has had losses for several years. The market value of the noncash assets of the business is far less than book value ($90,000). In liquidation, the partnership sells these assets for $30,000, realizing a loss of $60,000. Crane's 20 percent share of this loss is $12,000. Because the loss exceeds his $10,000 capital balance, Crane's account has a $2,000 deficit. Crane is obligated to contribute personal funds to the business in order to meet this debt. Assume that Crane cannot erase the deficiency by contributing personal assets. Because of mutual agency, the other partners must absorb the deficiency before the final distribution of cash.

Because Aviron and Bloch share losses in the ratio of 3:1, Aviron absorbs three fourths of the deficiency $[3/(3 + 1) = 3/4]$ and Bloch absorbs one fourth $[1/(3 + 1) = 1/4]$. Aviron's share of Crane's $2,000 deficiency is $1,500 ($2,000 × 3/4), and Bloch's share is $500 ($2,000 × 1/4).

The journal entries to record the foregoing liquidation transactions are

Oct. 31	Cash	30,000	
	Aviron, Capital ($60,000 × .60)	36,000	
	Bloch, Capital ($60,000 × .20)	12,000	
	Crane, Capital ($60,000 × .20)	12,000	
	Noncash Assets		90,000
	To sell noncash assets in liquidation and allocate loss to partners.		
31	Liabilities	30,000	
	Cash		30,000
	To pay liabilities in liquidation.		
31	Aviron, Capital ($2,000 × 3/4)	1,500	
	Bloch, Capital ($2,000 × 1/4)	500	
	Crane, Capital		2,000
	To allocate Crane's capital deficiency to the other partners.		
31	Aviron, Capital ($40,000 − $36,000 − $1,500)	2,500	
	Bloch, Capital ($20,000 − $12,000 − $500)	7,500	
	Cash		10,000
	To disburse cash to partners in liquidation.		

The summary of transactions in Exhibit 13-3 includes a separate transaction (highlighted) to allocate Crane's deficiency to Aviron and Bloch.

DEFICIENT PARTNER ERASES DEFICIENCY. A partner may erase his or her deficiency by contributing cash or other assets to the partnership. Such contributions are credited to the deficient partner's account and then distributed to the other

EXHIBIT 13-3 *Partnership Liquidation—Deficient Partner Unable to Erase a Capital Deficiency*

	Cash	+ Noncash Assets	= Liabilities +	Aviron (60%) +	Bloch (20%) +	Crane (20%)
					Capital	
Balances before sale of assets...	$ 10,000	$ 90,000	$ 30,000	$ 40,000	$ 20,000	$ 10,000
Sale of assets and sharing of loss..................	30,000	(90,000)		(36,000)	(12,000)	(12,000)
Balances	40,000	-0-	30,000	4,000	8,000	(2,000)
Payment of liabilities.........:	(30,000)		(30,000)			
Balances	10,000	-0-	-0-	4,000	8,000	(2,000)
Sharing of Crane's deficiency by Aviron and Bloch.......				(1,500)	(500)	2,000
Balances	10,000	-0-	-0-	2,500	7,500	-0-
Disbursement of cash to partners	(10,000)			(2,500)	(7,500)	-0-
Balances	$ -0-	$ -0-	$ -0-	$ -0-	$ -0-	$ -0-

partners. Suppose Crane erases his deficiency by investing $2,000 cash in the partnership.

The journal entries to record Crane's contribution and the disbursement of cash to the partners are

Oct. 31	Cash	2,000	
	Crane, Capital		2,000
	Crane's contribution to erase his capital deficiency in liquidation.		
31	Aviron, Capital..................................	4,000	
	Bloch, Capital.................................	8,000	
	Cash		12,000
	To disburse cash to partners in liquidation.		

In this case, the summary of transactions, beginning with the balances after payment of the liabilities, appears in Exhibit 13-4.

EXHIBIT 13-4 *Partnership Liquidation—Partner Erases Capital Deficiency*

	Cash	+ Noncash Assets	= Liabilities +	Aviron (60%) +	Bloch (20%) +	Crane (20%)
					Capital	
Balances after payment of liabilities	$ 10,000	$ -0-	$ -0-	$ 4,000	$ 8,000	$(2,000)
Crane's contribution to erase his deficiency	2,000					2,000
Balances	12,000	-0-	-0-	4,000	8,000	-0-
Disbursement of cash to partners ..	(12,000)			(4,000)	(8,000)	
Balances	$ -0-	$ -0-	$ -0-	$ -0-	$ -0-	$ -0-

Partnership Financial Statements

Partnership financial statements are much like those of a proprietorship. However, a partnership income statement includes a section showing the division of net income to the partners. For example, the partnership of Gray and Hayward might report its income statement for the year ended June 30, 19X6, as follows:

Gray and Hayward **Income Statement** **For the Year Ended June 30, 19X6**	
Sales revenue	$381,000
Net income	$ 79,000
Allocation of net income:	
M. Gray	$ 36,600
L. Hayward	42,400
Total	$ 79,000

Large partnerships may not find it feasible to report the net income of every partner. Instead, the firm may report the allocation of net income to active and retired partners and average earnings per partner. For example, the CPA firm of Arthur Andersen & Company reported the following:

The Arthur Andersen Worldwide Organization **Combined Statement of Earnings** **For the Year Ended August 31, 19X0**	
Dollar amounts in thousands	
Fees for Professional Services	$805,492
Earnings for the year	$181,880
Allocation of earnings:	
To partners active during the year—	
Resigned, retired, and deceased partners	$ 9,901
Partners active at year end	160,270
To retired and deceased partners—retirement and death benefits	4,310
Not allocated to partners—retained for specific partnership purposes	7,399
	$181,880
Average earnings per partner active at year end (1,170 partners)	$137

Exhibit 13-5 summarizes the financial statements of a proprietorship and a partnership.

EXHIBIT 13-5 *Financial Statements of a Proprietorship and a Partnership*

Income Statements
For the Year Ended December 31, 19X1

Proprietorship		Partnership		
Revenues.	$460	Revenues.		$460
Expenses	(270)	Expenses		(270)
Net income	$190	Net income		$190
		Allocation of net income:		
		To Smith	$114	
		To Jones.	76	$190

Statements of Owner Equity
For the Year Ended December 31, 19X1

Proprietorship		Partnership	Smith	Jones
Capital, December 31, 19X0	$ 90	Capital, December 31, 19X0	$ 50	$ 40
Additional investments . . .	10	Additional investments . . .	10	—
Net income	190	Net income	114	76
Subtotal.	290	Subtotal.	174	116
Drawings	(120)	Drawings	(72)	(48)
Capital, December 31, 19X1	$170	Capital, December 31, 19X1	$102	$ 68

Balance Sheets
December 31, 19X1

Proprietorship		Partnership	
		Assets	
Cash and other assets	$170	Cash and other assets.	$170
		Equities	
		Smith, capital	$102
		Jones, capital	68
Smith, capital	$170	Total capital	$170

Summary Problem for Your Review

The partnership of Prolux, Roberts, and Satulsky is liquidating. Its accounts have the following balances after closing:

Cash.....................	$ 22,000	Liabilities.................	$ 77,000
Noncash assets	104,000	Prolux, capital.............	23,000
		Roberts, capital............	10,000
		Satulsky, capital	16,000
		Total liabilities	
Total assets	$126,000	and capital..............	$126,000

The partnership agreement allocates profits to Prolux, Roberts, and Satulsky in the ratio of 3 : 4 : 3. In liquidation, the noncash assets were sold in a single transaction for $64,000 on May 31, 19X7. The partnership paid the liabilities the same day.

Required

1. Journalize the liquidation transactions. The partnership books remain open until June 7 to allow Roberts to make an additional $4,000 contribution to the business in view of her capital deficiency. This cash is immediately disbursed to the other partners. Use T-accounts if necessary.
2. Prepare a summary of the liquidation transactions, as illustrated in the chapter. Roberts invests cash of $4,000 in the partnership in partial settlement of her capital deficiency. The other partners absorb the remainder of Roberts's capital deficiency.

SOLUTION TO REVIEW PROBLEM

Requirement 1
(Liquidation journal entries)

May 31	Cash.......................................	64,000	
	Prolux, Capital [($104,000 − $64,000) × .30]	12,000	
	Roberts, Capital [($104,000 − $64,000) × .40]	16,000	
	Satulsky, Capital [($104,000 − $64,000) × .30]......	12,000	
	Noncash Assets		104,000
	To sell noncash assets in liquidation and distribute loss to partners.		
31	Liabilities	77,000	
	Cash....................................		77,000
	To pay liabilities in liquidation.		
June 7	Cash.......................................	4,000	
	Roberts, Capital..........................		4,000
	Roberts's contribution to erase part of her capital deficiency in liquidation.		

After posting the entries, Roberts's capital account still has a $2,000 deficiency, indicated by its debit balance:

Roberts, Capital			
Loss on sale	16,000	Bal.	10,000
		Investment	4,000
Bal.	2,000		

Prolux and Satulsky must make up Roberts's remaining $2,000 deficiency. Since Prolux and Satulsky had equal shares in the partnership profit-and-loss ratio (30 percent each), they divide Roberts's deficiency equally.

June 7 Prolux, Capital ($2,000 × ½) 1,000
        Satulsky, Capital ($2,000 × ½)...................... 1,000
            Roberts, Capital   2,000
        To allocate Roberts's capital deficiency to the other partners.

At this point, the capital accounts of Prolux and Satulsky appear as follows:

Prolux, Capital				**Satulsky, Capital**		
Loss on sale	12,000	Bal.	23,000	Loss on sale	12,000	Bal.	16,000
Loss on Roberts	1,000			Loss on Roberts	1,000		
		Bal.	10,000			Bal.	3,000

The final disbursement entry is

June 7 Prolux, Capital................................. 10,000
        Satulsky, Capital 3,000
            Cash   13,000
        To disburse cash to partners in liquidation.

Activity in the Cash account appears as follows:

Cash			
Bal.	22,000	Payment of liabilities	77,000
Sale of assets	64,000		
Roberts's contribution	4,000		
Bal.	13,000	Final distribution	13,000

Requirement 2.   (Summary of liquidation transactions)

			Noncash			**Capital**		
	Cash	+	Assets	=	Liabilities +	Prolux (30%) +	Roberts (40%) +	Satulsky (30%)
Balances before sale of assets......	$ 22,000		$ 104,000		$ 77,000	$ 23,000	$ 10,000	$ 16,000
Sale of assets and sharing of loss...	64,000		(104,000)			(12,000)	(16,000)	(12,000)
Balances.....................	86,000		-0-		77,000	11,000	(6,000)	4,000
Payment of liabilities	(77,000)				(77,000)			
Balances.....................	9,000		-0-		-0-	11,000	(6,000)	4,000
Roberts's investment of cash to erase part of her deficiency......	4,000						4,000	
Balances.....................	13,000		-0-		-0-	11,000	(2,000)	4,000
Sharing of Roberts's deficiency by Prolux and Satulsky						(1,000)	2,000	(1,000)
Balances.....................	13,000		-0-		-0-	10,000	-0-	3,000
Disbursement of cash to partners ..	(13,000)					(10,000)		(3,000)
Balances.....................	$ -0-		$ -0-		$ -0-	$ -0-	$ -0-	$ -0-

Summary

A *partnership* is a business co-owned by two or more persons for profit. The characteristics of this form of business organization are its *ease of formation, limited life, mutual agency, unlimited liability,* and *no partnership income taxes.*

A written *partnership agreement,* or *articles of partnership,* establishes procedure for admission of a new partner, withdrawals of a partner, and the sharing of profits and losses among the partners.

When a new partner is admitted to the firm or an existing partner withdraws, the old partnership is *dissolved,* or ceases to exist. A new partnership may or may not emerge to continue the business.

Accounting for a partnership is similar to accounting for a proprietorship. However, a partnership has more than one owner. Each partner has an individual capital account and a withdrawal account.

Partners share net income or loss in any manner they choose. Common sharing agreements base the *profit-and-loss ratio* on a stated fraction, partners' capital contributions, and/or their service to the partnership. Some partnerships call the cash withdrawals of partners *salaries* and *interest,* but these amounts are not expenses of the business. Instead, they are merely ways of allocating partnership net income to the partners.

An outside person may become a partner by purchasing a current partner's interest or by investing in the partnership. In some cases the new partner must pay the current partners a bonus to join. In other situations the new partner may receive a bonus to join.

When a partner withdraws, partnership assets may be reappraised. Partners share any gain or loss on the asset revaluation based on their profit-and-loss ratio. The withdrawing partner may receive payment equal to, greater than, or less than, his or her capital book value, depending on the agreement with the other partners.

In *liquidation,* a partnership goes out of business by selling the assets, paying the liabilities, and disbursing any remaining cash to the partners. Any partner's capital deficiency, which may result from sale of assets at a loss, must be absorbed before remaining cash is distributed.

Partnership *financial statements* are similar to those of a proprietorship. However, the partnership income statement commonly reports the allocation of net income to the partners.

Self-Study Questions

Test your understanding of the chapter by marking the best answer for each of the following questions.

1. Which of these characteristics does *not* apply to a partnership? *(p. 496)*
   - a. Unlimited life
   - b. Mutual agency
   - c. Unlimited liability
   - d. No business income tax

2. A partnership records a partner's investment of assets in the business at *(p. 498)*
   - a. The partner's book value of the assets invested
   - b. The market value of the assets invested
   - c. A special value set by the partners
   - d. Any of the above, depending upon the partnership agreement

3. The partnership of Lane, Murdock, and Nu divides profits in the ratio of 4:5:3. During 19X6 the business earned $40,000. Nu's share of this income is *(p. 499)*
   - a. $10,000
   - b. $13,333
   - c. $16,000
   - d. $16,667

4. Suppose the partnership of Lane, Murdock, and Nu in the preceding question lost $40,000 during 19X6. Murdock's share of this loss is *(p. 499)*
   - a. Not determinable because the ratio applies only to profits
   - b. $13,333
   - c. $16,000
   - d. $16,667

5. Placido, Quinn, and Rolfe share profits and losses ⅕, ⅙, and ¹⁹⁄₃₀. During 19X3 the first year of their partnership, the business earned $120,000, and each partner withdrew $50,000 for personal use. What is the balance in Rolfe's capital account after all closing entries? *(p. 504)*
   a. Not determinable because Rolfe's beginning capital balance is not given
   b. Minus $10,000
   c. $26,000
   d. $70,000

6. Fuller buys into the partnership of Graff and Harrell by purchasing a one-third interest for $55,000. Prior to Fuller's entry, Graff's capital balance was $46,000, and Harrell's balance was $52,000. The entry to record Fuller's buying into the business is *(p. 507)*

   a. Cash 55,000
          Fuller, Capital   55,000

   b. Graff, Capital 27,500
      Harrell, Capital 27,500
          Fuller, Capital   55,000

   c. Cash 55,000
          Fuller, Capital   51,000
          Graff, Capital   2,000
          Harrell, Capital . . .   2,000

   d. Cash 51,000
      Graff, Capital   2,000
      Harrell, Capital   2,000
          Fuller, Capital   55,000

7. Thomas, Valik, and Wollenberg share profits and losses equally. Their capital balances are $40,000, $50,000, and $60,000, respectively, when Wollenberg sells her interest in the partnership to Valik for $90,000. Thomas and Valik continue the business. Immediately after Wollenberg's retirement, the total assets of the partnership are *(p. 510)*
   a. Increased by $30,000
   b. Increased by $90,000
   c. Decreased by $60,000
   d. The same as before Wollenberg sold her interest to Valik

8. Prior to Hogg's withdrawal from the partnership of Hogg, Hamm, and Bacon, the partners' capital balances were $140,000, $110,000, and $250,000, respectively. The partners share profits and losses ⅓, ¼, and ⁵⁄₁₂. The appraisal indicates that assets should be written down by $36,000. Hamm's share of the write-down is *(p. 510)*
   a. $7,920   b. $9,000   c. $12,000   d. $18,000

9. Closing the business, selling the assets, paying the liabilities, and disbursing remaining cash to the owners is called *(p. 513)*
   a. Dissolution   c. Withdrawal
   b. Forming a new partnership   d. Liquidation

10. A and B have shared profits and losses equally. Immediately prior to the final cash disbursement in a liquidation of their partnership, the books show:

Cash	= Liabilities	+ A, Capital	+ B, Capital
$100,000	$ -0-	$60,000	$40,000

How much cash should A receive? *(p. 514)*
   a. $40,000   b. $50,000   c. $60,000   d. None of the above

Answers to the self-study questions are at the end of the chapter.

Accounting Vocabulary

articles of partnership *(p. 496)*,   capital deficiency *(p. 516)*,   dissolution *(p. 496)*,   liquidation *(p. 513)*,   mutual agency *(p. 496)*,   partnership agreement *(p. 496)*,   unlimited personal liability *(p. 497)*.

ASSIGNMENT MATERIAL _____

Questions

1. What is another name for a partnership agreement? List eight items that the agreement should specify.

2. Montgomery, who is a partner in M&N Associates, commits the firm to a contract for a job within the scope of its regular business operations. What term describes Montgomery's ability to obligate the partnership?

3. If a partnership cannot pay a debt, who must make payment? What term describes this obligation of the partners?

4. How is partnership income taxed?

5. Identify the advantages and disadvantages of the partnership form of business organization.

6. Randall and Smith's partnership agreement states that Randall gets 60 percent of profits and Smith gets 40 percent. If the agreement does not discuss the treatment of losses, how are losses shared? How do the partners share profits and losses if the agreement specifies no profit-and-loss-sharing ratio?

7. Are salary and interest allocated to partners expenses of the business? Why or why not?

8. What determines the amount of the credit to a partner's capital account when the partner contributes assets other than cash to the business?

9. Do partner withdrawals of cash for personal use affect the sharing of profits and losses by the partner? If so, explain how. If not, explain why not.

10. Name two events that can cause the dissolution of a partnership.

11. Briefly describe how to account for the purchase of an existing partner's interest in the business.

12. Malcolm purchases Brown's interest in the Brown & Kareem partnership. What right does Malcolm obtain from the purchase? What is required for Malcolm to become Kareem's partner?

13. Assissi and Carter each have capital of $75,000 in their business and share profits in the ratio of 55:45. Denman acquires a one-fifth share in the partnership by investing cash of $50,000. What are the capital balances of the three partners immediately after Denman is admitted?

14. When a partner resigns from the partnership and receives assets greater than her capital balance, how is the excess shared by the other partners?

15. Why are the assets of a partnership often revalued when a partner is about to withdraw from the firm?

16. Distinguish between dissolution and liquidation of a partnership.

17. Name the three steps in liquidating a partnership.

18. Why does the cash of a partnership equal the sum of its partner capital balances after the business sells its noncash assets and pays its liabilities?

19. The partnership of Ralls and Sauls is in the process of liquidation. How do the partners share (a) gains and losses on the sale of noncash assets and (b) the final cash disbursement?

20. Fernandez, Garcia, and Estrada are partners, sharing profits and losses in the ratio of 3:2:1. In liquidation, Estrada's share of losses on the sale of assets exceeds his capital balance. What becomes of Estrada's capital deficiency if Estrada cannot make it up?

21. Compare and contrast the financial statements of a proprietorship and a partnership.

22. Summarize the situations in which partnership allocations are based on (a) the profit-and-loss ratio and (b) the partners' capital balances.

Exercises

Exercise 13-1 *Recording a partner's investment*

Ann Clinton has operated an apartment-locater service as a proprietorship. She and Amanda Doss have decided to reorganize the business as a partnership. Ann's investment in the partnership consists of cash, $8,100; accounts receivable, $13,600 less allowance for uncollectibles, $800; office furniture, $2,700 less accumulated depreciation, $1,100; a small building, $55,000 less accumulated depreciation, $27,500; accounts payable, $3,300; and a note payable to the bank, $10,000.

To determine Ann's equity in the partnership, she and Amanda hire an independent appraiser. This outside party provides the following market values of the assets and liabilities that Ann is contributing to the business: cash, accounts receivable, office furniture and related accumulated depreciation, accounts payable, and note payable—the same as Ann's book value; allowance for uncollectible accounts, $2,900; building, $70,000 less accumulated depreciation, $35,000; and accrued expenses payable (including interest on the note payable), $1,200.

Required

Make the entry on the partnership books to record Ann's investment.

Exercise 13-2 *Preparing a partnership balance sheet*

On October 31, 19X9, Alpha and Beta agree to combine their proprietorships as a partnership. Their balance sheets on October 31 are as follows:

Assets	Alpha's Business		Beta's Business	
	Book Value	Current Market Value	Book Value	Current Market Value
Cash......................	$ 8,000	$ 8,000	$ 3,700	$ 3,700
Accounts receivable (net)	13,000	11,800	22,000	20,200
Inventory...................	34,000	35,100	51,000	46,000
Plant assets (net).............	53,500	57,400	121,800	123,500
Total assets	$108,500	$112,300	$198,500	$193,400
Liabilities and Capital				
Accounts payable	$ 9,100	$ 9,100	$ 23,600	$ 23,600
Accrued expenses payable	800	800	2,200	2,200
Notes payable	—	—	75,000	75,000
Alpha, capital	98,600	102,400		
Beta, capital.................			97,700	92,600
Total liabilities and capital	$108,500	$112,300	$198,500	$193,400

Required

Prepare the partnership balance sheet at October 31, 19X9.

Exercise 13-3 *Computing partners' shares of net income*

Roy Dean and Joe Edwards form a partnership, investing $30,000 and $60,000, respectively. Determine their shares of net income or net loss for each of the following situations:

a. Net loss is $69,000, and the partners have no written partnership agreement.
b. Net income is $84,000, and the partnership agreement states that the partners share profits and losses based on their capital contributions.

c. Net loss is $63,000, and the partnership agreement states that the partners share profits based on their capital contributions.

d. Net income is $105,000. The first $40,000 is shared based on the partner capital contributions. The next $30,000 is based on partner service, with Dean receiving 30 percent and Edwards receiving 70 percent. The remainder is shared equally.

Exercise 13-4   *Computing partners' capital balances*

Roy Dean withdrew cash of $52,000 for personal use, and Joe Edwards withdrew cash of $60,000 during the year. Using the data from situation d in Exercise 13-3, journalize the entries to close the (a) income summary account and (b) the partners' drawing accounts. Explanations are not required.

Indicate the amount of increase or decrease in each partner's capital balance. What was the overall effect on partnership capital?

Exercise 13-5   *Admitting a new partner*

Jack Phillips is admitted to a partnership. Prior to the admission of Phillips, the partnership books show Susan Reckers's capital balance at $80,000 and Lewis Schmitz's capital balance at $40,000. Compute the amount of each partner's equity on the books of the new partnership under each of the following plans:

a. Phillips pays $30,000 for Schmitz's equity. Phillips's payment is not an investment in the partnership but instead goes directly to Schmitz.

b. Phillips invests $30,000 to acquire a one-fifth interest in the partnership.

c. Phillips invests $60,000 to acquire a one-fourth interest in the partnership.

Exercise 13-6   *Recording the admission of a new partner*

Make the partnership journal entry to record the admission of Phillips under plans a, b, and c in Exercise 13-5. Explanations are not required.

Exercise 13-7   *Withdrawal of a partner*

After closing the books, T&W's partnership balance sheet reports capital of $50,000 for T and $70,000 for W. T is withdrawing from the firm. The partners agree to write down partnership assets by $30,000. They have shared profits and losses in the ratio of one third to T and two thirds to W. If the partnership agreement states that a withdrawing partner will receive assets equal to the book value of his owner's equity, how much will T receive?

W will continue to operate the business as a proprietorship. What is W's beginning capital on the proprietorship books?

Exercise 13-8   *Withdrawal of a partner*

Lana Brown is retiring from the partnership of Brown, Green, and White on May 31. After the books are closed on that date, the partner capital balances are Brown, $36,000; Green, $51,000; and White, $22,000. The partners agree to have the partnership assets revalued to current market values. The independent appraiser reports that the book value of the inventory should be decreased by $8,000, and the book value of the building should be increased by $32,000. The partners agree to these revaluations. The profit-and-loss ratio has been 5:3:2 for Brown, Green, and White, respectively. In retiring from the firm, Brown receives $25,000 cash and a $25,000 note from the partnership. Journalize (a) the asset revaluations and (b) Brown's withdrawal from the firm.

Exercise 13-9   *Liquidation of a partnership*

Marsh, Ng, and Orsulak are liquidating their partnership. Before selling the noncash assets and paying the liabilities, the capital balances are Marsh, $23,000; Ng, $14,000; and Orsulak, $11,000. The partnership agreement divides profits and losses equally.

a. After selling the noncash assets and paying the liabilities, the partnership has cash of $48,000. How much cash will each partner receive in final liquidation?

b. After selling the noncash assets and paying the liabilities, the partnership has cash of $45,000. How much cash will each partner receive in final liquidation?

Exercise 13-10   *Liquidation of a partnership*

Prior to liquidation, the accounting records of Pratt, Qualls, and Ramirez included the following balances and profit-and-loss-sharing percentages:

					Capital	
	Cash +	Noncash Assets	= Liabilities +	Pratt (40%)	Qualls (30%)	Ramirez (30%)
Balances before sale of assets...	$8,000	$57,000	$19,000	$20,000	$15,000	$11,000

The partnership sold the noncash assets for $73,000, paid the liabilities, and disbursed the remaining cash to the partners. Complete the summary of transactions in the liquidation of the partnership. Use the format illustrated in the chapter.

(Group A)

Problems

Problem 13-1A   *Investments by partners*

Geraci and Hutton formed a partnership on March 15. The partners agreed to invest equal amounts of capital. Hutton invested her proprietorship's assets and liabilities (credit balances in parentheses):

	Hutton's Book Value	Current Market Value
Accounts receivable...............	$ 12,000	$ 12,000
Allowance for doubtful accounts	(740)	(1,360)
Inventory	43,850	51,220
Prepaid expenses	2,400	2,400
Store equipment.................	36,700	31,000
Accumulated depreciation..........	(9,200)	(7,800)
Accounts payable................	(22,300)	(22,300)

On March 15 Geraci invested cash in an amount equal to the current market value of Hutton's partnership capital, which was $65,160. The partners decided that Hutton would earn 70 percent of partnership profits because she would manage the business. Geraci agreed to accept 30 percent of profits. During the period ended December 31, the partnership earned $55,000. Geraci's drawings were $12,000, and Hutton's drawings were $36,000.

Required

1. Journalize the partners' initial investments.
2. Prepare the partnership balance sheet immediately after its formation on March 15.
3. Journalize the December 31 entries to close the income summary account and the partner drawing accounts.

Problem 13-2A *Computing partners' shares of net income and net loss*

J. Warner, S. Deitmer, and R. Mullaney have formed a partnership. Warner invested $20,000, Deitmer $40,000, and Mullaney $60,000. Warner will manage the store, Deitmer will work in the store three quarters of the time, and Mullaney will not work in the business.

Required

1. Compute the partners' shares of profits and losses under each of the following plans. Use this format for your answer:

	Warner	Deitmer	Mullaney	Total

Total net income (net loss). . . . .
Allocation to the partners:
   Warner. . . . .
   Deitmer . . . .
   Mullaney . . . .
     Total. . . . .
Net income (loss) left for allocation. . . . .
Add a line for "Net income allocated to partners" as necessary.

   a. Net income is $27,000, and the articles of partnership do not specify how profits and losses are shared.

   b. Net loss is $47,000, and the partnership agreement allocates 45 percent of profits to Warner, 35 percent to Deitmer, and 20 percent to Mullaney. The agreement does not discuss the sharing of losses.

   c. Net income is $104,000. The first $50,000 is allocated based on salaries of $34,000 for Warner and $16,000 for Deitmer. The remainder is allocated based on partner capital contributions.

   d. Net income for the year ended September 30, 19X4, is $81,000. The first $42,000 is allocated based on partner capital contributions. The next $30,000 is based on service, with $20,000 going to Warner and $10,000 going to Deitmer. Any remainder is shared equally.

2. Revenues for the year ended September 30, 19X4, were $621,000, and expenses were $540,000. Under plan d, prepare the partnership income statement for the year.

Problem 13-3A *Recording changes in partnership capital*

Red River Resort is a partnership, and its owners are considering admitting Greg Lake as a new partner. On July 31 of the current year the capital accounts of the three existing partners and their shares of profits and losses are as follows:

	Capital	Profit-and-Loss Ratio
Ellen Urlang	$48,000	1/6
Amy Sharp	64,000	1/3
Bob Hayes.	88,000	1/2

Required

Journalize the admission of Lake as a partner on July 31 for each of the following independent situations:

1. Urlang gives her partnership share to Lake, who is her nephew.
2. Lake pays Hayes $50,000 cash to purchase one half of Hayes's interest.
3. Lake invests $50,000 in the partnership, acquiring a one-fifth interest in the business.

4. Lake invests $40,000 in the partnership, acquiring a one-eighth interest in the business.
5. Lake invests $30,000 in the partnership, acquiring a 15 percent interest in the business.

Problem 13-4A   *Recording changes in partnership capital*

Boat Town is a partnership owned by three individuals. The partners share profits and losses in the ratio of 30 percent to Golden, 40 percent to Miller, and 30 percent to Ramos. At December 31, 19X6, the firm has the following balance sheet:

Cash................		$ 25,000	Total liabilities........	$103,000
Accounts receivable ...	$ 16,000			
Less allowance for				
uncollectibles.....	1,000	15,000		
Inventory...........		51,000	Golden, Capital.......	23,000
Equipment..........	130,000		Miller, Capital........	41,000
Less accumulated			Ramos, Capital	24,000
depreciation......	30,000	100,000	Total liabilities and	
Total assets		$191,000	capital	$191,000

Golden withdraws from the partnership on this date.

Required

Record Golden's withdrawal from the partnership under the following plans:

1. Golden gives his interest in the business to Wilson, his son-in-law.
2. In personal transactions, Golden sells his equity in the partnership to Meyers and Sloan, who each pay Golden $15,000 for one half of his interest. Miller and Ramos agree to accept Meyers and Sloan as partners.
3. The partnership pays Golden cash of $5,000 and gives him a note payable for the remainder of his book equity in settlement of his partnership interest.
4. Golden receives cash of $10,000 and a note for $20,000 from the partnership.
5. The partners agree that the equipment is worth $150,000 and that accumulated depreciation should remain at $30,000. After the revaluation, the partnership settles with Golden by giving him cash of $10,000 and inventory for the remainder of his book equity.

Problem 13-5A   *Liquidation of a partnership*

The partnership of Yagoda, Kelly, and Dobbs has experienced operating losses for three consecutive years. The partners, who have shared profits and losses in the ratio of Yagoda 15 percent, Kelly 60 percent, and Dobbs 25 percent, are considering the liquidation of the business. They ask you to analyze the effects of liquidation under various possibilities about the sale of the noncash assets. They present the following condensed partnership balance sheet at December 31, end of the current year:

Cash..................	$ 18,000	Liabilities	$ 74,000
Noncash assets	163,000	Yagoda, Capital............	19,000
		Kelly, Capital.............	66,000
		Dobbs, Capital.............	22,000
Total assets	$181,000	Total liabilities and capital ...	$181,000

Required

1. Prepare a summary of liquidation transactions (as illustrated in the chapter) for each of the following situations:

a. The noncash assets are sold for $175,000.
b. The noncash assets are sold for $133,000.
c. The noncash assets are sold for $63,000, and the partner with a capital deficiency is personally bankrupt.
d. The noncash assets are sold for $60,000, and the partner with a capital deficiency pays cash of $1,500 to the partnership to erase part of the deficiency.
2. Make the journal entries to record the liquidation transactions in requirement 1d.

Problem 13-6A *Liquidation of a partnership*

RMG & Company is a partnership owned by Ryan, Morales, and Goldberg, who share profits and losses in the ratio of 1 : 3 : 4. The adjusted trial balance of the partnership (in condensed form) at June 30, end of the current fiscal year, follows.

RMG & Company		
Adjusted Trial Balance		
June 30, 19XX		
Cash	$ 14,000	
Noncash assets	116,000	
Liabilities		$100,000
Ryan, capital		22,000
Morales, capital		41,000
Goldberg, capital		62,000
Ryan, drawing	24,000	
Morales, drawing	35,000	
Goldberg, drawing	54,000	
Revenues		108,000
Expenses	90,000	
Totals	$333,000	$333,000

Required

1. Prepare the June 30 entries to close the revenue, expense, income summary, and drawing accounts.
2. Insert the opening capital balances in the partner capital accounts, post the closing entries to the capital accounts, and determine each partner's ending capital balance.
3. The partnership liquidates on June 30 by selling the noncash assets for $100,000. Using the ending balances of the partner capital accounts, prepare a summary of liquidation transactions (as illustrated in the chapter). Any partner with a capital deficiency is unable to contribute assets to erase the deficiency.

(Group B)

Problem 13-1B *Investments by partners*

On June 30 McMinn and Carrico formed a partnership. The partners agreed to invest equal amounts of capital. McMinn invested her proprietorship's assets and liabilities (credit balances in parentheses).

On June 30 Carrico invested cash in an amount equal to the current market value of McMinn's partnership capital, which was $46,250. The partners decided that McMinn would earn two thirds of partnership profits because she would manage the business. Carrico agreed to accept one third of profits. During the remainder of the year, the partnership earned $48,000. McMinn's drawings were $35,200, and Carrico's drawings were $14,000.

	McMinn's Book Value	Current Market Value
Accounts receivable...................	$ 8,100	$ 8,100
Allowance for doubtful accounts........	(-0-)	(1,050)
Inventory...........................	22,340	29,000
Prepaid expenses....................	1,700	1,700
Office equipment....................	45,900	41,400
Accumulated depreciation	(15,300)	(13,800)
Accounts payable	(19,100)	(19,100)

Required

1. Journalize the partners' initial investments.
2. Prepare the partnership balance sheet immediately after its formation on June 30.
3. Journalize the December 31 entries to close the income summary account and the partner drawing accounts.

Problem 13-2B   *Computing partners' shares of net income and net loss*

D. Hogan, E. Stanford, and S. Reichlin have formed a partnership. Hogan invested $6,000, Stanford $18,000, and Reichlin $36,000. Hogan will manage the store, Stanford will work in the store half time, and Reichlin will not work in the business.

Required

1. Compute the partners' shares of profits and losses under each of the following plans. Use this format for your answer:

	Hogan	Stanford	Reichlin	Total
Total net income (net loss)................				
Allocation to the partners:				
Hogan				
Stanford............................				
Reichlin				
Total...............................				
Net income (loss) left for allocation........				

Add a line for "Net income allocated to partners" as necessary.

   a. Net loss is $51,600, and the articles of partnership do not specify how profits and losses are shared.
   b. Net loss is $70,000, and the partnership agreement allocates 40 percent of profits to Hogan, 25 percent to Stanford, and 35 percent to Reichlin. The agreement does not discuss the sharing of losses.
   c. Net income is $88,000. The first $40,000 is allocated based on salaries, with Hogan receiving $28,000 and Stanford receiving $12,000. The remainder is allocated based on partner capital contributions.
   d. Net income for the year ended January 31, 19X8, is $132,000. The first $75,000 is allocated based on partner capital contributions, and the next $36,000 is based on service, with Hogan receiving $28,000 and Stanford receiving $8,000. Any remainder is shared equally.

2. Revenues for the year ended January 31, 19X8, were $872,000, and expenses were $740,000. Under plan d, prepare the partnership income statement for the year.

Problem 13-3B   *Recording changes in partnership capital*

Englewood Consulting Associates is a partnership, and its owners are considering admitting Hilda Newton as a new partner. On March 31 of the current year the capital accounts of the three existing partners and their shares of profits and losses are as follows:

	Capital	Profit-and-Loss Percent
Jim Zook.................	$ 40,000	15%
Richard Land..............	100,000	30
Jennifer Lim..............	160,000	55

Required

Journalize the admission of Newton as a partner on March 31 for each of the following independent situations:

1. Land gives his partnership share to H. Newton, who is his daughter.
2. Newton pays Lim $145,000 cash to purchase Lim's interest in the partnership.
3. Newton invests $60,000 in the partnership, acquiring a one-sixth interest in the business.
4. Newton invests $60,000 in the partnership, acquiring a one-fifth interest in the business.
5. Newton invests $40,000 in the partnership, acquiring a 10 percent interest in the business.

Problem 13-4B   *Recording changes in partnership capital*

Pediatric Associates is a partnership owned by three individuals. The partners share profits and losses in the ratio of 31 percent to Turman, 38 percent to Herron, and 31 percent to Tyler. At December 31, 19X7, the firm has the following balance sheet.

Cash................		$ 31,000	Total liabilities........		$ 94,000
Accounts receivable ...	$ 22,000				
Less allowance for uncollectibles.....	4,000	18,000	Turman, capital.......		61,000
Office equipment......	$310,000		Herron, capital........		72,000
Less accumulated depreciation......	70,000	240,000	Tyler, capital .... Total liabilities and		62,000
Total assets		$289,000	capital		$289,000

Herron withdraws from the partnership on December 31, 19X7, to establish her own medical practice.

Required

Record Herron's withdrawal from the partnership under the following plans:

1. Herron gives her interest in the business to Zagat, her niece.
2. In personal transactions, Herron sells her equity in the partnership to Grimes and Hirsh, who each pay Herron $50,000 for one half of her interest. Turman and Tyler agree to accept Grimes and Hirsh as partners.
3. The partnership pays Herron cash of $15,000 and gives her a note payable for the remainder of her book equity in settlement of her partnership interest.
4. Herron receives cash of $10,000 and a note for $70,000 from the partnership.
5. The partners agree that the office equipment is worth only $280,000 and that its accumulated depreciation should remain at $70,000. After the revaluation, the partnership settles with Herron by giving her cash of $10,600 and a note payable for the remainder of her book equity.

Problem 13-5B   *Liquidation of a partnership*

The partnership of Monet, Dixon, and Palma has experienced operating losses for three consecutive years. The partners, who have shared profits and losses in the ratio of Monet 20 percent, Dixon 30 percent, and Palma 50 percent, are considering the liquidation of the business. They ask you to analyze the effects of liquidation under various possibilities about the sale of the noncash assets. They present the following condensed partnership balance sheet at December 31, end of the current year:

Cash......................	$ 27,000	Liabilities.................	$131,000
Noncash assets	202,000	Monet, capital.............	13,000
		Dixon, capital	39,000
		Palma, capital	46,000
Total assets	$229,000	Total liabilities and capital ...	$229,000

Required

1. Prepare a summary of liquidation transactions (as illustrated in the chapter) for each of the following situations:
   a. The noncash assets are sold for $212,000.
   b. The noncash assets are sold for $194,000.
   c. The noncash assets are sold for $122,000, and the partner with a capital deficiency pays cash to the partnership to erase the deficiency.
   d. The noncash assets are sold for $124,000, and the partner with a capital deficiency is personally bankrupt.
2. Make the journal entries to record the liquidation transactions in requirement 1d.

Problem 13-6B   *Liquidation of a partnership*

BP&O is a partnership owned by Bell, Pastena, and O'Donnell, who share profits and losses in the ratio of 5:3:2. The adjusted trial balance of the partnership (in condensed form) at September 30, end of the current fiscal year, follows.

BP&O Adjusted Trial Balance September 30, 19XX		
Cash.............................	$ 7,000	
Noncash assets	177,000	
Liabilities..........................		$135,000
Bell, capital		57,000
Pastena, capital		44,000
O'Donnell, capital...................		18,000
Bell, drawing.......................	45,000	
Pastena, drawing....................	37,000	
O'Donnell, drawing.................	18,000	
Revenues		211,000
Expenses	181,000	
Totals.............................	$465,000	$465,000

Required

1. Prepare the September 30 entries to close the revenue, expense, income summary, and drawing accounts.
2. Insert the opening capital balances in the partner capital accounts, post the closing entries to the capital accounts, and determine each partner's ending capital balance.
3. The partnership liquidates on September 30 by selling the noncash assets for $132,000. Using the ending balances of the partner capital accounts, prepare a summary of liquidation transactions (as illustrated in the chapter). Any partner with a capital deficiency is unable to contribute assets to erase the deficiency.

Decision Problem—Disagreements Among Partners

Clay Grant invested $20,000 and Elaine Marsh invested $10,000 in a public relations firm that has operated for 10 years. Neither partner has made an additional investment. They have shared profits and losses in the ratio of 2 : 1, which is the ratio of their investments in the business. Grant manages the office, supervises the 16 employees, and does the accounting. Marsh, the moderator of a television talk show, is responsible for marketing. Her high profile generates important revenue for the business. During the year ended December 19X4 the partnership earned net income of $87,000, shared in the 2 : 1 ratio. On December 31, 19X4, Grant's capital balance was $120,000, and Marsh's capital balance was $80,000.

Required

Respond to each of the following situations:

1. What explains the difference between the ratio of partner capital balances at December 31, 19X4, and the 2 : 1 ratio of partner investments and profit sharing?
2. Marsh believes the profit-and-loss-sharing ratio is unfair. She proposes a change, but Grant insists on keeping the 2 : 1 ratio. What two factors may underlie Marsh's unhappiness?
3. During January 19X5 Grant learned that revenues of $18,000 were omitted from the reported 19X4 income. He brings this to Marsh's attention, pointing out that his share of this added income is two thirds, or $12,000, and Marsh's share is one third, or $6,000. Marsh believes they should share this added income based on their capital balances—60 percent, or $10,800, to Grant and 40 percent, or $7,200, to Marsh. Which partner is correct? Why?
4. Assume the 19X4 $18,000 omission was an account payable for an operating expense. How would the partners share this amount?

Answers to Self-Study Questions

1. a
2. b
3. a ($40,000 × 3/12 = $10,000)
4. d ($40,000 × 5/12 = $16,667)
5. a
6. c [($46,000 + $52,000 + $55,000) × 1/3 = $51,000; $55,000 − $51,000 = $4,000; $4,000 ÷ 2 = $2,000 each to Graff and Harrell]
7. d
8. b ($36,000 × 1/4 = $9,000)
9. d
10. c

Corporations: Organization, Paid-In Capital, and the Balance Sheet

---

LEARNING OBJECTIVES

After studying this chapter, you should be able to

1 Identify the characteristics of a corporation

2 Record the issuance of stock

3 Prepare the stockholders' equity section of a corporation balance sheet

4 Account for the incorporation of a going business

5 Allocate dividends to preferred and common stock

6 Distinguish among various stock "values"

The corporation is the dominant form of business organization in the United States. Although proprietorships and partnerships are more numerous, corporations transact more business and are larger in terms of total assets, sales revenue, and number of employees. Most well-known companies, such as CBS, General Motors, IBM, and Pillsbury, are corporations. Their full names include *Corporation* or *Incorporated* (abbreviated *Corp.* and *Inc.*) to indicate that they are corporations, for example, CBS, Inc. and General Motors Corporation. This chapter and the next three discuss corporations and how to account for them.

Characteristics of a Corporation

Why is the corporation form of business so attractive? We now look at the features that distinguish corporations from proprietorships and partnerships.

Separate Legal Entity

A **corporation** is a business entity formed under state law. The state grants a **charter,** which is the document that gives the state's permission to form a corporation.

A corporation is a distinct entity from a legal perspective. We may consider the corporation as an artificial person that exists apart from its owners, who are called **stockholders** or **shareholders.** The corporation has many of the rights that a person has. For example, a corporation may buy, own, and sell property. Assets

OBJECTIVE 1

Identify the characteristics of a corporation

and liabilities in the business belong to the corporation. The corporation may enter into contracts, sue, and be sued.

The owners' equity of a corporation is divided into shares of **stock.** A person becomes a stockholder by purchasing the stock of the corporation. The corporate charter specifies how much stock the corporation can issue (sell) and lists the other details of its relationship with the state.

Continuous Life and Transferability of Ownership

Most corporations have continuous lives regardless of changes in the ownership of their stock. Stockholders may transfer stock as they wish. They may sell or trade the stock to another person, give it away, bequeath it in a will, or dispose of it in any other way they desire. The transfer of the stock does not affect the continuity of the corporation. Proprietorships and partnerships, on the other hand, terminate when their ownership changes.

No Mutual Agency

Mutual agency of the owners is *not* present in a corporation. The stockholder of a corporation cannot commit the corporation to a contract (unless he or she is also an officer in the business). For this reason, a stockholder need not exercise the care that partners must in selecting co-owners of the business.

Limited Liability of Stockholders

A stockholder has **limited liability** for corporation debts. He or she has no personal obligation for corporation liabilities. The most that a stockholder can lose on an investment in a corporation's stock is the cost of the investment. Recall that proprietors and partners are personally liable for the debts of their businesses.

The combination of limited liability and no mutual agency means that persons can invest limited amounts in a corporation without fear of losing all their personal wealth because of a business failure. This feature enables a corporation to raise more capital from a wider group of investors than proprietorships and partnerships.

Separation of Ownership and Management

Stockholders own the business, but a board of directors—elected by the stockholders—appoints corporate officers to manage the business. Thus stockholders may invest $1,000 or $1 million in the corporation without having to manage the business or disrupt their personal affairs.

However, this separation between owners—stockholders—and management may create problems. Corporate officers may decide to run the business for their own benefit and not to the stockholders' advantage. Stockholders may find it difficult to lodge an effective protest against management policy because of the distance between them and management.

Corporate Taxation

Corporations are separate taxable entities. They pay a variety of taxes not borne by proprietorships or partnerships. These taxes include an annual franchise tax levied by the state. The franchise tax is paid to keep the corporation charter in force and enables the corporation to continue in business. Corporations also pay federal and state income taxes. Corporate earnings are subject to **double taxation.** First, corporations pay their own income taxes on corporate income. Then, the stockholders pay personal income tax on the cash dividends that they receive from corporations. This is different from proprietorships and partnerships, which pay no business income tax. Instead, the tax falls solely on the owners.

Government Regulation

Strong government regulation is an important disadvantage to the corporation. Because stockholders have only limited liability for corporation debts, outsiders doing business with the corporation can look no further than the corporation itself for any claims that may arise against the business. To protect persons who loan money to a corporation or who invest in its stock, states monitor the affairs of corporations. This government regulation consists mainly of ensuring that corporations disclose the business information that investors and creditors need to make informed decisions. For many corporations, this government regulation is expensive.

Organization of a Corporation _____

Creation of a corporation begins when its organizers, called the **incorporators,** obtain a charter from the state. The **charter** includes the authorization for the corporation to issue a certain number of shares of stock, which are shares of ownership in the corporation. The incorporators pay fees, sign the charter, and file the required documents with the state. Then the corporation comes into existence. The incorporators agree to a set of **bylaws,** which act as the constitution for governing the corporation.

The ultimate control of the corporation rests with the stockholders, who receive one vote for each share of stock they own. The stockholders elect the members of the **board of directors,** which sets policy for the corporation and appoints the officers. The board elects a **chairperson,** who usually is the most powerful person in the corporation. The board also designates the **president,** who is the chief operating officer in charge of managing day-to-day operations. Most corporations also have vice-presidents in charge of sales, manufacturing, accounting and finance, and other key areas. Often the president and one or more vice-presidents are also elected to the board of directors. Exhibit 14-1 shows the authority structure in a corporation.

Most corporations have an annual meeting at which the stockholders elect directors and make other stockholder decisions. Stockholders unable to attend this annual meeting may vote on corporation matters by use of a **proxy,** which is a legal document that expresses the stockholder's preference and appoints another person to cast the vote.

The structure of proprietorships, partnerships, and corporations is similar in that all three types of business have owners, managers, and employees. In proprietorships and partnerships, policy decisions are usually made by the owners—the proprietor and the partners. In a corporation, however, the managers who set policy—the board of directors—may or may not be owners (stockholders).

A corporation keeps a subsidiary record of its stockholders. The business must notify the stockholders of the annual stockholder meeting and mail them dividend payments (which we discuss later in this chapter). Large companies use a

EXHIBIT 14-1 *Authority Structure in a Corporation*

registrar to maintain the stockholder list and a transfer agent to issue stock certificates. Banks provide these registration and transfer services. The transfer agent handles the change in stock ownership from one shareholder to another.

Capital Stock

A corporation issues stock certificates to its owners in exchange for their investments in the business. The basic unit of capital stock is called a *share*. A corporation may issue a stock certificate for any number of shares it wishes—one share, one hundred shares, or any other number. Exhibit 14-2 depicts an actual stock certificate for one share of IBM stock. The certificate shows the company name, the stockholder name, the number of shares, and the par value of the stock (which we discuss later).

Stock in the hands of a stockholder is said to be **outstanding.** The total number of shares of stock outstanding at any time represents 100 percent ownership of the corporation. Because stock represents the corporation's capital, it is often called capital stock.

Stockholders' Equity

The balance sheet of a corporation reports assets and liabilities in the same way as a proprietorship or a partnership. However, owners' equity of a corporation—called **stockholders' equity**—is reported differently. State laws require corpora-

EXHIBIT 14-2   *Stock Certificate*

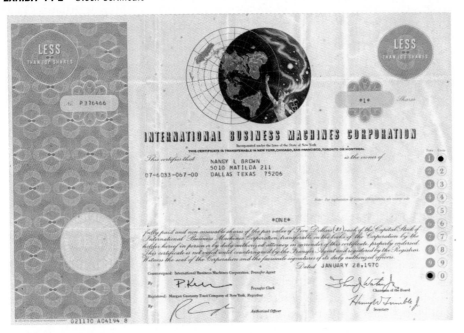

tions to report the sources of their capital. The two most basic sources of capital are investments by the stockholders, called **paid-in capital** or **contributed capital,** and capital earned through profitable operation of the business, called **retained earnings.** Exhibit 14-3 outlines a simplified corporation balance sheet to show how to report these categories of stockholders' equity.

An investment of cash or any other asset in a corporation increases its assets and stockholders' equity. The corporation's entry for receipt of a $20,000 stockholder investment in the business is

Oct. 20	Cash	20,000	
	Capital Stock		20,000
	Investment by stockholders.		

Capital stock is paid-in capital. It is regarded as the permanent capital of the business because it is *not* subject to withdrawal by the stockholders.

Profitable operations produce income, which increases stockholders' equity through an account called Retained Earnings. At the end of the year, the balance

EXHIBIT 14-3   *Simplified Corporation Balance Sheet*

Assets.................	$600,000	Liabilities	$240,000
		Stockholders' Equity	
		Paid-in capital:	
		Capital stock	200,000
		Retained earnings......	160,000
		Total stockholders' equity	360,000
		Total liabilities and	
Total assets.............	$600,000	stockholders' equity.....	$600,000

of the Income Summary account is closed to Retained Earnings. For example, if net income is $95,000, Income Summary will have a $95,000 credit balance. The closing entry will debit Income Summary to transfer net income to Retained Earnings as follows:

Dec. 31	Income Summary............................	95,000	
	Retained Earnings		95,000
	To close Income Summary by transferring net *income* to Retained Earnings.		

If operations produce a net *loss* rather than net income, the Income Summary account will have a debit balance. Income Summary must be credited to close it. With a $60,000 loss, the closing entry is:

Dec. 31	Retained Earnings	60,000	
	Income Summary.........................		60,000
	To close Income Summary by transferring net *loss* to Retained Earnings.		

A large loss may cause a debit balance in the Retained Earnings account. This condition—called a Retained Earnings **deficit,** or accumulated deficit—is reported on the balance sheet as a negative amount in stockholders' equity. Assume a $50,000 deficit:

Stockholders' Equity

Paid-in capital:	
Capital stock	$200,000
Deficit............................	(50,000)
Total stockholders' equity..............	$150,000

If the corporation has been profitable and has sufficient cash, a distribution of cash may be made to the stockholders. Such distributions—called **dividends**—decrease both the assets and the retained earnings of the business. The balance of the Retained Earnings account at any time is the sum of earnings accumulated since incorporation, minus any losses, and minus all dividends distributed to stockholders. Retained Earnings is entirely separate from the paid-in capital invested in the business by the stockholders.

Some people think of Retained Earnings as a fund of cash. It is not, because Retained Earnings is an element of stockholders' equity, representing a claim against all assets resulting from earnings that have not been distributed to the owners.

Stockholder Rights _____

The ownership of stock entitles stockholders to four basic rights, unless specific rights are withheld by agreement with the stockholders.

1. The right to participate in management by voting on matters that come before the stockholders. This is the stockholder's sole right to a voice in the management of the corporation. Each share of stock entitles the owner to one vote.

2. The right to receive a proportionate part of any dividend. Each share of stock in a particular class receives an equal dividend.

3. The right to receive a proportionate share (based on number of shares held) of any assets remaining after the corporation pays its liabilities in liquidation.

4. The right to maintain one's proportionate ownership in the corporation. Suppose you own 5 percent of a corporation's stock. If the corporation issues 100,000 new shares of stock, it must offer you the opportunity to buy 5 percent (5,000) of the new shares. This right, called the **preemptive right,** is usually withheld from the stockholders.

Classes of Stock

Corporations issue different types of stock to appeal to a wide variety of investors. The stock of a corporation may be either common or preferred and either par or no-par.

Common and Preferred Stock

Every corporation issues **common stock,** the most basic form of capital stock. Unless designated otherwise, the word *stock* is understood to mean "common stock." Common stockholders have the four basic rights of stock ownership, unless a right is specifically withheld. For example, some companies issue Class A common stock, which usually carries the right to vote, and Class B common stock, which may be nonvoting. (Classes of common stock may also be designated Series A, Series B, and so on.) The general ledger has a separate account for each class of common stock. In describing a corporation, we would say the common stockholders are the owners of the business.

Owners of **preferred stock** also have the four basic stockholder rights, unless a right is specifically denied. Often the right to vote is withheld from preferred stockholders. Preferred stock gives its owners certain advantages over common stockholders. These benefits include the priority to receive dividends before the common stockholders and the priority to receive assets before the common stockholders if the corporation liquidates. Because of the priorities that preferred stockholders have, we see that common stock represents the residual ownership in the corporation's assets after subtracting the liabilities and the claims of preferred stockholders. Companies may issue different classes of preferred stock. (Class A and Class B or Series A and Series B, for example). Each class is recorded in a separate account.

Par Value and No-Par Stock

Stock may be par value stock or no-par stock. **Par value** is an arbitrary amount assigned to a share of stock. Most companies set the par value of their common stock quite low. J.C. Penney's common stock par value is 50¢ per share, Bethlehem Steel's common stock par value is $8 per share, and Ralston Purina's common stock par value is 41⅔¢ per share. Par value of preferred stock is often higher; $100 per share is typical, but some preferred stocks have par value of $25 and $10. Par value is used to compute dividends, as we shall see. **No-par** stock does not have par value, but some no-par stock has a *stated value,* which makes it similar to par value stock.

Issuing Stock

The charter that the incorporators receive from the state includes an **authorization** for the business to issue—that is, to sell—a certain number of shares of stock. Corporations may sell the stock directly to the stockholders or they may use the service of an *underwriter*, such as the brokerage firms Merrill Lynch and Dean Witter. An underwriter agrees to buy all the stock it cannot sell to its clients.

The corporation need not issue all the stock that the state allows. Management may hold some stock back and issue it later if the need for additional capital arises. The stock that the corporation does issue to stockholders is called issued stock. Only by issuing stock—not by receiving authorization—does the corporation increase the asset and equity amounts on its balance sheet.

The price that the stockholder pays to acquire stock from the corporation is called the issue price. Often the issue price bears no relation to the stock's par value because the par value was intentionally set quite low. A combination of market factors, including the company's comparative earnings record, financial position, prospects for success, and general business conditions, determines issue price. Investors will not pay more than market value for the stock. The following sections show how to account for the issuance of stock.

Issuing Common Stock

Issuing Common Stock at Par.   Suppose Medina Corporation issues 500 shares of its $10 par common stock for cash equal to its par value. The stock issuance entry is

OBJECTIVE 2

Record the issuance of stock

Jan. 8	Cash (500 × $10)	5,000	
	Common Stock		5,000
	To issue common stock at par.		

The amount invested in the corporation, $5,000 in this case, is called paid-in capital or contributed capital. The credit to Common Stock records an increase in the paid-in capital of the corporation.

Issuing Common Stock at a Premium.   A corporation usually issues its common stock for a price above par value. The excess amount above par is called a **premium.** Assume Medina issues $10 par common stock for a price of $25. The $15 difference is a premium. This sale of stock increases the corporation's paid-in capital by $25, the total issue price of the stock. Both the par value of the stock and the premium are part of paid-in capital. A premium on the sale of stock is not gain, income, or profit to the corporation, because the entity is dealing with its own stockholders. This illustrates one of the fundamentals of accounting: a company cannot earn a profit, nor can it incur a loss, when it sells its stock to, or buys its stock from, its own stockholders.

Suppose Medina Corporation issues 4,000 shares of its $10 par common stock for $25 per share—a total of $100,000 (4,000 × $25). The premium per share is $15 ($25 − $10), and the entry to record the issuance of the stock is

Jan. 23	Cash (4,000 × $25)	100,000	
	Common Stock (4,000 × $10)		40,000
	Paid-in Capital in Excess of Par—Common		
	(4,000 × $15)		60,000
	To issue common stock at a premium.		

Account titles that could be used in place of Paid-in Capital in Excess of Par—Common are Additional Paid-In Capital—Common and Premium on Common Stock. Since both par value and premium amounts increase the corporation's capital, they appear in the stockholders' equity section of the balance sheet.

At the end of the first year, Medina Corporation would report stockholders' equity on its balance sheet as follows, assuming the corporate charter authorizes 20,000 shares of common stock and retained earnings is $85,000:

Stockholders' Equity

Paid-in capital:	
Common stock, $10 par, 20,000 shares authorized, 4,500 shares issued	$ 45,000
Paid-in capital in excess of par	60,000
Total paid-in capital	105,000
Retained earnings	85,000
Total stockholders' equity	$190,000

We determine the dollar amount reported for common stock by multiplying the total number of shares *issued* (500 + 4,000) by the par value per share. The *authorization* reports the maximum number of shares the company may issue under its charter.

Issuing Common Stock at a Discount. Stock issued at a price below par is said to be issued at a **discount.** For example, the issuance of $5 par common stock for $3 creates a $2 discount per share. The entry to record 1,000 shares of $5 par common stock issued for $3 per share is

Feb. 18	Cash (1,000 × $3)	3,000	
	Discount on Common Stock (1,000 × $2)	2,000	
	Common Stock (1,000 × $5)		5,000
	To issue common stock at a discount.		

What is the paid-in capital in this case? It is $3,000, the amount invested by the stockholders. The discount is reported in the stockholders' equity section of the balance sheet immediately after the stock account (as just shown for reporting a premium). However, the discount account—because it has a debit balance—is subtracted from the credit-balance par value of the stock issued to figure the capital amount.

The issuance of stock at a discount is rare. In fact, it is illegal in most states. When stock is sold at a discount, the stockholder has a *contingent liability* for the discount amount. If the corporation later liquidates, its creditors can require the original stockholder to pay the discount amount. Many companies set the par value of their common stock very low to avoid this contingent liability. A company is not likely to issue its stock at a price below an already low par value.

Issuing No-Par Common Stock. The contingent liability on common stock issued at a discount may explain why some state laws allow companies to issue no-par stock. If the stock has no par value, there can be no discount and thus no contingent liability. A recent survey of 600 companies revealed that they had 108 issues of no-par stock.

When no-par stock is issued, the asset received is debited and the stock account is credited. Glenwood Corporation issues 300 shares of no-par common stock for $20 per share. The stock issuance entry is

Aug. 14   Cash (300 × $20)   6,000
                   Common Stock   6,000
              To issue no-par common stock.

Regardless of the stock's price, Cash is debited and Common Stock is credited for the amount of cash received. There is no Paid-in Capital in Excess of Par for true no-par stock.

   Assume that the charter authorizes Glenwood to issue 5,000 shares of no-par stock and the company has $3,000 in retained earnings. The corporation would report stockholders' equity as follows:

Stockholders' Equity

Paid-in capital:
   Common stock, no-par, 5,000 shares authorized, 300 shares issued $6,000
Retained earnings... 3,000
Total stockholders' equity $9,000

Issuing No-par Common Stock with a Stated Value.   Accounting for no-par stock with a stated value is identical to accounting for par value stock. The premium account for no-par common is entitled Paid-in Capital in Excess of *Stated* Value — Common.

Issuing Common Stock for Assets Other Than Cash.   When a corporation issues stock in exchange for assets other than cash, it debits the assets received for their current market value and credits the capital accounts accordingly. The assets' prior book value does not matter because the stockholder will demand stock equal to the market value of the asset given. Assume Kahn Corporation issues 15,000 shares of its $1 par common stock for equipment worth $4,000 and a building worth $120,000. The entry is

Nov. 12   Equipment..................................   4,000
              Building.................................... 120,000
                   Common Stock (15,000 × $1)   15,000
                   Paid-in Capital in Excess of Par — Common
                       ($124,000 − $15,000)   109,000
              To issue common stock in exchange for equipment
              and a building.

Paid-in capital increases by the amount of the assets' current market value, $124,000 in this case.

Issuing Common Stock through Subscriptions.   Established companies usually issue stock and receive the full price in a single transaction. New corporations, to gauge their ability to raise capital, often take subscriptions for their stock. A **stock subscription** is a contract that obligates an investor to purchase the corporation's stock at a later date. Because a contract exists between the two parties, the corporation acquires an asset, Subscription Receivable, when it receives the subscription. The investor gains an equity in the corporation by promising to pay the subscription amount. Depending on the subscription agreement, the subscriber may pay the subscription in a lump sum or in installments.

Assume Medina Corporation receives a subscription on May 31 for 1,000 shares of $10 par common stock. The subscription price is $22 per share. The subscriber makes a down payment of $6,000 and agrees to pay the $16,000 balance in two monthly installments of $8,000 each. Medina Corporation will issue the stock when the subscriber pays in full. The entry to record receipt of the subscription is

May 31	Cash	6,000	
	Subscription Receivable—Common		
	($22,000 − $6,000)	16,000	
	Common Stock Subscribed (1,000 × $10)		10,000
	Paid-in Capital in Excess of Par—Common		
	(1,000 × $12)		12,000
	To receive common stock subscription at $22 per share.		

Subscription Receivable—Common, is a current asset if collection is expected within one year. Otherwise it is long-term and is reported in the Other Assets category on the balance sheet. Common Stock Subscribed is an element of stock-holders' equity, reported immediately beneath Common Stock (and above Paid-in Capital in Excess of Par—Common) on the balance sheet. The "Subscribed" label will be dropped when the subscription is paid off and the stock is issued. Paid-in Capital in Excess of Par—Common is the same premium account that is credited when stock is sold for cash at a price in excess of par. The entries to record receipt of the two installments and issuance of the stock are

June 30	Cash ($16,000 × ½).	8,000	
	Subscription Receivable—Common		8,000
	To collect first installment on common stock subscription.		
July 31	Cash ($16,000 × ½).	8,000	
	Subscription Receivable—Common		8,000
	To collect second installment on common stock subscription.		
31	Common Stock Subscribed.	10,000	
	Common Stock		10,000
	To issue common stock under subscription agreement.		

The last entry is needed to transfer the par value of the stock from the Subscribed account to Common Stock.

Because the subscription is a legally binding contract, subscribers must pay their subscriptions in full. If they fail to do so, state laws govern the settlement between the corporation and the defaulting subscriber.

Issuing Preferred Stock

Not all corporations issue preferred stock. A recent survey of 600 companies indicated that only 213 had preferred stock outstanding. Accounting for pre-ferred stock follows the pattern illustrated for common stock. Assume the Medina Corporation charter authorizes issuance of 5,000 shares of 5 percent, $100 par preferred stock. On July 31 the company issues 400 shares at a price of $110.

(Preferred stock often sells at its par value or at a premium but seldom at a discount.) The issuance entry is

July 31	Cash (400 × $110)	44,000	
	Preferred Stock (400 × $100)		40,000
	Paid-in Capital in Excess of Par—Preferred		
	(400 × $10)		4,000
	To issue preferred stock at a premium.		

Observe that the Paid-in Capital in Excess of Par account title includes the word Preferred. A corporation lists separate accounts for Paid-in Capital in Excess of Par on Preferred Stock and on Common Stock to differentiate the two classes of equity.

Accounting for *no-par preferred stock* follows the pattern illustrated for no-par common stock.

Let's review the first half of this chapter by showing the stockholder's equity section of Medina Corporation's balance sheet. (Assume that all figures, which are arbitrary, are correct.) Note the two sections of stockholders' equity: paid-in capital and retained earnings. Also observe the order of the equity accounts: preferred stock at par value, paid in capital in excess of par on preferred stock, common stock at par value, common stock subscribed, and paid in capital in excess of par on common stock. If Medina had a Preferred Stock Subscribed account, it would appear after Preferred Stock and before Paid-in Capital in Excess of Par—Preferred (corresponding to the order illustrated for the common stock accounts).

Stockholders' Equity

Paid-in capital:	
Preferred stock, 5% $100 par, 5,000 shares authorized, 400 shares issued	$ 40,000
Paid-in capital in excess of par—preferred	4,000
Common stock, $10 par, 20,000 shares authorized,	
4,500 shares issued	45,000
Common stock subscribed, 1,000 shares	10,000
Paid-in capital in excess of par—common	72,000
Total paid-in capital	171,000
Retained earnings	85,000
Total stockholders' equity	$256,000

OBJECTIVE 3

Prepare the stockholders' equity section of a corporation balance sheet

---

Summary Problems for Your Review

1. Test your understanding of the first half of this chapter by answering whether each of the following statements is true or false.

_____ a. A stockholder may bind the corporation to a contract.

_____ b. The policy-making body in a corporation is called the board of directors.

_____ c. The owner of 100 shares of preferred stock has greater voting rights than the owner of 100 shares of common stock.

_____ d. Par value stock is worth more than no-par stock.

_____ e. Issuance of 1,000 shares of $5 par value stock at $12 increases contributed capital by $12,000.

_____ f. The issuance of stock at a discount occurs less frequently than issuance of stock at a premium.

_____ g. The issuance of no-par stock with a stated value is fundamentally different from issuing par value stock.

_____ h. A corporation issues its preferred stock in exchange for land and a building with a combined market value of $200,000. This transaction increases the corporation's owner equity by $200,000 regardless of the assets' prior book value.

_____ i. Receipt of a subscription contract does not increase the stockholders' equity of the corporation unless the subscriber makes a down payment.

_____ j. Common Stock Subscribed is a part of stockholders' equity.

2. Adolph Coors Company is a leading brewery. The company has two classes of common stock. Note that only the Class A common stockholders are entitled to vote. The company's balance sheet included the following presentation:

Shareholders' Equity

Capital stock	
Class A common stock, voting, $1 par value, authorized and issued 1,260,000 shares	$ 1,260,000
Class B common stock, non-voting, no-par value, authorized and issued 46,200,000 shares	11,000,000
	12,260,000
Additional paid-in capital	2,011,000
Retained earnings	872,403,000
	$886,674,000

Required

a. Record the issuance of the Class A common stock. Assume the additional paid-in capital amount relates to the Class A common stock. Use the Coors account titles.

b. Record the issuance of the Class B common stock. Use the Coors account titles.

c. Rearrange the Coors stockholders' equity section to correspond to the following format:

Shareholders' Equity

Paid-in Capital:	
Class A common stock	$
Paid-in capital in excess of par — Class A common stock	
Class B common stock	
Total paid-in capital	
Retained earnings	
Total shareholders' equity	$

d. What is the total paid-in capital of the company?

e. How did Coors withhold the voting privilege from their Class B common stockholders?

SOLUTIONS TO SUMMARY PROBLEMS

1. Answers to true-false statements:

a. False   b. True   c. False   d. False   e. True

f. True   g. False   h. True   i. False   j. True

2. a. Cash 3,271,000

            Class A Common Stock 1,260,000

            Additional Paid-in Capital 2,011,000

     To record issuance of Class A common stock
     at a premium.

b. Cash 11,000,000

            Class B Common Stock 11,000,000

     To record issuance of Class B common stock.

c. Shareholders' Equity

     Paid-in Capital:

         Class A common stock, voting, $1 par value, authorized

         and issued 1,260,000 shares . . . . $ 1,260,000

         Paid-in capital in excess of par—Class A common stock .   2,011,000

         Class B common stock, non-voting, no par value, autho-

         rized and issued 46,200,000 shares   11,000,000

         Total paid-in capital   14,271,000

     Retained earnings   872,403,000

     Total shareholders equity $886,674,000

d. Total paid-in capital is $14,271,000, as shown in the answer to c.

e. The voting privilege was withheld from stockholders by specific agreement with them.

Donated Capital _____

Corporations occasionally receive gifts, or donations. For example, city council members may offer a company free land to encourage it to locate in their city. Cities in the southern United States have lured some companies away from the North using this offer. The free land is called a donation. Also, a stockholder may make a donation to the corporation in the form of cash, land, or other assets or stock that the corporation can resell.

A donation is a gift that increases the assets of the corporation. However, the donor (giver) receives no ownership interest in the company in return. A transaction to receive a donation does not increase the corporation's revenue, and thus it does not affect income. Instead, the donation creates a special category of stockholders' equity called **donated capital.** The corporation records a donation by debiting the asset received at its current market value, and by crediting Donated Capital, a stockholders' equity account.

Suppose Burlington Industries receives 100 acres of land as a donation from the city of Raleigh, North Carolina. The current market value of the land is $150,000. Burlington records receipt of the donation as follows:

Apr. 18   Land 150,000

            Donated Capital 150,000

     To receive land as a donation from the city.

Donated capital is reported on the balance sheet after the stock accounts in the paid-in capital section of stockholders' equity.

Incorporation of a Going Business

You may dream of having your own business someday, or you may currently be a business proprietor or partner. Businesses that begin as a proprietorship or a partnership often incorporate at a later date. By incorporating a going business, the proprietor or partners avoid the unlimited liability for business debts. And as we discussed earlier, incorporating also makes it easier to raise capital.

To account for the incorporation of a going business, we close the owner equity accounts of the prior entity and set up the stockholder equity accounts of the corporation. Suppose Santa Fe Travel Associates is a partnership owned by Joe Brown and Monica Lee. The partnership balance sheet, after all adjustments and closing entries, reports Joe Brown, Capital, of $50,000, and Monica Lee, Capital, of $70,000. They incorporate the travel agency as Santa Fe Travel Company, Inc., with an authorization to issue 200,000 shares of $1 par common stock. Joe and Monica agree to receive common stock equal in par value to their partnership owner equity balances. The entry to record the incorporation of the business is

Feb. 1	Joe Brown, Capital	50,000	
	Monica Lee, Capital	70,000	
	Common Stock		120,000
	To incorporate the business, close the capital accounts of the partnership, and issue common stock to the incorporators.		

OBJECTIVE 4
Account for the incorporation of a going business

Organization Cost

The costs of organizing a corporation include legal fees, taxes and fees paid to the state, and charges by promoters for selling the stock. These costs are grouped in an account titled Organization Cost, which is an asset because these costs contribute to a business's start-up. Suppose Mary Kay Cosmetics, Inc., pays legal fees of $15,000 and the state of Texas incorporation fee of $500 to organize the corporation. In addition, a promoter charges a fee of $24,000 for selling the stock and receives the corporation's no-par stock as payment. Mary Kay's journal entries to record these organization costs are

Mar. 31	Organization Cost ($15,000 + $500)	15,500	
	Cash		15,500
	Legal fees and state incorporation fee to organize the corporation.		
Apr. 3	Organization Cost	24,000	
	Common Stock		24,000
	Promoter fee for selling stock in organization.		

Organization Cost is an *intangible asset,* reported on the balance sheet along with patents, trademarks, goodwill, and any other intangibles. We know that an intangible asset should be amortized over its useful life, and organization costs will benefit the corporation for as long as the corporation operates. But how long will that be? We cannot know in advance, but we still must expense these costs over some period of time. The Internal Revenue Service tax laws allow corporations to use a minimum 5-year useful life for amortization. GAAP allows a maximum 40-year useful life. Companies therefore amortize organization costs over a period between 5 and 40 years. Assume a 10-year life, and the preceding organization cost of $39,500 ($15,500 + $24,000) would be amortized by a debit to Amortization Expense and a credit to Organization Cost for $3,950 ($39,500/10) each year.

Dividends on Preferred and Common Stock _____

A corporation must declare a dividend before paying it. The board of directors alone has the authority to declare a dividend. The corporation has no obligation to pay a dividend until the board declares one, but once declared, the dividend becomes a legal liability of the corporation. Declaration of a cash dividend is recorded by debiting Retained Earnings and crediting Dividends Payable as follows:

June 19	Retained Earnings	XXX	
	Dividends Payable		XXX
	To declare a cash dividend.		

Payment of the dividend, which usually follows declaration by a few weeks, is recorded by debiting Dividends Payable and crediting Cash:

July 2	Dividends Payable	XXX	
	Cash.		XXX
	To pay a cash dividend.		

Dividends Payable is a current liability. When a company has issued both preferred and common stock, the preferred stockholders receive their dividends first. The common stockholders receive dividends only if the total declared dividend is large enough to pay the preferred shareholders first.

Pine Industries, Inc., in addition to its common stock, has approximately 9,000 shares of preferred stock outstanding. Preferred dividends are paid at the annual rate of $1.75 per share. Assume Pine declares an annual dividend of $150,000. The allocation to preferred and common stockholders is

<table>
<tr><td></td><td style="text-align:right">Total Dividend
of $150,000</td></tr>
<tr><td>Preferred dividend (9,000 shares × $1.75 per share) . . . .</td><td style="text-align:right">$ 15,750</td></tr>
<tr><td>Common dividend (remainder: $150,000 − $15,750). . . . .</td><td style="text-align:right">134,250</td></tr>
<tr><td>Total dividend. . . . .</td><td style="text-align:right">$150,000</td></tr>
</table>

OBJECTIVE 5

Allocate dividends to preferred and common stock

If Pine declares only a $20,000 dividend, preferred stockholders receive $15,750, and the common stockholders receive $4,250 ($20,000 − $15,750).

This example illustrates an important relationship between preferred stock and common stock. To an investor, the preferred stock is safer because it receives dividends first. For example, if Pine Industries earns only enough net income to pay the preferred stockholders' dividends, the owners of common stock receive no dividends at all. However, the earnings potential from an investment in common stock is much greater than from an investment in preferred stock. Preferred dividends are usually limited to the specified amount, but there is no upper limit on the amount of common dividends.

We noted that preferred stockholders enjoy the advantage of priority over common stockholders in receiving dividends. The dividend preference is stated as a percentage rate or a dollar amount. For example, preferred stock may be "6 percent preferred," which means that owners of the preferred stock receive an annual dividend of 6 percent of the par value of the stock. If par value is $100 per share, preferred stockholders receive an annual cash dividend of $6 per share (6 percent of $100). The preferred stock may be "$3 preferred," which means that stockholders receive an annual dividend of $3 per share regardless of the preferred stock's par value. The dividend rate on no-par preferred stock is stated in a dollar amount per share.

Cumulative and Noncumulative Preferred Stock

The allocation of dividends may be complex if the preferred stock is *cumulative.* Corporations sometimes fail to pay a dividend to their preferred stockholders. This occurrence is called *passing the dividend,* and the passed dividends are said to be **in arrears.** The owners of **cumulative preferred stock** must receive all dividends in arrears before the corporation pays dividends to the common stockholders.

The preferred stock of Pine Industries is cumulative. Suppose the company passed the 19X4 preferred dividend of $15,750. Before paying dividends to its common stockholders in 19X5, the company must first pay preferred dividends of $15,750 for both 19X4 and 19X5, a total of $31,500. *Preferred stock is cumulative in the eyes of the law unless it is specifically labeled as noncumulative.*

Assume that Pine Industries passes its 19X4 preferred dividend. In 19X5 the company declares a $50,000 dividend. The entry to record the declaration is

Sep. 6	Retained Earnings	50,000	
	Dividends Payable, Preferred ($15,750 × 2)		31,500
	Dividends Payable, Common		
	($50,000 − $31,500)......................		18,500
	To declare a cash dividend.		

If the preferred stock is **noncumulative,** the corporation is not obligated to pay dividends in arrears. Suppose that the Pine Industries preferred stock was noncumulative, and the company passed the 19X4 preferred dividend of $15,750. The preferred stockholders would lose the 19X4 dividend forever. Of course, the common stockholders would not receive a 19X4 dividend either. Before paying any common dividends in 19X5, the company would have to pay the 19X5 preferred dividend of $15,750.

Having dividends in arrears on cumulative preferred stock is *not* a liability to the corporation. (A liability for dividends arises only after the board of directors declares the dividend.) Nevertheless, a corporation must report cumulative preferred dividends in arrears. This information alerts common stockholders as to how much in cumulative preferred dividends must be paid before any dividends will be paid on the common stock. This gives the common stockholders an idea about the likelihood of receiving dividends and satisfies the disclosure principle.

Dividends in arrears are often disclosed in notes, as follows (all dates and amounts assumed). Observe the two references to Note 3 in this section of the balance sheet. The "6 percent" after "Preferred stock" is the dividend rate.

Preferred stock, 6 percent, par $50, 2,000 shares issued (Note 3). $100,000
Retained earnings (Note 3)   414,000

> Note 3—Cumulative preferred dividends in arrears. At December 31, 19X2, dividends on the company's 6 percent preferred stock were in arrears for 19X1 and 19X2, in the amount of $12,000 (6% × $100,000 × 2 years).

Participating and Nonparticipating Preferred Stock

The owners of **participating preferred stock** may receive—that is *participate in*—dividends beyond the stated amount or stated percentage. Assume that the corporation declares a dividend. First, the preferred stockholders receive their dividends. If the corporation has declared a large enough dividend, then the common stockholders receive their dividends. If an additional dividend amount remains to be distributed, common stockholders and participating preferred stockholders share it. For example, the owners of a $4 preferred stock must receive the specified annual dividend of $4 per share before the common stockholders receive any dividends. Then a $4 dividend is paid on each common share. The participation feature takes effect only after the preferred and common stockholders have received the specified $4 rate. Payment of an extra *common* dividend of, say, $1.50 is accompanied by a $1.50 dividend on each preferred share.

Participating preferred stock is rare. In fact, preferred stock is nonparticipating unless it is specifically described as participating on the stock certificate and in the financial statements. Therefore, if the preferred stock in our example is nonparticipating (the usual case), the largest annual dividend that a preferred stockholder will receive is $4.

Convertible Preferred Stock

Convertible preferred stock may be exchanged by the preferred stockholders, if they choose, for another class of stock in the corporation. For example, the Pine Industries preferred stock may be converted into the company's common stock. A note to Pine's balance sheet describes the conversion terms as follows:

> The . . . preferred stock is convertible at the rate of 6.51 shares of common stock for each share of preferred stock outstanding.

If you owned 100 shares of Pine's convertible preferred stock, you could convert it into 651 (100 × 6.51) shares of Pine common stock. Under what condition would you exercise the conversion privilege? You would do so if the market value of the common stock that you could receive from conversion exceeded the market value of the preferred stock that you presently held. This way, you as an investor could increase your personal wealth.

Pine Industries preferred stock has par value of $100 per share, and the par value of the common stock is $1. The company would record conversion of 100 shares of preferred stock, issued previously at par, into 651 shares of common stock as follows:

Mar 7	Preferred Stock (100 × $100)	10,000	
	Common Stock (651 × $1)		651
	Paid-in Capital in Excess of Par—Common		9,349
	Conversion of preferred stock into common.		

If the preferred stock was issued at a premium, Paid-in Capital in Excess of Par—Preferred must also be debited to remove its balance from the books.

Preferred stock, we see, offers alternative features not available to common stock. Preferred stock is cumulative or noncumulative, participating or nonparticipating, and convertible or not convertible.

Different Values of Stock

The business community refers to several different *stock values* in addition to par value. These values include market value, redemption value, liquidation value, and book value.

> **OBJECTIVE 6**
> Distinguish among various stock "values"

Market Value

A stock's **market value** is the price for which a person could buy or sell a share of the stock. The issuing corporation's net income, financial position, its future prospects, and the general economic conditions determine market value (also called market price). Daily newspapers report the market price of many stocks. In almost all cases, stockholders are more concerned about the market value of a stock than any of the other values discussed below. A stock listed at (an alternative term is *quoted at*) 29¼ sells for, or may be bought for, $29.25 per share. The purchase of 100 shares of this stock would cost $2,925 ($29.25 × 100), plus a commission. If you were selling 100 shares of this stock, you would receive cash of $2,925 less a commission. The commission is the fee an investor pays to a stockbroker for buying or selling the stock.

Redemption Value

Preferred stock's fixed dividend rate makes it somewhat like debt. However, companies do not get a tax deduction for preferred dividend payments. Thus they may wish to buy back, or redeem, their preferred stock to avoid paying the dividends. Preferred stock that provides for redemption at a set price is called redeemable preferred stock. In some cases, the company has the *option* of redeeming its preferred stock at a set price. In other cases, the company is *obligated* to redeem the preferred stock. The price the corporation agrees to pay for the stock, which is set when the stock is issued, is called **redemption value**.

The preferred stock of Pine Industries, Inc., is "redeemable at the option of the Company at $25 per share." Beginning in 1992, Pine is "required to redeem annually 6,765 shares of the preferred stock ($169,125 annually)." Pine's annual redemption payment to the preferred stockholders will include this redemption value plus any dividends in arrears.

Liquidation Value

Liquidation value, which applies only to preferred stock, is the amount the corporation agrees to pay the preferred stockholder per share if the company liquidates. Great Northern Nekoosa Corporation, a large paper company, has preferred stock with "a preference of $50 in liquidation." Dividends in arrears are added to liquidation value in determining the payment to the preferred stockholders if the company liquidates.

Book Value

The **book value** of a stock is the amount of owners' equity on the company's books for each share of its stock. Corporations often report this amount in their annual reports. If the company has only common stock outstanding, its book value is computed by dividing total stockholders' equity by the number of shares outstanding. A company with stockholders' equity of $180,000 and 5,000 shares of common stock outstanding has book value of $36 per share ($180,000/5,000 shares).

If the company has both preferred and common stock outstanding, the preferred stockholders have the first claim to owners' equity. Ordinarily, preferred stock has a specified liquidation or redemption value. The book value of preferred is its redemption value plus any cumulative dividends in arrears on the stock. Its book value *per share* equals the sum of redemption value and any cumulative dividends in arrears divided by the number of preferred shares outstanding. After the corporation figures the preferred shares' book value, it computes the common stock book value per share. The corporation divides the common equity (total stockholders' equity minus preferred equity) by the number of common shares outstanding.

Assume that the company balance sheet reports the following amounts:

Stockholders' Equity

Paid-in capital:	
Preferred stock, 6%, $100 par, 5,000 shares authorized,	
400 shares issued	$ 40,000
Paid-in capital in excess of par—preferred	4,000
Common stock, $10 par, 20,000 shares authorized,	
4,500 shares issued	45,000
Common stock subscribed, 1000 shares	10,000
Paid-in capital in excess of par—common	72,000
Total paid-in capital	171,000
Retained earnings	85,000
Total stockholders' equity	$256,000

Suppose that four years (including the current year) of cumulative preferred dividends are in arrears and preferred stock has a redemption value of $130 per share.

Book value computations treat subscribed stock as though it were issued stock. The book value per share computations for this corporation follow.

Preferred:	
Redemption value (400 shares × $130)	$ 52,000
Cumulative dividends ($40,000 × .06 × 4)	9,600
Stockholders' equity allocated to preferred	$ 61,600
Book value per share ($61,600/400 shares)	$ 154.00

Common:

Total stockholders' equity	$256,000
Less stockholders' equity allocated to preferred.....................	61,600
Stockholders' equity allocated to common	$194,400
Book value per share [$194,400/(4,500 shares + 1,000 shares)].........	$35.35

How is book value per share used in decision making? Companies may agree to buy a corporation based on the book value of its stock. Corporations may settle up with a stockholder, agreeing to pay the book value of the person's stock in the company. In general, however, book value is not directly related to the market value of stock.

Summary Problems for Your Review

1. Use the following accounts and related balances to prepare the classified balance sheet of Whitehall, Inc., at September 30, 19X4. Use the account format of the balance sheet.

Common stock, $1 par, 50,000 shares authorized, 20,000 shares issued	$ 20,000	Long-term note payable	$ 74,000
		Inventory................	85,000
Dividends payable	4,000	Property, plant, and equipment, net..........	225,000
Cash	9,000	Donated capital............	18,000
Accounts payable	28,000	Accounts receivable, net.....	23,000
Stock subscription receivable —common	2,000	Preferred stock, $3.75, no-par, 10,000 shares, authorized, 2,000 shares issued.................	24,000
Retained earnings	56,000		
Paid-in capital in excess of par —common	115,000	Common stock subscribed 3,000 shares............	3,000
Organization cost, net	1,000	Accrued liabilities	3,000

2. The balance sheet of Trendline Corporation reported the following at March 31, 19X6, end of its fiscal year. Note that Trendline reports paid-in capital in excess of par or stated value after the stock accounts.

Stockholders' Equity

Preferred stock, 4%, $10 par, 11,000 shares authorized (redemption value, $110,000)	$110,000
Common stock, no-par, $5 stated value, 100,000 shares authorized	250,000
Common stock subscribed	17,500
Paid-in capital in excess of par or stated value:	
Common stock..	214,000
Donated capital	55,000
Retained earnings	330,000
Total stockholders' equity	$976,500

Required

a. Is the preferred stock cumulative or noncumulative? Is it participating or nonpartici-pating? How can you tell?

b. What is the total amount of the annual preferred dividend?

c. How many shares of preferred stock and common stock has the company issued?

d. How many shares of common stock are subscribed?

e. What was the market value of the assets donated to the corporation?

f. Compute the book value per share of the preferred stock and the common stock. No prior year preferred dividends are in arrears, but Trendline has not declared the current-year dividend.

SOLUTIONS TO REVIEW PROBLEMS

1.

Whitehall, Inc.
Balance Sheet
September 30, 19X4

Assets			**Liabilities**	
Current:			Current:	
Cash........................	$ 9,000		Accounts payable	$ 28,000
Accounts receivable, net..........	23,000		Dividends payable	4,000
Stock subscription receivable–			Accrued liabilities	3,000
common.....................	2,000		Total current liabilities	35,000
Inventory.....................	85,000		Long-term note payable...........	74,000
Total current assets	119,000		Total liabilities	109,000
Property, plant, and equipment, net ..	225,000			
Intangible assets:			**Stockholders' Equity**	
Organization cost, net............	1,000		Paid-in capital:	
			Preferred stock, $3.75, no-par,	
			10,000 shares authorized, 2,000	
			shares issued	$ 24,000
			Common stock, $1 par, 50,000	
			shares authorized, 20,000 shares	
			issued	20,000
			Common stock subscribed, 3,000	
			shares......................	3,000
			Paid-in capital in excess of par—	
			common....................	115,000
			Donated capital.................	18,000
			Total paid-in capital	180,000
			Retained earnings	56,000
			Total stockholders' equity.......	236,000
			Total liabilities and	
Total assets	$345,000		stockholders' equity...........	$345,000

2. Answers to Trendline Corporation questions:

a. The preferred stock is *cumulative* and *nonparticipating* because it is not specifically labeled otherwise.

b. Total annual preferred dividend: $4,000 ($100,000 × .04)

c. Preferred stock issued: 10,000 shares ($100,000/$10 par)
Common stock issued: 50,000 shares ($250,000/$5 stated value)

d. Common stock subscribed: 3,500 shares ($17,500/$5 stated value)

e. Market value of donated assets: $55,000

f. Book values per share of preferred and common stock:

Preferred:

Redemption value	$110,000
Cumulative dividend for current year ($100,000 × .04)	4,000
Stockholders' equity allocated to preferred	$114,000
Book value per share ($114,000/10,000 shares)	$11.40

Common:

Total stockholders' equity	$976,500
Less stockholders' equity allocated to preferred.....................	114,000
Stockholders' equity allocated to common	$862,500
Book value per share [$862,500/(53,500 shares = 50,000 shares issued + 3,500 shares subscribed)]	$16.12

Summary

A corporation is a separate legal and business entity. *Continuous life,* the ease of raising large amounts of capital and transferring ownership, and *limited liability* are among the advantages of the corporate form of organization. An important disadvantage is *double taxation.* Corporations pay *income taxes,* and stockholders pay tax on dividends. *Stockholders* are the owners of corporations. They elect a *board of directors,* which elects a chairperson and appoints the officers to manage the business.

Corporations may issue different classes of stock: *par value, no-par value, common,* and *preferred.* Stock is usually issued at a *premium*—an amount above par value. Also, corporations may issue stock under a *subscription* agreement. The balance sheet carries the capital raised through stock issuance under the heading Paid-in Capital or Contributed Capital in the stockholders' equity section.

Corporations may receive *donations* from outsiders or from stockholders. Donated Capital is a stockholders' equity account.

Only when the board of directors declares a *dividend* does the corporation incur the liability to pay dividends. Preferred stock has priority over common stock as to dividends, which may be stated as a percentage of par value or as a dollar amount per share. In addition, preferred stock has a claim to dividends in arrears if it is *cumulative* and a claim to further dividends if it is *participating. Convertible* preferred stock may be exchanged for the corporation's common stock.

A stock's *market value* is the price for which a share may be bought or sold. *Redemption value, liquidation value, and book value*—the amount of owners' equity per share of company stock—are other values that may apply to stock.

Self-Study Questions

Test your understanding of the chapter by marking the best answer for each of the following questions.

1. Which of the following is a *disadvantage* of the corporate form of business organization? *(p. 537)*
   a. Limited liability of stockholders
   b. Government regulation
   c. No mutual agency
   d. Transferability of ownership

2. The person with the most power in a corporation is the *(p. 537)*
   a. Incorporator
   b. Chairman of the board
   c. President
   d. Vice-president

3. The dollar amount of the stockholder investments in a corporation is called *(p. 539)*
   a. Outstanding stock
   b. Total stockholders' equity
   c. Paid-in capital
   d. Retained earnings

4. The arbitrary value assigned to a share of stock is called *(p. 541)*
   a. Market value
   b. Liquidation value
   c. Book value
   d. Par value

5. Which is the most widely held class of stock? *(p. 541)*
   a. Par value common stock
   b. No-par common stock
   c. Par value preferred stock
   d. No-par preferred stock

6. Mangum Corporation receives a subscription for 1,000 shares of $100 par preferred stock at $104 per share. This transaction increases Mangum's paid-in capital by *(pp. 545, 546)*
   a. $0 because the corporation received no cash
   b. $4,000
   c. $100,000
   d. $104,000

7. Organization cost is classified as a (an) *(p. 549)*
   a. Operating expense
   b. Current asset
   c. Contra item in stockholders' equity
   d. None of the above

8. Trade Days, Inc., has 10,000 shares of $3.50, $50 par preferred stock, and 100,000 of $4 par common stock outstanding. Two years' preferred dividends are in arrears. Trade Days declares a cash dividend large enough to pay the preferred dividends in arrears, the preferred dividend for the current period, and a $1.50 dividend to common. What is the total amount of the dividend? *(p. 550)*
   a. $255,000   b. $220,000   c. $150,000   d. $105,000

9. The preferred stock of Trade Days, Inc., in the preceding question was issued at $55 per share. Each preferred share can be converted into 10 common shares. The entry to record the conversion of this preferred stock into common is *(pp. 552, 553)*

   a. Cash 550,000
      Preferred Stock............................   500,000
      Paid-in Capital in Excess of Par—Preferred Stock   50,000

   b. Preferred Stock............................ 500,000
      Paid-in Capital in Excess of Par—Preferred Stock 50,000
      Common Stock...............................   550,000

   c. Preferred Stock............................ 500,000
      Paid-in Capital in Excess of Par—Preferred Stock 50,000
      Common Stock...............................   400,000
      Paid-in Capital in Excess of Par—Common Stock   150,000

   d. Preferred Stock............................ 550,000
      Common Stock...............................   400,000
      Paid-in Capital in Excess of Par—Common Stock   150,000

10. When an investor is buying stock as an investment, the value of most direct concern is *(p. 553)*
    a. Par value   b. Market value   c. Liquidation value   d. Book value

Answers to the self-study questions are at the end of the chapter.

Accounting Vocabulary

additional paid-in capital *(p. 543)*, authorization of stock *(p. 542)*, board of directors *(p. 537)*, book value of stock *(p. 554)*, bylaws *(p. 537)*, chairperson of the board *(p. 537)*, charter *(pp. 535, 537)*, common stock *(p. 541)*, contributed capital *(p. 539)*, convertible preferred stock *(p. 542)*, cumulative preferred stock *(p. 551)*, deficit *(p. 540)*, discount on stock *(p. 543)*, dividends *(p. 540)*, dividends in arrears *(p. 551)*, donated capital *(p. 548)*, double taxation *(p. 537)*, incorporator *(p. 537)*, limited liability *(p. 536)*, liquidation value of stock *(p. 554)*, market value of stock *(p. 553)*, organization cost *(p. 549)*, outstanding stock *(p. 538)*, paid-in capital *(p. 539)*, par value *(p. 541)*, participating preferred stock *(p. 552)*, preemptive right *(p. 541)*, preferred stock *(p. 541)*, premium on stock *(p. 542)*, president *(p. 537)*, proxy *(p. 537)*, redemption value of stock *(p. 553)*, retained earnings *(p. 539)*, shareholder *(p. 535)*, stock *(p. 536)*, stockholders' equity *(p. 538)*, stock subscription *(p. 544)*.

ASSIGNMENT MATERIAL

Questions

1. Why is a corporation called a creature of the state?
2. Identify the characteristics of a corporation.
3. Explain why corporations face a tax disadvantage.
4. Briefly outline the steps in the organization of a corporation.
5. How are the structures of a partnership and a corporation similar and different?
6. Name the four rights of a stockholder. Is preferred stock automatically nonvoting? Explain how a right may be withheld from a stockholder.
7. Dividends on preferred stock may be stated as a percentage rate or a dollar amount. What is the annual dividend on these preferred stocks: 4 percent, $100 par; $3.50, $20 par; and 6 percent, no-par with $50 stated value?
8. Which event increases the assets of the corporation: authorization of stock or issuance of stock? Explain.
9. Suppose H. J. Heinz Company issued 1,000 shares of its 3.65 percent, $100 par preferred stock for $120. How much would this transaction increase the company's paid-in capital? How much would it increase Heinz's retained earnings? How much would it increase Heinz's annual cash dividend payments?
10. Give two alternative account titles for Paid-in Capital in Excess of Par—Common Stock.
11. Explain the contingent liability created by issuance of stock at a discount.
12. How does issuance of 1,000 shares of no-par stock for land and a building, together worth $150,000, affect paid-in capital?
13. Why does receipt of a stock subscription increase the corporation's assets and owners' equity?
14. Give an example of a transaction that creates donated capital for a corporation.
15. Journalize the incorporation of the Barnes & Connally partnership. The partners' capital account balances exceed the par value of the new corporation's common stock. (Omit amounts.)
16. Rank the following accounts in the order they would appear on the balance sheet: Common Stock, Organization Cost, Donated Capital, Preferred Stock, Common Stock Subscribed, Stock Subscription Receivable (due within six months), Retained Earnings, Dividends Payable. Also, give each account's balance sheet classification.
17. What type of account is Organization Cost? Briefly describe how to account for organization cost.

18. Mancini Inc. has 3,000 shares of its $2.50, $10 par preferred stock outstanding. Dividends for 19X1 and 19X2 are in arrears, and the company has declared no dividends on preferred stock for the current year, 19X3. Assume that Mancini declares total dividends of $35,000 at the end of 19X3. Show how to allocate the dividends to preferred and common (a) if preferred is cumulative and (b) if preferred is noncumulative.

19. As a preferred stockholder, would you rather own cumulative or noncumulative preferred? If all other factors are the same, would the corporation rather the preferred stock be cumulative or noncumulative? Give your reason.

20. How are cumulative preferred dividends in arrears reported in the financial statements? When do dividends become a liability of the corporation?

21. Distinguish between the market value of stock and the book value of stock.

22. How is book value per share of common stock computed when the company has both preferred stock and common stock outstanding?

Exercises

Exercise 14-1 *Issuing Stock*

Journalize the following stock issuance transactions of Washington Corporation. Explanations are not required.

Feb. 19 Issued 4,000 shares of $10 par common stock for cash of $12.50 per share

Mar. 3 Sold 300 shares of $2.25, no-par Class A preferred stock for $6,000 cash.

Mar. 11 Received inventory valued at $25,000 and equipment with market value of $16,000 for 3,300 shares of the $10 par common stock.

Mar. 15 Issued 1,000 shares of 5 percent, no-par Class B preferred stock with stated value of $50 per share. The issue price was cash of $55 per share.

Exercise 14-2 *Stockholders' equity section of a balance sheet*

The charter of Washington Corporation authorizes the issuance of 5,000 shares of Class A preferred stock, 1,000 shares of Class B preferred stock, and 10,000 shares of common stock. Prepare the stockholders' equity section of the Washington balance sheet for the transactions given in the preceding exercise. Retained Earnings has a balance of $63,000.

Exercise 14-3 *Stock subscriptions*

Betsy Ross Corporation has just been organized and is selling its stock through stock subscriptions. Record the following selected transactions that occurred during June 19X6.

June 3 Received a subscription to 200 shares of $1 par common stock at the subscription price of $20 per share. The subscriber paid one fourth of the subscription amount as a down payment. The corporation will issue the stock when it is fully paid.

June 18 Collected one half of the amount receivable from the subscriber.

July 3 Collected the remainder from the subscriber and issued the stock.

Exercise 14-4 *Paid-in capital for a corporation*

Errico Inc. has recently organized. The company issued common stock to an attorney who gave Errico legal services of $2,400 to help her in organizing the corporation. It issued common stock to another person in exchange for his patent with a market value of $40,000. In addition, Errico received cash both for 2,000 shares of its preferred stock at $110 per share and for 32,000 shares of its common stock at $15 per share. The city of Arlington donated 50 acres of land to the company as a plant site. The market value of the land was $180,000. Without making journal entries, determine the total paid-in capital created by these transactions.

Exercise 14-5 *Recording issuance of stock*

The actual balance sheet of Gulf Resources & Chemical Corporation reported the following stockholders' equity. Note that Gulf has two separate classes of preferred stock, labeled as Series A and Series B.

Stockholders' Investment
(same as stockholders' equity)

Preferred stock, $1 par, authorized 4,000,000 shares (Note 7)	
Series A	$ 58,451
Series B..	375,765
Common stock, $.10 par, authorized 20,000,000, [issued and]	
outstanding 9,125,390 shares................................	912,539
Capital in excess of par....................................	75,542,382

Note 7. Preferred Stock:	**Shares [Issued and]** **Outstanding**
Series A	58,451
Series B................................	375,765

Required

Assume that the Series A preferred stock was issued for $3 cash per share, the Series B preferred was issued for $20 cash per share, and the common was issued for cash of $69,198,484. Make the summary journal entries to record issuance of all the Gulf Resources stock. Explanations are not required.

Exercise 14-6 *Incorporating a partnership*

The Podunk Jaybirds are a semiprofessional baseball team that has been operated as a partnership by D. Robertson and G. Childres. In addition to their management responsibilities, Robertson also plays second base and Childres sells hot dogs. Journalize the following transactions in the first month of operation as a corporation:

May 14   The incorporators paid legal fees of $1,440 and state taxes and fees of $600 to obtain a corporate charter.

May 14   Issued 2,500 shares of $10 par common stock to Robertson and 1,000 shares to Childres. Robertson's capital balance on the partnership books was $30,000, and Childres's capital balance was $12,000.

May 18   The city of Podunk donated 20 acres of land to the corporation for a stadium site. The land value was $20,000.

Exercise 14-7 *Recording issuance of no-par stock*

Fanous, Inc., is an importer of European furniture and Oriental rugs. The corporation issues 10,000 shares of no-par common stock for $75 per share. Record issuance of the stock (a) if the stock is true no-par stock and (b) if the stock has stated value of $5 per share.

Exercise 14-8 *Computing dividends on preferred and common stock*

The following elements of stockholders' equity are excerpted from the balance sheet of Gulf Resources & Chemical Corporation.

Stockholders' Equity

Preferred stock, cumulative and nonparticipating, $1 par (Note 7)

Series A, 58,451 shares issued..	$ 58,451
Series B, 375,765 shares issued	375,765
Common stock, $.10 par, 9,125,390 shares issued.....................	912,539

Note 7. Preferred Stock:	Designated Annual Cash Dividend
Series A	$ .20
Series B...................................	1.30

Assume that the Series A preferred has preference over the Series B preferred and the company has paid all preferred dividends through 19X4.

Required

Compute the dividends to both series of preferred and to common for 19X5 and 19X6 if total dividends are $0 in 19X5 and $1,500,000 in 19X6. Round to the nearest dollar.

Exercise 14-9   *Stockholders' equity section of a balance sheet*

China Palace Corporation has the following selected account balances at June 30, 19X7. Prepare the stockholders' equity section of the company's balance sheet. (Not all accounts listed are part of stockholders' equity).

Common stock, no-par with $5 stated value, 500,000 shares authorized, 120,000 shares issued	$600,000	Preferred stock subscribed 1,000 shares.............	$ 20,000
		Inventory.................	112,000
		Machinery and equipment ...	109,000
Donated capital............	34,000	Preferred stock subscription	
Accumulated depreciation– machinery and equipment .	62,000	receivable...............	8,000
Retained earnings	119,000	Preferred stock, 5%, $20 par, 20,000 shares authorized,	
Paid-in capital in excess of		10,000 shares issued	200,000
par—preferred stock	60,000	Organization cost, net.......	3,000

Exercise 14-10   *Book value per share of preferred and common stock*

The balance sheet of International Graphics Corporation reported the following:

Redeemable preferred stock; redemption value $5,103,000............	$ 4,860,000
Common stockholders' equity 8,120,375 shares issued and outstanding...	216,788,000
Total stockholders' equity.......................................	$221,648,000

Assume that International has paid preferred dividends for the current year and all prior years (no dividends in arrears), and the company has 100,000 shares of preferred stock outstanding. Compute the book value per share of the preferred stock and the common stock.

Exercise 14-11   *Book value per share of preferred and common stock; preferred dividends in arrears*

Refer to Exercise 14-10. Compute the book value per share of the preferred stock and the common stock, assuming that three years' preferred dividends (including dividends for the current year) are in arrears. Assume the preferred stock is cumulative and its dividend rate is 6 percent.

Problems (Group A)

Problem 14-1A *Journalizing corporation transactions and preparing the stockholders' equity section of the balance sheet*

Greenlawn, Inc., was organized under the laws of the state of Delaware. The charter authorizes Greenlawn to issue 100,000 shares of $3, no-par preferred stock and 500,000 shares of common stock with $1 par value. During its start-up phase, the company completed the following transactions:

July 5 Paid fees and incorporation taxes of $1,500 to the state of Delaware to obtain the charter and file the required documents for incorporation.

6 Issued 500 shares of common stock to the promoters who organized the corporation. Their fee was $15,000.

7 Accepted subscriptions for 1,000 shares of common stock at $30 per share and received a down payment of one third of the subscription amount.

12 Issued 300 shares of preferred stock for cash of $18,000.

14 Issued 800 shares of common stock in exchange for land valued at $24,000.

31 Collected one half of the stock subscription receivable.

31 Earned a small profit for July and closed the $4,000 credit balance of Income Summary into the Retained Earnings account.

Required

1. Record the transactions in the general journal.
2. Prepare the stockholders' equity section of the Greenlawn balance sheet at July 31.

Problem 14-2A *Stockholders' equity section of the balance sheet*

The following summaries for Lopez, Inc., and Monroe Corporation provide the information needed to prepare the stockholders' equity section of the company balance sheet. The two companies are independent.

Lopez, Inc. Lopez, Inc., is authorized to issue 25,000 shares of $1 par common stock. All the stock was issued at $6 per share. The company incurred net losses of $30,000 in 19X1 and $14,000 in 19X2. It earned net incomes of $8,000 in 19X3 and $41,000 in 19X4. The company declared no dividends during the four-year period.

Monroe Corporation. Monroe's charter authorizes the company to issue 5,000 shares of 5 percent, $100 par preferred stock and 500,000 shares of no-par common stock. Monroe issued 1,000 shares of the preferred stock at $105 per share. It issued 200,000 shares of the common stock for $300,000. The company's retained earnings balance at the beginning of 19X4 was $120,000. Net income for 19X4 was $65,000, and the company correctly subtracted the 5 percent preferred dividend for 19X4 from retained earnings. No preferred dividends are in arrears.

Required

For each company, prepare the stockholders' equity section of its balance sheet at December 31, 19X4. Show the computation of all amounts. Entries are not required.

Problem 14-3A *Journalizing corporation transactions and preparing the stockholders' equity section of the balance sheet*

The partnership of Starr & Wagner needed additional capital to expand into new markets, so the business incorporated as Micro Devices, Inc. The charter from the state of Ohio authorizes Micro Devices to issue 50,000 shares of 5 percent, $20 par preferred stock and 100,000 shares of no-par common stock with a stated value of $5 per share. In its first month, Micro Devices completed the following transactions:

Dec. 1 Paid a charter fee of $500 and incorporation taxes of $2,100 to the state of Ohio and paid legal fees of $1,000 to organize as a corporation.

2 Issued 500 shares of common stock to the promoter for assistance with issuance of the common stock. The promotional fee was $3,000.

2 Issued 9,000 shares of common stock to Starr and 12,000 shares to Wagner in return for the net assets of the partnership. Starr's capital balance on the partnership books was $54,000, and Wagner's capital balance was $72,000.

4 Accepted subscriptions for 4,000 shares of common stock at $6 per share and received a down payment of 20 percent of the subscription amount.

8 Received a small parcel of land valued at $35,000 as a donation from the city of Akron.

10 Issued 400 shares of preferred stock to acquire a patent with a market value of $10,000.

16 Issued 600 shares of common stock for cash of $3,600.

30 Collected one third of the stock subscription receivable.

Required

1. Record the transactions in the general journal.
2. Prepare the stockholders' equity section of the Micro Devices balance sheet at December 31. Retained Earnings' balance is $19,970.

Problem 14-4A *Analyzing the stockholders' equity of an actual corporation*

The purpose of this problem is to familiarize you with the financial statement information of a real company. Bethlehem Steel Corporation is one of the nation's largest steel companies. Bethlehem included the following stockholders' equity on its balance sheet:

Stockholders' Equity	($ Millions)
Preferred stock—	
Authorized 20,000,000 shares in each class; issued:	
$5.00 Cumulative Convertible Preferred Stock, at $50.00 stated value,	
2,500,000 shares...	$ 125
$2.50 Cumulative Convertible Preferred Stock, at $25.00 stated value,	
4,000,000 shares...	100
Common stock—$8 par value—	
Authorized 80,000,000 shares; issued 48,308,516 shares	621
Retained earnings..	529
	$1,375

Observe that Bethlehem reports no Paid-in Capital in Excess of Par or Stated Value. Instead, the company reports these items in the stock accounts.

Required

1. Identify the different issues of stock Bethlehem has outstanding.
2. Is the preferred stock participating or nonparticipating? How can you tell?
3. Which class of stock did Bethlehem issue at par or stated value, and which class did it issue above par or stated value?
4. Rearrange the Bethlehem Steel stockholders' equity section to correspond, as appropriate, to the terminology and format illustrated on page 554. Assume Bethlehem is authorized to issue 20,000,000 shares of the $5 preferred stock and an additional 20,000,000 shares of the $2.50 preferred. Assume the total stockholders' equity of $1,375 million is correct. Report dollar amounts in millions, as Bethlehem does.
5. Suppose Bethlehem passed its preferred dividends for one year. Would the company have to pay these dividends in arrears before paying dividends to the common stockholders? Give your reason.

6. What amount of preferred dividends must Bethlehem declare and pay each year to avoid having preferred dividends in arrears?
7. Assume preferred dividends are in arrears for 19X5.
   a. Write Note 6 of the December 31, 19X5, financial statements to disclose the dividends in arrears.
   b. Journalize the declaration of a $60 million dividend for 19X6. An explanation is not required.

Problem 14-5A   *Computing dividends on preferred and common stock*

Heinz Company has 5,000 shares of 4 percent, $10 par value preferred stock and 100,000 shares of $1.50 par common stock outstanding. During a three-year period Heinz declared and paid cash dividends as follows: 19X1, $0; 19X2, $5,000; and 19X3, $34,000.

Required

1. Compute the total dividends to preferred stock and common stock for each of the three years if
   a. Preferred is noncumulative and nonparticipating.
   b. Preferred is cumulative and nonparticipating.
2. For case *1b*, record the declaration of the 19X3 dividends on December 22, 19X3, and the payment of the dividends on January 14, 19X4.

Problem 14-6A   *Analyzing the stockholders' equity of an actual corporation*

The balance sheet of Oak Manufacturing, Inc., reported the following:

Stockholders' Investment (same as stockholders' equity)	($ Thousands)
Cumulative convertible preferred stock	$ 45
Common stock, $1 par value, authorized 40,000,000 shares; issued 16,000,000 shares	16,000
[Additional] paid-in capital	176,000
Retained earnings	(77,165)
Total stockholders' investment	$114,880

Notes to the financial statements indicate that 9,000 shares of $1.60 preferred stock with a stated value of $5 per share were issued and outstanding. The preferred stock has a redemption value of $25 per share, and preferred dividends are in arrears for two years, including the current year. The additional paid-in capital was contributed by the common stockholders. On the balance sheet date, the market value of the Oak Manufacturing common stock was $7.50 per share.

Required

1. Is the preferred stock cumulative or noncumulative, participating or nonparticipating? How can you tell?
2. What is the amount of the annual preferred dividend?
3. What is the total paid-in capital of the company?
4. What was the total market value of the common stock?
5. Compute the book value per share of the preferred stock and the common stock.

Problem 14-7A   *Preparing a corporation balance sheet*

The following accounts and related balances of Texas Mesa Corporation are arranged in no particular order. Use them to prepare the company's classified balance sheet in the account format at November 30, 19X7.

Accounts payable	$ 47,000	Accounts receivable, net	$ 87,000
Stock subscription receivable, preferred	1,000	Preferred stock, 4%, $10 par, 25,000 shares authorized,	
Retained earnings	101,000	3,000 shares issued	30,000
Common stock, $5 par, 100,000 shares authorized,		Cash	41,000
		Inventory	176,000
42,000 shares issued	210,000	Property, plant, and	
Dividends payable	3,000	equipment, net.	328,000
Donated capital	109,000	Organization cost, net	6,000
Additional paid-in capital—		Prepaid expenses	13,000
common	73,000	Preferred stock subscribed	
Accrued liabilities	17,000	700 shares	7,000
Long-term note payable	86,000	Patent, net	31,000

(Group B)

Problem 14-1B *Journalizing corporation transactions and preparing the stockholders' equity section of the balance sheet*

Multipurpose Corporation received a charter from the state of Colorado. The company is authorized to issue 50,000 shares of 5 percent, $40 par preferred stock and 300,000 shares of no-par common stock. During its start-up phase, the company completed the following transactions:

Oct. 2 Paid fees of $800 and incorporation taxes of $2,000 to the state of Colorado to obtain the charter and file the required documents for incorporation.

4 Issued 900 shares of common stock to the promoters who organized the corporation. Their fee was $45,000.

5 Accepted subscriptions for 1,000 shares of common stock at $50 per share and received a down payment of one fourth of the subscription amount.

9 Issued 1,000 shares of common stock in exchange for equipment valued at $50,000.

14 Issued 600 shares of preferred stock for cash of $44 per share.

30 Collected one third of the stock subscription receivable.

31 Earned a small profit for October and closed the $6,100 credit balance of Income Summary into Retained Earnings.

Required

1. Record the transactions in the general journal.
2. Prepare the stockholders' equity section of the Multipurpose balance sheet at October 31.

Problem 14-2B *Stockholders' equity section of the balance sheet*

Stockholders' equity information is given for Baker Corporation and Wang, Inc. The two companies are independent.

Baker Corporation. Baker Corporation is authorized to issue 10,000 shares of $5 par common stock. All the stock was issued at $8 per share. The company incurred a net loss of $12,000 in 19X1. It earned net incomes of $5,000 in 19X2 and $21,000 in 19X3. The company declared no dividends during the three-year period.

Wang, Inc. Wang's charter authorizes the company to issue 7,500 shares of $2.50 preferred stock with par value of $50 and 120,000 shares of no-par common stock. Wang issued 800 shares of the preferred stock at $60 per share. It issued 20,000 shares of the common stock for a total of $240,000. The company's retained earnings balance at the beginning of 19X3 was $72,000, and net income for the year was $49,000. During 19X3 the company correctly subtracted the specified dividend on preferred and a $.50 per share dividend on common from retained earnings. No preferred dividends are in arrears.

Required

For each company, prepare the stockholders' equity section of its balance sheet at December 31, 19X3. Show the computation of all amounts. Entries are not required.

Problem 14-3B *Journalizing corporation transactions and preparing the stockholders' equity section of the balance sheet*

The partners who owned Wolfson & Stauffer wished to avoid the unlimited personal liability of the partnership form of business, so they incorporated the partnership as Financial Consultants, Inc. The charter from the state of Arizona authorizes the corporation to issue 10,000 shares of 6 percent, $100 par preferred stock and 250,000 shares of no-par common stock with a stated value of $2 per share. In its first month, Financial Consultants completed the following transactions:

Dec. 1   Paid incorporation taxes of $900 and a charter fee of $1,100 to the state of Arizona and paid legal fees of $1,900 to organize as a corporation.

     3   Issued 750 shares of common stock to the promoter for assistance with issuance of the common stock. The promotion fee was $7,500.

     3   Issued 4,100 shares of common stock to Wolfson and 3,800 shares to Stauffer in return for the net assets of the partnership. Wolfson's capital balance on the partnership books was $41,000, and Stauffer's capital balance was $38,000.

     5   Accepted subscriptions for 5,000 shares of common stock at $10 per share and received a down payment of 25 percent of the subscription amount.

     7   Received a small parcel of land valued at $42,000 as a donation from the city of Phoenix.

     12   Issued 1,000 shares of preferred stock to acquire a patent with a market value of $110,000.

     22   Issued 1,500 shares of common stock for $10 cash per share.

     28   Collected 20 percent of the stock subscription receivable.

Required

1. Record the transactions in the general journal.
2. Prepare the stockholders' equity section of the Financial Consultants balance sheet at December 31. Retained Earnings balance is $20,820.

Problem 14-4B *Analyzing the stockholders' equity of an actual corporation*

The purpose of this problem is to familiarize you with the financial statement information of a real company, U and I, Inc. U and I included the following stockholders' equity on its year-end balance sheet at February 28:

Stockholders' Equity	($ Thousands)
Voting Preferred Stock, 5.5% cumulative—par value $23 per share; authorized 100,000 shares in each class:	
Class A—issued 75,473 shares	$ 1,736
Class B—issued 92,172 shares	2,120
Common stock—par value $5 per share; authorized 5,000,000 shares;	
issued 2,870,950 shares	14,355
[Additional] Paid-in Capital.	5,548
Retained earnings.	8,336
	$32,095

Required

1. Identify the different issues of stock U and I has outstanding.
2. Is the preferred stock participating or nonparticipating? How can you tell?
3. Give the summary entries to record issuance of all the U and I stock. Assume that all the stock was issued for cash and that the additional paid-in capital applies to the common stock. Explanations are not required.
4. Rearrange the U and I stockholders' equity section to correspond, as appropriate, to the format and terminology illustrated on page 554. Assume the total stockholders' equity of $32,095,000 is correct.
5. Suppose U and I passed its preferred dividends for one year. Would the company have to pay these dividends in arrears before paying dividends to the common stockholders? Give your reason.
6. What amount of preferred dividends must U and I declare and pay each year to avoid having preferred dividends in arrears?
7. Assume preferred dividends are in arrears for 19X8.
   a. Write Note 5 of the February 28, 19X8, financial statements to disclose the dividends in arrears.
   b. Record the declaration of a $500,000 dividend in the year ended February 28, 19X9. An explanation is not required.

Problem 14-5B   *Computing dividends on preferred and common stock*

Continental Corporation has 10,000 shares of $4.25, no-par preferred stock and 40,000 shares of no-par common stock outstanding. Continental declared and paid the following dividends during a three-year period: 19X1, $10,000; 19X2, $80,000; and 19X3, $265,000.

Required

1. Compute the total dividends to preferred stock and common stock for each of the three years if
   a. Preferred is noncumulative and nonparticipating.
   b. Preferred is cumulative and nonparticipating.
2. For case 1b, record the declaration of the 19X3 dividends on December 28, 19X3, and the payment of the dividends on January 17, 19X4.

Problem 14-6B   *Analyzing the stockholders' equity of an actual corporation*

The balance sheet of St. Louis Drilling Company reported the following:

Shareholders' Investment
(same as stockholders' equity)

Redeemable non-voting preferred stock, no-par (Redemption value $358,000)	$320,000
Common stock, $1 par value, authorized 60,000 shares; issued 28,000 shares	28,000
[Additional] paid-in capital	231,000
Retained earnings	7,000
Total shareholders' investment	$586,000

Notes to the financial statements indicate that 8,000 shares of $3.90 preferred stock with a stated value of $40 per share were issued and outstanding. Preferred dividends are in arrears for three years, including the current year. The additional paid-in capital was contributed by the common stockholders. On the balance sheet date, the market value of the St. Louis common stock was $4.50 per share.

Required

1. Which class of stockholders controls the company? Give your reason.
2. Is the preferred stock cumulative or noncumulative, participating or nonparticipating? How can you tell?
3. What is the amount of the annual preferred dividend?
4. What is the total paid-in capital of the company?
5. What was the total market value of the common stock?
6. Compute the book value per share of the preferred stock and the common stock.

Problem 14-7B   *Preparing a corporation balance sheet*

The following accounts and related balances of Kentucky Coal and Iron, Inc., are arranged in no particular order. Use them to prepare the company's classified balance sheet in the account format at June 30, 19X2.

Trademark, net	$ 9,000	Inventory	$122,000
Organization cost, net	14,000	Dividends payable	9,000
Preferred stock, $.65, no-par,		Retained earnings	48,000
10,000 shares authorized,		Accounts payable	53,000
2,700 shares issued	27,000	Property, plant, and	
Stock subscription receivable		equipment, net	167,000
—common	3,000	Common stock, $.50 par,	
Cash	19,000	500,000 shares authorized,	
Accounts receivable, net	34,000	214,000 shares issued	107,000
Paid-in capital in excess of		Prepaid expenses	10,000
par—common	19,000	Common stock subscribed	
Accrued liabilities	26,000	22,000 shares	11,000
Long-term note payable	72,000	Donated capital	6,000

Decision Problem

Evaluating Alternative Ways Of Raising Capital

J. McDade and M. Fineberg have written a computer program for a video game that they believe will rival Nintendo. They need additional capital to market the product, and they plan to incorporate their partnership. They are considering alternative capital structures for the corporation. Their primary goal is to raise as much capital as possible without giving up control of the business. The partners plan to receive 120,000 shares of the corporation's common stock in return for the net assets of the partnership. After the partnership books are closed and the assets adjusted to current market value, McDade's capital balance is $65,000 and Fineberg's balance is $55,000.

The corporation's plans for a charter include an authorization to issue 5,000 shares of preferred stock and 500,000 shares of $1 par common stock. McDade and Fineberg are uncertain about the most desirable features for the preferred stock. Prior to incorporating, the partners have discussed their plans with two investment groups. The corporation can obtain capital from outside investors under either of the following plans:

Plan 1.   Group 1 will invest $75,000 to acquire 600 shares of $5, no-par preferred stock and $100,000 to acquire 100,000 shares of common stock. Each preferred share receives 50 votes on matters that come before the stockholders. The investors in Group 1 would attempt to control the corporation if they have the majority of the corporate votes.

Plan 2.   Group 2 will invest $150,000 to acquire 1,000 shares of 6 percent, $100 par nonvoting, noncumulative, participating preferred stock.

Required

Assume the corporation is chartered.

1. Journalize the issuance of common stock to McDade and Fineberg.
2. Journalize the issuance of stock to the outsiders under both plans.
3. Assume net income for the first year is $130,000 and total dividends of $19,800 are properly subtracted from retained earnings. Prepare the stockholders' equity section of the corporation balance sheet under both plans.
4. Recommend one of the plans to McDade and Fineberg. Give your reasons.

Financial Statement Problem

Stockholder's equity

The Gulf+Western balance sheet appears in Appendix C. Answer these questions about the company's common stock.

1. What class of stock does the balance sheet report? What is its par value? How many shares are authorized? How many shares were outstanding at October 31, 1987?
2. Under what title does Gulf+Western report paid-in capital in excess of par? Give another title for this account.
3. Total stockholders' equity is not labeled. What is its amount at October 31, 1987?
4. Journalize the issuance of 50,000 shares of Gulf+Western common stock for cash of $68 per share. Use Gulf+Western terminology. No explanation is required.
5. The Selected Financial Data on page 24 show book value per common share of $35.05 at October 31, 1987. Show this book value computation. (Note G mentions preferred stock that is not reported on the balance sheet. You may ignore the preferred stock.)

Answers to Self-Study Questions

1. b
2. b
3. c
4. d
5. a
6. d (1,000 shares × $104 = $104,000)
7. d Intangible asset
8. a [(10,000 × $3.50 × 3 = $105,000) + (100,000 × $1.50 = $150,000) = $255,000]
9. c
10. b

Corporations: Retained Earnings, Dividends, Treasury Stock, and the Income Statement

Chapter 14 introduced the corporate form of business. Chapter 15 continues our discussion of corporation retained earnings and cash dividends and also considers stock dividends, treasury stock, and the corporate income statement.

Retained Earnings and Dividends

We have seen that the equity section on the corporation balance sheet is called stockholders' equity or shareholders' equity. The paid-in capital accounts and retained earnings make up the stockholders' equity section.

Retained Earnings is the corporation account that carries the balance of the business's net income from operations accumulated over the corporation's lifetime less its net losses and any declared dividends. *Retained* means "held on to." Retained Earnings is accumulated income to cover dividends and any future losses. Because Retained Earnings is an owners' equity account, it normally has a credit balance. Corporations may use other labels for Retained Earnings, among them Earnings Reinvested in the Business and Retained Income.

A debit balance in Retained Earnings, which arises when a corporation's expenses exceed its revenues, is called a *deficit*. This amount is subtracted from the sum of the credit balances in the other equity accounts on the balance sheet to determine total stockholders' equity. In a recent survey, 37 of 600 companies (6.2 percent) had a retained earnings deficit.

At the end of each accounting period, the Income Summary account—which carries the balance of net income for the period—is closed to the Retained Earnings account. Assume the following amounts are drawn from a corporation's temporary accounts.

Income Summary

Dec. 31, 19X1	Expenses	750,000	Dec. 31, 19X1	Revenues	850,000
			Dec. 31, 19X1	Bal.	100,000

This final closing entry transfers net income from Income Summary to Retained Earnings:

19X1

Dec. 31	Income Summary	100,000	
	Retained Earnings		100,000
	To close net income to Retained Earnings.		

If 19X1 was the corporation's first year of operations, the Retained Earnings account now has an ending balance of $100,000:

Retained Earnings

			Jan.	1, 19X1 Bal.	-0-
			Dec.	31, 19X1 Net income	100,000
			Dec.	31, 19X1 Bal.	100,000

A $60,000 net loss for the year would produce this debit balance in Income Summary:

Income Summary

Dec. 31, 19X3	Expenses	470,000	Dec. 31, 19X3	Revenues	410,000
Dec. 31, 19X3	Bal.	60,000			

To close a $60,000 loss, we would credit Income Summary and debit Retained Earnings, as follows:

19X3

Dec. 31	Retained Earnings	60,000	
	Income Summary...........................		60,000
	To close net loss to Retained Earnings.		

After posting, Income Summary's balance is zero, and the Retained Earnings balance is decreased by $60,000.

Remember that the account title includes the word *earnings. Credits to the Retained Earnings account arise only from net income.* When we examine a corporation income statement and want to learn how much net income has the corporation earned and retained in the business, we turn to Retained Earnings.

After the corporation has earned net income, its board of directors may declare and pay a cash dividend to the stockholders. The entry on January 15, 19X2, to record the declaration of a $35,000 dividend is

19X2

Jan. 15	Retained Earnings...............................	35,000	
	Dividends Payable		35,000
	To declare a cash dividend.		

After the dividend declaration is posted, the Retained Earnings account has a $65,000 credit balance:

Retained Earnings

Jan. 15, 19X2	Dividend	35,000	Jan. 1, 19X2	Bal.	100,000
			Jan. 15, 19X2	Bal.	65,000

The Retained Earnings account is not a reservoir of cash waiting for the board of directors to pay dividends to the stockholders. Instead, Retained Earnings is an owners' equity account representing a claim on all assets in general and not on any asset in particular. Its balance is the cumulative, lifetime earnings of the company less its cumulative losses and dividends. In fact, the corporation may have a large balance in Retained Earnings but not have the cash to pay a dividend because the company purchased a building or the company may have abundant cash from borrowing but very little retained earnings. To *declare* a dividend, the company must have an adequate balance in Retained Earnings. To *pay* the dividend, it must have the cash. Cash and Retained Earnings are two entirely separate accounts sharing no necessary relationship.

Dividend Dates

Three relevant dates for dividends are

1. **Declaration date.** On the declaration date, the board of directors announces the intention to pay the dividend. The declaration creates a liability for the corporation. Declaration is recorded by debiting Retained Earnings and crediting Dividends Payable.
2. **Date of record.** The people who own the stock on the date of record receive the dividend. The corporation announces the record date, which follows the declaration date by a few weeks, as part of the declaration. The corporation makes no journal entry on the date of record because no transaction occurs. Nevertheless, much work takes place behind the scenes to properly identify the stockholders of record on this date because the stock is being traded continuously.
3. **Payment date.** Payment of the dividend usually follows the record date by two to four weeks. Payment is recorded by debiting Dividends Payable and crediting Cash.

Stock Dividends

A **stock dividend** is a proportional distribution by a corporation of its own stock to its stockholders. Stock dividends are fundamentally different from cash dividends because stock dividends do not transfer the assets of the corporation to the stockholders. Cash dividends are distributions of the asset cash, but stock dividends cause changes *only* in the stockholders' equity of the corporation. The effect of a stock dividend is an increase in the stock account and a decrease in Retained Earnings. Because both of these accounts are elements of stockholders' equity, total stockholders' equity is unchanged. There is merely a transfer from one stockholders' equity account to another, and no asset or liability is affected by a stock dividend.

The corporation distributes stock dividends to stockholders in proportion to the number of shares they already own. For example, suppose you owned 300 shares of Xerox Corporation common stock. If Xerox distributed a 10 percent common stock dividend, you would receive 30 (300 $\times$ .10) additional shares. You would now own 330 shares of the stock. All other Xerox stockholders would receive additional shares equal to 10 percent of their prior holdings. You would all be in the same relative position after the dividend as you were before.

In distributing a stock dividend, the corporation gives up no assets. Why, then, do companies issue stock dividends?

Reasons for Stock Dividends

A corporation may choose to distribute stock dividends for the following reasons:

1. To continue dividends but conserve cash. A company may want to keep cash in the business in order to expand, buy inventory, pay off debts, and so on. Yet the company may wish to continue dividends in some form. To do so, the corporation may distribute a stock dividend. The debit to Retained Earnings also conserves cash by decreasing the Retained Earnings available for the declaration of future cash dividends. Stockholders pay tax on cash dividends but not on stock dividends.

2. To reduce the market price per share of its stock. Many companies pay low cash dividends and grow by reinvesting their earnings in operations. As they grow, the company's stock price increases. If the price gets high enough, eventually some potential investors may be prevented from purchasing the stock. Distribution of a stock dividend may cause the market price of a share of the company's stock to decrease because of the increased supply of the stock.

Suppose the market price of a share of stock is $50. If the corporation doubles the number of shares of its stock outstanding by issuing a stock dividend, the market price of the stock would drop by approximately one half, to $25 per share. The objective is to make the stock less expensive and thus attractive to a wider range of investors.

Entries for Stock Dividends

The board of directors announces stock dividends on the declaration date. The date of record and the distribution date follow. (This is the same sequence of dates used for a cash dividend.) The declaration of a stock dividend does *not* create a liability because the corporation is not obligated to pay assets. (Recall that a liability is a claim on *assets.*) Instead, the corporation has declared its intention to distribute its stock. Assume General Lumber Corporation has the following stockholders' equity prior to the dividend:

Stockholders' Equity

Paid-in capital:	
Common stock, $10 par, 50,000 shares authorized,	
20,000 shares issued.	$200,000
Paid-in capital in excess of par—common.	70,000
Total paid-in capital	270,000
Retained earnings.	85,000
Total stockholders' equity	$355,000

The entry to record a stock dividend depends on the size of the dividend. Generally accepted accounting principles (GAAP) distinguish between **small stock dividends** (less than 25 percent of the corporation's issued stock) and **large stock dividends** (25 percent or more of issued stock).

Assume General Lumber Corporation declares a 10 percent (small) common stock dividend on November 17. The company will distribute 2,000 (20,000 × .10) shares in the dividend. On November 17 the market value of its common stock is $16 per share. GAAP requires small stock dividends to be accounted for at market value. Therefore, Retained Earnings is debited for the market value of the 2,000 dividend shares. Common Stock Dividend Distributable is credited for par value, and Paid-in Capital in Excess of Par is credited for the remainder. General Lumber makes the following entry on the declaration date:[1]

Nov. 17	Retained Earnings (20,000 × .10 × $16)............	32,000	
	Common Stock Dividend Distributable		
	(20,000 × .10 × $10).....................		20,000
	Paid-in Capital in Excess of Par—Common ...		12,000
	To declare a 10 percent common stock dividend.		

OBJECTIVE 1
Account for stock dividends

On the distribution (payment) date, the company records issuance of the dividend shares as follows:

Dec. 12	Common Stock Dividend Distributable.............	20,000	
	Common Stock		20,000
	To issue common stock in a stock dividend.		

Common Stock Dividend Distributable is an owner's equity account. (It is *not* a liability because the corporation has no obligation to pay assets.) If the company prepares financial statements after the declaration of the stock dividend but before issuing it, Common Stock Dividend Distributable is reported in the stockholders' equity section of the balance sheet immediately after Common Stock and Common Stock Subscribed and before Paid-in Capital in Excess of Par—Common. However, this account holds the par value of the dividend shares only from the declaration date to the date of distribution.

The following tabulation shows the changes in stockholders' equity caused by the stock dividend:

Stockholders' Equity	Before the Dividend	After the Dividend	Change
Paid-in capital:			
Common stock, $10 par, 50,000 shares authorized, 20,000 shares issued	$200,000		
22,000 shares issued		$220,000	**up by $20,000**
Paid-in capital in excess of par—common	70,000	82,000	**up by $12,000**
Total paid-in capital...............	270,000	302,000	**up by $32,000**
Retained earnings	85,000	53,000	down by $32,000
Total stockholders' equity	$355,000	$355,000	**Unchanged**

[1] Committee on Accounting Procedure, "Accounting Research Bulletin No. 43," *Restatement and Revision of Accounting Research Bulletins* (New York: AICPA, 1961,) chap. 7, sec. B, pars. 10–14.

Compare stockholders' equity before and after the stock dividend. Observe the increase in the balances of Common Stock and Paid-in Capital in Excess of Par—Common and the decrease in Retained Earnings. Also observe that total stockholders' equity is unchanged from $355,000.

Amount of Retained Earnings Transferred in a Stock Dividend.   Stock dividends are said to be *capitalized retained earnings* because they transfer an amount from retained earnings to paid-in capital. The paid-in capital accounts are more permanent than retained earnings because they are not subject to owner withdrawals through dividends. As we saw in the preceding illustration, the amount transferred from Retained Earnings in a *small* stock dividend is the market value of the dividend shares because the effect on the market price of each share of the company's stock is likely to be small. Therefore, many stockholders view small stock dividends as distributions of earnings.

A *large* stock dividend, though, significantly increases the number of shares available in the market and so is likely to decrease the stock price significantly. Because of the drop in market price per share, a large stock dividend is not likely to be perceived as a distribution of earnings. GAAP does not require that large stock dividends be accounted for at a specific amount. A common practice is to use the par value of the dividend shares.

Suppose General Lumber declared a 50 percent common stock dividend. The declaration entry is

Dec. 7	Retained Earnings (20,000 × .50 × $10)	100,000	
	Common Stock Dividend Distributable		100,000
	To declare a 50 percent common stock dividend.		

Issuance of the dividend shares on the payment date is recorded by this entry:

Dec. 22	Common Stock Dividend Distributable	100,000	
	Common Stock		100,000
	To issue common stock in a stock dividend.		

Once again, total stockholders' equity is unchanged. For a large stock dividend, the increase in Common Stock is exactly offset by the decrease in Retained Earnings.

Stock Splits

A large stock dividend may decrease the market price of the stock. The stock then becomes attractive to more people. A stock split also decreases the market price of stock—with the intention of making the stock more attractive. A **stock split** is an increase in the number of outstanding shares of stock coupled with a proportionate reduction in the par value of the stock. For example, if the company splits its stock 2 for 1, the number of outstanding shares is doubled and each share's par value is halved. Most leading companies in the United States—IBM, Ford Motor Company, Borg-Warner Corporation, Giant Food, Inc., and others—have split their stock.

Assume that the market price of a share of IBM common stock is $120 and that the company wishes to decrease the market price to approximately $30. IBM decides to split the common stock 4 for 1 in order to reduce the stock's market price from $120 to $30. A 4-for-1 stock split means that the company would have four times as many shares of stock outstanding after the split as it had before and that each share's par value would be quartered. Assume IBM had 150 million shares of $5 par common stock issued and outstanding before the split.

Stockholders' Equity	($ Millions)
Paid-in capital:	
Common stock, **$5 par,** 900 million shares authorized,	
150 million shares issued.	$ 750
Paid-in capital in excess of par—common.	5,200
Total paid-in capital.	5,950
Retained earnings.	20,000
Total stockholders' equity	$25,950

After the 4-for-1 stock split, IBM would have 600 million shares (150 million shares × 4) of $1.25 par ($5/4) common stock outstanding. Total stockholders' equity would be exactly as before the stock split. Indeed, the balance in the Common Stock account does not even change. Only the par value of the stock and the number of shares authorized and issued change. Compare the highlighted figures in the two stockholders' equity presentations.

Stockholders' Equity	($ Millions)
Paid-in capital:	
Common stock, $1.25 par, 3.6 billion shares authorized,	
600 million shares issued.	$ 750
Paid-in capital in excess of par—common.	5,200
Total paid-in capital.	5,950
Retained earnings.	20,000
Total stockholders' equity	$25,950

Because the stock split affects no account balances, no formal journal entry is necessary. Instead, the split is recorded in a memorandum entry such as the following:

Aug. 19   Called in the outstanding $5 par common stock and distributed four shares of $1.25 par common stock for each old share previously outstanding.

Stock Dividends and Stock Splits

A stock dividend and a stock split both increase the number of shares of stock owned per stockholder. Also, neither a stock dividend nor a stock split changes the investor's total cost of the stock owned. For example, assume you paid $3,000 to acquire 150 shares of Avon Products common stock. If Avon distributes a 100 percent stock dividend, your 150 shares increase to 300, but your total cost is still $3,000. Likewise, if Avon distributes a 2-for-1 stock split, your shares increase in number to 300, but your total cost is unchanged. Neither type of stock action is taxable income to the investor.

Both a stock dividend and a stock split increase the corporation's number of shares outstanding. For example, a 100 percent stock dividend and a 2-for-1 stock split both double the outstanding shares and cut the stock's market price per share in half. They differ in that a stock *dividend* shifts an amount from retained earnings to paid-in capital, leaving par value per share unchanged. A stock *split*

OBJECTIVE 2

Distinguish stock splits from stock dividends

EXHIBIT 15-1   *Effects on Total Stockholders' Equity*

	Declaration	Payment of Cash or Distribution of Stock
Cash dividend	Decrease	None
Stock dividend	None	None
Stock split	None	None

Source: Adapted from Beverly Terry.

affects no account balances whatsoever but instead changes the par value of the stock.

Exhibit 15-1 summarizes the effects of dividends and stock splits on total stockholders' equity.

Treasury Stock[2]

Corporations may purchase their own stock from their shareholders for several reasons. (1) The company may have issued all its authorized stock and need the stock for distributions to officers and employees under bonus plans or stock purchase plans. (2) The purchase may help support the stock's current market price by decreasing the supply of stock available to the public. (3) The business may be trying to increase net assets by buying its shares low and hoping to sell them for a higher price later. (4) Management may gather in the stock to avoid a takeover by an outside party.

A corporation's own stock that it has issued and later reacquired is called **treasury stock.** (In effect, the corporation holds the stock in its treasury.) For practical purposes, treasury stock is like unissued stock: neither category of stock is outstanding in the hands of shareholders. The company does not receive cash dividends on its treasury stock, and treasury stock does not entitle the company to vote or to receive assets in liquidation. The difference between unissued stock and treasury stock is that treasury stock has been issued and bought back.

The purchase of treasury stock decreases the company's assets and its stockholders' equity. The size of the company literally decreases, as shown on the balance sheet. The Treasury Stock account has a debit balance, which is the opposite of the other owners' equity accounts. Therefore, Treasury Stock is a contra stockholders' equity account.

Purchase of Treasury Stock

We record the purchase of treasury stock by debiting Treasury Stock and crediting the asset given in exchange—usually Cash. Suppose that Southwest Drilling Company had the following stockholders' equity before purchasing treasury stock:

---

[2] In this book we illustrate the *cost* method of accounting for treasury stock because it is used most widely. Alternative methods are presented in intermediate accounting courses.

Stockholders' Equity

Paid-in capital:	
Common stock, $1 par, 10,000 shares authorized, 8,000 shares issued	$ 8,000
Paid-in capital in excess of par—common	12,000
Total paid-in capital	20,000
Retained earnings	14,600
Total stockholders' equity	$34,600

On November 22 Southwest purchases 1,000 shares of its $1 par common as treasury stock, paying cash of $7.50 per share. Southwest records the purchase as follows:

Nov. 22	Treasury Stock, Common (1,000 × $7.50)	7,500
	Cash	7,500
	Purchased 1,000 shares of treasury stock at $7.50 per share.	

Treasury stock is recorded at cost, without reference to the par value of the stock. The Treasury Stock account appears beneath retained earnings on the balance sheet, and its balance is subtracted from the sum of total paid-in capital and retained earnings, as follows:

> **OBJECTIVE 3**
> Account for treasury stock

Stockholders' Equity

Paid-in capital:	
Common stock, $1 par, 10,000 shares authorized, 8,000 shares issued . . .	$ 8,000
Paid-in capital in excess of par—common	12,000
Total paid-in capital	20,000
Retained earnings	14,600
Subtotal	34,600
Less Treasury stock (1,000 shares at cost)	**(7,500)**
Total stockholders' equity	$27,100

Observe that the purchase of treasury stock does not decrease the number of shares issued. The Common Stock, Paid in Capital in Excess of Par, and Retained Earnings accounts remain unchanged. However, total stockholders' equity decreases by the cost of the treasury stock. Also, shares of stock *outstanding* decrease from 8,000 to 7,000. To compute the number of outstanding shares, subtract the treasury shares (1,000) from the shares issued (8,000). Although the number of outstanding shares is not required to be reported on the balance sheet, this figure is important. Only outstanding shares have a vote, receive cash dividends, and share in assets if the corporation liquidates.

Sale of Treasury Stock

Sale of Treasury Stock at Cost. Treasury stock may be sold at any price agreeable to the corporation and the purchaser. If the stock is sold for the same price that the corporation paid to reacquire it, the entry is a debit to Cash and a credit to Treasury Stock for the same amount.

Sale of Treasury Stock above Cost. If the sale price is greater than reacquisition cost, the difference is credited to the account Paid-in Capital from Treasury

Stock Transactions. Suppose Southwest Drilling Company resold 200 of its treasury shares for $9 per share. The entry is

Dec. 7	Cash (200 × $9)	1,800	
	Treasury Stock, Common (200 × $7.50—the		
	purchase cost per share)		1,500
	Paid-in Capital from Treasury Stock Transactions ..		300
	To sell 200 shares of treasury stock at $9 per share.		

Paid-in Capital from Treasury Stock Transactions is reported with the other paid-in capital accounts on the balance sheet, beneath the Common Stock and Capital in Excess of Par accounts.

Sale of Treasury Stock below Cost. At times the resale price is less than cost. The difference between these two amounts is debited to Paid-in Capital from Treasury Stock Transactions. If the difference between resale price and cost is greater than the credit balance in Paid-in Capital from Treasury Stock Transactions, then the company debits Retained Earnings for the remaining amount. For example, Southwest Drilling records the sale of 400 shares of treasury stock at $5 per share in the following entry:

Dec. 23	Cash (400 × $5)	2,000	
	Paid-in Capital from Treasury Stock Transactions	300	
	Retained Earnings	700	
	Treasury Stock, Common (400 × $7.50—the		
	purchase cost per share)		3,000
	To sell 400 shares of treasury stock at $5 per share.		

Paid-in Capital from Treasury Stock Transactions receives only a $300 debit because that is the extent of this account's credit balance. (See the preceding example illustrating the sale of treasury stock above cost.) The remaining $700 is debited to Retained Earnings.

No Gain or Loss from Treasury Stock Transactions

The purchase and sale of treasury stock do not affect net income. Sale of treasury stock above cost is an increase in paid-in capital, not income. Likewise, sale of treasury stock below cost is a decrease in paid-in capital or Retained Earnings, not a loss. Treasury stock transactions take place between the business and its owner's, the stockholders. Because a company cannot earn a profit in dealing in its own stock with its owners, we credit Paid-in Capital from Treasury Stock Transactions for sale above cost and debit that account (and, if necessary, Retained Earnings) for a sale below cost. These accounts appear on the balance sheet, not on the income statement.

Does this mean that a company cannot increase its net assets by buying treasury stock low and selling it high? Not at all. Management often buys treasury stock because it believes the market price of its stock is too low. For example, a company may buy 500 shares of its stock at $10 per share. Suppose it holds the stock as the market price rises and resells the stock at $14 per share. The net assets of the company increase by $2,000 [500 shares × ($14 − $10 = $4 difference per share)]. This increase is reported as paid-in capital and not as income.

Summary Problem for Your Review

Simplicity Pattern Co., Inc., reported the following stockholders' equity:

Shareholders' Equity	($ Thousands)
Preferred stock, $1.00 par value	
Authorized—10,000,000 shares	
Issued—None	$ —
Common stock, 8 ⅓ cents par value	
Authorized, 30,000,000 shares	
Issued 13,733,229 shares.	1,144
Capital in excess of par value	48,122
Earnings retained in business	89,320
	138,586
Less treasury stock, at cost (1,919,000 common shares)	14,742
	$123,844

Required

1. What was the average issue price per share of the common stock?
2. Journalize the issuance of 1,200 shares of common stock at $4 per share. Use Simplicity's account titles.
3. How many shares of Simplicity's common stock are outstanding?
4. How many shares of common stock would be outstanding after Simplicity split its common stock 3 for 1?
5. Using Simplicity account titles, journalize the declaration of a stock dividend when the market price of Simplicity common stock is $3 per share. Consider each of the following stock dividends independently:
   a. Simplicity declares a 10 percent common stock dividend on the shares outstanding, computed in 3.
   b. Simplicity declares a 100 percent common stock dividend on the shares outstanding, computed in 3.
6. Journalize the following treasury stock transactions, assuming they occur in the order given:
   a. Simplicity purchases 500 shares of treasury stock at $8 per share.
   b. Simplicity sells 100 shares of treasury stock for $9 per share. Credit Paid-in Capital from Treasury Stock Transactions.
   c. Simplicity sells 100 shares of treasury stock for $5 per share.

SOLUTION TO SUMMARY PROBLEM

1. Average issue price of the common stock was $3.59 per share [($1,144,000 + $48,122,000)/13,733,229 shares = $3.59].

2.
Cash (1,200 × $4)	4,800	
Common Stock (1,200 × $.08⅓)		100
Capital in Excess of Par Value.		4,700
To issue common stock at a premium.		

3. Shares outstanding = 11,814,229 (13,733,229 shares issued minus 1,919,000 shares of treasury stock)

4. Shares outstanding after a 3-for-1 stock split = 35,442,687 (11,814,229 shares outstanding × 3)

5a.	Earnings Retained in Business		
	(11,814,229 × .10 × $3).....................	3,544,269	
	Common Stock Dividend Distributable		
	(11,814,229 × .10 × $.08⅓)..............		98,452
	Capital in Excess of Par Value..............		3,445,817
	To declare a 10 percent common stock dividend.		
b.	Earnings Retained in Business		
	(11,814,229 × $.08⅓).....................	984,519	
	Common Stock Dividend Distributable		984,519
	To declare a 100 percent common stock dividend.		
6a.	Treasury Stock (500 × $8).....................	4,000	
	Cash		4,000
	To purchase 500 shares of treasury stock at $8 per share.		
b.	Cash (100 × $9).............................	900	
	Treasury Stock (100 × $8).................		800
	Paid-in Capital from Treasury Stock		
	Transactions		100
	To sell 100 shares of treasury stock at $9 per share.		
c.	Cash (100 × $5).............................	500	
	Paid-in Capital from Treasury Stock Transactions		
	(balance from answer 6b)	100	
	Earnings Retained in Business...................	200	
	Treasury Stock (100 × $8).................		800
	To sell 100 shares of treasury stock at $5 per share.		

Retirement of Stock

A corporation may purchase its own common stock or preferred stock and retire it by canceling the stock certificates. The retired stock cannot be reissued. Companies usually retire their stock in order to replace it with another issue of stock or to liquidate shares when they go out of business. Retiring stock, like purchasing treasury stock, decreases the outstanding stock of the corporation. Unlike a treasury stock purchase, stock retirement decreases the number of shares issued. Assets are decreased by the amount paid to buy the shares being retired. In retiring stock, the corporation removes the balances from all paid-in capital amounts related to the retired shares, like Capital in Excess of Par.

A corporation may repurchase shares for retirement for a price that is below the stock's issue price (par value plus any capital in excess of par). This difference between purchase price and issue price is a credit to Paid-in Capital from Retirement of Common Stock (or Preferred Stock).

Assume that a corporation issued its $10 par common stock for $14, a $4 premium per share. If the company later purchases 500 shares of the stock for retirement at $13 per share, the retirement entry is

May 22	Common Stock (500 × $10)	5,000	
	Paid-in Capital in Excess of Par—Common (500 × $4)..	2,000	
	Cash (500 × $13)...............................		6,500
	Paid-in Capital from Retirement of		
	Common Stock............................		500
	To purchase and retire common stock.		

Paid-in Capital from Retirement of Common Stock is reported after Capital in Excess of Par—Common Stock, along with any other paid-in capital accounts related to the common.

If the corporation must pay more for the stock than its issue price, the excess is debited to Retained Earnings. Assume the corporation paid $16 per share to purchase the stock for retirement. The entry is

May 22	Common Stock (500 × $10)	5,000	
	Paid-in Capital in Excess of Par—Common (500 × $4)..	2,000	
	Retained Earnings	1,000	
	Cash (500 × $16)...............................		8,000
	To purchase and retire common stock.		

Retiring stock, like purchasing stock, is a transaction that does not affect net income. No gain or loss arises from stock retirement because the company is doing business with its owners. The entries we presented in illustrating stock retirement affect *balance sheet accounts,* not income statement accounts.

Restrictions on Retained Earnings

Dividends, purchases of treasury stock, and retirements of stock require payments by the corporation to its stockholders. In fact, treasury stock purchases and stock retirements are returns of paid-in capital to the stockholders. These outlays decrease the corporation's assets, so fewer assets are available to pay liabilities. Therefore, its creditors seek to restrict a corporation's dividend payments and treasury stock purchases. For example, a bank may agree to loan $500,000 only if the borrowing corporation limits dividend payments and purchases of its stock.

To ensure that corporations maintain a minimum level of stockholders' equity for the protection of creditors, state laws restrict the amount of its own stock that a corporation may purchase. The maximum amount a corporation can pay its stockholders without decreasing paid-in capital is its balance of retained earnings. Therefore, restrictions on dividends and stock purchases focus on the balance of retained earnings.

Companies usually report their retained earnings restrictions in notes to the financial statements. The following actual disclosure by RTE Corporation, a manufacturer of electronic transformers, is typical:

NOTES TO CONSOLIDATED FINANCIAL STATEMENTS
NOTE F—LONG-TERM DEBT

The . . . loan agreements . . . restrict cash dividends and similar payments to shareholders. Under the most restrictive of these provisions, retained earnings of $4,300,000 were unrestricted as of December 31, 19X3.

OBJECTIVE 4
Report restrictions of retained earnings

In another actual example, Chromalloy American Corporation could not declare dividends, purchase treasury stock, or purchase stock for retirement, as indicated by its Note 8:

> **NOTES TO CONSOLIDATED FINANCIAL STATEMENTS 8:**
> **LONG-TERM DEBT**
>
> The Company's loan agreements contain covenants which restrict the declaration or payment of cash dividends and the purchase . . . or retirement of capital stock. At December 31, 19X3, . . . all of the Company's [retained] earnings were restricted due to these convenants.

Appropriations of Retained Earnings

Appropriations are restrictions of Retained Earnings that are recorded by formal journal entries. A corporation may appropriate — segregate in a separate account — a portion of Retained Earnings for a specific use. For example, the board of directors may appropriate part of Retained Earnings for building a new manufacturing plant, for meeting possible future liabilities, or for other reasons. A debit to Retained Earnings and a credit to a separate account — Retained Earnings Appropriated for Plant Expansion — records the appropriation. This appropriated retained earnings account appears directly above the regular Retained Earnings account on the balance sheet.

An appropriation does *not* decrease total retained earnings. Any appropriated amount is simply a portion of retained earnings that is earmarked for a particular purpose. When the need for the appropriation no longer exists, an entry debits the Retained Earnings Appropriated account and credits Retained Earnings. This entry closes the Appropriation account and returns its amount back to the regular Retained Earnings account.

Retained earnings appropriations are rare. Corporations generally disclose any retained earnings restrictions in the notes to the financial statements. The notes give the corporation more room to describe the nature and amounts of any restrictions. Thus corporations satisfy the requirement for adequate disclosure.

Disclosing any restriction on retained earnings is important to stockholders and possible investors because the restricted amounts may not be used for dividends. A corporation with a $100,000 balance in Retained Earnings and a $60,000 restriction may declare a maximum dividend of $40,000 — if the cash is available and the board of directors so decides.

Variations in Reporting Stockholders' Equity _____

Real-world accounting and business practices may use terminology and formats in reporting stockholders' equity that differ from our general examples. We use a more detailed format in this book to help you learn the components of the stockholders' equity section. Companies assume that readers of their statements already understand the omitted details.

One of the most important skills you will learn in this course is the ability to understand the financial statements of actual companies. Thus we present in Exhibit 15-2 a side-by-side comparison of our general teaching format and the format that you are more likely to encounter in real-world balance sheets. Note the following points in the real-world format:

1.   The heading Paid-in Capital does not appear. It is commonly understood that Preferred Stock, Common Stock, and Additional Paid-in Capital are elements of paid-in capital.

EXHIBIT 15-2 *Stockholders' Equity*

General Teaching Format		Real-World Format	
Stockholders' Equity		**Stockholders' Equity**	
Paid-in capital:		Preferred stock, 8%, $10 par, 30,000 shares authorized and issued	$ 310,000
Preferred stock, 8%, $10 par, 30,000 shares authorized and issued	$ 300,000	Common stock, $1 par, 100,000 shares authorized, 60,000 shares issued	60,000
Paid-in capital in excess of par—preferred	10,000	Additional paid-in capital...........	2,160,000
		Retained earnings (Note 7)..........	1,565,000
Common stock, $1 par, 100,000 shares authorized, 60,000 shares issued	60,000	Less treasury stock, common (1,400 shares at cost)	(42,000)
			$4,053,000
Paid-in capital in excess of par—common....................	1,940,000		
Paid-in capital from treasury stock transactions, common	9,000		
Paid-in capital from retirement of preferred stock...............	11,000		
Donated capital–plant site	200,000		
Total paid-in capital	2,530,000		
Retained earnings appropriated for contingencies..................	400,000		
Retained earnings–unappropriated...	1,165,000		
Total retained earnings	1,565,000		
Total.....................	4,095,000	Note 7—*Restriction on retained earnings.*	
Less treasury stock, common (1,400 shares at cost)	(42,000)	At December 31, 19XX, $400,000 of retained earnings is restricted by the company's board of directors to absorb	
Total stockholders' equity.......	$4,053,000	the effect of any contingencies that may arise. Accordingly, possible dividend declarations are restricted to a maximum of $1,165,000 ($1,565,000 − $400,000).	

2. Preferred stock is often reported in a single amount that combines its par value and premium.

3. For presentation in the financial statements, all additional paid-in capital—from capital in excess of par on common stock, treasury stock transactions, stock retirement, and donated capital—appears as a single amount labeled Additional Paid-in Capital. Additional Paid-in Capital belongs to the common stockholders, and so it follows Common Stock in the real-world format.

4. Often, total stockholders' equity ($4,053,000 in the exhibit) is not specifically labeled.

Corporation Income Statement _____

A corporation's net income receives more attention than any other item in the financial statements. Net income measures the business's ability to earn a profit and answers the question of how successfully the company has managed its operations. To stockholders, the larger the corporation's profit, the greater the likelihood of dividends. To creditors, the larger the corporation's profit, the better able it is to pay its debts. Net income builds up a company's assets and owners' equity. It also helps to attract capital from new investors who hope to receive dividends from future successful operations.

Suppose you are considering investing in the stock of two manufacturing companies. In reading their annual reports and examining their past records, you learn that the companies showed the same net income figure for last year and that each company has increased its net income by 15 percent annually over the last five years. You observe, however, that the two companies have generated income in different ways.

Company A's income has resulted from the successful management of its central operations (manufacturing). Company B's manufacturing operations have been flat for two years. Its growth in net income has resulted from selling off segments of its business at a profit. Which company would you invest in?

Company A holds the promise of better future earnings. This corporation earns profits from continuing operations. We may reasonably expect the business to match its past earnings in the future. Company B shows no growth from operations. Its net income results from one-time transactions, the selling off of its operating assets. Sooner or later, Company B will have sold off the last of its assets used in operations. When that occurs, the business will have no means of generating income. Based on this reasoning, your decision is to invest in the stock of Company A.

This example points to two important investment considerations: the *trend* of a company's earnings and the *makeup* of its net income. The probability of making intelligent investment decisions is improved if the income statement separates the results of central, continuing operations from special, one-time gains and losses. We now discuss the components of the corporation income statement. We will see how the income statement reports the results of operations in a manner that allows statement users to get a good look at the business's operations. Exhibit 15-3 will be used throughout these discussions. The items of primary interest are highlighted for emphasis.

Continuing Operations

We have seen that income from a business's continuing operations helps financial statement users make predictions about the business's future earnings. In the income statement of Exhibit 15-3, the top-most section reports income from continuing operations. This part of the business is expected to continue from period to period. We may use this information to predict that Electronics Corporation will earn income of approximately $54,000 next year.

Note that income tax expense has been deducted in arriving at income from continuing operations. The tax that corporations pay on their income is a significant expense. The federal income tax rate for corporations varies from time to time, and the current maximum rate is 34 percent. For computational ease, let's use an income tax rate of 40 percent in our illustrations. This is a reasonable estimate of combined federal and state income taxes. The $36,000 income tax expense in Exhibit 15-3 equals the pretax income from continuing operations multiplied by the tax rate ($90,000 \times .40 = $36,000$).

Discontinued Operations

Most large corporations engage in several lines of business. For example, General Mills, Inc., best known for its food products, also has retailing and restaurant operations. Sears, Roebuck & Co., in addition to its retail stores, has a real estate

EXHIBIT 15-3 *Corporation Income Statement*

OBJECTIVE 5
Identify the elements of a corporation income statement

Electronics Corporation
Income Statement
For the Year Ended December 31, 19X5

Sales revenue		$500,000
Cost of goods sold		240,000
Gross margin		260,000
Operating expenses (detailed)		181,000
Operating income.		79,000
Other gains (losses)		
Gain on sale of machinery.		11,000
Income from continuing operations before income tax . .		90,000
Income tax expense.		36,000
Income from continuing operations		54,000
Discontinued operations:		
Operating income, $30,000, less income tax		
of $12,000	$18,000	
Gain on disposal, $5,000, less income tax of		
$2,000	3,000	21,000
Income before extraordinary items		75,000
Extraordinary flood loss.	(10,000)	
Less income tax saving.	4,000	(6,000)
Net income		$ 69,000
Earnings per share of common stock (30,000 shares outstanding):		
Income from continuing operations		$1.80
Income from discontinued operations		.70
Income before extraordinary items.		2.50
Extraordinary loss.		(.20)
Net income.		$2.30

subsidiary, an insurance company, and a savings and loan enterprise. We call each significant part of a company a **segment of the business.**

A company may sell a segment of its business. Such a sale is not a regular source of income because a company cannot keep on selling its segments indefinitely. The sale of a business segment is viewed as a one-time transaction. The income statement carries information on the segment that has been disposed of under the heading Discontinued Operations. This section of the income statement is divided into two components: (1) operating income or (loss) on the segment that is disposed of and (2) any gain (or loss) on the disposal. Income and gain are taxed at the 40 percent rate and reported as follows:

Discontinued operations:
Operating income, $30,000, less income tax, $12,000 . . . . $18,000
Gain on disposal, $5,000, less income tax, $2,000   3,000
                                                                      $21,000

Trace this presentation to Exhibit 15-3.

It is necessary to separate discontinued operations into these two components because the company may operate the discontinued segment for part of the year.

This is the operating income (or loss) component. Then, usually a gain (or loss) on the disposal of the segment occurs.

Discontinued operations are common in business. The Black and Decker Manufacturing Company disposed of its gasoline chain saw business. Purolator, Inc., sold its armored-car segment, and RJR Nabisco disposed of its fast-food business, including Kentucky Fried Chicken. Each of these items was disclosed as discontinued operations in the company's income statement.

Extraordinary Gains and Losses

Extraordinary gains and losses, also called extraordinary items, are both unusual for the company and infrequent. Losses from natural disasters (like earthquakes, floods, and tornadoes) and the taking of company assets by a foreign government (expropriation), are extraordinary.

Extraordinary items are reported along with their income tax effect. Assume Electronics Corporation lost $10,000 of inventory in a flood. This flood loss, which reduces income, also reduces the company's income tax. The tax effect of the loss is computed by multiplying the amount of the loss by the tax rate. The tax effect decreases the net amount of the loss in the same way that the tax effect of income reduces the amount of net income. An extraordinary loss is reported along with its tax effect as follows:

Extraordinary flood loss...............	$(10,000)	
Less income tax saving...............	4,000	$(6,000)

Trace this item to the income statement in Exhibit 15-3. An extraordinary gain is reported the same way, net of the income tax on the gain.

Gains and losses due to employee strikes, the settlement of lawsuits, discontinued operations, and the sale of plant assets are *not* extraordinary items. They are considered normal business occurrences. However, because they are outside the business's central operations, they are reported on the income statement as other gains and losses. An example is the gain on sale of machinery in Exhibit 15-3.

Earnings Per Share (EPS)

The final segment of a corporation income statement presents the company's earnings per share, abbreviated as EPS. In fact, GAAP requires that corporations disclose EPS figures on the income statement.

Earnings per share is the amount of a company's net income per share of its outstanding common stock. EPS is a key measure of a business's success. Consider a corporation with net income of $200,000 and 100,000 shares of common stock outstanding. Its EPS is $2 ($200,000/100,000). A second corporation may also have net income of $200,000 but only 50,000 shares of common stock outstanding. Its EPS is $4 ($200,000/50,000).

Just as the corporation lists separately its different sources of income — from continuing operations, discontinued operations, and so on — it lists separately the EPS figure based on different income sources. Consider that Electronics Corporation had $54,000 in income from continuing operations, $21,000 in income from discontinued operations, and an extraordinary loss of $6,000. Net income was $69,000 ($54,000 + $21,000 − $6,000). Electronics had 30,000 common shares outstanding for the entire accounting period. The company's EPS is reported on the income statement as follows:

Earnings per share of common stock (30,000 shares outstanding):

Income from continuing operations ($54,000/30,000)...................	$1.80
Income from discontinued operations ($21,000/30,000)	.70
Income before extraordinary items ($75,000/30,000)...................	2.50
Extraordinary loss ($6,000/30,000)	(.20)
Net income ($69,000/30,000)	$2.30

The income statement user can understand the sources of the business's EPS amounts when presented in this detail.

Exhibit 15-3 presents the detailed income statement of Electronics Corporation for the year ended December 31, 19X5. The income statement is in multiple-step format.

Weighted Average Number of Shares of Common Stock Outstanding. Computing EPS is straightforward if the number of common shares outstanding does not change over the entire accounting period. For many corporations, however, this figure varies over the course of the year. Consider a corporation that had 100,000 shares outstanding from January through November, then purchased 60,000 shares as treasury stock. This company's EPS would be misleadingly high if computed using 40,000 (100,000 − 60,000) shares. To make EPS as meaningful as possible, corporations use the weighted average number of common shares outstanding during the period.

Let's assume the following figures for Diskette Demo Corporation. From January through May the company had 240,000 shares of common stock outstanding; from June through August, 200,000 shares; and from September through December, 210,000 shares. We compute the weighted average by considering the outstanding shares per month as a fraction of the year:

Number of Common Shares Outstanding		Fraction of Year		Weighted Average Number of Common Shares Outstanding
240,000	×	5/12	(January through May)	= 100,000
200,000	×	3/12	(June through August)	= 50,000
210,000	×	4/12	(September through December)	= 70,000
			Weighted average number of common shares outstanding during the year	220,000

The 220,000 weighted average would be divided into net income to compute the corporation's EPS.

Preferred Dividends. Throughout the EPS discussion we have used only the number of shares of common stock outstanding. Holders of preferred stock have no claim to the business's income beyond the stated preferred dividend. However, preferred dividends do affect the EPS figure. Recall that EPS is earnings per share of *common* stock. Also recall that dividends on preferred stock are paid first. Therefore, preferred dividends must be subtracted from income subtotals (income from continuing operations, income before extraordinary items, and net income) in the computation of EPS. Preferred dividends are not subtracted from income or loss from discontinued operations, and they are not subtracted from extraordinary gains and losses.

If Electronics Corporation had 10,000 shares of preferred stock outstanding, each with a $1.50 dividend, the annual preferred dividend would be $15,000 (10,000 × $1.50). The $15,000 would be subtracted from each of the different income subtotals, resulting in the following EPS computations for the company:

Earnings per share of common stock (30,000 shares outstanding):

Income from continuing operations ($54,000 − $15,000)/30,000 . . . . $1.30
Income from discontinued operations ($21,000/30,000) 70
Income before extraordinary items ($75,000 − $15,000)/30,000 . . . .   2.00
Extraordinary loss ($6,000/30,000) . . . .   (.20)
Net income ($69,000 − $15,000)/30,000 . . . . $1.80

Dilution.   Some corporations make their preferred stock more attractive to investors by offering convertible preferred stock. Holders of convertible preferred may exchange the preferred stock for common stock. If in fact the preferred stock is converted to common stock, then the EPS will be *diluted*—reduced—because more common stock shares are divided into net income. Because convertible preferred can be traded in for common stock, the common stockholders want to know the amount of the decrease in EPS if the preferred stock is converted into common. To provide this information, corporations present two sets of EPS amounts: EPS based on outstanding common shares (primary EPS), and EPS based on outstanding common shares plus the number of additional common shares that would arise from conversion of the preferred stock into common (diluted EPS).

EPS is the most widely used accounting figure. Many income statement users place top priority on EPS. Also, a stock's market price is related to the company's EPS. By dividing the market price of a company's stock by its EPS, we compute a statistic called the price-to-earnings ratio. *The Wall Street Journal* reports the price to-earnings ratios (listed as P/E) daily for more than 3,000 companies.

Statement of Retained Earnings

Retained earnings may be a significant portion of a corporation's owner's equity. The year's income increases the retained earnings balance, and dividends decrease it. Retained earnings are so important that corporations draw up a financial statement outlining the major changes in this equity account, much as the statement of owner's equity presents information on changes in the equity of a proprietorship. The statement of retained earnings for Electronics Corporation appears in Exhibit 15-4.

Some companies report income and retained earnings on a single statement. Exhibit 15-5 illustrates how Electronics would combine its income statement and its statement of retained earnings.

EXHIBIT 15-4   *Statement of Retained Earnings*

Electronics Corporation
Statement of Retained Earnings
For the Year Ended December 31, 19X5

Retained earnings balance, December 31, 19X4	$130,000
Net income for 19X5	69,000
	199,000
Dividends for 19X5	(21,000)
Retained earnings balance, December 31, 19X5	$178,000

EXHIBIT 15-5 *Statement of Income and Retained Earnings*

Electronics Corporation Statement of Income and Retained Earnings For the Year Ended December 31, 19X5	
Sales revenue..	$500,000
Cost of goods sold.....................................	240,000
Net income for 19X5....................................	69,000
Retained earnings, December 31, 19X4...................	130,000
	199,000
Dividends for 19X5.....................................	(21,000)
Retained earnings, December 31, 19X5..................	$178,000
Earnings per share of common stock (30,000 shares outstanding):	
Income from continuing operations............................	$1.80
Income from discontinued operations	.70
Income before extraordinary items............................	2.50
Extraordinary loss	(.20)
Net income...	$2.30

Prior Period Adjustments

OBJECTIVE 6

Account for prior period adjustments

What happens when a company makes an error in recording revenues or expenses? Detecting the error in the period in which it occurs allows the company to make a correction before preparing that period's financial statements. But failure to detect the error until a later period means that the business will have reported an incorrect amount of income on its income statement. After closing the revenue and expense accounts, the Retained Earnings account will absorb the effect of the error, and its balance will be wrong until the error is corrected.

Corrections to the beginning balance of Retained Earnings for errors of an earlier period are called **prior period adjustments.** The correcting entry includes a debit or credit to Retained Earnings for the error amount and a debit or credit to the asset or liability account that was misstated. The prior period adjustment appears on the corporation's statement of retained earnings to indicate to readers the amount and the nature of the change in the Retained Earnings balance.

Assume that McDonald Corporation recorded income tax expense for 19X4 as $30,000. The correct amount was $40,000. This error resulted in understating 19X4 expenses by $10,000 and overstating net income by $10,000. A bill from the government in 19X5 for the additional $10,000 in taxes alerts the McDonald management to the mistake. The entry to record this prior period adjustment in 19X5 is

19X5

June 19	Retained Earnings	10,000	
	Income Tax Payable		10,000
	Prior period adjustment to correct error in recording income tax expense of 19X4.		

The debit to Retained Earnings excludes the error correction from the income statement of 19X5. Recall the matching principle. If Income Tax Expense is debited when the prior period adjustment is recorded in 19X5, then this $10,000 in taxes would appear on the 19X5 income statement. This would not be proper since the expense arose from 19X4 operations.

This prior period adjustment would appear on the statement of retained earnings, as follows:

McDonald Corporation Statement of Retained Earnings For the Year Ended December 31, 19X5	
Retained earnings balance, December 31, 19X4, **as originally reported**	$390,000
Prior period adjustment – debit to correct error in recording income tax expense of 19X4	(10,000)
Retained earnings balance, December 31, 19X4, **as adjusted**	380,000
Net income for 19X5	114,000
	494,000
Dividends for 19X5	(41,000)
Retained earnings balance, December 31, 19X5	$453,000

Our example shows a prior period adjustment for additional expense. To make a prior period adjustment for additional income, retained earnings is credited and the misstated asset or liability is debited.

Summary Problem for Your Review

The following information was taken from the ledger of Kraft Corporation:

Loss on sale of discontinued operations	$ 20,000	Selling expenses	$ 78,000
Prior period adjustment— credit to Retained Earnings	5,000	Common stock, no-par, 45,000 shares issued	180,000
Gain on sale of plant assets	21,000	Sales revenue	620,000
Cost of goods sold	380,000	Interest expense	30,000
Income tax expense (saving)		Extraordinary gain	26,000
Continuing operations	32,000	Operating income, discontinued operations	30,000
Discontinued operations:		Loss due to lawsuit	11,000
Operating income	12,000	General expenses	62,000
Loss on sale	(8,000)	Preferred stock, 8%, $100 par, 500 shares issued	50,000
Extraordinary gain	10,000	Paid-in capital in excess of par—preferred	7,000
Treasury stock, common (5,000 shares at cost)	25,000	Retained earnings, beginning, as originally reported	103,000
Dividends	16,000		

Required

Prepare a single-step income statement and a statement of retained earnings for Kraft Corporation for the current year ended December 31. Include the earnings per share presentation and show computations. Assume no changes in the stock accounts during the year.

SOLUTION TO SUMMARY PROBLEM

Kraft Corporation
Income Statement
For the Year Ended December 31, 19—

Revenue and gains:		
Sales revenue................................		$620,000
Gain on sale of plant assets		21,000
Total revenues and gains		641,000
Expenses and losses:		
Cost of goods sold	$380,000	
Selling expenses	78,000	
General expenses	62,000	
Interest expense	30,000	
Loss due to lawsuit	11,000	
Income tax expense..........................	32,000	
Total expenses and losses..................		593,000
Income from continuing operations..............		48,000
Discontinued operations:		
Operating income	$30,000	
Less income tax...........................	12,000	18,000
Loss on sale of discontinued operations	20,000	
Less income tax saving	8,000	(12,000)	6,000
Income before extraordinary items		54,000
Extraordinary gain	26,000	
Less income tax............................	10,000	16,000
Net income		$ 70,000

Earnings per share:

Income from continuing operations [($48,000 − $4,000)/40,000 shares].....	$1.10
Income from discontinued operations ($6,000/40,000 shares)	.15
Income before extraordinary items ($54,000 − $4,000)/40,000 shares]......	1.25
Extraordinary gain ($16,000/40,000 shares)..........................	.40
Net income [($70,000 − $4,000)/40,000 shares]	$1.65

Computations:

$$EPS = \frac{\text{Income} - \text{Preferred dividends}}{\text{Common shares outstanding}}$$

Preferred dividends: $50,000 × .08 = $4,000
Common shares outstanding: 45,000 shares issued − 5,000 treasury shares = 40,000 shares outstanding

Kraft Corporation
Statement of Retained Earnings
For the Year Ended December 31, 19—

Retained earnings balance, beginning, as originally reported	$103,000
Prior period adjustment–credit	5,000
Retained earnings balance, beginning, as adjusted....................	108,000
Net income for current year.......................................	70,000
	178,000
Dividends for current year..	(16,000)
Retained earnings balance, ending	$162,000

Summary _____

Retained Earnings carries the balance of the business's net income accumulated over its lifetime, less its declared dividends and any net losses. *Cash dividends* are distributions of corporate assets made possible by earnings. *Stock dividends* are distributions of the corporation's own stock to its stockholders. Stock dividends and *stock splits* increase the number of shares outstanding and lower the market price per share of stock.

Treasury stock is the corporation's own stock that has been issued and reacquired and is currently held by the company. The corporation may sell treasury stock for its cost or for more or less than cost. *Retirement* of stock cancels the designated shares, which cannot then be reissued.

Retained earnings may be *restricted* by law or contract or by the corporation itself. An *appropriation* is a restriction of retained earnings that is recorded by formal journal entries.

The corporate *income statement* lists separately the various sources of income — *continuing operations,* which include other gains and losses, *discontinued operations,* and *extraordinary gains and losses.* The bottom line of the income statement reports *net income* or *net loss* for the period. *Income tax expense* and *earnings-per-share* figures also appear on the income statement, likewise divided into different categories based on the nature of income. The *statement of retained earnings* reports the causes for changes in the Retained Earnings account. This statement may be combined with the income statement.

Self-Study Questions

Test your understanding of the chapter by marking the best answer for each of the following questions.

1. A corporation has total stockholders' equity of $100,000, including retained earnings of $19,000. The cash balance is $35,000. The maximum cash dividend the company can declare and pay is *(p. 573)*
   a. $19,000
   b. $35,000
   c. $65,000
   d. $100,000

2. An entry debiting Dividends Payable and crediting Cash is recorded on the *(p. 573)*
   a. Declaration date
   b. Date of record
   c. Payment date
   d. None of the above

3. Meyer's Thrifty Acres has 100,000 shares of $20 par common stock outstanding. The stock's market value is $37 per share. Meyer's board of directors declares and distributes a 1 percent common stock dividend. Which of the following entries shows the full effect of declaring and distributing the dividend? *(p. 575)*

   a. Retained Earnings 37,000
       Common Stock Dividend Distributable 20,000
       Paid-in Capital in Excess of Par—Common 17,000

   b. Retained Earnings 20,000
       Common Stock..................................... 20,000

   c. Retained Earnings 17,000
       Paid-in Capital in Excess of Par—Common 17,000

   d. Retained Earnings 37,000
       Common Stock..................................... 20,000
       Paid-in Capital in Excess of Par—Common 17,000

4. Lang Real Estate Investment Corporation declared and distributed a 50 percent stock dividend. Which of the following stock splits would have the same effect on the number of Lang shares outstanding? *(pp. 577, 578)*
   a. 2 for 1
   b. 3 for 2
   c. 4 for 3
   d. 5 for 4

5. A company purchased 10,000 of its $1.50 par common stock as treasury stock, paying $6 per share. This transaction *(p. 579)*
   a. Has no effect on company assets
   b. Has no effect on owners' equity
   c. Decreases owners' equity by $15,000
   d. Decreases owners' equity by $60,000

6. A restriction of retained earnings *(pp. 583, 584)*
   a. Has no effect on total retained earnings
   b. Reduces retained earnings available for the declaration of dividends
   c. Can be reported by a note or by appropriation of retained earnings, or both
   d. All of the above

7. Which of the following items is *not* reported on the income statement? *(p. 587)*
   a. Premium on stock
   b. Extraordinary gains and losses
   c. Income tax expense
   d. Earnings per share

8. The income statement item that is likely to be most useful for predicting income from year to year is *(p. 586)*
   a. Extraordinary items
   b. Discontinued operations
   c. Income from continuing operations
   d. Net income

9. In computing earnings per share (EPS), dividends on preferred stock are *(p. 589)*
   a. Added because they represent earnings to the preferred stockholders
   b. Subtracted because they represent earnings to the preferred stockholders
   c. Ignored because they do not pertain to the common stock
   d. Reported separately on the income statement

10. A corporation accidentally overlooked an accrual of property tax expense at December 31, 19X4. Accountants for the company detect the error early in 19X5 before the expense is paid. The entry to record this prior period adjustment is *(p. 591)*

a. Retained Earnings XXX
    Property Tax Expense.   XXX

c. Retained Earnings...... XXX
    Property Tax Payable.   XXX

b. Property Tax Expense .. XXX
    Property Tax Payable.   XXX

d. Property Tax Payable... XXX
    Property Tax Expense.   XXX

Answers to the self-study questions are at the end of the chapter.

Accounting Vocabulary

appropriation of retained earnings *(p. 584)*, date of record *(p. 573)*, declaration date *(p. 573)*, earnings per share (EPS) *(p. 588)*, extraordinary item *(p. 588)*, large stock dividend *(p. 575)*, payment date *(p. 573)*, prior period adjustment *(p. 591)*, segment of a business *(p. 587)*, small stock dividend *(p. 575)*, stock dividend *(p. 573)*, stock split *(p. 576)*, treasury stock *(p. 578)*.

ASSIGNMENT MATERIAL _____

Questions

1. Identify the two main parts of stockholders' equity.
2. Identify the account debited and the account credited from the last closing entry a corporation makes each year. What is the purpose of this entry?
3. Ametek, Inc., reported a cash balance of $73 million and a retained earnings balance of $162.5 million. Explain how Ametek can have so much more retained earnings than cash. In your answer, identify the nature of retained earnings and state how it ties to cash.
4. Briefly discuss the three important dates for a dividend.
5. A friend of yours receives a stock dividend on an investment. He believes stock dividends are the same as cash dividends. Explain why this is not true.

6. Give two reasons for a corporation to distribute a stock dividend.

7. A corporation declares a stock dividend on December 21 and reports Stock Dividend Payable as a liability on the December 31 balance sheet. Is this correct? Give your reason.

8. What percentage distinguishes a small stock dividend from a large stock dividend? What is the main difference in accounting for small and large stock dividends?

9. To an investor, a stock split and a stock dividend have essentially the same effect. Explain the similarity and difference to the corporation between a 100 percent stock dividend and a 2-for-1 stock split.

10. Give four reasons why a corporation may purchase treasury stock.

11. What effect does the purchase of treasury stock have on the (a) assets, (b) issued stock, and (c) outstanding stock of the corporation?

12. What is the normal balance of the Treasury Stock account? What type of account is Treasury Stock? Where is Treasury Stock reported on the balance sheet?

13. Revell Inc. purchased treasury stock for $25,000. If Revell sells half the treasury stock for $15,000, what account should it credit for the $2,500 difference? If Revell sells half the treasury stock for $9,000, what accounts should be debited for the $3,500 difference?

14. What effect does the purchase and retirement of common stock have on the (a) assets, (b) issued stock, and (c) outstanding stock of the corporation?

15. Why do creditors wish to restrict a corporation's payment of cash dividends and purchases of treasury stock?

16. What are two ways to report a retained earnings restriction? Which way is more common?

17. Identify three items on the income statement that generate income tax expense. What is an income tax saving, and how does it arise?

18. Why is it important for a corporation to report income from continuing operations separately from discontinued operations and extraordinary items?

19. Give two examples of extraordinary gains and losses and four examples of gains and losses that are *not* extraordinary.

20. What is the most widely used of all accounting statistics? What is the price-to-earnings ratio? Compute the price-to-earnings ratio for a company with EPS of $2 and market price of $12 per share of common stock.

21. What is the earnings per share of a company with net income of $5,500, issued common stock of 12,000 shares, and treasury common stock of 1,000 shares.

22. What account do all prior period adjustments affect? On what financial statement are prior period adjustments reported?

Exercises

Exercise 15-1 *Journalizing dividends and reporting stockholders' equity*

Eatmore Hamburger System, Inc., is authorized to issue 300,000 shares of $1 par common stock. The company issued 100,000 shares at $6 per share, and all 100,000 shares are outstanding. When the retained earnings balance was $300,000, Eatmore declared and distributed a 50 percent stock dividend. Later, Eatmore declared and paid a $.20 per share cash dividend.

Required

1. Journalize the declaration and distribution of the stock dividend.
2. Journalize the declaration and payment of the cash dividend.
3. Prepare the stockholders' equity section of the balance sheet after both dividends.

Exercise 15-2 *Journalizing a stock dividend and reporting stockholders' equity*

The stockholders' equity for Tick Tock Jewelry Corporation on September 30, 19X4—end of the company's fiscal year—follows.

Stockholders' Equity

Common stock, $10 par, 100,000 shares authorized, 50,000 shares issued..........	$500,000
Paid-in capital in excess of par—common...	50,000
Retained earnings......................	280,000
Total stockholders' equity	$830,000

On November 16 the market price of Tick Tock's common stock was $15 per share and the company declared a 10 percent stock dividend. Tick Tock issued the dividend shares on November 30.

Required

1. Journalize the declaration and distribution of the stock dividend.
2. Prepare the stockholders' equity section of the balance sheet after the stock dividend.

Exercise 15-3 *Journalizing treasury stock transactions*

Journalize the following transactions of Shoe Renewry, Inc., a national chain of shoe repair shops:

May 19   Issued 3,000 shares of no-par common stock at $12 per share.
Aug. 22 Purchased 600 shares of treasury stock at $14 per share.
Nov. 11 Sold 200 shares of treasury stock at $15 per share.
Dec. 28 Sold 100 shares of treasury stock at $11 per share.

Exercise 15-4 *Journalizing treasury stock transactions and reporting stockholders' equity*

Northwest Distributing Company had the following stockholders' equity on November 30:

Stockholders' Equity

Common stock, $5 par, 500,000 shares authorized, 50,000 shares issued.............	$250,000
Paid-in capital in excess of par	150,000
Retained earnings......................	220,000
Total stockholders' equity	$620,000

On December 19 the company purchased 1,000 shares of treasury stock at $6 per share. Journalize the purchase of the treasury stock and prepare the stockholders' equity section of the balance sheet at December 31.

Exercise 15-5 *Reporting stockholders' equity after a stock split*

Assume Northwest Distributing Company (the business in the preceding exercise) split its $5 par common stock 4 for 1 on December 10. Make the memorandum entry to record the stock split, and prepare the stockholder's equity section of the balance sheet immediately after the split. Assume the number of authorized shares increases to 2,000,000.

Exercise 15-6 *Reporting a retained earnings restriction*

The agreement under which Brookview Sales, Inc., issued its long-term debt requires the restriction of $351,000 of the company's retained earnings balance. Total retained earnings is $609,000, and total paid-in capital is $822,000.

Required

Show how to report stockholders' equity (including retained earnings) on Brookview's balance sheet, assuming:

a. Brookview discloses the restriction in a note. Write the note.
b. Brookview appropriates retained earnings in the amount of the restriction and includes no note in its statements.

Exercise 15-7 *Preparing a multiple-step income statement*

The ledger of a corporation contains the following information for 19X7 operations:

Cost of goods sold	$45,000	Income tax saving—loss on	
Loss on discontinued		discontinued operations	$ 20,000
operations	50,000	Extraordinary gain	12,000
Income tax expense—		Sales revenue	130,000
extraordinary gain	4,800	Operating expenses (including	
		income tax)	60,000

Required

Prepare a multiple-step income statement for 19X7. Omit earnings per share.

Exercise 15-8 *Computing earnings per share*

Benavides Inc. earned net income of $56,000 for the second quarter of 19X6. The ledger reveals the following figures:

Preferred stock, $2.50 per year, no-par, 1,400 shares issued and	
outstanding	$ 50,000
Common stock, $10 par, 32,000 shares issued	320,000
Treasury stock, common, 2,000 shares at cost	36,000

Required

Compute EPS for the quarter, assuming no changes in the stock accounts during the quarter.

Exercise 15-9 *Preparing a statement of retained earnings with a prior period adjustment*

Posen Inc., a soft-drink company, reported a prior period adjustment in 19X9. An accounting error caused net income of prior years to be overstated by $3.8 million. Retained earnings at January 1, 19X9, as previously reported, stood at $395.3 million. Net income for 19X9 was $78.1 million, and dividends were $39.8 million. Prepare the company's statement of retained earnings for the year ended December 31, 19X9.

Exercise 15-10 *Preparing a combined statement of income and retained earnings*

The Kroger Company, a large grocery company, had retained earnings of $792.6 million at the beginning of 19X3. The company showed these figures at December 31, 19X3:

	($ Millions)
Increases in retained earnings:	
Net income	$127.1
Decreases in retained earnings:	
Cash dividends—preferred	2.3
common	85.2
Debit to retained earnings due to purchase of preferred stock	11.3

Required

Beginning with net income, prepare a combined statement of income and retained earnings for the Kroger Company for 19X3. The debit to Retained Earnings was caused by

Kroger's paying $11.3 more to retire its preferred stock than the original issue price of the stock.

Exercise 15-11   *Computing earnings per share*

Greenlawn Supply had 40,000 shares of common stock and 10,000 shares of $10 par, 5 percent preferred stock outstanding on December 31, 19X8. On April 30, 19X9, the company issued 9,000 additional common shares and ended 19X9 with 49,000 shares of common stock outstanding. Income from continuing operations of 19X9 was $106,200, and loss on discontinued operations was $8,280. The company had an extraordinary gain of $50,600.

Required

Compute Greenlawn's EPS amounts for 19X9, starting with income from continuing operations.

Problems   (Group A)

Problem 15-1A   *Journalizing dividend and treasury stock transactions*

Pecos Corporation completed the following selected transactions during the current year:

Jan. 9   Discovered that income tax expense of the preceding year was overstated by $8,000. Recorded a prior period adjustment to correct the error.

Feb. 10   Split common stock 2 for 1 by calling in the 20,000 shares of $10 par common and issuing 40,000 shares of $5 par common.

Mar. 18   Declared a cash dividend on the 5 percent, $100 par preferred stock (1,000 shares outstanding). Declared a $.20 per share dividend on the 40,000 shares of common stock outstanding. The date of record was April 2, and the payment date was April 23.

Apr. 23   Paid the cash dividends.

July 30   Declared a 10 percent stock dividend on the common stock to holders of record August 21, with distribution set for September 11. The market value of the common stock was $21 per share.

Sep. 11   Issued the stock dividend shares.

Sep. 26   Purchased 3,000 shares of the company's own common stock at $18 per share.

Nov. 8   Sold 1,000 shares of treasury common stock for $20 per share.

Dec. 13   Sold 500 shares of treasury common stock for $17 per share.

Required

Record the transactions in the general journal.

Problem 15-2A   *Journalizing prior period adjustments and dividend and treasury stock transactions; reporting retained earnings and stockholders' equity*

The balance sheet of Abilene, Inc., at December 31, 19X1, reported the following stockholders' equity:

Paid-in capital:
Common stock, $10 par, 100,000 shares au-
    thorized, 20,000 shares issued $200,000
Paid-in capital in excess of par—common. . .   300,000
    Total paid-in capital   500,000
Retained earnings.   240,000
    Total stockholders' equity. $740,000

During 19X2 Abilene completed the following selected transactions:

Jan. 11 Discovered that income tax expense of 19X1 was understated by $14,000. Recorded a prior period adjustment to correct the error.

Apr. 30 Declared a 10 percent stock dividend on the common stock. The market value of Abilene common stock was $24 per share. The record date was May 21, with distribution set for June 5.

June 5 Issued the stock dividend shares.

July 29 Purchased 2,000 shares of the company's own common stock at $19 per share.

Nov.13 Sold 1,000 shares of treasury common stock for $24 per share.

Nov.27 Declared a $.30 per share dividend on the 21,000 shares of common stock outstanding. The date of record was Dec. 17, and the payment date was January 7, 19X3.

Dec. 31 Closed the $103,000 credit balance of Income Summary to Retained Earnings.

Required

1. Record the transactions in the general journal.
2. Prepare a retained earnings statement at December 31, 19X2.
3. Prepare the stockholders' equity section of the balance sheet at December 31, 19X2.

Problem 15-3A *Journalizing dividend and treasury stock transactions and reporting stockholders' equity*

The balance sheet of Sausalito Sales Company at December 31, 19X5, reported 100,000 shares of no-par common stock authorized, with 30,000 shares issued and a Common Stock balance of $180,000. Sausalito Sales also had 5,000 shares of 5 percent, $10 par preferred stock authorized and outstanding. The preferred stock was issued in 19X1 at par. Retained Earnings had a credit balance of $65,000. During the two-year period ended December 31, 19X7, the company completed the following selected transactions:

19X6

Mar. 15 Purchased 2,000 shares of the company's own common stock for the treasury at $5 per share.

July 2 Declared the annual 5 percent cash dividend on the preferred stock and a $.75-per-share cash dividend on the common stock. The date of record was July 16, and the payment date was July 31.

July 31 Paid the cash dividends.

Nov.30 Declared a 20 percent stock dividend on the *outstanding* common stock to holders of record December 21, with distribution set for January 11, 19X7. The market value of Sausalito common stock was $10 per share.

Dec. 31 Earned net income of $60,000 for the year.

19X7

Jan. 11 Issued the stock dividend shares.

June 30 Declared the annual 5 percent cash dividend on the preferred stock. The date of record was July 14, and the payment date was July 29.

July 29 Paid the cash dividends.

Aug. 2 Purchased and retired all the preferred stock at $14 per share.

Oct. 8 Sold 800 shares of treasury common stock for $12 per share.

Dec. 19 Split the no-par common stock 2 for 1 by issuing two new no-par shares for each old no-par share previously issued. The corporation had issued 35,600 shares, so after the split it had 71,200 shares issued. (Stock splits affect all issued stock, including treasury stock as well as stock that is outstanding.)

31 Earned net income of $81,000 during the year.

Required

1. Record the transactions in the general journal. Explanations are not required.
2. Prepare the stockholders' equity section of the balance sheet at two dates: December 31, 19X6, and December 31, 19X7.

Problem 15-4A *Preparing a single-step income statement and a statement of retained earnings; reporting stockholders' equity on the balance sheet*

The following information was taken from the ledger and other records of Rivera Corporation at September 30, 19X6.

Loss on sale of plant assets	$ 8,000	Interest revenue	$ 4,000
Sales returns	9,000	Extraordinary loss	30,000
Income tax expense (saving):		Operating loss, discontinued segment	15,000
Continuing operations	72,000	Loss on insurance settlement	12,000
Discontinued segment:		General expenses	113,000
Operating loss	(6,000)	Preferred stock, $3, no-par 10,000 shares	
Gain on sale	8,000	authorized, 5,000 shares issued	200,000
Extraordinary loss	(12,000)	Paid-in capital in excess of par—common	20,000
Sales revenue	903,000	Retained earnings, beginning, as originally	
Treasury stock, common (1,000 shares at		reported	88,000
cost)	11,000	Selling expenses	136,000
Dividends	35,000	Common stock, $10 par, 25,000 shares	
Gain on sale of discontinued segment	20,000	authorized and issued	250,000
Prior period adjustment—credit to Retained		Sales discounts	18,000
Earnings	6,000	Interest expense	11,000
Contributed capital from treasury stock		Cost of goods sold	420,000
transactions	7,000		

Required

Prepare a single-step income statement and a statement of retained earnings for Rivera Corporation for the fiscal year ended September 30, 19X6. Also prepare the stockholders' equity section of the balance sheet at that date. Include the earnings-per-share presentation, and show computations.

Problem 15-5A *Preparing a corrected combined statement of income and retained earnings*

Monica Hearn, accountant for International Food Incorporated, was injured in a skiing accident. Another employee prepared the income statement on the following page for the fiscal year ended December 31, 19X3.

The individual amounts listed on the income statement are correct. However, some accounts are reported incorrectly, and others do not belong on the income statement at all. Also, income tax (40 percent) has not been applied to all appropriate figures. International issued 52,000 shares of common stock in 19X1 and held 2,000 shares as treasury stock during 19X3. The retained earnings balance, as originally reported at December 31, 19X2, was $92,000.

Required

Prepare a corrected combined statement of income and retained earnings for 19X3. Prepare the income statement in single-step format.

International Foods Incorporated
Income Statement
19X3

Revenue and gains:		
Sales		$349,000
Prior period adjustment–credit.		14,000
Gain on retirement of preferred stock (issued for		
$100,000; purchased for $93,000).		7,000
Paid-in capital in excess of par—common		80,000
Total revenues and gains.		450,000
Expenses and losses:		
Cost of goods sold	$145,000	
Selling expenses.	76,000	
General expenses.	61,000	
Sales returns.	11,000	
Dividends.	7,000	
Sales discounts.	6,000	
Income tax expense	20,000	
Total expenses and losses		326,000
Income from operations		124,000
Other gains and losses:		
Gain on sale of discontinued operations	10,000	
Flood loss	(20,000)	
Operating loss on discontinued segment	(15,000)	
Total other losses		(25,000)
Net income.		$149,000
Earnings per share.		$2.98

Problem 15-6A *Using actual-company data to record transactions and report earnings per share*

The following items were taken from the financial statements of actual companies that showed amounts in millions and rounded to the nearest $100,000.

The General Tire & Rubber Company declared and paid cash dividends of $35.2 million to its common stockholders and also declared and issued a 2 percent stock dividend on its 23.6 million common shares outstanding. The par value of General's common stock was $.30 per share, and the market value of the stock at the time of the stock dividend was $60 per share.

Required

1. Journalize the declaration and payment of the cash dividend.
2. Journalize declaration and issuance of the stock dividend.

At the beginning of the year, IU International Corporation had a treasury stock balance of $288.3 million. During the year, IU paid $2.2 million to purchase treasury stock. The company also sold treasury stock for $79.9 million. The cost of the treasury stock sold was $68.3 million. In addition, IU paid $19.6 million to purchase and retire preferred stock with par value of $18.8 million. The preferred stock had been issued at par in previous years.

Required

3. Journalize the purchase and the sale of treasury stock.

4. Compute the ending balance of the Treasury Stock account.
5. Journalize the purchase and retirement of preferred stock.

Chesapeake Corporation of Virginia, a paper company, reported a $4.0 million extraordinary gain that resulted from issuing 200,000 shares of its $5 par common stock and giving $4.5 million in cash to pay off long-term debt of $16.5 million. Chesapeake's income before the extraordinary item was $8.5 million, and the company had 6.4 million shares of common stock outstanding.

Note: An extraordinary gain or loss is recorded exactly as any other gain or loss, but with "Extraordinary" in its account title.

Required

6. Journalize the transaction.
7. Show how Chesapeake reported earnings per share for the year.

Problem 15-7A *Computing earnings per share and reporting a retained earnings restriction*

The capital structure of Montpelier Gardens at December 31, 19X6, included 20,000 shares of $1.25 preferred stock and 44,000 shares of common stock. Common shares outstanding during 19X7 were 44,000 January through May, 50,000 June through August, and 60,500 September through December. Income from continuing operations during 19X7 was $47,440. The company discontinued a segment of the business at a loss of $6,630, and an extraordinary item generated a gain of $33,660. Montpelier's board of directors restricts $60,000 of retained earnings for contingencies.

Required

1. Compute Montpelier's earnings per share. Start with income from continuing operations.
2. Show two ways of reporting Montpelier's retained earnings restriction. Assume total retained earnings is $190,000 and total paid-in capital is $230,000.

(Group B)

Problem 15-1B *Journalizing dividend and treasury stock transactions*

El Paso Corporation completed the following selected transactions during 19X6:

Jan. 13 Discovered that income tax expense of 19X5 was understated by $11,000. Recorded a prior period adjustment to correct the error.

Jan. 21 Split common stock 3 for 1 by calling in the 10,000 shares of $15 par common and issuing 30,000 shares of $5 par common.

Feb. 6 Declared a cash dividend on the 4,000 shares of $2.25, no-par preferred stock. Declared a $.50 per share dividend on the 30,000 shares of common stock outstanding. The date of record was February 27, and the payment date was March 20.

Mar. 20 Paid the cash dividends.

Apr. 18 Declared a 50 percent stock dividend on the common stock to holders of record April 30, with distribution set for May 30. The market value of the common stock was $11 per share.

May 30 Issued the stock dividend shares.

June 18 Purchased 2,000 shares of the company's own common stock at $12 per share.

Nov. 14 Sold 800 shares of treasury common stock for $10 per share. Debited Retained Earnings for the difference between sale price and cost because there was no Paid-in Capital from Treasury Stock Transactions.

Dec. 22 Sold 1,000 shares of treasury common stock for $16 per share.

Required
Record the transactions in the general journal.

Problem 15-2B *Journalizing prior period adjustments and dividend and treasury stock transactions; reporting retained earnings and stockholders' equity*

The balance sheet of Odessa Corporation at December 31, 19X3, presented the following stockholders' equity:

Paid-in capital:

Common stock, $1 par, 250,000 shares authorized, 50,000 shares issued	$ 50,000
Paid-in capital in excess of par—common	350,000
Total paid-in capital.	400,000
Retained earnings	110,000
Total stockholders' equity	$510,000

During 19X4, Odessa completed the following selected transactions:

Jan. 7 Discovered that income tax expense of 19X3 was overstated by $7,000. Recorded a prior period adjustment to correct the error.

Mar. 29 Declared a 50 percent stock dividend on the common stock. The market value of Odessa common stock was $9 per share. The record date was April 19, with distribution set for May 19.

May 19 Issued the stock dividend shares.

July 13 Purchased 5,000 shares of the company's own common stock at $6 per share.

Oct. 4 Sold 3,000 shares of treasury common stock for $9 per share.

Dec. 27 Declared a $.20 per share dividend on the 73,000 shares of common stock outstanding. The date of record was January 17, 19X5, and the payment date was January 31.

     31 Closed the $62,000 credit balance of Income Summary to Retained Earnings.

Required

1. Record the transactions in the general journal.
2. Prepare the retained earnings statement at December 31, 19X4.
3. Prepare the stockholders' equity section of the balance sheet at December 31, 19X4.

Problem 15-3B *Journalizing dividend and treasury stock transactions and reporting stockholders' equity*

The balance sheet of Carmel Service Company at December 31, 19X7, reported 10,000 shares of $.50, no-par preferred stock authorized and outstanding. The preferred was issued in 19X1 at $8 per share. Carmel also had 500,000 shares of $1 par common stock authorized with 100,000 shares issued. Paid-in Capital in Excess of Par—Common had a balance of $300,000. Retained Earnings had a balance of $18,000, and the preferred dividend for 19X7 was in arrears. During the two-year period ended December 31, 19X9, the company completed the following selected transactions:

19X8

Feb. 15 Purchased 5,000 shares of the company's own common stock for the treasury at $3 per share.

Apr. 2 Declared the cash dividend on the preferred stock in arrears for 19X7 and the current cash dividend on preferred. The date of record was April 16, and the payment date was May 1.

May 1 Paid the cash dividends.

May 2 Purchased and retired all the preferred stock at $7.50 per share.

Dec. 31 Earned net income of $45,000 for the year.
19X9

Mar. 8 Sold 2,000 shares of treasury common stock for $4 per share.

Sep. 28 Declared a 5 percent stock dividend on the *outstanding* common stock to holders of record October 15, with distribution set for October 31. The market value of Carmel Common stock was $5 per share.

Oct. 31 Issued the stock dividend shares.

Nov. 5 Split the common stock 2 for 1 by calling in the 104,850 shares of old $1 par common stock and issuing 209,700 shares of $.50 par common. (Stock splits affect all issued stock, including treasury stock and stock that is outstanding.)

Dec. 31 Earned net income of $62,000 during the year.

Required

1. Record the transactions in the general journal. Explanations are not required.
2. Prepare the stockholders' equity section of the balance sheet at two dates: December 31, 19X8, and December 31, 19X9.

Problem 15-4B *Preparing a single-step income statement and a statement of retained earnings and reporting stockholders' equity on the balance sheet*

The following information was taken from the ledger and other records of Mancini Corporation at June 30, 19X5:

Treasury stock, common (2,000 shares at cost)	$ 28,000	Sales revenue	$559,000
General expenses	71,000	Retained earnings, beginning, as originally reported	63,000
Loss on sale of discontinued segment	8,000	Selling expenses	87,000
Prior period adjustment–debit to Retained Earnings	4,000	Common stock, no-par, 22,000 shares authorized and issued	350,000
Cost of goods sold	319,000	Sales discounts	7,000
Interest expense	23,000	Paid-in capital from retirement of preferred	
Gain on settlement of lawsuit	8,000	stock	16,000
Sales returns	15,000	Interest revenue	5,000
Income tax expense (saving):		Extraordinary gain	27,000
Continuing operations	16,000	Operating loss, discontinued segment	9,000
Discontinued segment:		Loss on sale of plant assets	10,000
Operating loss	(3,600)	Dividends on preferred stock	?
Loss on sale	(3,200)	Preferred stock, 6%, $25 par, 20,000	
Extraordinary gain	10,800	shares authorized, 4,000 shares issued	100,000
Dividends on common stock	12,000		

Required

Prepare a single-step income statement and a statement of retained earnings for Mancini Corporation for the fiscal year ended June 30, 19X5. Also prepare the stockholders' equity section of the balance sheet at that date. Include the earnings-per-share presentation and show computations.

Problem 15-5B *Preparing a corrected combined statement of income and retained earnings*

Leslie Gose, accountant for Stinnett Catering Company, was injured in a sailing accident. Another employee prepared the following income statement for the fiscal year ended June 30, 19X4:

Stinnett Catering Company
Income Statement
June 30, 19X4

Revenues and gains:		
Sales..		$522,000
Gain on retirement of preferred stock (issued		
for $50,000; purchased for $48,000)		2,000
Paid-in capital in excess of par—common		100,000
Total revenues and gains		624,000
Expenses and losses:		
Cost of goods sold.................................	$233,000	
Selling expenses	103,000	
General expenses	74,000	
Sales returns	22,000	
Prior period adjustment–debit........................	4,000	
Dividends	15,000	
Sales discounts	10,000	
Income tax expense.................................	32,000	
Total expenses and losses		493,000
Income from operations		131,000
Other gains and losses:		
Extraordinary gain.................................	30,000	
Operating income on discontinued segment..............	25,000	
Loss on sale of discontinued operations	(40,000)	
Total other gains		15,000
Net income		$146,000
Earnings per share		$7.30

The individual amounts listed on the income statement are correct. However, some accounts are reported incorrectly, and others do not belong on the income statement at all. Also, income tax (40 percent) has not been applied to all appropriate figures. Stinnett issued 24,000 shares of common stock in 19X1 and held 4,000 shares as treasury stock during the fiscal year 19X4. The retained earnings balance, as originally reported at June 30, 19X3, was $56,000.

Required

Prepare a corrected combined statement of income and retained earnings for fiscal year 19X4. Prepare the income statement in single-step format.

Problem 15-6B   *Using actual-company data to record transactions and report earnings per share*

The following items were taken from actual financial statements that reported amounts in millions, rounded to the nearest $100,000.

Hampton Industries, Inc., declared and paid cash dividends of $.1 million to preferred stockholders and also declared and issued a 10 percent stock dividend on its 2.0 million common shares outstanding. The par value of Hampton's common stock was $1.00 per share, and the market value of the stock at the time of the stock dividend was $6.50 per share.

Required

1. Journalize the declaration and payment of the cash dividend.
2. Journalize the declaration and issuance of the stock dividend.

At the beginning of the period, the Louisiana Land and Exploration Company had a treasury stock balance of $1.2 million. During the period, Louisiana paid $212.8 million to purchase treasury stock, and the company also sold treasury stock for $.6 million. The cost of the treasury stock was $.5 million.

Required

3. Journalize the purchase and the sale of treasury stock.
4. Compute the ending balance of the Treasury Stock account.

Crown Cork & Seal Company, Inc., purchased and retired 800,000 shares of its common stock at a cost of $40 per share. Assume that par value was $1 per share and that the common stock was issued for $9 per share.

Required

5. Journalize the purchase and retirement of the common stock.

G. C. Murphy Company reported a $1.3 million extraordinary gain on the issuance of treasury stock, which cost $3.4 million, to pay off long-term debt of $4.7 million. Murphy's income before extraordinary item was $17.0 million, and the company had 4.1 million shares of common stock outstanding.
Note: An extraordinary gain or loss is recorded exactly as any other gain or loss, but with "Extraordinary" in its account title.

Required

6. Journalize the transaction.
7. Show how Murphy reported earnings per share for the year.

Problem 15-7B   *Computing earnings per share and reporting a retained earnings restriction*

Tradewinds Travel's capital structure at December 31, 19X2, included 5,000 shares of $2.50 preferred stock and 130,000 shares of common stock. Common shares outstanding during 19X3 were 130,000 January through February; 119,000 during March; 121,000 April through October; and 128,000 during November and December. Income from continuing operations during 19X7 was $349,655. The company discontinued a segment of the business at a gain of $69,160, and an extraordinary item generated a loss of $49,510. The board of directors of Tradewinds has restricted $240,000 of retained earnings for expansion of the company's office facilities.

Required

1. Compute Tradewinds's earnings per share. Start with income from continuing operations.
2. Show two ways of reporting Tradewinds's retained earnings restriction. Assume total retained earnings is $739,800 and total paid-in capital is $947,610.

Decision Problem

Analyzing Cash Dividends and Stock Dividends
Pacific Union Corporation had the following stockholders' equity on June 30 of the current year:

Common stock, no-par, 100,000 shares issued...........................	$ 750,000
Retained earnings.....................	830,000
Total stockholders' equity..............	$1,580,000

In the past, Pacific Union has paid an annual cash dividend of $1.50 per share. Despite the large retained earnings balance, the board of directors wished to conserve cash for expansion. The board delayed the payment of cash dividends by one month and in the meantime distributed a 20 percent stock dividend. During the following year, the company's cash position improved. The board declared and paid a cash dividend of $1.25 per share.

Suppose you own 1,000 shares of Pacific Union common stock, acquired three years ago. The market price of the stock was $24 per share before any of the above dividends.

Required

1. How does the stock dividend affect your proportionate ownership in the company? Explain.
2. What amount of cash dividends did you receive last year? What amount of cash dividends will you receive after the above dividend action?
3. Immediately after the stock dividend was distributed, the market value of Pacific Union stock decreased from $24 per share to $20 per share. Does this represent a loss to you? Explain.
4. Suppose Pacific Union announces at the time of the stock dividend that the company will continue to pay the annual $1.50 cash dividend per share, even after the stock dividend. Would you expect the market price of the stock to decrease to $20 per share as in 3 above? Explain.

Financial Statement Problem

Treasury Stock, Retained Earnings, and the Corporation Income Statement

Use the Gulf+Western financial statements in Appendix C to answer these questions.

1. How many shares of common stock did Gulf+Western have outstanding at October 31, 1987? How many shares were in the treasury? How many shares had Gulf+Western issued through October 31, 1987?
2. Gulf+Western uses a method of accounting for treasury stock that is different from the method discussed in this chapter. Nevertheless, you can determine from the Statement of Changes in Stockholders' Equity the company's cost of treasury stock acquired during fiscal 1987. It is the total reduction in stockholders' equity. What was this amount?
3. What was the retained earnings balance at October 31, 1987? In Note F, how much of retained earnings was unrestricted as to the payment of cash dividends? How much was restricted?
4. What transactions caused the extraordinary items during fiscal 1986? Identify each individual item as a gain or a loss and give its net amount. Show the total amount reported on the income statement.
5. What transaction caused the earnings from discontinued operations during fiscal 1985? Show all the components of this item, including the related income tax amounts.
6. Income taxes for fiscal 1985 include the $83.6 million reported on the income statement plus the income tax effects of discontinued operations given in Note B. What was Gulf+Western's total income tax expense for fiscal 1985? Gulf+Western refers to income tax expense as "Provision for income taxes," a common title.

Answers to Self-Study Questions

1. a   3. d   5. d   7. a   9. b
2. c   4. b   6. d   8. c   10. c

Mathematical Presentations

This appendix reviews some of the mathematical presentations in the book. You may find it helpful to refer to this appendix as you use the text.

Fractions, Decimals, Percentages, and Ratios _____

There are four ways to describe mathematically a specific portion of something: as a fraction, a decimal, a percentage, and a ratio. These expressions are interchangeable, as the following discussion shows.

Delwood Plaza, a shopping center, consists of 40 stores. Thirty of the stores are occupied. Ten are vacant. We can describe the portions of the shopping center that are occupied and vacant in four ways:

	Portion of the Shopping Center	
	Occupied	**Vacant**
Fraction	$30/40 = 3/4$	$10/40 = 1/4$
Decimal	$3/4 = 3 \div 4 = .75$	$1/4 = 1 \div 4 = .25$
Percentage	$.75 = 75\%$	$.25 = 25\%$
Ratio	$3:4$	$1:4$

Fractions, decimals, percentages, and ratios are based on the relationship between two numbers. In this example, we are expressing the relationship between (a) the portion of the shopping center that is occupied (or vacant) and (b) the total shopping center.

As another example, suppose your daily drive to college is six miles. After driving two miles, you could describe your progress as $2/6 = 1/3$, or as .333, or as $33\frac{1}{3}\%$, or as $1:3$. They all carry the same meaning. In this example, we are expressing the relationship between (a) the portion of the drive completed and (b) the total distance to be driven.

In all cases, there is a key question to ask before computing fractions, decimals, percentages, and ratios: What is the base amount? That is, what is the denominator in the computation? For example, if a percentage is to be computed, the base amount is the number that represents 100 percent (40 stores in the shopping center and 6 miles in the daily drive to college).

Percentage Changes _____

In business, percentage changes are widely used to measure achievement. For example, a company's total assets may increase from $200,000 to $240,000. This is a 20 percent increase, computed as follows:

Total assets now	$240,000	120%
Total assets previously..............	200,000	100
Increase in total assets	$ 40,000	20%
Percentage increase in total assets:		
Increase divided by previous amount		
($40,000 ÷ $200,000)		20%

Suppose that during the next period total assets decrease to $180,000. The decrease is 25 percent, computed in exactly the same manner:

Total assets now	$180,000	75%
Total assets previously	240,000	100
Decrease in total assets	$ 60,000	25%
Percentage decrease in total assets:		
Decrease divided by previous amount		
($60,000 ÷ $240,000).............		25%

Dollar Signs and Double Underlines

In this book we show monetary figures by placing a dollar sign ($) with the first amount in each column and with each total that is underlined twice. This is the method used in companies' published annual reports. The preceding section, Percentage Changes, gives two examples.

Dollar signs are *not* used for amounts debited and credited in journals and ledgers. It is understood that these are monetary figures. However, we often use dollar signs in parenthetical explanations to aid your understanding of a particular entry. For example, two cash purchases of supplies for $50 and $40 could be combined into one entry:

	Amount	
	Debit	Credit
Supplies ($50 + $40)	90	
Cash.....................		90

The ledger also omits dollar signs:

Supplies	Cash
90	90

Double underlines indicate a final total, as presented in the Percentage Changes section.

Positive and Negative Amounts

In most mathematical presentations, the plus sign (+) denotes a positive amount, and the minus sign (−) denotes a negative amount: for example, $7 + 5 - 3 = 9$. In a columnar presentation it would be cumbersome to use a + or a − sign for each number. Accountants use a short-cut method that omits the plus sign for positive amounts and uses parentheses to denote negatives, as follows:

$$
\begin{array}{r}
7 \\
5 \\
\underline{(3)} \\
\underline{\underline{9}}
\end{array}
$$

Not all negative amounts are presented with parentheses, however. Parentheses are often omitted where the description clearly indicates that a subtraction occurs, as follows:

Males	7
Plus: Females	5
Less: Children	$\underline{3}$
Total adults	$\underline{\underline{9}}$

Reversing Entries

This appendix shows how accountants use a special technique called *reversing entries* to ease the burden of bookkeeping.

Accrued Expenses and the Related Liabilities _____

Some expenses accrue day by day (or even hour by hour), but they are paid at regular, longer intervals, often weekly or monthly. Many times the payment does not occur on the financial statement date. Therefore, at the end of the period the business must make an adjusting entry to record the expenses that have built up to that time but that will not be paid until later. Without an adjustment, the business's financial statements will overstate net income and owner's equity (because expenses and liabilities will be understated). These built-up expenses are called accrued expenses (or accrued liabilities because their recording includes a credit to a liability account). Examples include property taxes, interest on notes payable, and employee salaries and wages.

Assume that at December 27, 19X1—near the end of the accounting period—Salary Expense has a debit balance of $185,000 from salaries paid during the year. At year end the business owes employees $3,000 for their service during the last three work days of the year. This amount will be paid on January 3, the next payday, along with $2,000 in salaries for the first two work days of the new year. The next weekly payroll amount will be $5,000. However, to present the complete financial picture, the $3,000 in salaries incurred in 19X1 must be included in the 19X1 statements. Accordingly, the business makes the following adjusting entry on December 31:

Adjusting Entries

19X1

Dec. 31   Salary Expense.................................   3,000

                   Salary Payable............................   3,000

After posting, the Salary Payable and Salary Expense accounts appear as follows:

Salary Payable

	19X1		
	Dec. 31	Adj.*	3,000
	Dec. 31	Bal.	3,000

Salary Expense

19X1				
Year's total through				
Dec. 27		185,000		
Dec. 31	Adj.	3,000		
Dec. 31	Bal.	188,000		

After the adjusting entry, the 19X1 *income statement* reports salary expense of $188,000, and the *balance sheet* at December 31, 19X1, reports Salary Payable, a liability, of $3,000. The $188,000 debit balance of Salary Expense will be eliminated by a closing entry at December 31, 19X1, as follows:

Closing Entries

19X1

Dec. 31   Income Summary   188,000

                   Salary Expense.........................   188,000

After posting, Salary Expense appears as follows:

Salary Expense

Year's total through					
Dec. 27		185,000			
Dec. 31	Adj.	3,000			
Dec. 31	Bal.	188,000	Dec. 31	Clo.	188,000

* Entry explanations used throughout this appendix are
Adj. = Adjusting entry
Bal. = Balance
Clo. = Closing entry
CP   = Cash payment entry
CR   = Cash receipt entry
Rev. = Reversing entry, explained later in the appendix

Reversing Entries

Reversing entries are special types of entries that ease the burden of accounting after adjusting entries have been made in a preceding period. Let's see how reversing entries work. Suppose you are the accountant who records cash payments for salaries. In the normal course of recording salary payments during the year, you make the following payroll entry:

Salary Expense	5,000	
Cash..		5,000

However, suppose that payday does not land on the day the accounting period ends and that you have made an adjusting entry to accrue salary payable of $3,000, as we have just seen. On January 3, 19X2, you record the weekly payroll of $5,000. You credit Cash for $5,000, but what account—or accounts—do you debit? The cash payment entry is

19X2

Jan. 3	Salary Payable	3,000	
	Salary Expense	2,000	
	Cash.......................................		5,000

This method of recording the cash payment is *inefficient* because you must refer back to the adjusting entries of December 31, 19X1. Otherwise, you do not know the amount of the required debit (in this example, $3,000) to Salary Payable. Searching the preceding year's adjusting entries takes time, and in business, time is money. To avoid having to analyze the payment entry and having to separate the debit into two accounts, accountants have devised a technique called reversing entries.

Making a Reversing Entry. A **reversing entry** switches the debit and the credit of a previous adjusting entry. The reversing entry is dated the first day of the period following the adjusting entry.

Let's continue with our example of the end-of-period cash payment of $5,000 in salaries. On December 31, 19X1, the accountant made the following entry to accrue Salary Payable:

Adjusting Entries

19X1

Dec. 31	Salary Expense..................................	3,000	
	Salary Payable		3,000

The reversing entry simply flip-flops the position of the debit and the credit:

Reversing Entries

19X2

Jan. 1	Salary Payable	3,000	
	Salary Expense		3,000

Notice that the reversing entry is dated the first day of the new period. It is the exact opposite of the December 31 adjusting entry. Ordinarily, the accountant who makes the adjusting entry also prepares the reversing entry at the same time.

OBJECTIVE 1

Make a reversing entry for an accrued expense

She postdates the reversing entry to January 1 of the next period, however, so that it affects the new period. Note how the accounts appear after the accountant posts the reversing entry:

Salary Payable

19X2				19X1		
Jan. 1	**Rev.**	**3,000**		Dec. 31	Bal.	**3,000**

Zero balance

Salary Expense

19X1				19X1		
Dec. 31	Bal.	188,000		Dec. 31	Clo.	188,000
				Zero balance		
				19X2		
				Jan. 1	**Rev.**	**3,000**

The arrow shows the transfer of the $3,000 credit balance from Salary Payable to Salary Expense. This credit balance in Salary Expense does not mean that the entity has negative salary expense, as might be suggested by a credit balance in an expense account. Instead, the odd credit balance is merely a temporary result of the reversing entry. The credit balance is eliminated on January 3, 19X2, when the $5,000 cash payment for salaries is debited to Salary Expense in the customary manner:

19X2			
Jan. 3	Salary Expense	5,000	
	Cash.		5,000

Then this cash payment entry is posted:

Salary Expense

19X2				19X2		
Jan. 3	CP	5,000		Jan. 1	Rev.	3,000
Jan. 3	Bal.	2,000				

Now Salary Expense has its correct debit balance of $2,000, which is the amount of salary expense incurred thus far in 19X2. The $5,000 cash disbursement also pays the liability for Salary Payable. Thus the Salary Payable account has a zero balance which is correct, as shown at the top of this page.

The adjusting and reversing process is repeated year after year. Cash payments for salaries are debited to Salary Expense, and these amounts accumulate in that account. At the end of the year, the accountant makes an adjusting entry to accrue salary expense incurred but not yet paid. At the same time, the accountant also makes a reversing entry, which allows her to record all payroll entries in the customary manner—by routinely debiting Salary Expense. Even in computerized systems, making reversing entries is more efficient than writing a program to locate the amount accrued from the preceding period and making the more complicated journal entry.

Reversing entries deserve emphasis. Accountants often must deal with hundreds or even thousands of repetitive transactions. With reversing entries, accountants don't have to worry that a cash payment might apply in part to an accrued liability recognized at the end of the preceding period. Reversing entries allow them to debit an expense for the full cash expense payment. Reversing entries may be made for all types of accrued expenses. However, they are optional, and some companies do not use them.

Accrued Revenues and the Related Assets _____

Certain revenues, such as interest earned on notes receivable, accrue with the passage of time, just as expenses do. However, a business usually does not record *accrued revenues* daily, weekly, or even monthly. Instead, it records them when it receives cash. Thus at the end of the accounting period, the business may have earned revenue that it has not yet recorded.

Assume the business has a note receivable on which it receives cash interest on February 1 and August 1. Interest accumulates at $200 per month. During 19X3 the business receives $1,200 of interest on August 1, and that amount is the balance in Interest Revenue at December 31, 19X3, before any adjustments. Suppose that between August 1 and December 31 the business has earned additional interest revenue of $1,000, which it will receive February 1, 19X4, along with $200 of interest revenue for January 19X4. The year-end adjusting entry on December 31, 19X3 is

Adjusting Entries

19X3			
Dec. 31	Interest Receivable...............................	1,000	
	Interest Revenue		1,000

After posting, the accounts appear as follows:

Interest Receivable

19X3				
Dec. 31	Adj.	1,000		
Dec. 31	Bal.	1,000		

Interest Revenue

			19X3		
			Aug. 1	CR	1,200
			Dec. 31	Adj.	1,000
			Dec. 31	Bal.	2,200

The 19X3 income statement reports interest revenue of $2,200, and the balance sheet reports interest receivable of $1,000.

Receipt of $1,200 cash interest on February 1, 19X4, eliminates the $1,000 receivable. This receipt also includes $200 interest revenue earned during January 19X4. A reversing entry, dated January 1, 19X4, avoids having to account for these dual effects. The reversing entry is

Reversing Entries

OBJECTIVE 2

Make a reversing entry for an accrued revenue

19X4			
Jan. 1	Interest Revenue......................................	1,000	
	Interest Receivable		1,000

After posting the reversing entry, Interest Receivable and Interest Revenue appear as follows:

Interest Receivable

19X3				19X4			
Dec. 31	Bal.	1,000		Jan. 1	**Rev.**	**1,000**	

Zero balance

Interest Revenue

19X3				19X3			
Dec. 31	Clo.	2,200		Dec. 31	Bal.	2,200	

Zero balance

19X4			
Jan. 1	**Rev.**	**1,000**	

The arrow shows the transfer of the debit balance from Interest Receivable to Interest Revenue. This debit will be eliminated on February 1, 19X4, when the business receives cash interest of $1,200. The cash receipt entry is then routinely recorded:

19X4			
Feb. 1	Cash	1,200	
	Interest Revenue.............................		1,200

After posting, the Interest Revenue account has the correct credit balance of $200, which is the amount of interest revenue earned in 19X4:

Interest Revenue

19X4				19X4			
Jan. 1	Rev.	1,000		Feb. 1	CR	1,200	
				Feb. 1	Bal.	200	

Accountants use reversing entries for all types of accrued revenues, but they are optional.

Summary Problem for Your Review

The fiscal year accounting period of Blue Bell, Inc., maker of Wrangler jeans, ends on September 30. After going through the accounting process, including the adjusting entries, Blue Bell reported its *accrued liabilities* on a recent balance sheet as follows. These accrued liabilities resulted directly from the adjusting entries.

Liabilities

Notes payable—Banks and other	$135,419,000
Current maturities of long-term debt	3,664,000
Accounts payable, principally trade	120,697,000
Dividends payable	5,756,000
Accrued liabilities:	
Compensation [salaries and wages]	**23,620,000**
Pension and profit sharing	**4,981,000**
Income taxes	**21,624,000**
Taxes—Other than income	**8,028,000**
Interest	**3,534,000**
Other	**7,983,000**
Total	$335,306,000

The company's accrued liability for compensation is its unpaid compensation expense for the year ended September 30.

Required

1. Journalize adjusting entries like those that Blue Bell made at September 30 to record accrued compensation expense and accrued interest expense.
2. Journalize the related reversing entries. Date them appropriately.
3a. Set up ledger accounts for Compensation Payable and Compensation Expense, on September 30, prior to the adjusting entries in Requirement 1. Compensation Payable had a zero balance and Compensation Expense had a debit balance of $380,000,000.
   b. Journalize the closing entry for Compensation Expense at September 30.
   c. Assume Blue Bell paid compensation of $25 million on October 3. Journalize this cash payment, assuming a reversing entry was made.
   d. Post the adjusting, closing, reversing, and cash payment entries to Compensation Payable and Compensation Expense. Use the appropriate dates and label adjusting entries as Adj., closing entries as Clo., reversing entries as Rev., and cash payments as CP.
   e. After all postings, what is the balance in Compensation Payable? What does this mean? What is the balance in Compensation Expense? What does this balance mean?

SOLUTION TO REVIEW PROBLEM

1. Adjusting entries at September 30:

Adjusting Entries

Sep. 30	Compensation Expense	23,620,000	
	Compensation Payable...........		23,620,000
30	Interest Expense	3,534,000	
	Interest Payable................		3,534,000

2. Reversing entries at October 1:

Reversing Entries

Oct. 1	Compensation Payable................	23,620,000	
	Compensation Expense...........		23,620,000
1	Interest Payable.....................	3,534,000	
	Interest Expense		3,534,000

3a. Ledger accounts and balances prior to September 30 adjusting entries:

Compensation Payable

Compensation Expense

CP		
CP		
Sep. 30 Bal.	380,000,000	

b. Closing entry at September 30:

Closing Entries

Sep. 30	Income Summary ($380,000,000 + $23,620,000).....................	403,620,000	
	Compensation Expense		403,620,000

c. Cash payment for compensation at October 3:

Oct. 3	Compensation Expense	25,000,000	
	Cash		25,000,000

d. Ledger accounts posted:

Compensation Payable

Oct. 1	Rev.	23,620,000	Sep. 30	Adj.	23,620,000

Zero balance

Compensation Expense

	CP		ζ			
	CP		ζ			
			380,000,000			
Sep. 30	Adj.		23,620,000			
Sep. 30	Bal.		403,620,000	Sep. 30	Clo.	403,620,000
Oct. 3	CP		25,000,000	Oct. 1	Rev.	23,620,000
Oct. 3	Bal.		1,380,000			

e. The balance in Compensation Payable is zero. This means Blue Bell has no compensation liability. The debit balance in Compensation Expense is $1,380,000. This amount is the portion of the October 3 payment that is compensation expense of the new year.

Prepaid Expenses

Prepaid expenses are advance payments of expenses. Prepaid Insurance, Prepaid Rent, Prepaid Advertising, and Prepaid Legal Cost are prepaid expenses. Supplies that will be used up in the current period or within one year are also accounted for as prepaid expenses.

OBJECTIVE 3
Record prepaid expenses in two ways

When a business prepays an expense—rent, for example—it can debit an *asset* account (Prepaid Rent) as follows:

Prepaid Rent XXX
    Cash. XXX

Alternatively, the accountant can debit an *expense* account in the entry to record this cash payment, as follows:

Rent Expense. XXX
    Cash. XXX

Regardless of the account debited, the business must adjust the accounts at the end of the period. Making the adjustment allows the business to report the correct amount of expense for the period and the correct amount of asset at the period's end.

Prepaid Expense Recorded Initially as an Asset

Prepayments of expenses provide a future benefit to the business, so it is logical to record the prepayment by debiting an *asset* account. Suppose on August 1, 19X6, the business prepays one year's rent of $6,000 ($500 per month). The cash payment is recorded:

19X6
Aug. 1 Prepaid Rent 6,000
         Cash. 6,000

On December 31, the end of the accounting period, five months' prepayment has expired and must be accounted for as *expense.* The adjusting entry is

Adjusting Entries

19X6

Dec. 31   Rent Expense ($6,000 $\times$ 5/12).   2,500
                   Prepaid Rent   2,500

The adjusting entry transfers $2,500 of the original $6,000 prepayment from Prepaid Rent to Rent Expense. This leaves a $3,500 debit balance in Prepaid Rent, which is seven months' rent still prepaid. After posting, the accounts appear as follows:

Prepaid Rent

19X6			19X6		
Aug. 1	CP	6,000	Dec. 31	Adj.	2,500
Dec. 31	Bal.	3,500			

Rent Expense

19X6				
Dec. 31	Adj.	2,500		
Dec. 31	Bal.	2,500		

The $2,500 balance of Rent Expense is closed to Income Summary, along with all other expenses and revenues, at the end of the accounting period.

No reversing entry is used under this approach. The asset account Prepaid Rent has a debit balance to start the new period. This is consistent with recording prepaid expenses initially as assets.

The balance sheet at December 31, 19X6, reports Prepaid Rent of $3,500 as an asset. The 19X6 income statement reports Rent Expense of $2,500 as an expense, which is the expired portion of the initial $6,000 rent prepayment. Keep this reporting result in mind as you study the next section.

Prepaid Expense Recorded Initially as an Expense

Prepaying an expense creates an asset. However, the asset may be so short-lived that it will expire in the current accounting period—within one year or less. Thus the accountant may decide to debit the prepayment to an expense account at the time of payment. Continuing with the rent example, the $6,000 cash payment on August 1 may be debited to Rent Expense:

19X6

Aug. 1   Rent Expense.   6,000
                   Cash.   6,000

At December 31 only five months' prepayment has expired, leaving seven months' rent still prepaid. In this case, the accountant must transfer 7/12 of the original prepayment of $6,000, or $3,500, to Prepaid Rent. The adjusting entry decreases the balance of Rent Expense to 5/12 of the original $6,000, or $2,500. The December 31 adjusting entry is

Adjusting Entries

19X6

Dec. 31   Prepaid Rent ($6,000 × 7/12)   3,500

Rent Expense   3,500

After posting, the two accounts appear as follows:

Prepaid Rent

19X6			
Dec. 31	Adj.	3,500	
Dec. 31	Bal.	3,500	

Rent Expense

19X6			19X6		
Aug. 1	CP	6,000	Dec. 31	Adj.	3,500
Dec. 31	Bal.	2,500			

The balance sheet for 19X6 reports Prepaid Rent of $3,500, and the income statement for 19X6 reports Rent Expense of $2,500. Whether the business initially debits the prepayment to an asset account or to an expense account, the financial statements report the same amounts for prepaid rent and rent expense. The Rent Expense's balance is closed at the end of the period.

During the next accounting period, the $3,500 balance in Prepaid Rent will expire and become expense. It is efficient on the beginning date of the new year to make a *reversing entry* that transfers the ending balance of Prepaid Rent back to Rent Expense:

Reversing Entries

19X7

Jan. 1   Rent Expense.   3,500

Prepaid Rent   3,500

> **OBJECTIVE 4**
> Reverse the adjustment for a prepaid expense recorded initially as an expense

This reversing entry avoids later worry about what prepayments become expenses. The arrow shows the transfer of the debit balance from Prepaid Rent to Rent Expense after posting:

Prepaid Rent

19X6			19X7			
Dec. 31	Bal.	3,500	Jan.	1	**Rev.**	**3,500**

Zero balance

Rent Expense

19X6			19X6			
Aug. 1	CP	6,000	Dec. 31	Adj.	3,500	
Dec. 31	Bal.	2,500	Dec. 31	Clo.	2,500	
19X7						
Jan.	1	**Rev.**	**3,500**			

After the reversing entry, the $3,500 amount is lodged in the expense account. This is consistent with recording prepaid expenses initially as expenses. Because this $3,500 amount will become expense during 19X7, no additional adjustment is needed. Subsequent expense prepayments are debited to Rent Expense and then adjusted at the end of the period as outlined here. Reversing entries ease the work of the accounting process for all types of prepaid expenses that are recorded initially as expenses. Reversing entries are *not* used for prepaid expenses that are recorded initially as assets.

Comparing the Two Approaches to Recording Prepaid Expenses

In summary, the two approaches to recording prepaid expenses are similar in that the asset amount reported on the balance sheet and the expense amount reported on the income statement are the same. They differ, however, in the prepayment entries and the adjusting entries. When a prepaid expense is recorded initially as an asset, (1) the adjusting entry transfers the *used* portion of the asset to the expense account and (2) no reversing entry is used. When a prepaid expense is recorded initially as an expense, (1) the adjusting entry transfers the *unused* portion of the expense to the asset account and (2) a reversing entry transfers the amount of the asset account back to the expense account to start the new accounting period.

Unearned (Deferred) Revenues _____

Unearned (deferred) revenues arise when a business collects cash in advance of earning the revenue. The recognition of revenue is *deferred* until later when it is earned. Unearned revenues are liabilities because the business that receives cash owes the other party goods or services to be delivered later.

Recall the prepaid expense examples listed on p. 1131—insurance, rent, advertising, and so on. Prepaid expenses create assets for the business that pays the cash. The business that receives the cash in advance, however, faces a liability. For example, the landlord who receives a tenant's rent in advance must provide future service to the tenant. This is a liability, and the cash the landlord receives is unearned rent revenue. Similarly, unearned revenue arises as magazine publishers sell subscriptions, colleges collect tuition, airlines sell tickets, and attorneys accept advance fees.

When a business receives cash before earning the related revenue, the business debits Cash. It can credit either a *liability* account or a *revenue* account. In either case, the business must make adjusting entries at the end of the period to report the correct amounts of liability and revenue on the financial statements.

Unearned (Deferred) Revenue Recorded Initially as a Liability

Receipt of cash in advance of earning revenue creates a liability, so it is logical to debit Cash and credit a *liability* account. Assume an attorney receives a $7,200 fee in advance from a client on October 1, 19X2. The attorney will earn this amount at the rate of $800 per month during the nine-month period ending June 30, 19X3. The attorney's cash receipt entry is

OBJECTIVE 5

Record unearned revenues in two ways

19X2			
Oct. 1	Cash	7,200	
	Unearned Legal Revenue......................		7,200

On December 31, 19X2, the end of the law firm's accounting period, three months of the fee agreement have elapsed. The attorney has earned 3/9 of the $7,200, or $2,400. The adjusting entry to transfer $2,400 to the revenue account is

Adjusting Entries

19X2
Dec. 31   Unearned Legal Revenue ($7,200 × 3/9)   2,400
                  Legal Revenue   2,400

After posting, the liability and revenue accounts are

Unearned Legal Revenue

19X2			19X2		
Dec. 31	Adj.	2,400	Oct. 1	CR	7,200
			Dec. 31	Bal.	4,800

Legal Revenue

			19X2		
			Dec. 31	Adj.	2,400
			Dec. 31	Bal.	2,400

The law firm's 19X2 income statement reports legal revenue of $2,400, while its balance sheet reports unearned legal revenue of $4,800 as a liability. During 19X3 the attorney will earn the remaining $4,800 and will then make an adjusting entry to transfer $4,800 to the Legal Revenue account. No reversing entry is used. The balance in the liability account is consistent with recording the unearned revenue initially as a liability.

Unearned (Deferred) Revenue Recorded Initially as a Revenue

Receipt of cash in advance of earning the revenue can be credited initially to a *revenue* account. If the business has earned all the revenue within the period during which it received the cash, no adjusting entry is necessary. However, if the business earns only a part of the revenue at the end of the period, it must make adjusting entries.

Suppose on October 1, 19X2, the law firm records the nine-month advance fee of $7,200 as revenue. The cash receipt entry is

19X2
Oct. 1   Cash   7,200
                  Legal Revenue   7,200

At December 31 the attorney has earned only 3/9 of the $7,200, or $2,400. Accordingly, the firm makes an adjusting entry to transfer the unearned portion (6/9 of $7,200, or $4,800) from the revenue account to a liability account.

Adjusting Entries

19X2
Dec. 31   Legal Revenue ($7,200 × 6/9)   4,800
                  Unearned Legal Revenue   4,800

The adjusting entry leaves the earned portion (³/₉, or $2,400) of the original amount in the revenue account. After posting, the total amount ($7,200) is properly divided between the liability account ($4,800) and the revenue account ($2,400), as follows:

Unearned Legal Revenue

		19X2		
		Dec. 31	Adj.	4,800
		Dec. 31	Bal.	4,800

Legal Revenue

19X2			19X2		
Dec. 31	Adj.	4,800	Oct. 1	CR	7,200
			Dec. 31	Bal.	2,400

The attorney's 19X2 income statement reports legal revenue of $2,400, and the balance sheet at December 31, 19X2, reports as a liability the unearned legal revenue of $4,800. Whether the business initially credits a liability account or a revenue account, the financial statements report the same amounts for unearned legal revenue and legal revenue.

The law firm will earn the $4,800 during 19X3. On January 1, 19X3, it is efficient to make a reversing entry in order to transfer the liability balance back to the revenue account. By making the reversing entry, the accountant avoids having to reconsider the situation one year later, when the 19X3 adjusting entries will be made. The reversing entry is

OBJECTIVE 6

Reverse the adjustment for an unearned revenue recorded initially as a revenue

Reversing Entries

19X3			
Jan. 1	Unearned Legal Revenue............................	4,800	
	Legal Revenue.................................		4,800

After posting, the liability account has a zero balance. The $4,800 credit is now lodged in the revenue account because it will be earned during 19X3. The arrow in the following example shows the transfer from the liability account to the revenue account.

Unearned Legal Revenue

			19X2		
			Dec. 31	Adj.	4,800
19X3			19X2		
Jan. 1	**Rev.**	**4,800**	Dec. 31	Bal.	4,800

Zero balance

Legal Revenue

19X2			19X2		
Dec. 31	Adj.	4,800	Oct. 1	CR	7,200
Dec. 31	Clo.	2,400	Dec. 31	Bal.	2,400
			19X3		
			Jan. 1	**Rev.**	**4,800**

Subsequent advance receipts of revenue are credited to the Legal Revenue account. The year-end adjusting process is the same for every period.

Comparing the Two Approaches to Recording Unearned (Deferred) Revenues

The two approaches to recording unearned revenue are similar in that the liability amount reported on the balance sheet and the revenue amount reported on the income statement are the same. The approaches differ, though, in how adjustments are handled. When unearned revenues are recorded initially as liabilities, (1) the adjusting entry transfers to the revenue account the amount of the advance collection that has been *earned* during the period, and (2) *no* reversing entry is used. When unearned revenues are recorded initially as revenue, (1) the adjustment transfers to the liability account the amount of the advance collection that is still *unearned,* and (2) a reversing entry transfers the balance of the liability account to the revenue account to begin the next accounting period.

Summary Problem for Your Review

Pizza Time Theatre, Inc., reported prepaid expenses of $429,380 on a recent balance sheet. Assume that during the year the company paid cash in the amount of $1 million for prepaid insurance, rent, and so on.

Required

Record the company's prepaid expense transactions and related adjusting, closing, and reversing entries, assuming the company records prepaid expenses initially as (1) an asset and (2) an expense. Record entries in a single Prepaid Expense account and a single Expense account.

SOLUTION TO REVIEW PROBLEM

1. Prepaid expense recorded initially as an *asset*:
   Cash payment of $1,000,000:

Prepaid Expense............................	1,000,000	
Cash		1,000,000

   Year-end adjusting entry:

Expense ($1,000,000 − $429,380)...............	570,620	
Prepaid Expense........................		570,620

Year-end closing entry:

Income Summary	570,620	
Expense		570,620

Reversing entry: None

2. Prepaid expense recorded initially as an *expense*:
   Cash payment of $1,000,000:

Expense	1,000,000	
Cash		1,000,000

Year-end adjusting entry:

Prepaid Expense	429,380	
Expense		429,380

Year-end closing entry:

Income Summary	570,620	
Expense		570,620

Reversing entry dated January 1 of new year:

Expense	429,380	
Prepaid Expense		429,380

Summary

Accrual entries may be accompanied by *reversing entries,* which eliminate the need to refer back to the adjusting entries of the preceding period when recording the cash payments and receipts of a new period. They are the exact opposite of the related adjusting entry. An efficiency device, they eliminate the need to refer back to a preceding period's adjusting entries when making cash entries in the next period. However, they are optional.

Prepaid expenses may be recorded initially in an *asset* account or an *expense* account. When prepaid expenses are recorded initially as an asset, no need exists for a reversing entry because the asset account balance will be adjusted at the end of the next period. However, when prepaid expenses are recorded initially as an expense, a reversing entry eases accounting for the expense of the new period. Regardless of the approach taken, the financial statements should report the same amount of asset and expense.

Unearned (deferred) revenues may be recorded initially as a *liability* or a *revenue.* Recording unearned revenues initially as liabilities causes no need for a reversing entry. However, when recording them initially as revenues, a reversing entry eases accounting. Either recording approach is acceptable as long as the *financial statements* report the *correct* amounts.

Self-Study Questions

Test your understanding of this appendix by marking the best answer for each of the following questions.

1. The reversing entry for a $900 accrual of salary expense is *(p. 615)*

   a. Salary Expense.. 900
       Salary Payable.................................... 900
   b. Salary Expense.. 900
       Cash.. 900
   c. Salary Payable.. 900
       Cash.. 900
   d. Salary Payable.. 900
       Salary Expense.................................... 900

2. Reversing entries are dated *(p. 615)*
   a. The date on which the entry is made
   b. The beginning of the next period
   c. The end of the period
   d. Any of the above

3. The benefit of reversing entries is that they *(p. 617)*
   a. Eliminate the need for adjusting entries
   b. Close out the balances in all the revenues and expenses
   c. Streamline the accounting for transactions in a period following an adjusting entry
   d. Increase the amounts of assets and decrease the amounts of liabilities reported on the balance sheet

4. Which of the following entries would it be helpful to reverse? *(pp. 617–18, 623)*

   a. Interest Receivable.................................... XXX
       Interest Revenue XXX
   b. Rent Expense XXX
       Prepaid Rent XXX
   c. Cash... XXX
       Interest Receivable.............................. XXX
   d. Supplies XXX
       Supplies Expense................................ XXX

   d. Both a and b
   e. Both a and d
   f. None of the above

5. Recording a prepaid expense initially as an asset *(pp. 621, 624)*
   a. Has no effect on the amount of asset and expense reported in the financial statements so long as the correct adjusting entry is made at the end of the period.
   b. Leads to reporting the correct amount of asset and expense in the financial statements.
   c. Leads to reporting an incorrect amount of asset and expense in the financial statements.
   d. Is illogical. It is more logical to record the prepaid expense initially as an expense.

Answers to the self-study questions are at the end of the appendix.

Accounting Vocabulary

reversing entry *(p. 615)*.

ASSIGNMENT MATERIAL _____

Questions

1. What are the identifying characteristics of a reversing entry? What is the practical value of reversing entries?
2. The title Accrued Expenses does not include the word *liability* or *payable*. Why are accrued expenses liabilities?
3. What are the two ways to initially record a prepaid expense? How are they similar? How are they different?
4. Explain why recording a prepaid expense initially as an expense calls for a reversing entry.
5. Unearned revenues are also called deferred revenues. Why?
6. Suppose your company receives cash from customers in advance of earning the revenue. Which approach to recording the unearned revenue would you take and why?
7. Which approach to recording unearned (deferred) revenues calls for a reversing entry?
8. Each of the following adjusting entries is incomplete. Indicate the account debited or credited in the other half of the entry.

Accounts Receivable	XXX	
a		XXX
b		XXX
Wage Payable		XXX
Supplies Expense	XXX	
c		XXX
Unearned Revenue	XXX	
d		XXX

9. Indicate whether each of the following accounts is (a) an asset, (b) a liability, (c) a revenue, or (d) an expense: Unearned Legal Revenue, Interest Receivable, Prepaid Rent, Sales Revenue, Insurance Expense, Supplies, Salary Expense, Income Tax Expense, Property Tax Payable, Deferred Subscription Revenue, Service Fees Earned.
10. Where is the ultimate emphasis in financial accounting? How do adjusting entries tie into this emphasis?

Exercises

Exercise B-1   *Journalizing and posting wage payment and accrual transactions*

During 19X2 London Sales Company pays wages of $40,800 to its employees. At December 31, 19X2, the company owes accrued wages of $900 that will be included in the $1,200 weekly payroll payment on January 4, 19X3.

Required

1. Open T-accounts for Wage Expense and Wage Payable.
2. Journalize all wage transactions for the year, including adjusting, closing, and reversing entries. Record the $40,800 amount by a single debit to Wage Expense.
3. Post amounts to the two T-accounts, showing their balances at January 4, 19X3. Denote cash payment entries by CP, adjusting entries by Adj., closing entries by Clo., reversing entries by Rev., and balances by Bal.

Exercise B-2   *Recording supplies transactions two ways*

At the beginning of the year supplies of $1,490 were on hand. During the year the business paid $3,300 cash for supplies. At the end of the year the count of supplies indicates the ending balance is $1,260.

Required

1. Assume the business records supplies by initially debiting an *asset* account. Therefore, place the beginning balance in the Supplies T-account and record the above entries directly in the accounts without using a journal.
2. Assume the business records supplies by initially debiting an *expense* account. Therefore, place the beginning balance in the Supplies Expense T-account and record the above entries directly in the accounts without using a journal.
3. Compare the ending account balances under the two approaches. Are they the same or different? Why?

Exercise B-3   *Recording unearned revenues two ways*

At the beginning of the year the company owed customers $6,450 for unearned sales collected in advance. During the year the business received advance cash receipts of $10,000. At year end the unearned revenue liability is $3,900.

Required

1. Assume the company records unearned revenues by initially crediting a *liability* account. Open T-accounts for Unearned Sales Revenue and Sales Revenue and place the beginning balance in Unearned Sales Revenue. Journalize the cash collection and adjusting entries and post their dollar amounts. As references in the T-accounts, denote a balance by Bal., a cash receipt by CR, and an adjustment by Adj.
2. Assume the company records unearned revenues by initially crediting a *revenue* account. Open T-accounts for Unearned Sales Revenue and Sales Revenue and place the beginning balance in Sales Revenue. Journalize the cash collection and adjusting entries and post their dollar amounts. As references in the T-accounts, denote a balance by Bal., a cash receipt by CR, and an adjustment by Adj.
3. Compare the ending balances in the two accounts. Explain why they are the same or different.

Exercise B-4   *Using reversing entries to account for unearned revenues*

One approach to recording unearned revenue in Exercise B-3 calls for a reversing entry. Identify that approach. Journalize and post the entries required in Exercise B-3 and also the closing and reversing entries. The end of the current period is December 31, 19X1. Use dates for all entries and postings except the cash collection, which is a summary of the year's transactions. As references in the ledger accounts, denote a balance by Bal., cash receipts by CR, adjusting entries by Adj., closing entries by Clo., and reversing entries by Rev.

Exercise B-5   *Recording accrued revenues with and without reversing entries*

Columbus Corporation receives a note receivable on November 1, 19X5. During the remainder of the year, Columbus earns accrued interest revenue of $3,000. This amount will be collected on May 1, 19X6, along with $6,000 of interest revenue for 19X6.

Required

1. Open T-accounts for Interest Receivable and Interest Revenue. Journalize and post the interest accrual and cash collection transactions and the closing entry, assuming reversing entries are not used. As references in the ledger accounts, denote a balance by Bal., cash receipts by CR, adjusting entries by Adj., closing entries by Clo., and reversing entries by Rev.
2. Repeat requirement 1, assuming reversing entries are used.
3. Compare the account balances achieved in requirements 1 and 2.

Exercise B-6 *Identifying transactions from a ledger account*

McGraw Company makes its annual insurance payment on June 30. Identify each of the entries (a) through (e) to the Insurance Expense account as a cash payment, an adjusting entry, a closing entry, or a reversing entry. Also give the other account debited or credited in each entry.

Insurance Expense

Date	Item	Debit	Credit	Balance Debit	Balance Credit
19X4					
Jan. 1	(a)	800		800	
June 30	(b)	1,240		2,040	
Dec. 31	(c)		410	1,630	
Dec. 31	(d)		1,630	—	
19X5					
Jan. 1	(e)	410			410

Problems   *(Group A)*

Problem B-1A   *Recording prepaid rent and revenue collected in advance two ways*

DeGroot Sales and Service completes the following transactions during 19X4:

Aug. 31   Pays $9,000 store rent covering the six-month period ending February 28, 19X5.

Dec.   1   Collects $2,200 cash in advance from customers. The service revenue will be earned $550 monthly over the period ending March 30, 19X5.

Required

1. Journalize these entries by debiting an asset account for Prepaid Rent and by crediting a liability account for Unearned Service Revenue. Explanations are unnecessary.
2. Journalize the related adjustments at December 31, 19X4.
3. Post the entries to the ledger accounts and show their balances at December 31, 19X4. Posting references are unnecessary.
4. Repeat Requirements 1 through 3. This time debit Rent Expense for the rent payment and credit Service Revenue for the collection of revenue in advance.
5. Compare the account balances in Requirements 3 and 4. They should be equal.

Problem B-2A   *Journalizing adjusting and reversing entries*

Vidmar Company's accounting records reveal the following information before adjustments at December 31, 19X3, the end of the accounting period:

a. Wages owed to hourly employees total $3,400. Total salaries owed to salaried employees are $2,790. These amounts will be paid on the next scheduled payday in January 19X4.
b. On October 31 Vidmar loaned $40,000 to another business. The loan agreement requires the borrower to pay Vidmar interest of $2,400 on April 30, 19X4. One third of this interest is earned in 19X3.
c. Vidmar routinely debits Sales Supplies when it purchases supplies. At the beginning of 19X3 supplies of $800 were on hand, and during the year the company purchased supplies of $6,700. At year end the count of sales supplies on hand indicates the ending amount is $950.
d. Vidmar collects revenue in advance from customers and credits such amounts to Sales Revenue because the revenue is usually earned within a short time. At December 31,

19X3, however, the company has a liability of $6,840 to customers for goods they paid for in advance.

e. Rentals cost the company $1,000 per month. The company prepays rent of $6,000 each May 1 and November 1 and debits Rent Expense for such payments.

f. On December 23 Vidmar Company received a property tax bill from the city. The total amount, due on February 1, 19X4, is $4,600. Half of this amount is property tax expense for 19X3.

g. The company prepaid $3,500 for television advertising that will run daily for two weeks—December 27, 19X3 through January 9, 19X4. Vidmar debited Prepaid Advertising for the full amount on December 1.

Required

1. Journalize the adjusting entry needed for each situation at December 31, 19X3, identifying each entry by its corresponding letter.

2. Journalize reversing entries as needed. Use the corresponding letters for references. Date the entries appropriately.

3. Use the first situation that calls for a reversing entry to explain the practical value of the reversal.

Problem B-3A   *Preparing an adjusted trial balance; journalizing reversing entries*

The year-end trial balance of Retton Company at July 31 of the current year appears as follows:

Retton Company
Trial Balance
July 31, 19XX

Account Title	Balance Debit	Balance Credit
Cash..............................	$ 3,960	
Accounts receivable	14,700	
Note receivable	78,330	
Prepaid rent........................	6,000	
Prepaid insurance		
Furniture	9,600	
Accumulated depreciation		$ 4,200
Accounts payable		16,090
Wage payable		
Salary payable......................		
Interest payable.....................		
Unearned service revenue		
Notes payable		30,000
M. L. Retton, capital		48,490
M. L. Retton, withdrawals	46,000	
Service revenue.....................		129,000
Advertising expense	3,000	
Wage expense	31,750	
Salary expense......................	26,300	
Rent expense.......................		
Utilities expense	3,640	
Depreciation expense		
Insurance expense...................	2,400	
Interest expense.....................	2,100	
Total.............................	$227,780	$227,780

The accounting records reveal the following additional data at July 31, 19XX.

a. Accrued wages of $1,400 and accrued salaries of $640 at July 31.
b. Retton records advance collections from customers by crediting Service Revenue. At July 31, $2,400 of the balance of Service Revenue has still not been earned. This amount of revenue will be earned early in August.
c. Prepaid rent expired during the year, $5,300. When Retton pays rent, he debits Prepaid Rent.
d. Insurance expense for the year, $2,100. When Retton pays insurance, he debits Insurance Expense.
e. Depreciation on furniture for the year, $1,200.
f. Accrued interest expense at July 31, $430.

Required

1. Write the trial balance on a sheet of paper, enter the adjustments in adjacent columns, and prepare the adjusted trial balance at July 31 of the current year.
2. Journalize the reversing entries, as appropriate, at August 1.

Problem B-4A *Identifying adjustments and the related reversing entries*

The unadjusted and adjusted balances are shown below for selected accounts. Journalize the adjusting entries that were made and posted at May 31, 19X5, the end of the accounting period. Where appropriate, also journalize the reversing entries at June 1, 19X5.

	Unadjusted Balance	Adjusted Balance
Interest receivable	$ —	$ 1,465
Prepaid rent.	4,500	1,500
Supplies	—	940
Accumulated depreciation	12,900	15,300
Salary payable	—	3,090
Property tax payable	—	1,300
Unearned sales revenue	—	790
Sales revenue	98,870	98,080
Interest revenue	3,590	5,055
Salary expense	49,550	52,640
Rent expense	—	3,000
Supplies expense	5,560	4,620
Property tax expense	2,110	3,410
Depreciation expense	—	2,400

Problem B-5A *Recording supplies and unearned revenue transactions two ways*

The accounting records of Stone Company reveal the following information about sales supplies and unearned sales revenue for 19X5:

Sales Supplies

19X5		
Jan. 1	Beginning amount on hand	$ 420
Mar. 16	Cash purchase of supplies	3,740
Dec. 31	Ending amount on hand	290

Unearned Sales Revenue

19X5

Jan. 1	Beginning amount on advance collections	6,590
July 22	Advance cash collection from customer	16,480
Nov. 4	Advance cash collection from customer	38,400
Dec. 31	Advance collections earned during the year.	52,160

Required

1. Assume Stone Company records (a) supplies by initially debiting an asset account and (b) advance collections from customers by initially crediting a liability account
   a. Open T-accounts for Sales Supplies, Sales Supplies Expense, Unearned Sales Revenue, and Sales Revenue. Insert the beginning balances in the appropriate accounts.
   b. Record the cash transactions during 19X5 directly in the accounts.
   c. Record the adjusting and closing entries at December 31, 19X5, directly in the accounts.
   d. If appropriate, record the reversing entries at January 1, 19X6, directly in the accounts.
2. Assume Stone Company records (a) supplies by initially debiting an expense account and (b) advance collections by initially crediting a revenue account. Perform Steps *a* through *d* as in Requirement 1.
3. Using the following format, compare the amounts that would be reported for the above accounts in the 19X5 balance sheet and income statement under the two recording approaches of Requirements 1 and 2. Explain any similarity or difference.

	Requirement 1	Requirement 2
Balance sheet at December 31, 19X5 reports:		
Sales supplies.	$_____	$_____
Unearned sales revenue	_____	_____
Income statement for year ended December 31, 19X5, reports:		
Sales revenue.	_____	_____
Sales supplies expense.	_____	_____

(Group B)

Problem B-1B   *Recording prepaid rent and revenue collected in advance two ways*

McGraw Service Company completes the following transactions during 19X7:

Oct. 31 Pays $4,200 store rent covering the six-month period ending April 30, 19X8.
Nov. 1 Collects $1,800 cash in advance from customers. The service revenue will be earned $600 monthly over the period ending January 31, 19X8.

Required

1. Journalize these entries by debiting an asset account for Prepaid Rent and by crediting a liability account for Unearned Service Revenue. Explanations are unnecessary.
2. Journalize the related adjustments at December 31, 19X7.
3. Post the entries to the ledger accounts and show their balances at December 31, 19X7. Posting references are unnecessary.
4. Repeat Requirements 1 through 3. This time debit Rent Expense for the rent payment and credit Service Revenue for the collection of revenue in advance.
5. Compare the account balances in Requirements 3 and 4. They should be equal.

Problem B-2B   *Journalizing adjusting and reversing entries*

The accounting records of Conner Company reveal the following information before adjustments at December 31, 19X6, the end of the accounting period.

a. On December 29 the company prepaid $2,200 for newspaper advertising that will run for 10 days beginning December 29, 19X6. Conner debited Prepaid Advertising for the full amount.
b. On July 31 Conner deposited $25,000 in a savings account. The bank will pay Conner interest of $1,200 on January 31, 19X7. Of this amount, five sixths is earned in 19X6.
c. On November 29 Conner Company received a property tax bill from the city. The total amount, due on January 15, 19X7, is $3,900. Three fourths of this amount is property tax expense of 19X6.
d. Commissions owed to sales employees at December 31 are $2,565, and salaries owed to home office employees are $1,870.
e. Conner collected revenue of $12,400 in advance from customers during the year. The company expected to earn the revenue during the year, so it credited Sales Revenue for the full amount. However, at December 31, the company has not yet shipped $3,169 of these goods.
f. On December 1 the company paid $4,500 rent for December, January, and February. It is company practice to debit Rent Expense for such prepayments.
g. Conner routinely debits Sales Supplies when it purchases supplies. At the beginning of 19X6 supplies of $380 were on hand, and during the year the company paid $4,000 for supplies. At year end, supplies of $510 are on hand.

Required

1. Journalize the adjusting entry needed for each situation at December 31, 19X6, identifying each entry by its corresponding letter.
2. Journalize reversing entries as needed. Use the corresponding letters for references. Date the entries.
3. Use the first situation that calls for a reversing entry to explain the practical value of the reversal.

Problem B-3B   *Preparing an adjusted trial balance; journalizing reversing entries*

The year-end trial balance of Saxman Company at June 30 of the current year appears as shown on the following page.
    The accounting records reveal the following additional data at June 30, 19XX:

a. Accrued wages of $970 and accrued salaries of $880 at June 30.
b. Saxman records advance collections from customers by crediting Service Revenue. At June 30, $1,780 of the balance of Service Revenue has still not been earned.
c. Prepaid rent expired during the year, $1,400. When Saxman pays rent, she debits Prepaid Rent.
d. Insurance expense for the year, $3,640. When Saxman pays insurance, she debits Insurance Expense.
e. Depreciation on furniture for the year, $2,600.
f. Accrued interest expense at June 30, $560.

Required

1. Write the trial balance on a sheet of paper, enter the adjustments in adjacent columns, and prepare the adjusted trial balance at June 30 of the current year.
2. Journalize the reversing entries, as appropriate, at July 1.

Saxman Company
Trial Balance
June 30, 19XX

Account Title	Debit	Credit
	Balance	
Cash.............................	$ 4,120	
Accounts receivable	23,800	
Note receivable	91,030	
Prepaid insurance		
Prepaid rent........................	1,500	
Furniture	14,700	
Accumulated depreciation		$ 6,280
Accounts payable		24,630
Wage payable		
Salary payable.......................		
Interest payable.....................		
Unearned service revenue		
Notes payable		42,000
Betty Saxman, capital		55,170
Betty Saxman, withdrawals	41,000	
Service revenue......................		136,000
Advertising expense	3,750	
Wage expense	40,900	
Salary expense.......................	31,200	
Rent expense........................		
Utilities expense	4,200	
Depreciation expense		
Insurance expense....................	3,880	
Interest expense......................	4,000	
Total..............................	$264,080	$264,080

Problem B-4B *Identifying adjustments and the related reversing entries*

The unadjusted and adjusted balances are shown below for selected accounts. Journalize the adjusting entries that were made and posted at January 31, 19X2, the end of the accounting period. Where appropriate, also journalize the reversing entries at February 1, 19X2.

	Unadjusted Balance	Adjusted Balance
Interest receivable...................	$ —	$ 780
Prepaid insurance	3,400	860
Supplies...........................	—	1,195
Accumulated depreciation	32,600	39,100
Wage payable	—	2,285
Income tax payable...................	—	2,860
Unearned sales revenue	—	2,390
Sales revenue	134,670	132,280
Interest revenue....................	3,300	4,080
Wage expense	24,660	26,945
Insurance expense...................	—	2,540
Depreciation expense	—	6,500
Supplies expense....................	7,990	6,795
Income tax expense.................	11,800	14,660

Problem B-5B   *Recording prepaid expense and unearned revenue transactions two ways*

The accounting records of Waco Publications reveal the following information about prepaid insurance and unearned subscription revenue for 19X7:

Prepaid Insurance

19X7

Jan. 1	Beginning prepaid amount......................	$ 2,000
Aug. 31	Cash payment of insurance premiums	4,050
Dec. 31	Ending prepaid amount	2,700

Unearned Subscription Revenue

19X7

Jan. 1	Beginning liability for unearned subscriptions	9,640
June 30	Advance cash collections from customers...........	48,500
Dec. 31	Advance cash collections from customers...........	51,980
Dec. 31	Subscription revenue earned during the year........	97,410

Required

1. Assume Waco records (a) prepaid insurance by initially debiting an asset account and (b) advance collections of subscriptions from customers by initially crediting a liability account.
   a. Open accounts for Prepaid Insurance, Insurance Expense, Unearned Subscription Revenue, and Subscription Revenue. Insert the beginning balances in the appropriate accounts.
   b. Record the cash transactions during 19X7 directly in the accounts.
   c. Record the adjusting and closing entries at December 31, 19X7, directly in the accounts.
   d. If appropriate, record the reversing entries at January 1, 19X8, directly in the accounts.
2. Assume Waco records (a) prepaid insurance by initially debiting an expense account and (b) advance collections on subscriptions by initially crediting a revenue account. Perform Steps *a* through *d* as in Requirement 1.
3. Using the following format, compare the amounts that would be reported for the above accounts in the 19X7 balance sheet and income statement under the two recording approaches of Requirements 1 and 2. Explain any similarity or difference.

	Requirement 1	Requirement 2
Balance sheet at December 31, 19X7, reports:		
Prepaid insurance	$_____	$_____
Unearned subscription revenue	_____	_____
Income statement for year ended December 31, 19X7, reports:		
Subscription revenue..........................	_____	_____
Insurance expense	_____	_____

Answers to Self-Study Questions

1. d   2. b   3. c   4. e   5. a

C

Published
Financial Statements

STOCKHOLDERS AND BOARD OF DIRECTORS
GULF+WESTERN INC.

We have examined the consolidated balance sheet of Gulf+Western Inc. as of October 31, 1987 and 1986, and the related consolidated statements of earnings, changes in stockholders' equity and cash flows for each of the three years in the period ended October 31, 1987. Our examinations were made in accordance with generally accepted auditing standards and, accordingly, included such tests of the accounting records and such other auditing procedures as we considered necessary in the circumstances.

In our opinion, the financial statements referred to above present fairly the consolidated financial position of Gulf+Western Inc. at October 31, 1987 and 1986, and the consolidated results of its operations and cash flows for each of the three years in the period ended October 31, 1987, in conformity with generally accepted accounting principles applied on a consistent basis.

Ernst + Whinney

New York, New York
December 18, 1987

GULF+WESTERN INC.

Gulf+Western Inc.

1 9 8 7   SELECTED FINANCIAL DATA

The table below summarizes recent financial information for Gulf+Western. For further information, refer to the audited financial statements and the notes thereto contained elsewhere herein.

Year Ended or at October 31	1987	1986	1985	1984	1983
	(Dollar amounts in millions, except per share)				
Revenues	$4,681.1	$3,781.1	$3,320.7	$2,818.3	$2,522.3
Net revenues	2,903.6	2,093.8	1,860.8	1,582.3	1,436.5
Earnings from continuing operations before income taxes	608.7	386.3	235.2	213.3	277.7
Earnings from continuing operations before extraordinary items	356.1	228.7	151.6	137.4	185.5
Net earnings (loss)	356.1	267.4	247.8	235.9	(191.7)
Earnings (loss) per share					
From continuing operations before extraordinary items	5.76	3.66	2.15	1.93	2.39
Net earnings (loss)	5.76	4.28	3.51	3.32	(2.54)
Cash dividends declared per common share	1.125	.90	.90	.90	.788
Working capital	776.3	492.0	614.5	1,018.5	1,033.0
Total assets	4,928.9	4,243.4	4,064.1	4,202.6	4,553.7
Notes payable and current maturities of long-term debt	64.9	29.8	121.9	72.1	213.1
Long-term debt, net of current maturities	1,334.9	1,260.8	1,076.1	894.1	1,001.7
Stockholders' equity	2,106.6	1,902.1	1,737.7	1,875.7	1,958.0
Book value per common share	35.05	30.85	27.91	26.75	25.32
Capital expenditures	57.1	73.6	62.8	68.9	49.3
Number of stockholders					
Common Stock	31,000	34,000	39,000	46,000	49,000
Preferred stock	3,000	3,000	3,000	3,000	4,000

Reference is made to Note B to the consolidated financial statements for a description of the Company's discontinued operations.

Gulf+Western Inc.

CONSOLIDATED STATEMENT OF EARNINGS

Year Ended October 31	1987	1986	1985
	(In millions, except per share)		
Revenues..	**$4,681.1**	$3,781.1	$3,320.7
Less revenues of unconsolidated finance subsidiary — Note A	**1,777.5**	1,687.3	1,459.9
Net Revenues	**2,903.6**	2,093.8	1,860.8
Earnings of unconsolidated finance subsidiary before income taxes — Note A............	**324.1**	289.5	251.0
	3,227.7	2,383.3	2,111.8
Cost of goods sold	**1,753.5**	1,215.8	1,178.2
Selling, general and administrative expenses	**751.8**	671.3	576.2
	2,505.3	1,887.1	1,754.4
Operating Income	**722.4**	496.2	357.4
Other expense	**(1.0)**	(2.4)	(6.0)
Interest expense — net — Note J...	**(112.7)**	(107.5)	(116.2)
Earnings from Continuing Operations Before Income Taxes	**608.7**	386.3	235.2
Provision for income taxes — Notes A and H.......................................	**252.6**	157.6	83.6
Earnings from Continuing Operations Before Extraordinary Items	**356.1**	228.7	151.6
Extraordinary items — Note C..		38.7	
Earnings from discontinued operations — Note B			96.2
Net Earnings...	**$ 356.1**	$ 267.4	$ 247.8
Dividends on preferred stock	**$ 0.8**	$ 0.8	$ 0.8
Average common and common equivalent shares outstanding — Note A.................	**61.7**	62.3	70.3
Earnings per share — Note A			
From continuing operations before extraordinary items	**$ 5.76**	$ 3.66	$ 2.15
Net earnings..	**5.76**	4.28	3.51

See notes to consolidated financial statements.

25

Gulf+Western Inc.

⬛⬛⬛⬛ FINANCIAL REPORTING BY BUSINESS SEGMENTS

A summary description of the Company's business segments and Consumer/Commercial Finance operations is as follows:

Entertainment
Produces, finances and distributes motion pictures, television programming and prerecorded videocassettes and operates motion picture theatres and sports and entertainment facilities.

Publishing/Information
Publishes and distributes hardcover, mass market and trade paperback books, consumer information and special interest books, educational textbooks and materials, and business and professional information and services.

Consumer/Commercial Finance
Provides consumer finance (including direct installment and revolving credit loans and other consumer finance services) and commercial finance (including transportation and industrial equipment financing) and related insurance products.

REVENUES AND OPERATING INCOME

Year Ended October 31	Revenues 1987	1986	1985	Operating Income 1987	1986	1985
	(In millions)					
Business Segments						
Entertainment	$1,829.6	$1,144.8	$1,062.6	$297.3	$128.8	$ 69.1
Publishing/Information	1,074.0	949.0	798.2	161.5	140.5	103.7
Total	2,903.6	2,093.8	1,860.8	458.8	269.3	172.8
Consumer/Commercial Finance	1,777.5	1,687.3	1,459.9	324.1	289.5	251.0
Corporate Expenses.				(60.5)	(62.6)	(66.4)
	$4,681.1	$3,781.1	$3,320.7	$722.4	$496.2	$357.4

Net revenues by business segment include revenues that are directly associated with a particular segment. Revenues between business segments (amounts are insignificant), which are accounted for on substantially the same basis as revenues from unaffiliated customers, have been eliminated. No single customer accounts for 10% or more of the consolidated net revenues.

Export sales to unaffiliated customers were $365.8, $206.4 and $223.8 million, respectively, for the three years ended October 31, 1987, 1986 and 1985. These sales were principally made in the following foreign geographic areas: Europe, the Far East, Canada and Latin America.

See Note K for additional disclosures related to business segments.

Gulf+Western Inc.

Management's Discussion and Analysis of Financial Condition and Results of Operations

RESULTS OF OPERATIONS

Entertainment

Operating income increased in both fiscal 1987 and fiscal 1986 from fiscal 1985. Results for the current year reflected the box office success of *Beverly Hills Cop II, Fatal Attraction* and *The Untouchables,* the outstanding performances of *Top Gun, Star Trek IV: The Voyage Home, The Golden Child, "Crocodile" Dundee* and *Children of a Lesser God* in both theatrical release and the videocassette market, as well as videocassette sales of *Indiana Jones and the Temple of Doom* and *Ferris Bueller's Day Off.* Television operations increased significantly, primarily because of the domestic syndication of *Cheers* and *Family Ties.* In addition to the above, fiscal 1987 results benefited from the availability of *Witness* and *Ferris Bueller's Day Off* for pay cable and the gain from the sale of Hughes Television Network. Partially offsetting these results was a modest adjustment to domestic syndication bad debt reserves in the first quarter of 1987. The theatre operations reflected record revenues from the Canadian theatre chain due to higher attendance levels and concession sales as well as contributions to earnings from the acquired domestic theatre operations. Operating income for Madison Square Garden declined because of the absence of income earned in the prior-year period from Rangers' playoff games and Hughes Television Network.

Results for fiscal 1986 reflect increases from all operations. The substantial improvement in revenues from theatrical releases was attributable primarily to the blockbuster performance of *Top Gun* and the outstanding results of *Ferris Bueller's Day Off* and *"Crocodile" Dundee.* The recognition of income related to licensing of *Raiders of the Lost Ark, Trading Places, 48 Hours* and *Flashdance* to network television, network profits resulting from the higher domestic syndication sales levels and network license fees of *Family Ties, Cheers* and *Webster,* and the continued growth of the home video operations, which benefited from the strong sales of *Beverly Hills Cop, Witness* and the cassettes included in Paramount's holiday season promotion program, also contributed to the improved results. These increases more than offset the lower syndication income resulting from the timing of renewals of library products. In addition, Madison Square Garden Network and Madison Square Garden Center reported improved earnings. The MSG Network benefited from growth in subscriber revenues, the increased number of events televised, including Rangers' playoff games, and lower programming costs, while Madison Square Garden Center benefited from an expanded schedule of concerts and increased attendance at sporting events. Theatre operations showed improvement as a result of higher concession sales and increased attendance. Fiscal 1986 also reflects the absence of operating losses sustained in the prior year from the coin-operated video game business, which had been shut down.

Publishing/Information

Operating income increased in fiscal 1987 and fiscal 1986 compared with fiscal 1985. Results of the elementary and secondary groups increased in fiscal 1987 because of strong sales performances, which were partially offset by the inclusion in the first six months of fiscal 1987 of the expected seasonal losses of Silver Burdett Company, which was acquired in May 1986. The consumer publishing group registered a significant increase primarily in trade operations, which benefited from such titles as *The Closing of the American Mind, The Great Depression of 1990, Women Who Love Too Much, Dark Angel* and *Veil: The Secret Wars of the CIA 1981–1987.* The international group's operations increased principally as a result of growth in the Asian, Canadian and United Kingdom markets. The professional information group's operating income declined as a result of higher expenses related to tax reform act supplements and increased business development spending. The higher education group posted an increase in operating results due to strong college book sales.

Elementary and secondary publishing operations made the largest contribution to the fiscal 1986 increase as compared with fiscal 1985, benefiting from the acquisition of Silver Burdett Company. The higher education operations increased principally because of revenues from college book and technical publications, while the professional information group benefited from acquired product lines and product enhancements. The international operations' improvement is primarily a result of growth in both the Canadian and United Kingdom markets. These increases more than offset the decline in the consumer publishing operations, which benefited from growth of its direct marketing operations and strong sales of *Hollywood Husbands, A Matter Of Honor* and *The Road Less Traveled* but which were adversely affected by a sluggish market that reduced profit margins in the paperback operations.

Results for the above periods were augmented by the acquisitions of Prentice-Hall, Inc. in December 1984, Ginn & Company in June 1985 and Silver Burdett Company in May 1986 as well as by the operating efficiencies attained through the consolidation of these operations.

Consumer/Commercial Finance

Operating income increased in both fiscal 1987 and fiscal 1986 compared with fiscal 1985 because of the increase in finance charge revenue resulting from the growth of net finance receivables (15.6% in 1987 and 8.4% in 1986) and increases in insurance sales, primarily to commercial finance customers. Consumer operations benefited from increased real estate-secured lending and improved results in mortgage banking and related real estate services as well as from its strong credit card portfolio. Commercial finance gains were achieved primarily in the heavy-duty truck portfolio as a result of receivables growth, while both operations continued to benefit from strict control of operating costs. Interest expense increased for fiscal 1987 and 1986 as a result of the higher average debt outstanding, due to an increased finance receivables portfolio, which was partially offset by a decline in average interest rates. The average interest margin was 8.54%, 8.87% and 8.66% for the years ended October 31, 1987, 1986 and 1985, respectively. Like other consumer finance businesses, the consumer/commercial finance unit experienced a higher level of credit losses during fiscal 1987 compared with fiscal 1986. As a result of a recent Financial Accounting Standards Board pronouncement, the Company will be required to consolidate its consumer/commercial finance subsidiary beginning in fiscal 1989. Separate financial statements for these operations are presented elsewhere herein.

Interest Expense — Net

In addition to the results of the operating units, earnings for fiscal 1987 reflect an increase in interest costs after a decrease in fiscal 1986 versus fiscal 1985. The increase in fiscal 1987 results from an increase in average debt outstanding and a decrease in average short-term investments that more than offset the effect of lower interest rates. The decrease for fiscal 1986 reflects a lower average of debt outstanding during the year as well as lower average interest rates.

LIQUIDITY AND CAPITAL RESOURCES

The Company depended primarily upon internal cash flow and external borrowings to finance its operations during the three years ended October 31, 1987. During fiscal 1987, the Company borrowed $250 million under long-term revolving loan agreements and received $222 million from the sale of certain entertainment receivables with the proceeds used to reduce commercial paper borrowings. During the year ended October 31, 1987, the Company purchased an additional 1.8 million shares of its Common Stock under a 12-million share repurchase program announced in October 1985. Subsequent to October 31, 1987, the Company purchased an additional 1.1 million shares of its Common Stock through December 10, 1987, leaving 0.8 million remaining shares authorized under the program. The Company may authorize an additional share repurchase program in 1988. Total debt as a percentage of total capitalization was 40% at October 31, 1987 and 1986.

At October 31, 1987, available long-term revolving loan agreements were $564 million which were used to support outstanding commercial paper and long-term revolving loan agreement borrowings. In the past, the Company has been able to increase its borrowings as required and expects to be able to continue to do so.

Capital expenditures amounted to $57 million in 1987, $74 million in 1986 and $63 million in 1985.

Effects of Change in Accounting for Income Taxes

The Financial Accounting Standards Board has issued a rule which will materially change the accounting and reporting for income taxes. The Company will be required to comply with its provisions in fiscal 1990.

Recognition of the provisions of the rule may result in a reduction in stockholders' equity not exceeding $80 million depending on the ultimate effect of tax planning alternatives developed prior to the time of adoption. This charge would reflect the elimination of certain deferred tax assets which would not meet the asset recognition requirements of the rule. The rule provides that the reduction in stockholders' equity may be accounted for by a one-time charge to earnings in the year the rule becomes effective or by restatement of prior years' financial statements.

Effects of Inflation and Changing Prices

The Company has, as a result of a restructuring program launched in 1983, divested itself of capital-intensive businesses and has expanded, through acquisitions and internal growth, its non-capital-intensive operations in the entertainment, publishing/information and consumer/commercial finance fields. While inflation affects all companies, its impact on those that are not heavily invested in fixed assets is mitigated because there is less potential for earnings to be inflated by understated depreciation charges or for significant understatement of the current value of assets. Furthermore, the impact of inflation on entertainment and publishing inventories is generally less than that in other industries due to the rapidity of their turnover, the uniqueness of product and the manner in which they are produced.

Helping to offset inflation's impact is the Company's maintenance of a net monetary liability position, since these liabilities will be paid with dollars of decreased purchasing power during inflationary times. Management believes that as a result of its concentration in non-capital-intensive operations, along with various Company programs designed to ensure the efficient utilization of resources and the control of costs, it has taken the necessary steps to minimize the effects of inflation on its operations.

Gulf+Western Inc.

CONSOLIDATED BALANCE SHEET

October 31	1987	1986
ASSETS	(In millions)	
Current Assets		
Cash and cash equivalents	$ 365.0	$ 61.5
Trade receivables, net of allowance for doubtful accounts of $51.8 million in 1987 and $29.0 million in 1986	642.6	540.3
Inventories — Notes A and D	324.6	277.6
Prepaid expenses, income taxes and other — Note J	405.1	390.8
Total Current Assets	1,737.3	1,270.2
Property, Plant and Equipment — Note A		
Land	93.7	90.7
Buildings	244.1	231.2
Machinery, equipment and other	182.5	192.2
	520.3	514.1
Less allowance for depreciation	142.2	121.5
	378.1	392.6
Other Assets		
Investment in affiliated companies — Notes A, B and E	1,463.2	1,016.0
Noncurrent receivables and inventories — Notes A and D	286.2	369.5
Intangible assets, net of accumulated amortization of $67.0 million in 1987 and $43.2 million in 1986 — Note A	863.7	1,039.2
Deferred costs and other — Note A	200.4	155.9
	2,813.5	2,580.6
	$4,928.9	$4,243.4
LIABILITIES AND STOCKHOLDERS' EQUITY		
Current Liabilities		
Current maturities of long-term debt	$ 64.9	$ 29.8
Trade accounts payable	122.9	95.4
Accrued expenses and other liabilities — Note J	741.0	643.1
Income taxes payable	32.2	9.9
Total Current Liabilities	961.0	778.2
Deferred Liabilities	526.4	302.3
Long-Term Debt, net of current maturities — Notes A and F	1,334.9	1,260.8
Stockholders' Equity — Note G		
Common Stock, recorded at $1.00 par value; 300,000,000 shares authorized; shares outstanding, 60,110,377 at October 31, 1987 (excluding 28,126,877 shares held in treasury) and 61,657,498 at October 31, 1986 (excluding 26,339,687 shares held in treasury)	60.1	61.7
Paid-in surplus	505.8	508.1
Retained earnings — Notes E, F and H	1,548.0	1,363.7
Cumulative translation adjustments	(7.3)	(31.4)
	2,106.6	1,902.1
	$4,928.9	$4,243.4

See notes to consolidated financial statements.

29

Gulf+Western Inc.

1 9 8 7 CONSOLIDATED STATEMENT OF CHANGES IN STOCKHOLDERS' EQUITY

Three Years Ended October 31, 1987	Common Stock	Paid-in Surplus	Retained Earnings	Cumulative Translation Adjustments	Total Stockholders' Equity
			(In millions)		
Balance at October 31, 1984, net of treasury	$ 70.1	$ 534.9	$ 1,329.8	$ (59.1)	$ 1,875.7
Common Stock issued					
Exercise of stock options and grants to employees	1.0	28.8			29.8
Dividend reinvestment and stock purchase plan	0.1	2.3			2.4
Conversion of debentures	0.1	3.2			3.3
Acquisition of stock for the treasury	(9.0)	(71.0)	(317.2)		(397.2)
Cash dividends					
Common Stock ($.90 per share)			(63.1)		(63.1)
Preferred stock			(0.8)		(0.8)
Translation adjustments				6.0	6.0
Realization upon sale of businesses				33.8	33.8
Net earnings for the year			247.8		247.8
Balance at October 31, 1985, net of treasury	62.3	498.2	1,196.5	(19.3)	1,737.7
Common Stock issued					
Exercise of stock options and grants to employees	0.4	16.6			17.0
Dividend reinvestment and stock purchase plan	0.1	2.2			2.3
Acquisition of stock for the treasury	(1.1)	(8.9)	(43.8)		(53.8)
Cash dividends					
Common Stock ($.90 per share)			(55.6)		(55.6)
Preferred stock			(0.8)		(0.8)
Translation adjustments				(12.1)	(12.1)
Net earnings for the year			267.4		267.4
Balance at October 31, 1986, net of treasury	61.7	508.1	1,363.7	(31.4)	1,902.1
Common Stock issued					
Exercise of stock options and grants to employees	**0.2**	**10.5**			**10.7**
Dividend reinvestment and stock purchase plan		**2.3**			**2.3**
Acquisition of stock for the treasury	**(1.8)**	**(15.1)**	**(102.4)**		**(119.3)**
Cash dividends					
Common Stock ($1.125 per share)			**(68.6)**		**(68.6)**
Preferred stock			**(0.8)**		**(0.8)**
Translation adjustments				**24.1**	**24.1**
Net earnings for the year			**356.1**		**356.1**
Balance at October 31, 1987, net of treasury	**$60.1**	**$505.8**	**$1,548.0**	**$ (7.3)**	**$2,106.6**

See notes to consolidated financial statements.

30

Gulf+Western Inc.

CONSOLIDATED STATEMENT OF CASH FLOWS

Year Ended October 31	1987	1986	1985
	(In millions)		
Cash Flows from Continuing Operating Activities			
Earnings from continuing operations before extraordinary items.	$ 356.1	$ 228.7	$ 151.6
Non-cash expenses			
Depreciation	30.0	25.8	23.3
Deferred income taxes.	32.6	83.9	30.2
Amortization of intangible assets	24.0	21.6	20.2
Amortization of plate costs	30.1	24.1	23.7
Gross cash flows provided from continuing operating activities	472.8	384.1	249.0
Undistributed net earnings of unconsolidated affiliates	(135.7)	(104.7)	(72.2)
Theatrical and television inventories			
Gross additions	(477.5)	(381.0)	(366.0)
Amortization	503.8	314.6	324.2
Network features and syndication licenses	10.1	35.0	18.9
Net (increase) decrease in receivables, inventories (other than theatrical and television), payables and other	143.8	(116.5)	(178.2)
Net cash flows provided from (used for) continuing operating activities	517.3	131.5	(24.3)
Cash Flows from Investment and Other Activities			
Expenditures for property, plant and equipment	(57.1)	(73.6)	(62.8)
Proceeds on disposal of property, plant and equipment.	8.8	107.5	1.4
Purchase price of acquired businesses	(107.0)	(398.0)	(808.5)
Increase in investment in affiliated companies	(20.6)	(40.6)	(28.2)
Proceeds on sale of businesses	17.6	100.1	1,113.7
Discontinued operations.			74.1
Decrease in noncurrent receivables	28.9	11.5	13.9
Net cash flows provided from (used for) investment and other activities	(129.4)	(293.1)	303.6
Cash Flows from Financing Activities			
Proceeds of long-term debt		272.6	850.1
Payments of long-term debt	(51.0)	(241.2)	(691.6)
Increase in commercial paper and other borrowings classified as long-term debt	142.3	11.1	106.2
Issuance of Common Stock.	13.0	19.3	32.2
Acquisition of stock for the treasury	(119.3)	(53.8)	(397.2)
Dividends.	(69.4)	(56.4)	(63.9)
Net cash flows used for financing activities	(84.4)	(48.4)	(164.2)
Increase (Decrease) in Cash and Cash Equivalents	303.5	(210.0)	115.1
Cash and Cash Equivalents at Beginning of Year	61.5	271.5	156.4
Cash and Cash Equivalents at End of Year.	$ 365.0	$ 61.5	$ 271.5

See notes to consolidated financial statements.

Gulf+Western Inc.

1 9 8 7 NOTES TO CONSOLIDATED FINANCIAL STATEMENTS

NOTE A — SIGNIFICANT ACCOUNTING POLICIES

Principles of Consolidation

The consolidated financial statements include the accounts of Gulf+Western Inc. ("Company") and its significant majority-owned affiliates other than its consumer/commercial finance subsidiary. The Company's investments in its unconsolidated finance subsidiary and 20–50% owned investees are carried on the equity basis. The income taxes of the unconsolidated finance subsidiary and investees are included in the provision for income taxes.

Certain amounts in the consolidated financial statements for periods prior to fiscal 1987 have been reclassified to conform to current presentation for comparative purposes.

Inventories

Inventories are generally determined using the lower of cost (first-in, first-out or average cost method) or net realizable value.

Theatrical and Television Inventories, Revenues and Costs

Feature films are produced or acquired for distribution normally first in the theatrical market followed by, in usual order of priority, videocassettes, pay cable, network television and syndicated television. On average, the length of the revenue cycle for feature films approximates four years. Television series produced for the networks are licensed first to television networks and foreign markets; the more successful ones are later syndicated in domestic markets. Television series produced for syndication or other non-network (first-run) markets are generally licensed to domestic and foreign markets concurrently. The length of the revenue cycle for television series will vary depending on the number of seasons a series remains in active production.

Theatrical revenues from domestic and foreign markets are recognized as films are exhibited. Revenues arising from television license agreements are recognized in the year that the films or television series are available for telecast. Revenues from the sale of videocassettes are recognized upon delivery of the merchandise.

Inventories related to theatrical and television product (which include direct production costs, production overhead, capitalized interest and acquisition costs) are stated at the lower of cost less amortization or net realizable value. Inventories are amortized and profit participations and residuals are accrued on an individual product basis in the proportion that current revenues bear to the estimated remaining total lifetime revenues. Estimates of total lifetime revenues and expenses are periodically reviewed. The costs of feature and television films are classified as current assets to the extent such costs are expected to be recovered through the respective primary markets. Other costs relating to film production are classified as noncurrent.

The Company estimates that approximately 95% of unamortized film costs at October 31, 1987 will be amortized within the next three years.

Property, Plant and Equipment

Property, plant and equipment are carried at cost. Provision for depreciation on substantially all depreciable assets is computed using the straight-line method over the estimated useful lives of the assets.

Intangible Assets

Intangible assets primarily arose from the excess of cost of purchased businesses over the value of their net underlying assets (goodwill) and are being amortized by the straight-line method over appropriate periods not exceeding forty years.

Deferred Costs and Other

Deferred costs and other includes plate costs, which consist of certain prepublication costs being amortized by the straight-line method over appropriate periods not exceeding four years.

Unamortized Debt Discount

Debt discount is amortized over the term of the related debt using the interest method.

Income Taxes

Provision for income taxes includes deferred taxes which represent future tax effects of items reported for income tax purposes in periods different than for financial purposes. Investment tax credits are recognized as a reduction in the income tax provision using the flow-through method.

Pension Plans

Pension expense includes amortization of prior service cost over periods of thirty to forty years. The Company's funding policy varies; however, it generally follows the requirements of government regulations.

Earnings Per Share

Earnings per share amounts are based on the weighted average common and dilutive common equivalent (stock options) shares outstanding during the respective periods. Earnings per share are computed by dividing the average common and, where dilutive, common equivalent shares outstanding into the earnings applicable to such shares.

NOTE B — ACQUISITION AND DISPOSITION OF BUSINESSES

Acquisitions

In December 1984, the Company completed the purchase of Prentice-Hall, Inc., one of the nation's largest publishers of books, business information services and educational materials, for approximately $710 million. In June 1985, the Company completed the purchase of Ginn & Company, a leading elementary and secondary textbook publisher, for approximately $110 million. In May 1986, the Company completed the purchase of Silver Burdett Company, an elementary textbook publisher, for approximately $125 million. In October 1986 and December 1986, the Company purchased Mann

Theatres Corporation and Festival Enterprises, motion picture theatre circuits, for approximately $220 million and $50 million, respectively. The acquisitions have been accounted for as purchases and the financial statements include the results of their operations from the dates of acquisition.

The following table summarizes, on a pro forma basis, the combined results of operations as though Silver Burdett, Mann Theatres and Festival Enterprises had been acquired on November 1, 1985. It includes estimated interest expense, amortization of intangible assets and related income taxes. These pro forma results do not necessarily reflect the actual results of operations had the acquisitions taken place on that date, nor are they necessarily indicative of future results.

Year Ended October 31	1987	1986
	(In millions, except per share) (Unaudited)	
Revenues.	**$4,681.1**	$3,918.0
Earnings from continuing operations before extraordinary items	**356.3**	200.9
Net earnings	**356.3**	239.6
Earnings per share		
From continuing operations before extraordinary items	**5.76**	3.21
Net earnings	**5.76**	3.83

Dispositions

In September 1985, the Company completed the sale of its Consumer and Industrial Products Group to Wickes Companies, Inc. for approximately $1 billion cash and a five-year option to purchase two million shares of Wickes common stock at $30.00 per share. The Consumer and Industrial Products Group comprised the Company's Apparel and Hosiery, Manufacturing, Bedding and Home Furnishings, and Automotive Parts Distribution segments. The sale resulted in a gain, net of taxes payable, of approximately $120 million. However, the elimination of previously deferred foreign exchange losses and tax benefits applicable to such businesses reduced the gain for accounting purposes to approximately $15 million.

Net revenues and operating results to date of disposition and gain on disposal of discontinued operations for the year ended October 31, 1985 are as follows (in millions):

Net revenues	$2,001.9
Earnings from operations before income taxes	$ 140.3
Provision for income taxes	(59.1)
	81.2
Gain on sale before income taxes	105.0
Provision for income taxes	(90.0)
	15.0
Earnings from discontinued operations	$ 96.2

In February 1987, the Company entered into an agreement in principle with Warner Communications Inc. ("Warner") under which Warner will acquire a 50% interest in the Company's domestic motion picture theatre operations for approximately half of the Company's purchase price. The transaction is expected to close in January 1988 and, after closing, is subject to the approval of the United States District Court for the Southern District of New York pursuant to the 1951 Warner consent judgment. Accordingly, the results of these operations have been deconsolidated.

During fiscal 1987, 1986 and 1985, the Company also acquired or sold certain other businesses, the results of which are included in continuing operations. The contributions of these businesses in the aggregate were not significant to the Company's results of operations for the years presented, nor are they expected to have a material effect on the Company's results on a continuing basis.

NOTE C — EXTRAORDINARY ITEMS

During the fourth quarter of fiscal 1986, the Company sold real estate, which was not used in its business, for cash of $100 million. This sale resulted in a gain of $58.9 million, net of applicable taxes of $30.6 million. In addition, the Company redeemed 80.5% of its $12^3/8$% Subordinated Notes due 1995 for $1,202.50 per $1,000 principal amount and terminated an interest rate obligation due 1990 through a cash payment of $20.5 million. These financing transactions resulted in a loss of $20.2 million, net of income tax benefits of $17.2 million.

NOTE D — INVENTORIES

Inventories as described in Note A are stated as follows (in millions):

October 31	1987	1986
Current		
Lower of cost or net realizable value		
Finished goods	**$142.0**	$143.1
Work in process	**24.8**	14.1
Materials and supplies	**28.2**	22.5
	195.0	179.7
Theatrical and television productions	**129.6**	97.9
	324.6	277.6
Noncurrent		
Theatrical and television productions	**146.9**	204.9
	$471.5	$482.5

NOTE E — INVESTMENT IN AFFILIATED COMPANIES

Investment in affiliated companies at October 31, 1987 includes $1,074.2 million ($943.9 million at October 31, 1986) applicable to the Company's ownership of all of the outstanding capital stock of Associates First Capital Corporation (First Capital). Also included in this caption are net receivables from First Capital of approximately $22.1 million at October 31, 1987 ($6.0 million net payables at October 31, 1986). The Company's investment in First Capital is $141.5 million greater than the underlying equity in the net assets of such company. This difference, which arose prior to November 1, 1970, is not being amortized because, in the opinion of management, it is considered to have a continuing value. The Company received dividends of $84.0 million, $80.5 million and $82.5 million from First Capital in fiscal 1987, 1986 and 1985, respectively. Separate financial statements of First Capital are presented elsewhere herein.

In addition, investment in affiliated companies at October 31, 1987 includes $281.6 million applicable to the Company's domestic motion picture theatre operations (see Note B).

Included in consolidated retained earnings at October 31, 1987 is $714.5 million of undistributed earnings principally attributable to First Capital.

NOTE F — LONG-TERM DEBT

Long-term debt includes:

October 31	1987	1986
	(In millions)	
Notes payable to institutional investors, interest 8.75% to 9.55%, averaging 9.49%, due 1988 to 1999	$ 103.8	$ 114.8
8 1/2% senior notes due 1996	99.5	99.4
9 3/4% senior debentures due 2016	173.3	173.3
11 5/8% senior notes due 1992	124.6	124.5
12 1/8% Eurodollar notes due 1989	100.0	100.0
7% subordinated debentures due 2003, net of unamortized discount of $66.0 million at October 31, 1987 and $67.5 million at October 31, 1986 (effective average interest rate of 11%)	165.5	163.9
12 3/8% subordinated notes due 1995	19.4	19.4
6% subordinated debentures due 1988	12.1	26.0
Revolving loan agreement borrowings, interest at variable short-term market rates	250.0	
Commercial paper supported by unused long-term revolving loan agreements	235.6	343.3
Other notes and debentures, interest 4% to 12%, averaging 9.58%, due 1988 to 2002	51.2	65.6
Obligations under capital leases	64.8	60.4
	1,399.8	1,290.6
Less current maturities	64.9	29.8
	$1,334.9	$1,260.8

Maturities of long-term debt (including the present value of obligations under capital leases as set forth in Note I) during the five years ending October 31, 1992 are (in millions):

1988	$ 64.9
1989	117.5
1990	263.9[1]
1991	97.4[1]
1992	156.2[1]

[1]Includes $245.6, $75.0 and $15.0 million in 1990, 1991 and 1992, respectively, of unused long-term revolving loan agreements supporting commercial paper and revolving loan agreement borrowings, which are expected to be extended.

At October 31, 1987, the Company had $564 million of unused long-term revolving loan agreements used to support outstanding commercial paper and long-term revolving loan agreement borrowings.

The Company has complied with restrictions and limitations required under terms of various loan agreements. Consolidated retained earnings unrestricted as to the payment of cash dividends was $845 million at October 31, 1987.

At October 31, 1987, approximately $377 million of net assets of subsidiaries, including $299 million of the retained earnings of the Company's unconsolidated finance subsidiary, were restricted as to the payment of dividends and loans to the Company, primarily as the result of these subsidiaries' debt agreements.

NOTE G — CAPITAL STOCK

The authorized capital stock of the Company includes 10,000,000 shares of Cumulative Preferred Stock (nonconvertible), of which 600,000 shares are designated as Series A 12% (all issued and held by a subsidiary of the Company), 400,000 shares are designated as Series B 8% and 9,000,000 shares are undesignated. In addition, 20,000,000 shares of Cumulative Convertible Preferred Stock are authorized, all of which are undesignated.

The Company has outstanding $5.75 Sinking Fund Preferred Stock, which has an annual dividend rate of $5.75 a share. At October 31, 1987 and 1986, 471,981 and 479,262 shares, respectively, of $5.75 Sinking Fund Preferred Stock were authorized. At October 31, 1987, 145,611 shares, excluding 89,668 shares held in treasury, were outstanding and at October 31, 1986, 145,611 shares, excluding 96,949 shares held in treasury, were outstanding. The carrying value of such $5.75 Sinking Fund Preferred Stock was $14.6 million at October 31, 1987 and 1986.

Common Stock outstanding at October 31, 1987 does not include 86,377 shares reserved under the 1964 Stock Option Incentive Plan; 116,500 shares reserved under the 1973 Key Employees Stock Purchase Plan; 4,483,456 shares reserved under the 1984 Stock Option Plan; and 1,907,855 shares reserved under the Long-Term Performance Plan.

The Company's 1964 Stock Option Incentive Plan provided for the issuance of options to key employees to purchase Common Stock of the Company at a price not less than fair market value on the date of grant. Options granted under this plan were exercisable on a cumulative basis over a four-year period beginning one year from the date of grant at the rate of 25% of the original grant each year. In August 1985, the Company made all outstanding options under this plan immediately exercisable.

The Company's 1973 Key Employees Stock Purchase Plan provided for the issuance of options to key employees to purchase shares of the Company's Common Stock at a price not less than fair market value on the date of grant. Options granted under this plan are exercisable for a period of ten years from the date of grant.

The Company's 1984 Stock Option Plan provides for the issuance of options to key employees to purchase Common Stock of the Company at a price not less than fair market value on the date of grant. Options may not be granted under this plan that expire more than ten years from the date of grant. The Company may establish installment exercise terms for a stock option so that the option becomes fully exercisable in a series of cumulative portions. The Company may also accelerate the period for the exercise of any stock option or portion thereof. In December 1985, the Company made substantially all outstanding options under this plan immediately exercisable.

Transactions involving outstanding stock options under these plans were:

	Number of Common Shares			Option Price	
	1964 Plan	1973 Plan	1984 Plan	Per Share	Aggregate
					(in millions)
Outstanding at October 31, 1984	769,681	223,375	771,398	$ 8.88–$27.88	$45.2
Granted			483,256	27.25– 41.38	19.2
Upon exercise					
Issued	(430,072)	(78,725)	(140,210)	8.88– 34.50	(15.0)
Rescinded		(15,650)	(27,151)	8.88– 30.75	(1.0)
Rescinded	(58,239)		(28,347)	15.50– 40.38	(2.2)
Outstanding at October 31, 1985	281,370	129,000	1,058,946	9.40– 41.38	46.2
Granted			846,741	46.31– 63.38	52.7
Upon exercise					
Issued	(139,593)	(12,500)	(152,344)	12.46– 40.38	(8.8)
Rescinded			(2,125)	30.75– 40.38	(0.1)
Rescinded	(10,045)		(45,449)	13.13– 40.38	(1.8)
Outstanding at October 31, 1986	131,732	116,500	1,705,769	9.40– 63.38	88.2
Granted			48,836	63.44– 78.00	3.3
Issued	(45,355)		(194,714)	27.13– 63.38	(10.1)
Rescinded			(10,350)	30.75– 63.38	(0.6)
Outstanding at October 31, 1987	86,377	116,500	1,549,541	9.40– 78.00	$80.8
Exercisable at					
October 31, 1986	131,732	116,500	1,605,269		
October 31, 1987	86,377	116,500	1,457,124		
Reserved for future grants at					
October 31, 1986			2,972,401		
October 31, 1987			2,933,915		

In November 1987, the Company granted options under the 1984 Plan to purchase an additional 900,926 shares of the Company's Common Stock at a total price of $61.0 million.

The Company follows the practice of recording amounts received upon the exercise of options by crediting Common Stock and paid-in surplus. No charges are reflected in the consolidated statement of earnings as a result of the grant or exercise of stock options. The Company records compensation expense related to stock appreciation rights of the 1973 Plan and 1984 Plan and share unit features of the 1973 Plan based on the change in the quoted market price of the Common Stock for the period. The exercise prices of options are subject to anti-dilution provisions.

During fiscal 1985, 1986 and November 1987, 335,000, 50,000 and 100,000 shares, respectively, of Common Stock of the Company were granted to certain key employees subject to restrictions which will lapse on certain dates through fiscal 1993. The average market price of these shares on the date on which they were granted ranged from $27.25 to $67.75. Compensation expense is being recorded over the period during which services are to be performed.

During the year ended October 31, 1986, 92,415 shares of Common Stock of the Company were granted to employees at an average market price of $58.70 under the terms of the Company's Long-Term Performance Plan. At October 31, 1987 and 1986, there were 1,907,855 shares of Common Stock reserved for future grants under this plan.

NOTE H — INCOME TAXES

Provision (benefit) for income taxes on continuing operations includes (in millions):

Year Ended October 31	1987	1986	1985
Current			
Federal	$142.8	$ 26.7	$16.6
Foreign	58.8	35.1	20.2
State and other	18.4	11.9	16.6
	220.0	73.7	53.4
Deferred			
Federal	33.4	84.0	31.3
Foreign	(0.8)	(3.1)	4.7
State and other		3.0	(5.8)
	32.6	83.9	30.2
	$252.6	$157.6	$83.6

Deferred taxes of continuing operations reflect the tax effect of recognition of various income and expense items in different periods for financial reporting than for income tax purposes including charges (credits) of (in millions):

Year Ended October 31	1987	1986	1985
Costs of motion picture and television production	$31.1	$28.5	$44.7
Income on motion picture and television production	(5.1)	(10.7)	4.1
Valuation of inventories	(15.4)	4.6	(3.3)
One-time life insurance reserves adjustment			(8.0)
Leasing transactions	31.4	40.8	10.0
Employee compensation and other payroll related expenses	(2.5)	(7.2)	(6.1)
Income on consumer finance receivables	(2.5)	16.6	0.4
Provisions for bad debts	(22.6)	6.7	(4.9)
Other	18.2	4.6	(6.7)
	$32.6	$83.9	$30.2

The following summarizes the components of earnings from continuing operations before income taxes (in millions):

Year Ended October 31	1987	1986	1985
Domestic	$528.8	$330.1	$190.9
Foreign	79.9	56.2	44.3
	$608.7	$386.3	$235.2

A reconciliation between the statutory Federal income tax rate and the effective rate of income tax expense to earnings from continuing operations before income taxes for the three years ended October 31, 1987 is as follows:

	% of Earnings Before Income Taxes		
	1987	1986	1985
Statutory rate	42.0%	46.0%	46.0%
Increase (decrease) in taxes arising from effect of			
Foreign earnings	0.7	(3.1)	(2.0)
Investment tax credits	(7.5)	(5.0)	(7.5)
U.S. state and local income taxes	1.8	2.1	2.6
Special deductions relating to life insurance companies		(1.4)	(1.7)
One-time life insurance reserves adjustment			(4.2)
Other	4.5	2.2	2.3
Effective tax rate	41.5%	40.8%	35.5%

The Company's share of the undistributed earnings of subsidiaries not included in its consolidated Federal income tax return, which could be subject to additional income taxes if remitted, was approximately $530 million at October 31, 1987. No provision has been made for taxes which could result from the remittance of such undistributed earnings since the Company intends to reinvest these earnings indefinitely.

NOTE I — COMMITMENTS AND CONTINGENCIES

Total rental expense of continuing operations was $52.0, $48.3 and $48.3 million, respectively, for the three years ended October 31, 1987, 1986 and 1985. Contingent rental expense (primarily based on revenues) included therein for 1987, 1986 and 1985 was $10.7, $9.5 and $10.7 million, respectively.

At October 31, 1987, the minimum lease payments under capital leases and noncancellable operating leases were as follows (in millions):

Year Ending October 31	Capital Leases	Operating Leases
1988	$ 14.2	$ 35.5
1989	14.4	31.2
1990	13.8	27.1
1991	13.1	24.2
1992	12.9	22.0
Thereafter	49.1	188.6
Total minimum lease payments	117.5	$328.6
Less amounts representing interest	52.7	
Present value of net minimum lease payments	$ 64.8	

Many of the leases also require the lessee to pay property taxes, insurance and ordinary repairs and maintenance.

Effective January 1, 1987, the Company established a new pension plan to cover substantially all permanent employees. The assets and liabilities of the Company's former pension plans, including those of its unconsolidated finance subsidiary and those pension plans covering retired employees of certain of its discontinued operations that had been retained by the Company, were merged into this plan.

Pension expense from continuing operations excluding the Company's unconsolidated finance subsidiary was $24.8, $10.6 and $6.9 million, respectively, for the three years ended October 31, 1987, 1986 and 1985. As of the most recent valuation dates, the actuarially computed value of accumulated benefits under the Company's merged pension plans and the market value of net fund assets were as follows (in millions):

October 31	1987	1986
Accumulated benefits		
Vested	$279.0	$37.9
Nonvested	17.9	4.3
	$296.9	$42.2
Net fund assets available for benefits	$386.6	$67.8

The interest rate used in determining the actuarially computed value of accumulated benefits was primarily 8.5%.

In addition to providing pension benefits, the Company provides certain health care and life insurance benefits for retired employees. Substantially all of the Company's employees may become eligible for those benefits when they reach normal retirement age while working for the Company. The cost of health care and life insurance benefits is recognized as insurance premiums are paid or as claims are paid for those uninsured benefits. Such costs were not material.

The Company is a defendant in various lawsuits wherein substantial amounts are claimed. In the opinion of counsel, these suits should not result in judgments which in the aggregate would have a material adverse effect on the Company's financial condition.

NOTE J — SUPPLEMENTAL INFORMATION

The details of certain balance sheet accounts are as follows (in millions):

October 31	1987	1986
Prepaid expenses, income taxes and other		
Income taxes	$221.9	$240.5
Other	183.2	150.3
	$405.1	$390.8
Accrued expenses and other liabilities		
Accrued compensation and other employee benefit related items	$ 77.7	$ 67.4
Participations payable and accrued syndication expenses	226.9	203.8
Deferred television contracts income	62.3	43.8
Royalties	45.5	43.8
Unexpired subscriptions and advanced subscription payments	47.9	43.9
Other	280.7	240.4
	$741.0	$643.1

The details of interest expense — net are as follows (in millions):

Year Ended October 31	1987	1986	1985
Interest expense			
Interest on indebtedness and other	$143.5	$147.7	$155.5
Interest paid to unconsolidated finance subsidiary	3.8	5.4	9.0
Imputed interest on long-term liabilities	6.7	8.0	8.0
Less capitalized interest	(5.4)	(5.4)	(6.2)
	148.6	155.7	166.3
Interest income			
Interest on investments	17.8	24.5	26.4
Imputed interest on long-term receivables	18.1	23.7	23.7
	35.9	48.2	50.1
	$112.7	$107.5	$116.2

Imputed interest relates principally to network and syndication licenses of motion picture and television products.

Capitalized interest relates to projects under construction and theatrical and television productions in process, of which $5.9, $6.1 and $8.3 million was amortized as a charge to earnings in 1987, 1986 and 1985, respectively.

NOTE K — FINANCIAL REPORTING BY BUSINESS SEGMENTS

A summary description of the Company's business segments and their respective Revenues and Operating Income for 1987, 1986 and 1985 is set forth on page 26.

Depreciation, capital expenditures and identifiable assets were as follows (in millions):

Year Ended or at October 31	Depreciation			Capital Expenditures			Identifiable Assets		
	1987	1986	1985	1987	1986	1985	1987	1986	1985
Business Segments									
Entertainment	$17.8	$15.9	$13.1	$37.2	$57.7[1]	$51.5[2]	$1,360.9	$1,298.7	$ 925.6
Publishing/Information	9.3	7.1	7.2	16.6	10.6	8.1	1,706.4	1,537.8	1,489.2
Total	27.1	23.0	20.3	53.8	68.3	59.6	3,067.3	2,836.5	2,414.8
Investment in Consumer/Commercial Finance							1,096.3	937.9	811.7
Corporate and Other Non-Segment Items	2.9	2.8	3.0	3.3	5.3	3.2	765.3	469.0	815.8
	$30.0	$25.8	$23.3	$57.1	$73.6	$62.8	$4,928.9	$4,243.4	$4,042.3[3]

[1]Includes the purchase of various previously leased theatres in Canada.
[2]Includes the purchase of lease and related rights as well as the land under Madison Square Garden Center.
[3]In addition there were $21.8 million of identifiable assets related to discontinued operations.

Identifiable assets are those which can be directly identified or associated with the segments. Amounts reflected for consumer/commercial finance represent the Company's net investment in those operations. Corporate and other non-segment items principally include cash and cash equivalents, prepaid and deferred income taxes and corporate property and equipment.

NOTE L — QUARTERLY RESULTS (UNAUDITED)

The following summarizes the quarterly operating results of the Company for the fiscal years ended October 31, 1987 and 1986 (in millions, except per share):

	Quarter Ended							
	January 31		April 30		July 31		October 31	
	1987	1986	1987	1986	1987	1986	1987	1986
Revenues	$1,087.7	$862.0	$989.9	$863.9	$1,150.1	$1,044.4	$1,453.4	$1,010.8
Net revenues	656.6	460.8	558.8	438.4	695.4	618.7	992.8	575.9
Cost of goods sold	418.1	286.2	339.2	250.9	388.4	343.1	607.8	335.6
Operating income	146.4	81.6	118.5	102.6	206.5	170.5	251.0	141.5
Earnings from continuing operations before income taxes	119.5	57.0	90.9	74.0	176.8	140.8	221.5	114.5
Earnings from continuing operations before extraordinary items	69.3	34.2	52.7	45.7	102.6	82.1	131.5	66.7
Extraordinary items								38.7
Net earnings	69.3	34.2	52.7	45.7	102.6	82.1	131.5	105.4
Earnings per share								
From continuing operations before extraordinary items	1.11	.55	.86	.73	1.66	1.31	2.13	1.07
Net earnings	1.11	.55	.86	.73	1.66	1.31	2.13	1.69

Glossary

Terms for all 28 chapters of **Accounting** appear here, with their page numbers.

Accelerated depreciation. A type of depreciation method that writes off a relatively larger amount of the asset's cost nearer the start of its useful life than does the straight-line method *(p. 389)*.

Account. The detailed record of the changes that have occurred in a particular asset, liability, or owner equity during a period *(p. 39)*.

Account format of the balance sheet. Format that lists the assets at the left, with liabilities and owner equity at the right *(p. 143)*.

Account payable. A liability that is not written out. Instead, it is backed by the reputation and credit standing of the debtor *(p. 11)*.

Account receivable. An asset, a promise to receive cash from customers to whom the business has sold goods *(p. 11)*.

Accounting. The system that measures business activities, processes that information into reports and financial statements, and communicates the findings to decision makers *(p. 2)*.

Accounting controls. Methods and procedures that safeguard assets, authorize transactions, and ensure the accuracy of the financial records *(p. 265)*.

Accounting cycle. Process by which accountants produce an entity's financial statements for a specific period *(p. 125)*.

Accounting information system. The combination of personnel, records, and procedures that a business uses to meet its need for financial data *(p. 215)*.

Accounting rate of return. The remainder of average annual net cash inflow from operations minus annual depreciation, divided by average amount invested in the business. This is the most widely used measure of profitability. The higher the accounting rate of return, the better the investment *(p. 1020)*.

Accounts receivable turnover. Ratio of net credit sales to average net accounts receivable. Measures ability to collect cash from credit customers *(p. 753)*.

Accrual-basis accounting. Accounting that recognizes (records) the impact of a business event as it occurs, regardless of whether the transaction affected cash *(p. 86)*.

Accrued expense. An expense that has been incurred but not yet paid in cash *(p. 94)*.

Accrued revenue. A revenue that has been earned but not yet received in cash *(p. 95)*.

Accumulated depreciation. The cumulative sum of all depreciation expense from the date of acquiring a plant asset *(p. 93)*.

Acid-test ratio. Ratio of the sum of cash plus short-term investments plus net current receivables to current liabilities. Tells whether the entity could pay all its current liabilities if they came due immediately. Also called the quick ratio *(p. 751)*.

Additional paid-in capital. Another name for Paid-in capital in excess of par *(p. 543)*.

Adjusted gross income. Total income minus specified adjustments (deductions) equals adjusted gross income, an amount that exists only in the tax law *(p. 1043)*.

Adjusted trial balance. A list of all the ledger accounts with their adjusted balances *(p. 99)*.

Adjusting entry. Entry made at the end of the period to assign revenues to the period in which they are earned and expenses to the period in which they are incurred. Adjusting entries help measure the period's income and bring the related asset and liability accounts to correct balances for the financial statements *(p. 89)*.

Administrative controls. Plan of organization, methods, and procedures that help managers achieve operational efficiency and adherence to company policies *(p. 265)*.

Aging of accounts receivable. A way to estimate bad debts by analyzing individual accounts receivable according to the length of time they have been due *(p. 316)*.

Allocation base. Logical common denominator for assigning a given cost to two or more departments of a business *(p. 976)*.

Allowance for doubtful accounts. A contra account, related to accounts receivable, that holds the estimated amount of collection losses. Also called Allowance for uncollectible accounts *(p. 313)*.

Allowance for uncollectible accounts. Another name for Allowance for doubtful accounts *(p. 313)*.

Allowance method. A method of recording collection losses based on estimates prior to determining that the business will not collect from specific customers *(p. 312)*.

Amortization. Expense that applies to intangible assets in the same way depreciation applies to plant assets and depletion applies to natural resources *(p. 401)*.

Annuity. Stream of equal periodic amounts *(p. 1022)*.

Appropriation of retained earnings. Restriction of retained earnings that is recorded by a formal journal entry *(p. 584)*.

Articles of partnership. Agreement that is the contract between partners specifying such items as the name, location, and nature of the business, the name, capital investment, and duties of each partner, and the method of sharing profits and losses by the partners. Also called the partnership agreement *(p. 496)*.

Asset. An economic resource a business owns that is expected to be of benefit in the future *(p. 10)*.

Auditing. The examination of financial statements by outside accountants, the most significant service that CPAs perform. The conclusion of an audit is the accountant's professional opinion about the financial statements *(p. 7).*

Authorization of stock. Provision in a corporate charter that gives the state's permission for the corporation to issue—that is, to sell—a certain number of shares of stock *(p. 542).*

Average cost method. Inventory costing method based on the average cost of inventory during the period. Average cost is determined by dividing the cost of goods available for sale by the number of units available *(p. 348).*

Bad debt expense. Another name for Uncollectible accounts expense *(p. 311).*

Balance sheet. List of an entity's assets, liabilities, and owner equity as of a specific date. Also called the statement of financial position *(p. 18).*

Balancing the ledgers. Establishing the equality of (a) total debits and total credits in the general ledger, (b) the balance of the accounts receivable control account in the general ledger and the sum of individual customer accounts in the accounts receivable subsidiary ledger, or (c) the balance of the accounts payable control account in the general ledger and the sum of individual creditor accounts in the accounts payable subsidiary ledger *(p. 238).*

Bank collection. Collection of money by the bank on behalf of a depositor *(p. 273).*

Bank reconciliation. Process of explaining the reasons for the difference between a depositor's records and the bank's records about the depositor's bank account *(p. 273).*

Bank statement. Document for a particular bank account showing its beginning and ending balances and listing the month's transactions that affected the account *(p. 271).*

Batch processing. Computerized accounting for similar transactions in a group or batch *(p. 220).*

Beginning inventory. Goods left over from the preceding period *(p. 345).*

Board of directors. Group elected by the stockholders to set policy for a corporation and to appoint its officers *(p. 537).*

Bond discount. Excess of a bond's maturity (par) value over its issue price *(p. 611).*

Bond indenture. Contract under which bonds are issued *(p. 624).*

Bond premium. Excess of a bond's issue price over its maturity (par) value *(p. 611).*

Bond sinking fund. Group of assets segregated for the purpose of retiring bonds payable at maturity *(p. 624).*

Bonds payable. Groups of notes payable (bonds) issued to multiple lenders called bondholders *(p. 609).*

Bonus. Amount over and above regular compensation *(p. 431).*

Book value of a plant asset. The asset's cost less accumulated depreciation *(p. 93).*

Book value of stock. Amount of owners' equity on the company's books for each share of its stock *(p. 554).*

Book value per share of common stock. Common stockholders' equity divided by the number of shares of common stock outstanding *(p. 760).*

Branch accounting. System for separating the accounts of a branch of a business from the accounts of the home office *(p. 981).*

Branch-factor ledger control. Account in the home office ledger that represents the home office investment in, or receivable from, a branch of the business *(p. 982).*

Branch ledger. The part of a general ledger kept by a branch of the business, separate from the home office ledger *(p. 981).*

Break-even analysis. Another name for Cost-volume-profit analysis *(p. 825).*

Break-even point. Amount of unit sales or dollar sales at which revenue equals expenses *(p. 825).*

Budget. Management's tool for forecasting a business's future in amounts, including the quantities of products to be sold and their expected selling prices, the numbers of employees and their pay, and a host of other amounts that are ultimately expressed in dollars *(p. 787).*

Budget committee. Group that prepares the master budget; includes representatives from all departments of the business *(p. 787).*

Budget formula. The heart of a flexible budget, shows how to compute the budget amounts *(p. 938).*

Budgeted factory overhead rate. Budgeted total overhead cost divided by the budgeted rate base *(p. 871).*

Budgeting. Setting of goals for a business, such as its sales and profits, for a future period *(p. 7).*

Bylaws. Constitution for governing a corporation *(p. 537).*

Byproduct. Output of a joint production process with minor sales value in comparison to the main product *(p. 917).*

Callable bonds. Bonds that the issuer may call or pay off at a specified price whenever the issuer wants *(p. 625).*

Capital. Another name for the owner equity of a business *(p. 11).*

Capital budgeting. Formal means of making long-range decisions for investments such as plant locations, equipment purchases, additions of product lines, and territorial expansions *(p. 1017).*

Capital deficiency. Debit balance in a partner's capital account *(p. 516).*

Capital expenditure. Expenditure that increases the capacity or efficiency of an asset or extends its useful life. Capital expenditures are debited to an asset account *(p. 404).*

Capital expenditures budget. Plan for purchases of property, plant, and equipment and other assets that management uses to produce revenues over a long time *(p. 790).*

Capital gain. Special category of gain (or loss) defined in the tax law that results from the disposal of property such as investments in stocks, bonds, and real estate, and personal assets *(p. 1045).*

Capital lease. Lease agreement that meets any one of four criteria: (1) The lease transfers title of the leased asset to the lessee. (2) The lease contains a bargain purchase option. (3) The lease term is 75 percent or more of the estimated useful life of the leased asset. (4) The present value of the lease payments is 90 percent or more of the market value of the leased asset *(p. 629).*

Capital loss. Special category of loss (or gain) defined in the tax law that results from the disposal of property such as investments in stocks, bonds, and real estate, and personal assets *(p. 1045).*

Cash-basis accounting. Accounting that records only transactions in which cash is received or paid *(p. 86)*.

Cash budget. Details the way a business intends to go from the beginning cash balance to the desired ending balance. Also called the Statement of budgeted cash receipts and disbursements *(p. 796)*.

Cash disbursements journal. Special journal used to record cash disbursements by check *(p. 232)*.

Cash equivalent. Highly liquid short-term investments that can be converted into cash with little delay *(p. 698)*.

Cash flows. Cash receipts and cash payments (disbursements) *(p. 695)*.

Cash receipts journal. Special journal used to record cash receipts *(p. 225)*.

Central processing unit (CPU). The brain of a computer. It performs mathematical and logical operations and controls the other components of the computer system *(p. 1078)*.

Certified Public Accountant (CPA). A professional accountant who earns this title through a combination of education, experience, and an acceptable score on a written national examination *(p. 4)*.

Chairperson of the board. Elected person on a corporation's board of directors, usually the most powerful person in the corporation *(p. 537)*.

Change in accounting estimate. A change that occurs in the normal course of business as a company alters earlier expectations. Decreasing uncollectible account expense from 2 percent to 1½ percent of sales and changing the estimated useful life of a plant asset are examples *(p. 472)*.

Change in accounting principle. A change in accounting method, such as from the LIFO method to the FIFO method for inventories and a switch from the sum-of-years-digits depreciation method to the straight-line method *(p. 472)*.

Chart of accounts. List of all the accounts and their account numbers in the ledger *(p. 56)*.

Charter. Document that gives the state's permission to form a corporation *(pp. 535, 537)*.

Check. Document that instructs the bank to pay the designated person or business the specified amount of money *(p. 271)*.

Check register. Special journal used to record all checks issued in a voucher system *(p. 287)*.

Closing entries. Entries that transfer the revenue, expense, and owner withdrawal balances from these respective accounts to the capital account *(p. 138)*.

Closing the accounts. Step in the accounting cycle at the end of the period that prepares the accounts for recording the transactions of the next period. Closing the accounts consists of journalizing and posting the closing entries to set the balances of the revenue, expense, and owner withdrawal accounts to zero *(p. 136)*.

Collection method. Method of applying the revenue principle by which the seller waits until cash is received to record the sale. This method is used only if the receipt of cash is uncertain *(p. 468)*.

Commission. Employee compensation computed as a percentage of the sales that the employee has made *(p. 431)*.

Common-size statement. A financial statement that reports only percentages (no dollar amounts); a type of vertical analysis *(p. 745)*.

Common stock. The most basic form of capital stock. In describing a corporation, the common stockholders are the owners of the business *(p. 541)*.

Comparability principle. Specifies that accounting information must be comparable from business to business and that a single business's financial statements must be comparable from one period to the next *(p. 466)*.

Completed-contract method. Method of applying the revenue principle by a construction company by which all revenue earned on the project is recorded in the period when the project is completed *(p. 470)*.

Conservatism. Concept that underlies presenting the gloomiest possible figures in the financial statements *(p. 356)*.

Consignment. Transfer of goods by the owner (consignor) to another business (consignee) who, for a fee, sells the inventory on the owner's behalf. The consignee does not take title to the consigned goods *(p. 347)*.

Consistency principle. A business must use the same accounting methods and procedures from period to period *(p. 353)*.

Consolidation method for investments. A way to combine the financial statements of two or more companies that are controlled by the same owners *(p. 661)*.

Constraint. Item that restricts production or sales. Also called the Limiting factor *(p. 1012)*.

Contingent liability. A potential liability *(p. 325)*.

Continuous budget. Systematically adds a month or a quarter as the month or quarter just ended is deleted. Also called a Rolling budget *(p. 801)*.

Contra account. An account with two distinguishing characteristics: (1) it always has a companion account, and (2) its normal balance is opposite that of the companion account *(p. 93)*.

Contra asset. An asset account with a credit balance. A contra account always has a companion account and its balance is opposite that of the companion account *(p. 93)*.

Contract interest rate. Interest rate that determines the amount of cash interest the borrower pays and the investor receives each year. Also called the Stated interest rate *(p. 612)*.

Contributed capital. Another name for Paid-in capital *(p. 539)*.

Contribution margin. Excess of sale price over variable expenses *(p. 826)*.

Contribution margin income statement. Separates expenses into variable costs and fixed costs and highlights the contribution margin, which is the excess of sales over variable expenses *(p. 838)*.

Contribution margin percentage. Sales of 100 percent minus the variable expense percentage *(p. 827)*

Control account. An account whose balance equals the sum of the balances in a group of related accounts in a subsidiary ledger *(p. 224)*.

Controllable overhead variance. Another name for the Flexible budget overhead variance *(p. 950)*.

Controlling (majority) interest. Ownership of more than 50 percent of an investee company's voting stock *(p. 661)*.

Conversion cost. Short-hand term that includes direct labor and overhead *(p. 859)*.

Convertible bonds. Bonds that may be converted into the common stock of the issuing company at the option of the investor *(p. 626)*.

Convertible preferred stock. Preferred stock that may be exchanged by the preferred stockholders, if they choose, for another class of stock in the corporation *(p. 552)*.

Copyright. Exclusive right to reproduce and sell a book, musical composition, film, or other work of art. Issued by the federal government, copyrights extend 50 years beyond the author's life (*p. 402*).

Corporation. A business owned by stockholders that begins when the state approves its articles of incorporation. A corporation is a legal entity, an "artificial person," in the eyes of the law (*p. 9*).

Cost accounting. The branch of accounting that determines and controls a business's costs (*p. 7*).

Cost allocation. Assignment of various costs to the departments of a business. (*p. 976*).

Cost behavior. Description of how costs change in response to a shift in the volume of business activity (*p. 821*).

Cost method for investments. The method used to account for short-term investments in stock and for long-term investments when the investor holds less than 20 percent of the investee's voting stock. Under the cost method, investments are recorded at cost and reported at the lower of their cost or market value (*p. 658*).

Cost of a plant asset. Purchase price, sales tax, purchase commission, and all other amounts paid to acquire the asset and to ready it for its intended use (*p. 384*).

Cost of goods manufactured. Manufacturers' counterpart to the Purchases account. Cost of goods manufactured takes the place of purchases in the computation of cost of goods sold (*p. 857*).

Cost of goods sold. The cost of the inventory that the business has sold to customers, the largest single expense of most merchandising businesses. Also called Cost of sales (*p. 177*).

Cost of sales. Another name for Cost of goods sold (*p. 177*).

Cost principle. States that assets and services are recorded at their purchase cost and that the accounting record of the asset continues to be based on cost rather than current market value (*p. 467*).

Cost-volume-profit analysis. Expresses the relationships among a business's costs, volume, and profit or loss. An important part of a budgeting system that helps managers predict the outcome of their decisions (*p. 821*).

Coupon bonds. Bonds for which the owners receive interest by detaching a perforated coupon (which states the interest due and the date of payment), from the bond and depositing it in a bank for collection (*p. 610*).

CPU. Abbreviation of Central processing unit (*p. 1078*).

Credit. The right side of an account (*p. 43*).

Credit memorandum. Document issued by a seller to indicate having credited a customer's account receivable account (*p. 234*).

Creditor. The party to a credit transaction who sells a service or merchandise and obtains a receivable (*p. 309*).

Cumulative preferred stock. Preferred stock whose owners must receive all dividends in arrears before the corporation pays dividends to the common stockholders (*p. 551*).

Current asset. An asset that is expected to be converted to cash, sold, or consumed during the next twelve months, or within the business's normal operating cycle if longer than a year (*p. 142*).

Current cost. Present cost of replacing an asset's particular service potential or usefulness (*p. 669*).

Current cost accounting. Accounting model that uses the current cost of a company's assets and expenses in place of their historical cost (*p. 670*).

Current liability. A debt due to be paid within one year or one of the entity's operating cycles if the cycle is longer than a year (*p. 143*).

Current portion of long-term debt. Amount of the principal that is payable within one year (*p. 426*).

Current ratio. Current assets divided by current liabilities (*p. 751*).

CVP analysis. Abbreviation of Cost-volume-profit analysis (*p. 821*).

Date of record. Date on which the owners of stock to receive a dividend are identified (*p. 573*).

Days' sales in receivables. Ratio of average net accounts receivable to one day's sales. Tells how many days' sales remain in Accounts Receivable awaiting collection (*p. 754*).

Debentures. Unsecured bonds, backed only by the good faith of the borrower (*p. 611*).

Debit. The left side of an account (*p. 42*).

Debit memorandum. Business document issued by a buyer to state that the buyer no longer owes the seller for the amount of returned purchases (*p. 236*).

Debt ratio. Ratio of total liabilities to total assets. Tells the proportion of a company's assets that it has financed with debt (*p. 755*).

Debtor. The party to a credit transaction who makes a purchase and creates a payable (*p. 309*).

Decision model. A method or technique for evaluating and choosing among alternative courses of action (*p. 1017*).

Declaration date. Date on which the board of directors announce the intention to pay a dividend. The declaration creates a liability for the corporation (*p. 573*).

Default on a note. Failure of the maker of a note to pay at maturity. Also called Dishonor of a note (*p. 326*).

Deferred revenue. Another name for Unearned revenue (*p. 427*).

Deficit. Debit balance in the retained earnings account (*p. 540*).

Dependent. Person who receives more than half of his or her support from another taxpayer (*p. 1041*).

Depletion. That portion of a natural resource's cost that is used up in a particular period. Depletion expense is computed in the same way as units of production depreciation (*p. 401*).

Deposit in transit. A deposit recorded by the company but not yet by its bank (*p. 273*).

Depreciation. Expense associated with spreading (allocating) the cost of a plant asset over its useful life (*p. 92*).

Direct expense. Expense that is conveniently identified with and traceable to a particular department of a business (*p. 976*).

Direct labor. Cost of salaries and wages for the employees who physically convert materials into the company's products (*p. 858*).

Direct material. Material that becomes a physical part of a finished product and whose cost is separately and conveniently traceable through the manufacturing process to finished goods (*p. 858*).

Direct method. Format of the operating activities section of the statement of cash flows that lists the major categories of operating cash receipts (collections from customers and receipts of interest and dividends) and cash disbursements (payments to suppliers, to employees, for interest and income taxes) (*p. 698*).

Direct write-off method. A method of accounting for bad

debts by which the company waits until the credit department decides that a customer's account receivable is uncollectible and then records uncollectible account expense and credits the customer's account receivable *(p. 311)*.

Disclosure principle. Holds that a company's financial statements should report enough information for outsiders to make knowledgeable decisions about the company *(p. 471)*.

Discount on stock. Excess of the par value of stock over its issue price *(p. 543)*.

Discount rate. Management's minimum desired rate of return on an investment, used in a present value computation *(p. 1022)*.

Discounting a note payable. A borrowing arrangement in which the bank subtracts the interest amount from the note's face value. The borrower receives the net amount *(p. 424)*.

Discounting a note receivable. Selling a note receivable before its maturity *(p. 324)*.

Dishonor of a note. Another name for Default on a note *(p. 326)*.

Disk drive. Computer input device that reads data and instructions from magnetic disks *(p. 1077)*.

Diskette. Thin 5¼-inch diameter round magnetic disk enclosed in a square plastic envelope. Also called a Floppy diskette *(p. 1077)*.

Dissolution. Ending of a partnership *(p. 496)*.

Dividend yield. Ratio of dividends per share of stock to the stock's market price per share *(p. 760)*.

Dividends. Distributions by a corporation to its stockholders *(p. 540)*.

Dividends in arrears. Cumulative preferred dividends that the corporation has failed to pay *(p. 551)*.

Donated capital. Special category of stockholders' equity created when a corporation receives a donation (gift) from a donor who receives no ownership interest in the company *(p. 548)*.

Double-declining-balance (DDB) method. An accelerated depreciation method that computes annual depreciation by multiplying the asset's decreasing book value by a constant percentage, which is two times the straight-line rate *(p. 389)*.

Double taxation. Corporations pay their own income taxes on corporate income. Then, the stockholders pay personal income tax on the cash dividends that they receive from corporations *(p. 537)*.

Doubtful account expense. Another name for Uncollectible account expense *(p. 311)*.

Earnings per share (EPS). Amount of a company's net income per share of its outstanding common stock *(p. 588)*.

Effective interest rate. Another name for market interest rate *(p. 612)*.

Effective tax rate. A taxpayer's income tax amount divided by taxable income *(p. 1052)*.

Efficiency variance. Difference between the quantity of inputs (materials and labor) actually used and the quantity that should have been used (the flexible budget) for the actual output achieved, multiplied by the standard unit price of the input. Also called the Usage variance and the Quantity variance *(p. 946)*.

Electronic fund transfer. System that accounts for cash

transactions by electronic impulses rather than paper documents *(p. 289)*.

Ending inventory. Goods still on hand at the end of the period *(p. 345)*.

Entity. An organization or a section of an organization that, for accounting purposes, stands apart from other organizations and individuals as a separate economic unit. This is the most basic concept in accounting *(p. 9)*.

EPS. Abbreviation of Earnings per share of common stock *(p. 588)*.

Equity. A legal and economic claim to the assets of a business. Equities are divided between outsider claims (liabilities) and insider claims (owner equity or capital) *(p. 11)*.

Equity method for investments. The method used to account for investments in which the investor can significantly influence the decisions of the investee. Under the equity method, investments are recorded initially at cost. The investment account is debited (increased) for ownership in the investee's net income and credited (decreased) for ownership in the investee's dividends *(p. 660)*.

Equivalent units. Measure of the number of complete units that could have been manufactured from start to finish using the costs incurred during the period *(p. 901)*.

Estimated residual value. Expected cash value of an asset at the end of its useful life. Also called Residual value, Scrap value and Salvage value *(p. 387)*.

Estimated useful life. Length of the service that a business expects to get from an asset, may be expressed in years, units of output, miles, or other measures *(p. 387)*.

Expense. Decrease in owner equity that occurs in the course of delivering goods or services to customers or clients *(p. 14)*.

Expense allocation. Assignment of various expenses to the departments of a business *(p. 976)*.

Extraordinary item. A gain or loss that is both unusual for the company and infrequent *(p. 588)*.

Extraordinary repair. Repair work that generates a capital expenditure *(p. 404)*.

Factory ledger. A branch ledger for a manufacturing plant *(p. 981)*.

Factory overhead. All manufacturing costs other than direct materials and direct labor *(p. 858)*.

FICA tax. Federal Insurance Contributions Act (FICA) or Social Security tax which is withheld from employees' pay *(p. 433)*.

FIFO. The First-in, first-out inventory method *(p. 348)*.

Financial accounting. The branch of accounting that provides information to people outside the business *(p. 8)*.

Financial budget. Projects the means of raising money from stockholders and creditors and plans cash management *(p. 790)*.

Financial statements. Business documents that report financial information about an entity to persons and organizations outside the business *(p. 18)*.

Financing activity. Activity that obtains the funds from investors and creditors needed to launch and sustain the business. A section of the statement of cash flows *(p. 697)*.

Finished goods inventory. Completed goods that have not yet been sold *(p. 857)*.

First-in, first-out (FIFO) method. Inventory costing

method by which the first costs into inventory are the first costs out to cost of goods sold. Ending inventory is based on the costs of the most recent purchases (p. 348).

Fixed cost. Cost that does not change in total as volume changes (p. 822).

Fixed expense. Expense that does not change in total as volume changes (p. 822).

Flexible budget. Set of budgets covering a range of volume rather than a single level of volume (p. 937).

Flexible budget overhead variance. Difference between total actual overhead (fixed and variable) and the flexible budget amount for actual production volume. Also called the Controllable variance (p. 950).

Flexible budget variance. Difference between an amount in the flexible budget and the actual results for the corresponding item (p. 940).

FOB destination. Terms of a transaction that govern when the title to the inventory passes from the seller to the purchaser—when the goods arrive at the purchaser's location (p. 347).

FOB shipping point. Terms of a transaction that govern when the title to the inventory passes from the seller to the purchaser—when the goods leave the seller's place of business (p. 347).

Franchises and licenses. Privileges granted by a private business or a government to sell a product or service in accordance with specified conditions (p. 402).

Fringe benefits. Employee compensation, like health and life insurance and retirement pay, which the employee does not receive immediately in cash (p. 432).

Gain. An increase in owner equity that does not result from a revenue or an investment by an owner in the business (p. 476).

Generally accepted accounting principles (GAAP). Accounting guidelines, formulated by the Financial Accounting Standards Board, that govern how businesses report their financial statements to the public (p. 6).

General journal. Journal used to record all transactions that do not fit one of the special journals (p. 222).

General ledger. Ledger of accounts that are reported in the financial statements (p. 223).

Going concern concept. Accountants' assumption that the business will continue operating in the foreseeable future (p. 464).

Goods available for sale. Beginning inventory plus net purchases (p. 345).

Goodwill. Excess of the cost of an acquired company over the sum of the market values of its net assets (assets minus liabilities) (p. 403).

Gross income. In taxation, total income minus exclusions (p. 1043).

Gross margin. Excess of sales revenue over cost of goods sold. Also called gross profit (p. 169).

Gross margin method. A way to estimate inventory based on a rearrangement of the cost of goods sold model: Beginning inventory + Net purchases = Cost of goods available for sale. Cost of goods available for sale − Cost of goods sold = Ending inventory. Also called the Gross profit method (p. 359).

Gross pay. Total amount of salary, wages, commissions, or any other employee compensation before taxes and other deductions are taken out (p. 432).

Gross profit. Excess of sales revenue over cost of goods sold. Also called gross margin (p. 169).

Gross profit method. Another name for the gross margin method of estimating inventory cost (p. 359).

Hardware. Equipment that makes up a computer system (p. 219).

High-low method. Method of separating a mixed cost into its variable and fixed components (p. 836).

Home office ledger. The part of a general ledger kept by the home office, separate from the branch ledger, which the branch keeps (p. 981).

Home-office ledger control. Account in the branch ledger that represents an owner equity of, or branch payable to, the home office (p. 982).

Horizontal analysis. Study of percentage changes in comparative financial statements (p. 740).

Imprest system. A way to account for petty cash by maintaining a constant balance in the petty cash account, supported by the fund (cash plus disbursement tickets) totalling the same amount (p. 283).

Income from operations. Gross margin (sales revenue minus cost of goods sold) minus operating expenses. Also called Operating income (p. 184).

Income statement. List of an entity's revenues, expenses, and net income or net loss for a specific period. Also called the Statement of operations (p. 18).

Income summary. A temporary "holding tank" account into which the revenues and expenses are transferred prior to their final transfer to the capital account (p. 139).

Income tax. A general-purpose tax levied on the income of a taxpayer. Entirely separate from all other taxes, it is the federal government's largest source of revenue (p. 1039).

Income tax allocation. Process of accruing income taxes during the period that the related income occurs, with the goal of matching the period's expenses—including income tax expense—against the period's revenues, regardless of when the income tax is paid (p. 1053).

Incorporators. Persons who organize a corporation (p. 537).

Indirect expense. Expense that is not traceable to a single department of a business; an expense other than a direct expense. Often indirect expenses arise from activities that serve more than one department simultaneously (p. 976).

Indirect labor. Factory labor costs other than direct labor. Indirect labor costs, which are difficult to trace to specific products, include the pay of forklift operators, janitors, and plant guards (p. 859).

Indirect materials. Manufacturing materials whose cost cannot easily be traced directly to particular finished products (p. 859).

Indirect method. Format of the operating activities section of the statement of cash flows that starts with net income and shows the reconciliation from net income to operating cash flows. Also called the Reconciliation method (p. 713).

Inflation. Increase in the general price level (p. 669).

Information system design. Identification of an organization's information needs, and development and implementation of the system to meet those needs (p. 7).

Installment method. Method of applying the revenue principle in which gross profit (sales revenue minus cost of goods sold) is recorded as cash is collected (p. 468).

Intangible asset. An asset with no physical form, a special right to current and expected future benefits (p. 383).

Integrated software. Computer program that includes modules handling different functions. Coordinates the output of the various modules *(p. 1079)*.

Interest. The revenue to the payee for loaning out the principal, and the expense to the maker for borrowing the principal *(p. 322)*.

Interest coverage ratio. Another name for the Times-interest-earned ratio *(p. 756)*.

Interest period. The period of time during which interest is to be computed, extending from the original date of the note to the maturity date *(p. 322)*.

Interest rate. The percentage rate that is multiplied by the principal amount to compute the amount of interest on a note *(p. 322)*.

Internal auditing. Auditing that is performed by a business's own accountants to evaluate the firm's accounting and management systems. The aim is to improve operating efficiency and to ensure that employees follow management's procedures and plans *(p. 7)*.

Internal control. Organizational plan and all the related measures adopted by an entity to safeguard assets, ensure accurate and reliable accounting records, promote operational efficiency, and encourage adherence to company policies *(p. 265)*.

Inventory cost. Price paid to acquire inventory—not the selling price of the goods. Inventory cost includes its invoice price, less all discounts, plus sales tax, tariffs, transportation fees, insurance while in transit, and all other costs incurred to make the goods ready for sale *(p. 347)*.

Inventory profit. Difference between gross margin figured on the FIFO basis and gross margin figured on the LIFO basis *(p. 352)*.

Inventory turnover. Ratio of cost of goods sold to average inventory. Measures the number of times a company sells its average level of inventory during a year *(p. 752)*.

Investing activity. Activity that increases and decreases the assets that the business has to work with. A section of the statement of cash flows *(p. 697)*.

Invoice. Seller's request for payment from a purchaser. Also called a bill *(p. 171)*.

Itemized deduction. In taxation, a particular category that includes medical expenses, interest expense, charitable contributions, taxes paid, casualty losses, and miscellaneous deductions *(p. 1043)*.

Job cost record. Document used to accumulate and control cost in a job order system *(p. 864)*.

Job order costing. Accounting system used by companies that manufacture products as individual units or in batches, each of which receives varying degrees of attention and skill *(p. 863)*.

Joint product. Goods identified as individual products only after a juncture in the production process called the split-off point *(p. 916)*.

Journal. The chronological accounting record of an entity's transactions *(p. 45)*.

Labor time ticket. Document that identifies an employee, the amount of time the employee spent on a particular job, and the employee's labor cost charged to the job *(p. 868)*.

Large stock dividend. A stock dividend of 25 percent or more of the corporation's issued stock *(p. 575)*.

Last-in, first-out (LIFO) method. Inventory costing method by which the last costs into inventory are the first costs out to cost of goods sold. This leaves the oldest costs—those of beginning inventory and the earliest purchases of the period—in ending inventory *(p. 348)*.

LCM rule. The Lower-of-cost-or-market rule *(p. 356)*.

Lease. Rental agreement in which the tenant (lessee) agrees to make rent payments to the property owner (lessor) in exchange for the use of the asset *(p. 627)*.

Leasehold. Prepayment that a lessee (renter) makes to secure the use of an asset from a lessor (landlord) *(p. 402)*.

Ledger. The book of accounts *(p. 39)*.

Lessee. Tenant in a lease agreement *(p. 627)*.

Lessor. Property owner in a lease agreement *(p. 627)*.

Leverage. Another name for Trading on the equity *(p. 758)*.

Liability. An economic obligation (a debt) payable to an individual or an organization outside the business *(p. 11)*.

LIFO. The Last-in, first-out inventory method *(p. 348)*.

Limited liability. No personal obligation of a stockholder for corporation debts. The most that a stockholder can lose on an investment in a corporation's stock is the cost of the investment *(p. 536)*.

Limiting factor. Item that restricts production or sales. Also called the Constraint *(p. 1012)*.

Liquidation. The process of going out of business by selling the entity's assets and paying its liabilities. The final step in liquidation of a business is the distribution of any remaining cash to the owners *(p. 513)*.

Liquidation value of stock. Amount a corporation agrees to pay a preferred stockholder per share if the company liquidates *(p. 554)*.

Liquidity. Measure of how quickly an item may be converted to cash *(p. 142)*.

Long-term asset. An asset other than a current asset *(p. 142)*.

Long-term investment. Separate asset category reported on the balance sheet between current assets and plant assets *(p. 632)*.

Long-term liability. A liability other than a current liability *(p. 143)*.

Loss. A decrease in owner equity that does not result from an expense or a distribution to an owner of the business *(p. 477)*.

Lower-of-cost-or-market (LCM) rule. Requires that an asset be reported in the financial statements at the lower of its historical cost or its market value (current replacement cost) *(p. 356)*.

Mainframe. Computer system characterized by a single computer *(p. 219)*.

Majority interest. Another name for a Controlling ownership interest in another business *(p. 661)*.

Maker of a note. The person or business that signs the note and promises to pay the amount required by the note agreement. The maker is the debtor *(p. 321)*.

Management accounting. The branch of accounting that generates confidential information for internal decision makers of a business, such as top executives *(p. 8)*.

Management by exception. Management strategy by which executive attention is directed to the important deviations from budgeted amounts *(p. 973)*.

Margin of safety. Excess of expected sales over break-even sales *(p. 833)*.

Market interest rate. Interest rate that investors demand in order to loan their money. Also called the Effective interest rate *(p. 612)*.

Market value of stock. Price for which a person could buy or sell a share of stock *(p. 553)*.

Marketable security. Another name for Short-term investment, one that may be sold any time the investor wishes *(p. 657)*.

Master budget. Budget that includes the major financial statements and supporting schedules. The master budget can be divided into the operating budget, the capital expenditures budget, and the financial budget *(p. 787)*.

Matching principle. The basis for recording expenses. Directs accountants to identify all expenses incurred during the period, to measure the expenses, and to match them against the revenues earned during that same span of time *(p. 88)*.

Materiality concept. States that a company must perform strictly proper accounting only for items and transactions that are significant to the business's financial statements *(p. 475)*.

Materials inventory. Materials on hand and intended for use in the manufacturing process. Also called Raw materials inventory *(p. 857)*.

Materials requisition. Request for materials prepared by manufacturing personnel, the document that sets a manufacturing process in motion *(p. 866)*.

Maturity date. The date on which the final payment of a note is due. Also called the Due date *(p. 322)*.

Maturity value. The sum of the principal and interest due at the maturity date of a note *(p. 322)*.

Menu. List of options for choosing computer functions *(p. 1079)*.

Menu-driven. Type of computer software that offers a list of options for doing various functions *(p. 1079)*.

Microcomputer. A computer small enough for each employee (work station) to have its own *(p. 219)*.

Minicomputer. Small computer that operates like a large system but on a smaller scale *(p. 219)*.

Minority interest. A subsidiary company's equity that is held by stockholders other than the parent company *(p. 665)*.

Mixed cost. Cost that is part variable and part fixed *(p. 823)*.

Mixed expense. Expense that is part variable and part fixed *(p. 823)*.

Modified Accelerated Cost Recovery System (MACRS). Special tax depreciation method *(p. 1052)*.

Monetary asset. Asset whose value is stated in a fixed number of dollars. This amount does not change, regardless of inflation *(p. 672)*.

Monetary liability. Liability stated in a fixed number of dollars. This amount does not change, regardless of inflation *(p. 672)*.

Monitor. Computer output device that resembles a television and allows the user to view data being processed and to receive messages from the program being run *(p. 1078)*.

Mortgage. Borrower's promise to transfer the legal title to certain assets to the lender if the debt is not paid on schedule *(p. 627)*.

Multiple-step income statement. Format that contains subtotals to highlight significant relationships. In addition to net income, it also presents gross margin and income from operations *(p. 188)*.

Mutual agency. Every partner can bind the business to a contract within the scope of the partnership's regular business operations *(p. 496)*.

Net earnings. Another name for Net income or Net profit *(p. 15)*.

Net income. Excess of total revenues over total expenses. Also called Net earnings or Net profit *(p. 15)*.

Net loss. Excess of total expenses over total revenues *(p. 15)*.

Net monetary assets. Excess of monetary assets over monetary liabilities *(p. 672)*.

Net monetary liabilities. Excess of monetary liabilities over monetary assets *(p. 672)*.

Net pay. Gross pay minus all deductions, the amount of employee compensation that the employee actually takes home *(p. 432)*.

Net present value. Method of computing the expected net monetary gain or loss from a project by discounting all expected cash flows to the present value, using a desired rate of return. A zero or positive net present value indicates that the investment should be purchased. A negative net present value indicates that the investment should be rejected *(p. 1021)*.

Net profit. Another name for Net income or Net earnings *(p. 15)*.

Net purchases. Purchases less purchase discounts and purchase returns and allowances *(p. 174)*.

Net realizable value. Sales value less the cost of selling the item *(p. 917)*.

Net sales. Sales revenue less sales discounts and sales returns and allowances *(p. 177)*.

Nominal account. Another name for a temporary account —revenues and expenses—that are closed at the end of the period. In a proprietorship the owner withdrawal account is also nominal *(p. 137)*.

Nonmonetary asset. Asset whose price may change during inflation, such as inventory, land, buildings, and equipment *(p. 672)*.

Non-sufficient funds check. A "hot" check, one for which the payer's bank account has insufficient money to pay the check *(p. 273)*.

Note payable. A liability evidenced by a written promise to make a future payment *(p. 11)*.

Note receivable. An asset evidenced by another party's written promise that entitles you to receive cash in the future *(pp. 11, 310)*.

NSF check. A non-sufficient funds check *(p. 273)*.

Objectivity principle. Another name for the Reliability principle *(p. 466)*.

Off-balance-sheet financing. Acquisition of assets or services with debt that is not reported on the balance sheet *(p. 629)*.

On-line processing. Computerized accounting for transaction data on a continuous basis, often from various locations, rather than in batches at a single location *(p. 220)*.

Operating activity. Activity that creates revenue or expense in the entity's major line of business. Operating activities affect the income statement. A section of the statement of cash flows *(p. 697)*.

Operating budget. Sets the target revenues and expenses, and thus net income, for the period *(p. 790)*.

Operating expenses. Expenses, other than cost of goods sold, that are incurred in the entity's major line of business—rent, depreciation, salaries, wages, utilities, property tax, and supplies expense *(p. 184)*.

Operating income. Another name for Income from operations *(p. 184)*.

Operating lease. Usually a short-term or cancelable rental agreement *(p. 627)*.

Operation costing. The most popular hybrid costing system, combining features from job costing and process costing, used to account for the manufacture of goods that have some common features plus some individual characteristics *(p. 913)*.

Opportunity cost. Maximum available profit contribution forgone (rejected) by using limited resources for a particular purpose. It is the cost of the forsaken next best alternative *(p. 1015)*.

Ordinary repair. Repair work that creates a revenue expenditure, which is debited to an expense account *(p. 404)*.

Organization cost. The costs of organizing a corporation, including legal fees, taxes and fees paid to the state, and charges by promoters for selling the stock. Organization cost is an intangible asset *(p. 549)*.

Other expense. Expense that is outside the main operations of a business, such as a loss on the sale of plant assets *(p. 184)*.

Other receivables. A miscellaneous category that includes loans to employees and branch companies, usually long-term assets reported on the balance sheet after current assets and before plant assets. Other receivables can be current assets *(p. 310)*.

Other revenue. Revenue that is outside the main operations of a business, such as a gain on the sale of plant assets *(p. 184)*.

Outstanding check. A check issued by the company and recorded on its books but not yet paid by its bank *(p. 273)*.

Outstanding stock. Stock in the hands of a stockholder *(p. 538)*.

Overapplied overhead. Credit balance in the factory overhead account, results when applied overhead exceeds the actual overhead cost *(p. 874)*.

Owner equity. The claim of an owner of a business to the assets of the business. Also called Capital *(p. 11)*.

Paid-in capital. A corporation's capital from investments by the stockholders. Also called Contributed capital *(p. 539)*.

Par value. Arbitrary amount assigned to a share of stock *(p. 541)*.

Parent company. An investor company that owns more than 50 percent of the voting stock of a subsidiary company *(p. 661)*.

Participating preferred stock. Preferred stock whose owners may receive — that is participate in — dividends beyond the stated amount or stated percentage *(p. 552)*.

Partnership. A business with two or more owners *(p. 8)*.

Partnership agreement. Another name for the Articles of partnership *(p. 496)*.

Patent. A federal government grant giving the holder the exclusive right for 17 years to produce and sell an invention *(p. 402)*.

Payback. Length of time it will take to recover, in net cash inflow from operations, the dollars of a capital outlay. The shorter the payback period the better the investment, and vice versa *(p. 1018)*.

Payee of a note. The person or business to whom the maker of a note promises future payment. The payee is the creditor *(p. 321)*.

Payroll. Employee compensation, a major expense of many businesses *(p. 431)*.

Pension. Employee compensation that will be received during retirement *(p. 629)*.

Percentage-of-completion method. Method of applying the revenue principle by a construction company by which revenue is recorded as the work is performed *(p. 470)*.

Period cost. Operating expenses which are never traced through the inventory accounts *(p. 861)*.

Periodic inventory system. The business does not keep a continuous record of the inventory on hand. Instead, at the end of the period the business makes a physical count of the on-hand inventory and applies the appropriate unit costs to determine the cost of the ending inventory *(p. 360)*.

Permanent accounts. The assets, liabilities, and capital accounts. These accounts are *not* closed at the end of the period because their balances are not used to measure income *(p. 138)*.

Perpetual inventory system. The business keeps a continuous record for each inventory item to show the inventory on hand at all times *(p. 361)*.

Personal exemption. A tax deduction that is a set amount allowed for a taxpayer, the taxpayer's spouse, and each person who qualifies as a dependent *(p. 1044)*.

Petty cash. Fund containing a small amount of cash that is used to pay minor expenditures *(p. 282)*.

Plant asset. Long-lived assets, like land, buildings, and equipment, used in the operation of the business *(pp. 92, 383)*.

Postclosing trial balance. List of the ledger accounts and their balances at the end of the period after the journalizing and posting of the closing entries. The last step of the accounting cycle, the postclosing trial balance ensures that the ledger is in balance for the start of the next accounting period *(p. 141)*.

Posting. Transferring of amounts from the journal to the ledger *(p. 46)*.

Preemptive right. A stockholder's right to maintain a proportionate ownership in a corporation *(p. 541)*.

Preferred stock. Stock that gives its owners certain advantages over common stockholders, such as the priority to receive dividends before the common stockholders and the priority to receive assets before the common stockholders if the corporation liquidates *(p. 541)*.

Premium on stock. Excess of the issue price of stock over its par value *(p. 542)*.

Prepaid expense. A category of miscellaneous assets that typically expire or get used up in the near future. Examples include prepaid rent, prepaid insurance, and supplies *(p. 90)*.

Present value. Amount a person would invest now to receive a greater amount at a future date *(p. 612)*.

President. Chief operating officer in charge of managing the day-to-day operations of a corporation *(p. 537)*.

Price/earnings ratio. Ratio of the market price of a share of common stock to the company's earnings per share *(p. 759)*.

Price variance. Difference between the actual unit price of an input (materials and labor) and a standard unit price, multiplied by the actual quantity of inputs used *(pp. 945–946)*.

Prime costs. Direct materials plus direct labor *(p. 859)*.

Principal amount. The amount loaned out by the payee and borrowed by the maker of a note *(p. 321)*.

Prior period adjustment. Correction to retained earnings for an error of an earlier period is a prior period adjustment *(p. 591)*.

Private accountant. Accountant who works for a single business, such as a department store or General Motors *(p. 4)*.

Process costing. System for assigning costs to goods that are mass-produced in a continuous sequence of steps *(p. 897)*.

Product cost. Cost identified with goods purchased or manufactured for resale *(p. 860)*.

Production cost report. Summary of the activity in a processing department for a period *(p. 912)*.

Production volume overhead variance. Difference between the flexible budget for actual production and standard overhead applied to production *(p. 951)*.

Pro forma data. Carefully formulated expression of predicted results, such as projections of future income and income tax *(p. 1054)*.

Program. Set of instructions that tell the computer what to do *(p. 1076)*.

Promissory note. A written promise to pay a specified amount of money at a particular future date *(p. 321)*.

Proprietorship. A business with a single owner *(p. 8)*.

Proxy. Legal document that expresses a stockholder's preference and appoints another person to cast the vote *(p. 537)*.

Public accountant. Accountant who serves the general public and collects fees for work, which includes auditing, income tax planning and preparation, and management consulting *(p. 4)*.

Purchase discount. Reduction in the cost of inventory that is offered by a seller as an incentive for the customer to pay promptly. A contra account to purchases *(p. 173)*.

Purchase returns and allowances. Decrease in a buyer's debt from returning merchandise to the seller or from receiving from the seller an allowance from the amount owed. A contra account to purchases *(p. 174)*.

Purchases. The cost of inventory that a firm buys to resell to customers in the normal course of business *(p. 170)*.

Purchases journal. Special journal used to record all purchases of inventory, supplies, and other assets on account *(p. 230)*.

Purchasing power gain (or loss). A purchasing power gain occurs during inflation because a company is able to pay its liabilities with dollars that are cheaper than the dollars borrowed. A purchasing power loss occurs during inflation when a creditor receives dollars that are worth less than the dollars lent *(p. 672)*.

Quantity variance. Another name for the efficiency variance used to control materials and labor costs in a standard cost system *(p. 946)*.

Quick ratio. Another name for the Acid-test ratio *(p. 751)*.

Rate of return on common stockholders' equity. Net income minus preferred dividends, divided by average common stockholders' equity. A measure of profitability. Also called return on common stockholders' equity *(p. 758)*.

Rate of return on net sales. Ratio of net income to net sales.

A measure of profitability. Also called Return on sales *(p. 756)*.

Rate of return on total assets. The sum of net income plus interest expense divided by average total assets. This ratio measures the success a company has in using its assets to earn a profit. Also called Return on assets *(p. 757)*.

Raw materials inventory. Another name for Materials inventory *(p. 857)*.

Real account. Another name for a Permanent account — asset, liability, and capital — that are *not* closed at the end of the period *(p. 138)*.

Receivable. A monetary claim against a business or an individual, acquired mainly by selling goods and services and by lending money *(p. 309)*.

Reciprocal accounts. Two or more accounts that have the same offsetting balances and are used to control a general ledger that is kept in two or more locations *(p. 981)*.

Reconciliation method. Another name for the indirect method of formatting the operating activities section of the statement of cash flows *(p. 713)*.

Redemption value of stock. Price a corporation agrees to pay for stock, which is set when the stock is issued *(p. 553)*.

Registered bonds. Bonds for which the owners receive interest checks from the issuing company *(p. 610)*.

Relative sales value method. Allocation technique for identifying the cost of each asset purchased in a group for a single amount *(p. 385)*.

Relevant information. Expected future data that differ between alternative courses of action *(p. 1005)*.

Relevant range. Band of activity or volume in which actual operations are likely to occur. Within this range, a particular relationship exists between revenue and expenses *(p. 824)*.

Reliability principle. Requires that accounting information be dependable (free from error and bias). Also called the Objectivity principle *(p. 466)*.

Report format of the balance sheet. Format that lists the assets at the top, with the liabilities and owner equity below *(p. 143)*.

Residual value. Same as Estimated residual value *(p. 387)*.

Responsibility accounting. System for evaluating the progress of managers based on activities under their supervision *(p. 972)*.

Responsibility center. Any subunit of an organization needing control, the basic unit in a responsibility accounting system. The three common types of responsibility center are the cost center, the profit center, and the investment center *(p. 972)*.

Retail method. A way to estimate inventory cost based on the cost of goods sold model. The retail method requires that the business record inventory purchases both at cost and at retail. Multiply ending inventory at retail by the cost ratio to estimate the ending inventory's cost *(p. 359)*.

Retained earnings. A corporation's capital that is earned through profitable operation of the business *(p. 539)*.

Return on assets. Another name for Rate of return on total assets *(p. 757)*.

Return on common stockholders' equity. Another name for Rate of return on common stockholders' equity *(p. 758)*.

Return on sales. Another name for Rate of return on net sales *(p. 756)*.

Revenue. Increase in owner equity that is earned by delivering goods or services to customers or clients *(p. 13)*.

Revenue expenditure. Expenditure that merely maintains an asset in its existing condition or restores the asset to good working order. Revenue expenditures are expensed (matched against revenue) *(p. 404)*.

Revenue principle. The basis for recording revenues, tells accountants when to record revenue and the amount of revenue to record *(p. 87)*.

Reversing entry. An entry that switches the debit and the credit of a previous adjusting entry. The reversing entry is dated the first day of the period following the adjusting entry *(p. 615)*.

Rolling budget. Another name for a continuous budget *(p. 801)*.

Salary. Employee compensation stated at a yearly, monthly, or weekly rate *(p. 431)*.

Sales discount. Reduction in the amount receivable from a customer, offered by the seller as an incentive for the customer to pay promptly. A contra account to Sales revenue *(p. 176)*.

Sales journal. Special journal used to record credit sales *(p. 222)*.

Sales method. Method of applying the revenue principle in which revenue is recorded at the point of sale. This method is used for most sales of goods and services *(p. 468)*.

Sales mix. Combination of products that make up total sales *(p. 834)*.

Sales returns and allowances. Decrease in the seller's receivable from a customer's return of merchandise or from granting the customer an allowance from the amount the customer owes the seller. A contra account to Sales revenue *(p. 176)*.

Sales revenue. Amount that a merchandiser earns from selling inventory before subtracting expenses *(p. 169)*.

Sales volume variance. Difference between a revenue, expense, or operating income amount in the flexible budget and the corresponding revenue, expense, or income amount in the static (master) budget *(p. 940)*.

Salvage value. Another name for residual value or estimated residual value *(p. 387)*.

Segment of a business. A significant part of a company *(p. 587)*.

Serial bonds. Bonds that mature in installments over a period of time *(p. 610)*.

Sevice charge. Bank's fee for processing a depositor's transactions *(p. 273)*.

Shareholder. Another name for stockholder *(p. 535)*.

Short presentation. A way to report contingent liabilities in the body of the balance sheet, after total liabilities but with no amount given *(pp. 429, 430)*.

Short-term note payable. Note payable due within one year, a common form of financing *(p. 424)*.

Short-term self-liquidating financing. Debt incurred to buy inventories that will be sold and with the cash collections used to pay the debt *(p. 800)*.

Single-step income statement. Format that groups all revenues together and then lists and deducts all expenses together without drawing any subtotals *(p. 188)*.

Slide. An accounting error that results from adding one or more zeroes to a number, or from dropping a zero. For example, writing $500 as $5,000 or as $50 is a slide. A slide is evenly divisible by 9. *(p. 145)*.

Small stock dividend. A stock dividend of less than 25 percent of the corporation's issued stock *(p. 525)*.

Social Security tax. Another name for FICA tax *(p. 433)*.

Software. Set of programs or instructions that cause the computer to perform the work desired *(pp. 145, 219)*.

Specific cost method. Inventory cost method based on the specific cost of particular units of inventory *(p. 348)*.

Split-off point. Juncture in the production process after which joint products are specifically identified *(p. 916)*.

Spreadsheet. Integrated software program that can be used to solve many different kinds of problems. An electronically prepared work sheet *(p. 145)*.

Stable monetary unit concept. Accountants' basis for ignoring the effect of inflation and making no adjustments for the changing value of the dollar *(p. 465)*.

Standard cost. Predetermined cost that management believes the business should incur in producing an item *(p. 943)*.

Standard cost system. Designed to control costs by analyzing the relationship between actual costs and standard costs *(p. 943)*.

Standard deduction. A set amount of tax deduction that varies depending on the individual's filing status: single, married filing jointly, or head of household. The standard deduction is an alternative to itemizing tax deductions *(p. 1044)*.

Stated interest rate. Another name for the Contract interest rate *(p. 612)*.

Statement of budgeted cash receipts and disbursements. Another name for the Cash budget *(p. 796)*.

Statement of cash flows. Reports cash receipts and cash disbursements classified according to the entity's major activities: operating, investing, and financing *(p. 695)*.

Statement of financial position. Another name for the Balance sheet *(p. 18)*.

Statement of operations. Another name for the Income statement *(p. 18)*.

Statement of owner equity. Summary of the changes in the owner equity of an entity during a specific period *(p. 18)*.

Static budget. A budget prepared for only one level of activity *(p. 937)*.

Stock. Shares into which the owners' equity of a corporation is divided *(p. 536)*.

Stock dividend. A proportional distribution by a corporation of its own stock to its stockholders *(p. 573)*.

Stock split. An increase in the number of outstanding shares of stock coupled with a proportionate reduction in the par value of the stock *(p. 573)*.

Stock subscription. Contract that obligates an investor to purchase the corporation's stock at a later date *(p. 544)*.

Stockholder. A person who owns the stock of a corporation *(p. 9)*.

Stockholders' equity. Owners' equity of a corporation *(p. 538)*.

Straight-line method. Depreciation method in which an equal amount of depreciation expense is assigned to each year (or period) of asset use *(p. 387)*.

Subsequent event. An event that occurs after the end of a company's accounting period but before publication of its financial statements and which may affect the interpretation of the information in those statements *(p. 473)*.

Subsidiary company. An investee company in which a parent company owns more than 50 percent of the voting stock *(p. 661)*.

Subsidiary ledger. Book of accounts that provides supporting details on individual balances, the total of which appears in a general ledger account *(p. 224)*.

Sum-of-years-digits (SYD) method. An accelerated depreciation method by which depreciation is figured by multiplying the depreciable cost of the asset by a fraction. The denominator of the SYD fraction is the sum of the years' digits of the asset's life. The numerator of the SYD fraction starts with the asset life in years and decreases by one each year thereafter *(p. 390)*.

Sunk cost. Actual outlay incurred in the past and is present under all alternative courses of action. Sunk cost is irrelevant because it makes no difference to a current decision *(p. 1015)*.

Surtax. An additional tax often designed to shift more of the tax burden to high-income taxpayers *(p. 1046)*.

Tax avoidance. Structuring of business transactions in order to pay the least amount of income tax at the latest possible time permitted by the law *(p. 1054)*.

Tax credit. Amount that is subtracted directly from the amount of tax owed to the government *(p. 1047)*.

Tax-deferred compensation. Compensation that postpones the payment of taxes until the employee draws the money. Also called Tax-sheltered compensation *(p. 1058)*.

Tax evasion. Illegal activity designed to reduce tax *(p. 1054)*.

Tax return. Document on which each taxpayer reports income and shows the computation of income tax *(p. 1041)*.

Tax-sheltered compensation. Another name for Tax-deferred compensation *(p. 1058)*.

Taxable income. Earnings amount on which the income tax is based. It is the figure that is multiplied by the tax rate to compute the amount of income tax *(p. 1045)*.

Temporary accounts. The revenue and expense accounts which relate to a particular accounting period are closed at the end of the period. For a proprietorship, the owner withdrawal account is also temporary *(p. 137)*.

Term bonds. Bonds that all mature at the same time for a particular issue *(p. 610)*.

Time and a half. Overtime pay computed as 150 percent (1.5 times) the straight-time rate *(p. 432)*.

Time period concept. Ensures that accounting information is reported at regular intervals *(p. 465)*.

Time value of money. The fact that one can earn income by investing money for a period of time *(p. 1021)*.

Times-interest-earned ratio. Ratio of income from operations to interest expense. Measures the number of times that operating income can cover interest expense. Also called the Interest-coverage ratio *(p. 756)*.

Total income. In taxation, all income from whatever source derived *(p. 1043)*.

Total manufacturing cost. Sum of direct materials used, direct labor, and factory overhead. Total manufacturing cost is used to compute cost of goods manufactured, which is part of cost of goods sold *(p. 860)*.

Trade discount. A purchase discount that provides a lower price per item the larger the quantity purchased *(p. 173)*.

Trademarks and trade names. Distinctive identifications of a product or service *(p. 402)*.

Trading on the equity. Earning more income than the borrowed amount, which increases the earnings for the owners of a business. Also called leverage *(p. 631)*.

Transaction. An event that affects the financial position of a particular entity and may be reliably recorded *(p. 11)*.

Transposition. An accounting error that occurs when digits are flip-flopped. For example, $85 is a transposition of $58. A transposition is evenly divisible by 9 *(p. 145)*.

Treasury stock. A corporation's own stock that it has issued and later reacquired *(p. 578)*.

Trial balance. A list of all the ledger accounts with their balances *(p. 50)*.

Uncollectible account expense. Cost to the seller of extending credit. Arises from the failure to collect from credit customers *(p. 311)*.

Underapplied overhead. Debit balance remaining in the factory overhead account after overhead is applied, means that actual overhead cost exceeded the amount applied to jobs *(p. 874)*.

Underwriter. Organization that purchases the bonds from an issuing company and resells them to its clients, or sells the bonds for a commission, agreeing to buy all unsold bonds *(p. 610)*.

Unearned revenue. A liability created when a business collects cash from customers in advance of doing work for the customer. The obligation is to provide a product or a service in the future. Also called deferred revenue *(p. 96)*.

Unemployment compensation tax. Payroll tax paid by employers to the government, which uses the money to pay unemployment benefits to people who are out of work *(p. 435)*.

Units-of-production (UOP) method. Depreciation method by which a fixed amount of depreciation is assigned to each unit of output produced by the plant asset *(p. 389)*.

Unlimited personal liability. When a partnership (or a proprietorship) cannot pay its debts with business assets, the partners (or the proprietor) must use personal assets to meet the debt *(p. 497)*.

Usage variance. Another name for the Efficiency variance used to control materials and labor costs in a standard cost system *(p. 946)*.

Useful life. Same as Estimated useful life *(p. 387)*.

Voucher. Document authorizing a cash disbursement *(p. 284)*.

Voucher register. Special journal used to record all expenditures in a voucher system, similar to but more comprehensive than the purchases journal *(p. 287)*.

Voucher system. A way to record cash payments that enhances internal control by formalizing the process of approving and recording invoices for payment *(p. 283)*.

Wages. Employee pay stated at an hourly figure *(p. 431)*.

Withheld income tax. Income tax deducted from employees' gross pay *(p. 432)*.

Work sheet. A columnar document designed to help move data from the trial balance to the financial statements *(p. 126)*.

Index

Boldface indicates an Accounting Vocabulary term and the page in the text where it is defined. These terms are also defined in the Glossary.